NATIONAL HEALTH INSURANCE

PUBLIC DOCUMENTS SERIES

Series Editors: Tyrus G. Fain, with Katharine C. Plant and Ross Milloy

Federal Reorganization: The Executive Branch
The Intelligence Community: History, Organization, and Issues
National Health Insurance

NATIONAL HEALTH INSURANCE

Public Documents Series

Compiled and Edited by Tyrus G. Fain
in collaboration with
Katharine C. Plant and Ross Milloy

With an Introduction by
Senator Edward M. Kennedy

R. R. BOWKER COMPANY
New York & London, 1977

Published by R. R. Bowker Company
1180 Avenue of the Americas, New York, N.Y. 10036
Copyright © 1977 by Xerox Corporation
All rights reserved
Printed and bound in the United States of America

Library of Congress Cataloging in Publication Data
Main entry under title:

National health insurance.

(Public documents series)
Bibliography: p.
Includes index.
1. Insurance, Health—United States—Addresses, essays, lectures.
2. Medical care—United States—Addresses, essays, lectures.
I. Fain, Tyrus G. II. Plant, Katharine C. III. Milloy, Ross. IV. Series.
HD7102.U4N257   368.3′82′0973   77-22947
ISBN 0-8352-0960-1

CONTENTS

PART I
ISSUES AND INITIATIVES

PART II
U.S. HEALTH CARE INDUSTRY: KEY FACTS
ON COMPONENTS AND COSTS

PREFACE

This edited volume of contemporary government documents on national health insurance is the third title in the Public Documents Series. The series examines issues of major and topical public policy concern and seeks to make government documents more accessible to the public.

National health insurance has generated much controversy in American politics and is a subject of immediate significance, both to policymakers and to the public. The United States is the most affluent, technologically advanced society in the history of Western civilization; but, the American people pay increasingly high prices for health care, which many argue, is inferior in comparison to other industrialized, and less prosperous, nations. The high price of medical care and an inflationary economy have created a political momentum for reviewing our health system, and the Congress is now confronted with the renewed task of defining a national health policy that is economically feasible, equitable, and humane.

An idea which created a brief polemical debate over socialized medicine in the time of Harry Truman has come of age. A new president, with new advisers, is beginning his term of office and is pledged to a platform which explicitly endorses national health insurance. The organization and the delivery of health service in this country are about to undergo profound changes. Legislation pending in the Congress and the outcome of the 1976 national elections clearly suggest that the lives of everyone—patients, professionals, and paramedics—are about to be touched by these changes.

The current debate is over the form of the national health insurance to be enacted: whether the insurance be mandatory or optional; whether the federal government pay all, or part, of the cost; whether the insurance companies, the states, or the federal government administer the program; whether the professionals police themselves or whether a new cadre of health regulators emerge. These issues are but a few elements of the debate. The stakes are high, both for the public and the health industry. That industry has grown to be the third largest in the nation, involving over $100 billion per year, and its spokespersons are skilled, articulate defenders of its interests.

The diversity of political forces at play in the deliberations and debate over national health insurance represent politically charged opinions—expressed by both the advocates and opponents of the various approaches. As the debate focuses on specific courses to be taken, there is a need to consider national health insurance proposals within the context of the contemporary realities of health care and, also, other nations' experiences with health care.

The editors of the Public Documents Series have compiled this reference tool to inform the public about the subject of national health insurance and to make available in a single volume the documents used by decision-makers and legislators. They have assembled this material from a diverse body of documents appearing in thirty-eight separate volumes and reports, consisting of over 15,000 pages. The book contains core documents that are of special significance or that offer useful background summaries of longer, more complex materials. The documents included serve as a foundation upon which future proposals and legislation will be considered. The purpose of the compilation is to provide a documentary introduction to the public literature on national health insurance and to make available to the public materials which are ordinarily unavailable through commercial distribution channels. Most of the documents have appeared in government publications and are either out of print or difficult to obtain, and most were issued by the government without indexes or other bibliographic controls. No effort has been made to include commercial literature available in periodicals and books. It is assumed that the normal procedures employed in good scholarship will lead the researcher to those materials. Most libraries offer easily identifiable articles and monographs pertaining to the subject of health policy. To delve into that material would duplicate efforts.

The scope of the book encompasses a body of official reports, hearings, and studies concerning national health insurance, released by the government from 1970 to 1976. It was in 1970 that Senator Ralph Yarborough introduced his comprehensive national health insurance bill, and a broad-based coalition of health insurance advocates began forming. The Yarborough initiative was picked up by Edward Kennedy, his successor as chairman of the Health Subcommittee in the Senate. The focus of the book is on the issues of the debate over national health insurance, national health systems in other countries, and a view of the present health care industry in the United States, and its expenditures.

The volume is organized into two parts. Part I provides different perspectives on national health insurance issues, presented by a variety of persons, ranging from the principal authors of congressional legislation to lobbyists and representatives of particular interest groups. There is a chapter on the budgetary impact of a national health insurance program and a discussion of the estimated costs of alternative plans. The final chapter in Part I addresses the experiences of other nations that have some form of national health insurance. Virtually all industrialized nations of the world offer government supervised health care coverage to their people; many countries have operated a national health insurance program for over half a century. Germany began in the time of Bismarck and some of the socialist countries had national health systems prior to their respective revolutions. The United States, which is the exception, can benefit from their accumulated experience.

Part II represents a factual, largely statistical, synopsis of health care in the United States and includes an analysis of the trends on health facilities, manpower, and patients, as well as a review of private health insurance and public programs. A chapter on health care costs provides useful data and a profile of the nation's health care industry at mid-decade.

The material on specific legislation introduced presents a special problem regarding timeliness. Since legislation must be reintroduced in each Congress, the bills presented for consideration in 1975–1976, for example, died at the end of the 94th Congress in October 1976. The analysis and debate concerning them becomes somewhat out of date when they are reintroduced—as the bills are usually modified, the bill number changed, and, sometimes, their sponsorship and identifying name change as well. For instance, the Kennedy-Griffiths bill of the 93rd Congress became the Kennedy-Corman bill in the 94th. Rather than concentrate on the detailed features of each piece of legislation, the editors have sought to include overall descriptions of major proposals and comparisons of key provisions. Attention has been focused on the treatment of basic approaches and issues. The principal national health measures introduced in the 93rd and 94th Congresses are described in more detail in Appendix 2 of this volume.

For further reference on new legislation and amendments, the reader should consult the *Congressional Record* and reports of committee actions as they are released. There are, in addition, a number of fine information products available that address the subject on a current awareness basis. These include indexes and abstracts from *CSI Reports* (Capitol Services, Inc.), the *Predicasts Federal Index*, the *Congressional Quarterly*, the *Congressional Monitor*, and publications of the Congressional Information Service. Many of these publications are available in the larger public and academic libraries.

Acknowledgments for assistance in compiling and editing this volume should begin by recognizing the work of the federal officials and congressional committee staffs who authored most of the material included. By tradition, the names of government authors are seldom identified, so this expression of gratitude must, of necessity, be general. A number of people assisted in locating the documents, reviewing organization and format, and making suggestions for improvement. Foremost among them was Alice Keefer, the Public Documents Series library consultant. Her skill, perseverance, and good humor were exemplary. Thanks are also due to Bernadine Hiduski of the Joint Committee on Printing, Max Fine of the Health Security Action Council, Kay Cavalier of the Library of Congress, Clark Reid of the Senate Subcommittee on Health, Edmund Wise, and James Klick for thier suggestions and guidance. To Nancy Volkman, of R. R. Bowker, special thanks are due for her skill, patience, and diligence throughout the sometimes trying process of editing and revising. Finally, my associates Kate Plant and Ross Milloy deserve particular recognition and appreciation for their contributions to this book. They have worked continually and with dedication in assembling the Public Documents Series, and their efforts have been invaluable.

TYRUS G. FAIN

GUIDE TO USE

The documents in this volume were edited and, at times, abridged; where abridgment occurs, it is because of space limitations or because the editors sought to reduce redundancy—in an attempt to offer the most apposite information. Like the sources from which the text was drawn, there are inevitably gaps and inconsistencies in the style or format of the book. The editors have provided explanatory bridging narrative to facilitate transition between the documents, to lend continuity, and to elucidate the material. This narrative is set apart from the documents by horizontal lines. The editors have also provided notes and references at the end of five of the book's nine chapters, to give background on and perspective to the documents. The boldface numbers in the margin of the text (e.g., N1, N2, N3) refer to these notes and references.

The source of each document has been identified by the bracketed number appearing with the headings in chapters. The number, which is followed by the page numbers in the original source, refers to the numbered documents listed in the bibliography. Ellipses points have been inserted by the editors to indicate deletions of nonpertinent material from the original document. Because of these deletions, there are gaps in the numbering of the original document's footnotes.

The volume concludes with a bibliography; appendixes containing a list of acronyms and descriptions and summaries of national health insurance bills; an index of included documents; and a subject and name index.

INTRODUCTION

National health insurance has long been a major focus of debate among lawmakers and the medical and insurance communities. Recently, however, a new awareness concerning this vital issue has been dawning on the public in general. Citizens and citizen groups are starting to examine the issue of a national health insurance program more carefully because of our problems in providing decent health care to our people.

For a nation with one of the highest per capita incomes in the world, and where new heights are continually being reached in medical research and knowledge, the statistics reveal just how far behind we are in providing quality health care, compared to other industrialized nations of the world.

The latest statistics show that the United States ranks 12th in the world for infant mortality, with 16.7 deaths per 1,000 live births. Our nation ranks 10th in the world for the maternal mortality rate, with 18.8 deaths per 100,000 live births. The United States ranks 21st in the world for longevity in males, who have a life expectancy of 67.4 years. For females, the United States ranks 9th in the world, with a longevity rate of 75 years.

More and more of our money is being spent on rising health care costs, yet the statistics have not shown any major improvement during the last few years. The Department of Health, Education and Welfare recently conducted a study which showed that for fiscal year 1975, total health care costs for Americans was $122.2 billion, representing a per capita cost of $546.35. The preliminary statistics for fiscal year 1976 project health care costs will be $139.3 billion, or a per capita cost of $638. The 1976 health care bill represents a 14 percent increase over the previous year.

Compared to our neighbor Canada, which has had a national health care program for the past ten years, the United States has not fared as well. The per capita cost for health care in Canada for 1975 was $295, or roughly half of that for the United States. Only six years ago, the United States and Canada were both spending approximately 6 percent of their Gross National Products (GNP) for health care. However, between 1971 and 1975, Canada's health care costs have remained between 6.1 percent and 7 percent of its GNP, while the health care costs in the United States have climbed to 8.6 percent of the GNP in 1976. And the end is not in sight. The Congressional Budget Office estimates that by 1980 the cost of health care in the United States will be in the neighborhood of $252 billion per year.

The plight of Americans dependent on weekly paychecks, colliding with the skyrocketing impact of insurance premiums and of doctor and hospital bills, is becoming increasingly difficult. Even the poor, the disabled, and elderly, who are protected by state and federal programs, are finding they must pay more and more out of their own pockets. And even for millions of working Americans with group health insurance, serious or prolonged illness can mean more than a trip to the hospital. It can lead to the poorhouse. The simple fact is, continuing inflation is driving health care costs to prohibitive levels for more and more Americans.

Recent statistics reveal that nearly 40 million Americans have no health insurance and that millions of additional working people and their families lack the security of knowing their hospital and medical costs will be paid during layoffs and periods of unemployment. Two-thirds of those who are covered by health insurance plans still have to pay for office visits to their doctors and almost none are covered for preventive health care.

I believe that quality health care is as essential to our national well-being as sound education.

Since 1969, when I first submitted a national health insurance bill, I have felt that health care in our society must be a right—the same as the right to a decent education. Health care is more to Americans than a "good thing." We have come to see it as fundamental to the kind of life we cherish. We have been willing to invest heavily in research and education in order to bring the best possible medicine to the bedside. I believe that this same set of values is now behind the movement to make quality health care a legal right—to guarantee its availability to every member of our society.

We, as a people, place a high value on the individual—on personal opportunity to develop our abilities to the fullest—and on individual freedom. Nothing seems more tragic to us than lives filled with suffering, limited by disability, or lost too soon from illness or injury. By nature of our very humanity, the personal opportunity and individual freedom we cherish in our nation can become hollow promises in the face of injury or illness. But, if the illness or injury could have been prevented, corrected, or cured, the tragedy is compounded. For a child to grow up with needlessly twisted limbs or a clouded mind offends our most basic sense of fairness and equity. For a family to be bound in poverty by needless illness or disability is a denial of what we cherish most for our people.

The sad and tragic fact is that many citizens suffer needlessly in our nation. We have the resources and the know-how to offer adequate health care to every citizen. And since we can do it, I am convinced that we must.

Health care should be a "right" in the sense that, to the greatest practical extent, society guarantees quality health care to each citizen under law. We should make it a right individuals can claim from society, regardless of their income, jobs, residence, age, medical history, or any other factor. We should eliminate every contingency under our control that deprives any citizen of quality care.

In simple terms, health should be viewed like education—as a need too basic to depend on a person's income. A national consciousness of the parity between health and education is dawning on this country, and it would be shameful not to encourage it to the limit of our resources. In short, our national health policy, like our education policy, must express this growing belief that health care is a right. The logical step toward making health care a right is enactment of a national health insurance program. It is only a step, but a major step toward removing financial barriers and improving our health care system for every American.

To bring the facts concerning the national health insurance proposals before the general public, the R. R. Bowker Company has published this Public Documents Series volume. This publication contains the same documents and studies that are at the disposal of policy advisers in the federal government, including a comparison of the major national health insurance proposals now under consideration, economic impact of the national health insurance proposals, and other pertinent facts concerning this vital issue.

SENATOR EDWARD M. KENNEDY

PART I

ISSUES AND INITIATIVES

Introduction

Part I of this volume serves as an introduction to the public policy issues on national health insurance and addresses the following questions: What is being advocated? What is the political and economic context in which initiatives are being considered, and what are the experiences of other nations which may guide consideration of alternative programs?

The approach to a national health insurance program has yet to be defined by the United States government. The debate over the form of the first comprehensive national health insurance program centers on how such a program is to be financed, the extent of the coverage, the role, if any, of private insurance carriers as administrators, and the impact on the economy. Legislative proposals vary on each of these points and the advocates of each proposal draw upon domestic and foreign experience in other systems to advance their cases in the continuing debate. The chapters in Part I focus upon alternative proposals being considered by the Congress, their economic impact, and the health systems in use in other countries. (Detailed data on the health care industry in the United States is addressed in Part II of this volume.)

Chapter 1 sets forth four principal approaches for a national health insurance program, which have received serious attention by the Congress. National health insurance is a dynamic issue, whose handling by the policymakers is subject to a variety of influences, both political and economic. The choice of material included in this chapter has been tempered by that fact. Rather than focus on text pertaining to the details of specific bills, an effort has been made to organize the material around general themes and overall approaches.

The four specific measures summarized in Chapter 1 by their sponsors are intended to illustrate the range of alternatives under consideration. Each of these bills is described in more detail in Appendix 2 of this volume. These and future bills are subjected to amendment and modification from the day they were introduced, but they are representative of the principal approaches.

The political forces at play in the debate of a national health program are also dynamic, affected by the compromise and accommodation characteristic of a pluralistic, democratic society. Testimony drawn from various congressional hearings on national health insurance is presented which reflects a range of perspectives, articulated by health industry lobbyists and spokespersons representing segments of American society. Although the testimony sometimes addresses specific pending bills, the selection of reprinted statements includes general points of view, which will most likely persist throughout the debate.

Chapter 2 deals with the economic issue which permeates the national health insurance debate. There is widespread concern that the U.S. economy, as it stands in the mid-seventies, cannot stand the impact of a federally financed, comprehensive, mandatory health insurance system. While there are advocates of a broad cradle-to-grave program as the ''right'' of every citizen, there are those who argue that the economic costs would cause havoc on the economy. The outcome of the debate on this issue will probably depend, in large part, on the overall performance of the U.S. economy in future years. The parameters of the budgetary issue, along with an analysis of the four archtypal bills (presented in Chapter 1) are treated in Chapter 2.

Chapter 3 summarizes the current health systems in nine foreign countries. Most industrialized nations of the world have some form of national health insurance, and the success or failure of their systems should have bearing on what the United States does as it confronts health care issues. The different systems vary as to the manner in which benefits are financed, services are included, and so forth. While the summaries provided do not offer an evaluation of the programs or analyses of their applicability in the U.S. context, they do provide factual perspectives in understanding health care in other nations.

BACKGROUND ON THE ISSUES ([38], pp. 1–3)

ISSUE DEFINITION

Over the past 30 years, Congress has considered a succession of legislative proposals intended to substantially alter the role of the Federal Government in providing personal health care services to the American people. These measures are loosely classified as "national health insurance," and include specific proposals having the endorsement of widely divergent groups and representing a variety of philosophies. Each plan would give the National Government more responsibility, in varying degrees, for the financing of care, the regulation of health providers, and, in some instances, the organization of the health delivery system.

BACKGROUND AND POLICY ANALYSIS

The debate over national health insurance entails examination and consideration of several interrelated issues and problems. There is, for example, a great deal of concern about the spiraling costs of medical care and about the economic burden resulting from such costs. There is also an awareness of the difficulties that many Americans have in obtaining health services even when finances are no problem. There is much discussion of the strengths and weaknesses of the various ways of organizing the delivery of medical care and developing additional health resources to meet the demands of the public for more and higher quality health care.

Renewed interest in the subject of national health insurance has developed in a growing climate of seemingly widespread public discontent with the present status of the country's health system. Major sources of this apparent dissatisfaction are: (1) sharply escalating medical care prices, (2) incomplete and partial protection against medical care expenses paid for by private health insurance, (3) inadequate protection against the costs of care associated with catastrophic illness or disease, (4) the uneven distribution of health resources and services, and (5) the absence within the health industry of incentives to improve the efficiency and effectiveness of scarce health resources. Each of these issues is discussed briefly below.

In recent years, annual expenditures in the United States for health purposes have reached astronomical proportions: $118.5 billion in FY75 (8.3% of the gross national product), which represented per capita expenditures of $547 for every man, woman, and child in the country. The national health bill has risen so rapidly that in 6 years it has nearly doubled; in 15 years, more than quadrupled; and, in the 25 years since 1950, increased more than nine-fold.

Traditionally, expenditures for health in the United States have been financed from private sources. However, beginning in FY67 with the advent of the Medicare and Medicaid programs, the trend has been toward increased public financing of health. In FY75 this trend continued, with government outlays rising two and one-half times as fast as those from private sources (22.2% compared with 7.7%). As a result, the government (Federal, State and local) share of the Nation's health bill is now more than two-fifths; in 1966, it was about one-fourth.

Following the expiration of the Economic Stabilization Program on Apr. 30, 1974, medical care prices experienced a sharp increase. For the post-control period ending December 1974, the medical care component of the Consumer Price Index rose at an annualized rate of 14.1%. In contrast, prices for all goods and services measured by the CPI moved upward at a 12.1% annualized rate. Between May and December, the composite hospital service charges index rose at a 20.2% annualized rate, with physicians' fees increasing at a 14.4% annualized rate.

Although private health insurance has grown over the years, many Americans still have relatively little, if any, protection. In 1974, 78% of the civilian population had some form of private coverage against the cost of in-patient hospital care. While 74% of the population had private coverage for the costs in in-hospital physician visits, only 60% were insured for physician care rendered in the home or office. Some 67% had insurance for out-of-hospital drugs, but only 33% were insured for any form of nursing home care, and 16% for dental care. Although many persons not covered under private insurance plans receive assistance for their health care expenses through public programs such as Medicare, Medicaid, and the Veterans Administration, an estimated 22 million people, or 12% of the American population, have no health insurance protection under either public or private programs.

Consumer expenditures for private health insurance in 1974 totalled $28.4 billion in premiums and subscription charges, up 12% from 1973; 8% of premium income in 1974 was returned in benefits, with 14% of the premium dollar going for operating expenses and a net underwriting loss of 1.3% of premium income.

Despite the extent of participation in private plans, private health insurance met only 40% of consumer expenditures for personal health care in 1974. In the case of hospital care, private insurance covered considerably more--77% of all consumer expenditures. But only 51% of consumer costs for physicians' care and 7% of consumer expenditures for other types of care were paid for by private insurance.

Health care costs of a catastrophic nature are among the most difficult to protect against. Although slightly more than half the population under 65 is covered under a major medical or comprehensive health plan, many of these plans contain limits on maximum benefits per episode or per lifetime that prove inadequate in the face of long-term illness or the need for exotic medical treatments. Persons without major medical or comprehensive coverage are even more vulnerable to economic ruin in the face of such expenses.

The allocation and distribution of health resources in the United States are most uneven. In some communities, virtually no hospital facilities are available to serve the public. Elsewhere, there may be a surplus of beds and other scarce manpower and equipment resources. Many institutions are old and badly in need of modernization or repair. In 133 counties of the United States, there is no active physician engaged in providing care to patients. Nearly half a million Americans reside in these counties. Generally speaking, low-income inner city areas have relatively fewer physicians than the suburbs, the rural areas less than the urban, and the poorer States less than the wealthier.

The health industry is one of the largest in the Nation, and it is also believed by its critics to be one of the most inefficient. Increasing specialization and other factors have established requirements for greater and greater numbers and kinds of manpower. There is concern over the possibly excessive use of costly hospital resources to treat persons who could be equally and more economically served in other ways. There has been criticism that the methods used to pay for health care contain little in the way of incentives for the economical and efficient use of facilities, manpower, and special services.

The array of national health insurance proposals reflect divergent viewpoints as to what should be considered the priority problem areas to be resolved under a national health insurance program. Most of the bills concentrate on meeting the cost problem through improved and expanded public and/or private health insurance. Other proposals incorporate provisions that would reform and restructure the health delivery system.

Several major policy questions have been raised:

(1)   What is the proper role of the Federal Government in financing and administering health insurance?

(2)   What portion of the population should be covered under such a program?

(3)   How should the program be financed--through multiple public and private sources, or through a single channelling of funds through the public sector?

(4)   What should be the nature and scope of benefits to be insured?

(5)   To what extent should the private health insurance industry be involved in the program?

(6)   What is the potential effect of the program on the organization and delivery of health services throughout the country?

In addition to these basic questions, other pertinent issues include such matters as the reimbursement methods and cost controls to be devised for providers of health services, provisions for consumer participation and control, and the need for quality-control procedures.

The proposals before the 94th Congress include measures that would: (1) entitle all Americans to comprehensive health benefits, federally financed and administered, (2) make the Government responsible for financing health care only for the high risks in society--the aged, poor, disabled, and persons experiencing catastrophic illness costs, (3) provide federally financed economic incentives toward the purchase of private health insurance plans, or (4) mandate employers to purchase adequate private health insurance plans for employee groups. Proponents of a federalized health insurance approach maintain that the Government is not only the appropriate, but perhaps the only institution through which universal coverage and equitable financing can be achieved and leverage can be exerted upon the health system to control costs and improve quality and efficiency in services. Supporters of more decentralized approaches advocate pluralistic financing and administration of health insurance, and would seek to minimize Government intervention in the health system.

Chapter 1
The Debate: Selected Perspectives

LEGISLATIVE ADVOCATES OF NATIONAL HEALTH INSURANCE

The sponsors of four congressional measures regarding a national health insurance program present their positions in Chapter 1. The sponsors are Senator Edward Kennedy, Representative Al Ullman, Representative Richard Fulton, and Senators Russell Long and Abraham Ribicoff. These four measures were selected among dozens because they represent different approaches to national health insurance and because these particular proposals have received significant attention. They are likely to be the basic approaches to a program of national health insurance. In the simplest terms, they represent: public financing with no direct charge to the patient; mixed public and patient financing; tax incentives for individuals and employees to secure coverage; and coverage of catastrophic illnesses and medical indigents through government intervention and private initiative. The reprinted text which follows is drawn from the *Congressional Record* of the 94th Congress. Further details on each of these bills is provided in Appendix 2 of this volume.

Public Financing: Senator Edward Kennedy ([18], pp. S42–S45)

Senator Edward Kennedy is chairman of the Subcommittee on Health of the Senate Labor and Public Welfare Committee. He was a cosponsor in the 92nd Congress, along with then Senator Ralph Yarborough, of the first major national health insurance bill to receive significant attention. Since then, the Health Security Act, or the "Kennedy bill" as it is popularly known, has changed in many details. Similar companion bills were introduced in the House of Representatives by Representative Martha Griffiths in the 93rd Congress and by Representative James Corman in the 94th Congress. The basic approach in the Kennedy bill is a government run, government funded program covering the entire population with no direct payment required of the benefited patient. It would be financed by a federal payroll tax on employers and employees, a tax on earned income, and from general federal revenue. Administered by the Department of Health, Education, and Welfare, the overall program includes reorganization of health planning and health delivery systems, as well as increasing the nation's supply of health manpower and treatment facilities. Senator Kennedy's Health Security Act was supported by a majority of organized labor, consumer organizations, and a broad spectrum of independent professionals and academic experts who constituted a Committee on National Health Insurance. It is by far the most comprehensive national health insurance initiative pending. Kennedy's statement, presented on the floor of the Senate on January 15, 1975, follows.

Mr. KENNEDY. I am today introducing in this body, S. 3, the Health Security Act of 1975. In several weeks I will submit to the Senate a list of cosponsors who I believe will constitute a coalition for national health insurance sufficient to enact legislation in this Congress. I am anxious, however, that this bill be brought before the American people on this, the 1st day of the 94th Congress.

This bill proposes to establish a program that will assure health security to all Americans even as legislation of the 1930's assured them social security. The bill would cover every resident of this Nation with health insurance for the vast majority of essential health services. This insurance coverage would be provided regardless of where a person lives, where he works, his medical history, his income, the size of his family, or any other factor.

Moreover, he would pay for this insurance according to his ability to pay. Contrary to present insurance practice, he would not pay a flat premium regardless of income. He would not pay more if he or his family have a history of medical problems. He would not pay more if he has a dangerous job—or lives in a bad neighborhood.

This proposed legislation is the answer to providing good health insurance to every American on an equitable basis. It is also the answer to controlling the skyrocketing costs of health care and to assuring that quality health services are available and nearby when we need them, and to organizing health services in ways that help us to find the right doctor or the right service to fit our particular need.

This legislation, in other words, not only seeks to provide every American with enough insurance to enable him to purchase whatever health care he needs—it seeks also to assure that good health services are actually made available to each of us where and when we need them, and in a form that we can understand and use.

In accomplishing these goals the bill protects the rights of both doctor and patient—both provider and consumer of services. It assures that services are available by offering providers the resources and incentives to make them available. Indeed, the bill would usher in a new era of opportunity for provider and consumer alike.

THE LESSONS OF MEDICARE AND MEDICAID

This is the only national health insurance legislation before Congress which extends insurance coverage to all Americans on so equitable a basis, and couples this with so serious an effort to reform our health care system to assure that good services are actually available. The history of medicare and medicaid has taught us that attempts to offer health insurance on a piecemeal basis to segments of our population—without major efforts to expand and reform our health care system—result in increased inflation which robs Americans of much of the benefit of the new insurance. Medicare today covers less than half of the health care costs of the elderly, due in part to rising health care costs stimulated by passage of the medicare program. Many elderly Americans today, in fact, pay more for health care under medicare than they paid before the program was passed.

This legislation which I introduce today, the health security program, does not make this same mistake. It couples increased purchasing power through improved insurance with expanded and improved services. Moreover, it establishes budgeting mechanisms designed to bring the cost of health services in America under reasonable control.

This program will ultimately assure every American of the good health care he needs at a cost he can afford—and it will do this for less cost to our Nation than our present system, or any other pending health insurance proposal.

THE HEALTH CARE CRISIS

We are in the midst of a crisis in health care in America. There are many aspects to this crisis. But the aspect known best by every American is the crisis in costs.

THE CRISIS IN COSTS

Hospital costs have risen. Doctor bills have risen. And insurance premiums have risen to keep pace. Every American family feels the pressure of this inflation. The average wage earner works 1 month a year just to pay his health care and health insurance bills.

And there is no limit in sight. There is nothing at present built into our health care system that will assure an end to this inflation. Unless our Nation takes action to slow this progress, health care will cost Americans more and more each year.

The answer to this problem is not to cut back on benefits, to raise insurance premiums even more, or to simply offer more insurance to more Americans. The answer is to reform our health care system and bring these costs under control.

THE COST OF HEALTH SECURITY

There has been a great deal of debate about the costs of national health insurance. Opponents of the health security program which I introduce today have argued the program will cost too much—as if "cost" means what appears in the Federal budget.

Well, it is true that under the health security program more money will pass through the Federal budget than under other proposals. But, that is because the Federal Government under this proposal becomes the health insurance agent for the Nation. The billions of dollars that are currently paid to insurance companies would be paid to the Federal Government under the program. Likewise, since this program covers all essential health services without deductibles, coinsurance, or limitations, billions of dollars that Americans currently pay to doctors, hospitals, laboratories, dentists, drugstores, and other providers would also be paid to the Government.

The Government would collect these funds and serve as Americans' agent in paying these bills. Yes, the funds would flow through the Federal budget in this process. But, cost is not what appears in the Federal budget. Any American family will tell you that cost is what comes out of his paycheck—or out of his pocketbook.

Under the Health Security Act American will pay no more health insurance premiums, little or no doctor bills, little or no hospital bills, fewer dental bills, fewer drug bills, and less of many other health care costs.

Instead, Americans will pay taxes geared to their income. The average family, in the early years of the program, will pay the Government roughly the same amount for health care that it is currently paying the insurance companies, the doctors and others. The difference is, the average family will have a far better insurance policy and will get broader services for their money. Moreover, as the cost controls in the health security program take hold, the health security program will cost less than our present system would cost, even with its poorer services.

This cost saving is effected through strong budget controls over the health care system—and through such efficiencies as have been demonstrated in health maintenance organizations. A GAO study of health facility construction costs said:

Various studies have shown that prepaid group practice members compared with traditional insurance plan members (1) have substantially lower hospital use rates, generally at least 20 percent less, (2) have lower surgery rates, and (3) compare favorably on other measures of health care.

The same study indicated these organizations reduce the need for hospital beds by 20 percent.

By offering incentives to providers to form health maintenance organizations, the health security program will save millions of dollars on expensive hospital care. Organizations, through these savings, can offer good care to Americans at far lower cost than under the current system.

The fact is that the health security program will cost far less out of the workingman's paycheck and pocketbook. It will cost far less to our Nation in terms of gross expenditures for health care. These are the real costs that both the average family and this Government need to come to terms with and face up to. These are the costs that will be brought under control by the health security program.

COMMUNITIES WITHOUT DOCTORS

But the health care crisis in America is not a matter of inflation and rising costs alone. The crisis is also evident to the 5,000 American communities that have no doctor, and to patients who wait in city hospital emergency rooms 6 or 8 hours for help because they have no doctor or because they cannot reach him after hours. This legislation sets aside funds, establishes planning procedures, and creates incentives to attract health professionals and build facilities accessible to every community—and to allow imaginative professionals to offer health care in new ways designed to meet the special needs of these rural and urban communities.

THE CRISIS OF DISORGANIZATION

The crisis is also evident to patients who spend hours waiting at the doctor's office only to be sent to a laboratory for tests, then waiting at a specialist's office perhaps only to be sent to yet another laboratory for more tests, then perhaps back to the first doctor or to a hospital or a drugstore. Each stop involves waiting, some involve traveling across town and back, and some involve making appointments way in advance. All in all, it can take days or weeks to complete the process; it can cost extra dollars for repeated tests and duplicate records, and worst of all, it can discourage the elderly, the infirm, or the poor from completing the course.

And the whole process is geared more to responding to the patient for a specific disease, than to viewing the patient as a whole with the intention of preventing diseases and keeping him well.

The health security legislation encourages health professionals to reorient their efforts toward preventative care, and to offer more tightly organized forms of health care to Americans who choose it. It does this by building in long-term economic incentives to professionals who start health maintenance organizations, foundations, and other new forms of care—as well as offering the resources needed to underwrite the startup and initial operating losses of some organizations.

THE CRISIS IN QUALITY OF CARE

The crisis is evident, too, to Americans who suffer needlessly because they can not get to the skilled services or facilities they need, or because they receive less than the best quality care. The fact is that the quality of health care varies greatly in America. There is too much unnecesary or ill-advised surgery performed. There are too many missed diagnoses. It is not necessarily due to greed, to incompetence, or to carelessness. It is simply that our Nation is trying to offer sophisticated 20th century medical care through 19th century organizations.

We have created scores of new and interrelated specialties but continue to think the physician can operate on his own with no close formal relations to other physicians of other specialties. Most physicians practice solo or in groups of the same specialty. The patient medical records, like his physicians, are scattered all over town, and sometimes it is the patient who decides what specialist he needs for a given problem. It seems clear that, in this fragmented system, a patient is likely to be treated by the specialist he chooses from the perspective of that specialty. A surgeon, for example, is more likely to pursue a surgical solution to a problem than would an internist, if other approaches are possible—especially if consultation between the specialists is cumbersome and there is no real incentive to explore all possible solutions. The delay and clumsiness of referral and consultation can also lead to missed diagnoses—as can the absence of a complete medical record to the doctor who is making the diagnosis.

Moreover, we have for the most part continued to license health professionals on a once and for all basis, while medical knowledge has literally exploded during recent decades. We have not required continuing education of physicians whose training was completed decades ago—and more importantly, we have made minimal efforts to establish continuing programs to meet these physicians' particular needs and problems.

This health security program establishes national licensure and coninuing education requirements—as well as the resources for conducting these programs. It also establishes a National Quality of Care Commission in the Department of Health, Education, and Welfare to gather statistics, establish guidelines, and set standards of quality based on the advice of health professionals and it strengthens local peer review organizations to review services in their area in the light of these standards. The program further establishes referral requirements that assure a variety of treatments are considered before a patient is subjected to lengthy or costly procedures. All of these features are aimed at providing the incentives and resources to health professionals to reorganize health care in a way consistent with the enormous complexity of modern medicine—and assuring every American that he is getting the best health care possible whenever he encounters our health care system.

THE CRISIS OF INADEQUATE HEALTH INSURANCE

But perhaps the crisis in health care is most obvious to Americans whose health insurance has run out, who cannot get insurance because of their medical history, or who simply cannot afford to buy good insurance. Many Americans of all incomes have been bankrupted by health care costs which continue after their insurance runs out. They then join the ranks of Americans whose medical history makes it impossible to buy good insurance at all, and millions of other Americans of low income who are not eligible for group plans and cannot afford decent insurance.

For these Americans who have no decent insurance every illness can turn into a financial disaster. Since every penny comes out of an already limited income, they weigh every decision as to whether or not to seek a doctor—and sometimes they wait too long and suffer needless pain.

There is no way to tell how many children grow up in America with needlessly twisted limbs, dulled minds, or other handicaps simply because fear of the cost kept his parents away from the doctor for too long. There is no way to tell how many Americans suffer needless pain and even early death simply because good health costs too much. It is clear, however, that these things can and do happen all too often for a country as advanced as America.

The problem is our hopelessly fragmented health insurance system which encourages insurance companies in the name of profit to exclude Americans who need care the most, or to limit their policies to the most profitable benefits that they can market. This crazy-quilt system also frustrates the providers of care. Doctors and hospitals are faced with providing expensive services to millions of Americans whose insurance may or may not pay—knowing frequently that if the insurance does not come through there is little hope of the patient being able to pay the bill.

The provider deserves a fair fee for his services. The answer to our health insurance dilemma is not to require the provider to offer free care—it is to create an insurance system that assures that every American is covered for basic health care. If we insist that health professionals should offer help to everyone who needs it, and Americans do insist on that, then we should make sure that every American is covered by an insurance policy that will pay the provider a fair fee for his service.

Nor should insurance coverage influence the provider's method of treatment. Too often providers are encouraged to hospitalize a patient in order that insurance will cover the cost. Insurance should be comprehensive enough to cover whatever course of treatment the physician considers medically appropriate.

The health security program assures this by covering all Americans with comprehensive health insurance coverage from the Federal Government. When this legislation is passed—

No American family will be bankrupted by the cost of care;

No American will be kept from needed care for fear of the cost;

Doctors and hospitals will not be forced to write off bills or hire bill collectors. They will bill one source on one form and know in advance that they will be paid; and

Providers will be freed to offer care in the most medically accepted way, without regard to insurance coverage.

This program will free the patient to seek health care, and it will free the provider to be a physician and healer rather than an accountant.

THE FEDERAL GOVERNMENT AS INSURANCE CARRIER

The health security program makes the Federal Government the insurance agent for all Americans. This is essential to the program. It is essential in order to assure that all Americans have the same comprehensive insurance coverage at a cost they can afford. It is essential also to bringing about reform in our health care system, because this role as the insurance carrier is the lever we need to control costs and improve the way health care is organized and delivered in our Nation. I say "we," because I conceive of this lever as an instrument that providers and customers of health care alike will use to establish the incentives and set aside the resources necessary to bring about change. This national program will be shaped by the best thinking and in the best interests of both providers and consumers.

I believe that the private health insurance industry has failed us. It fails to control costs. It fails to control quality. It provides partial benefits, not comprehensive benefits; acute care, not preventive care. It ignores the poor and the medically indigent.

Despite the fact that private health insurance is a giant $20 billion industry, despite more than three decades of enormouth growth, despite massive sales of health insurance by thousands of private companies competing with each other for the health dollar of millions of citizens, health insurance benefits today pay only 40 percent of the total cost of individuals covered by private health care, leaving 60 percent to be paid out of pocket by the patient at the time of illness or as a debt thereafter, at the very time when he can least afford it.

Nearly all private health insurance is partial and limited. For most citizens, their health insurance coverage is more loophole than protection.

Too often, private carriers pay only the cost of hospital care. They force doctors and patients alike to resort to wasteful and inefficient use of hospital facilities, thereby giving further impetus to the already soaring cost of hospital care and unnecessary strains on health manpower.

Valuable hospital beds are used for routine tests and examinations which, under any rational health care system, would be conducted on an outpatient basis.

Unnecessary hospitalization and unnecesarily extended hospital care are encouraged for patients for whom any rational system would provide treatment in other, less elaborate facilities.

There is no way we can use the private health insurance industry to offer all Americans the protection they need. There is no way the Nation can use this industry as a lever to encourage change and reform in the health care system.

It is for these reasons that this legislation proposes to make the Federal Government the health insurance agent in a national program of health security.

GUARANTEES TO THE NATION'S DOCTORS
AND OTHER PROVIDERS

America's health professionals are the backbone of health care in the Nation. Without their strong and creative efforts, we will never solve any of our health care problems in America. I intend to protect the rights of America's providers, and assure them their rightful leadership role in any efforts Congress makes to improve our health care system.

The health care crisis in our Nation is as apparent to providers as to the patient. Providers are concerned with disorganization of services, with quality of care, with inadequate and fragmented insurance coverages, and with the shortage and maldistribution of health professionals and facilities. These problems frustrate providers' attempts to serve the people who need care the most. They involve them in a tangle of cumbersome referrals and cross-referrals. They occasionally have him without proper facilities and associates. And the insurance redtape frequently turns the physician into a bookkeeper.

The health security program does not aim at taking responsibility for reform away from the providers. Rather, it offers providers the incentives and resources they need to bring about the reform both they and their patients so badly need. Indeed, the program creates a lever which I hope providers will help to use responsibly to bring about change.

The program's intent is to in fact free providers of some of the constraints that limit them. For example,

The Health Security Act allows all varieties of medical practice—whether solo, fee-for-service practice; or prepaid group practice; or anything in between. It is not the program's intent to stifle any form of practice. Instead, we want to encourage all forms of practice that improve efficiency and quality.

Let me offer a series of guarantees to protect the fundamental principles important to American physicians.

The first guarantee is that the Federal Government in this Nation must not own the hospitals or employ the physicians. I do not want to build a British health care system in the United States. I do not want socialized medicine in America.

I believe in maintaining the free enterprise system in this country and in American medicine. In fact, I would like to see even more variety, and more competition in the health care system between different forms of health care. I look forward to a day when physicians can practice in solo practice, in HMO's, in medical foundations, in large groups, or in any other way that is efficient and beneficial to the patients and doctors, too. I believe we can create a uniquely American health care system that will preserve free enterprise for the doctors, and still offer your patients the financial support and adequate care they need.

The second guarantee is that Americans must not be assigned as patients to one physician or another, or to one organization or another for their health care. I want Americans to have maximum choice in this regard. Only in this way can we produce a system that is fair to doctors and patients alike.

My third guarantee is that the Federal Government must not make medical judgments or interfere in the clinical decisions between a doctor and his patient. What we must do is encourage physicians to take the actions necessary to assure Americans that they are receiving the finest possible care that American medicine can offer.

My fourth guarantee is that we must not create an overarching Federal agency in Washington, telling every area and community in this Nation exactly how they must offer health care. What we must do is to set national guidelines and standards, within which local agencies can develop the best possible health care programs for the doctors and patients in their areas.

I subscribe completely to these guarantees, and I am confident that they will be at the heart of any national health care legislation which Congress may enact.

COMPARISONS WITH OTHER NATIONS

The know-how exists to create a better organized system of health care in America. Other nations have in fact gone ahead of us in this regard. The United States is the only major industrial nation in the world without a system of national health insurance or a national health service. While none of these systems seem suited to America's values and society, they have, in fact, succeeded in moving their nations ahead of our country in many important areas.

In infant mortality, among the major industrial nations of the world, the United States today trails behind 19 other countries, including all the Scandinavian nations, most of the British Commonwealth, Japan, and East Germany. Half of these nations were behind us in the early 1950's.

We trail six other nations in the percentage of mothers who die in childbirth. In the early 1950's, we had the lowest rate of any industrial nation.

Tragically, the infant mortality rate for nonwhites in the United States is nearly twice the rate for whites. And nearly five times as many nonwhite mothers die in childbirth as whites—shameful evidence of the ineffective prenatal and postnatal care our minority groups receive.

The story told by other health indicators is equally dismal. The United States trails 27 other nations in life expectancy for males at age 45, and 11 other nations in life expectancy for females.

In fact, our Nation has the potential for higher levels of health than any of these nations because of our far vaster health care resources, and the brilliant record of American medical research. I believe the health security program is a uniquely American approach to organizing health care that will capitalize on these strengths and preserve the basic values of doctor and patient alike.

THE DEVELOPMENT OF THE HEALTH SECURITY PROGRAM

Walter Reuther, the late president of the United Auto Workers, was among the first to see that financing programs like medicare and medicaid or extensions of private health insurance could not resolve the crisis of disorganization and the spiraling cost of health care. Walter Reuther understood that the Nation needed to take a bold step forward. In November 1968, he announced the formation of the Committee of One Hundred for National Health Insurance. As he said, in establishing the mandate of the committee:

I do not propose that we borrow a national health insurance system from any other nation. No nation has a system that will meet the peculiar needs of America. I am confident that we have in America the ingenuity and the social inventiveness needed to create a system of national health insurance that will be uniquely American—one that will harmonize and make compatible the best features of the present system, with maximum freedom of choice, within the economic framework and social structure of a national health insurance system.

Joining Walter Reuther on that committee were Dr. Michael E. deBakey, president of Baylor College of Medicine; Mrs. Mary Lasker, president of the Albert and Mary Lasker Foundation; Mr. Whitney M. Young, Jr., executive director of the National Urban League; and other outstanding citizens from the fields of medicine, public health, industry, agriculture, labor, education, the social services, youth, civil rights, religious organizations, and consumer groups. I have had the honor of serving on that committee, along with my former Senate colleagues, Ralph Yarborough, John Sherman Cooper, and William Saxbe.

In its efforts over the past 4 years, the committee has worked to develop a sound program for improving the organization, financing and delivery of health services to the American people. The committee's deliberations were based upon the premise that progress toward a more rational health system should be orderly and evolutionary. The members of the committee felt that a better system of health care for America should rest upon the positive motivations and interests of both consumers and providers of health services. They believed that no system could succeed if it were imposed by fiat through rigid legislation and administrative regulations.

Throughout its deliberations, the committee has been guided by the work of its distinguished technical subcommittee, chaired by Dr. I. S. Falk, professor emeritus of public health of Yale University and the most eminent authority in the field of health economics in the Nation. The committee consulted extensively with representatives of professional associations, consumer organizations, labor unions, business groups, and many other interested organizations. The health security program is the result of these efforts, and it gives careful consideration to the recommendations of all of these groups.

In August 1970, Senators Cooper, Saxbe, Yarborough, and I, together with 11 other Senators, introduced the original version of the health security program as S. 4297 in the 91st Congress.

At the time the bill was originally introduced, Congresswoman Martha Griffiths of Michigan had already introduced legislation in the House of Representatives to create a national health insurance program similar in overall concept to the health security program, and her bill had received the strong endorsement of the AFL–CIO, under the leadership of President George Meany.

These two bills were combined into a strong new Health Security Act of 1971, which was introduced in the 92d Congress as S. 3 and H.R. 22.

THE HEALTH SECURITY ACT OF 1975

The revised Health Security Act of 1975 is the product of this long and arduous process of refinement. Improvements have been made in the areas of care in the home. Other refinements increase the equity of the tax support for the program by increasing the limit on the wage base for the social security tax from $15,000 to $20,000. Essentially, however, this new bill retains the basic principles of the bill first introduced in the 92d Congress.

The 94th Congress faces the greatest need in decades for a program of comprehensive national health insurance. Inflation is driving health care costs to prohibitive levels for more and more Americans, and unemployment will leave millions more without health insurance coverage.

The health security program, S. 3, goes further than any other proposal to control health care costs and assure every American family the health care it needs as a matter of right. Since its design by the Committee of One Hundred, health security has become the standard by which all national health insurance proposals are judged. The proposal has been further improved for the 94th Congress by the Committee for National Health Insurance and the leadership of America's trade union movement.

Health security's principles can unite the Nation better than any other bill. The concept of comprehensive care for all Americans under social security as a matter of right enjoys the broadest popular support of any national health insurance proposal.

I believe it is imperative that we begin our discussion of national health insurance in the 94th Congress with the high standard set by health security. During the last Congress, I introduced a bill designed to implement as much of the health security program as was possible in the 93d Congress. I believe the 94th Congress can do much more, and I hope my colleagues will join me in supporting health security as their legislative goal.

Mixed Public and Private Programs: Representative Al Ullman ([17], pp. H40–H42)

Representative Al Ullman is chairman of the House Ways and Means Committee. His proposal of a national insurance system, introduced first in the 92nd Congress and resubmitted subsequently with modifications, contains the element of "user financing." The proposal, as presented in the 94th Congress, involves three elements: (1) a federally funded insurance plan for the aged, low-income persons, and the medically indigent, to be administered by private insurance carriers under federal contract; (2) a program whereby employers would be required to offer specified, minimum private health insurance coverage to their employees and their families; (3) a plan for coverage of any individual wishing to finance his or her participation. The Ullman bill was supported by the American Hospital Association. Representative Ullman's statement, presented on the floor of the House of Representatives on January 14, 1975, when he introduced his bill, follows.

Mr. ULLMAN. Mr. Speaker, I am submitting to the Congress today legislation titled the "National Health Care Services Reorganization and Financing Act." Its aim is to create a better health-care system for the Nation, and it is a new version of a bill I originally introduced in the 92d Congress. The basic principles and philosophy of the bills are identical. The objectives—to reorient our system of health delivery and to bring into being a more equitable system of financing health services for all the population—remain unchanged.

In recent years, the imperatives and pressures for the enactment of such a measure have increased. Economic stringencies and governmental controls over the health-care industry, however temporary, further revealed the gaps and inequities in the present system. For the sake of the immediate future and for generations to come, these serious problems must not be left unattended. I am personally persuaded, as a result of hearings on national health insurance in the Ways and Means Committee during the last two Congresses, and after months of weighing the provisions and implications of my own proposal, that the Congress can no longer postpone major decisions to assure the availability of health services to all persons in the United States.

I continue to regard my proposal, as I would any legislative proposal, to be an invitation to comment and thought, providing a direction and philosophy I firmly believe to be right. I trust that it will draw the attention and interest of the Congress, the health industry, and the general public. It contains an important new concept, an administrative entity known as the health care corporation or HCC. The HCC, as the coordinator of community health resources, represents an exciting new concept of responsible localism. As a member of the Advisory Commission on Intergovernmental Relations, I have been deeply concerned with the strengthening of State and local resources in the administration of Federal programs.

In my opinion, the National Health Care Services Reorganization and Financing Act offers the most realistic solution to health care delivery, regulation and financing among the dozen or so that have been proposed. It is implementable now because the structure it defines is based on existing resources but with the guidelines and incentives for putting an end to the present fragmentation and duplication of services, their uneven distribution, and their lack of accessibility in many rural and urban areas. It provides for considerable expansion of outpatient services and their broader utilization.

None of the other proposals for national health insurance could fulfill this potential. Either they are attempts to resolve the serious problems of health services in a piecemeal fashion, or they would create a monolithic, bureaucratic system which in the end would be prohibitive in cost. Most do not interweave provisions for financing health care with incentives for restructuring the delivery of services. And some, worse still, would only perpetuate existing inadequacies and infuse more money into outmoded mechanisms.

We need desperately to pull it all together, to approach the development of a better health system anew, to resolve the problems of financing and delivery of services interrelatedly. If we fail to bring about this convergence, we will fail to better serve the public interest, and I believe that in the long run we will have wasted human, financial, and material resources.

I am impressed not only with mounting public concern over the cost and delivery of health services, but also with the sincere concern of health professionals and professional organizations. Many are striving for a more effective health services delivery system even though changes and controls would unquestionably impose complications on their activities.

The American Hospital Association has been most helpful in the realistic establishment of goals, concepts and methods, and has provided technical staff assistance in designing the total concept of a coordinated, equitably financed system.

The bill calls for the consolidation of the major Federal health programs and the incorporation of medicare and medicaid within a program of national health insurance. It also provides for a new Department of Health, to be headed by a Secretary for Health responsible to the President. In addition, it includes greater detail and necessary technical information for changes in the financing of health services. It emphasizes the responsibility of the individual for his own health, but provides the framework for better health care and financing for everyone.

Certain principles of the bill I am introducing today deserve special mention, beginning with the recognition of health care as an inherent right of every person. Others, without order of priority, include the following:

Health services and the delivery system, as well as its financing, must be pluralistic, inclusive of both private and public sectors of the health field, and must be predicated on carefully designed Federal incentives and subsidies to assist and assure the cooperation of the various components of the health industry;

The rights of every individual to choose among providers of health services and underwriters of health insurance benefits must be preserved;

The same scope of comprehensive health benefits must be available to all;

The same high level of quality of care must be available to all; and

The Federal Government must assume responsibility for the cost of health care for first, the nonworking poor, second, the elderly, and third, to the extent needed to assure their capability to purchase services, the working poor, but with assurances that the program does not create disincentives to productive employment.

Inherent in each of these principles, whether in terms of use of health services or payment for them, is the principle that every individual has a responsibility for the maintenance of his own health and, to the extent that he is able, to contribute to his share of the cost of care. There are numerous corollary principles, which I shall not describe here, such as those relating to the dignity of the individual, and the relationship of health and the environment.

The health care corporation which would be the coordinating unit of the system at the local level would provide a geographically based system for synthesizing and coordinating local health resources. These corporations would be built upon the existing delivery system, but with mandatory reorganization and reorientation to meet local needs, under the supervision of newly mandated State health commissions.

HCC's would be organized in a variety of ways, determined largely by community needs, custom, and precedent. They would grow out of the community, providing for citizen or consumer representation on their governing boards and being accountable to the public. It is expected that they would primarily be organized by health care providers—hospitals, doctors, dentists, as well as nursing homes and community health organizations—working with the community to establish a more effective, coordinated system.

Every HCC would have to provide, within a State plan administered by the State health commission and approved by the Secretary of the Department of Health, a comprehensive benefit program for all persons in its service area who wished to register. After the first 5 years of operation, it would be required to offer as an option to its registrants, services on a capitation basis of payment, or so much per person per year, a method of payment that requires providers of service to accept a direct responsibility for utilization and cost of services. Among its responsibilities, the HCC would be charged with encouraging the development and use of outpatient services, and for seeing that the most appropriate service would be provided for patients in the most effective, least costly way.

Every employer would be required to purchase for his employees and their families a comprehensive level of benefits as prescribed in the legislation and within regulations issued by the Secretary of Health, paying at least 75 percent of the premium costs. The employees would pay a maximum of 25 percent. For individuals and their families who registered with HCC's, the Federal Government would contribute 10 percent of premium costs To assist the self-employed and small employers in meeting premium payments, my proposal also includes a special tax credit mechanism.

Newly formed independent State health commissions, appointed by State Governors, would approve HCC's for operation and approve charges for service. These same commissions would develop State health plans subject to the approval of the Secretary; control the rates charged by health care providers and health insurance carriers; issue certificates of need and approve health service areas; and review and approve provider budgets. Thus State government would play a central role in the national program, obviating a large bureaucratic operation in Washington.

I should like to emphasize that the legislation provides for multiple sources of financing to assure a basic level of health care benefits for all persons, including catastrophic health insurance benefits. For persons unable to pay, in part or in full, the Federal Government would purchase the specified level of coverage established for all persons through general Federal revenues, with individual contributions scaled inversely to income levels and family size. Health services to the aged would continue to be financed through a combination of the social security tax mechanism and general Federal revenues. Since parts A and B of the medicare program would be merged, premium contributions by individuals for part B would be eliminated. Payroll financing, therefore, would be restricted approximately to its present levels, with additional costs paid through general Federal revenues.

In sum, this bill would meet the following objectives, upon a 5-year implementation of the national program following congressional enactment:

All persons, regardless of age or income, would be entitled to the same broad package of benefits:

Everyone would be insured against the cost of catastrophic illness;

The Federal Government would pay for the health care costs of the poor and the elderly, and part of the costs for all others;

Special benefits for children up to age 12 would be provided—medical, dental, and eye care;

Outpatient care would be emphasized in order to relieve the burden of unnecessary use of costly inpatient care facilities;

Through the capitation method of payment for care, incentives for keeping costs down would be broadly introduced at the community level;

Health education programs, in support of the principle that the individual has a responsibility for the maintenance of his own health, would be available through health care corporations in every geographic service area in the national effort to raise health levels, increase knowledge about nutrition, and bring better understanding of the management of illness in the family.

How such a national program would affect American families is, of course, the most important question. Any legislative proposal can itemize what its author believes needs to be done, but this hardly assures that what is envisioned can take place. However, I believe that this legislation, since its objectives are based on existing resources and on developments in the delivery of health services already in the making, is totally realistic. Health care providers in recent decades have increasingly concerned themselves with how to contain costs yet at the same time keep pace with the numerous advances of medical science and strive for an increasing volume of services of higher quality. They have struggled, against steep odds, and without a coordinated national effort, to plan sensibly so that our legacy to coming generations will neither be a system inadequate to the needs nor one so uncoordinated as to be costly beyond bounds.

From the public's point of view there also are many problems to be faced, the foremost being the increasing cost of health care and the inaccessibility for many to needed services. The public generally finds it anomalous that in a Nation founded on democratic ideals and in which resources are plentiful, there continue to be serious gaps in health care. The public seeks a stronger voice in how health services should be provided. However, it is fair to say, recognizing the lack of a coordinated system is in large part to blame, that public awareness of health is far less than it could be and that a sizable educational program is needed if individuals are to avail themselves of health services in the most timely, effective, and consequently, most economical way. We have by no means put to use all of the health knowledge that is at hand, nor can we claim to have practiced what we know.

To conclude, I wish again to acknowledge the complexity of my proposal, but also to say that it must necessarily be so, for there is no simple solution to the Nation's health problems. Then I would like to draw attention to the legislation's provisions, following enactment, for a 5-year period for the development of State plans, the establishment of HCC's, and the establishment of a department of health. This would be a period of development and experimentation with the various organizational forms of health care corporations, time for the combining of parts A and B of medicare and the incorporation at the Federal level of medicaid.

The legislation I propose would coordinated our health services in a way that would bring improved health care for all Its aim, immediate as well as long range, is the containment of health care costs and the removal of the real possibility that a family's resources can be totally depleted as a result of the cost of serious illness.

I believe that this bill is the most flexible of all of the major health proposals that you will be considering this session. I trust that its flexibility will attract your interest and support, and, above all, your participation in its development.

Tax Incentives for Health Coverage: Representative Richard Fulton ([19], pp. H3117–H3118)

Representative Richard Fulton serves on the House Ways and Means Committee. His proposed Comprehensive Health Care Insurance Act of 1975 was introduced in the 94th Congress with the endorsement of the American Medical Association. His plan for a national health insurance would give tax credits to participating employers and individuals for participation in a program consisting of: (1) employee coverage in which employers would offer specified private health insurance protection to their employees; (2) continued coverage under employee plans if the individual receives unemployment benefits; (3) access to coverage by the self-employed and nonemployed on a voluntary basis. Representative Fulton's statement, presented on the floor of the House of Representatives on April 22, 1975, follows.

Mr. FULTON. Mr. Speaker, one of the more current cliches has it that nothing is so inevitable as an idea whose time has come. People are particularly prone these days to apply this bromide to national health insurance—an idea whose time has come.

But ideas are like babies: a good deal happens between the moment of conception and the child's readiness to enter this troubled world.

Off and on, the Government and the Nation have been considering, rejecting, and shelving the idea of national health insurance since the days of Presidents Roosevelt and Truman.

During the past decade, the Congress has detected a fetal heartbeat. It has now reached the point where the labor pains are coming more frequently and we are about to put the water on to boil, preparatory to our role as legislative midwives.

I must confess to occasional impatience during these long, arduous years of deliberation, debate, and copious testimony before the responsible congressional committees. It has seemed, at times, as if nothing more could be said, much less should be said.

The bound record of the testimony that has been given before the Ways and Means Committee, for example, is exhaustive.

And yet this long, drawn-out process has been of tremendous value.

We are now at the point where almost all of us agree that national health insurance is needed. We have resisted the proposition—less prevalent these days than it used to be—that any form of national health insurance would be better than what we have today.

For it is not true, Mr. Speaker, our present system of health care delivery brings more high quality medical care to more people than any system in any other nation in the history of the world. As Bert Seidman of the AFL–CIO has observed, in its scientific and clinical aspects, medicine in America "has no peer."

The system is nonetheless flawed. It falls short in such areas as manpower shortages and maldistribution; cost that prices it beyond the means of many; ease of access for many more of our citizens; and so on.

Aware of these problems, we have been frequently tempted to legislate the needed reforms in one fell swoop. I am glad we have resisted that temptation, for it boils down to this:

The right kind of NHI can accomplish a world of good. The wrong kind can do irreparable damage.

It seems to me that certain principles are essential to any law we pass if we are to make NHI a success in the delivery of quality care to everyone—rich, poor or middle-income—without bankrupting the Nation.

First, the benefits of any plan must be comprehensive. They must include care inside the hospital or out of it; skilled nursing facilities; emergency and out-patient services; across-the-board medical care, whether it be diagnostic, therapeutic or preventive; home health services; full dental care for children and emergency dental care for everyone; ambulance services; institutional and out-patient psychiatric care; well-baby care; immunizations; X-ray, laboratory and anesthesiology services.

Second, a responsible NHI bill must be comprehensive in its coverage. There are still Americans who do not receive adequate medical care because they cannot pay for it.

And there are still American families going bankrupt because a father, a mother or a child is unfortunate enough to undergo a long-time, expensive illness. This must be stopped, and the sooner the better.

Third, we must build on the very diversity of our present system, which I view as its great strength, not its weakness. Americans receive their health and medical care through a variety of delivery methods: private practitioners, closed panel clinics, HMOs, and so forth.

No single method of delivering care can fit every community, every circumstance, every patient's need. The one-size-fits-all approach can never work in a nation so large for a population whose requirements differ so vastly.

Fourth, we must build on the structure of group health insurance which is to-day—right now—providing sound basic coverage for a vast majority of Americans at no cost to the Government. It is easier to remedy whatever deficiencies exist in this mechanism than to junk it in favor of a new and elaborate Government structure that would have to be created from scratch. I say it is easier, Mr. Speaker. It would also be considerably less traumatic for Americans to remain with a familiar system than to adjust to a new program designed and operated by the Federal Government.

According to Consumers Union, it would "take years" for any new Federal HNI agency—numbering an estimated 70,000 employees—to achieve full, efficient operation. Furthermore, there is no evidence that such an agency would be one whit more efficient than private insurers in the handling of claims.

The fifth principle we must incorporate into any national health insurance law is particularly timely at this point in our history:

Can we afford the plan we devise?

Members may reply that we must afford it because action by the Government is so clearly called for; and because without that action we will not rectify the inadequacies of the present system.

I am completely sympathetic to those who call for action. If I were not, I would not be introducing the bill I am describing for you today. But I remind my friends that unemployment is frighteningly high, inflation remains unchecked, the economy is in the doldrums, a large deficit in the budget is staring us in the face, and the Congress has been sufficiently alarmed to cut taxes by $22.8 billion.

So I say that whether or not we can afford the actions we take in the creation of an NHI program is very much to the point.

Democrats and Republicans alike are fond of expressing their allegiance to the maxim attributed to Abraham Lincoln. He held, as all of us recall, that it was the duty of government to do for the people what the people could not, or could not do so well, for themselves.

The majority of Americans can and do manage to afford the purchase of comprehensive health insurance from private insurers. Good for them. These are not the people who are at the heart of our concern.

Which brings us to the concept of need. It is essential, in my view, that we use our Federal resources to help those who need help the most. The measure I am introducing would do just that: it would focus on those with the greatest need.

Now, Mr. Speaker, bearing those five principles in mind, I invite my colleagues to test the proposal I am introducing against the yardsticks of comprehensive benefits, comprehensive coverage of our population, diversity in the means through which care would be provided, use of the present system to the degree that this is desirable, and the affordability of what we propose to do. . . .

I alluded earlier in my remarks to the mass of testimony given before the Ways and Means Committee and the continuing scrutiny and debate which has occupied Congress over the years in its considerations of national health insurance.

Members may recall that I have been a principal sponsor of an NHI measure called medicredit, which embodied the thinking of the Nation's physicians.

The bill I introduce today is one that again reflects the thinking of the Nation's doctors. But it is substantively different from medicredit, one of whose main provisions relied heavily on the use of tax credits, applied on a sliding scale, to help our citizens defray the costs of buying their own health insurance.

The tax credit provision of the bill I introduce today is, by comparison, very modest. So this is not simply a tinkered-with version of medicredit. On the other hand: it represents the evolution of the doctors' thinking on this complex subject; and it demonstrates that the continuing process of discussion and debate has influenced the doctors as, indeed, it has influenced the thinking of Congress.

Covering Catastrophic Illnesses: Senators Russell Long and Abraham Ribicoff ([20], pp. S17449–S17451, S17453–S17457)

Senator Russell Long is chairman of the Senate Finance Committee and Senator Abraham Ribicoff was the Secretary of Health, Education, and Welfare under President John F. Kennedy. During the 94th Congress, they introduced the Catastrophic Health Insurance and Medical Assistance Reform Act of 1975 (a companion bill was introduced in the House of Representatives by Representative Joe Waggoner). Their measure was to provide benefits to persons who incurred unusually large health expenses or whose economic status made health service fees a burden. Administration of the program would be similar to that of the Medicare program and would be supervised by the Department of Health, Education, and Welfare. Private health insurance carriers and plans would be subjected to federal certification. Provisions for employer tax contribution and for state and local participation would account for about one half of the costs involved; the remainder would be borne by general federal revenue. When this bill was introduced, Senator Long spoke first and then Senator Ribicoff. Their statements, presented on the floor of the Senate on October 3, 1975, follow.

Mr. LONG . . . . I am proud to introduce today proposed legislation which we believe represents a major step forward toward the provision of adequate protection against the high costs of health care. This bill represents a middle-of-the-road bipartisan approach toward meeting the health care financing needs of the American people.

The Catastrophic Health Insurance and Medical Assistance Reform Act of 1975 is designed to accomplish three objectives. First, to develop a means of assuring all Americans that they will not be bankrupted by the devastating effects of serious illness; second, to eliminate the widespread inequities of the medicaid program by replacing it with a program providing equal benefits to all Americans at the lower end of the income scale; and third, the provisions of the bill would assure the actual availability of adequate basic private health insurance to those many millions of hard-working, middle-income Americans as a floor of protection above which they would be covered by catastrophic health insurance.

The thrust of the bill is to assign a large area of responsibility to the private health insurance industry of this country, establishing benchmarks against which the success of their efforts will be measured. Obviously, to the extent private health insurance effectively meets the basic needs of a large segment of our population, further expansion of governmental programs would not be necessary.

The present bill, while essentially similar to S. 2513, which we introduced in the last Congress, does have some significant changes which we believe make a good bill even better. Perhaps the most important change is to include a role for the private health insurance sector in the provision of catastrophic health insurance—where they can provide those benefits on a basis identical with those of the Government catastrophic health insurance plan.

To those of us who have worked with medicare, medicaid, and the other Federal health care financing programs, it has become quite clear that there are limits to the Government's administrative capacity. It seemed to us rather foolhardy to pile upon that limited capacity further responsibility which could not be met effectively. Therefore, we have consciously chosen an approach which, in the areas of catastrophic health insurance and basic private health insurance, builds upon the strengths of the private sector while correcting weaknesses.

The Long-Ribicoff health insurance proposal has three essential parts. The proposal is incremental—that is, each part is phased in over a period of time in the interest of administrative efficiency and manageable new costs.

The first part consists of catastrophic insurance coverage for all Americans. Each year hundreds of thousands of Americans are stricken by catastrophic illnesses or accidents. In addition to suffering the terrible physical consequences of these events, these individuals and their families also suffer the often devastating financial effects of these illnesses.

The bill would establish a catastrophic health insurance program which would cover all American citizens after they had incurred medical expenses of $2,000 or been hospitalized for 60 days. The benefits covered under the program would be the same as those covered under the medicare program without any upper limits on hospital days. It is this catastrophic portion of the bill that has been modified in a most significant fashion—called for a totally Federal public catastrophic health insurance program. This year's bill provides an option. An employer can either choose to cover his employees for catastrophic costs through private health insurance, or, alternatively, he can choose to obtain such coverage through the Federal program. Our expectation is that the vast majority of employers would choose to obtain such coverage through private health insurers. The Federal program would serve primarily to insure those who are not in a permanent employment situation. Under the bill, the private catastrophic program would have to be fully as comprehensive as the public plan.

The public catastrophic program would be administered by the Social Security Administration using carriers and intermediaries as in the present medicare program. Private catastrophic programs would, of course, be administered by the private insurance companies.

The catastrophic program would be financed through a 1-percent payroll tax on employers. There would be no tax on employees. Employers who chose the private insurance option would subtract from their 1-percent payroll tax liability approved premiums paid for private catastrophic insurance policies. In addition, all employers would receive a 50-percent tax credit—or rebate—against their overall 1-percent payroll tax liability. This would be in lieu of a deduction for catastrophic health insurance premiums and would tend to equalize treatment between small employers and large employers.

The total cost of the catastrophic illness plan including both Federal costs and the costs of private catastrophic insurance purchased by employers, is estimated at $3.6 billion in the first full year of operation. The catastrophic provision would take effect January 1, 1977, so that the legislation would have no budgetary impact at all until the last half of fiscal 1977, thus, in fiscal year 1977 the total costs of the program would be about $1 billion.

Aside from the addition of the private insurance option, there are two other changes in the catastrophic program which I should mention briefly. First, under this year's proposal, all citizens would be covered, rather than just those covered under social security, as in last year's bill. Second, under the new bill, patients would not be liable for any co-insurance payments after meeting the deductible amounts, in contrast to the 20-percent coinsurance liability in last year's bill.

The second part of the bill consists of an entirely new basic health benefits program for low-income individuals and families. While most middle-income families can afford and can obtain reasonably adequate private health insurance coverage toward the costs of their first 60 days of hospitalization and first $2,000 of medical expenses, many millions of low-income individuals and families cannot afford or do not have such basic private health insurance protection available to them.

The present Federal-State program providing health benefits to the poor—medicaid—does not generally cover low-income workers who are not on welfare. It is basically provided only to welfare families and, even then, benefit and eligibility levels vary substantially and significantly from State to State. In most States medicaid is limited to poor aged, blind, and disabled persons or fatherless families.

Because of economic difficulties, several States have, and others are considering, cutbacks in already inadequate medicaid programs.

Today, for example, in one State a disabled person with $1,800 annual income might not be eligible for medicaid whereas, in another State, he would be. Further, that same disabled person might be covered for only 15 days of hospitalization under medicaid in one State while, in another, he would be eligible for unlimited hospitalization. Now, that just does not make sense, does it?

Aside from those obvious inequities in treatment of the poor, there is another inequity developing with implementation of the supplemental security income plan for aged, blind, and disabled persons, where thousands of people in a State would be eligible for medicaid and other thousands in the same State, and with the same income, would not. An in no State is medicaid coverage available to a hard-working couple or small intact family with low income.

The new program which we propose would provide, effective July 1, 1977, basic health benefits coverage with uniform national eligibility standards for all low-income individuals and families, whether they are on welfare or working. It would thereby eliminate the major inequities in the current medicaid program. It would be administered by the Social Security Administration.

Coverage under the new program would be available to all individuals and families with annual incomes at or below the following levels: First, an individual with income at or under $2,400; second, a two-person family with income at or under $3,600; and third, a family of four with an income at or under $4,800. For each family member above the first four, the eligibility limit is increased by $400. In addition, families with incomes slightly above the eligibility levels would be eligible for benefits if their medical expenses reduced their income to these levels. For example, a family of four with an income of $5,200 would become eligible after they had expended $400 for medical expenses, including any health insurance premiums. Of course, no person presently eligible for medicaid would lose entitlement to benefits because of the new program.

The basic benefits provided under the low-income plan are designed to mesh with the deductibles under the catastrophic program.

The benefits covered by the plan would include 60 days of hospital care and all medically necessary physicians' services, laboratory and X-ray services, home health services and care in skilled nursing homes and intermediate care facilities. A copayment of $3 would be required on patient-initiated services, such as visits to a doctor's office, but copayments could not exceed $30 per individual or family during a year. These copayments would not apply to well-baby care or with respect to family planning services.

The plan would also afford catastrophic insurance coverage to those low-income families who are not covered under the catastrophic plan.

States would be free to provide additional benefits—such as drugs and dental services—with the Federal Government assuming one-half of the cost.

For millions of older Americans with low incomes, the Long-Ribicoff bill would pick up their part B medicare premiums—presently $6.70 per month—as well as paying their medicare deductibles and coinsurance amounts. In addition, it would provide them with all medically necessary hospital, skilled nursing facility, and intermediate care facility services. Home health care would also be available without limitation.

Mr. President, the low-income plan would not only help the poor, it would aid hospitals, physicians, and State governments. With respect to hospitals, the program would virtually eliminate their problems with bad debts. With respect to physicians, the program would call for reimbursement at medicare levels—rather than at the often substandard medicaid rates. With respect to State governments, the plan would afford very substantial fiscal relief. States would make a fixed contribution toward the cost of the low-income plan based upon each State's level of spending for medicaid and general assistance health care in the year prior to the effective date of the plan, July 1, 1977. For example, if a State spent $100 million of its own funds under medicaid for the types of care covered under the new low-income plan, it would contribute that $100 million to the low-income fund during the first and in each succeeding year. Additionally, the State would contribute 50 percent of the estimated amount of State and local expenditures in the year before the low-income plan effective date for health care services to people ineligibile for medicaid, but who would be eligible for those types of services under the new low-income plan.

The estimated annual cost of the low-income plan is $5.3 billion in general revenues above present Federal-State expenditures for medicaid.

Mr. President, the third part of our bill consists of a new and voluntary certification program for private basic health insurance policies. With this new program, private insurers could, of their own volition, submit any or all of their basic health insurance policies to the Secretary for certification. This certification would be based upon certain minimum criteria specified in the bill relating to adequacy of coverage, ratio of benefits paid to premium income, and conditions of eligibility.

Insurers could advertise the certification in promoting their policies. Three years after enactment of this bill, carriers and intermediaries under the medicare program would be expected to offer one or more certified policies to the general public in areas where they sold policies.

In addition, the bill contains provisions designed to facilitate arrangements whereby basic health insurance policies meeting minimum standards could be offered through private insurance "pools" established by groups of private insurers.

The bill also directs the Secretary of Health, Education, and Welfare to report to Congress after 3 years as to the extent to which private health insurance meeting the criteria is actually and generally available in each State.

In any area of the country where certified basic health insurance was not generally and actually available to the entire population, the Secretary is also authorized to make such coverage available at cost through social security.

Mr. President, this bill does not constitute a "be all—endall" approach, but it does provide an opportunity to provide significant assistance to many millions by closing major gaps in the financing of necessary health care. We believe that careful building and improving upon the present system through this major initiative is the only feasible alternative to the potentially disruptive and bankrupting effects involved in proposals which would radically alter and almost scrap existing structures and mechanisms. The variables are too uncontrollable and the chances of error too great for us to risk the magnitude of any mistakes in the total takeover approach. What Senator RIBICOFF and I propose to do is what we know needs to be done and can be done.

We firmly believe that the thrust of the catastrophic health insurance and the Medical Assistance Reform Act is the direction in which we should proceed. Both Senator RIBICOFF and I expect that our proposal will certainly benefit from additional constructive efforts during the course of legislative consideration.

Mr. President, I believe that those who have joined in cosponsoring this measure with us have made a significant and impressive contribution. These are Senators who, through the years, have made their suggestions and sponsored their own bills, indicating ways that they believed we could solve the problem of providing better health care for America. Having worked in this area, we were proud that some of them saw fit to join our efforts and coalesce on a bill which we believe the Senate could pass.

We are extremely proud to have them in this effort. We believe that by moving in this fashion, trying to take the suggestions of each Senator on the Finance Committee as well as each Senator who has worked in this area through the years up to this point, we can contribute to shaping a bill in the best national interests and a bill that can be passed and one which we believe will serve the Nation.

Mr. President, I now send the Catastrophic Health Insurance and Medical Assistance Reform Act to the desk. . . .

Mr. RIBICOFF. Mr. President, today I join with the distinguished chairman of the Senate Finance Committee (Mr. LONG) in introducing the Catastrophic Health Insurance and Medical Assistance Reform Act of 1975.

It was almost 2 years ago to the day that we first presented our health care concept to the Senate. We felt at that time, and still feel, that our proposal is realistic, workable and meets the most important health care needs in America at a cost which the American people can afford.

In the last few years the economic climate of America has changed and the attitude of most Americans toward government has undergone an evolution. We are in the midst of a recession which has severely curtailed the ability of our Government to implement new and expensive programs, however meritorious.

Moreover, Congress and the American people are beginning to doubt the ability of Government to provide the services which have been promised under law. And with good reason. It takes no expert to see that the medicare system—which covers little over 20 million people—is awash with problems ranging from reimbursement to cost and quality controls, to a host of other issues. Other programs such as SSI, medicaid, welfare, and food stamps are also beset with bureaucratic problems.

All of this experience dictates one thing—caution. We must not move ahead faster than we are able to. Let us meet the most pressing health needs first, building upon the experience we have had in medicare and medicaid. Building on our successes. Learning from our failures. Expanding the program only as fast as we are actually able to implement it.

Although we do not have the capacity to administer a full cradle-to-grave national health insurance proposal at this time, there are still a number of problems which must be met now.

For more and more Americans health care is a problem. We do not have to be poor to be staggered by health costs. Almost anyone can find his life savings depleted, his house sold out from under him, educational opportunities for his children lost—all because of major illness or injury.

Low-income individuals are hurt most of all, but middle-class Americans can be financially destroyed almost as easily.

It is easy to describe the problems facing us in health care but it is much more difficult to propose an adequate and workable solution.

In developing our proposal we have consulted with every sector of the health care field—consumers, physicians, insurers, hospitals, administrators, labor leaders, and others. All of them have contributed and all of them have had constructive suggestions. The interest on health care is evidenced by the many health insurance proposals now pending before Congress.

We believe our bill best meets the needs of the American people and provides a workable and financially realistic mechanism. It is not perfect. No proposal is. In the weeks and months ahead we look forward to receiving constructive ideas to improve our proposal.

The Long-Ribicoff bill represents an approach which has attracted broad bipartisan support. The three parts of the proposal—catastrophic, low income, and private health insurance standards—are all designed to bring about availability, equity and adequacy of insurance coverage through building upon the existing system.

The proposal is incremental—that is, each part is phased in over a period of time in the interest of administrative efficiency and manageable new costs rather than trying to do everything at once and thereby overwhelming the administrative system.

The bill also recognizes the reality of our present economic situation. The legislation would have no budgetary impact until the last half of fiscal 1977 when the catastrophic portion of the bill takes effect. When fully effective the Long-Ribicoff bill will cost approximately $9 billion above existing law.

The bulk of these funds—more than $5 billion—goes toward relieving States of ever-increasing medicaid expenditures. At a time when States are facing severe fiscal burdens, the provisions of this bill will hold States harmless against increasing medicaid costs—and help reduce their fiscal burdens.

The bill is divided into three basic sections.

Title I protects all Americans against the large or catastrophic costs associated with prolonged illness, disease or injury. In effect, it places a ceiling on almost every American family's medical costs. We have an obligation to assure that no one goes into bankruptcy because of prolonged illness or injury. Under this title a family's medical costs would be assumed by the social security fund once it had incurred 60 days of hospital costs and/or $2,000 of medical bills. An employer would have the option to buy a catastrophic plan in the private sector.

Title II establishes a medical assistance plan with a uniform national program of medical benefits for low-income persons. It replaces the costly, inefficient, and inadequate Federal-State medicaid programs and provides health protection for 34 million Americans, including 12 million working poor persons who were ineligible for medicaid. The coverage of this plan would provide basic benefits to mesh with the catastrophic program. That is, this program would pay for the first $2,000 and 60 days of hospital and the catastrophic plan would assume costs above those limits. By requiring the States to pay only what they paid for medicaid in the year prior to enactment, States will save millions of dollars. Without this bill their costs would have continued to climb.

Title III of this bill makes it possible for any other American not eligible for the low-income plan to purchase at a reasonable price a private insurance policy. It sets standards for these policies to assure that they mesh with the catastrophic program. Insurers who elect to participate in this program and whose policies meet the basic standards set in this bill would be eligible to have their policies certified as meeting the proper standards. The Secretary of Health, Education, and Welfare would study the operation of this title for 3 years to see if this insurance was being made available. Any insurer not meeting the standards after 3 years would be ineligible to serve as a medicare carrier or intermediary. In addition, if a private policy meeting these standards is not available after 3 years, a similar policy would be made available at cost from the Social Security Administration.

TITLE I—CATASTROPHIC HEALTH INSURANCE PROGRAM

The catastrophic health insurance proposal provides health insurance once a family has incurred $2,000 of medical costs or 60 days of hospital coverage.

It is intended to supplement private health insurance which many Americans have today in one form or another. For those who do not have such basic coverage, a second title provides coverage for the poor and a third title in the bill would make available to everyone a private health insurance policy at reasonable cost.

The catastrophic insurance title is modeled on the medicare experience.

Basically, the bill would provide protection to all those who are currently and fully insured under social security, their spouses and dependents, and to all social security beneficiaries. This year we have expanded coverage so that those not now covered under social security would also be protected.

Federal employees remain eligible for major medical catastrophic protection under the Federal Employees Health Benefit Act, and State and local employees could buy into the catastrophic program established under this bill.

It contains deductibles of $2,000 per family for physicians' benefits and 60 days hospitalization deductible per individual for hospitalization benefits. In other words, benefits would be payable for a family's medical bills beyond $2,000 and hospitalization would be covered from the 61st day of an individual's hospitalization.

The types of services covered under the catastrophic plan would be similar to those currently covered under parts A and B of medicare except that there would be no limitation on hospital days or home health visits.

Present medicare part A coverage includes 90 days of hospital care, 100 days of posthospital extended care, and 100 home health visits. Present part B coverage include physician's services, laboratory and X-ray services, physical therapy services, and other medical and health items and services. Unlike medicare which provides basic insurance coverage, people would be responsible for payment for the first 60 days of hospital care and the first $2,000 in medical expenses in a year.

Families could insure themselves through the use of present private health insurance arrangements against their basic health care costs, including the first 60 days of hospitalization and the first $2,000 of medical bills. For those families without the resources to obtain this basic private health insurance coverage, I believe the Federal Government should play a role in assuring availability of such basic coverage, as we already do for many of the poor through medicaid. Title II of the bill assures this basic coverage for the poor and title III provides it for the nonpoor.

The catastrophic program would be administered along with medicare by the Social Security Administration, and it would incorporate all of medicare's quality, cost, and utilization controls.

Under a new provision of our bill, we have provided an option with respect to catastrophic health insurance which allows employers to opt for insurance by a qualified health insurance plan, if he chooses not to take the social security administered plan. In order to qualify, the private plan must offer benefits which are at a minimum identical with those available under the public plan.

Under the private option, the catastrophic plan would be administered by the private insurance company of the employer's choice.

The employer's premium for private catastrophic would be deducted from his 1-percent payroll tax liability. In addition, the employer would be eligible for the tax credit of 50 percent of his 1-percent payroll tax liability.

The private option for catastrophic insurance was developed to recognize two significant factors. First, private catastrophic health insurance coverage is growing rapidly and need not be displaced where it is adequate. Second, at a time of $70 billion deficits it is the more prudent course to develop a health insurance plan with as small an impact on the Federal budget as possible.

TITLE II—MEDICAL ASSISTANCE PLAN

While title I protects virtually all Americans against medical costs above $2,000 in medical bills and/or 60 days of hospital care, most Americans cannot even afford to spend those amounts. Titles II and III address themselves to this problem.

For low-income Americans the problem of paying for medical care is espe-cially acute. While approximately three-quarters of the American people are covered by some form of health insurance, the poor and the minority groups are less likely to have health insurance. Slightly less than half of those white Americans with incomes under $5,000 and slightly more than one-third of the minority race population under $5,000 have insurance. But 90 percent of the white population and 86.9 percent of the minority population over $10,000 in income have insurance. The following table, based on a survey by the National Center for Health Statistics, illustrates the point.

I ask unanimous consent that it be printed in the RECORD at this point.

There being no objection, the table was ordered to be printed in the RECORD, as follows:

HEALTH INSURANCE: WHO HAS COVERAGE

[Percent of persons under 65 years of age with hospital insurance coverage, by color, income, and age: 1970]

Age	White			Black and others		
	Under $5,000	$5,000 to $9,999	$10,000 and over	Under $5,000	$5,000 to $9,999	$10,000 or more
All ages under 65 years	49.9	81.9	90.3	38.3	70.7	86.9
Under 17 years	37.1	79.6	89.7	31.1	66.0	86.7
17 to 24 years	59.9	77.1	83.5	49.7	67.2	78.4
25 to 44 years	47.5	83.5	91.9	42.8	74.6	88.9
45 to 64 years	57.3	87.3	92.6	43.6	81.0	92.4

Mr. RIBICOFF. Mr. President, even these figures tend to exaggerate insurance protection. They are limited to hospital protection. Even fewer people have insurance to protect against the costs of physician services, X-ray, laboratory, and other services. And they do not take into account the fact that most insurance coverage is subject to deductibles and copayments. As a result, health insurance met only 42 percent of all health care costs in 1971.

Title II of the bill would establish a medical assistance plan, effective July 1, 1977, for low-income individuals and families. The plan would provide federally administered basic health benefits coverage with uniform national eligibility standards.

The basic benefits provided under the plan are designed to mesh with those under the catastrophic health insurance plan. It is aimed in large part at providing coverage to low-income working individuals and families, in addition to replacing the current medicaid program. This means that some 34 million Americans, including 12 million working poor not now covered by medicaid, would have health insurance protection. It would eliminate the present inequities in medicaid whereby people with the same income and needs are eligible for medicaid in one State but ineligible in another, as well as the extensive variations in benefits between States. The administration would be more efficient and more adequate both from the provider's side and the patient's side. The plan would also result in substantial fiscal relief to State and local governments whose expenditures would be fixed at no higher than what they spent under medicaid during the year prior to the effective date of this program.

ELIGIBILITY

Coverage would be available to all individuals and families having an income at or below the following levels: $2,400 for an individual; $3,600 for a two-person family; $4,200 for a three-person family; $4,800 for a four-person family; and $400 additional for each additional family member.

To be eligible for benefits, persons would have to be resident citizens of the United States or aliens lawfully admitted for permanent residence, or otherwise legally residing in the United States.

Eligible individuals would file an application—or have an application filed in their behalf. Upon approval of an application, each individual would be issued a health benefits eligibility card.

To enhance administrative simplicity, eligibility would be certified on an annual basis with a coverage year generally beginning on April 1, and with the income determinations generally being upon the previous year's income. Provisions are included to allow entrance into the program, where appropriate, at any point during the year. In such cases, eligibility would be redetermined on the following April 1. In addition, the plan provides for prospective earnings estimates, where appropriate, in determination of eligibility.

Individuals' or families' eligibility would generally continue throughout the coverage year unless their income increased to more than 20 percent above the eligibility level. In determining eligibility, a family is defined as two or more individuals related by blood, marriage or adoption, and residing in a place maintained by one or more of them as their home. Also, in determining eligibility, income would include both earned and unearned income, including welfare payments, pensions, or social security payments, support and alimony payments, gifts, rents, dividends, and interest. The plan includes lesser income limits for Puerto Rico, the Virgin Islands, and Guam. Additionally, there would be special rules established by the Secretary to deal with cases where the gross income of an individual or family from a trade or business—including farming—would be considered sufficiently large to cause the family not to be regarded as "low income."

The plan contains a "grandfather" provision to guarantee that no current medicaid recipient would be disadvantaged by this program.

BENEFITS

The plan would cover medically necessary inpatient hospital services for up to 60 days during a benefit period, as well as all medically necessary skilled nursing facility care, intermediate facility care, and home health services. Additionally, the plan would cover all medically necessary medical and other health services—including physicians' services and laboratory and X-ray services—as well as prenatal and well-baby care, family planning counseling services and supplies and, for children under 18, periodic screening, diagnosis, and treatment. Additionally, the plan would make payments for part B medicare premiums for eligible individuals.

Mental health care would be covered on an inpatient basis to the extent that it consisted of active care and treatment provided in an accredited medical institution, and outpatient mental health services would be covered without limitation if provided in a qualified community mental health center. Additionally, the plan would cover up to five visits to a psychiatrist. Additional visits would be authorized upon a finding that the patient would require institutionalization in the absence of such care.

For individuals who are also entitled to benefits under the catastrophic health insurance plan, the medical assistance plan would pay any coinsurance required under the catastrophic plan. For persons not eligible for benefits under the catastrophic plan, the medical assistance plan would make payments for benefits covered under the catastrophic plan. The plan would also cover routine immunizations.

DEDUCTIBLES AND COINSURANCE

In view of the fact that the medical assistance plan is aimed at providing benefits to individuals and families without adequate resources to purchase medical care, there would generally be no deductible or coinsurance payments required.

However, to assist in controlling patient-initiated utilization, there would be a $3 per visit copayment for each of the first 10 outpatient physicians' visits per family, but no copayment would be applicable for visits for well-baby care and family planning services.

There would be one other circumstance in which a copayment would be required. This would be applicable in those situations where a person, without dependents, is in a long-term care facility or more than 60 days. In such cases, the individual—usually an elderly person in a nursing home—would retain $50 of his monthly income and any income in excess of $50 would be required as a copayment.

PAYMENTS AND ADMINISTRATION

Payments made to providers and practitioners under this program would be subject to the same reimbursement, quality, health and safety standards, and utilization controls as are applicable under the medicare program. Reimbursement controls would limit payments to not more than audited "reasonable costs" to participating institutions and agencies, and "reasonable charges" to practitioners and other suppliers.

Payments made under this program, along with any required copayment, would have to be accepted by providers and practitioners as payment in full for the services rendered, and no person accepting such payment could charge amounts in excess of the payment for the individual receiving the service.

Benefits under the program would be residual and amounts payable under this program would be reduced by amounts payable under any other public or private insurance plan under which the individual was covered with the exception of a State program designed to supplement this program.

In addition, amounts otherwise payable under this program would be reduced by not more than $250 in a benefit period if an eligible employed individual failed to enroll in an employer-sponsored health insurance plan for which the employer paid 75 percent or more of the premium cost. No employer could exclude an otherwise eligible employee from participation in a health insurance plan solely on account of the employee's eligibility for benefits under the medical assistance plan.

The utilization and quality of services would be reviewed by utilization review committees established in hospitals and skilled nursing facilities, and by the Professional Standards Review Organizations established under Public Law 92–603.

The program utilizes the same administrative mechanisms used for the administration of medicare, including where appropriate, medicare's carriers, intermediaries and public health agencies. The program also would encompass use of medicare's statutory quality standards, in that the same conditions of participation which apply to institutions participating in medicare would apply to those institutions participating in this program.

Primary policy, operating and general administrative responsibility for the program is specifically assigned to the Social Security Administration, basically involving personnel and facilities employed in the Bureau of Health Insurance.

FINANCING

The low-income plan would be financed from general revenues, just as the Federal share of the current medicaid program is now financed, and also with State funds. A medical assistance trust fund would be established to make payments for benefits under the program. The fund would receive appropriations from general revenues and State contributions.

States would contribute a fixed amount which would be equivalent to their total expenditures from State funds under medicaid for the types of benefits covered under this plan during the year prior to the effective date of this program. Additionally, a State would also pay 50 percent of the estimated amount that the State and local governments had expended in that same base year for provision of these types of services to people not covered under medicaid who would, however, be covered under the new plan. State contributions in future years would be limited to the initial contribution amount.

The State contribution would be reduced by an amount equal to one-half the amount expended by the State from non-Federal funds in providing types of services not covered under this program, but which could have been matched under the medicaid program. This provision would encourage States to offer or to continue providing optional services, such as drugs, dental services, and eyeglasses.

The additional first full-year Federal cost above present medicaid expenditures, is estimated at $5.3 billion.

CONCLUSION

An estimated 34 million people throughout the United States would be eligible for benefits under this program in any given year though, of course, not all of these people will receive services in a given year. The current medicaid program covers some 22 million people. The additional people covered under this new program represent primarily the working poor who, until this time, have been ineligible for federally supported medical assistance.

TITLE III

While title I protects all Americans against extraordinarily high health bills and title II provides basic health care for low-income families, title III assures the availability of private health insurance coverage to the rest of the population. While the private health insurance industry has made strides in recent years in making better insurance protection more widely available to more Americans, more needs to be done to encourage this expansion.

Finally one-quarter of the American population still has no hospital insurance protection. Even fewer people have nonhospital protection as the following chart indicates:

Percent of civilian population covered

Hospital care	76.9
Physicians' services:	
Surgical services	74.2
In-house visits	72.3
X-rays and lab	70.7
Office and home visits	46.6
Dental care	7.5
Out-of-hospital prescribed drugs	52.1
Private-duty nursing	51.0
Visiting nurse service	53.6
Nursing home care	18.8

For those people not eligible for the low-income plan we propose to assure that a private health insurance policy is available at a reasonable rate to anyone who wishes to purchase it.

Title III, therefore, describes a model basic private health insurance policy which meshes with the catastrophic program and establishes a mechanism whereby companies can voluntarily have their policies certified by the Secretary of HEW as meeting at least the minimum definition of adequate basic health insurance.

The standards for such a package would include coverage for 60 days of hospital care, $2,000 of medical expenses. Other criteria ban exclusions, waivers of liability and waiting periods in group policies and, with respect to individual policies, limit medical exclusion to preexisting pregnancy and waiting periods for other preexisting conditions to not more than 90 days. Additional requirements deal with opportunities for enrollment including at least an annual open enrollment period.

The Government-certified policies would have to be sold at reasonable rates. In determining reasonableness the primary factor would be the ratio of benefits paid out to premiums collected. Reasonable ratios of benefit payments to premiums or defined in terms of average ratios for group policies generally underwritten by insurers.

While these standards provide needed flexibility in rate determination by insurers they would put an end to the health policies which pay out only 30 or 40 cents for each dollar of premium collected.

No one could be denied the opportunity to buy a policy because of preexisting conditions or because he or she is a bad risk. In order to facilitate the offering of such policies the insurers would be authorized to offer such policies on a "pooled" basis with a proportionate sharing of risks and rewards.

During the first 3 years of the operation of title III the Secretary of HEW would study the extent to which private health insurance meeting the definition of adequacy is actually and generally available. He would report his findings to Congress.

After that date no company or organization could serve as a medicare carrier or intermediary unless it offered a policy certified by the Secretary as meeting the model definition.

This title, then, would encourage private health insurers to upgrade their pay-out ratio, thus making available better private health insurance to the average person.

And it would provide the Congress in 3 years with an accurate picture of the extent to which private health insurance is providing adequate coverage to the general population.

The private health insurance industry will have a real incentive and real standards toward which they can work in meeting the needs of the majority of the population who are presently covered for better or worse under private health insurance.

Title III is a means of saying to the broad population that it is our expectation and hope that private health insurance will provide the opportunity to secure insurance coverage for the first 60 days of hospitalization and the first $2,000 of medical expenses, after which the Government catastrophic health insurance program would take over.

I believe that this legislation is a major step in protecting all Americans against rising health costs. It puts a ceiling on every American's medical bills, assures health protection to those who can't afford it and encourages the private health insurance industry to make available the best possible policies at reasonable rates. At the same time it allows employees the flexibility necessary to bargain with their employers for broad health care protection.

We can wait no longer to reform our health care system. We have the opportunity today to make health care a right for all Americans—not just a privilege for the few.

I join my distinguished colleague, the chairman of the Senate Finance Committee in urging the Members of this body to help us make health care reform a reality.

INTEREST GROUPS AND INTERESTED PARTIES

Hundreds of individual citizens and numerous organizations have submitted views on national health insurance proposals to the congressional committees having jurisdiction over the study of national health. Most of that material has been reprinted as transcripts of hearings and exhibits, and was issued by the committees involved (see [14] through [35], [40], and [41]). From that vast documentation of opinions and advocacy, several selections have been chosen for inclusion in the section which follows. These particular selections were chosen because they represent active participants in the debate over national health and because their points of view are well presented. For the most part, the documents are the product of organized lobbies representing the interests of specific constituencies who prefer one or another course of action be taken or avoided. As such, these interested groups or parties are advocates, rather than objective analysts and their testimony should be examined from that point of view. Further, it should be noted that there is a public relations element in the statements of the lobbyists. Some lobbyists seem to endorse a position in public only to oppose it when wielding influence in private. For example, Professor Pierre de Vise, whose testimony follows, contends that the American Medical Association's seeming acceptance of a national health insurance concept is of that order. Finally, the viewpoints of these organizations and individuals are in a state of evolution due to the changing political and economic conditions; therefore, the positions expressed at the time of the hearings may very well have since been revised.

The Sixty-Year Debate Over National Health Insurance ([35], pp. 135–149)

Professor Pierre de Vise is a member of the Urban Sciences College at the University of Illinois. He has studied national health policy from a historical and comparative cross-national view. Participating in a panel discussion on national health insurance organized by the House Ways and Means Committee, Professor de Vise made the following statement: "The only thing preventing a workable national health insurance program for the United States is that our doctors would not accept it, and our citizens would not impose it on recalcitrant doctors at the present time. We must resign ourselves to an unworkable national health plan that will so exacerbate the present dilemma of poor access and runaway costs that either the doctors or the citizens will have a change of heart, and decide to join the rest of the Western world in making health care part of the public interest." At the conclusion of his remarks during the panel discussion, de Vise submitted the following paper. It is reprinted here to provide a historical perspective on the evolution of a national health insurance concept, as well as to give voice to a widely held view that organized medicine has and will continue to thwart any major shift in national health policy which would drastically alter the manner in which private medicine is practiced.

THE GOVERNMENT SEEN AS SANTA CLAUS TO MISCHIEVOUS DOCTORS, AND OTHER VIEWS OF THE ROLE OF GOVERNMENT IN AMERICAN HEALTH: AN INTERPRETATION OF THE SIXTY-YEAR DEBATE ON MEDICARE AND NATIONAL HEALTH INSURANCE

Underlying any new social legislation is a concept of how to bring desired change to our social structure. Compulsory health insurance is the idea behind a half dozen national health bills now before Congress. The basic idea of pooling resources in order to spread the economic risks of illness goes back to ancient Greece and does not exactly qualify as a new idea. But compulsory national health insurance is essentially a twentieth century idea·

Compulsory insurance was first enacted in Prussia in 1854 and extended by Bismarck to the new German nation in 1883. It soon spread to other European countries after the passage of British National Health Insurance in 1911. Today all industrial nations, with the important exception of the United States, have some form of compulsory national health insurance as part of their social insurance programs or as a national health sevice. A more affluent and larger scale national economy and philosophical and constitutional antecedents help explain the peculiar resistance of Americans to the idea of compulsory national health insurance, or social insurance in general. The Social Security Act of 1935, the Hill-Burton Hospital Construction Act of 1946, the Kerr-Mills Act of 1960, and the Social Security Amendments of 1965 and 1972 are major milestones in the progress toward health insurance in the United States. A brief review of the long legislative history of these programs is instructive for an outlook of future developments.

A few feeble attempts were made by the Federal Government before the New Deal to intervene in health care but most of these were aborted within a few years. The yellow fever epidemic of 1793 led to the Act of 1796 requiring Federal revenue officers to oversee state enforcement of quarantine laws on the grounds that epidemics ignored state borders and therefore constituted interstate commerce.

The act was found unconstitutional by Chief Justice Marshall who reasserted state authority. The 1813 act providing for the free distribution of cowpox vaccine was similarly construed as an attack on states' rights and was repealed in 1822. Another yellow fever epidemic led to the creation in 1879 of the National Board of Health to study better ways to control epidemics and design a national quarantine system. The Board's charter was not renewed in 1884. The Sheppard-Towner Act of 1922, providing Federal subsidies for state programs of child and maternal health, was denounced by the American Medical Association as unwarranted Federal intervention in private medical matters and the act was repealed in 1929.

Before the New Deal of the 1930's Congress and the Supreme Court held that the constitution places responsibility for health and welfare matters with the states. Yet the states were unwilling or unable to finance costly welfare measures unless all states were required to do so. Thus, the Federal Government was the only government that could achieve a broad social insurance program. The Social Security Act of 1935 represents the first milestone in the New Federal role in social insurance. But health insurance was not included because of fear that the A.M.A.'s "unyielding opposition" might jeopardize the passage of the entire social security package. The health insurance amendments (Titles 18 and 19) took 30 years, and national health insurance will probably take 42 years after passage of the original Social Security Act.

It took a great shift in public philosophy during the Depression and New Deal to permit responsibility in social insurance to pass from the states to the Federal

Government. In terms of health insurance, the shift is still far from complete. The population covered is limited to the aged and the indigent, and the government enjoys the privilege of funding the programs without effective quality and cost controls assumed by other national governments in their health insurance programs. In both Europe and the United States, health systems emerged in the context of economic resources, from political and social values, and from the influence of pressure groups.

Until relatively recently, the American middle class was large and affluent enough to support the health system with private funds through direct payments from private patients and through philanthrophy for the poor. Advances in medical technology led to a shift of care from physicians offices to large and expensively equipped hospitals. But hospitals grouped together into Blue Cross hospital insurance plans, and in the decade between 1940 and 1950, provided hospital insurance to a majority of Americans. Government health sevices and funds expanded greatly to insure major classes of the uninsured culminating with the passage of Medicare and Medicaid in 1965. But the extension of government programs to the self-supporting segment of the population was not in tune with political and social values.

Perhaps no other nation in the Western World had a sufficiently large and affluent middle class to support a health system for the poor and the working class.[1] Hence most European nations turned to NHI, first to underwrite the care of the poor and eventually to insure most of the population.

MEDICARE AND ITS AFTERMATH

Organized medicine fought vigorously against Medicare and Medicaid in the fear that this legislation was the "opening wedge" to NHI. And indeed the authors of Medicare regarded this legislation as the first step in insuring all social security beneficiaries. The HEW bureaucrats were confident that Medicare and Medicaid would convince doctors and hospitals that government funding of private health services could work smoothly. However these hopes were not realized. The demand for health services on the part of the elderly and the poor exceeded expectations and a outpaced growth in the supply of services. Price inflation at 150 percent the rate of the general price level resulted, and more Medicare and Medicaid funds were absorbed by inflated doctors' fees and hospital bills than by increased services. Cost control became the new strategy—cost control not only in public programs but in the private sector as well since Medicare and Mediaid charges are at the prevailing market. A whole battery of cost control modalities came into being—Health Maintenance Organizations (HMOs), Certificate of Need for hospital construction, Utilization Review (UR), and Professional Standards Review Organizations (PSROs), to name a few.

The Comprehensive Health Planning Act and the Regional Medical Program Services Act were enacted in 1966 in attempts to monitor new health services stimulated by expanded federal programs. These proved ineffective and were superseded by the Health Planning and Resource Development Act of 1975.

Although the original Medicare strategy backfired, an even more compelling need to bring the Frankenstein monster under control is propelling us to NHI legislation. The federal role in health care was irreversibly committed by Medicare and Medicaid. In the ten years since 1965, the government share of all health care payments rose from 25 percent to 40 percent. Government payments for physicians services jumped from 7 to 26 percent, and payments to hospitals rose from 36 to 49 percent. Federal health programs mushroomed from 100 to 300 in ten years.

Overall, health care costs rose from $38.9 to $104.2 billion in the ten years between 1965 and 1974. In this period, public expenditures increased more than fourfold—from $9.8 to $41.3 billion. The slice of health care costs out of the GNP grew from 5.9 to 7.7 percent. Higher prices caused half of the ten-year growth as medical care inflation rose 50 percent faster than the consumer price index.

The expanded federal role in health care must also be seen in the context of the growth in public spending. Government now takes 30 percent of the GNP and is projected to grow to 40 percent in the next ten years. The trend is definitely toward Sweden where government takes half of the GNP.

The inexorable progress toward the Welfare State may suggest the renunciation of formerly cherished values of laissez-faire and checks and balances. But it is more likely the result of long-term processes of industrialisation and urbanization than of basic changes in political philosophy. The increasingly complex economic forces here and abroad have forced us to regulate more and more of the economy. The Great War followed by the Great Depression and a second World War were the spectacular breakdowns in the existing international social order that led the United States and other nations to follow the path to the Welfare State.

Unfortunately, increased government controls over economic life have not totally prevented inflation and unemployment, anymore than controls over health

---

[1] Odin W. Anderson, *The Uneasy Equilibrium* (New Haven, Conn.: College and University Press, 1968).

care have prevented skyrocketing costs, maldistribution of resources, and a dual care system. But there is no question of retreating. We are irreversibly committed to increasing government controls because of the increasing complexity of economic life. We must simply learn to do better in achieving our goals of social policy, which may mean more experimentation, perhaps in the direction of more controls.

WHY DOCTORS OPPOSE NATIONAL HEALTH INSURANCE

Most economic and cost-benefit analyses reveal that doctors and other health care vendors were the major beneficiaries of Medicare—Medicaid and other federal health programs that doctors and other vendors fought so vigorously against. Similarly, projections of cost-benefits would show vendors to be major beneficiaries of the vast redistribution of income that would result from national health insurance. Conventional political analysis would suggest that a pressure group like the AMA would lobby for rather than against the passage of Medicare—Medicaid and National Health Insurance, in anticipation that such programs would add $10,000 a year to the average income of a physician. This is certainly the characteristic of traditional distributive policies where various interest groups ask the government for public lands, income subsidies, pensions, river and harbor improvements and other assistance. The amazing and almost un-American resistance of doctors to programs designed to make them richer and their patients healthier is truly baffling.

Ideological differences and fear of government controls and their impact on income and freedom of practice are the main explanations given for the opposition of doctors to federal health programs. We propose to review the historical development of the stuggle of organized medicine against government action in health care. But first we propose a theoretical framework within w\`ich we can place this struggle in the context of national changes in resources and subsequent shifts in demands on government and decisional systers.

THE THREE R's OF HEALTH POLICY DEVELOPMENT: RESOURCES, REDISTRIBUTION AND REGULATION

We repeat that resources of wealth, urbanization and industrialisation are the major variables in demands for new legislation. There are three criteria for judging the effect of a new policy—group benefits, equity, and consensus. Four policy types may be identified—distributive, redistributive, self-regulating, and regulatory. Groups making demands on government may be scaled on a continuum ranging from fragmentation to integration measured by the scope, diversity and compatibility of demands made as well as by the unity of activity among groups making them.[2]

With urbanization has come a shift from fragmented to integrated groups as large organized interest groups have allied with one another according to shared ideologies. The two major political parties are the ultimate integrated groups. However, industrialization and technological advances lead to specialization of function, interest and demand. We are thus faced with a paradox of increasing aggregation of demands diluted by specialty induced proliferation in interests and demand.

Fragmentation of demand, which characterized traditional American politics, leads to decisional systems based on consensus and to policies of distribution and self-regulation. The U.S. system has become more integrative bringing shifts to policies of redistribution and regulation. But fragmentation has grown apace of integration. Thus, there are pressures to turn policies of regulation and redistribution back to policies of self-regulation and distribution.

In the case of medical care, the AMA is a highly integrated group that seeks a policy of self-regulation. Although doctors would reap the main benefits of a redistribution policy in health care, the AMA vigorously opposes it because other groups such as employers and labor unions that might be adversely affected could easily enter the decisional system and push for a policy of regulation. Alongside the integrated AMA, there are literally hundreds of fragmented specialty interest groups that make distributive demands on government. We now have over 300 categorical health programs resulting from the demands of these groups.

On the side of the decisional system, we have the White House which seeks an integrated policy doing battle with the Federal bureaucracy and Congress which often promote distributive and self-regulating policies on behalf of the fragmented interest groups. These interest groups are out for all they can get, whereas the White House has the responsibility for allocating a fixed budget in a manner that corresponds to the optimum satisfaction of all demands on government, and to the optimum application of cost/benefit ratios.

Both Secretary Richardson and Secretary Weinberger sought mightily to rein the categorical interests entrenched in the HEW bureaucracy. The attempts to reorder priorities and budgets included reorganization of the health bureaucracy,

[2] Robert H. Salisbury, "The Analysis of Public Policy: A Search for Theories and Roles," in Austin Ranney (ed.) *Political Science and Public Policy* (Chicago: Markham Publishing Company, 1968).

shifting all the power from the Surgeon General to the Assistant Secretary for Health, decentralization to regional offices, special revenue sharing, the application of efficiency criteria, and impoundment of appropriations. The latest attempts at controlling categorical interests are the Professional Standard Review Organizations (PSROs) and the Health Systems Agencies (HSAs). Both sets of agencies are designed to respond to demands of integrated groups and both have authority to say no to spending by categorical interests.

THE A.M.A. AND THE PUBLIC INTEREST

Both the highly integrated A.M.A. and the fragmented categorical interests represent providers' with minimal input from consumers, even though, in the aggregate, government intervention (or non-intervention) may grievously affect the interests of consumers.

Health consumer groups and labor unions have been remarkably ineffective in counteracting the pressure from providers. Even if we grant that the A.M.A. is rational in opposing medical care subsidy programs out of fear that adversely affected groups will press for regulation, there remains the puzzling question: How does the A.M.A.'s will prevail against the public interest? A.M.A. membership counts less than 200,000. Yet the A.M.A. has challenged much larger groups like the AFL–CIO, the American Legion, and the Democratic Party. It has frustrated health care programs of such popular Presidents as Franklin Roosevelt, Truman, Eisenhower and Kennedy.

The answer to this mismatch probably lies in the concept of imbalanced political interests. This concept holds that concentrated groups will be more effective in the political process than diffuse ones. Health care programs vitally affect the livelihood of doctors but may mean insignificant benefits or costs to individuals whatever the aggregate level of those benefits and costs. The related concept of imbalanced political markets tells us that informed voters and rich voters are more influential than the uninformed and the poor.[3]

THE A.M.A. AND MEDICAL INFLATION

Medical inflation at a rate 50 percent higher than the rise of the general price level was brought about in part by expanded federal subsidies. It has resulted in escalating some diffuse interests into concentrated interests. Examples are medicaid costs to states and the Federal Government, Social Security payroll taxes to employers, and the proportion of fringe benefits absorbed by health insurance to labor unions. The prognosis is that National Health Insurance with an unregulated fee-for-service system is likely to further exacerbate medical inflation. However, the payment structure is still much to decentralized to deal effectively with medical inflation. Present Federal and state strategies are to cut down on health services to the poor rather than directly confront the concentrated interest of doctors in a self-regulating policy that leads to medical inflation.

The self-regulating policy of organized medicine has contributed to medical inflation through the monopoly power of doctors and hospitals. This power has been used to artificially limit the supply of doctors, to discourage the use of salaried doctors, to restrict the activities of osteopaths, chiropractors, nurses, and other physician substitutes, and to hamper the effective monitoring of costs and appropriate utilization.

The three major responses of government to medical inflation are (1) to improve market behavior through coinsurance, deductibles and HMOs, (2) to establish public utility regulation dealing with facility construction and rates; and (3) to create a monopsony of consumers to deal on equal terms with the monopoly of vendors through a strong national health system of the kind proposed in the Kennedy-Corman bill.[3] It will probably take a combination of all three approaches to tame the monster of medical inflation.

To recapitulate, the long gestation of the National Health Insurance idea is due in part to the fact that the large and affluent middle class was able to subsidize the care of the poor until recently. It is also due in part to three strong political traditions—the Jeffersonian view that "that government is best which governs least," the *laissez-faire* doctrine which assigns government responsibility for ensuring maximum freedom for private enterprise, and the public philosophy of "social Darwinism" which limits government social welfare programs for fear of frustrating the "survival of the fittest" mechanism by which society progresses. The debate over national health insurance has also been prolonged by the determined opposition of the A.M.A. ever since the idea first took root in the 1910's and down to the 1970's and the A.M.A.'s two national health insurance bills.

THE A.M.A. AND NATIONAL HEALTH INSURANCE

The welfare state in Britain and the New Deal in the United States mark the evolution of nineteenth century liberal political philosophies of Stuart Mill and the Manchester School, and of Thomas Jefferson and the Federalists in the

---

[3] Theodore Marmor, "Politics, Public Policy, and Medical Inflation" (in press, 1975).

two countries. The fewer groups that still voice these political philosophies are now regarded as conservatives, and many of their expressions are derided as reactionary and callous. Three such denigrated slogans of twentieth century conservatism are:

"The business of America is business."

"What is good for General Motors is good for the country."

"Health care is not a right but a privilege."

These political expressions made by the Presidents of the United States, General Motors and the A.M.A. would have been perfectly in tune with nineteenth century libertarian principles of least government, *laissez-faire*, and social Darwinism. But they are no longer considered appropriate in most sectors of society and the economy today, with the flagrant exception of health care.

There is a possible explanation why physicians hold onto these nineteenth century dogmas. Because of their years of demanding training and hard work and their daily exposure to suffering, physicians often become callous to ordinary human feelings. They also become fierce believers in free enterprise, hard work, and self-reliance. In their tendency to value individuals by these standards, doctors develop an image of women and children as the ignorant and the incompetent dependents of men.

Doctors have particularly rigid attitudes about "morals" and people "getting something for nothing." Free health care for children and mothers raises the image and unwed mothers and illegitimate children, guilty on both counts of morals and dependency in the distorted catechism of doctors. These social values explain in part the opposition of the A.M.A. to the Sheppard-Towner Act in the 1920's. It also explains the belief that health care is a privilege, not a right.

An interesting elucidation of the latter concept as recently provided by medical society spokesmen at a national conference on Partnership for Health Planning held in Nashville in February, 1969. These statements were made by B. G. Mitchell, M.D., of Memphis, and reported by the *American Medical News* of March 17, 1969, to represent the feeling of the medical community:

"With the passage of the Medicare law our nation witnessed for the first time a system of taxation of younger working people to provide health care for a segment of our population, whether they needed help or not. The medical profession vigorously opposed this plan and we shall oppose such plans in the future."

"Beware of free medical services or any type of service that creates a feeling of irresponsibility in the public. This is resulting in moral decadence, overutilization, and a something-for-nothing attitude which is difficult to combat. Some element of this moral decay may even spread to the providers of service."

The views reflected in these comments are not often expressed so frankly anymore, but the fact that this was unquestionably the prevailing attitude of the medical profession in the United States for many years has certainly influenced the organization of medical and health services for the last 30 years and is thus a contributing cause, at least, of some of the disjunctions for which the health services are so widely criticized today.

The transformation of the A.M.A. role from a liberal-social guardian to that of a conservative-economic protectionist occurred during the Depression and New Deal of the 1930's. Its nineteenth century values failed to keep pace with the great shift in American political values in the period. Furthermore, debate over national health insurance between 1916 and 1922 converted the A.M.A. from a professional association to a partisan labor union.

Actually, the A.M.A. showed little interest in Federal and state action between the time of its founding in 1846 and the 1870's when it created a section of state medicine and hygiene, which distinguished community health care from private and curative medicine, and which defined public hygiene as the control of contagious disease. The A.M.A. set up its House of Delegate structure in 1901, with members chosen by state societies. The Council on Medical Education was organized in 1904 and produced, in collaboration with the Carnegie Foundation, the Flexner report of 1910, which was to revolutionize medical education. Dr. Flexner's final list approved 66 of 135 schools. Twenty-nine schools were closed between 1910 and 1914.

THE SIX ROUNDS IN THE NATIONAL HEALTH INSURANCE DEBATE

We can identify six rounds in the sixty-year debate over National Health Insurance: 1916–22: In its successful fight against state insurance plans, the A.M.A. transforms itself from a liberal professional association into a conservative protectionist labor union. 1939–49: The A.M.A. defeats Murray-Wagner-Dingell, Taft-Smith-Ball, Truman and Ewing health bills. 1953: A.M.A. defeats Eisenhower's Reinsurance Bill. 1957: A.M.A. defeats Forand bill, a precursor of Medicare. 1960–65: A.M.A. accedes to Wilbur Mills' compromises of Kerr-Mills (1960) and Medicare-Medicaid (1965). 1970s: Administration, Kennedy, and A.M.A. bills are major contenders among a dozen National Health Insurance bills that attempt to repair damage done by Medicare-Medicaid.

Until the late 1960's, the business community and the Republican Party were allies of the A.M.A. But the more than doubling of medical costs since 1965 made cost-containment the major new political strategy in health care. Thus, the traditional debate between the National Health Insurance proponents among

Democrats and the A.M.A. opposition is now joined by the administration and its cost-containment policy. But it is not certain that the administration and A.M.A. plans would not bankrupt us or the Kennedy plan would assure health care to all.

THE FIRST DEBATE ON NATIONAL HEALTH INSURANCE: 1916–1922

The British National Health Insurance Act of 1911 set the stage for the first great debate on insurance. At first the response was favorable to health insurance. It was endorsed in 1912 by the Progressive Party and its candidate, Theodore Roosevelt. The American Association for Labor Legislation (AALL), founded by economists at the University of Wisconsin in 1906, developed a model health insurance bill in 1915. By 1917 twelve state legislatures were considering the bill, eight had appointed study commissions, with the first three to report coming out in favor of the bill. Even the A.M.A. joined the bandwagon. Its Social Insurance Committee, headed by Dr. Alexander Lambert of the AALL, recommended compulsory state-run health insurance in 1916. The next year the House of Delegates approved principles of government health insurance.

The Armistice brought disenchantment and reaction in the United States, not only about the League of Nations but about health insurance as well. The very month after the Armistice, California voters defeated a health insurance plan, and the following April the New York State Assembly defeated a similar bill.

By 1919 the current of reaction which began with the Senate rejection of President Wilson's Peace Treaty became a tidal wave against all social innovation. Health insurance was tagged with both extreme right and left labels—the defeated "Hun" and "Bolshevism." By 1920 the A.M.A. House of Delegates repudiated both its president, Dr. Lambert, and its earlier resolution by coming out in "unequivocal opposition" to health insurance. The insurance and pharmaceutical industries joined the A.M.A. in public campaigns against health insurance. In 1920 and again in 1922 the House of Delegates declared itself against state medicine; "Any form of medical treatment provided, conducted, controlled or subsidized by the federal, or any state government or municipality." Only the Army, Navy, Merchant Marines and U.S. Public Health Service were exempted. The A.M.A. disapproved the Sheppard-Towner Act of 1922 giving grants-in-aid to state programs of maternal and child health. (The program was discontinued in 1929.)

THE COMMITTEE ON THE COST OF MEDICAL CARE

Under the auspices of the Carnegie and five other foundations, the Committee on the Cost of Medical Care (CCMC) was established in 1927. Chaired by Ray Lyman Wilbur, President of Stanford, the CCMC set out five areas for study: (1) incidence of disease and disability; (2) existing facilities; (3) expenditures for services; (4) income of providers; and (5) chronic care facilities. A research staff of 75 under the direction of Harry Moore, University of Chicago economist, produced 27 field studies and a final report in 1932 approved by 39 of the 50 committee members. The sweeping recommendations included the following: "Medical service should be furnished by group practice physicians organized around a hospital to render complete office and hospital care. Costs of care should be placed on a group payment basis, through insurance or taxation or both." The minority members strongly opposed hospital-based group practice. In their report, they argued that medicine was personal service, not mass production; and that the role of government should be limited to the care of indigents, public health, and the armed forces—"everything else belongs to private practice." The minority report urged that the general practitioner be restored to his central place in medical practice—"The GP can treat 85 percent of all illnesses and injuries with very simple equipment." Insurance was secondary: it should be attached to general practice and be under the control of county or state medical societies.

The Journal of the A.M.A. attacked the majority report in an editorial dated December 3, 1932, concluding in these words: "The alignment is clear—on the one side the forces representing the great foundations, public health officialdom, social theory—even socialism and communism—inciting to revolution; on the other side, the organized medical profession urging principles of sound practice of medicine."

In 1933, the American Hospital Association endorsed hospital insurance as "one of the most effective ways to offset the increasing demand for more radical and dangerous forms of state medicine." Vountary hospital insurance which the CCMC report had passed over lightly, became the "opening wedge."

THE NEW DEAL AND THE SOCIAL SECURITY ACT

In the midst of the Great Depression, Franklin Delano Roosevelt was elected in a landslide in 1932. Early in 1934, FDR appointed a Committee on Economic Security to make recommendations for a program against "misfortunes which cannot be wholly eliminated." Illness was one of the misfortunes. The Committee was composed of the Secretaries of Labor, Treasury, Agriculture, the Attorney General and Harry Hopkins. Many advisory committees were set up, including one on medical care. The original Social Security Bill that was developed by the Committee said that the Social Security Board should study the problem of health insurance. But so many telegrams descended on Congress that the entire Social Security program seemed endangered. In an editorial, J.A.M.A. said some felt the A.M.A. should oppose the entire program. It did not take long for this innocuous reference to be struck out of the bill. But Title V restored the Sheppard Towner Act that had lapsed in 1929. The Social Security Act was passed in August, 1935.

MEETING THE CHALLENGE OF THE PHYSICIAN SURPLUS

The Great Depression further polarized organized medicine and government. While the government met the challenge of economic chaos with the revolutionary New Deal, the A.M.A. responded by greatly increasing its restrictive control over medical schools, particularly their programs, curriculums, and admissions policies. In the first three decades of the twentieth century, restrictions on the supply of physicians were a by-product of the A.M.A.'s successful attack on low-quality medical schools and low admission standards. In the 1930's and 1940's, however, the desire to prevent undue competition and ward off "socialized medicine" became paramount issues. Restrictive policies directed at medical school admissions standards resulted in a steady reduction of medical school admissions during these two decades.

Dr. Walter Bierrin, A.M.A. President in 1934, was the first in a long list of officials to warn of the "social dangers of an oversupply of physicians." In a series of J.A.M.A. articles he called for "real courage and tenacity" on the part of medical societies to "bend" the medical schools to the "urgent social and economic needs of the changing order. He foresaw that the principal function of medical service would be to cut down by half the number of medical schools and physicians. Dr. Bierring confidently predicted that "a fine piece of educational work could well be done if we were to use only half of the 70-odd medical schools in the United States." [4]

Dr. Bierring and his associates might well have succeeded in halving the number of medical graduates had the Depression continued long enough. There was an 18 percent drop in the number of admissions between 1933 and 1938, in spite of an increase in applicants. As it was, the tighter admission requirements did result in halving the number of admissions per 1,000 applicants through the 1930 and 1940 decades. Thus, there were fewer admissions in 1950 than in 1930, though the number of applicants had doubled in the interim.

Attempts by governments, providers, and consumers to ease the physician shortage were consistently opposed by the A.M.A. in this period. In a series of delaying actions and strategic retreats in the 1930's and 1940's, the A.M.A. in turn opposed voluntary health insurance plans, compulsory health insurance legislation, federal aid for medical education, and prepaid group practice programs

THE SECOND DEBATE: 1939–1949, THE A.M.A. VERSUS FDR, TRUMAN, EWING, AND WAGNER

The Social Security Administration was charged with studying and recommending legislation on old age pensions, unemployment compensation, and "related subjects." Many studies on the related subject of health insurance were carried out by the Bureau of Research and Statistics, drawing in part on the massive field studies of the CCMC and of the National Health Survey of 1935–36 based on interviews of 737,000 households.

FDR appointed the Interdepartmental Committee to coordinate Health and Welfare Activities in 1936. The Technical Committee on Health Care, set up the next year, found existing health care inadequate and called for a national comprehensive heatlh program. This call for action resulted in the First National Conference of Health convened in Washington in July, 1938. It was attended by 176 health care professionals and leaders.

The Second World War set the next stage for the great insurance debate. The A.M.A. successfully opposed the Wagner National Health Bill of 1939 (S. 1620), the Eliot Bill in 1942 (H.R. 7354), the Murray-Wagner-Dingell National Health Bill of 1943 (S. 1161) and 1945) S. 1606), the Taft-Smith-Ball Medical Indigency Bill of 1946, President Truman's National Health Program (1947, 1949), and Federal Security Administrator Ewing's ten-year National Health Insurance plan.

FDR asked for better medical care in Messages to Congress in 1939, 1941, 1942 and 1953. Truman started supporting National Health Insurance in his 1946 Message to Congress. Oscar Ewing called for a second National Conference on Health in May 1948. The National Health Assembly was attended by 800 people. Ewing told them that "we cannot continue to use the purchasing power demand as our exclusive criterion of the adequacy of supply." In 1948, 40 percent of the population was covered for hospital insurance, 23 percent for surgical insurance, and 9 percent for physicians' office services. Ewing predicted that no more than half of the population would ever be insured voluntarily.

President Truman's 1948 election victory panicked the A.M.A. Its House of Delegates met in emergency session and voted an assessment of $25 per member to prevent "the enslavement of the medical profession." The public relations

---

[4] W. L. Bierring. "The Family Doctor and the Changing Order," *Journal of American Medical Association,* Vol. 144 (1934), 1997.

firm of Whitaker and Baxter was hired and a $4.5 million campaign was launched to combat national health insurance and "creeping socialism."

The A.M.A. made a complete turnabout and vigorously espoused the "Voluntary way" of insurance as the "American way" in its campaign to defeat the Truman compulsory health insurance legislation. But as late as 1949, A.M.A. officials were still lobbying to cut down congressional bills designed to stimulate medical school enrollment. In a throwback to 1919 A.M.A. spokesmen linked compulsory health insurance with revolutionary and un-American tags. The A.M.A. claimed credit for the defeat of four senators and for the victory of eight new senators in the 1950 election.

Meanwhile, back at the fort, Truman established the President's Commission on the Health Needs of the Nation in 1951. Paul Magnuson, M.D., of the Northwestern Medical School, was chairman, and Lester Breslow, M.D., of the California Health Department, was staff director. Within a year, the Commission produced its report and recommendations: Government should prod and promote, assist financially but not control or operate health services. Health is a basic human right, and society must assure access to health care and provide health education. Then can personal action reach its full potential, the majority members concluded. They also urged that all methods of private and public financing be given a chance. This time, it was the liberal members who constituted the minority. They protested that states should not have the option not to enter into a federal-state health insurance system.

The A.M.A. claimed victory and concluded its four-year campaign against national health insurance in 1952. Its successful campaign was reflected by the omission of national health insurance in the Democratic Platform of 1952 and candidate Eisenhower's repudiation of it. Years later President Truman was to single out the one-sided debate on national health insurance as his most bitter disappointment.

THE THIRD ROUND: 1953–1957; THE A.M.A. VERSUS EISENHOWER AND THE AMERICAN LEGION

In the 1952 Presidential campaign, Eisenhower said: "American medicine outstripped the world on a voluntary basis and on that basis the needs of Americans will most adequately be met." Eisenhower assured the A.M.A. in 1953 that he continued to oppose socialized medicine and would keep government out of the existing structure of medicine. By that year, 60 percent of the population was covered by hospital insurance. Half of all hospital charges were paid by insurance.

In his State of the Union Message of 1954, Eisenhower proposed the concept of reinsurance. This entailed underwriting and supporting companies that would insure high risk and low income groups. But the A.M.A. would not buy it. Its president, David Allman, M.D., called it the familiar opening wedge and said government should stay out of health insurance completely. The A.M.A. board claimed reinsurance involved not only subsidization of voluntary health insurance but federal regulation and control as well.

The Reinsurance bill was defeated 238 to 134 in July 1954. Eisenhower reasserted his support of the concept in his State of the Union Message of 1955. That year, Marion Folsom succeeded Oveta Culp Hobby as HEW Secretary. In an interview in the New York Times of August 24, 1955, Folsom called reinsurance the keystone of the Eisenhower health program. But he hinted that the policy would be dropped because "liberals say it can't do the job, won't reach lower income people, and doctors don't want the government to do anything." Reinsurance indeed was dropped after 1956. It was replaced by an emphasis on grants-in-aid for facilities and personnel, and to states for medical assistance to indigents.

After 1954, the A.M.A. became increasingly unhappy over the Veterans Administration policy of giving free care to veterans for nonservice connected disabilities. The VA network of hospitals was the great exception to government reluctance to provide direct health services. By 1954, 60 percent of VA medical care was for nonservice connected illness. Thus it came to pass that the A.M.A. and the American Legion, those two bastions of conservatism, came to blows on the issue of misguided patriotism. The A.M.A. asserted that the Legion was unwittingly planting the seeds of socialization when it continued to foster free medical care for veterans. "It would be unfortunate indeed," a JAMA editorial warned, "that if in our efforts to reward patriotism we were responsible for the creation of a system of government medicine against the will of the majority.

THE FOURTH ROUND: 1957–1960; THE A.M.A. VERSUS THE AFL–CIO AND THE FARMERS UNION

The bell for the fourth round of the debate was sounded by the Forand Bill in 1957, to provide health insurance for the elderly on social security. This time the A.M.A. hired the public relations firm of Braun and Co. and was joined by the insurance and drug industries in opposition to the first Medicare bill. The fight in this round was a little more even, with the AFL–CIO, the National Farmers' Union and the American Nurses Association in support of the bill. Although the bill was defeated in committee by a two-to-one margin in 1960, the simple fact that it was brought to a vote was a signal victory for its supporters.

Moreover, the A.M.A. had suffered its first defeat in 1956 by unsuccessfully opposing aid to the totally and permanently disabled elderly beneficiaries under Social Security. The next year the Social Security Amendments of 1957 permitted states to use federal grants-in-aid to pay providers of health services for public assistance recipients.

THE FIFTH ROUND: 1960–1965; THE A.M.A. VERSUS MEDICARE

In the summer of 1960 the stage was set for the fifth round and first real showdown on the floor of the Senate. On one side of the aisle was the Republican subsidy bill endorsed by Presidential candidate Nixon; on the other was a diluted version of the Forand bill endorsed by the Democratic candidate Kennedy. In the middle was a compromise bill endorsed by Representatives Mills, Senator Kerr, and the A.M.A. The Republican and Democratic bills were defeated 67–28 and 51–44. The minimal Kerr-Mills-A.M.A. bill then swept through 91–2.

The Kerr-Mills Act provided between 50 and 80 percent of funds states used in medical aid to the aged. But states had an option to determine eligibility and benefits. Thus by 1953, only 32 of the states had programs in effect. Five states— California, New York, Massachusetts, Michigan and Pennsylvania—with 32 percent of the aged were receiving 90 percent of the Kerr-Mills funds.

In the 1960 election both Nixon and Kennedy promised to strengthen the Kerr-Mills Act if elected. President Kennedy's victory signaled the fifth round in the debate; the A.M.A. launched an all-out effort against "the most deadly challenge ever faced by the medical profession." The grim prospect that the Federal government might ensure the health of the nation's aged, blind, and disabled would be challenged by a 70-man speakers' bureau and a newly-created American Medical Political Action Committee (AMPAC). In the first two months of Kennedy's administration a Presidential task force recommended Medicare; the President endorsed it in a message to Congress; and the King-Anderson bill was introduced. The bill was immediately attacked by the A.M.A.: "Medicare is really Fedicare— a costly concoction of bureaucracy, bad medicine—and an unbalanced budget." After nine days of hearings in August 1961, the bill was allowed to die in committee. More hearings were held in 1962 and 1963 resulting in 14,000 pages of testimony but no votes.

Some consumer groups were now adding their weight to the debate. The National Council of Senior Citizens was formed in 1961 with AFL–CIO support and counted 600,000 members by 1962. In 1964, the AFL–CIO, over 13 million members strong, spent $1 million in the 1964 elections, and another $1 million for lobbying the following year through its Committee on Political Education (COPE). A.M.A.'s AMPAC also spent a $1 million in 1965.

The November 1964 elections gave the Democrats 32 new seats in the House, for a ratio of better than 2 to 1. The Ways and Means Committee shifted from 15 Democrats and 10 Republicans to 17 Democrats and 8 Republicans and Rep. Mills promised Medicare action in early 1965.

The administration introduced H.R. 1 and S. 1 in January. It did not cover physicians services, an omission pounced upon by the A.M.A. The A.M.A. suddenly proposed its own "Eldercare," administered by the states but including physician care. Eldercare was held to be more comprehensive than Medicare which was projected to cover only a fourth of the health care expenses of the elderly. The A.M.A. trotted out a survey showing that two-thirds of the respondents preferred physician care and selective coverage of the indigent. Rep. Byrnes introduced the Eldercare bill.

At that point, Rep. Mills asked HEW's Wilbur Cohen to merge the two bills. Cohen's resulting "three-layer cake" included Medicare, private insurance for physician care, and an expanded Kerr-Mills for the poor. These became Title 18, Parts A and B, and Title 19.

The new bill passed the House in April 1965. In June, the Senate yielded to the American Hospital Association position that hospital specialists should be covered under Part A (hospital services) rather than Part B (physician services). This threw the A.M.A. House of Delegates into an uproar. The A.H.A. was accused by the A.M.A. President with seizing upon this bill to seek "ever-widening dominion over doctors." An A.M.A. pamphlet predicted that Medicare would result in "a complete takeover of medical practice by A.H.A. and the Federal government." The delegations from nine states voted to refuse to participate in Medicare. Fortunately the Senate-House committee set up to reconcile differences between the two bills put the hospital specialists back in Part B and the signout threat was over. The reconciled bill passed the Senate in July 1965 and the Social Security Amendments of 1965 (Medicare and Medicaid) became the law of the land.

Thus did the United States finally join the rest of the western world in insuring the health of its aged and indigent.

TOWARD NATIONAL HEALTH INSURANCE IN THE 1970'S

The expansion of Medicare/Medicaid insurance to the total working population is the agenda for the current (sixth) round in the insurance debate. The first decisive blows in this round are the Social Security Amendments of 1972 (H.R. 1), which somewhat extend, and somewhat restrict Medicare and Medicaid. In a cut-down version of a catastrophic illness insurance bill, Social Security benefits are extended to 1.7 million people under 65 who are victims of chronic kidney disease. But victims of other crippling diseases are not covered. Private physicians have lost the vendor monopoly, a major cause of the inflationary effect of Medicare and Medicaid, and beneficiaries may now choose to receive their care from an HMO. Perhaps the major impact of the new law is to allow states to greatly reduce Medicaid benefits because of camplaints of waste, fraud, and overutilization in the program. A more effective cost and utilization review mechanism is imposed in the form of PSROs to be made up of peer physicians.

As in the 1960's the two major national health insurance bills are linked with the names of Nixon and Kennedy. But as in 1960, these bills are so divergent ($6.5 versus $8.3 billion the first year according to HEW) that a compromise bill will probably win the day again. Indeed such a compromise bill was attempted by the Ways and Means Committee in August 1974. But the committee could not agree on such issues as financing catastrophic insurance out of payroll taxes or general revenue and on mandatory or optional employee participation.

As in 1965, the A.M.A. has come up with its own alternative plans. The first, "Medicredit," was a voluntary plan financed out of sliding income tax credits. The second plan, introduced in April 1975, called for mandatory employer coverage but voluntary employee participation, and would be financed largely out of general revenues.

WHY THE A.M.A. STILL OPPOSES NATIONAL HEALTH INSURANCE

Organized medicine's fear of the effects of National Health Insurance on freedom, practice, and income of physicians is probably as unfounded today as it was in earlier decades. Physicians were by far the major beneficiaries of Medicaid and Medicare in spite of their opposition. They will likewise be the major beneficiaries of National Health Insurance. By the end of the 1970's organized medicine will likely control even the HMO's and PSRO's that now seem to threaten them.

The opposition of the A.M.A. to social programs that are supposed to enhance the efficiency, quality, and income of physicians may make little sense on the face of it. Various people have accused the A.M.A. of being regressive and reactionary, of being unrepresentative of American doctors, or of shamming protest to disarm potential critics of the huge Federal subsidies of doctors flowing out of Medicare and Medicaid. Some of the A.M.A.'s opposition may indeed be seen as an irrational counterproductive rear guard action for the preservation of the social values of a bygone age. That is due in part to the hard training of doctors and their strong adherence to the work ethic. It is also due to the inability of doctors to accept the advice of nondoctors such as association executives, lawyers, politicians, lobbyists and public relations experts. Evidence of this are the tenuous working relations between the A.M.A. staff and the committees, and the reported low morale of the staff.

But it is hard to question the representativeness of the A.M.A. or impugn its sincerity. It apparently speaks for the great majority of America's physicians, and it speaks honestly for them. Survey after survey confirm the misgivings and anguish of doctors at the prospect of National Health Insurance. In one of the most comprehensive such surveys, reported by *Medical Economics* in August 1971, most doctors (80 percent) believe National Health Insurance is inevitable; 60 percent think patients should pay part of each bill, but 60 percent think poor people should get free care, and a third think old people should not pay; two-thirds prefer the A.M.A.'s "Medicredit" tax credit financing method. Only 12 percent of the doctors think they will gain financially and 40 percent think they will lose income. One-third would refuse to join a group practice required to do so for reimbursement. Two-thirds fear National Health Insurance will worsen medical care; only one-tenth believe care will be improved. Three-fourths would accept physician peer-review boards sponsored by their medical society; one-fourth would accept such boards under hospital sponsorship, and six percent would accept such boards under government auspices. While 60 percent of the surveyed doctors would accept National Health Insurance, 35 percent would retire, 10 percent would shift from practice to research or administration, 10 percent would leave medicine altogether, and 5 percent each would go on strike, leave the country, and take other desperate actions. (These add up to more than 100 because of multiple answers).

A more recent survey of 2,713 senior physicians was reported in the May 1975 issue of *Medical Care*. Despite the fact that 56 percent of the respondents were in favor of some form of National Health Insurance, almost three-fourths said most doctors they knew were opposed. Over three-fourths of the doctors felt that NHI was inevitable. Over half preferred the tax-credit financing method, and 37 percent preferred payroll taxes. With respect to reimbursement, three-fourths favored fee-for-service, only one fourth favored capitation, and merely 14 percent favored salary. Two-thirds felt NHI would adversely affect their work; only 17 percent thought it would improve quality of care, about half predicted NHI would result in unnecessary hospitalization and doctors' services.

Over a fourth thought they would earn less money, and 14 percent thought they would earn more. One fifth said the A.M.A. represented their opinion on most matters, half on some matters, and another fifth, on hardly any matters.

In a sense the A.M.A. is looking after the inteersts of its constituency in the well-established American labor union tradition. The A.M.A. is probably wrong in fearing National Health Insurance would destroy private practice, but it is not wrong in thinking that the technological and social forces underlying social insurance would vastly affect doctor-political relationships. Even in the absence of social insurance measures like Medicare, the revolution in medical technology would have made huge demands on the amount and organization of capital and specialized manpower and resulted in greatly expanding the role of what Robert Cunningham calls the third world of medicine—medical schools, hospitals, private insurance, group practice, and the drug industry.[5] That organized medicine has managed to shape and control these forces, as well as the forces of social insurance, is testimony to both the high social credit of physicians and to the success of their past political and propaganda campaigns. According to most opinion surveys, physicians generally occupy the top position among professions and occupations in public esteem, altrusm, and credibility. If television program values are any indication, physicians vie with policemen as the most revered contemporary occupations. What other profession could have maintained this stance after decades of ranting against health programs for the aged, blind, disabled, and indigent mothers and children, and after half a decade of charges of financial exploitation and other abuses in the medical care provided these classes?

How then do we explain organized medicine's continuing paranoia and paroxysm of fear and distrust elicited by the interposition of government and hospitals in the expansion of corporatism and of social insurance? Two reasons are that the business community and the Republican Party are no longer on the side of the A.M.A. in the insurance debate. There are indeed no longer two sides, but rather at least three sides in the current debate on National Health Insurance.

This is the very development that the A.M.A. sought to prevent. In the context of the earlier discussion, the A.M.A. fought against the redistribution policy of Medicare in fear that government and employers would become adversely affected as payers for excessive services at inflated prices and would consequently try to check inflated demand and prices with a policy of regulation.

THREE FACTIONS IN THE CURRENT DEBATE

It is the inflationary effect of Medicare-Medicaid, produced by ineffective cost and utilization controls insisted upon the A.M.A., that broke up the coalition. Up to 1965, the National Association of Manufacturers, the U.S. Chamber of Commerce, and the Republican leadership were generally allies of the A.M.A. But concern over escalating costs of medical care in the United States—which more than doubled since the onset of these programs in 1965—made cost-containment the major new political strategy in health care, and the Federal Administration and the business community its principal proponents.[6] The administration's new cost-containment policy first found expression in the "health cost effectiveness amendments" presented to Congressional committees in October 1969, which culminated in the Social Security Amendments of 1972 already discussed. Big business for its part voiced its disenchantment with the A.M.A. through such manifestoes as the January 1970 issue of *Fortune Magazine* on "our ailing medical system" and such spokesmen as the chairman of I.B.M. As quoted by the Washington editor of *Medical Economics*, Thomas J. Watson, Jr. recanted his former stance "as a dyed-in-the-wool free trader, free enterprise, and hater of bureaucracy," and declared: 'We do not need National Health Insurance as a political football in 1972; we need a new National Health Insurance law, and we need it now. Indeed, I hope the Administration will put this at the top of its priority list." [7]

The vastly expanded authority of states to reduce Medicaid benefits and PSRO's to cut down on unnecessary medical care and financial abuses are but the first step in the administration's cost-containment strategy. The President in 1973 called for a major shakedown of health programs that are "too fat, too bloated," and assigned the task to Casper ("Cap the Knife") Weinberger, who was moved from Budget to H.E.W. Although the Democrats are identified with the more inflationary Kennedy bill, both Democratic and Repulican platforms in 1972 emphasized cost containment. "Incentives and controls to curb inflation in health care platforms. But the Democrats sought "Universal National Health

[5] Robert M. Cunningham, *The Third World of Medicine* (New York: McGraw-Hill, 1958).
[6] Pierre de Vise, "The Social Pressures: Health Care Plans Proposed by the Federal Government, by Corporations, and by Labor Unions May be Regarded as Declarations of Independence from America's Medical Dictatorship," *Hospitals,* Vol. 45 (February 1, 1971), 51–55.
[7] J. A. Reynolds, "Inside Washington: The Net Tightens Around Doctors," *Medical Economics* (April 12, 1971), 230–240.

Insurance" with free choice for both provider and consumer, and at an affordable cost, whereas Republicans opposed "nationalized compulsory health insurance" because it would triple health care costs and deny free choice. These differences are incorporated in two of the major insurance bills—the Administration's Comprehensive Health Insurance Plan (CHIP) and the Kennedy-Corman Bill.

N1

The major participants in the present debate have been identified as the purchasers of care (the Administration and insurance carriers), the providers of care (physicians and hospitals), and consumers (the labor unions.)[8, 9] Each of these participants has an insurance plan—the Administration, the Health Insurance Association, A.M.A., A.H.A., AFL–CIO, and the UAW-sponsored Kennedy-Corman Plan. The three leading plans represent the three major parties at stake—the Administration Plan speaks for purchasers of care; the A.M.A. Plan for the providers of care; and the Kennedy-Corman Plan comes the closest to representing the consumers of care.

The purposes, costs, and effects on doctors vary in the three plans according to their underlying goals and objectives. Major priorities in the Administration Plan are economy and efficiency, and mandatory PSRO's and optional HMO's are designed to penalize waste and reward efficiency. The A.M.A. would prefer no plan at all, but if a plan is inevitable, then the objective is to assure income for treating indigents within the existing fee-for-service, private practice system. The A.M.A. Plan is strictly a financing mechanism, with voluntary employee participation and no change in the delivery system. Consumers are concerned about both access to care and costs. Labor unions, which are the best organized health consumers, are especially distressed by the increasing proportion of fringe benefits and payroll deductions eaten up by health insurance. Thus, the Kennedy-Corman Plan goes the farthest in overhauling of the existing delivery system, with built-in controls on costs and quality.

CONCLUSIONS

In addition to differences between these three plans that may be hard to reconcile, there is great uncertainty as to whether any of the plans could actually fulfill their stated objectives. Based on the disastrous experience of Medicare and Medicaid, there is good reason to believe that the modest Administration and A.M.A. plans would further shift medical manpower from poor to middle-class areas and that the more ambitious Kennedy Plan would bankrupt us. But it is not even certain that the Administration and A.M.A. plans would *not* bankrupt us or that the Kennedy Plan *would* assure quality for care and control costs.

These proposals can work only if effective price and mode of delivery controls of the three types already discussed can be implemented. There is no doubt that under "free" competition, subsidies for the medical care of families above the poverty level would result in further shifts of physicians from poverty to non-poverty communities, raise private practice fees, and force up medical insurance rates.

Federal controls on medical prices and delivery systems are justified even now with respect to the $40 billion expended on health care by government in 1974. They would become mandatory if the government were to increase its health budget to $50 billion by subsidizing National Health Insurance. Without these controls Federal subsidies would drive up medical expenditures to levels that would not be tolerated by Americans. Within three years health care could take 10 percent of our gross national product, hospital beds would cost $150 per day, a physician's office visit would cost $25, a diagnostic visit $100, and physicians would earn $80,000 a year on the average. If that day should come about, there is no doubt that the pressure on government to nationalize hospital and medical services would become overwhelming.

The challenge for American government is not to spend more but to spend better—to channel current annual expenditures of $40 billion into more efficient and accessible health delivery systems made possible by medical technology advances and national health plans. In other parts of the western world, indeed in parts of the United States covered by prepaid group practice plans, comprehensive care is provided to all the population for a fraction of what the American government currently pays for fractionated care for the nation's old and poor.

The only thing preventing a workable National Health Insurance program for the United States is that our doctors would not accept it and our citizens would not dictate it on recalcitrant doctors at the present time. We must resign ourselves to an unworkable National Health Plan that will so exacerbate the present dilemma of poor access and runaway costs that either the doctors or the citizens will have a change of heart, and decide to join the rest of the western world in making health care part of the public interest.

---

[8] S. W. Olson, "Health Insurance for the Nation," *New England Journal of Medicine,* Vol. 284 (1971), 525–533.
the Light of Contemporary Policy Issues," *Inquiry,* Vol. 8, No. 2 (1971), 20–36.
[9] R. M. Battistella, "National Health Insurance: An Examination Leading Proposals in

The American Medical Association in 1975 ([36], Part I, pp. 507–520)

The American Medical Association (AMA) is generally credited with having one of the most effective national lobbying organizations in the United States. Its offices in Washington, D.C. employ dozens of analysts and experts whose job is to stay abreast of developments in government which affect the private practices of medicine. While the AMA historically has been associated with public opposition to national health insurance, as Professor de Vise noted, of late it has assumed a new posture. In his statement read to the House Ways and Means Committee in 1975, Dr. Max Parrott, then AMA president, set forth AMA's support of the Fulton bill (involving tax credits) and its opposition to other forms of government supervision and payment of fees.

STATEMENT OF MAX H. PARROTT, M.D., PRESIDENT, AMERICAN MEDICAL ASSOCIATION, ACCOMPANIED BY RICHARD E. PALMER, M.D., PRESIDENT-ELECT; AND HARRY N. PETERSON, DIRECTOR, DEPARTMENT OF LEGISLATION

Dr. PARROTT. Thank you, Mr. Chairman. I am Max H. Parrott, president of the American Medical Association. I am a practicing physician from Portland, Oreg., and with me today in presenting association testimony on this important subject of national health insurance is Richard E. Palmer, M.D., president-elect of the American Medical Association from Alexandria, Va.

Incidentally, we are both practicing physicians, I in the field of obstetrics and gynecology, Dr. Palmer in pathology. Also with us is Harry N. Peterson, director of our department of legislation at the American Medical Association.

Mr. Chairman, we are pleased to have this opportunity to appear again before you to express our views on national health insurance. The subject of this legislation has been raised many times during the past three Congresses. Once again national health insurance is under close scrutiny by interested Congressmen, committees, administration officials, and the public. I will take the liberty of not reading the whole text which is before you because of time constraints.

Mr. ROSTENKOWSKI. Without objection, we will place your entire text in the record.

Dr. PARROTT. The extended discussion on national health insurance which has taken place during the past years has been beneficial in many respects in analyzing the issues and in evaluating the impact upon society.

We have observed a shift in attitude toward such a national program with an increased awareness and concern on the part of most interested parties as to the magnitude of the problems involved. These problems have been brought into better focus as a result of evidence of the effects of governmentally administered and controlled programs both here and abroad.

Our national priorities have also shifted because of the effects of the changing economy, and the devastating effects of inflation on all segments of our society.

The public has expressed among its major priorities a concern with inflation, with the state of the economy, and with crime. National polls have indicated that national health insurance is of low concern.

During this same period of time significant changes have taken place in our health system through increased manpower programs, increased facilities construction, increased levels of private health insurance coverage, and a variety of other programs. There is fuller realization and acknowledgment that this country's health system—

under attack by many in the course of the national health insurance debate—is indeed superior to any other in the world.

Mr. Chairman, we will amplify on these points as we proceed in our testimony.

Improvements in our health system are continually occurirng, and the system is increasingly effective in responding to the needs of our society. Individuals who have recently testified before you have urged deliberation and caution in considering any national health plan. This will assure that our excellent system will continue to improve and will not suffer the stifling effects experienced in other countries.

When considering a national plan for this country it is necessary to take cognizance of the strengths of our method of health care delivery. I would like to review briefly some of those strengths with you at this time.

First: American medical service and medical technology have developed at an unparalleled rate, along with American scientific achievement in general. This has all happened since World War II. Presently in this country there is more and better medical technology than anywhere else in the world. And that technology has been fostered and achieved in the absence of a national health insurance program.

Second: There are more physicians being graduated from medical schools at this time than at any other time in our history. The estimated number of graduates for this year is nearly 13,000, a 72-percent increase in 10 years. In addition, approximately 50 percent of those entering graduate medical education, that is, specialty training; are now in medical specialties considered as primary care—a goal which was not expected to be achieved for several years [see attachment 1].

Dr. Parrott. This is being accomplished in the absence of national health insurance or Federal controls.

Third: More medical schools have opened in the past 10 years than were opened in the previous 20 years. We now have 114 medical schools as compared with only 88 in 1965 and this is illustrated in attachment No. 2 attached to our testimony.

Dr. Parrott. Many of these schools are emphasizing primary care and are located in nonmetropolitan or physician shortage areas. This, too, has been done in the absence of a national health insurance program.

Fourth: Statistics show that presently the private sector has made available to the population basic health insurance benefit policies covering 80 percent of the total population. In addition that same private sector provides catastrophic benefits for three out of every four persons in this country. The bulk of the remaining population has access to medicare/medicaid. A very small percentage represents people who, unfortunately, do not now have such insurance. Of significance, we note what while there is an increasing amount of private insurance, the total percentage of health care expenditures for private insurance benefits for the under-65 population has steadily increased from 1966, also, total out-of-pocket personal expenditures, which include premium payments, have decreased during that time. Moreover, this massive private health insurance coverage has occurred without stimulus of a national health insurance program.

It is also necessary to point out that if we had adopted programs similar to those of other countries our present strengths would have N2 been compromised and jeopardized.

Mr. Chairman, these great strengths which we see in the health care system of this country are the ones upon which we believe it is most appropriate to build any program of national health insurance. It is both reasonable and obvious that these aspects must be accentuated rather than adopt a program suggested by some which not only would impose a system of Federal administration upon our health system but would also attempt, for some reason still unclear to us, to restructure the entire system.

[Attachment No. 1]

CHANGES IN "PRIMARY CARE" RESIDENCY PROGRAMS AND 1ST-YEAR POSITIONS 1968-73

Specialty	Number of approved programs			Number of 1st year positions filled			1st year positions filled, number of United States and Canadian graduates		Positions filled, number of FMG's		Percent FMG's	
	1968	1973	Percent change 1968–73	1968	1973	Percent change 1968–73	1968	1973	1968	1973	1968	1973
Family practice	0	206	----	----	766	----	----	720	----	46	----	6
General practice	154	51	−67	254	176	−31	116	33	143	143	56	81
Internal medicine	419	433	+3	2,589	4,139	+60	1,801	3,154	788	985	30	23
Obstetrics/gynecology	358	347	−3	759	1,003	+33	433	675	326	328	43	32
Pediatrics	260	274	+5	1,002	1,699	+69	651	1,141	406	588	41	33
Total	1,191	1,311	+9	4,604	7,783	+69	3,001	5,723	1,663	2,090	36	27

Note: U.S. graduates: 1968, 7,973; 1973, 11,613.

[Attachment No. 2]

STUDENTS AND GRADUATES IN MEDICAL AND BASIC SCIENCE SCHOOLS, 1930–75 [1]

Year	Number schools [2]	Total enrollment	1st year	Intermediate years	Graduates
1930–31	76	21,982	6,456	10,791	4,735
1935–36 [3]	77	22,564	6,605	10,776	5,183
1940–41 [3]	77	21,379	5,837	10,267	5,275
1945–46	77	23,216	6,060	11,330	5,826
1950–51	79	26,186	7,177	12,874	6,135
1955–56	82	28,639	7,686	14,108	6,845
1956–57	85	29,130	8,014	14,320	6,796
1957–58	85	29,473	8,030	14,582	6,861
1958–59	85	29,614	8,128	14,626	6,860
1959–60	85	30,084	8,173	14,830	7,081
1960–61	86	30,288	8,298	14,996	6,994
1961–62	87	31,078	8,483	15,427	7,168
1962–63	87	31,491	8,642	15,585	7,264
1963–64	87	32,001	8,772	15,893	7,336
1964–65	88	32,428	8,856	16,163	7,409
1965–66	88	32,835	8,759	16,502	7,574
1966–67	89	33,423	8,964	16,716	7,743
1967–68	94	34,538	9,479	17,086	7,973
1968–69	99	35,833	9,863	17,911	8,059
1969–70	101	37,669	10,401	18,901	8,367
1970–71	103	40,487	11,348	20,165	8,974
1971–72	108	43,650	12,361	21,738	9,551
1972–73	112	47,546	13,726	23,429	10,391
1973–74	114	50,886	14,185	25,088	11,613
1974–75	114	54,074	14,963	26,397	12,714

[1] To appear in "JAMA" in final issue of 1975.
[2] Prior to 1956–57, schools in development were not included.
[3] For the years 1931–32 through 1941–42, 2 schools reported total enrollment and graduates only.

We do, of course, recognize that there are some weaknesses within the present health care system. But we would hasten to point out that weaknesses are in the process of being rectified by our present responsive system without the need for a national health insurance program.

Manpower shortages are being overcome, alternative delivery systems are under experimentation, new types of providers are being utilized on an increasing scale, greater health education is being carried on by many groups, and new public awareness of the impact of total environment upon health is being aroused.

However, one significant problem which does remain, and which appears to us as a primary concern of the public, is the one of financial access to care, particularly in view of advanced medical technology and increasing health care costs, as well as the state of our economy.

As you hear testimony from advocates of those programs which would attempt to restructure the system as well as to provide financing mechanisms, I would urge you to keep in mind not only the foregoing essential consideration, but also the following basic thoughts concerning medical care in the United States today.

First: The need for catastrophic coverage is to assure that if such expenses do occur the individual will be able to pay from a source other than his own pocket. Nevertheless, this insurance for most people under 65 in reality is only an assurance for peace of mind since for most of them, the catastrophic occasion will never occur. The major need remains access to full care.

Second: Preventive health care, touted by many supporters of other bills as achieving a superior state of health if enacted, is limited in its effectiveness under any health insurance program. National health insurance cannot correct many conditions leading to serious illnesses and to suggest otherwise amounts to overpromise. For example, how would any physician stop his patient from smoking? What will convince anyone not to overeat or not to pursue an improper diet? Who can be forced to exercise? What will be done to assure adequate housing, clean air, proper working conditions, and a healthful environment? What about boredom, indifference, depression, lack of family attachments? Who will stop drug addiction and/or alcoholism? What about injuries and deaths caused by accidents? We could continue to enumerate many other issues which, whether generally recognized or not, are a part of preventive health care which have a definite, direct bearing upon life styles, quality of life and of health, but which cannot be ameliorated by any national health insurance program.

Third: It must be pointed out that one of the very basic reasons for present concern over the high cost of care can be directly traced to the success of medicine in recent years in the development of new technology. The elderly live longer today because of better medical technology. The seriously ill or injured are kept alive and eventually returned to normal life through the intervention of more highly skilled personnel and more complex equipment. Organs are transplanted, and people are able to carry on their lives. Today we treat and maintain the chronically ill and the seriously ill and the injured beyond what could even be imagined 20 or 30 years ago. In addition, health facilities are expensive because of the necessity to comply with present statutes and regulations intended to foster quality care. In addition, labor, equipment, and supply costs are higher. Although some costs might be reduced through a system of strict rationing, we must pose the question as to whether Congress would desire such a system at the expense of continued development and application of medical technology.

All of these points which I have reviewed with you strongly mitigate against a restructuring of our present system.

With these concepts in mind, I would urge you to look to the fundamental issues in the proposed national health insurance plans particularly in the methods of financing and administration.

In these two elements the plans vary considerably.

Some plans would tax payrolls through social security taxes to fund a program administered and controlled by social security. Others would more realistically rely upon the present strong points in our system by requiring employer coverage and insurance carrier administration in the private sector.

This latter type plan recognizes the important role of the private sector as well as the administrative limitations and shortcomings of the Federal bureaucracy. It also recognizes the fact that administration of a national health insurance program is better performed in the private sector. Administration in the private sector is more realistic when one considers the mounting evidence of problems arising in national programs which are prototypes for proposals now advanced involving government administration.

We need only call attention to European national health insurance programs as examples. When their central government took over the responsibilities for financing and administering programs, the growth and development of facilities, particularly and technology to a lesser extent were frozen at the level at which central government took control. Since that time the governments have been faced with increasingly antiquated facilities, with a growing dissatisfaction with the government system by both providers and patients, with an exodus of trained personnel to other countries, with increasing tax liability, with increase in costs, with waiting lists of 1 or more years, and which the inability of government to cope with rationing of health care. And it must be remembered that these problems have occurred in countries which are, as compared with the United States, small in area, compact, and homogeneous in population. Factors which should really help to assure success and where the population is inclined to look to the central government for assistance in many areas.

In our own country, the program which comes closest to an example of a national health insurance program for the public is medicare, a program which has benefited the elderly. However, this program has been characterized by overzealous bureaucratic control. In fact, its method of administration cautions against adopting any such similarly administered program for the general public.

As a final cautionary note, we would urge you to consider the inflationary impact upon the economy of a governmentally financed and administered program. We are all aware of the present difficulties through which our economy has been passing during the past 2 years. The Federal budget has been near the breaking point with a scope of deficit spending which is staggering in comprehension. Federal spending has arrived at the point at which the public is unable to withstand the two-pronged assault on it of inflation caused by deficit spending and of high taxes imposed in order to support Federal programs.

Mr. Chairman, in order to appraise the factors leading to rising costs in health care, this association is convening a national commission on the cost of medical care to be composed of individuals representing various sectors of the health care field and of the public.

In the meantime, however, Mr. Chairman, in order not to increase inflationary pressures and deficit spending, nor to hinder medical technology and the forward strides taking place in health care development, we must caution against any federally controlled and administered national health insurance program. Should we rush into such a system, the result will be a decrease in quality care and in availability.

We would also caution that no national health insurance system can achieve its goals without the support and commitment of providers of services. Artificial and unrealistic limitations on reimbursement or interferences with the practice of medicine will curtail availability of service and defeat the purpose of the program.

Mr. Chairman, this concludes my statement. At this time, I will call on Dr. Richard Palmer to continue with our testimony.

Dr. PALMER. Thank you.

Mr. Chairman, members of the subcommittee, the health care system of this country is a pluralistic one, a composite of various private initiatives and public programs. It is a system which encourages innovation and competition by providing incentives for organizational change and offers opportunity for improvement of quality care.

The public interest would be better served if we examine the goals of NHI within the context of the existing system and direct our energies toward perfection of this system in meeting the health care needs of this Nation.

Needed improvements can be brought about without gambling on a whole new medical health system whose effects and efficiencies, in the main, are unpredictable. We offer our plan for maximum health services for all persons through comprehensive insurance protection under a proven system which provides the finest health care in the world, and which can be financed in the private sector with a minimum of Federal support. This is the "Comprehensive Health Care Insurance Act of 1975" (H.R. 6222).

N3

H.R. 6222 would establish a program to assure that every person has equal access to high quality medical and health care regardless of ability to pay. For the poor and for the affluent alike it provides identical coverage and includes protection against both the ordinary and catastrophic expenses of illness that an individual or family encounter.

Coverage would be provided for all inpatient and outpatient hospital care, 100 inpatient days a year in a skilled nursing facility, and all home health care services. It also provides: full physician services including all medical care provided under this direction; a full range of preventive services including physical examinations, immunizations and inoculations; well-balanced care; X-ray and laboratory services; ambulance services; and full psychiatric care. Children under age 7 will be fully covered for dental care, and this age limit will be raised each year until all persons under the age of 18 are covered; adults would be covered for emergency dental care.

Cost-sharing will apply as a safeguard against abuse, but will apply in moderation so as not to deny benefits to persons in need of care who cannot meet such costs. There is no deductible in our plan—no fixed amount is required to be paid before benefits begin. Benefits will begin immediately, with coinsurance set at 20 percent with the full amount of coinsurance being related to income. However, a fixed ceiling on the amount of coinsurance that any individual or any family will be required to pay in a year will apply to all persons. The poor, however, will not have to pay any coinsurance.

Most Americans are currently covered by employment-based insurance, and the premium is paid in full by the employer or shared between employer and employee; the total cost is thus paid in the private sector and without Government involvement. H.R. 6222 mandates the employer to offer coverage for employees and their families, thereby continuing a method of protection with which they all are familiar and which can be readily put into operation. The mandate gives legislative assurance that the full coverage will be provided, that the employer will pay at least 65 percent of the premium and, accordingly, that the employee will have only a limited participation in premium cost.

Those who are unemployed or poor will be entitled to Federal participation in the premium but they—like all others—will still have a choice of private coverage—an insurance policy, if you will, a Blue-Cross/Blue Shield plan, a group prepayment plan (including HMO), or any other plan meeting the program standards of adequate coverage. The amount of Federal contribution would be scaled according to income of the insured—and the Government would pay the full premium for the poor. On the same basis, Federal participation would assist medicare eligibles in obtaining supplemental coverage to bring their benefits up to the level contemplated by the new insurance program.

Simple mechanisms built into the program facilitate the Government's premium participation without resort to a cumbersome means test. A premium participation table enables the individual to assess readily the amount to which he is entitled. He may buy his insurance, pay the full premium and claim the Government share as a credit against tax on his income tax return. Or he may arrange to pay only his share of the premium, if any, prepare a claim form, and have the carrier bill the Government for the premium balance.

Most Americans believe that the role of Government financing in health insurance should be directed toward making quality care accessible to those who cannot afford to meet the expenses of such care. This is an underlying precept in our program of private insurance through employment—financed primarily in the private sector—and premium assistance by Government for the poor and the lederly. It is in sharp contrast to the financing in H.R. 21 that would impose on our tax system—already strained—the burden of some $50 billion in new social security taxes and the matching from general revenues of an additional $50 billion in order to support a federally controlled and administered health care system under which all services would be supplied by providers and professional practitioners under contract to the Government.

There is no basis for assuming that health care financing can be better or more economically adminstered in the governmental sector than in the private sector. On the contrary, Government administration has been shown to be more costly. We agree with a former Secretary of HEW that elimination of the profit factor, through the Social Security handling of health insurance finances, will not bring economies and efficiencies, the financing of health care is too important to the American people to turn over to a Federal bureaucracy.

If we allow Federal administration, we risk creating a national program which is unresponsive to particular needs and lacking in sufficient stability and innovation. We need a health care system that has room for and will reinforce the strengths of private initiative, not one that will stifle them under piles of paperwork and Federal regulation. It is our firm conviction, therefore, that any national health insurance program should be administered through the private sector.

If in the view of Congress an urgent need for national health legislation exists, we commend for your specific approval H.R. 6222, which would preserve the flexibility of our medical system, and build on the real accomplishments of American medicine. It stresses the major contribution made by the private sector of the economy and takes advantage of private institutions and industries. It attempts to hold to a minimum its demands upon Government, both for tax dollars and for the inevitable controls that go with them and does not thrust upon the Government a tremendous program of health spending to be financed primarily through new taxes.

We see, on the other hand, in some of the other proposals now before the Congress, elements which threaten the existing system of health care delivery and the high quality of care it affords. We shall touch on only a few of these.

N5   We have already indicated our strong opposition to H.R. 21. We also strongly oppose a public utility approach to health care delivery as conceived in H.R. 1. Newly created entities—health care corporations (HCC's)—would be operating under franchise of the State Health Commission (SHC), in designated areas within a State, and would provide services directly or through affiliates within their franchised areas. Each State Health Commission would be under mandate to divide the State into health care corporation areas and blanket the State with health care corporations. The State Health Commission would also have ratemaking authority. In addition to the special Federal subsidies for the development and operation of health care corporations, provision is made for special premium subsidies for health care corporation enrollees. In the interest of good medical care, we have advocated a policy of pluralism which affords an individual or family a variety of health care delivery methods, and a choice of the kind of care they will receive. We must, therefore, reject the discriminatory Federal funding in support of a single method of health care delivery. We reject also, as undesirable and unnecessary, the State franchising of health care operations and public utility regulation.

H.R. 1 specifically requires that services of certain physicians (such as radiologists and pathologists) be paid as hospital services, thus making them subject to the institutional ratemaking provisions. This is highly objectionable. Any plan should properly recognize the physician's professional service as being distinct from hospital services, and any provisions for institutional reimbursement should not be interpreted to include the professional services irrespective of the setting in which the professional services are provided. This differentiation from hospital services should apply to physicians services under any bill, including H.R. 6222.

N6   Another bill, H.R. 10028—identical with S. 2470, the Long-Ribicoff bill in the Senate—emphasizes catastrophic coverage. Revised from its form in the previous Congress, it now provides in part for the use of private insurance, and in this respect we are pleased that it does indeed recognize one of the strengths of the present system.

However, the total program contemplated in the bill H.R. 10028 is unacceptable. This is a program of catastrophic insurance for all—with benefits for medical services to begin after a family has incurred $2,000 of medical expenses, for hospital care benefits to begin after 60 days of hospital confinement. Coverage would be provided either under a public plan, administered in parallel with medicare, and subject to medicare conditions and limitations on payment of services, or under an elective employer plan providing private insurance for employees and their families. Such private coverage would be administered by the carriers. Underlying the public plan for catastrophic insurance would be basic coverage for low-income persons under a federalized medicaid program administered in the same manner as medicare and financed from Federal general revenues and State contributions. Providers and practitioners would be required to accept as reimbursement in full for their services only those amounts designated as payments from the plan.

In examining the need for such a program we observe that, in 1974, 135 million persons under age 65 had major medical insurance. This is the most rapidly growing form of health insurance in the Nation, and the trend for such added coverage is fostered by an increasing public awareness. Consequently, we must question the need to impose on the American taxpayer and consumer a costly universal Federal program of freestanding catastrophic health insurance.

We believe that the benefits under any health care program should be uniform, and our bill does provide for basic health care needs as well as catastrophic needs. Our bill recognizes that catastrophic protection should be a part of total comprehensive benefits. Free standing catastrophic coverage is made to appear attractive because it requires less financing, but this is because it is a program of very limited benefits and makes no provision for the fundamental health care needs of the majority. Catastrophic insurance alone is not a solution to the problem of meeting the health care problems of all persons. For this reason we have opposed such a measure.

There are additional objections to H.R. 10028 which we might point out, however. For one, the proposal will operate to enlarge the sphere of federally financed and controlled insurance coverage while severely reducing insurance in the private sector. Under a system of HEW certification of private insurance, private carriers will be induced to tailor their policies to provide basic coverage with limits adequate to meet the deductibles contained in Federal catastrophic insurance. This will have the net effect of transferring insurance coverage from the private sector to the tax-financed public program. It is easy to observe, moreover, that further Government invasion into the insurance field may be achieved through the simple device of reducing the catastrophic insurance deductible.

In our concern for erosion of the present health care system, we must look upon this program as an incremental approach to complete governmental domination of the health care system. The danger is real, and with accession of bureaucratic control the course of complete domination becomes more difficult to reverse.

The American citizen, as both taxpayer and patient would be ill-served by transferring the functions now performed by the private insurance system to a federally controlled and operated system.

In conclusion, we submit H.R. 6222 as the health insurance program best suited for fulfilling the national need. We urge your favorable consideration of H.R. 6222 as being based upon these principles on which any national health insurance program must be founded.

Mr. Chairman, we will be pleased to respond to any questions which the subcommittee may have. We wish again to state our appreciation for the opportunity to appear before you and present our views. Please be assured that it is our desire to be of assistance to the subcommittee as it considers this and other legislation affecting the health care of our citizens. [AMA plan. . .follow:]

A NATIONAL HEALTH INSURANCE PLAN DESIGNED BY AMERICA'S PHYSICIANS

1. WHY PHYSICIANS SUPPORT NATIONAL HEALTH INSURANCE

As the ones responsible for caring for patients every day, physicians know how essential quality medical care is to the health and well-being of an individual. They are also very much aware that the cost of health and medical care has become a financial burden for certain segments of our population. Even for those with substantial incomes, a long or serious illness can create serious financial problems.

These are the concerns that led physicians, through the American Medical Association, to develop their own national health insurance plan. It is called the Comprehensive Health Care Insurance Act of 1975 (H.R. 6222) and was introduced in Congress April 22, 1975.

2. THE UNDERPINNINGS OF THE PLAN

In formulating the plan, the physicians established a *comprehensive list* of medical and health services that would be available to everyone, incorporated a set of principles to assure *quality care*, and based the entire program on a *sound, realistic financing mechanism*.

Integral to the plan is the belief that federal financial help should be provided to those who need it most, and that everyone should be free to choose his or her own physician and health insurance plan. Further, physicians believe any program of national health insurance should be built on the best of the present system—a system which is already providing more and better health care to more people than in any other country.

3. HERE'S HOW THE PHYSICIANS' PLAN WOULD WORK

The program would provide a complete package of benefits essential to good health care, as well as to protect against the cost of catastrophic illness—without limits. Realistic preventive care benefits would also be included. Importantly, the plan is designed to keep red tape and bureaucracy to a minimum.

The actual health care protection would be furnished entirely by a private health insurance policy or plan. Coverage would be available through the present system of employer-employee group health insurance plans; or through a program for the self-employed and non-employed. Supplemental coverage would be available to those eligible for Medicare to raise the level of benefits to equal those of the physicians' plan. Individuals currently receiving Medicaid benefits would receive them through this new program.

Benefits

Under the physicians' plan, approved protection would have to provide payment of expenses for both basic and catastrophic health care needs. This would be true whether an individual participates in the employer-empoyee program, the program for the self-employed and non-employed, or the supplemental coverage for Medicare beneficiaries. All insurance plans offered would be approved by the respective states to assure that benefits met the comprehensive national standards.

Benefits for a 12-month period would have to include:
365 days of hospital inpateient care.
100 days of inpateint care in a skilled nursing care facility.
All emergency and outpateint services.
All physicians care (diagnostic, therapeutic, and preventive, regardless of where it is provided) and other health services.
All home health services.
All dental care for children.
Emergency dental care for everyone.
Ambulance service.
Institutional and outpatient psychiatric care.
Well-baby care.
Immunization.
Physical examinations.
X-ray and laboratory services.
Anesthesiology services.

Employer coverage

Most people would receive their health care protection as they do now—through the current system of employer-employee group health insurance. The employer would be required to offer the insurance but participation by the employee would be voluntary. At least 65% of the health insurance cost would have to be paid by the employer, the rest would be paid by the employee. Financial assistance will be provided for small businesses.

Self-Employed, Non-Employed, and Medicare-Eligibles

Individuals or families in these categories could buy qualified health care insurance. The insurance plan would have to meet the established national standards of benefits and policy conditions. The federal government would contribute toward the cost of the policy according to the individual's or family's ability to pay. The amount for a given year is measured according to how much the individual or family paid in income tax the preceding year.

For example, a family of four earning $4,850 a year would pay no income tax. Therefore, the federal government would pay the entire cost of the health insurance premium.

For a family of four earning $6,040 a year, the income tax would be $159. The federal government would pay 84% of the cost of the family's health insurance premium.

For a family of four with an annual income of $10,349, the income tax would be $891. For this category (and any individual or family paying more than $891 income tax), the federal government would pay 10% of the cost of the family's health insurance premium.

The financial assistance would be in the form of an income tax credit or a certificate to be given to the insurance company toward payment of the premium.

Unemployed

Unemployed persons, while eligible for federal or state unemployment compensation, would continue to be covered by their previous employer-sponsored insurance. Premiums would be paid by the federal government. If unemployment compensation expired before new employment, the government would continue to cover health insurance premiums for the rest of the year. At the beginning of the new calendar year, the individual would immediately be eligible for the non-employed subsidy program (described in previous paragraphs). Because of this provision, there would be no interruption in coverage.

Coinsurance

As with any program that offers as many benefits as the medical profession's plan, financial safeguards must be included, otherwise the program would be too expensive for the taxpayers to afford. In this program there would be cost-sharing in the form of coinsurance.

Although the amounts are small, cost-sharing between citizens and the government would help keep the total cost of the program at a reasonable level. It would help prevent policy holders from going to a physician "just because it's paid for" or entering a hospital "because it's more convenient."

Coinsurance would be 20% of the cost of all covered benefits—except for the poor. But in no case could coinsurance exceed $1,500 for an individual or $2,000 for a family, regardless of income. As soon as an individual or family reaches the limit on coinsurance, the catastrophic portion of the plan would take over.

Coinsurance would be 20% of the cost of all covered benefits, but not more than a specified ceiling limit related to income. The poor would pay no coinsurance.

This coinsurance maximum (the most an individual or family would pay) would be equal to 10% of the individual or family income after a "coinsurance deduction" has been subtracted. The coinsurance deduction is figured according to family size. For example, the deduction is $4,200 for a family of four. So if a family of four earns $10,000, the coinsurance limit (or total cost) for a 12-month period would be $580, or 10% of $5,800 (salary of $10,000 minus deduction of $4,200). The family would not have to pay more than $580 for all of the medical services provided in that year, even if there were expenses of a catastrophic size.

In no case could coinsurance exceed $1,500 for an individual or $2,000 for a family, regardless of income.

As soon as a family or individual reaches the limit on coinsurance, the catastrophic portion of the plan would take over.

4. WILL NATIONAL HEALTH INSURANCE REALLY SOLVE AMERICA'S HEALTH PROBLEMS

Unfortunately, no—because many of America's health problems do not have purely medical solutions. Many of these problems can be solved only when our society commits itself to eliminating the root causes, such as poor housing and sanitation, malnutrition, smoking, lack of exercise. A basic, and essential step in accomplishing this objective is the dissemination of good, sound health information to the public.

Over the years, America's physicians, through the AMA, have been deeply involved in health education. The AMA has on-going programs to educate the public about drug abuse, venereal disease, proper nutrition, and exercise.

The AMA is also working hard to increase the capability of our health care system by encouraging and supporting the expansion of the allied health professions and increasing the number of physicians. The AMA is particularly gratified that the total enrollment in U.S. medical schools has increased from 32,500 in 1965 to 53,000 in 1975. An equally important development is the increasing numbers of medical students entering the primary care areas of family practice, internal medicine, obstetrics and gynecology, and pediatrics. In 1973 alone, nearly 50% of the graduating students entered residency training in these areas.

The AMA has also been a very active and positive force in the passage of constructive health and medical care legislation for the public. It has strongly supported such federal legislation as maternal and child health programs; protection of human beings in medical research; drug abuse education; medical devices safety standards; cancer research; assistance for allied health personnel, public health personnel and nurses training. In addition, the AMA has authored and introduced legislation to develop community emergency medical services programs, to improve rural health care delivery, and to upgrade health care for American Indians.

Many years ago, physicians, themselves, pioneered peer review programs, and set up safeguards to ensure that all patients receive quality medical and health care.

Even though our present system provides more and better health care to more people than in any other country, physicians are aware that the American system is not perfect. And they are as concerned as anyone about its improvement. The

Comprehensive Health Care Insurance Act is only one of many AMA programs that represents the physicians' active campaign to improve health care and its delivery in America.

The Health Insurance Industry ([23], pp. 1328–1340)

The health insurance industry has great stakes at play in any formulation of a national health insurance program. The industry (of private insurance carriers) is willing to support a national program as long as private carriers are involved in its administration. Various representatives from the industry have appeared before congressional committees on behalf of their interests. The largest private carrier is the Blue Cross–Blue Shield organization, and one of its most articulate spokespersons is William Ryan, who assumed the presidency of the National Association of Blue Shield Plans in 1976. He testified in February of that year before the House Committee on Interstate and Foreign Commerce, as did his Blue Cross counterpart, Walter McNerney (see [23], pp. 1323–1361). While the Health Insurance Association of America, which is a trade association for the private health insurance carriers, endorsed the Burleson-McIntyre National Health Care Act of 1975 (H.R. 5990 and S. 1438 of the 94th Congress, described in Chapter 2), it seems clear from Ryan's testimony that his association is intent on exerting a continuing role in administration of insurance plans—no matter what legislation might be enacted.

STATEMENT OF WILLIAM E. RYAN, PRESIDENT DESIGNATE,
NATIONAL ASSOCIATION OF BLUE SHIELD PLANS

Mr. Chairman, I am William E. Ryan, President Designate of the National Association of Blue Shield Plans. The Association consists of 71 locally based, not-for-profit medical care prepayment Plans, employing 55,000 people and covering 72 million private subscribers and an additional 12 million as agents for government programs. All told, two of every five Americans look to Blue Shield for financial protection against health care expense.

I am privileged to appear before you today to testify on national health insurance. Blue Shield respects the members of this Subcommittee for recognizing the evolutionary nature of the debate over national health insurance and for your efforts to explore every aspect of this subject before taking action.

We have followed with interest through the years and have been an active participant in the national health insurance debate. Even before the issue reached national prominence, we were dedicated to identifying areas in which health coverage could be improved and working to seek appropriate answers. We are continuing this effort.

The private sector carriers have done much to reduce the economic risk resulting from health care services expenses for the majority of Americans. Today more than 90 percent of all Americans under the age 65 are covered by some form of health care coverage. This number is increasing each year. The role of the private carrier in America has been absolutely unique in the world. No other country has developed a strong, viable private insurance system as America has created.

Notwithstanding these efforts, there continue to be problems that private carriers have not been able to solve. Some of these will only be resolved through the active participation of government. Some will require the effort of the whole society, because, Mr. Chairman, they trace directly to society itself.

The concept of a single, all-encompassing bill to redirect the health system, identifying its deficiencies and channeling its dollar flow to effect the necessary remedies, has been a magnificent goal. It is an illusion. The health system is too complex. Its evolution is too rapid. The demands upon it are too varied and conflicting.

With some understanding of and great sympathy for the Subcommittee's problem, Mr. Chairman, we respectfully suggest that the Congress cannot move effectively on too broad a front. We believe, on the other hand, that major problems do exist that can only be solved with Congress' help. These will be handled well, in our view, in direct proportion to Congress' willingness to isolate and define those problems, prioritize them, and address them on their own merits with regard for their impact upon other elements of the system.

In general, the problems to be solved by national health insurance are not those traceable to the health system itself. Rather, they are those caused by the inability or unwillingness of some people to purchase adequate health care coverage. And, in honesty, there are characteristics of the health insurance system which should be corrected or improved. Government can be highly effective in these area, if it directs its efforts at the specific problems and applies its financing and regulatory authorities selectively.

The nature of these problems can be stated rather simply:

1. The poor and near poor are unable to purchase coverage for themselves. They will need public assistance.

2. The temporarily unemployed should be offered coverage during their period of unemployment.

3. Long-term medical care services should be provided to the aged, who are for the most part on fixed incomes.

4. Everyone should have access to protection against insolvency due to catastrophic medical expense, even though relatively few are so affected.

5. Those now classed as "uninsurable" should be able to purchase coverage at reasonable rates.

6. Coverage should be as available to all individuals and small groups as it is now to large groups.

7. The quality of coverage should be assured, and effective carrier performance incentives should be implemented.

If federal involvement is to be successful, government's response must be appropriate. Too narrow a response is wasted. On the other hand, over-reaction that creates unnecessary confusion, unneeded bureaucracy and unwarranted interference with health care may do even more harm. In short, federal initiatives should be tailored to meet the identified needs. We believe that federal action should proceed in a working relationship with our industry and in accord with a few basic principles, which we would suggest as:

1. There should be maximum participation by the private sector, which has developed nearly all of the capacity which now exists in the actual administration of health benefits. To get the greatest benefit from the health financing industry, excessive regulation and controls not directed at quality and efficiency of coverage should be avoided at all costs.

2. There should be free choice between provider and patient and a competitive market among carriers, within the constraints of standards for benefits and administration.

3. The public should have free choice of health care delivery systems.

4. Federal financing will be required for coverage of the poor and the medically indigent. The private sector has no capacity to provide such financing without legislation.

5. Effective regulation of carriers with respect both to benefits and retentions is necessary. Traditionally, this has been a state function, and regulations should continue to be implemented by the states. However, federal guidelines will be needed, and the federal government should have intervention authority if the states fail to act.

6. There should be minimum standards for basic coverage and an opportunity for those groups and individuals who wish protection beyond the minimum level to purchase complementary coverage.

7. There should be opportunity to integrate supplemental coverage with the basic coverage and administer it as one program, for economy and efficiency, and in order to provide first dollar benefits and the advantages of physician participation as an alternative to cost sharing through coinsurance and deductibles.

8. Catastrophic coverage must be coordinated with basic coverage and should not be implemented as a "free-standing" program. In the absence of such coordination, it is essentially impossible to define the point of catastrophe, and there is potential for enormous duplication of administrative effort.

9. An NHI program should be understandable from the outset in terms of its systems requirements, in order to facilitate design of appropriate systems for its implementation. However, implementation should be phased in, with maximum possible lead time, to permit orderly accommodation of the staffing, training, software and hardware problems which will accompany implementation, and which would be considerably exacerbated by a sudden massive eligibility for new benefits.

Any legislation will ultimately have to deal with at least five basic issues which can be resolved in a number of ways. How the Congress does resolve them will essentially dictate the form of the final legislation. These issues include eligibility for benefits; financing; means of administration; cost containment; and benefit structure. We would like, Mr. Chairman, to comment on each of these issues.

Health insurance is one of the most widely purchased items in our society. According to the Health Insurance Association of America over 160 million Americans had, in 1974, some form of hospital benefits through a Blue Cross Blue Shield Plan or a commercial insurance company. Over 150 million Americans had some form of surgical benefits for the same period. The Social Security Administration reported that beginning the first of July, 1974, there were over 23 million enrolled in Medicare Part A and over 22 million enrolled in Part B. There were 24 million actual recipients of Medicaid in this last fiscal year. Total eligibility is unknown, but was obviously higher. The Social Security Administration, calculated to eliminate those with duplicate coverage as much as possible, estimates that approximately 87 percent of the population had some form of health care coverage as of December 31, 1973.

Regardless of which statistics one accepts, between 87 percent and 97 percent of the American people appear to be eligible for some health care coverage. This does not include those eligible for direct services from the federal government such as the military, American native Indians, etc. The case is weak that government must finance a health insurance program for the population at large. The vast majority of Americans have health insurance.

This is not to say that government should not play a role in assuring that all Americans are eligible for health insurance. However, the vast regulatory and taxing power of government should be used judiciously. It should be tailored to the real problems. A national health insurance program should support, upgrade and complement the existing health insurance system. The government's role should be a combination of regulation in the interest of those who are covered, and financial assistance where it is necessary. The health insurance problem for the general, working, self-supporting population is not eligibility for coverage, but rather assurance that coverage is reasonably priced, adequate, and not unduly discriminatory against individuals and small groups, high risks, and the unemployed.

While health insurance coverage is almost a common denominator among the population, some people are not financially able to secure adequate health insurance. The medical expenses of others are of such a catastrophic nature that they are threatened by financial ruin. The financing of the medical expenses of these people is a problem for society in general. The affected families cannot cope with it alone. The government can, and in many instances already has, used tax revenues to assure that those who cannot afford adequate health care insurance have the financial means to secure care. Government should continue its efforts in this area, and any national health insurance program should assure that the poor, the near-poor and the catastrophically ill have access to adequate health care coverage. Government can make an important contribution by assuring that a basic benefit structure reflecting the minimum coverage needed by an American family is identified for and available to the entire population.

One criticism leveled at the present health insurance industry is that setting premiums by the experience of "groups" encourages employers to discriminate against older, handicapped and high risk workers. The real impact is questionable. Many of these workers are protected from discriminatory hiring practices by federal legislation. Even if such discrimination exists, questions of productivity, worker morale and basic social prejudice are probably more responsible than the impact on the health insurance premium rate.

Blue Shield historically resisted experience rating, and we are not now one of its major advocates. We are, however, sensitive to the point that a collectively-bargained premium is a form of compensation, and should at least arguably be related to an employer or an industry.

If such potential discrimination is a problem, it can be eliminated through the government's use of its regulatory and legislative powers. Requiring all groups below a given size to be community rated, limiting differentials in premium, and further legislation assuring nondiscriminatory hiring practices could be appropriate.

Another population group with special problems is the temporarily unemployed. Extended unemployment would eventually make these people eligible for programs for low income individuals and families. In most cases, however, unemployment is a temporary situation, and these individuals and their families have established standards of living compatible with their previous income. Temporarily unemployed individuals will tend to apply cash assets to ongoing obligations, assuming that employment-related health coverage will be available again before illness strikes. If illness should occur during the period of unemployment, they could find their assets quickly depleted, aggravating an already unfortunate situation.

It has been argued that the social costs of unemployment, including continuation of health insurance coverage, should be the responsibility of employers. But it is unfair to the employer not to limit his liability. Society should share some of the burden.

A national health insurance program could require each employer to continue health insurance coverage under his existing program for a period of 30 days after an employee's termination, whether voluntary or involuntary. If after this period the unemployed individual had not found employment or were not eligible for coverage under a working spouse's health program, the state unemployment agency could become responsible for certifying the eligibility of the individual and his or her dependents' health coverage under a state plan for the temporarily unemployed. Financing would be through state or state and federal revenues, administered by carriers.

Terminated employees who are eligible for continued coverage through health care welfare trust funds would not be eligible for the unemployed health care program until the expiration of such coverage. A temporarily unemployed individual with a spouse eligible for or enrolled in an employee health care plan would not be eligible for the unemployed health care program to the extent that the spouse could provide him with coverage as a dependent.

PROGRAM AND BENEFIT DESIGN

Most NHI proposals currently before Congress have focused on two approaches: the voluntary and the compulsory. The voluntary approach (illustrated by mandated provisions) eliminates financial access barriers to assure that everyone—regardless of financial or health status—will have access to coverage. The compulsory approach (illustrated by tax-funding and government administration provisions) provides every person with "insurance" automatically.

Our present health insurance combines the best features of both voluntary and compulsory coverage. The methods should be applied to meet specific objectives and needs and should not be imposed on the entire population without regard to the vast differences in its needs, capacities, and preferences. Therefore, Mr. Chairman, we recommend the following characteristics for a program to accomplish the objectives of assuring access to adequate health coverage while preserving the best features of the voluntary and compulsory methods.

A mandated access program should be implemented by requiring all employers to offer both a basic program and catastrophic coverage (with a specific level and scope of benefits) to all their employees and pay at least a percentage of the premium with the employee paying the difference, if any.

Participation by the employee would be voluntary. In addition, the basic program with required catastrophic coverage would also be offered to the self-employed at a premium not to exceed a specified percentage (e.g. 125 percent) of the group plan rate.

Employers could elect to offer self-insured plans, but should be subject to the same requirements, standards, and regulations as qualified carriers.

Employees now covered through employee health and welfare trust funds could continue such arrangements provided their plans were certified.

This would be necessary in order to provide continuity of coverage for certain individuals who work for multiple employers over relatively short periods of time.

Each employer required to provide a "certified" health care plan would have to offer an option to membership in a qualified health maintenance organization in the areas in which the employees reside, if such an entity exists in the areas. The Secretary, by regulation, would define qualification requirements for HMO's. The requirements for qualification under the HMO Act of 1973 (PL 93–222) would not apply for this program. This law was written for specific experimental purposes and would be inappropriate to a national health insurance program.

Employers would not be required to pay more for an employee's health benefits under the health maintenance organization option than they would otherwise spend on behalf of the employee under the mandated Employee Health Care Plan.

POOR AND NEAR POOR

Some people are not financially able to secure adequate health insurance. The financing of medical expenses for the poor and near poor is a problem for society in general, as these people cannot cope with it alone. Government should continue to finance the medical expenses for this sector of the population replacing the Medicaid program and using qualified carriers to administer the new program. This would assure uniformity of benefits, simplify administration, and eliminate certain inequities when a recipient moves from one state to another. Federal and state revenues as well as premium contributions based on income and family size should finance the program. However, states should not be required to pay more than they were paying at the time of enactment as a contribution to basic benefits under Title XIX.

The beneficiary of the program for the poor should have a choice among carriers. Providing the beneficiary with an opportunity to elect a carrier periodically (perhaps every two years) permits him to exercise judgment regarding the effectiveness of service provided by the carrier. Government and carriers are also provided with a measure of carrier performance that is truly based upon ultimate results. In order to participate, carriers, would be required to operate within acceptable cost parameters.

MEDICARE

Medicare (Title XVIII) should remain essentially unchanged. However, long-term benefits should be expanded. Limits should be placed on cost sharing which, once fulfilled, would entitle the patient to catastrophic protection. The program could be more effectively administered if the federal government would test carrier performance by results, without forcing itself into the internal decision-making of the carrier. The recommendations of the DHEW's Advisory Committee on Medicare Administration, Contracting and Subcontracting are appropriate in this respect.

CATASTROPHIC AND SUPPLEMENTAL COVERAGE

There should be an opportunity for each group or individual to purchase supplemental coverage, such as coverage to fill the deductible and co-insurance amounts, integrated with basic coverage and administered as one program.

Catastrophic coverage should be coordinated with the basic program and should not be implemented as a "free-standing" program. Each group or individual should have good basic coverage. This basic program should pay for in-hospital medical services and surgical services without upper limits as long as the service is medically necessary. We have had cases under the basic Federal Employee Program where as much as $100,000 has been covered for one patient.

In addition to the basic program, the patient should have additional coverage to pay for benefits such as drugs, blood, physical and occupational therapy expenses, etc. It should be clear to the patient, the provider, and the carrier that if a particularly medically necessary service were rendered which was not a basic benefit, it would be covered under the catastrophic program or a supplemental policy.

Having basic coverage provide discrete benefits is far more efficient and economical than interposing an artificial dollar limit. The dollar limit undermines the ability of the carrier to exercise controls, by interrupting its pricing and utilization review processes. It forces the expensve re-creation of history and eligibility files. It creates further expense in confirming incurred expenditures. It imposes conflicting pricing patterns on the same episode of care. It confuses the patient, the provider and the carrier, and compounds the confusion by making the patient responsible for determining his own eligibility.

Perhaps most importantly, the free-standing catastrophic approach may encourage a sense of false security in the patient, leading him to self-insure amounts which may, in themselves, be catastrophic. A free-standing catastrophic program might well result in many patients having less effective coverage than they currently hold, without appreciating the fact. The realization would come when they were least able to cope with the problem and totally unable to share it actuarially.

OTHER PROGRAM PROVISIONS

Employers should be permitted to offer benefits in addition to those required under the mandated program, and to pay more than the required percentage of premium for a certified health care plan. In the absence of a collective bargaining agreement, the employer should not be permitted to require employees to contribute to additional benefits in order to receive the mandated program.

Lawfully designated collective bargaining agents would be allowed to negotiate, accept or reject an employer's health care plan offer on behalf of all employees within the bargaining unit.

No carrier should be allowed to offer coverage supplemental to a "certified" plan unless it also offer certified coverage. In the absence of such a requirement, carriers which responsibly make coverage available, regardless of risk, could be put on a competitive disadvantage by less responsible carriers which avoid the requirements of certification. This would tend to raise the rates for subscribers of certified carriers.

BENEFIT DESIGN

The design of a benefit package must take into consideration: (1) the objectives of the program; (2) the population to be covered; (3) the health resources available; and (4) the financial resources available to pay for these benefits.

The national health program should be implemented in phases with respect to specific benefit increments, so as not to place a sudden additional burden on the health system and on those who must pay for benefits. The phasing in should be planned with the ultimate goal of reaching comprehensive health coverage for the entire nation. However, effective and economical systems planning requires that the ultimate design of each program be spelled out at the time the program is initially legislated.

The benefit design of the various programs will affect demand for certain services. Induced demand should not be phased into a system until there is adequate capacity to absorb it. Therefore, careful analysis of system capacity, growth expectations, and social purpose should be an integral part in establishing a benefit structure.

To a considerable extent, the scope of benefits of a mandated program, particularly in its first phases, is dependent upon the Congress' evaluation of the practical economic impact. The following benefits for necessary care could be phased in at a rate geared to the availability of funds for public programs and Congress' determination of the ability of the private sector to assume additional responsibilities. These benefits represent medical coverage only. Obviously any national health insurance program should also include hospitalization and other essential services which will need to be integrated with this list.

1. Medical care and supplies (including laboratory, X-ray and ambulance service) for: all accidents; surgical and medical emergencies; complications

of pregnancy, but not normal obstetrical care or delivery; Inpatient professional care for: non-emergency illness and surgery; radiation and physical therapy; and chronic illness, other than renal dialysis; Out of hospital surgical,
diagnostic X-ray and laboratory, and radiation service; and Obstetrical care
include pre- and post-natal care and newborn care.

2. Well baby care including immunization prior to 13 months of age.

3. Physician home and office care, except psychiatric care, but including mul-
tiphasic screening, immunization and radiation therapy.

4. Physical examination at frequency rate related to the age and condition
of the patient.

5. Children's care to age 14 for dentistry, vision and hearing, including periodic physical examinations.

6. Care for drug addiction, alcoholism, in-patient mental disorders.

7. Full psychiatric care for children to age 18 and emergency psychiatric
treatment for adults, subject to weekly recertification of emergency need.

**8. Rehabilitation care under the supervision of a physician including care
in specialized institutions and including necessary prosthetic appliances.**

9. Psychiatric care other than emergency care, subject to cost sharing and
periodic recertification.

10. Rental and purchase of durable medical equipment.

11. Prescription drugs.

12. Private duty nursing for in-hospital care upon physician certification
except where intensive care facilities are available.

13. Private duty nursing in the home following institutionalized care upon
certification of need, and private duty nursing in the home by certified VNA
nurses in lieu of institutional care upon physician certification of need.

Item one represents the majority of economically threatening health care
expense for professional services. It is now in force in most reasonably comprehensive programs, and represents a core of benefits which should, in our
view, be universally held.

Items two through thirteen are desirable coverages, the priority of which
will vary somewhat from group to group. They are not of equal actuarial
value. Not all of these benefits should necessarily be part of the initially mandated core coverage.

Each program should provide to each of its subscribers health care coverage
that is at least equivalent to the basic coverage stipulated in the program. This
would include a required minimum core of benefits (Category 1), plus a minimum value of additional benefits selected from an approved list (Category
II). Category II benefits would be assigned relative actuarial values. Every
program should be required to contain benefits from this list which cumulative-
ly total a predetermined point value.

The rationale for Category II is to permit the group to choose benefits most
appropriate to its needs and desires. The mandatory benefits of Category I
guard against selecting away from universally needed benefits with significant
economic implications in order to limit expenditures at the expense of adequacy of protection. Coverage of any deductibles or coinsurance for Category
I benefits should be available among Category II benefits. In addition, a certified health care plan would have to offer catastrophic coverage as a mandated
adjunct to the basic coverage.

State and local government bodies should be considered "employers" for purposes of this program. However, the federal government, which has developed
a highly successful health benefits program within a complex environment,
could maintain that program. Congress, in its dual role as employer and legislative branch, already exercises control over coverage for federal employees.

Private employers who have negotiated health care plans with employees or
their representatives before this law is enacted should be allowed to continue
the health care program until it expires, for a maximum period of three years
after enactment date.

FINANCING

The method of financing goes to the very heart of the whole national health
insurance question. The administration of an NHI program, the role of the
government and of the private sector and the voluntary or compulsory nature
of national health insurance are to some extent determined by the financing
mechanism.

The bulk of health insurance financing is presently lodged in the private
sector of our economy. Individuals and corporations each contribute significantly to the private health insurance coverage which is so pervasive in our
society. Both the scope and level of benefits and the percentage of premium
payments have been a significant part of collective bargaining, resulting in
broader benefits and more substantial and, in many cases complete, contributions toward the employee's premiums by corporations. Non-union workers have
also received expanded health benefits.

In recent years, the federal and state governments, through Medicare and
Medicaid, have made significant contributions to the financing of health care
for specific segments of the population. Our present health care financing is not
dependent upon one source, but derived from multiple sources.

We have already noted that there are certain segments of the population which require financial support to secure health insurance benefits. Such support can most effectively be secured through government and the use of tax revenues. Society cannot afford to allow those with low incomes not to have access to health care insurance. However, in view of the broad coverage that exists in the general population, we can find no compelling rationale to increase taxes to purchase health insurance for the general population. In fact, such a course would be extremely dangerous because it injects the federal government into the health care industry far more than is necessary or desirable. There is a grave danger that total control of the program by the government would lead to inflexibility and unresponsiveness in the health care industry. It would also eliminate the advantage of private market competition and alternative choices by the public. This type of proposal would virtually eliminate private underwriting of basic services, thus destroying the back-up systems before it could possibly demonstrate its own effectiveness. It would be an irrevocable commitment to a federal administration that has not, in our view, been shown to be either necessary or desirable.

In addition, we do not believe that the use of federal taxes to support health insurance is the most effective use of tax revenues, nor the best approach to health. Other problems, such as housing, sanitation, diet, and education, which all have impact on the overall health of the American people, may be far more responsive to the federal interest. Sadly, the provision of health services alone to those whose health problems arise from substandard conditions of living serves largely to recycle the problems.

Mr. Chairman, some current NHI proposals rely substantially upon private sources for financing national health insurance. Others rely totally upon the Social Security system to finance the entire NHI program. In addition to our other concerns about using the tax structure to support universal health insurance, the Social Security tax seems particularly inappropriate. The use of this financing mechanism would have at least four adverse effects.

First, it would change significantly the purpose of Social Security as it was enacted, and as it has developed until now. The concept of Social Security is one of establishing a floor of benefits, whether for income or for health services, below which people will not be permitted to fall when they leave the labor market. Neither benefit is extended to the working population, except by accident of circumstances. Social Security is not intended as, and should not become, a program for the currently employed population.

Second, any program to finance health services primarily from Social Security taxes would have a profound effect upon the total tax base available for other national needs. We do not believe that this would serve the national interest. Neither do we detect any feeling on the part of the public that this particular need warrants so much priority in the tax structure.

Third, Social Security financing would seriously impinge upon the right of the people to make choices, and to spend in accordance with their own priorities and needs. Government should respect, for example, the rights of the purchaser who can afford to buy better coverage than would be offered under a Social Security program, and who finds real advantage in the carrier's administration of broader coverage. Groups would be prohibited from their traditional practice of balancing service, cost effectiveness, and a scope of benefits tailored to their requirements. There is no need for government to impinge so heavily upon the right of its citizens to choose.

Fourth, Social Security financing would tend to freeze the financing system for health. Government is necessarily interested in fiscal accountability. It does not characteristically respond to new and experimental ways of delivering services in a wide disparity of geographic and social circumstances. Congress recently expressed its support of the health maintenance organization. Health maintenance organizations would never have developed in this country if they had had to meet the fiscal requirements of pre-existing law. The cost of errors of judgment or failure to respond to new ideas is multiplied enormously in a monolithic system. If there are a hundred carriers in the business, one can be found to support any reasonable experiment. If it proves successful, the other carriers will be impelled by competition to recognize its success. But if a government monopoly makes the same error, the absence of alternatives will bury the opportunity.

ADMINISTRATION

The objectives of a national program for better access to care can best be met, to the extent that they require financing of personal health services, through underwritten coverage using private carriers. The health insurance industry has been able to bring good quality health care within financial reach of the vast majority of the people of this nation. Government funds should not be used to pay for services which the private sector is well able to buy selectively in an open and highly competitive market. The purchase of services by government becomes necessary only when the private sector lacks financial resources to deliver a needed service. Health services for the poor are one clear example. To use tax dollars to finance all health care, and to impose government administration, would not only eliminate a proven and successful industry, but would also use tax dollars to do what is already being done.

Some NHI legislative proposals express the assumption that government can administer more economically and efficiently than the private sector. Mr. Chairman, this assumption has no solid foundation. We have found no evidence to support the contention that government can administer health insurance better than the best of the private sector. We have found some significant evidence to the contrary.

Mr. John Krizay, Research Director of the Twentieth Century Fund, undertook to examine the allegation that the Medicare program had been operated more economically than private insurance. His findings were published in the Congressional Record of June 7, 1973 (page S10602). We strongly commend this information to your attention.

Mr. Krizay concedes that Medicare and the Blue Cross Blue Shield Federal Employee Program are not totally comparable. However, he states that FEP is as comparable a program as can be found in private industry. He notes that Medicare's reported costs are not accurate, in that government accounting does not recognize many true costs which private industry must report. He examines the experience of the two programs in 1968, 1969 and 1970, and finds that "Blue Shield, in particular, demonstrates a decided superiority over Medicare Part B (in terms of operating cost)." "Contrary to Senator Kennedy's claim," reports Mr. Krizay, "it is more likely that the private sector has demonstrated superior operating efficiency in administering comparable programs." He concludes that "it is clear that one cannot make a persuasive case for a public-sector operated universal health insurance program on the theory that its operating cost would be lower. The claim that the Medicare experience offers such proof is unquestionably outlandish."

The Advisory Committee on Medicare Administration, Contracting and Subcontracting, more commonly known as the Perkins Committee, made an exhaustive study of the carrier role in government programs. One significant finding was that the better Part B carriers have been inhibited in their performance by over-administration on the part of government. The Committee recommended that government should reduce its role in carrier decision making, and rely on its capacity to test carrier performance by results. In other words, the best capacities of the private sector have not been shown in Medicare, partly because government has not given it the opportunity.

There are essentially no basic ideas in government programs that were not originally developed by the private sector. We view the allegation that government administration is more efficient and more economical as unproven and unprovable, and we reject it.

We strongly recommend that private carriers be used to the fullest extent possible, and that private funds be used where possible to finance health care needs.

REGULATION

Clearly, use of the private carriers does require guarantees that certain standards are met and that carriers act responsibly. Therefore, a realistic system of qualification should be developed for carriers desiring to underwrite or furnish benefits for any NHI program.

The regulation of carriers has historically been accomplished at the state level. Unless the states fail to act responsibly, there is no valid reason to place this obligation elsewhere. Regulation is more effective if it is at the local level, as it often involves a need to consider specific situations. Nevertheless, we support the concept of minimum federal guidelines, and of federal authority to intervene if the states do not perform.

Carrier certification requirements should allow a reasonable amount of flexibility to meet the various needs of different population groups within the state. Each carrier, in order to have its policy certified, should offer catastrophic coverage as a mandated adjunct to basic coverage to each of its subscribers within the state. Catastrophic coverage should be uniformly rated within each carrier in a state. This would substantially mitigate the adverse effects of experience rating. However, different carriers should be permitted to offer different single catastrophic rates in order to maintain the advantages of competition.

States should be the regulatory and certifying authorities. Claims procedures should not be specified by any agency of government. In addition, each state should, as part of its regulatory requirements, provide a means whereby subscribers are protected in the event of insolvency or impairment of a carrier. Carriers should maintain reserves which are sufficient to protect the interest of their subscribers.

Carriers should also show evidence of effective utilization review and control designed to safeguard the interests of their subscribers. The subscribers' certificates should state clearly the benefits and the conditions under which the benefits will be provided. All exclusions, waiting periods, deductible provisions and other limitations should be clearly indicated. All promotional activities should be reasonable and avoid misleading statements. Accounting practices should conform with recognized accounting principles and afford a reliable financial statement. Premium rates should be reasonably related to benefit expenditures. Blue Shield Plans have imposed such regulation on their services for years.

The method or methods permitted for rate setting should also be subject to regulation. Rating regulations should be flexible enough to permit competition between carriers as well as reasonable freedom in program structure.

Employer groups with less than 50 employees would be covered under a small group plan and, at the carrier's option, be rated either on a community or experience basis. Individuals and families not eligible for group coverage would be covered under a non-group plan. This maintains maximum competition to benefit the subscriber; provides incentives for consciousness of cost controls; discourages over-utilization; and encourages employee health, education and safety programs.

Carriers should be permitted at their option to join together to form pools to extend coverage to individuals and groups of less than 50 persons. Any law or regulatory agency rulings which restrict such activity should be overridden by federal legislation.

Carriers would be required to have an open enrollment period at least once every 12 months and accept all persons who apply. Individuals who leave an employer group plan should be immediately eligible for non-group coverage with the same carrier without regard to health status.

States should be prohibited from requiring carriers to reduce surplus or qualifying reserves to less than three months of benefit payments plus operating expenses. They should also provide for public disclosure by carriers regarding their administrative expenses in relation to benefits paid out.

Each carrier's rates should be subject to review by the appropriate state agency as being reasonable in relation to the benefits provided; in the relationship between rate determination classifications: and in any geographical variances in charges or cost per unit of service and in utilization factors; and as reflecting separate rate determinations for individuals and for families. Without the requirement for individual carrier determination of premium rates, the efficient and capable carrier is forced to participate in the losses of less capable carriers. This denies its subscribers benefits which should be available to them through careful consumer choice.

We would further recommend that the state require that all group health care plans provide employees for a minimum of 30 days following termination of employment entitlement to the group benefits at the group premium rates, with the same degree of employer contribution. Further, that such health care plans must also provide for extension of group coverage to the totally disabled employee during the period of such total disability following employment for a reasonable period following termination of employment; and that coordination of benefit provisions be included in all health care plans and individual health benefits policies in order to avoid duplicate payments for the same service.

The self-insured employer should also be required to provide the extensions of benefits to left employees outlined above. After the required extension of benefits period has been exhausted by the left employee, self-insured employers must guarantee that such employee have access to similar coverage on a non-group basis by a carrier, for a reasonable time thereafter. We would further recommend that self-insured employers be required to establish fiscal reserves for health benefits on a basis reasonably consistent with the basis utilized by carriers. Otherwise, the carriers' subscriber would be forced to bear the loss in the case of failure by the self-insured employer.

Almost every NHI proposal before Congress includes some type of cost sharing provisions. Deductibles and coinsurance have been proposed for two purposes: (1) to hold down the cost of the program (that is, the amount of premium or tax) and (2) to further reduce cost by discouraging over-utilization.

Cost-sharing, of course, need not be at the point of service. The patient can participate at the time he pays his premium, or at the time he receives service (by use of copayments, deductibles and coinsurance) or after the service has been received through post-payment provisions.

There is no doubt that participation by the patient at the time of service does lead to reduced premium cost. However, this apparent saving to the patient is frequently offset by later expenses which can seldom be anticipated with accuracy, and which may be severe.

Deductible provisions are also relatively difficult to administer, especially in a highly mobile society. The cumulative administrative cost of deductible complications to the provider and carrier, when combined with what the patient pays, very possibly exceeds the savings which could accrue to the program. Any decrease in utilization which this method may yield will almost necessarily impact hardest on low-income families, where it may be least desirable. While this type of cost-sharing does keep premium cost down, the total cost of the service is still a reality. In the long run, it must be paid by the patient, often at a time when he is least able to do so.

While carriers rely on deductibles and coinsurance as a primary control on utilization, other carriers consider them essentially substitutes for more effective methods. They have had extensive experience writing first dollar coverage and have developed mechanisms to control unnecessary utilization, which are more effective because they are based on analysis of objective experience rather than subjective decisions of the patient.

In no event should carriers be required to carry deductibles forward from one NHI program to another. Neither should carriers be required to transfer deductible amounts already paid when an individual changes carriers.

One of the truly substantive areas of competition between health care carriers has been the personal financial liability the insured must assume under his contract. This competition should remain permissible, through coinsurance and copayments. Exercise of the option will reduce premium cost of a program, but will place the burden of additional financial liability for the deductibles, coinsurance and copayments on the insured. The election of full payment for covered services which we have recommended as a Category II benefit would provide the alternative of sharing these risks actuarially.

Cost sharing by those subscribers who elect it could be handled by allowing two alternatives: (1) the traditional method whereby carriers pay the provider the insured amount, with the subscriber paying the provider any cost sharing amounts; or (2) post-payment reimbursement, which would permit subscribers to contract with carriers to pay the provider the insured amount as well as any cost sharing amounts. Carriers would be permitted to offer and the subscribers would be free to elect a delayed payment plan (with appropriate and reasonable administrative and interest charges). State or local laws or regulations which would prohibit any qualified NHI carrier from implementing this option should be overridden by the federal NHI Act.

Deductible provisions should not be used as a basis for mandating the use of a health credit card or its equivalent. There are two reasons for this. First, the recommended benefit pattern provides enough flexibility for a group to tailor benefits to its needs and desires, including a choice between deductibles and full payment coverage. One of the alternatives is that, under agreed-upon conditions, the employee can make premium contributions so that his employer can purchase an improved program without increasing the employer's cost. To the extent that the employee's premium contribution reduces deductible, coinsurance and copayment provisions, it amounts to an actuarial sharing of the risk of these costs.

Secondly, the recommended override of restrictions on post-payment would create a competitive advantage for those carriers which elect to offer deferred payment, if the public finds the alternative attractive. Given the availability of several means of achieving the same end (expanding benefits without necessarily expanding premium), a mandate to use only one method is unnecessary and unduly restrictive invasion of consumer choice.

HEALTH CARE COST

A statement regarding national health insurance would not be complete without addressing health care costs.

It is important to be realistic in this area. In a literal sense, health care cost cannot be contained, nor would it be desirable to do so. The advance of medical technology cannot be stopped, nor can the health care industry be isolated from general inflation of the economy. On the contrary, the United States has traditionally placed high social priority on expanding the capacity of medical science and distributing its benefits to the people. Both objectives, however desirable, are inherently inflationary. The observation that other countries with the same objectives but with quite different financing systems are experiencing similar increases in health costs supports this conclusion.

It is important to define health care cost in this context. It is far easier, for example, to contain the liability of a program that it is to contain total health care cost. As an example, a report of the Special Committee on Aging, U.S. Senate, issued June 24, 1975, states that "the proportion of an aged's medical expenses reimbursed by Medicare has fallen from 45.5 percent in fiscal 1969 to 38.1 percent in 1974." This means more out-of-pocket expenses for medical care are being paid by the elderly. Clearly, a contributing factor has been a series of limits on program liability, which have failed to address the issue of total cost.

In Medicare there is nowhere else to turn. The private carriers have been driven from the basic benefit market for the elderly. However, a great deal of the coverage held by the working population is full payment coverage, a quite different product from Medicare indemnification. It is unlikely that those who hold this coverage would willingly accept a cutback to indemnity coverage. Since the competitive market for health coverage does not permit a carrier to limit its liability for covered services in a full-payment contract without regard to total cost, we are accustomed to thinking in those terms.

It is our experience that health care cost is too broad an issue to attack frontally. Rather, it must be divided into its components: the cost of a given service; the number of services rendered; and the intensity of service applied to a particular case. Intensity is illustrated by the substitution of computerized axial tomography for X-rays in certain diagnostic applications. The tomography represents neither an additional service nor an increase in the cost of the X-ray. In the proper circumstances, it is more effective and more expensive, representing greater intensity rather than greater utilization.

We believe, given the inflationary pressures upon health services, that a realistic objective is to make health care cost more predictable and more carefully justified, by influencing the elements of unit cost, utilization, and intensity, and by strengthening the commitment and management capacity of the carriers to achieve these purposes. Blue Shield Plans have been addressing these issues for years, with emphasis on these key result areas:

1. Assurance that the review and pricing processes brought to bear on individual claims and patterns of practice are cost-effective, and are used to the limit of their cost-effectiveness.

2. Assurance that the relationship between the carrier and the medical profession is being used to benefit the subscriber, particularly in the identification and application of criteria for medical necessity and the propriety of charges.

3. Assurance to the subscriber that he has the degree of predictability called for in his contract and, where indicated, an effective advocate in any dispute concerning his liability for "unnecessary utilization" or "unreasonable charges".

4. Assurance to the buyers of coverage that increases in cost are justified on the basis of reasonableness of unit cost; active consideration of intensity of service; and an acceptable relationship between incidence and the quality of care.

5. Assurance to the public at large that the method of contracting and paying for service reinforces (or at least fails to inhibit) constructive evolution of the delivery system, with particular reference to the proper modality of treatment, the provision of alternative means of delivery, and the use of carrier technology to support the review and examination of medical practice.

Blue Shield has built a substantial program in pursuit of these results. We believe it has been generally effective. It has not held health care costs at a constant level, and it will not do so. This is beyond the realistic capacity of any financing system, private or governmental, so long as health costs are so substantially influenced by general inflation; the development of clinical medicine; substantial increases in the production of physicians and other health personnel; the effects of the malpractice crisis upon professionals' overhead and upon defensive utilization; provider concern with the unsettled regulatory and political climate; and, perhaps most importantly, a better educated public with higher expectations.

NATIONAL HEALTH POLICY

Before any proposal is put into effect, the nation needs a rational method of arriving at orderly priorities for the evolution and development of the health delivery and financing systems. These priorities should be realistically structured and priced, in accordance with specific objectives. They should lead to a defined national health policy, not fixed and rigid, but modified progressively as priorities change, capacities increase, and new objectives emerge.

The national health policy should consider the relative costs and benefits of programs involving the production of health personnel; public health management and reporting; environmental factors influencing health; assurance of adequate family income; health education; and the financing of personal health services. It should also explore the potential of new approaches to health care, and consider such special needs as custodial care.

A National Council on Health Policy should be established. Members of the Council would be appointed by the President, and would serve at his pleasure. Care would be taken to represent the interests of consumers, purchasers, carriers, practicing physicians, hospitals and other providers of health care, both nationally and through local liaison arrangements.

The Council would develop and submit to the President a statement of national health priorities, based upon specific objectives for promoting the nation's health. It would also submit a legislative program, with recommended appropriations, which would be discussed in open hearings. The program would include an inventory and assessment of the strengths and weaknesses of the delivery and financing systems as they exist from time to time, and would be aimed at achieving specific results through an orderly process of innovation and development.

Thank you for this opportunity to present our views on these most important issues.

Consumer Interests

The consumer's interest in national health insurance proposals is not organized into any single coherent body with designated spokespersons. Almost everyone who has testified on the subject claims to have the medical consumer's interest at heart. From the dozens of statements presented to congressional committees by individuals and groups representing consumer interests, three have been selected for inclusion here. They were chosen because they have actively participated in consumer interest debates and because their points of view are well presented. They are: president of United Auto Workers (UAW), Leonard Woodcock, representing the labor-funded, broad-based "citizens' lobby" (the Health Security Action Council), which supports the Kennedy bill; attorney and consumer advocate, Ralph Nader; and then president of the National Consumers League, Esther Peterson. Mrs. Peterson was White House Consumer Affairs Adviser under President Johnson, and presently serves as special assistant to President Carter for consumer affairs.

HEALTH SECURITY ACTION COUNCIL ([36], Part 1, pp. 67–74)

The Health Security Action Council is a broad-based citizens' group which operates as a lobby for the kind of nationwide, government-financed, mandatory health insurance and health policy program encompassed in the Kennedy bill (involving public financing). The Council has its headquarters in Washington, D.C. and employs a full-time, professional staff. It has a prestigious membership which includes businessmen and women, health professionals, students, women's organizations, and labor leaders such as Leonard Woodcock, president of the UAW. Organized labor, especially the AFL-CIO and the UAW, has contributed heavily to the Council, as have individual philanthropists. It has become a significant lobbyist on behalf of the Kennedy measure and other liberal initiatives in health policy. Leonard Woodcock, accompanied by the Council's Executive Secretary, Max Fine, and several experts appeared before the House Ways and Means Committee; their testimony follows.

STATEMENT OF LEONARD WOODCOCK IN BEHALF OF HEALTH SECURITY ACTION COUNCIL, AND INTERNATIONAL UNION, UNITED AUTOMOBILE, AEROSPACE AND AGRICULTURAL IMPLEMENT WORKERS OF AMERICA, UAW

Mr. Chairman, members of the Health Subcommittee. My name is Leonard Woodcock and I appear before you today on behalf of the five million members of the United Auto Workers' families, and the 80 national organizations which comprise the Health Security Action Council. The members of these organizations number in the millions and represent a broad cross-section of American life. I understand that your Committee will take testimony directly from State and local representative groups of the Health Security Action Council later on in these hearings, and we commend you for opening your hearings to the people who will be most affected by what you do here.

With me today are Dr. I. S. Falk, Professor-Emeritus of Public Health, Yale University, who is Chairman of the Technical Committee of the Committee for National Health Insurance; Melvin A. Glasser, also a member of the Technical Committee and Director of the UAW Department of Social Security; and Max W. Fine, Executive Secretary of the Health Security Action Council.

Mr. Chairman, we are here to testify in support of the Health Security Act (H.R. 21) and about other health care proposals under consideration. We have already testified extensively before the Ways and Means Committee and two Committees of the United States Senate about why we support the Health Security Act. We are grateful to the more than 100 members of this body who are co-sponsoring this important and inevitable legislation. We stand for Health Security. We have fully put into the record why.

We have testified as to what Health Security is and what it is not. We have shown how it will produce urgently-needed changes in the health care delivery system. We have discussed its quality control features, the needs for which are growing even faster than malpractice insurance premium increases. We have provided data about its costs, cost controls and cost saving features, and we will continue to update these data and not be intimidated by those who are deliberately misinterpreting the costs of Health Security.

Your Committee has not yet acted on this urgent problem, but we have hope that the new round of hearings which you are now undertaking will finally produce a Health Security program for all Americans. We support your undertaking and we offer our assistance in helping you to clarify the issues so that your actions will be based on the facts as they exist and not on the imagination and distortions of Madison Avenue hucksters employed by the vested interests. As the problems have grown, so too have their efforts to convince us that no problems exist.

KEY ISSUES

As a result of the Administration's totally incomprehensible position on this issue, not much attention has been paid to the health care problems of the

American people in the past year. However, it has been a year in which the health care crisis has grown worse.

The problems of poor distribution of services, shortages of family physicians, and duplicated, disorganized and excessively high cost of services have all intensified.

It has been a year in which millions of American families played Russian Roulette with the lives and health of their children—a year in which 5.3 million of our 13.2 million preschool children were unprotected against the killing and crippling infectious diseases: polio, measles, rubella, diphtheria, whooping cough and tetanus.

It has been a year in which one-third of all pregnant women who delivered in public hospitals had no prenatal care and consequently ran high and unnecessary risks to themselves and their babies.

It has been a year in which millions of America's laid-off workers joined both the lines at the Unemployment Office and the swollen ranks of 40 million Americans who face disaster in the event of even a short acute illness or injury because they have no health insurance at all.

It has been a year of doctor strikes, public hospital overcrowding, private hospital and nursing home profiteering, and scandalous abuse of the weakest and least able of our senior citizens.

And it has been a year in which health costs have gone completely out of control, with physician fees escalating 40 percent faster than other items in the Consumer Price Index and hospital charges soaring 105 percent faster, while the hospitals placed the blame on their own employees whose wages still averaged under $7,800 per annum in all hospitals and at the poverty level of $5,800 in small hospitals.

Mr. Chairman, these are the types of problems with which your Committee must deal, and not merely the problem of which new financial patch to apply to a defective and already over-costly health care system. These are the problems which even the Administration has noted, and ignored on grounds that the Federal budget can absorb no new spending programs.

While we should be reaching out to assure that every child has access to immunizations, and the family the means to pay the costs, the Administration wants to tighten up and shift even part of the meager existing Federal support for these services to the States and to the family budgets. The Administration's policies would divert minimal Federal amounts in prevention and cause billions in the treatment costs to the States and families in future years. They would throw millions of additional Americans on to the medical dole.

Health is a great aspiration of the American people, but the budget cutters in the Administration suffer from severe buck fever when we face serious health problems. Although it has finally promulgated regulations on dual choice under the HMO legislation signed into law 20 months ago, the record is one of indecision and over-reliance on the private sector to which the Administration itself constantly offers magnificent opportunities for inaction.

Placing total reliance on the failing private insurance industry to solve our health care crisis, the Administration 11 months ago shelved for a year its own national health insurance plan. Whether or not the shelf life will be extended is not yet clear. What is clear is that the problems which caused an initial, if tardy, Administration response have not been solved and, indeed, have been more fully exposed to public view.

Sometimes it seems that the medical and medical insurance bureaucracies have ruled out compassion in dealing with people, but it is the fearful cost of health services that, rightly, draws most attention to the problems.

When the Committee for National Health Insurance was organized in 1968, Federal, State and local governments spent $20 billion for health purposes. Last year, costs of the same services escalated to $41 billion. Two years from now, the governmental budgets will be emptied of over $55 billion for health care unless changes are made in the system. Total costs, private and public, now are an estimated $118 billion annually and consume 8.3 percent of the GNP versus $54 billion and 6.5 percent of GNP in 1968.

It is, therefore, not a question as to whether the Congress should delay action on the issue of health care. The crisis has moved to such a stage that you will have no choice but to provide for an inordinate number of additional billions of dollars or say to the elderly and the poor, "We'll have to take back what we've given you."

In their recent national poll, the Cambridge Survey found that only 13 percent of the American people felt the present health care system was functioning relatively well, while 57 percent demanded a total national health insurance program as provided in the Health Security Act or even a complete Federal takeover of the entire system with doctors placed on salaries.

The depth of public dissatisfaction should be underestimated only at one's political peril, even though health may not command the urgency of the problems of the general economy and unemployment.

Federal employees will receive phantom pay raises next January because of 35-to-45 percent higher health insurance premiums which threaten to wipe out most of the five percent wage increase.

The situation is no less disturbing in the private sector where higher premiums also mean lower wages. We all purchase health services in the same sellers' market, and the prices there are completely out of control. To the extent that health care costs and health insurance premiums continue to absorb more of the hard-earned dollars of the American worker than of his foreign counterpart, the competitive position of American business and industry will continue to be weakened. Jobs as well as paychecks will be cut.

THE AMA BILL

The illness that afflicts the health care system is now generally diagnosed. In order to provide effective treatment, it should be clear that each of the causes must be dealt with, and dealt with concurrently.

Unfortunately, all but one of the major bills before your Committee, Mr. Chairman, choose to ignore most of the causes or even the symptoms of the illness.

An example is the plan developed by the American Medical Association, which resembles the previous Nixon and Ford plans. While it is generally agreed today that every American should have health insurance coverage, the AMA insists that coverage must be voluntary and not universal—or as they call it, "compulsory."

This bill (H.R. 6222) asks you to pass a law to mandate employers to offer second-rate private health insurance policies, purchased from carriers of the employers' choice, to all employees. However, the employee could be required to pay 35 percent of the premium costs. The marginally-employed and the low-income employed (for example, those hospital employees with incomes of only between $5,800 and $7,800 per annum) would be reluctant to pay about $350 a year for their share of the insurance. Many could not afford it. Others would not want it after they examined the policy and found that they and their families would still be liable for up to $2,000 per year in co-insurance payments, or up to $1,500 if they were single. Many services would be limited, others excluded entirely.

The AMA bill is typical of others which would mandate employer-employee insurance. These bills provide for the most inequitable financing of services. An employee earning $6,000 per annum would pay as much as an executive earning $60,000.

Since the AMA bill is totally lacking in cost controls, even greater escalation of medical costs than at present would occur should this approach be enacted.

Since quality controls would be absent and more dollars present, even greater incentives would be provided for over-utilization, over-prescribing and unnecessary surgery.

Mr. Chairman, doctors are not ogres. We believe that the large majority of physicians are dedicated, hard-working, competent and concerned individuals. Our quarrel is not with our doctors. Our quarrel is with a system which corrupts its own members and fails to meet the needs of the people—with a system which produces too few doctors, rewards inefficiency and ineffectiveness, leaves millions unserved in rural America and the inner cities and forces consumers to pay atronomical amounts for episodic care.

The AMA bill would not remove patient frustrations which plague the doctor-patient relationship.

It would only extract higher fees from patients and make solo practice, fee-for-service even more rewarding for doctors than at present. Health care would for the foreseeable future be locked into this corrupting system which lies at the root of many malpractice actions. Abuses would be ignored.

In the Health Security Bill (H.R. 21) which we support, provision is made to continue the fee-for-service system, but to introduce essentially needed controls on the cost and quality of the services delivered under this system.

Early in this century, in a preface to his book, "The Doctor's Dilemma," George Bernard Shaw wrote,

"That any sane nation, having observed that you could provide for the supply of bread by giving bakers a pecuniary interest in baking for you, should go on to give a surgeon a pecuniary interest in cutting off your leg, is enough to make one despair of political humanity."

LONG-RIBICOFF BILL

Those who believe that progress must be made incrementally regard the Long-Ribicoff Catastrophic Insurance Plan as an acceptable response to the health care crisis. We believe, however, that this bill has serious and even fatal flaws.

While the bill lacks any provision for representation of the consumer, it is clear that it would greatly strengthen the position of the private insurance companies.

A $30 billion industry which has failed to provide universal coverage, failed to control medical costs, failed to assure quality and which has enjoyed great success to date in defeating real national health insurance proposals would be further enriched by the Long-Ribicoff bill.

By law, the major share of the estimated $8.9 billion additional first-year costs of the program would flow through the insurance industry, which already retains $4 billion for its operating expenses and profits in ineffectually administering current health insurance plans. . . .

Mr. Chairman, catastrophic health insurance won't help people because it is based on a myth. The myth is that people already have good basic coverage but require protection only against catastrophic illness. The reality is that people do not have good basic coverage. Some do, most do not. In its "Forward Plan for Health," even the Administration concedes this point, as follows:

"The fact that most of the insured population has inadequate benefits is . . . troublesome. Most basic insurance policies exclude preventive care services, ambulatory care, and prescription drugs and medical devices, and many policies still exclude pre-existing conditions and congenital defects. In addition many policies include only limited coverage of other necessary services, such as mental health care. The usual protection against medical and financial catastrophes is also inadequate. About half of private policies limit total benefits in a lifetime to $10,000 or less, and almost two-thirds of current policies limit hospitalization to 60 days or less. In addition, virtually all policies have no upper limit on the amount of cost-sharing a patient is responsible for, regardless of how much has already been spent."

In other words, catastrophic insurance would be like building an archway with no foundation. Most people would be wiped out long before the trigger point for any benefits. Mostly the rich would benefit—rich providers, rich insurance executives and rich patients. Working people would pay the bills.

Catastrophic health insurance has deductibles of 60 hospital days and $2,000 in physician fees and medical expenses. This is a bill with a deductible of $11,500. (It is only in the rare situation that a patient would incur $2,000 in physician insurance fees in a year without a period of hospitalization).

Catastrophic health insurance will not provide any benefits at all to 99.5 percent of the American people, but it sounds good—like the organ grinder whose playing was supposed to soothe the people buried alive by the earthquake debris.

Mr. Chairman, there are other important reasons why we would oppose catastrophic health insurance as an alternative to comprehensive health insurance.

It would create greater imbalance and inflation in the health care system by adding to incentives for very expensive care and disincentives for preventive care.

It would distract the Congress and the public from serious consideration of a comprehensive national health insurance program on the theory that the most serious problems were being dealt with by providing coverage for catastrophic expenses.

It would invite providers of services to raise prices, especially for the seriously ill and dying, on the excuse that the family or individual would thereby become eligible for catastrophic benefits. The net result would be a price rise in all aspects of health care.

It would create incentives for longer hospitalization and other institutional care. There would be tremendous pressure to keep the patient in the hospital until the trigger point for catastrophic was reached.

It would weaken efforts to institute quality controls since catastrophic coverage would not take effect until after the 60th day of hospitalization (and consequently any controls written into the bill could not be instituted until after the 60th day of hospitalization).

Because of the high deductibles and the overwhelming emphasis on major illness, it would further distort the allocation of national health care resources, turning them further away from health maintenance, early diagnosis of disease, home health care, and other neglected aspects of the system.

It would strengthen the hand of the commercial insurance companies vis-a-vis national health insurance.

It would aggravate the maldistribution of services caused by economic factors since the major beneficiaries of catastrophic coverage would be those who are able to spend the deductible amounts.

It would further skew manpower away from rural and small town areas by increasing the funds available to pay lucrative specialists in the urban areas.

It would increase the cost of Medicaid and Medicare and other Government programs. (By pouring more money into the private sector, simultaneous acceleration of costs of public programs would occur).

It would increase the fragmentation and complexities of the financing system. . . .

HEALTH SECURITY

Mr. Chairman, we are convinced as are a majority of the American people, that our nation needs a universal, comprehensive national health insurance program. This country is one of the two or three top spenders on health care in the world. Yet the United States is the only industrialized nation in the world that does not have a national health program for its people.

We do not need to spend more money; we are already spending too much.

And we know from direct experience in our own Union that the cost problem is getting worse and worse.

Let me put it to you in terms of the average auto worker in Michigan whose family health insurance premium amounts to somewhere over one month's wages—monies he could have in the pay envelope if they were not diverted for this high priority need. By estimates of the Department of Health, Education and Welfare, unless there is intervention in the system, by 1980 he will have to forego two months' wages for the same benefits. We need to ask ourselves and we need to ask our elected representatives in the Congress whether this is a situation this nation can continue to tolerate. Similarly with Medicare and Medicaid. The OMB estimates that costs which totalled $10 billion in 1970 will increase to $25 billion in FY 1976 and total $52 billion in FY 1981.

Unless this Committee and this Congress does something about the health care system, there is no escaping the fact that you will have to provide the $27 billion more for the same inadequate health programs we have today.

But it would be wrong to look only at the dollar sign in terms of health care, It would be wrong to emphasize only that this country spends far more per capita on health care than any other nation in the world and that by most of the accepted indices of health studies we lag behind almost every other industrialized or semi-industrialized nation.

We need to look at the quality of the care we are getting. We need to ask ourselves whether the many studies and reports of needless surgery should produce action programs to correct the situation. We should be deeply disturbed by the large numbers of us who end up in hospitals each year as a result of reactions to prescribed drugs—some estimates indicating that as many as 80 percent of these reactions could have been avoided. We need to worry when we are told that as many as 30 percent of all the x-rays taken are either inaccurate or unreadable. We should be demanding far more aggressive measures to see to it that the large numbers of inaccurate or even wrong findings of laboratory tests are reduced sharply and possibly eliminated entirely. How on earth can we expect to get adequate treatment from the health care system if it is based on faulty tests?

In the interests of "economy", those who would do nothing advocate the incremental or step approach. They acknowledge the problems in health care to which I allude. But they say, "Let's try to get them fixed one by one. We should not try to do it all at once."

Mr. Chairman, creeping incrementalism will not shore up our collapsing health care delivery system. A complete breakdown would be the more likely result of adding catastrophic insurance and other incremental patches to the Medicare and Medicaid models.

The incremental approach is reminiscent to Huxley's frogs. He kept them in a tank and raised the temperature of the water very slowly, only about one degree a day. Within two months the frogs were boiled to death without knowing what was happening to them. If the temperature had been turned up rapidly, they would have jumped out of the water.

If we enact a national health plan which will generate real reforms, we can preserve the best in our present system and replace its worst features. If we add patches, the whole system may go under in a few years.

Those who favor incrementalism, completely abandon cost and quality controls, and systems improvements. Unless these are built into any plan, the plan will do nothing but exacerbate the problems it is trying to correct.

Incrementalism has been the approach which we have followed in the United States in the last 30 years. It is precisely this approach which has led us to the sad state of affairs in health today. The Health Security program through seeing all of the problems in relation to each other, and through using the leverage of large funds coming into the system, proposes to begin to integrate the necessary corrective measures in restructuring the system. It is admittedly evolutionary and it will take time to produce progressive change. But it sees the problem as a whole and deals with it in like manner.

Delivering health care to every American depends on the development and organization of the available resources, and an equitable financing system. It depends on the leverage and support of a national health insurance plan which will create the resources and provide the leverage needed for reforms. Health Security alone meets these standards.

Many national organizations—religious groups, labor, senior citizens, health professionals and others—have endorsed the principles of the Health Security Act as essential to the legislation you are considering. The first of these principles is health care as a right, unabridged by any means-tests, work earnings tests or any other requirements.

No greater observance of the nation's Bicentennial could be imagined than the enactment of a law which will make real the principle that every American has a right to health care.

We believe that the legislation enacted must:

Provide universal coverage, under one system.

Provide for comprehensive health care services, including preventive care as well as diagnosis, treatment and rehabilitation.

Provide payment in full for all costs of covered services, including the extraordinary costs of catastrophic illness.

Finance all covered services through a Trust Fund based on payroll taxes and general revenues, administered by the federal government.

Contain strong quality control mechanisms.

Establish prospective reimbursement of providers to control costs, eliminate duplication and reduce waste.

Assure effective consumer participation and public accountability.

Provide resources, development and distribution in a system responsive to community needs.

Of the bills before your Subcommittee, only the Health Security Act measures up to these essential principles.

CAN WE AFFORD HEALTH SECURITY?

The question of costs was well answered by Dr. Rashi Fein, Professor of Economics at Harvard Medical School, "New parks, roads or bombers represent money for things the people would otherwise not have. But medical care is different; we are already spending $104 billion, and private expenditures account for $63 billion of that total.

"So the issue is a non-issue. The question can we, as a people, afford national health insurance, really means can we afford to spend what we are already spending—and surely the answer is 'yes'."

Understandably, this Subcommittee is concerned about costs to the Federal budget, as well as costs to State and local governments, and to the family budgets.

Our consulting actuary has prepared an analysis of comparative costs of national health insurance programs for future years. Using the methodology developed by the Administration, including some assumptions with which we would not necessarily agree, the analysis shows nevertheless that H.R. 21 would, within four years, actually save $21 billion annually in national health expenditures in comparison with the catastrophic insurance program. It would save $25.5 billion in comparison with the Administration's own CHIP plan, which served as the blueprint for the new AMA bill. And it would save $11.6 billion in costs which would otherwise occur as a result of doing nothing.

The reasons for the savings are not complex. Under the Health Security bill, all costs would be anchored to budgets prepared and approved in advance. Under H.R. 21 system reorganization would be encouraged, with the concomitant savings in hospital utilization and provider costs which result from the team approach to the delivery of comprehensive benefits. Under other bills, payments to providers would remain open-ended.

We would like to submit this analysis for the record, it is in Appendix C.

With respect to the program costs of Health Security, Dr. Falk has updated the figures previously given to the Ways and Means Committee as a result of the astronomical increases in health costs which have occurred without Health Security. . . .

THE BUREAUCRATIC MYTH

Mr. Chairman, we feel the evidence is clear both in our own Social Security program and in the Canadian national health insurance program that administrative costs of national health insurance would be reduced by a Health Security-type program in comparison with the present system of hundreds of insurance companies, each with its own sales force, claims department, reserves, profits and battalions of underwriters and clerks.

Mr. Weinberger, the former Secretary of H.E.W., testified before the Ways and Means Committee last year that 45,000 to 49,000 additional employees would be required to administer H.R. 21. However, the Chairman of the Board of the Equitable Life Assurance Society of the United States has stated that 300,000 private health insurance employees would be put out of work if the Health Security Act were enacted. While I would be the last to wish to add to the unemployment rolls, we must surely ask whether we can continue to subsidize with limited numbers of health care dollars, the tremendous operating and administrative expenses of the health insurance industry.

Those who believe that the best defense is a strong offense, will continue to degrade the performance of the Social Security Administration.

The disclosures about SSI overpayments have strengthened the hand of those who would play upon the public's concern about "one more giant bureaucracy." Overpayments make headlines, causes of the problem are buried inside the newspapers.

This Subcommittee is aware of the causes of the SSI situation—a large program superimposed by political appointees upon an efficient agency which is denied the manpower required to administer it, given eleventh-hour orders changing essential characteristics of the program, and encumbered with deficient State data.

The problem is not that the Social Security Administration is inefficient or callous to public concerns about the expenditure of public funds. Social Security is a model of efficiency whose management practices could well be replicated by private insurance companies.

The problem is not that a new program recruited too many new employees to staff it. Too few are allowed by the political bosses of HEW.

The problem is not that we have a gigantic SNAFU caused by the bureaucracy. The SNAFU was caused by the political leadership. A director selected by former President Nixon with no experience in this field offered repeated public assurances that the SSI system was ready to go—the machines were in place, the manpower was adequate. After press disclosures of its inadequacies, he blamed the press, saying they were so preoccupied with Watergate that they failed to do their job of ferreting out and exposing the problems at an early stage.

Our Federal, State, and local governments employ millions of people who, Mr. Chairman, are willing to make our system work, if only they are provided the opportunity through quality leadership. They are by and large dedicated and industrious men and women. The leadership which was imposed on HEW over the past few years was another matter. Here was a leadership which was determined to prove itself incompetent, surrounding itself with free-swinging critics of government rather than able administrators, fond of crying out that government was unable to do anything, bent on fulfilling its own prophecy.

It's easy and often politically profitable to criticize governmental bureaucracy, but the members of the Ways and Means Committee know full well that the Social Security Administration suffered no SSI-type SNAFU's as long as its programs were run by dedicated public administrators and not politicians.

Mr. Chairman, I feel sure some of the members are concerned about press reports of the recent GAO analysis of administrative costs under Medicare. As you know, the GAO analysis was undertaken at the request of Chairman Mills in 1973, at a time when the Division of Direct Reimbursement of SSA was in the process of changing its claims reimbursement procedure. Accordingly, the costs per claim paid by the Division of Direct Reimbursement were substantially higher than Blue Cross or the commercial insurance intermediaries in that year.

However, I know you will be pleased to learn, as I was, that the data for the most current year FY 1975 show that the cost per claim for the Division of Direct Reimbursement was $4.11 as compared with $5.46 for the commercial insurance companies and $4.64 for the Blue Cross plans.

In conclusion, Mr. Chairman, let me say that we very much appreciate the initiatives you have taken in moving forward with these hearings and in seeking reasonable solutions to the problem of Congressional committee jurisdiction on the issue of national health insurance.

We appreciate the hard work you have undertaken and the personal commitment you have made to achieving a national health insurance plan which will benefit every American.

We urge you in the course of these hearings to hear from the people in their own surroundings and not only in Washington. We urge you also to visit Canada and to learn for yourselves what they have found to be good features and less desirable features of their national health insurance program. We should benefit from the Canadian experience.

Mr. Chairman, we thank you for the opportunity to present our views and are ready to answer questions about our testimony.

RALPH NADER ([31], pp. 3314–3322)

In the spring of 1974, Senator Edward Kennedy and Representative Wilbur Mills, then chairman of the House Ways and Means Committee, reached a compromise on a limited national health program designed to take a first step toward national mandatory coverage. For many who had supported the original and more comprehensive measure, the so-called Kennedy-Griffiths bill (Kennedy-Corman bill in the 94th Congress), this compromise was a step backwards. The Kennedy-Mills bill proposed member contributions, continued involvement of private insurance carriers, continuation of Medicare, and a number of provisions repugnant to Kennedy's liberal allies. (See [33], pp. 570–574 for a description of the Kennedy-Mills bill.) The measure got nowhere and Wilbur Mills lost his powerful position on the Ways and Means Committee in October 1974 as a result of a scandal. The proposal has not been revived by either Kennedy or Mills' successor on the committee, Representative Al Ullman. The degree to which the Kennedy-Mills compromise outraged supporters of the more comprehensive national health insurance is reflected in the testimony of Ralph Nader, presented before the House Ways and Means Committee in July 1974. Nader, as did many other consumer advocates, repudiated any idea of continued private control of health insurance administration and argued forcefully against makeshift measures. The more comprehensive Kennedy-Griffiths bill continued to receive support from Nader and other liberals. No legislation was enacted in the 93rd or 94th Congress, but the issues were clarified by the hearings held and the statements presented.

STATEMENT OF RALPH NADER, PUBLIC CITIZEN HEALTH RESEARCH GROUP, ACCOMPANIED BY SIDNEY WOLFE, M.D., DIRECTOR, AND ROBERT McGARRAH, ATTORNEY

Mr. BURKE. We welcome you to the committee, Mr. Nader. As I informed the other witnesses appearing just prior to your appearance, if the quorum bell rings, we will suspend and recess and move over to room H–208 in the Capitol.

You may identify yourself and your associates.

Mr. NADER. Thank you, Mr. Chairman.

On my left is Dr. Sidney Wolfe, the director of the Public Citizens Health Research Group; on my right is attorney Robert McGarrah.

Mr. BROTZMAN. I am sorry. What was the name?

Mr. NADER. Dr. Sidney Wolfe on my left and Robert McGarrah on my right.

Mr. Chairman, thank you for your invitation to comment on national health insurance.

Oftentimes when legislation gets bogged down over the years and proliferates in detail, it is important to step back in order to see the forest rather than have one's perspective too occluded by the trees.

It is also important to recognize the factor of legislative fatigue on the part of many Members of Congress who after 3 or 4 years are willing to settle not only for less but, unfortunately, for a system that will do nothing more than worsen the deficiencies of the present health care delivery economy, an economy it most decidedly is with all the behavioral patterns of profiteering, gouging, waste, and a master-servant relationship in reverse; that is, with the medical profession being the master instead of the servant of the patients for whom all this is supposed to be helpful.

Like an automobile manufacturer who systematically ignores safety and the energy crisis to build bigger and faster cars, Congress now seems ready to ignore the worst features of our health care system in order to build them into a national health insurance plan. Americans deserve and need comprehensive, accessible, quality medical care at a reasonable cost.

Mr. BURKE. Mr. Nader, we will have to interrupt you. We have to answer a quorum call so we will move over and meet in 15 minutes in room H–208 in the U.S. Capitol.

Mr. NADER. Thank you.

[A recess was taken.]

Mr. BURKE. The committee will be in order.

Mr. Nader, you may resume.

Mr. NADER. Of vital importance to the public and to the Congress is health care cost, presently in a convulsion of noncontrol. Americans already spend a greater percentage of our gross national product on health care expenditures—$94.1 billion [1] (or 7.7 percent of GNP) in 1973—than any other country in the world.

Our rate of health care inflation exceeds that of virtually every other section of our economy. And now that economic controls have been lifted, Government officials tell the public to expect costs to increase by 20 percent per year.

Physicians, for example, already the highest paid group in the country, are now urged to exercise "self-restraint" by keeping their annual fee increases below 20 percent.

It is interesting to note that the difference between what Americans spend on health care and what they spend on food is about 15 or 20 percent. That is the expenditures for health care are about 15 to 20 percent less than expenditures for food.

The person forced to pay every increased price—the average American worker—today must work for an entire month just to meet the

---

[1] National Health Insurance Resource Book, Committee on Ways and Means, U.S. House of Representatives. Apr. 11, 1974, p. 7.

health care expenses of his or her family. Yet such families still have seriously inadequate health services available.

While each employee loses an average of 6 days of work [1] due to illness every year—at an estimated total cost over $19.4 billion [2]— nearly every American who is covered finds himself limited to hospitalization insurance protection.

In other words, the greatest needs of the American people—comprehensive medical including all inpatient costs—are at present simply beyond their reach.

Whereas comprehensive health care includes coverage for hospitalization, outpatient services and drugs—without discrimination against the poor in the form of coinsurance and deductibles—comprehensive preventive health care adds a third component. Integrating programs of nutrition, immunization and occupational health surveillance, for example into community health care facilities, as fantasized if not realized by the term "health maintenance"—would be a significant advance toward better health at a lower cost.

The so-called national health plans with serious possibility of passage before this committee are a distortion and a perversion of this country's health care needs. They are in fact nothing more than congressional reactions to the needs of the health industry—not the American people. Each of them ignores the stark facts of our distorted health care system. Each of them designed as an add-on to the worst aspects of a system dangerously out of control.

In other words, the greatest needs of the American people are presently beyond their reach—reference is made to the so-called Nixon proposal and the downward revision called the Kennedy-Mills proposal.

There are no effective cost controls to a catastrophic illness plan. Each American's tax dollars will be spent on a relatively small number of people while millions of citizens go without basic preventive medical care outside the hospital that in the long run would protect them from catastrophic illness or disease. This is treadmill policymaking.

PREVENTIVE HEALTH INSURANCE

A major flow in the health care system is the fetish of doctors for the hospital. Everyone of the plans before this committee, except the Kennedy-Griffiths bill, ignores preventive medicine. Health care delivery today is so skewed toward hospital care that health insurance is practically synonymous with hospital coverage. [3]

Doctors have accordingly specialized to staff a multiplicity of hospital departments to the degree that today only 19 percent of all practicing physicians are in general practice. [4] As a result, despite the fact that patients enrolled in prepaid group practices, who have much easier access to better outpatient care, spend far fewer days in the hospital than patients with only hospital insurance, most doctors have obstinately clung to a wasteful fee-for-service system. [5]

Cost comparisons between prepaid health care systems with effective cost control and the most widespread fee-for-service oriented health care systems consistently show striking differences:

Per capita medical costs, 1960–65

Kaiser Permanente—up 19.1 percent.
Entire United States—up 43.5 percent. [6]

---

[1] National Health Insurance Resource Book, p. 89.
[2] Daniel N. Price, "Cash Benefits for Short-Term Sickness, 1948–72," Social Security Bulletin, vol. 37, No. 1, p. 19.
[3] National Health Insurance Resource Book, pp. 74–75. At the end of 1972, 78.7 percent of the population had some form of hospital insurance—the largest number of any type of health insurance coverage.
[4] National Health Insurance Resource Book, pp. 62–63.
[5] Ibid., pp. 80–81.
[6] Report of the National Advisory Commission in Health Manpower, vol. 2, Washington, D.C., Government Printing Office, November 1967, pp. 197–228.

Days of hospital utilization per 1,000 enrollees in 1968
  Prepaid group plans—429 days.
  Indemnity insurers—934 days.[1]

Surgical procedures per 1,000 enrollees
  Prepaid practice:
        Female surgery—4.8.
        Total surgery—34.
  Blue Shield:
        Female surgery—9.2.
        Total surgery—75.[1]

Thus, comparative studies strongly indicate that prepaid plans, devoid of fee for services incentives to "overutilize" patients, help to control costs and reduce unnecessary hospitalization and surgery without sacrificing the quality of care.

In the absence of such cost controls in any of the national health insurance plans presently under serious consideration, and with what is at best a token commitment to developing more HMO's in the form of the recently enacted HMO bill, these important lessons in cost and quality control are being virtually ignored.

It would be a verbal as well as a substantive travesty, Mr. Chairman, to characterize the Nixon proposal, for example, as a thrift bill. Because of its gross lack of quality control and cost control it will emerge, as the medicare experience before it shows, as a most wasteful aspect of Government spending. It should not camouflage in any other form.

Because of heavy emphasis on hospital care, doctor specialization and a profiteering drug and insurance business, the health care system's approach to disease is to spend massive sums on treatment of the dubious, as recent medical articles about overprescribing antibiotics and resultant fatalities show, and little on early detection or prevention.

As an example, I would like to point out the great progress we could have made in this country in detecting hypertension and doing something about it. That affects 25 million people. It is a simple test. It requires a popular based mobilization of public health resources and it is finally being considered by the Federal Government under the prodding of some of the more progressive physicians in the country.

Here for less than one-third of what it cost to build a nuclear submarine the entire country can be screened for hypertension and, with economic purchases of drugs, to treat the disease. The per-capita expenditure could be on the order of 7 cents per capita per year according to Dr. DeBakey. This is a perfect illustration of how a relatively small sum based on early detection and early treatment can undoubtedly save many thousands of lives from later cardiovascular diseases.

N10

An examination of changes in Federal spending for health over the last 2 years clearly indicates the increasing lack of attention to preventive program.[2]

From fiscal year 1973 to fiscal year 1975, HEW-funded health programs—including FDA, National Institute for Occupational Safety and Health, Center for Disease Control—had a decrease from $5.355 billion to $4.756 billion (a loss of $547 million or 10 percent) in funding.

It would be reassuring if this decrease reflected cost control and efficiency but unfortunately the significance of this detection is not that it reflects efficiency but it reflects a reduced fiscal commitment to these programs.

Agency decreases include less funding for lead poisoning programs, which affect children particularly, occupational safety and health

[1] Perrott, G. S.: The Federal Employees Health Benefits Program: Enrollment and Utilization of Health Services,, 1961–68. Washington, D.C.. Department of Health, Education, and Welfare, Health Services and Mental Health Administration, May 1971.
[2] House HEW appropriation hearings for 1975, pt. 2, p. 8.

training and research programs, immunization programs and other critical areas of prevention.

During the same interval (1973–75), funding for medicare and medicaid increased from $14.079 billion to $20.699 billion, an increase of more than $6 billion or almost 30 percent.

Thus, while critical programs to prevent illness are decreased, billions more are poured into programs without cost or quality control which, for a much higher price, are supposed to pay for preventable diseases after they occur.

The bills before this committee, particularly the catastrophic insurance approach, promise still more specialization and wasted funds which the workplaces, and the contaminated food, air and water around us continue to cause the very diseases we seek to treat.

Who was it said if we ignore history we would be condemned to repeat it?

This is what is in prospect for this kind of legislation if we ignoi the history of the past, particularly the history of the medicaid legislation and its implementation.

To take the worst features of what now passes for a health care system in the form of billions of dollars in annual retentions (profits and expenses) for private health insurance companies, billions wasted on unnecessary hospitalizations, inappropriate and useless drugs, and thousands of excess hospital beds—and then to add to this a so-called national health insurance plan which requires low wage earners to pay far more of their income than the rich through payroll taxes, deductibles and coinsurance [1]—is to perpetuate a fraud on the American public.

Confucious once said that if a person can name the proposal he can go a long way toward winning the battle. If this bill, such as the Nixon proposal, was called what it really should be called, as a corporate welfare proposal for the health, drug, and medical industries, then perhaps there would not be so many adherents and compromisers surrounding it.

Congress could just as well accomplish the same purpose by allocating $100 billion tax dollars in direct grants to private insurance companies, doctors, and hospitals.

Under either system, citizen needs for a rational comprehensive preventive health care system will go unmet. The absorptive capacity for money by institutional greed and monopolistic practices, closed to consumer involvement is almost infinite. It could substantially devour much more of the GNP.

In fact, I would like to advance the hypothesis that our health care delivery system surrounded by the health and insurance industry, the drug industry and the entire medical profession industry, could absorb the entire gross national product and still not produce much of anything better.

Indeed, at the present time it is absorbing that part of the gross national product, $100 billion, which is as large as the entire gross national product of mainland China which ministers to the needs of 800 million people in that country.

Also in terms of percentage of GNP we are far ahead of Western European countries in the expenditure on medical care. And on many indixes the health of our people such as mortality and disease is below that of countries in Europe.

Comprehensive preventive benefits must be available to the entire population. Today 30 million Americans have no health insurance at all and over 100 million Americans have no coverage for such basic services as doctor visits.[2]

[1] Edward V. Sparer, "Potential Disaster in National Health Plans," Just Economics, vol. 2, No. 5, pp. 3–4.
[2] Testimony of Leonard Woodcock before the Committee on Ways and Means, U.S. House of Representatives, May 22, 1974, p. 7.

The Nixon health insurance plan, Long-Ribicoff and the Mills-Kennedy bills all ignore these basic facts and impose regressive payroll taxes, with coinsurance and deductibles (ranging from $1,000–$2,000).

Who can dispute the legitimate and urgent needs of critically ill Americans? But can we afford to funnel our tax dollars into a system which at best inadequately assists some of the most dire cases only after they have spent hundreds if not thousands out of their own pockets?

There are millions of citizens in 5,000 U.S. communities who have no doctor at all. Access to medical services for medical care of any kind is so poor in America that we still rank 12th to 15th among all other countries in infant mortality.

Yet none of the national health insurance proposals before Congress would effectively redistribute the number of practicing physicians who today congregate around the most wealthy urban areas of this country. Nor would any of the proposals provide incentives or requirements for physicians to enter preventive family practice medicine. Health manpower legislation, now pending in the Senate, would provide incentives to relieve the problem of geographic maldistribution.

QUALITY AND PUBLIC ACCOUNTABILITY

Two further omissions undermine a real congressional opportunity to reform the health care system.

The first is quality control. Patients today play a game of Russian roulette when they select a doctor.[1] There are over 2 million unnecessary operations performed each year resulting in nearly 15,000 completely preventable deaths.

Other evidence indicates that more than 20 percent of all the antibiotics prescribed in hospitals each year are completely unnecessary. Without adequate and publicly accountable quality controls, any national health insurance plan which merely provides funds for more people is certain to enlarge the scope of these problems.

Prospects for the newly developing professional standards review organizations to prevent these abuses are not good at all, since they are required to adopt local standards of medical practice—undoubtedly the lowest common denominator of quality.

To be effective, then, any national health insurance plan must impose national standards and require public disclosure on the performance of all hospitals and doctors. Anything less would be to preserve present nonfunctioning peer review systems replete with conflicts of interest and secrecy.

Conflicts of interest and secrecy are the hallmark of our present health care delivery system as described by Prof. Sylvia Law in her book "Blue Cross: What Went Wrong" (New Haven: 1974, pp. 25–30).

Hospitals, doctors, and insurance companies have managed until now to convince the public that the citizen's role is only to pay without question. And today when the majority of citizens look to Congress for a comprehensive preventive health insurance plan,[2] they find the same groups who bear complete responsibility for the disastrous state of Amercan health care receiving not only all the benefits but actually **controlling every plan. Consumers, who must bear the tax weight of the national health insurance, are completely excluded from even the most innocuous role in decisions affecting their health.**

---

[1] Public Citizen's Health Research Group encountered massive opposition from Maryland doctors when it attempted to collect information on fees, office hours, credentials, and whether or not a physician accepted medicare or medicaid. Opposition was based on Maryland State law (art. 43, S. 129, Annotated Code of Maryland) which prohibits physicians from advertising. A first amendment challenge to the statute has been filed : *Public Citizen* v. *Commission on Medical Discipline of Maryland*, No. 74–56B (USCD D. Maryland).

[2] In a recent Harris poll, 54 percent of Americans favor passage of a national health insurance program combining Government, employer, and employee contributions into one Federal health insurance system that would cover all medical and health expenses. Boston Globe, June 19, 1974.

Whatever happened to consumer sovereignty, the supposed hallmark of our economic system?

There is no room in taxpayer funded national health insurance for private insurance companies. They have already proved they are far more concerned with their over $5 billion profits and retentions [1] than with providing low-cost comprehensive preventive health care.

You only have to look over the history of Metropolitan, Prudential, and other health and life insurance companies, particularly Metropolitan, which presumes to put out a lot of literature in this area, to see how little, and I might include Blue Cross here, to see how little attention is paid to preventive health care which reflects the ounce of prevention being worth the pound of cure.

That does not only include putting out pamphlets, it includes advocacy, it includes pushing with all their might, which is quite substantial for these kinds of changes.

Any role for private insurance companies, be it as fiscal intermediaries as in the Kennedy-Mills proposal, or as federally approved carriers of a federally mandated national health insurance plan such as the Nixon and Long-Ribicoff approach, must be completely rejected.

Canada initially used private insurance companies under its national health plan and later rejected their participation because of high costs.

S. 2513 (the Long-Ribicoff bill) section 1505 exempts private insurance carriers from prosecution under all Federal and State antitrust laws so the companies may pool risks to offer private insurance policies to the public pursuant to section 1502 of the bill.

The Long-Ribicoff bill is basically a catastrophic illness: It is a congressional illness. What happens when there is a legislative proposal and the process drags out year after year is that after a while fatigue sets in and legislators who know better, who indeed have written books and articles showing the need for a much stronger type of legislation, at least at the level of Kennedy-Griffiths, lose their energy, get fatigued, and settle for a rather innocuous, if not actually harmful, bill.

As we know, there are cycles to reform in every area of our country's economy and a piecemeal-type process that simply builds on the ingrained abuses of the health care delivery system and nourishes them is not only bad in and of itself but it weakens the effort for a much more funadmental change in the succeeding 5 or 10 years.

For the Long-Ribicoff bill to go further and exempt the private insurance carriers from the last discipline they have on them which is the market system, is an illustration of how extensive the process of surrender to calendar expediency can go.

My personal judgment here is that the best thing that Congress can do this year is not pass any health insurance plan and move forcefully next year to prepare the basis for a comprehensive plan that focuses on the critical elements of quality control, cost control, accessibility, preventive health care, and consumer participation at the grassroots level up to the hierarchy of the administration to Washington.

Congress should reject any plan designed to massively subsidize a private corporate insurance system whose primary objectives are increasing their wasteful ways and increasing profits derived from a captive consumer market.

What is needed therefore is a federally administered publicly accountable financing mechanism with revenues derived from progressive taxing mechanisms.

This is also an important point. The taxing system to fund these plans should not be regressive. It should be progressive in fact.

---

[1] Figures are the approximate retentions of Blue Cross-Blue Shield and other health insurance carriers. Social Security Bulletin (February 1974), p. 38.

Consumers must be afforded a majority role in administration of the program through local, State, and regional governing agencies whose activities and collected data are open to the public.

There should be no more situations, for example, under medicare where the inspection reports of nursing homes were considered secret until the Freedom of Information Act prevailed them to open them up.

The development of cooperative, prepaid health care institutions, clinics and hospitals alike, must be given first priority. I think more attention from some members of the committee to help develop cooperative hospital systems in the local community should be drawn.

Back in the 1920's the first cooperative hospital, in Elk City, Okla., bears scrutiny. This was a situation where a highly public interest oriented doctor led the way in developing the first cooperative hospital, basically paid for by contribution from families in Elk City, Okla., in return for rather comprehensive hospital care.

At the time he was fought all the way down by the medical establishment, but there are several cooperative hospitals, as distinguished from the Kaiser Permanente group prepaid plan, several cooperative hospitals in the country which are the essence of local control and local generation of funding and should be looked into.

I do not find any attention in the hearing records over the last few years to that option.

Congress should reject any plan designed to massively subsidize a private corporate insurance system whose primary objectives are increasing their wasteful ways and increasing profits derived from a congressionally mandated or encouraged captive consumer market.

Americans are now spending over $100 billion [1] annually for a health care delivery system whose inequities, costs, and quality is so deficient that almost every conceivable political faction now supports some concept of "national health insurance."

There is little doubt that a competent health system that serves consumers will not only advance the health of present and future generations but will also implement the economic wisdom that an ounce of prevention is worth a pound of cure.

We can't look at just what these bills supposedly cost. We have to look at what they will do. Whether we are wasteful is a function of what they will do. If they prevent wage loss of billions of dollars a year and if they prevent overapplication of drugs and if they prevent overutilization of medical and health facilities they are saving money for the economy.

They are thrift bills. I think that is the definition that should be brought to any final analysis of what these bills cost the people in this country.

It is readily apparent that citizens support comprehensive preventive national health insurance. It is Congress' responsibility to meet this need. It cannot be met by stopgap measures—catastrophic or otherwise—whose only result would be to fatten a system which is already a health and fiscal disaster.

NATIONAL CONSUMERS LEAGUE ([41], pp. 314–317)

Esther Peterson was president of the National Consumers League when she testified in May 1974 on national health insurance before the Senate Finance Committee. She had been consumer affairs adviser to President Johnson and a food chain executive in Washington, D.C., where she has pioneered in consumer-responsive marketing practices. She presently serves as a special assistant to President Carter for consumer affairs. Mrs. Peterson testified at the time the Kennedy-Mills bill was introduced, and it was this bill that caused

[1] Social Security Bulletin (February 1974), p. 3.

confusion over the direction to be taken by advocates of national health. In her statement to the committee, she stressed the importance of consumer participation in the day-to-day operations of a national health insurance program once it is established, and set forth a "bill of rights" to assure the users of the system's fair treatment.

STATEMENT BY THE NATIONAL CONSUMERS LEAGUE

The consumer wants in:

Much of the debate over national health insurance centers on issues of benefits, costs, coverage, administration and financing.

Of course, these are important. Omitted, however, and paramount to us and the cause of fiscal responsibility, is a central point:

Consumer participation in the governance of whatever national health insurance is constructed is essential. The people who get the benefits and pay for them should have a major voice in the setting of priorities and allocation of resources— taking on their shoulders the pains and agonies of making choices among worthy goals and of measuring goals against collective ability to pay.

The National Consumers League believes that any proposal lacking consumer participation in the making of policy and operating decisions is unacceptable.

All the measures before Congress are defective from this consumer viewpoint. The one we heartily endorse as closest to representing the consumer's needs, Health Security, is bold but not bold enough. You will look in vain in all the other major proposals for a dominant role for the consumer. Decisionmaking is left, alas, in the hands of insurers, providers, and their counterpart bureaucrats in government.

Strange to say, in an age so mistrustful of bureaucracy and the decoupling of power and responsiveness, all proposals but Health Security leave nothing or virtually nothing for grassroots Americans to say about the conduct and structure of their national health insurance.

We endorse Health Security's assignment to local and regional bodies having consumer majorities a key role in allocating funds and other resources among the providers of care. We believe, however, that this feature should be strengthened to provide for local and regional councils that are entirely made up of consumers. Further, and critically important, the consumers should be elected.

Providers should have their say through advisory bodies, but they should not be entrusted with the power to designate the allocation of consumer funds, except when they are under supervision of consumer-dominated boards of governors whose primary allegiance is to the public interest.

Lest a proposal based on bringing democracy into the health-care field appear revolutionary and without precedent, we mention a few steps already taken but not nearly bold enough.

1. There exist today 200 or more areawide and state comprehensive health planning agencies with consumer majorities mandated by law. (For the moment, we note solely their presence, not their strengths and weaknesses.)

2. We note the place accorded beneficiaries in the proposed long-term care portion of the Mills-Kennedy bill; it calls for one-half of the governing bodies of local community service agencies to be users or potential users, one-quarter to be elected, and one-quarter to be appointed by elected public officials.

3. The law on Health Maintenance Organizations requires that one-third of the governing bodies be composed of users.

4. We note the commitment to local self-determination in the Professional Standards Review Organization law, applicable to physicians, of course, not consumers. (Though we disapprove of the weak role accorded to public representatives to look into local and statewide PSROs, the concept of local physician self-determination under broad national guidelines is commendable.)

5. Finally, though the system has gone awry with cronyism and elitism, lay control over hospitals in the public interest must be noted. And, although evidence on effectiveness is wanting, steps toward consumer domination taken by Blue Cross plans warrant, at least initially, some applause.

When we survey the major NHI proposals, we find—except for Health Security—the same old pattern of condescension to the beneficiary. The person in whose name NHI is advanced, apparently exists in these legislative proposals as a passive "thing", to be ministered to but not to be considered seriously as the major actor in the new world.

The lack of a consumer counterweight in the Medicare program should be examined by the Congress. We suggest that the absence has embroiled Congress to an excessive degree in supervising the bureaucracies when it has far more important work to do. Medicare has lacked a dynamic in its governing structure that would resolve problems created by avoracious provider demands, that would resist the deliberate or unwitting creation of policies that serve the providers and the bureaucracies first and the consumer last.

We think the NHI proposals before Congress, again excepting Health Security, will retail Congress to death with petty problems. We urge the Congress to think wholesale.

The characteristics of a sound system of national health insurance—economical to the people and to the Congress in terms of money, time and emotion—would include:

A. There would be a centralized system for collecting contributions nationally. But there would also be a decentralized disbursement system operating under broad national guidelines.

B. Allocations to regional and local NHI governing boards would be made out of a national budget for health care. These periodically elected boards of consumers, well-staffed, would define a master plan for meeting the service needs of their populations. Advice of experts and provider representatives would be sought. The boards would receive prospective budgets from hospitals and other providers of care, offer them for public comment, and, in an open process, shape them according to the comments and master plan and then allocate the money. What we describe is essentially a legislative process applied to the health care economy.

C. The boards would decide among competing priorities, competing providers of care, and competing demands for service expressed by segments of the public. The boards would measure the effectiveness of programs, evaluate the efficiency of providers, and receive grievances from users of services; first, to be responsive to demands for fairness, and, second, to seek out systemic failures of the health-service system.

Through such means, with the power of the purse in the hands of locally elected consumers, the contemporary tendency of the health-care system to convenience the providers of care would be corrected.

Besides control over the purse, we suggest other specifications for a consumer-oriented national health insurance system. Benefits and services should be conceived of as a contract between the consumer boards and the beneficiaries. In effect, providers would be subcontractors of the boards. The rights of the health-care consumer would be stated, among them the rights to privacy, freedom of information, nonretaliatory grievance against the system, and prompt response. Every hospital, nursing home, HMO, PSRO, Independent Practice Association, and other organized service participating in national health insurance would have a patients' representative responsible for answering complaints and protecting patient interests. The NHI system should offer conciliation and arbitration services. Data collected through grievance processes should be available to help define human relations problems in institutions as well as matters of poor care, bad communications and needs for health education.

We turn now from rights and governance to substance. The system should cover, at once or shortly after initiation, all basic needs for health-services, including those of patients with long term nursing and psychiatric problems. The system should permit the experts in whose hands the consumer commits his or her health problems to make professional decisions unencumbered by a fractionated benefit structure or limited by the patient's ability to pay, race, religion, sex, age or national origin. Any system that maintains separate provisions for the poor is inherently discriminatory, as unhealthy in its way as racial discrimination in the schools. The sequestering of any part of our people from the main body of beneficiaries is bound to be inequitable in providing accessible, available, high quality care. And it is also bound to raise administrative costs.

We make these points in recognition of the tendency in the Congress and the Executive Branch—and in the States—to devise systems that limit governmental liability while exposing the people for whom the system was designed to unrestrained inflation. What else is one to make of the Nixon Administration's awesome complexity: it is a nonsystem aimed at avoiding federal liability and responsiveness. The same may be said of features of the Kennedy-Mills and Long-Ribicoff **proposals**.

We are pained by the approbation often attached to "incremental" approaches to national health insurance. Alas, incrementalism in this field will be inflationary, because it represents gradual encroachment on problems that intensify, as many cancers, unless they are cut out in one bold effort. Instead of the administrative economies and consumer conveniences of a single contribution covering all basic services, some NHI plans proliferate administration by setting up tests of age, income, kind of service, and type of illness. Providers are forced to cope with a variety of third-party payers or other income sources. The grand game is one in which providers try to place costs among payers to see who will absorb them and in which payers try to fend them off. Such is the complexity and apparent lack of equity that anger, fraud, frustration, and personal disaster become the hallmarks of incrementalism.

The desire to subdivide costs among a variety of payers also is costly in terms of administration and public credibility. Medicare beneficiaries often express anger at the unfairness of out-of-pocket payments they thought the system would cover, but doesn't. Copayments, deductibles, partial coverage, and exclusions bedevil the consumer and provider.

Almost every NHI proposal based on incrementalism and timidity will leap into a proliferation of billing without looking first. Yet, the consumer and the provider would do better without it. (The health insurance companies, of course, thrive on it. To end consumer billing would eliminate need for these companies' skills.)

Again, we urge Congress to go to wholesaling and reduce the administrative costs and improve the public satisfaction with NHI.

What the consumer wants is a simple, understandable, responsive system that is thrifty and effective.

The consumer wants "in" on the benefits and the hard choices. . . .

MODEL PATIENTS BILL OF RIGHTS

1. The maintenance of the health of its citizens is essential to the well being of the nation. Every person has the right to receive high-quality personal health services without regard to ability to pay, age, race, sex, religion, and national origin.

2. The right of privacy and protection against self-incrimination shall prevail during examination, diagnosis, and treatment. It shall govern the maintenance of all health records, verbal or recorded.

3. Except in emergencies, patients must be informed of treatment to be received, of who provides the treatment to be received, of risks and benefits to the extent known, and of whether or not the treatment is experimental. Patients have the right to withhold consent to treatment. If the patient is unable to give informed consent, it must be sought from next of kin or others responsible for the patient's rights, including the physician or institution, as a last resort.

4. The patient-provider relationship shall be free of any representatives of enforcement, investigative, financial, religious or social agencies, unless the patient, without duress, approves.

5. No person needing care shall be turned away or otherwise abandoned by providers of care.

6. No person shall be denied access to care because he or she has advocated or worked for change in the provision of health care.

7. Every person has a right to all information of a public nature on the quality of care, the administration of health services and their governance and economics.

8. Health care shall be organized to benefit the general public; therefore, elected consumer representatives under national health insurance shall have an ongoing role in decisionmaking with respect to local expenditures for health-care services, including services educational, preventive, curative, restorative and mental health.

9. Every citizen has the right to select and change physicians at will or to select a preferred system of medical care.

10. The right of health-care consumers to pursue complaints to a satisfactory conclusion shall not be denied.

Medical Educators ([41], pp. 179–184)

Dr. Leonard Cronkhite, Jr., appeared before the Senate Finance Committee in May 1974 on behalf of the Association of American Medical Colleges regarding national health insurance legislation. His statement reflects the views of medical educators and of those currently engaged in the study of medicine. In his testimony, Dr. Cronkhite set forth an indictment of the private health industry and called, in no uncertain terms, for adoption of a national health insurance program under tight federal supervision. While much of organized medicine, particularly the AMA, equivocates on key elements of a broad, compulsory, federally funded program, Dr. Cronkhite and his association came out clearly in favor of a comprehensive national health insurance. The impact on legislation from this quarter, however, is by no means as profound as that of the AMA.

PREPARED STATEMENT BY THE ASSOCIATION OF AMERICAN MEDICAL COLLEGES

Mr. Chairman and members of the Committee:

The Association of American Medical Colleges welcomes this opportunity to testify on legislation to establish a system of national health insurance in the United States.

Formed in 1876 to push for reforms in medical schools, the Association has broadened its activities over the years. Today it represents the whole complex of persons and institutions charged with the education of physicians and other health professionals, the conduct of biomedical research, and the provision of health services. The Association represents all 114 of the nation's operational medical schools and their students, 392 of the major teaching hospitals, and 60 academic societies and professional organizations.

The Association's member institutions educate all of the physicians, other than osteopathic physicians, in the United States. They play a major role in graduate medical education through programs carried out in the medical schools and in their affiliated teaching hospitals. Faculty members at these institutions conduct a substantial portion of the nation's biomedical research aimed at understanding the living process and the nature of disease and at developing more effective ways to prevent, diagnose, and treat disease.

Of direct interest to this Committee's consideration of national health insurance, the academic medical centers with their teaching hospitals are significant providers of acute inpatient and ambulatory medical services in the nation. AAMC-member teaching hospitals represent 6.5% of the total number of hospitals in the United States, contain over 23% of the total hospital beds, employ 29% of the total hospital personnel, and are responsible for 20% of all hospital admissions and 25% of all outpatient visits. By virtue of its size (usually over 300 beds) and location (often in an urban or metropolitan setting), the teaching hospital cares for a high percentage of patients from the immediate locality and the surrounding regions and maintains the resources of physical plant, skilled health personnel, complex equipment, and a spectrum of services necessary for comprehensive care of high quality. The teaching hospital has been characterized as the summit of the health care pyramid, the capstone of the nation's hospital system. High standards of clinical practice necessitate that the teaching hospital accept referrals from physicians in other hospitals involving patients who present difficult problems of diagnosis or who require treatment only available in the teaching hospital. In many cases patients seek out directly services offered in the teaching setting. The nation relies, then, on its teaching hospitals for the graduate education of physicians and other health manpower, the establishment of standards for the promotion of better health, the best care of the sick and injured, the continued advancement of medical knowledge, and the transfer of new technology to the patient's care.

It is in light of this major role Association members play as providers of health care, as educators of health manpower, and as biomedical and health service researchers, that the Association of American Medical Colleges today presents its views on legislation to establish a national health insurance system. On February 18, 1971, the Assembly of the Association, its highest legislative body, adopted a statement of policy urging the early enactment of a program of national health insurance. Although that statement still expresses the Association's policy on national health insurance in a general way, the renewed Congressional interest in the issue, as evidenced by the number of new proposals, and by these hearings, prompted the Association to appoint a Task Force to update and enlarge its national health insurance policy statement.

In its work, the Task Force did not set out to examine any particular legislative proposal for national health insurance, but instead to develop its own set of principles it believes any program of national health insurance that is enacted should follow. The Task Force first examined the present method of health care financing in the United States, assessed its deficiencies, and then determined what distortions in the present delivery system it believes can be attributed to the present system of health care financing. From these findings, the Task Force developed and the Association adopted positions on various issues involved in the consideration of programs of national health insurance. At this time the Association would like to share with the Committee these findings and positions:

FINDINGS

According to a recent Social Security Administration study, health spending in the United States in 1973 reached $94.1 billion. Funds to finance this health care bill came from three sources: 1) from individuals, as personal out-of-pocket medical expenditures; 2) from various forms of public or private insurance; and 3) from the general revenues, collected from taxpayers. In 1973, three-fifths of the nation's health care bill was paid from private sources, and two-fifths came from public sources. Total national expenditures for personal health care (excluding among other things expenditures for insurance premiums) totaled $76.5 billion in 1972 (the latest year for which data are available). Private health insurance met 25.5% of this amount, 35.6% came from direct out-of-pocket payments by consumers, and 37.5% was met by public funds.

Although health insurance met 42% of all consumer expenditures for personal health care in 1972, many individuals remained uncovered by any form of health insurance. In 1972, an estimated one-fifth of the population under age 65 had no financial protection against the hazards of illness. Still larger numbers had inadequate coverage. Three-fourths of the population had private insurance protection against some of the cost of hospital and surgical care; and 72% were covered for some of the cost of inpatient physicians' visits and outpatient radiologic and laboratory examinations; about 55% were covered for any part of their expenditures for prescription drugs, private duty nursing or visiting-nurse services; 22% for any nursing home care; and less than 9% for any dental care.

These statistics illustrate that the portion of the health care bill which the individual must now pay directly as a personal expenditure is large. The purpose of a national health insurance program is to transfer a large part of this personal financial responsibility to the insurance function. Most of the financial risk of illness should be shared by all in an approximately equal way through the insurance mechanism.

In the Association's view, then, the major purpose of national health insurance legislation is to create a better means of financing medical care. Although national health insurance per se may not effect a drastic restructuring of the health care delivery system, it should promote needed changes. To define and then bring about the ideal delivery system is too great a task to be accomplished in a single step. Yet national health insurance should both permit and strongly encourage changes in the present delivery system.

Accordingly, the Association makes the following findings of deficiencies in the present system of health care financing:

1. It acts as a barrier to accessibility to needed health care services.

2. It leaves too many uncovered costs to be borne inordinately by the individual as personal out-of-pocket expenditures.

3. It promotes and perpetuates a two-class system of patient care, because it leaves many individuals uncovered or inadequately covered.

4. The insurance component, unlike other insurance, does not cover the highest risks first, and often does not cover them at all.

Further, the Association makes the following findings of distortions in the present health care delivery system under the present health care financing mechanisms:

1. It interferes with professional judgment as to the use of expensive patient care where less expensive patient care would be appropriate.

2. It offers few incentives for efficiency.

3. It does not stimulate changes in the present delivery system.

4. It does not provide the risk capital necessary for innovation.

5. It stimulates the disproportionate distribution of health care resources to more affluent areas.

6. It provides inadequate financing for the provision of health services to the poor.

7. It provides inadequate incentives for distributing physicians by specialty according to the needs of society.

In light of these findings, the Association takes the following positions on the specific national health insurance issues of *scope of coverage, structure of covered benefits, consumer responsibility for cost-sharing, methods of financing the insurance system, regulation of the underwriter, regulation of providers, standards for provider reimbursement, development and distribution of resources,* and *effect on other programs.*

SCOPE OF COVERAGE

Because adequate health care has come to be recognized as a right and not a privilege of all Americans, any national health insurance system should have as its first priority the provisions of health insurance coverage for all. This goal of universal coverage will be attained by requiring as a matter of law not only that the opportunity to obtain adequate health insurance coverage must be made available to each individual, but also that he must take advantage of this opportunity. Voluntarism will never produce universal coverage, for there will always be those who will opt out due to ignorance, undue optimism, or neglect. A national health insurance program which does not provide universal coverage will unquestionably perpetuate the two-class system of patient care it is designed to eliminate, as afflicted individuals without health insurance protection will have to be treated on a charity basis.

BENEFIT STRUCTURE

A national health insurance plan should finance the most comprehensive package of health care benefits within the resources available. As a general rule, all necessary health care expenditures should be covered without quantity limits. Exclusion from coverage should be well-defined and well-reasoned. All exclusions should be periodically reviewed and re-evaluated in light of new federal initiatives and new developments in health care management and delivery. Any exclusion from coverage should fit into one of the following categories:

1. Services for which insufficient personnel and facilities exist for provision on a universal basis should be excluded. It would be irresponsible for the national health insurance legislation to create health care expectations that the delivery system could not meet.

2. Services not traditionally included in an individual's personal health care expenditures, and financed instead through general revenues as public health care expenditures, although important to good personal health, should initially be excluded from coverage under national health insurance. Because long-term

care for chronic mental illness, for example, is most often provided in state-operated institutions supported by public funds, this care would most efficiently be provided with federal assistance and in accord with federal quality standards through a separate state-operated system. The Medicaid program, which now finances long-term custodial care in nursing homes in many states, should be modified to have as its primary purpose the provision of this kind of care in accord with federal quality standards in all states for individuals who cannot pay for it as a personal health care expenditure.

3. Benefits which, if included, would pose unreasonable administrative burdens should be excluded from coverage under the national health insurance system.

Except for services excluded for these reasons, covered services should include, at a minimum and without limit, hospital services (including active treatment in psychiatric hospitals), physician services and other appropriate professional and paramedical services wherever provided, and diagnostic laboratory and diagnostic and therapeutic radiologic services wherever provided. Other covered benefits should include wherever provided such services as home health services, rehabilitation services, cost-beneficial preventive services, emergency medical services, and crisis-intervention mental health services.

COST-SHARING

A program of national health insurance is designed to provide ready financial access to the health care system and to shift the financial burden of health care from personal expenditures to insurance coverage, thus broadening the financial base available to support health care costs. The ideal health insurance program should therefore have no cost-sharing provisions. If a particular health insurance proposal includes such cost-sharing mechanisms as deductibles, coinsurance, or copayments, they should be held to minimum levels, and their effect on utilization should be evaluated. They should only be high enough to avoid over-utilization; they should not be burdensome in the aggregate to a family; they should be waived for low-income persons. Furthermore, they should not be applicable to essential minimum services, and the cost of administering the cost-sharing should not exceed the savings from avoided over-utilization. In addition, if a national health insurance plan utilizes cost-sharing, the provider, in order to promote efficiency, should not be involved in collecting the patient's share. The provider should not be required to determine at the point of delivery whether or not the patient has met cost-sharing obligations in the past or whether the patient can pay any new cost-sharing obligations that may arise.

FINANCING THE INSURANCE SYSTEM

The present system of health care financing leaves significant population groups without health insurance protection, and even larger groups with inadequate coverage. The individual's personal, out-of-pocket health bills too often exceed his financial ability to meet them and act as a barrier to needed care. Health insurance should meet more of the individual's health care expenses. The method used to finance the national health insurance system should mandate universal coverage and make certain that individuals are not caught in gaps of coverage with changes in employment or financial status. Each and every citizen must be assured of a uniform minimum package of benefits. The bills before the Committee achieve these objectives to varying degrees through a number of financing mechanisms. There are considerable differences of opinion within the Association's constituency about the relative merits of the various proposals now before the Congress. There is unanimous agreement on the criteria described here. The Association supports the financing provision of each bill that meets these criteria. The risk in S. 3286 is the prospect of an unwieldly, unresponsive, and inefficient bureaucracy. The problems with S. 2970 are the failure to assure universal coverage and the complexity of the regulatory procedures.

REGULATION OF THE INSURANCE UNDERWRITER

Regardless of the extent to which private health insurance is to be included in a national health insurance program, the federal government has a responsibility for safeguarding the public by effectively regulating the private insurers. Such regulation will be most effective if done by a single federal agency, independent of the agency charged with administering the national health insurance program, which will license, monitor, and otherwise regulate all health insurance underwriters. This agency should also be charged with the duty to promulgate standards governing carrier solvency, risk-selection, loss ratios, and premium rates.

REGULATION OF THE PROVIDER

Any regulation of the relationship between the underwriter or the intermediary and the provider must assure that the standards by which providers are reimbursed for their services are not only economically prudent but also fundamentally fair. Because there are substantial area-to-area variations, the regulation of provider reimbursement and health care costs would best be performed at the state or substate level under strong federal guidelines. Regulatory decisions in these areas must be rendered with due process, equity, and fairness, and there should be an effective mechanism for the appeal of such decisions.

PROVIDER REIMBURSEMENT STANDARDS

Any national health insurance system must establish a reimbursement policy which allows fair and reasonable payments for services and which stimulates efficiency and cost restraints as consistent with the promotion of high quality medical care.

A fair and reasonable reimbursement policy for physician services should provide payment for high quality professional medical services on an equal basis irrespective of the setting in which the services are provided. Such a reimbursement policy should not impede the training and education of medical students and residents, and should recognize the team approach to professional care in the teaching setting. The policy should not, for example, in setting conditions under which fee-for-service reimbursement of teaching physicians is to be made, require the kind of financial test and other conditions imposed by section 227 of the Social Security Amendments of 1972.

A reimbursement policy which is fair and reasonable also will meet the financial needs of the institutional providers of the services, including the replenishment of capital for the maintenance of an up-to-date facility. Allowable expenses for reimbursement under a national health insurance program should include the depreciation of capital assets, the amortization of debt, and the accumulation of an adequate operating margin. Furthermore, the reimbursement policy should reflect that there are valid differentials among the various types of providers in the cost of delivering care. The cost of services delivered in the teaching hospital, for example, will be greater for at least three reasons: (1) the severity of illness and complexity of diagnosis which patients bring to the teaching hospital; (2) the comprehensiveness and/or intensiveness of services provided by the teaching hospital; and (3) the teaching hospital's commitment to the incremental costs of providing the environment for medical and paramedical educational programs.

A reimbursement policy that stimulates efficiency and cost constraints consistent with the promotion of high quality medical care will not only mandate that the providers institute effective utilization review and quality control programs. It will also provide for an organized system of research and development of methods to insure that quality control and utilization control standards will be determined and implemented only on a valid statistical basis. Furthermore, because provider efforts to regulate and monitor quality and utilization are costly propositions, the cost of any such regulatory measure should be justified by its effectiveness and then treated as any other allowable cost for the purpose of reimbursement.

RESOURCE DEVELOPMENT AND DISTRIBUTION

While national health insurance should not be expected to correct all of the distortions in the present health care delivery system caused by the current system of health care financing, neither should its reimbursement policies encourage further distortions.

National health insurance is an appropriate mechanism for financing graduate medical education as a means of replenishing the health manpower pool. Graduate medical training includes important elements related to education and delivery of health services as integral parts of the training, and is thus appropriately financed by the health delivery system, both with respect to inpatient and ambulatory care. In its financing of graduate medical education, the national health insurance system may justifiably be used to influence the numbers and kinds of medical generalists and specialists that are trained. The problem of specialty distribution is currently under study by the Coordinating Council on Medical Education and the Institute of Medicine, and the findings and recommendations of such studies should be carefully considered in developing a method for dealing with the problem.

Similarly, national health insurance is an appropriate mechanism to assure the construction of resources that meet community needs. The special need for facilities for the education and training of health professionals by the medical schools and teaching hospitals must be given proper recognition in these determinations. The kind of approach to this problem taken by Section 1122 of the Social Security Act, which provides that providers constructing facilities determined to be unnecessary by a state's designated planning agency are not to receive federal reimbursement for depreciation and interest on those facilities, should be extended to reimbursements under a national health insurance program. Planning agencies should be strengthened to perform this additional function.

The federal government should have a coherent, rational, and unified role in the financing of health care. To date, public health care funds have been channeled into a variety of inadequate or overlapping federal programs, and the resulting fragmentation has been both costly and inefficient. Accordingly, separate federal programs that now exist, such as the Veterans Administration health care system, Public Health Service hospitals, the Indian Health Service, and the military dependents program, should be integrated into the national health insurance system. This integration will best be accomplished gradually, but nonetheless in accordance with a fixed timetable. To this end, the first priority should be the standardization of all benefits provided through all existing public programs to conform to the national health insurance benefit package standard. As this is accomplished, the other aspects of the separate public health care programs should be modified and meshed into the national health insurance system. If a program cannot feasibly be modified for integration into the national health insurance scheme, it should be gradually phased out.

These findings and positions on specific national health insurance issues comprise the Association's statement of policy on national health insurance as developed by the Task Force. The Association believes that these principles should govern any national health insurance program this Committee adopts. Of the bills now before this Committee, no single proposal exactly follows the Association's recommendations on these specific issues, although some bills follow more closely than others. The Association hopes that the Committee will use these principles to resolve the differing approaches to the issues in question taken by the various proposals now before the Committee.

National Association of Insurance Commissioners ([22], pp. 228–233)

William Huff III is Insurance Commissioner for the state of Iowa and is also an official of the National Association of Insurance Commissioners, an organization representing state level insurance officials. He testified before the House Committee on Interstate and Foreign Commerce during its hearings on national health insurance in February 1976. Huff is an advocate of decentralization in the administration of health insurance programs and supports the use of private carriers, supervised and controlled by existing—and perhaps expanded—state regulatory bodies. In the panoply of interest groups exerting influence on the outcome of the national health insurance debate, the Association is aligned with the private insurance industry and opposes a federally administered, federally funded program as proposed in the Kennedy-Corman bill. Following Huff's presentation, which is reprinted here, the committee heard from Melvin Glasser, director of the Social Security Department of UAW, who took issue with Huff's allegations on the cost effectiveness of the state-administered alternative. Glasser's testimony is not reprinted here but is available in [22], pp. 241–254.

SHOULD CONGRESS ENACT A FEDERALLY MANDATED COMPREHENSIVE NATIONAL HEALTH INSURANCE PROGRAM?

1. ECONOMIC BACKDROP

Today by far the greatest economic concern of the people of this country is the economy, inflation, and recession. In December 1973, "Survey of Public Attitudes" by Louis Harris and Associates for the U.S. Senate Subcommittee on Intergovernmental Relations it was found that 72 percent of those interviewed listed economics/inflation as one of the biggest problems facing the country. Yet, there has been proportionately little concern regarding the inflationary affect that a national health insurance poses. Broad benefits that include cradle-to-grave, first-dollar health care coverage for everyone is socially desirable when one ignores the ramifications of such a liberal benefit arrangement, but it cannot be ignored that such insurance benefits will bring about a sudden stimulant for demand of health care services.

The basic principles of economics have taught us that if you stimulate demand when supply is less than adequate, the expected result must be rapidly rising prices for the produce or service offered. Far too many of the national health insurance proposals give inadequate attention to the supply side of medical services. Certainly the creation of another Federal bureaucratic agency will not solve the limited supply problems that will become extremely critical under the popular national health insurance proposals that emphasize the broad benefits to be offered.

Inflation has become such a critical problem in this country that there is an uncertainty beginning to appear that questions the Government's ability to deal with the problem. Economics are reminding us that monetary and fiscal policy by the Federal Government has the most significant impact upon inflation. A major part of fiscal policy is Government's control over its own spending. A great deal of concern has recently arisen in view of the fact that the Federal Government budget is becoming a budget of previously committed funds, and as a result each year when Congress makes efforts to shape the expenditures for the next fiscal period they find that they have a smaller and smaller amount of uncommitted funds that can be influenced by their decisions.

This large segment of the budget is called uncontrollable outlays, and it is startling to find out for the fiscal year 1977, built-in costs for relatively uncontrollable program expenditure is estimated at $303 billion, or approximately 76 percent of total Federal budget expenditures this year. These percentages have increased from approximately 70 percent in 1973, 72 percent in 1974, 73 percent in 1975, and 72 percent in 1976 according to the budget of the U.S. Government fiscal year 1977.[1] There is no better example of these built-in commitments than our open-ended social security program. Furthermore, the gross Federal debt for 1977 is estimated at $719.5 billion, an 88-percent increase from $382.6 billion in 1970.[2]

The Federal Government refuses to take seriously the ever-rising national debt by calling the increased ceilings only temporary increases. It is clearly a game of charades and is another example of the built-in inflationary factors of which the Federal Government is rapidly losing control. The general public understands the adverse ramifications of hyperinflation and they are loudly proclaiming that they do not like it. Yet, there seems to be widespread unwillingness to attack the inflationary sources where the attack will be the most effective—that is, before legislative programs which have an ever-extending inflationary characteristic become law. A recently released trustees' report for the Social Security Administration shows that the present system's costs will exceed its income by the end of this decade and at that point the problem will become worse with each passing year. The Social Security Commissioner says this means that the financing of social security will have to be changed significantly in coming years in order to avoid bankruptcy.

When looking at the current national health insurance proposals from the viewpoint of a State insurance commissioner, it is incredibly difficult to believe that the national health insurance issue is receiving such a superficial evaluation regarding its economic impact over an extended period of time. We recognize that it is politically popular to advocate an insurance plan that stresses broad benefit coverage and ideally we all support the broadcast of benefits in our national health insurance benefit package. It is time, however, to be honest with the citizens of our country and explain the adverse effects of extremely liberal health insurance benefits without restructuring our entire health care system. They deserve to be told the entire story.

However, the proponents of a compulsory, comprehensive, Federal

---

[1] 94th Congress, 2d Session, House Document No. 94–343, at 354-355.
[2] Special Analysis, Budget of the United States Government, Fiscal Year 1977, at page 50.

national health insurance program simply maintain that adequate health care is the right of every citizen. This kind of national health insurance would provide every citizen with health services or the means to purchase such care. From the individual's viewpoint, the prospect of the Federal Government's assumption of the burden of medical bills is very appealing. Consequently, the national health insurance advocates are often well received.

Unfortunately, however, the issue as to whether Congress should enact a comprehensive national health insurance program cannot be considered in simplified isolation. National health insurance interrelates with the health care delivery system which, in turn, is only one facet of the total economic, sociopolitical environment within which all must function. If it is recognized that this Nation's economic resources are insufficient to meet all of this Nation's wants and desires, then priorities must be determined and resources allocated accordingly. In doing so, however, political as well as economic and social questions are raised. In short, the sheer magnitude of the national health insurance concept necessitates that it be considered in the context of other major problems rather than in an alluring isolation.

2. WASHINGTON SYNDROME

In recent years we have witnessed a tremendous concentration of power in the National Government. The magnitude of national power is now such that the very fundamental and constitutional concept of federalism is being seriously, perhaps fatally, undermined. As described above, the size and the uncontrollable nature of the Federal budget has limited the ability of the elected leaders to be responsive to the public's needs and concerns. In fiscal year 1977, 40 percent of the Federal budget is allocated for direct benefit payments to individuals.[1]

As a gigantic purchaser of goods and services, and as the employer of nearly 3 million of the Nation's civilian work force,[2] much of the public is dependent on the Federal Government. Such an economic dependence on a central government bodes ill for productivity and the continuance of a politically free citizenry.

Further, the Federal bureaucratic intervention into virtually every aspect of American life is questionable in terms of necessity and efficacy. The public has increasingly lost confidence in the ability of the Federal Government to govern on its behalf, despite the enormity of the taxes and other costs paid. The evidence is mounting that the public wants substantial authority and power returned to the State and local governments.

These various factors compel the conclusion that a Federal Government solution should not be sought for every problem. Making the National Government the insurer of the Nation's health would further undermine federalism to a very substantial degree as a viable element in our democratic system of government. Whatever the merits of national health insurance, this would be a terribly high price to pay, especially if there are other viable alternatives.

3. ALTERNATIVES

Other alternatives to a Federal Government health insurance program do exist. The private health insurance mechanism already covers 90 percent of the population to some degree and has shown willingness and capacity to provide protection to those currently without coverage or adequate coverage. Current experiences and the

---

[1] Office of Management and Budget, the United States Budget in Brief, Fiscal Year 1977.

[2] According to the Bureau of Labor Statistics in 1974, there were 2,874,000 civilian Federal employees. Handbook of Labor Statistics 1975, Reference Edition, page 119.

competitive nature of the private health insurance sector of the economy offers greater promise of efficiency over both the short and the long run in addressing the Nation's health insurance needs than does the Federal Government.

Furthermore, the private health insurance system is subject to State regulatory oversight. State insurance laws are designed to prevent abuse, improve the existing insurance markets, and stimulate industry responsiveness to the public's needs. State activity in the health insurance area in recent years has been impressive. Thus, the combination of the private health insurance mechanism as the basic provider of coverage and the State insurance regulatory system as the overseer and stimulator affords a viable alternative to a massive Federal national health insurance program. This alternative not only avoids the acceleration of the trend towards concentrating power in Washington—with all its attendant adverse consequences—but it avoids many of the multiple cost of a federally enacted comprehensive national insurance program.

4. MULIPLE COSTS OF A FEDERALLY MANDATED COMPREHENSIVE NATIONAL HEALTH INSURANCE PROGRAM

The cost of a federally funded and administered health insurance program, assumes a variety of forms. Ultimately, however, each is a cost which must be borne by the individual members of the American public.

(a) The dollar cost of the program benefits would be quite substantial for a comprehensive level of benefits and will mushroom as inflation takes its toll. Creating a mammoth Federal bureaucracy to administer the program will increase the dollar costs to even greater levels.

(b) As the size of Federal bureaucracy to administer the national health insurance program reaches gigantic proportions, people can be quite concerned over deterioration in the effective delivery of even the current level of Social Security benefits and services.

(c) The cost to the free enterprise system would be devastating. A large private industry would be destroyed. Hundreds of thousands of persons would lose their jobs with the resultant adverse impact on the economy as well. The precedent would be set for further Government takeovers of private industry.

(d) The cost to the States would be in the form of lost premium tax revenue—hence a reduction of State services—and/or marked reduction in State sovereignty.

(e) The cost to the individual members of the American public include reduced take-home pay, higher-priced goods and services, increased inflation, loss of jobs for some, potential deterioration in receipt of current Social Security benefits and services, reduced political and economic freedom, and loss of practical and effective recourse in the event of mistreatment by the Social Security or other federally administered system.

(f) As the uncontrollable portion of the Federal budget assumes an increasingly greater size—currently around 75 percent—due to open end spending commitments such as Social Security, the cost to Congress would be the lessened ability to respond to future problems and needs—thereby undermining the fabric of our democratic political system.

Thus, the price for a comprehensive federally financed and administered national health insurance program is a high one indeed, especially when other alternatives are available. Utilization of the private insurance mechanism under the supervision of the State insurance regulatory mechanism would eliminate or reduce many of the costs just summarized and yet at the same time address the Nation's health care problems.

5. COORDINATION OF FEDERAL-STATE ACTIVITIES

This is not to say that the Federal Government has no role. However, as the NAIC has urged, the States should develop and implement health care and insurance programs and that Congress and the Administration (should) coordinate their activities with those of the States.[1]

Obviously the third party payment mechanisms established within the private business sector possess the capacity and capability of serving the total health insurance needs of all citizens and, equally obvious, the State insurance regulatory system is well-equipped and has demonstrated its ability to safeguard the interests of the consuming public. The one element that has thus far escaped even minimally adequate control, however, is the health care delivery system itself, particularly with respect to the cost of health care services.

Few will refute the observation that the inflationary cost pattern generated by the health care delivery system is the fundamental crux of the existing dilemma. Indeed, one of the fundamnetal flaws in most national health insurance proposals that have received more than passing interest is their proccupation with the development of a mechanism to effect the payment for health care services whereas the prime focus needs to be development of viable means to control health care costs without adversely impacting on the quality or quantity of the delivery of needed care.

This is not to say the problem has been ignored, but it must be recognized that any attempt to impose effective health care cost controls through any third party payment medium is extremely self-limiting. For example, a State might well impose utilization review, prospective budget analysis, and even direct rate controls on hospitals either separately or as part of comprehensive health insurance legislation and, in fact, the current draft NAIC model bill contains requirements of this kind.

It is and must be recognized, however, that such provisions, though helpful, will be effective only to the extent that a hospital can actu-could be imposed on hospitals which would assure maximum economy and efficiency within the hospital itself but still not result in practically affordable charges because of the influence of competitive or minimum wage levels, inflation in the cost of equipment and supplies, pharmaceutical needs and other outside influences. The problem and its resolution, of course, becomes even more complex when considering individual health care providers as opposed to institutional provider charges.

The NAIC contends that the development and regulation of a comprehensive health insurance program distributed by the private insurance industry is not only a viable alternative to a federally inspired or mandated program but is, in fact, the most practical and will best serve the needs of the public. By utilizing the existing developmental, administrative, regulatory, and distribution system at the State level and within the private insurance industry, the Congress can free itself from consideration of counter-productive issues or solutions, eliminate a significant part of the budgetary considerations and direct its attention to the development of the technical expertise and resources needed to mount and sustain a meaningful attack on the causes of high cost, health care.

The variety of persons, institutions, localities and values require reliance on persons at the State and local level to experiment, develop, and implement policy aimed at improving the health care system and controlling its costs. At the same time, however, the Federal Government should focus on improving the supply of scarce manpower. HEW should serve as a source of advisory—not manda-

---

[1] Proceedings of the NAIC (1975).

tory—expertise to State and local groups on more effective delivery of health care. Perhaps Congress should target its financial assistance to helping lower income persons purchasing adequate health insurance. It is these types of roles that are the only necessary ingredients of any responsible national health insurance program that cannot be effectively undertaken wholly by the individual States.

In conclusion, Congress should refrain from enacting a national health insurance program at this time. The multiple costs—political, economic, and social—to the public, the current condition of our Nation's financial resources, and the alternative programs developed at the State level utilizing the private insurance system lead to these conclusions.

Congress should focus on those activities supplementing ongoing State and local activity rather than conflicting with or overriding these initiatives in the States. If at some time in the future the private insurance mechanism demonstrates either inability or unwillingness to respond to the health insurance needs of the public, Congress could then consider how best to remedy the defects if the States do not do so.

In any event, State insurance regulators should be vested with exclusive regulatory authority over the private insurance mechanism under any nationwide health insurance program.

Thank you very much.

The Ford Administration ([22], pp. 3–4, 6–7, 10–12, 18–20, 27–29)

Both Presidents Nixon and Ford were opposed to a nationwide, federally operated, mandatory health insurance program. Their administrations gave limited support to modifications in the current system, especially regarding provision of protection against financial burdens caused by catastrophic illness. Their lack of commitment to any significant change probably made enactment of any sweeping reform impossible in the early to mid-seventies. President Carter and the Democratic Party platform are both identified as advocating comprehensive national health insurance and may well succeed. In the 93rd Congress, S. 2970/H.R. 12684, the Comprehensive Health Insurance Program (CHIP), was presented on behalf of the Ford administration by Senator Robert Packwood and Representative Herman Schneebeli. (Further information on CHIP is provided in Chapter 2.) The CHIP bill was not reintroduced in the 94th Congress, nor was any legislative proposal on national health submitted by the Nixon and Ford administrations during the 94th Congress. The issue of health care, as viewed by the Ford administration, is presented here by HEW Secretary David Mathews. He testified before the Subcommittee on Health and the Environment of the House Interstate and Foreign Commerce Committee in February 1976. His remarks have been abridged to exclude digressions.

STATEMENT OF HON. DAVID MATHEWS, PH.D., SECRETARY, DE-
PARTMENT OF HEALTH, EDUCATION, AND WELFARE; ACCOM-
PANIED BY THEODORE COOPER, M.D., SECRETARY FOR HEALTH;
M. KEITH WEIKEL, PH.D., COMMISSIONER, MEDICAL SERVICES
ADMINISTRATION, SOCIAL AND REHABILITATION SERVICE;
STUART H. ALTMAN, PH.D., DEPUTY ASSISTANT SECRETARY
FOR HEALTH PLANNING; AND STEPHEN KURZMAN, ASSISTANT
SECRETARY FOR LEGISLATION

Secretary MATHEWS. Thank you very much.

I would like to introduce, if I might, my associates, because they have some comments to make on the particulars of my testimony.

Mr. ROGERS. Certainly.

Secretary MATHEWS. I think the committee is well-acquainted with Dr. Theodore Cooper, Assistant Secretary for Health.

Mr. Rogers. We are, and we welcome him again to the committee.

Secretary Mathews. Dr. M. Keith Weikel, who is the administrator of the Medical Services Administration, SRS.

Mr. Rogers. We welcome you.

Secretary Mathews. Dr. Stuart H. Altman, who is Deputy Assistant Secretary for Health Planning; and Mr. Stephen Kurzman, Assistant Secretary for Legislation.

Mr. Rogers. We welcome Mr. Kurzman and Mr. Altman.

Secretary Mathews. Mr. Chairman, I would first like to have the opportunity to describe for you the President's position on health care—his general philosophy—and I would like to comment on that philosophy as it is embodied in the bloc grant proposal.

I would also like to discuss the President's proposal for catastrophic protection under the medicare program and, as you have requested, make some remarks that are reflective of his position on the question of national health insurance.

In his state of the Union message, the President broadly outlined the Federal Government's role in health care financing, stating:

We cannot realistically afford federally dictated national health insurance providing full coverage for all 215 million Americans. The experience of other countries raises questions about the quality, as well as the cost, of such plans. But I do envision the day when we may use the private health insurance system to offer more middle-income families high quality health service at prices they can afford and shield them also from castastrophic illnesses.

He outlined a practical solution to correct current inequities and to improve existing programs that provide health benefits to beneficiaries under existing Federal programs.

These proposals will be placed in legislative form and introduced into the Congress shortly.

I must stress that the President's proposed reforms are needed now. These proposals should not be held in abeyance pending a resolution of the many complex, substantive financing issues in national health insurance. If our proposals are enacted, they will provide needed catastrophic health insurance under medicare by placing an annual limit on out-of-pocket expenditures for covered services. Also, under medicare, limits will be placed on amounts reimbursable to hospitals and physicians to help insure that the benefits available to medicare beneficiaries are not jeopardized by continued spiraling costs of care. Medicaid and 15 other Federal health programs will be consolidated and more responsibility will be placed at the State level to determine priorities in health care expenditures. . . .

Mr. Chairman, let me turn back to that portion of the President's statement refering to the future day when we may use the private health insurance system to offer more middle-income families protection against health care costs. The proposals I have been discussing are to improve programs for the low income, the disabled, and the aged. Certainly, they are the ones most vulnerable to the high costs of health care. However, there are millions more in our population who have little or no protection in the event of serious illness.

We are reviewing our data to determine more precisely the nature and extent of coverage among the general population and the extent to which the lack of coverage actually results in the failure to utilize services. We believe that closer study of this issue will help us better determine what further initiatives may need to be undertaken to provide better financial access to the entire population.

We would like to see additional improvements in the Nation's system of financing health care and we will be exploring alternative ways to do just that. The President proposed the Financial Assistance for Health Care Act as an example. There is no quick solution to the problems of health care financing, and attempts to find one before we fully understand the consequences could seriously impair the system we now have effectively serving the vast majority of our population.

I believe the measures we have taken to improve the existing system and the President's proposals in his state of the Union and budget messages are fiscally responsible and bode well for future efforts to improve financial protection against health costs.

I thank the committee for the opportunity to present these views and would now like to welcome any questions. . . .

Mr. ROGERS. Mr. Preyer.

Mr. PREYER. Thank you, Mr. Chairman. Mr. Mathews I would like to ask one back question and then, if I have time, a more specific one.

The back question is what do you invision as the purpose of national health insurance. The reason I asked is that the President in his state of the Union message, from which you quoted, said it would offer more middle income families high quality health services at prices they can afford. I think this is a good purpose for national health insurance. I am wondering if that is one of them, to offer more middle income families better medical services at lower prices, that is implied.

It seems to me middle income families may well pay in a different way under national health insurance, they may pay in the form of taxes rather than in fee for services, but they are going to pay as much or more than they are paying right now, and I wonder if we won't be building up some false expectations if we leave the impression one of the purposes of national health insurance is to make health care cheaper for middle income families.

So I would like to ask how is it going to reduce costs to middle income families and are there some other purposes behind national health insurance than just reducing costs to middle income families?

Secretary MATHEWS. Well, first of all, I would agree that we have to be very careful not to overstate what any system of national health insurance would do. It has been my personal concern in being introduced to this debate that not enough attention has been given to reporting to the public that a national health insurance system— even a very expensive one, an $80 or $90 billion system—would not really increase the supply of health care professionals. You have a system that spends that magnitude of money without buying one more tongue depressor or certainly without putting one more physician in the field. So, I think it is appropriate to be very cautious in stating what national health insurance might do.

I think it was the President's intent in this particular statement, in which he does say that these are the purposes that national health insurance could serve, to indicate that national health insurance can be a means of reducing the financial barriers to good health care.

At the same time, I think that it needs to be said, too, that a good system, a comprehensive system of national health care at some point in the future could be a means that would have the tangential effect of bringing some order into a system that plagues us all because it behaves in a way that is inconsistent with any other segment of our economy, in that its costs are extraordinarily above every other segment, and in a way that is frustrating to Congress, to our Department, to people in hospitals and to physicians. I think that—those in the medical profession—they are perhaps as unhappy or more so than anybody else about these problems.

Mr. PREYER. Well, I think that is a good response to that question. I am a little concerned that the general impression is getting abroad that by enacting national health insurance health care is suddenly going to be free or much less expensive for all of us, and I don't see that is going to be the case at all.

My specific question I would like to ask, Dr. Altman I think may be the one to respond to this, would be if he could briefly describe the CHIP program for us, at least in enough detail so we can deal with it in the coming months.

At the outset I would like to ask him, though, does the administration still favor this program?

Mr. ALTMAN. I think the President has indicated in his statement and the Secretary has indicated today that the President does favor over time an incremental approach toward national health insurance. In terms of basic outlines of the CHIP proposal, that of relying on the private sector, of relying where Governmental action is necessary primarily on the States and, in minimizing the role of the Federal Government and in controlling health care costs through a system of regulations on facilities and reimbursement, the basic principles of CHIP are still supported by the administration.

It is fair to say, however, that the President is looking quite consciously at whether all of the designs of CHIP are in fact the way he would like to go. In particular, he is concerned right now about adding a significant burden on the business community at a time when it is struggling to get out of a recession and the prospects of inflation are still significant.

We recognized when we wrote CHIP that we were adding a potential to the cost of business but spreading it along. At that time the economy was strong enough, in our view, to handle it. Now it is open to question. And so he is looking at that.

But I think in basic principle, yes, the administration still supports those underpinnings which went into the making of CHIP.

Mr. PREYER. So the conditions for approval of it now would be time, which is basically a budgetary matter, I suppose, and working out some more equitable distribution of the burden as far as employer and employee are concerned?

Mr. ALTMAN. Yes, and I would add the economy. I think when CHIP was designed in the early and middle seventies we had a much stronger economy. We had inflation at much lower rates and that is not the case now. . . .

Mr. ROGERS. When do you anticipate that a full national health insurance program should be enacted? When you make your long-term plans in the Department, as of what year do you anticipate enactment and implementation?

Secretary MATHEWS. I can only tell you what the President has said, which is, not this year. It seems to me his position is very much open.

Mr. ROGERS. I understand that. But I presume you have looked ahead with your advisors. That is why we have the Department, to plan ahead.

Now, what do your plans call for?

Secretary MATHEWS. If we were to make recommendations to the President for some future plan we would continue to make basically the same kind of recommendations as those under the CHIP proposal.

Mr. ROGERS. I understand that.

As of what time do you think it is feasible to ask for this program to be considered by the Congress? Should it be in 2 years, 3, 4, 5, 6, 7, 8, 9, 10? We are trying to get your thinking on that. Certainly I am sure you have looked at this since you had already presented a proposal for a national health insurance program before.

Secretary MATHEWS. Right. The President's position is that he will propose on national health insurance at a time when the economy allows him to do so. His position this year is that he does not feel the economy would allow such a proposal.

I don't think that the President, any more than any other President, would assert that he has the ability to predict exactly what the economy will do. As he said in his budget message, he would hope very much that within 3 years the state of the economy would be such that we can have a balanced budget.

Mr. ROGERS. I want to know, what are the economic factors that you in your planning have decided are key in determining when and whether we should move into this program? Must we have a balanced budget first? Must the inflation rate be at a given level, or what? What are those factors that this committee should use as a basis of judgment to make an intelligent decision? You and your experts we hope, are giving the President that advice. I would think you could give it to us.

Secretary MATHEWS. We don't advise the President on economic conditions, though.

Mr. ROGERS. In the health field?

Secretary MATHEWS. Only in the health field. It was his concern about the general economy that led him to the particular position on national health insurance. The position of the Department is that we are ready at any time; and, in fact, we continue to discuss with other agencies of the executive branch and with the President the design of a program. It is up to the President to make the judgment as to when he feels the time is appropriate, based on larger economy considerations that fall outside the purview of the Department to actually put such a proposal before the Congress.

I cannot tell you what those larger factors are that would trigger a national health insurance proposal on his part.

Mr. ROGERS. I understand that you have no control over the President's decision. What I am asking is, what do your planners project as to when we should enact national health insurance?

Secretary MATHEWS. Our planners do not deal with all the considerations that the President would be guided by. He would be looking at larger indications of the economy, I would presume. We look, as you point out, at the health industry and at the health economy, but it is neither within our mandate nor within our capacity to look at the kind of large economic considerations that he uses in making the determination.

Mr. ROGERS. In other words, if the President told you today we are going to move into national health insurance tomorrow your Department is now ready to do that?

Secretary MATHEWS. We would have proposals to make to him, yes.

Mr. ROGERS. Would they follow the CHIP approach?

Secretary MATHEWS. Yes.

Mr. ROGERS. That basically is your thinking?

Secretary MATHEWS. That is right.

Mr. ROGERS. Your recommendation for consideration of that approach to national health insurance simply depends on the time element?

Secretary MATHEWS. That is correct.

Mr. ROGERS. What are your proposals for controlling costs of health care? I noticed that you mentioned a lid of 4 percent on increases of doctors' fees in the medicare program, and a 7 percent limit on inflationary increases for hospitals. Do you have any other recommendations? What are those?

Secretary MATHEWS. Yes, we do. They are not all limited to financial controls. As a matter of fact, the point that I intended to make earlier is that, it seems to me one of the reasons people are having second thoughts about national health insurance is the well-founded conclusion that financial matters are not all that really determine good health care in the country. Certainly, we have proposals that we believe will make improvements in the health care delivery system.

Principally, I would mention the proposals that we are making to strengthen and proceed with the PSRO program. We feel that they get very much at some of the basic problems in the health care field.

We also have a major proposal for strengthening HMO's and for improving our capacity to deliver good health care. So, if you look at the President's proposal in its totality, there are both financial restraints and there are other features—reforms, if you will—which would improve the quality of care and which would also improve the scrutiny given to that care in cooperation with the health profession itself. There again I refer back to the PSRO organization. . . .

Mr. WAXMAN. My last question, Mr. Secretary—I am asked this often by constituents. It seems like almost every Western country has some form of comprehensive health insurance which provides access to health care systems as a matter of right rather than as a consequence of ability to pay for services.

This is the only country among so many others of Western democracies that does not give that protection to its people. Can you answer why the administration thinks the United States should lag so far behind these Western democracies? Also, do you see any prospects for a future in which we will grant this right to our people?

Secretary MATHEWS. Well, I think we need to note that the American people have also had a very different system for taking care of their health care needs, and I think it should be noted that this system has produced an extraordinarily fine program of health care as compared to other nations. We are obviously at work trying to improve it. The fact that some countries have opted for a national health care system often is a result of the difference between the way they have approached health care delivery generally and the way we have approached it in this country.

And I think you would want to consider, when you get to the point of considering a national health care system, looking at the indigenous way the American health care delivery system has developed, so that you make use of those things that are uniquely American.

It can also be pointed out that we are unique in the Western world in the way we do most everything.

Mr. WAXMAN. Do you believe that Government on all levels has responsibility to our citizens to provide them equal access to health care as a matter of right?

Secretary MATHEWS. I believe it is not necessary to define health care as a matter of right in order to address the problem of health care in the country. The question of "right" seems to me a fairly academic question, if I must say so.

When you use that term, you immediately raise questions as to whether you are drawing on the term as it was originally used in the 18th century to describe rights which were of a different sort and whether, in fact, that is applicable in this case.

It occurs to me that it is quite possible to view this matter philosophically in a great many different ways, but the important thing is whether you come to the conclusion that it is or is not important for the resources of Government—Federal and State—to address what is an obvious problem. And I don't think it takes any great philosophical contortions to come to the conclusion that it is proper. The proposals we advocate aim toward improving the health care delivery system are alleviating the plight of parts of our population which are especially victimized.

Mr. WAXMAN. Mr. Secretary, without going into the philosophical discussion of "rights" do you think Government has a responsibility to provide its citizens access to a quality care system, if they are sick, or do you think that this is some area which really ought to be left primarily within the private sector?

Secretary MATHEWS. I think the Federal Government does have a role and responsibility in this. Further, we need to constantly define and redefine that role so the Federal Government does what it can do best. I think, as I said earlier, any central system of government, in order to have a good society, whether in health or education or any other term, has to have as its allies a whole host of other institutions at other levels of government. I also believe it is the function of government not to retreat, not to withdraw, not to be less vigorous, but to be wise about what it does and to be equally wise about the necessity for partnerships with a whole host of other people that society is dependent upon to achieve what it wants to achieve.

That was a longer answer than you really wanted.

NOTES AND REFERENCES

1. The Comprehensive Health Insurance Program (CHIP) was the Nixon-Ford administrations' 1974 legislative proposal (S. 2970/H.R. 12684). It was introduced on behalf of the Ford administration by Senator Robert Packwood and Representative Herman Schneebeli in the 93rd Congress and was not reintroduced in the 94th. Further details on CHIP ([1]) follow the Rivlin-Altman-Mitchell discussion in Chapter 2.

2. A discussion of the health financing systems of selected foreign countries is found in Chapter 3.

3. A summary of H.R. 6222 appears in Appendix 2 of this volume.

4. A summary of H.R. 21 appears in Appendix 2.

5. A summary of H.R. 1 appears in Appendix 2.

6. The Long-Ribicoff/Waggonner bill (S. 2513 and H.R. 14079), introduced in the 93rd Congress, was reintroduced with modifications in the 94th Congress as S.2470/H.R. 10028. For a summary of S. 2470/H.R. 10028, refer to Appendix 2.

7. A discussion of Canada's health insurance system is found in Chapter 3.

8. The Kennedy-Mills bills (S. 3286 and H.R. 13870), introduced in the 93rd Congress, were not reintroduced in the 94th Congress.

9. The Kennedy-Griffiths bills (S. 3 and H.R. 22), introduced in the 93rd Congress, were reintroduced with modifications in the 94th Congress as the Kennedy-Corman bill (S. 3 and H.R. 21). For a summary of S. 3 and H.R. 21, refer to Appendix 2.

10. Dr. Michael DeBakey is a noted heart surgeon associated with the Baylor College of Medicine in Houston, Texas. He was an early advocate of a national health insurance program and testified before Senator Ralph Yarborough's Senate Health Subcommittee (of the Committee on Labor and Public Welfare) in support of the 1969–70 legislation introduced by Yarborough, Kennedy, and others. See [42], pp. 248 ff. for a transcript of his testimony.

Chapter 2
Financing National Health Insurance

BUDGETARY IMPACT

Enactment of a comprehensive, federally funded national health insurance program would have a significant effect on the national budget and, some argue, could have an adverse effect on efforts to control inflation. In addition, there have been steady increases in health expenditures under current federal programs, such as Medicare and Medicaid (140 percent over the past five years). These cost increases and inflation in the overall economy have created a climate of cautiousness regarding new federal initiatives in providing health care to the public. Parallel to these developments is a growing national awareness that even the affluent U.S. population is not well served by existing health systems and that despite the expansion of Medicare and Medicaid services, there are perhaps as many as forty million people earning under $10,000 per year who are ineligible for those services and have inadequate, if any, health insurance protection. Further, advocates of a federal health insurance program argue that the only way to check runaway costs of Medicare and Medicaid (most of which is due to an increase in fees) is to institute more, not less, federal control.

The conservatism of the Nixon and Ford administrations, combined with major inflation in the economy, has deterred the congressional advocates of national health insurance. While the Carter administration has adopted a more friendly posture and national health insurance is explicitly called for in the Democratic platform, the debate over the economic and budgetary impact of national health insurance in its varying forms has not been resolved. The need for holding down costs, especially inflationary costs (e.g., a rise in hospital room rates), while expanding health services, will continue to occupy the attention of national policymakers. This preoccupation is reflected in the testimony of two important figures in the congressional budgetmaking process during the Ford administration—Representative Brock Adams and Dr. Alice Rivlin.

Representative Adams was chairman of the House Budget Committee and Dr. Rivlin was head of the Congressional Budget Office (CBO) at the time they testified before the Subcommittee on Health and the Environment of the House Committee on Interstate and Foreign Commerce in February 1976. Adams is presently Secretary of Transportation and Rivlin continues as head of CBO. Subsequent to their testimony, which is reprinted here in part, they were both questioned by members of the subcommittee and were followed by Dr. Stuart Altman, a Ford administration spokesman from the Department of Health, Education, and Welfare. Portions of the Altman statement are also reprinted here, along with exchanges between witnesses and subcommittee members.

Representative Brock Adams, Chairman, House Budget Committee ([23], pp. 1161–1165, 1171–1174)

INTRODUCTION

I want to thank you, Mr. Chairman, for your invitation to present my views on some of the issues involved in the development of a national systems of health insurance. While I am appearing here because I am Chairman of the Committee on the Budget, I want to make it clear that the Committee as a whole has not taken a position on the enactment of national health insurance to date. My testimony, therefore, reflects my own views.

I have stated before and continue to believe that we must establish and implement a system of national health insurance which would achieve the following objectives: give all Americans access to good care, end financial hardship caused by illness, improve the efficiency and effectiveness of the health care delivery system, and provide licentives to both provider and consumer of health care to hold down costs.

The issue before this Subcommittee is, which arrangement of services, management, controls and financing can best achieve the objectives. While I will not address myself to specific legislative proposals which have been introduced, I will comment on a number of the issues—fiscal, budgetary and programmatic—which I feel must be considered in the development of NHI legislation.

TIMING OF NATIONAL HEALTH INSURANCE LEGISLATION

As Chairman of the House Budget Committee, it is one of my responsibilities to suggest ways in which we can achieve responsible long-term spending patterns. In keeping with this responsibility, I made a statement to the House on February 18th which outlined a possible approach to long-term spending policies within each of the functional categories of the budget. These suggested policies are designed to illustrate for my colleagues the types of decisions that will have to be made to bring the Federal budget into control. They do not represent policies to which I am rigidly committed. In considering new spending programs, as well as renewal or revision of programs that are already on the books, however, I do believe that we should follow the general economic and budgetary directions outlined in the statement.

On the economy:

"We must move steadily toward full employment and reasonable price stability. We can achieve that goal through a combination of existing job-creating programs, tax policies, a new program of employment in both the private and public sectors, and a series of structural reforms to reduce unemployment, improve productivity, and promote price stability;"

On the budget:

Overall spending for existing programs should be held below the amounts needed to carry out current levels of governmental activities and services. Achieving this objective will require that we institute program and management reforms which place increased emphasis on program simplification and reduced paperwork. We must also look to reduced spending for and elimination of lower-priority programs and activities in order to make room within available revenues for needed expansion of services.

If budgetary shifts similar to those I have recommended are made, I believe that there will become available funds that can be used to permit tax reductions, the expansion of worthwhile existing programs, and necessary new programs such as a national system of health insurance.

I strongly believe that we must have a system of national health insurance that is cost-effective and fair to all. As the members of this Subcommittee are well aware, all of the national health programs so far suggested are expensive and will have a significant impact on Federal spending. We are talking about a permanent program of immense importance to all Americans. I think we should adopt as a basic principle of national health insurance that it should not be financed as though it were a temporary or emergency measure. It must be treated as the permanent national commitment, which it will be, and should be paid for from available revenue. We must face the fact that we cannot afford a comprehensive national health insurance program until our available revenue expands significantly.

I do not think the day when that revenue is available is far off, and we need not be scared away from planning now for a full-fledged national health insurance program by groundless fiscal fears. I believe that by fiscal year 1980, the Federal budget will be in a position to implement fully such new initiatives as national health insurance. Further, I believe that fiscal year 1977 is an appropriate year for the basic enabling legislation to be passed. It is estimated that it will require two years from enactment of the law to develop the administrative structure and operating rules for a comprehensive program of national health insurance. On the basis of current estimates, we can authorize as much as $200 million for start-up costs upon enactment of the enabling legislation. The estimates also indicate that in fiscal year 1980, there will be available as much as $15 to $20 billion for new spending programs such as national health insurance.

At this point, it is imperative that the Subcommittee take note of the fact that the Budget Act requires that any authorizing legislaion to take effect in fiscal year 1977 must be reported from Committee before May 15, 1976.

Further, in considering the fiscal year 1980 budget, all "new spending" programs will be competing for any leeway that can develop in the budget. This means that the $15 to $20 billion "new spending" funds that we may be able to develop by fiscal year 1980 will not necessarily be available in its entirety for national health insurance, but that national health insurance will have to compete for those funds.

With your permission, Mr. Chairman, I will insert in the record at this point, 5-year projections of revenue and outlays developed by the staff of the Budget Committee which formed the basis for my statement on the 5-year budget proposal to the House on February 18, 1976, and which shows what can be expected in budgetary terms if the Congress follows the President's proposals, decides to simply continue current services as they are now, or decides to take actions similar to those outlined in my February 18 statement. (See insert #1)

COMPARISON OF 5-YEAR PROJECTIONS

[In billions of dollars]

	Fiscal year				
	1977	1978	1979	1980	1981
President's budget and projections [1]					
Outlays	394.2	429.5	455.7	482.5	509.9
Revenues	351.3	406.7	465.3	523.1	585.4
Deficit/surplus	−43.0	−22.8	+9.6	+40.6	+75.5
CBO current services (path B):					
Outlays [2]	424.1	463.9	495.1	530.5	564.0
Revenues	360.0	401.0	448.0	497.0	450.0
Deficit/surplus	−64.1	−62.9	−47.1	−33.5	−14.0
Recommended approach:					
Outlays	410.3	441.6	468.0	497.0	529.5
Revenues	360.7	420.2	464.0	523.2	588.7
Deficit/surplus	−49.6	−21.4	−4.0	+26.2	+59.2

[1] Budget of the U.S. Government fiscal year 1977 (p.28).
[2] Reflects CBO path B alternative for impact of inflation on highway program (function 400).

COST CONTROLS

A major concern in the entire area of health care, and especially in considering the development of a massive program of health insurance, is what can be done about keeping the cost of medical care at a reasonable level. This is the area in which the responsibilities of the Budget Committee and your Subcommittee most clearly overlap, and, I believe, is the area which will most certainly determine whether we can, in reality, support and maintain a reasonable level of health care for each of our citizens through a national health insurance program.

We already know the expensive consequences of establishing federal health insurance without adequate health controls. In the development of a Congressional budget, we have been constrained from advocating new health initiatives by the doubling in Federal outlays in Medicare and Medicaid, which have gone from $12.9 billion in 1972 to $25.8 billion in 1976, and are projected to increase to $48.5 billion in 1981 under the CBO current services estimates (ie: without any changes in program controls or benefits). Of that increase in Medicare and Medicaid costs over the past five years, $10.3 billion, or 80%, of the increase has resulted from higher costs for physician and hospital services. There is no question in my mind that the rising spiral in medical care prices has materially contributed to the delay in the enactment of a national system of health insurance, and that we must act now to curb the drastic annual increases in hospital costs and in physician fees. If we do not, the enactment of national health insurance will be further postponed. I would, therefore, recommend in the strongest possible terms that you pay particular attention to the impact of national health insurance on medical care prices and include in your final recommendations measures which would effectively keep these prices at a reasonable level. It is your Subcommittee, Mr. Chairman, which has the expertise to determine the health implications of various proposals and to determine which of the proposals will best meet the country's needs. I have reviewed a number of possible approaches to the question of cost control, however, and would like to comment on them.

As an interim measure to limit hospital price increases, the Federal government could establish a realistic and reasonable pricing policy for institutional care provided through Medicare and Medicaid. Under this proposal, price policy would not consist of rigid cost controls such as the President has proposed, but would instead establish reimbursement rates for hospitals and other institutions participating in Medicare and Medicaid that would be adjusted annually or semi-annually according to regional cost indices. Specifically, this proposal would establish Federal increases in reimbursements that are limited to 133% of each region's Consumer Price Index for all services. This approach would limit the increase in hospital reimbursements in FY 1977 to about 10%, declining to about 8½% in FY 1978. Further, the major private insurers of health care would be encouraged to adopt a similar reimbursement policy so that institutional providers do not simply pass on those costs disallowed by the Federal government to privately insured patients. The Administration's actuaries estimate that hospital costs will rise about 15% in 1977, while the Consumer Price Index is projected to rise about 6½%. We cannot permit hospital costs to increase 2½ times the general rate of inflation, and it is time that we insisted—through legislation—that hospital costs fall more into line with general prices, keeping in mind that improvements in quality and quantity of care must be recognized as resulting in some price increases. Such a flexible pricing increase limit policy could help accomplish this and would save about $600 million in FY 1977.

In the long term, we should consider establishing modifications of the present basic system of provider reimbursement, with emphasis on creating incentives to efficiency and economy which do not exist in the present cost reimbursement system. One approach to this would be to incorporate into a national health insurance system a prospective reimbursement scheme for each provider of health care. This system would require each provider to develop a budget for the subsequent year which, after approval by the appropriate reviewing agency, would serve as the basis for determining reimbursement rates for that provider. This approach to determining reimbursement on a prospective basis would permit the reviewing agency to examine and approve in advance capital expenditures, staff expansion, and new services. Such an approach would put us in the position of knowing before the fact what a unit of health services would cost.

The President has proposed a "cap" on physician fees. I do not believe this "cap" is equitable or effective. Under his proposal, the Federal government will limit increases in reimbursement to 4% above the prior year, but would permit the physician to pass on to his patients any amounts above the 4% limit. This approach simply shifts the burden of paying the higher costs from the Federal government to the aged and disabled beneficiary; it does nothing to limit the rate of increase in physician fees, unless the physician is compassionate and foregoes a portion of his increase for Medicare beneficiaries. The President's proposal would not work now and certainly is unacceptable in a national system of health insurance. As alternatives to this proposal, which I would encourage you to review carefully in your consideration of national health insurance, are a system of mandatory assignment which would require the physician to accept the reimbursement allowed by the program as the full cost of his service, or a system of fee schedules developed by local physician groups in conjunction with the national health insurance reviewing agency. . . .

In conclusion, Mr. Chairman, I would like to emphasize my view of the role of the Budget Committee. It is to give to the various authorizing Committees a bettter idea of the funds that will be available, now and in the future, to carry out programs under your jurisdiction. Quite clearly, your Subcommittee has the depth of experience and knowledge to determine the best mechanisms for using this money. I want to pledge to you the continued cooperation of the Budget Committee and its staff (especially to provide technical assistance to your staff in assuring consistency between the Budget Control Act requirements and the national health insurance legislation your Subcommittee may develop) in the effort to develop and pass national health insurance legislation which will be realistically funded and an effective instrument for bringing to all Americans the finest health care that medical science can provide. We can have no lesser goal, for the program that this Congress adopts will determine the health care that the American people will receive for many years to come. . . .

Mr. ROGERS. Mr. Scheuer.

Mr. SCHEUER. Thank you, Mr. Chairman.

I want to echo my colleague, Mr. Preyer's statement on the fine work you have been doing and great leadership you are giving the Budget Committee without which we wouldn't even begin to be able to grapple with the problem of getting a handle on the cost of health care as well as other social programs we are funding.

I know that in the beginning of your testimony you tell us that we cannot afford a comprehensive national health program until our available revenue expands significantly.

In other words, you are telling us that we cannot carve out of the existing pie and perhaps take a little slice off other programs and thereby fund a health program. You tell us on the next page that even when you get this new $15 billion or $20 billion, which I presume is the old fiscal dividend that got lost some years ago——

Mr. ADAMS. That is precisely right.

Mr. SCHEUER. When you are telling us you are holding up the warning signal, on the next page you are saying you don't think you could lay your hands on this $20 billion, because you are going to have to compete with all of the other programs that want to expand.

Aren't you telling us a national health program is "heads I win and tails you lose?" You won't let them compete against the other programs now, but you warn them they are going to have to compete in the future when you have the fiscal dividend available.

Isn't that sort of a "heads I win and tails you lose" deal?

Mr. Adams. No. I suggested that I was in support of the national health insurance program and that you could come in under the present fiscal year 1977 budget for your $100 to $200 million in implementation money. It is my understanding it takes 2 to 3 years before you will be up into the billion dollar range. Yes, you could start the program now.

I don't know of anybody that is proposing in fiscal year 1977 that you move in and compete with existing programs. What I am showing you is how, over 5 years, you do phase in national health insurance, not how you keep it out.

I would say this, that if you did come in with a very large program, it isn't a question of competing with the present programs, Mr. Scheuer. The question is how do you reduce the current services programs which are included on the chart in the second group at $424 billion next year, down enough that you can carve out a national health insurance program without raising the national debt up to $60 or $70 billion, which I think is going to be difficult to do.

I am just stating what the finite limits are; that is all.

Mr. Scheuer. If we try and control costs—as we must—in anticipation of national health insurance, do we do it on the public sector alone, or do we do it on the public and private sector?

If we do it on the public sector alone, wouldn't there be an immediate flow of professinal services away from the public sector and into the private sector where they can make uncontrolled dollars? Isn't this going to leave the elderly and the poor and the other people who depend upon the public services system holding the short end of the stick, again?

Mr. Adams. Yes; that is what I said to Mr. Waxman, and I again am not trying to tell the committee how I think they should solve that, because I don't feel I have the expertise to do that. I do agree with your conclusion that that kind of both-side control has to exist or, yes, you will get a flow.

Mr. Scheuer. Yes; if you, with all your hindsight and all your experience to date on the Budget Committee——

Mr. Adams. That is what we all have the most of.

Mr. Scheuer. We are all Monday morning quarterbacks.

If you were a Monday morning quarterback with all the experience you have had, both in your general disciplines of budget setting and with specific knowledge of medicaid and medicare, how would you write them differently today?

I don't mean in the details, but how would your philosophical or general fiscal cost controls approach differ from the approach taken a decade ago?

Mr. Adams. I would have used prospective budgeting and peer review and been very tough.

Mr. Scheuer. Well, that is short, sweet, and to the point. I think most of us up here agree with you.

Thank you very much, Mr. Chairman.

Mr. Rogers. I presume if we moved into an all public national health insurance program you would anticipate a tax increase because, obviously the cost would be rather heavy.

Mr. Adams. No, what I have stated in my statement was that you have a growth factor, as you have seen over the 5 years, and this pattern is: Our revenues rise because of additional numbers of people, and to a degree the inflation factor, which, under the progressive income tax, tends to produce more revenues and allows your revenues to go up without any changes in tax rate. That is what produces a potential surplus in fiscal year 1980 ranging from the $26 billion I suggest to the President's projection of about $40 billion and both getting up into the $50 to $60 billion range in fiscal year 1981. That is without any change in the rates, and it is with a $10 billion tax cut in about 1978–79 for those who have been pushed upward in the brackets through simple inflation.

Mr. ROGERS. I presume that does not anticipate additional programs?

Mr. ADAMS. It does not.

Mr. ROGERS. During that period of time?

Mr. ADAMS. And it also is conditioned, as I set forth at some length in the record, on restraint of existing programs. If we do not do this, we will never get to a surplus situation because the current services will continue to rise more rapidly than the revenues. Dr. Rivlin will describe this, I am sure, in more detail.

Mr. ROGERS. Yes. So it would seem to me that if we bring health care coverage from the private sector and place it in the public sector; if we want a national health insurance program which is all public: then I would anticipate you would require additional taxes.

Mr. ADAMS. Oh, yes.

Mr. ROGERS. I presume that would be true?

Mr. ADAMS. Yes.

Mr. ROGERS. If those taxes were provided that would ease your budget problem?

Mr. ADAMS. Oh, yes.

Mr. ROGERS. Would the Budget Committee think, then, that if we go to a public system it should be done as a packet, we should provide for a certain amount of taxes, general revenue taxes, or set aside a fund for those taxes to go into?

Mr. ADAMS. If you want it to go faster than phasing it in as your revenues grow, there isn't any other way to do it unless you use a partial private, partial public plan, so that the entire cost does not go into the budget. I assume what you are asking is the total amount in the Federal budget.

Mr. ROGERS. Yes.

Mr. ADAMS. Yes. And I might state that I am not a conservative, even though people state that. Realistically, we have tried to see what we could get in tax reform without going to the rate structure and the best we were able to do last year was nothing.

We are hopeful next year of $1.5 billion, depending upon what the Finance Committee does. If they accept the House bill, we could pick that up. But we are not talking in terms of $20 to $30 billion under any of the programs presently out.

I would like to see us pick up more through reform, but I want to state to the chairman that from the viewpoint of this member at this point, I can't see much surplus there until fiscal year 1980.

Mr. ROGERS. Suppose we were to mandate private insurance, which would cover a rather large portion of the population, and then provide public programs for the financially needy and perhaps the elderly.

What would be your reaction to some approach like that?

Mr. ADAMS. I think you could get it in place quicker than fighting for a tax increase. However, I would have to see your package and run it through an econometric model or the Congressional Budget Office to see what the economic impact is.

Mr. ROGERS. We are already spending a certain amount on medicaid and medicare. If we make improvements in those programs and then mandate private coverage of the middle sector, I presume we could move into a program like that more rapidly.

Mr. ADAMS. Now, and this is a personal view on that proposal, I think you must be very careful in the manner which you structure the mandate, because it could become very regressive. In other words, it is the same thing that applies with a payroll tax. For example if you are taking a certain percentage or a flat dollar figure from everybody across the board then the working poor and those that are less able to pay, pay a greater proportionate share.

Mr. ROGERS. Yes.

Mr. ADAMS. Without that factor in it, Mr. Chairman, yes, you do get a cheaper package in terms of Federal spending.

Mr. ROGERS. I anticipate this committee would want to draw the general outlines of an overall plan, even if parts of it were then phased in. Do you think that is wise, rather than just approaching the problem by enacting an increment here and an increment there as we go along? Do you think it is well for us to go ahead and outline the total plan, even though it may not be triggered until, say, 1980—to have the goal set, the outline of the plan set, even even though it may not all be triggered as of the date of enactment?

Mr. ADAMS. Yes, I think you should have a total package Mr. Chairman, because in that way you prepare the whole Congress and the Nation for getting into an overall program and they know what the overall costs are going to be and how you fit each piece together.

I think part of the problem we have now is that we are creating gaps in our health service by our categorical approach, both private and public, to health needs.

Dr. Alice Rivlin, Director, Congressional Budget Office ([23], pp. 1181–1187)

STATEMENT OF ALICE M. RIVLIN, PH.D., DIRECTOR, CONGRESSIONAL BUDGET OFFICE

Mr. Chairman and Members of the Committee: I appreciate having the opportunity to discuss with this subcommittee the financing and costs of national health insurance. I will talk first about medical care inflation, its causes and the effect it has on both public programs and private spending. Second, I will discuss national health insurance cost projections and compare them to current policy expenditures. Although my testimony today focuses on program costs and their budgetary impact, this should not imply that costs are the most important factor in considering national health insurance. The value of any additional expenditures must be judged by their effectiveness in improving individual financial protection and encouraging the efficient provision of high quality health services.

National expenditures for health care have been growing at a much more rapid rate than the general economy for the last two decades. In 1950, total health expenditures represented 4.6 percent of GNP. By 1975, this figure had increased to 8.3 percent. In large measure this growth is attributable to higher rates of inflation for medical care than for other services (see Table 1). Since 1964, the consumer price index has not quite doubled, but the cost per patient day in a hospital has quadrupled. While higher wages and prices have accounted for a large portion of this increase, close to 50 percent of the increase has resulted from treatments of significantly higher quality and effectiveness than were available a decade ago.

As a result of this sustained growth in inflation and service provided, public and private spending on health care and related activities will exceed $135 billion in this fiscal year. Almost one-third, or about $43 billion, will flow through the federal budget, largely as a result of Medicare and Medicaid. A decade ago, before the enactment of these programs, federal health expenditures were only $6 billion. Higher costs have produced most of the growth in Medicare expenditures. Since its inception, over 80 percent of the increase in program outlays can be attributed to higher costs, and only 20 percent to increases in the numbers of beneficiaries and their utilization of services.

Inflation has had a comparable impact on spending for health care in the private sector. Per capita health expenditures increased by 12 percent from 1974 to 1975, while per capita income went up by only 8 percent in the same period. Most people are aware of—and want to hold down—the increases in medical care costs that they pay directly. The impact of the higher employer-paid health insurance premiums on wage levels and on the price of goods and services is much less visible, but equally severe. For example, Ford and General Motors now spend between $125 and $150 per vehicle manufactured on health insurance premiums for their employees.

CAUSES OF INFLATION IN HEALTH SECTOR

The higher rates of inflation in the health sector have many causes, but they are clearly related in part to growth in third-party payments through public and private insurance plans. In 1955, 38 percent of the cost of personal health care services was met by public and private insurance. By 1974, insurance covered 63 percent of these expenditures. Hospital care is the most widely insured health service—in 1974 consumers paid only about 10 percent of hospital charges as a direct out-of-pocket expense.

The growth in insurance coverage has contributed to the growth in expenditures for health services in several ways.

First, the insured consumer tends to be less price conscious, because he often pays little or nothing from his own pocket at the time care is provided;

Second, because providers realize that patients will pay only a part of the bill directly, providers may not use resources efficiently and or try to minimize the cost of treatment;

Third, the wages of health care workers have experienced substantial gains over the last ten years as a result of higher demand for wage increases and more resources available to meet those demands; and

Fourth, the increased revenues resulting from greater insurance coverage have also made possible the provision of higher quality medical care through the acquisition of sophisticated equipment and the hiring of more and better trained personnel. These improvements add to cost.

In addition, the growth of "cost plus" reimbursement for hospitals has encouraged higher expenditures. Because a majority of hospital revenues are received on the basis of actual costs incurred, revenues rise automatically with expenses. Curtailing costs is therefore not generally a high priority.

EFFECT OF INFLATION ON PUBLIC PROGRAMS

If inflation in the general economy continues at historically high levels, as seems likely, it is reasonable to assume that medical care costs will also increase at near their present rate. This means that the cost of public programs will escalate at about 15 percent annually under current policy.

CBO estimates that if present policies are continued, Medicare outlays will total approximately $20.5 billion in FY 77 and that the cost of the federal share of Medicaid will be $9.5 billion. These programs alone will account for 85 percent of the expected $4.8 billion increase in federal health outlays (Budget Function 550) between FY 76 and FY 77. (This increase is for 15 months because of the transition quarter.)

By 1981 CBO estimates that under current policy Medicare expenditures will rise to $34.5 billion and Medicaid to $14.0. Higher costs is the principal cause for the growth in these program outlays. For example, 86 percent of the $14 billion projected increase in Medicare outlays from FY 77 to 81 is attributable to higher costs and only 14 percent to an expansion in the number of beneficiaries or higher rates of utilization.

In a period of tight budget constraints, the additional outlays needed to finance these higher costs at current service levels will absorb most of the funds which might otherwise be available to increase the number of beneficiaries or services covered. The growth in Medicare outlays to finance higher costs, $2.4 billion in the hospital insurance program alone from FY 76 to 77, exceeds the funding level for all categorical grant programs of the Public Health Service.

Congress could act to limit the budgetary impact of the increases in Medicare and Medicaid costs. The President has proposed such action in his FY 77 budget. Specifically, he recommends consolidating 15 categorical health service programs and Medicaid into a state block grant. Federal expenditures for Medicaid would thus be more easily controlled through the appropriations process, and by transferring the resource allocation decisions to the states.

The President also proposes three significant changes in the Medicare program. The first two changes, provider reimbursement limits and beneficiary cost-sharing, would reduce federal expenditures while the third, maximum beneficiary cost-sharing, would add to federal outlays.

This package of proposed Medicare changes will have the effect of simultaneously reducing federal outlays and protecting Medicare recipients against "catastrophic" expenditures. The majority of Medicare recipients would pay more out-of-pocket for health services than they would under current policy. This increased cost-sharing is intended to make Medicare recipients more cost-conscious.

There is a serious question, however, as to whether overall price increases in the health sector can be moderated by a program which controls reimbursements only for public program beneficiaries.

The unreimbursed hospital costs might instead be shifted to private patients. A serious danger, particularly if hospital controls are maintained for a long period of time, will be discrimination against Medicare and Medicaid patients through the provision of lower quality care. Physicians may bill patients directly to compensate for the lower increases in Medicare reimbursement.

The higher health care expenses which have driven up the cost of public and private insurance programs have created even more severe financial problems anxieties for people who are not insured or whose insurance is inadequate to deal with a very costly illness. The hardships faced by the uninsured, and by those for whom private coverage is becoming prohibitively expensive, have created pressures for the extension of existing public insurance programs or for the adoption of national health insurance.

NATIONAL HEALTH INSURANCE PROPOSALS

In considering whether or not to adopt national health insurance the following problem emerges. Past experience would indicate that broadening insurance coverage adds significantly to demand pressures and medical care inflation. Further improvements in individual financial protection risk more price inflation and greater inefficiencies in the use of resources.

The conflict between equally important social goals—providing broader financial assistance for health care and efficient use of health resources—poses a serious policy dilemma. It is hard to see how further augmentation of financial assistance for health care can be accomplished without a serious inflationary impact unless some form of effective price regulation is imposed. But the desirability and form of such regulation remains extremely controversial.

Regulatory proposals which have been suggested rane from hospital rate setting by states; to an extension of the type of controls used during Phase IV of the Economic Stabilization Period on all provider charges; to the imposition of global budget controls vore the entire health sector. In the latter instance, hospitals would be paid on a prospective budget basis and physicians would be reimbursed according to a government-set fee schedule or even by salary. Also, regulatory measures that assure proper utilization of hospital services could result in a reduction in expenditures.

As evidence of the fact that no consensus has yet emerged on the appropriate new role of the federal or state governments in the financing of services or regulation of the health industry, more than two dozen national health insurance bills have been introduced in this session of Congress. They have widely varying provisions with respect to population and benefit coverage, financing mechanisms and the degree of control imposed on the health care industry.

Different types of national health insurance plans would have different effects on the federal budget, on the general economy and on the health care delivery system. The key variables in assessing the probable budget impact of alternative proposals is whether the plan is primarily tax or premium financed, the range of benefits covered, the beneficiary cost-sharing requirements imposed and the plan's cost control features.

Because none of the bills has been reported out of a committee, CBO has not made formal cost estimates of specific proposals. However, in conjunction with the preparation of our annual report on the budget we have prepared five year projections of the cost of three basic approaches to providing national health insurance in order to analyze the effect each might have on total national spending for health services and on federal outlays, including tax expenditures.

Before discussing these projections, I would like to emphasize that prospective cost estimates of any national health insurance plan will be imprecise because of the lack of hard data in a number of important areas and limited knowledge of how consumers and providers will respond to new insurance coverage. The difficulty is compounded in attempting five year estimates because of the complex and far-reaching changes which these plans could produce in both the financing and delivery of health services.

However, as the projection problems are more or less common to all of the plans, useful comparisons can still be made among them. To assist in these comparisons, the cost estimates were made for all plans assuming full operation for the entire 1977 fiscal year. This does not mean we think it would be feasible to fully implement these plans in fiscal year 1977. Because some assumptions, such as the probable effectiveness of cost controls, are so uncertain, we felt it necessary to develop a "high" and "low" estimate series.

N1 FIRST FULL-YEAR COST ESTIMATES FOR PROTOTYPE NATIONAL HEALTH INSURANCE PLANS

Targeted Approach

The first of the three prototype plans might be labeled as a "targeted approach," since it would be aimed at providing coverage for all low-income families and universal protection against catastrophically high medical expenditures.

This prototype plan assumes that low-income families would be protected by a "federalized Medicaid" program with uniform national entitlement and benefit levels. We assumed income entitlement limits of $4,800 for a family of four, with "spend down" eligibility for families at higher income levels and state contributions to continue at their present level. The net additional cost of this part of the plan would be $6 to $7 billion in FY 77.

A number of plans have been proposed to provide protection against catastrophic medical costs. We assumed a fixed-benefit deductible plan which pays hospital costs after the first 60 days and medical expenses over the first $2,000. If a majority of employers choose to provide catastrophic protection through private insurance, the net new budget cost would be from $4 to $4.5 billion if the program were fully operational in FY 77.

Because of the possible reduction in categorical programs, the total additional costs of a catastrophic plan in which half the costs are borne by the federal government plus a uniform Medicaid program would be between $8.5 to $10.5 billion in FY 77 (see Table 2).

Comprehensive Premium Financed

The second prototype we examined was a comprehensive national health insurance plan with mixed public and private financing. We assumed that most of the population would be covered through employment-based private health insurance and that there would be public programs with comparable benefits for the poor and for high-risk individuals who could not purchase private insurance at acceptable rates. Medicare would be continued for the aged. If such a plan were fully operative in FY 77, it would result in additional federal outlays for health services of $13.5 to $15.5 billion (see Table 2).

Comprehensive Tax Financed

The third type of proposal for which we developed estimates is a tax-financed, publicly-administered health insurance plan with comprehensive benefits and no cost-sharing. Such a plan would absorb Medicare, Medicaid and most categorical health care programs. If fully operative in FY 77, a plan of this nature would result in additional federal outlays for health services of $74.5 to $77.5 billion (see Table 2).

ESTIMATES FOR FY 81 OF TOTAL NATIONAL SPENDING AND FEDERAL BUDGET COSTS UNDER THREE NATIONAL HEALTH INSURANCE PLANS

Each of the national health insurance plans I have described would have markedly different effects on federal outlays. While total national spending for health care would be roughly comparable in the first year under any of the proposals, it could vary substantially over time.

The similarity in the first year is because the existing health system is operating at close to capacity. Therefore, the greater potential demand generated by increased insurance coverage cannot be met initially. Furthermore, it is unlikely that prices will rise high enough to eliminate the shortage. However, as the capacity of the health system will adjust to the increased demand for services over time substantial differences in expenditures could be realized within five years.

Specifically, the increased demand for inpatient services produced by the targeted and premium-financed plans could probably be met in the first year of program operation and that of the tax-financed plan by the end of the second year. Physician shortages would be more serious in the early years and would be insufficient to meet full demand under all the plans for at least one year. Even after five years the availability of physicians might be insufficient to meet all demands generated by the tax-financed plan although the shortage will have been substantially reduced.

Because the impact of increased demand cannot be fully realized in "first year" projections and, similarly, because cost-containment provisions could not be assumed to have any substantial effect in the first year, we have estimated the cost of the three plans in 1981. This projection assumes five full years of program operation.

For each plan we have developed both "high" and "low" estimates. The "low series" assumes that cost control features proposed in a plan will be very effective in restraining inflation. The "high series" assumes that these measures will not be fully effective.

Two important point emerge from the five year projections which are not apparent in comparing intial-year program costs. First, strong cost controls, if they are effective, will yield substantially lower federal spending for these programs over time. Second, adoption of a national health insurance plan with rigid adherence to cost controls could actually reduce national spending on personal health services below the levels projected under current policy.

Targeted Approach

This plan offers only a limited opportunity to institute cost controls other than those which currently operate in the Medicaid program. Therefore, the five-year estimates for the targeted approach show a small range between the "high series" and "low series" estimates by 1981. Our projection for total national spending on personal health services under the targeted approach range from $249 to $256 billion in FY 81. Federal budget costs for health services in that same year would range from $74.5 to $79.5 billion. This compares with our current policy estimates of $238 billion for total national spending and $52 billion for federal budget costs for personal health services in 1981 (see Tables 2 and 3).

Comprehensive Premium Financed

Effective control of health prices through insurance reimbursement is difficult when there are multiple sources of funding as our present rate of inflation in the health sector would suggest. Therefore our "high series" estimates for the premium-financed comprehensive plan assume that present levels of inflation continue and are slightly accelerated in the early years by the increased demand new insurance coverage will generate. The low series projections for this plan assume that federal and/or state regulatory programs will reduce inflation levels under current policy.

These assumptions produce estimates of total national spending ranging from $235 to $256 billion in FY 81. The federal budget costs for health services would range from $71 to $81 billion in the same year (see Tables 2 and 3).

Comprehensive Tax Financed

Insurance financed directly through the tax system has the potential to provide the most effective means for controlling health costs through mechanisms such as prospective budgeting for hospitals and fee schedules for physicians. But if that potential is not fully realized, a tax-financed public plan could be far more inflationary than the present mixed system or than any of the other prototyes discussed.

Experience in other countries, most notably Canada, indicates that even a government-controlled tax-financed plan will have difficulty in controlling inflation. Alternatively in Great Britain, where controls have been successfully applied, under investment problems seem to have resulted because of the stringency of the controls.

In constructing the low-series estimate for this plan we assumed that a maximum federal budget would be adhered to and that spending would be limited to the amount of revenue generated by the payroll tax. The high series increased the expected inflation rates above the level anticipated for current policy. Under these widely varying assumptions the FY 81 budget cost for health care services of a tax-financed comprehensive plan could range from $157 to $192 billion. Total national spending in the same year could range from $217 to $273 billion (see Tables 2 and 3).

You will note that our low series estimate on total national spending under the tax-financed approach is about $20 billion less than our 1981 estimate for current policy. This reduction in projected expenditures could occur only if very severe controls are imposed on the health sector and are adhered to over the five year period. There is little in the history of public or private health insurance administration in this country to suggest that such a policy would be followed.

CONCLUSION

As I noted in opening this testimony, program costs will be only one aspect Congress considers when legislating national health insurance. Although my testimony has concentrated on the question of costs and their budgetary impact, I would repeat that it is equally important to take into account the benefits to be derived from each of the plans. It is not total costs alone that are important, but the value that we receive for those expenditures.

TABLE 1.—AVERAGE ANNUAL INCREASES IN OVERALL AND HEALTH CARE PRICES FOR SELECTED YEARS, 1955–75 AND FOR ECONOMIC STABILIZATION PERIOD (ESP)

Year	CPI all items	Medical care	Semiprivate room charge
1955	2.2	3.8	6.9
1960	2.0	4.0	6.3
1965	1.3	2.5	5.8
1967	2.9	7.1	19.8
1970	5.9	6.3	12.9
1975	8.5	10.0	19.1
ESP (August 1971–April 1974)	6.4	4.3	5.7

TABLE 2.—FEDERAL OUTLAYS FOR HEALTH SERVICES, 1977 AND 1981

[In billions of dollars]

	1977	1981
Current policy	$32.5	$52.0
Changes from current policy:		
Targeted approach	8.5–10.5	22.5–27.5
Premium financed	13.5–15.5	19.0–29.0
Tax financed	74.5–77.5	105.5–140.0

TABLE 3.—TOTAL NATIONAL SPENDING (PRIVATE AND PUBLIC) FOR PERSONAL HEALTH SERVICES, 1977 AND 1981

[In billions of dollars]

	1977	1981
Current policy	$142	$238
Targeted approach	148–149	249–256
Premium financed comprehensive national health insurance	152–153	235–256
Tax financed comprehensive national health plan	152–154	217–273

Mr. Rogers. Thank you very much, Doctor.

Would it be an imposition upon your time to ask if we could hear the other two presentations and then perhaps have questions for all of you at the end of that period?

Ms. Rivlin. That would be fine, Mr. Chairman.

Dr. Stuart Altman, Ford Administration ([23], pp. 1214–1217, 1302, 1218–1220)

Mr. Altman. Thank you, Mr. Chairman.

Mr. Rogers. We are anxious to hear your thinking, which I am sure forms the basis for any program the administration may present in the future.

Mr. Altman. Well, it is indeed a pleasure to have the opportunity to appear before the committee, especially today as a primary witness, rather than in a supporting role which I always enjoy. But this opportunity is especially appreciated.

What I really appreciate is the opportunity to sit back and listen to Dr. Rivlin and Dr. Mitchell talk about subjects that I have raised before this committee so many times in the last 5 years. It is nice to know that completely independent thinking on this subject arrives at rather similar conclusions.

As I have said many times, the cost of health care in this country is rising at such alarming rates that it really precludes many of the other activities that we would like to do in other human services, and I think I have never heard a better statement than what Congressman Adams articulated in that area.

I will not go over the figures reflecting these increases, painful as they are to recite, I am sure they are equally painful to hear.

I would like to indicate, however, that the problems of trying to control them are far from easy. Some of the cost increases, reflect increases in the general economy—I am reading from page 3 of my statement—and wage increases in this traditionally low paid industry, particularly hospital employees. An equal share, however, represents increases in the intensity of services; that is, increases in the number and kind of services performed. It is really this latter area that makes the control of rising health costs so difficult.

To the provider of health care, all or most of this added intensity represents needed quality improvements and, therefore, must be funded. To other observers, however, some of the spending is of questionable value and really results from a lack of budgeting constraints in the system.

I won't go through the economic stabilization program and the cost reductions that accompanied it except to say there are those who herald that activity as an indication that the Federal Government, when it does put its mind to doing something, can do it. To others it was the beginning of the end and if it had been allowed to continue the health care system in our country would have come crumbling down. Fortunately, or unfortunately, the Congress did not permit it to continue and so both sides can go undaunted arguing for their side of the issue.

To me, when you get it all down the key issue really continues to be the large and uncontrollable dollar flows available for medical care.

It strikes me, Mr. Chairman, that such programs—and I know how hard you and the members of your committee have worked on them—as PSRO, health planning, certificate of need, and HMO's can only be truly effective in an environment where the health care provider is forcde to face a limited budget. Without such a change in the reimbursement system, we put the regulator in the untenable position at times of having to say no when the provider says the care is necessary, when the patient believes he needs the care, and when the reimbursement system is ready to pay for it.

I don't have any easy solutions to offer, unfortunately. Moving toward prospective budgets for hospitals appears to be highly desirable. Setting limits on what physicians can be paid may ultimately be necessary. But I think it is critically important that we not impose rigid solutions or move to quickly as a Nation.

As I noted earlier in my prepared text, the medical marketplace does not in any sense exhibit the characteristics of the competitive market that would justify a completely unregulated environment, but neither has it completely broken down as some would allege.

Finally, I hardly need to remind this committee that governmental programs often look much better on paper than in their implementation. It is for these reasons that I strongly support the accelerated use of experimental authorities such as contained in section 222 of the social security amendments to see what works and what does not work.

Except for the poorest members of our society, I also believe that patient cost sharing is appropriate. Cost sharing provides a measure of patient and provider involvement in the decisionmaking process. It serves to remind everyone that care is not free. Any regulatory measure works best when it is consistent with the incentives of the patient and the provider.

Much has been said about the role of the provider in allocating medical resources, often to justify placing the full onus of cost control on him or her. I simply do not view it as an either/or situation.

Again, let me emphasize that unless we get all the actors in the health care scene to feel it is in their interest to control spending, I am afraid we are doomed to repeat the lessons of the past.

In 1974, the Department sent a report to Congress which provided estimates of the cost of the various national health insurance proposals then being considered. While the dollar amounts shown in this report are no longer accurate, the document is useful in making spending comparisons and examining sources of revenue by proposal. In arriving at the estimates contained in that report, we project anticipated 1975 expenditures under eight of the major proposals. We identified costs under each proposal as those which represented transferred costs and those which we called induced costs.

Transferred costs are shifts among sources of payment. Initially they do not in and of themselves represent any addition to spending but merely refer to transferring payment from one source to another, such as from the patient to a third-party payer, from private health insurance to public program, or within public programs from general revenues to payroll taxes.

However, having a third-party reimburse for what used to be out-of-pocket costs increases the demand for health services and hence induces greater spending for health case. An important consideration, therefore, in estimating costs of alternative proposals for national health insurance is to what extent out-of-pocket costs are lowered and greater health expenditures are induced.

While the exact magnitude of this so-called induced demand is the subject of much scholarly debate among actuaries and economists, its existence is not seriously question.

N2

The effect of covering kidney disease patients under medicare is one of the best examples of how health care expenditures are induced as a result of expanded insurance coverage. Prior to enactment of this program, total annual spending for renal dialysis and kidney transplanatation was $50 million. With the enactment of the program, more people were covered for more expensive services and we saw a dramatic increase in expenditures to $150 million in 1974.

Now in only its third year, spending for these new medicare beneficiaries is expected to exceed $450 million, and we estimate that the annual cost of this program will reach $1 billion before it levels off. As one would have expected, as the demand rose, so did the supply with the number of treatment centers increasing from 439 in 1973 to 580 in 1975.

I do not want to leave the committee with the impression that this added spending is bad. Certainly, the beneficiaries of this program are greatly helped by this expanded coverage, but the example does serve to illustrate how expanded coverage induces greater health spending.

In the Department's 1974 cost estimates, we estimated health spending under the Griffiths-Kennedy proposal at $116 billion in 1975, 12 percent higher than anticipated spending without any national health insurance proposal. This estimate was challenged both as being too low because it failed to reflect adequately the long-term systemic effects of a proposal.

I was both heartened and amused to see the spread of the estimates of the Congressional Budget Office. I think they were very realistic in indicating the magnitude of the difference between those high or low critics.

Mr. ROGERS. May I just ask here, in this Griffiths-Kennedy proposal, $116 billion covered everybody in the country?

Mr. ALTMAN. Yes, sir.

Mr. ROGERS. Actually we spent what?

Mr. ALTMAN. Well, at that time, if you will go to the last chart, chart 1, sitting there in 1974, when we were doing these estimates— expecting the Congress to continue the economic stabilization program—we were estimating $103 billion. Of course, things have changed and the spending turned out to be closer to $118 billion. So you have to compare the $116 billion to the $103 billion, not to what actually happened, because then the $116 billion would have been a lot higher.

Mr. ROGERS. Are you still using that figure?

Mr. ALTMAN. Well, I am not using it as an example of any number other than in relationship to the $103 billion.

Mr. ROGERS. All right. Thank you.

Mr. ALTMAN. If I am confusing the committee, I apologize.

Mr. ROGERS. I wondered if it had been costed out for 1975 at $116 billion; we would have perhaps saved $2 billion if it had been enacted?

Mr. ALTMAN. No, I don't think you can draw that conclusion.

Mr. ROGERS. That is what I wanted to make sure of. I didn't know if you were saying that.

Mr. ALTMAN. No, sir.

Mr. ROGERS. Thank you.

Mr. ALTMAN. Even the thought of my saying that—I think both these challenges to our estimates demonstrate the uncertainty inherent in predicting the induced costs of any proposal. This problem is especially acute in trying to estimate the longer term effects of a program.

Our 1974 estimates reflected only the short term costs of each of the major proposals. I believe these estimates were reasonably accurate as far as they went, but they did not adequately deal with the long term systemic effects of the different proposals.

Therefore, we felt it necessary to examine the long range—at least 5 years—spending effects of the various proposals. This is extremely difficult and is the reason we have been so long delayed in supplying new cost estimates for the various proposals.

As many of the committee know, we had planned to have new estimates by last October. However, we find ourselves today still without estimates and it may be several months yet before they are available.

One problem we have found in estimating longer run costs under national health insurance is that we not only have to look at historical experiences but we must make assumptions about the structure of each proposal and how spending will be affected in the years following enactment.

I have already cited the example of the increased spending associated with the renal dialysis program. Besides increases in the number of patients receiving care, once we created the funding source the behavior of both patients and health providers changed. Virtually all patients with end-stage renal disease now begin such therapy, rather than only those with the expectation of long term survival and rehabilitation as originally intended.

There has also been a shift in the proportion of patients seeking more expensive but less personally demanding care in a hospital or treatment center compared to home dialysis.

I would like to call the committee's attention to the table attached to my testimony entitled "Average Family Premium Rates by Type of Service." If you will just turn to that while I read, I think you might find it helpful when you reach your deliberations.

This table reflects estimates of fiscal year 1975 premium costs under the Administration's Comprehensive Health Insurance Plan, CHIP, introduced in the 93d Congress.

The first column of the table shows the estimated premium cost of each of the insured services using the CHIP cost sharing structure. Under CHIP, there was a $150 per person annual deductible for all covered services except drugs with 25 percent coinsurance up to a family out-of-pocket annual liability of $1,500. There was a separate $50 deductible for drugs and some additional restrictions on payment for mental health services. The total family premium required to insure the services and provide for administrative costs, State premium taxes, and other costs peripheral to health care delivery was estimated to be $600.

For purposes of comparison we have shown what the total costs of providing these services would have been with no deductible, but a flat 25 percent coinsurance and $1,500 limit on out-of-pocket liability. We have also added another column estimating the premium cost with no cost sharing at all.

Part of the added costs resulting from reductions in cost sharing are transferred costs. We would have simply been taking a portion of what had been paid out-of-pocket and transferring it to a new payment sources.

You can see, for example, with just a 25 percent coinsurance and no deductible that the added transferred costs would have been $182 and the added induced costs would have been $72 for a total premium of $854, compared to $600 under CHIP. With no cost sharing at all, the added transferred costs would have been $441 and the added induced costs would have been $156 for a total premium of $1,179.

I believe that by reviewing these data you can easily see how expanding third-party reimbursement can induce greater health spending. If the system can afford to pay the freight, it is fine to expand coverage by adding services or lowering cost sharing. But careful consideration will have to be given to how much of the load can be borne by the taxpayer if public monies are used for financing or

TABLE

AVERAGE FAMILY PREMIUM RATES
BY TYPE OF SERVICE (FY 1975)

Type of service	CHIP[1] Cost-Sharing Structure	25% coinsurance[2]			No Cost-Sharing		
		Total Premium	Add'l. Induced	Add'l. Transf'd.	Total Premium	Add'l. Induced	Add'l. Transf'd.
Total..............	$600	854	72	182	1179	156	441
Institutional:							
Hospital care...........	319	381	7	55	526	30	180
Nursing home care.........	8	8	0	0	13	2	3
Noninstitutional:							
Physicians' services.....	196	293	24	73	411	53	162
Dentists' services.......	2	12	4	6	16	6	8
Drugs................	23	36	6	7	55	15	17
Other services & supplies	52	124	31	41	173	50	71

1/ $150 deductible per person plus 25 percent coinsurance to a maximum family liability of $1500, maximum of 3 deductibles per family and separate $50 deductible per person for drugs.

2/ $1500 maximum liability maintained.

through the health insurance premium structure if private resources are used for financing.

Another effect of liberalizing cost sharing can be illustrated in the area of ambulatory care. Under the Griffiths-Kennedy proposal with no cost sharing, spending for services from outpatient clinics, physician offices, and outpatient departments in hospitals would increase by approximately 20 percent. Under a proposal with a $150 deductible and a 25 percent coinsurance rate applied to ambulatory care, the increase would be only about 10 percent.

I want to emphasize again that my statements in this regard, as in referring earlier to coverage for end-stage renal disease, should not be construed to mean I do not favor covering a benefit simply bcause it adds measurably to spending. I do believe, however, that benefits under any program of national health insurance, should be carefully designed in a way that does not distort ultimate spending patterns.

Finally, I would like to call the committee's attention to tab C which is attached to my testimony and which was derived from the 1974 report to which I referred earlier. You will note that 1975 spending on personal health care services without any national health insurance proposal was estimated to be $103 billion. From this no-national health insurance estimate we calculated the additional costs induced by each of the major national health insurance proposals. Personal health spending under each proposal is shown across the bottom of the chart. The bill with the lowest induced cost is the Long-Ribicoff proposal, with additional fiscal year 1975 aggregate spending estimated to be $4.3 billion or about 4 percent.

At the other end of the spectrum was the Griffiths-Kennedy proposal with induced costs estimated at $13 billion, or approximately 12 percent of total health spending. The reason for the difference was that the Griffiths-Kennedy proposal would have provided a third-party payment source for a much larger number of health services with little or no cost sharing to the patient.

The Long-Ribicoff proposal, on the other hand, was not a comprehensive national health insurance program, and except for very low-income persons, provided coverage only after $2,000 in medical bills had been incurred, or 60 days of hospital care had been used. The Administration's CHIP proposal fell in the middle of the two extremes and would have led to induced costs of $6.5 billion.

The chart also permits one to observe other important effects of the proposals' structures. For example, by design the Griffiths-Kennedy proposal would reduce the importance of private insurance to about three percent of total spending compared to 32 percent under the present insurance structure.

Under the Griffiths-Kennedy proposal, spending through private health insurance would have dropped almost to zero while under some of the proposals, such as those sponsored by AHA and AMA, there would have been an increase of up to approximately 40 percent.

Mr. SCHEUER. Could I ask a question, Mr. Chairman?

When you say on the bottom of page 11 that with $150 deductible and 25 percent coinsurance, you change effective demand from 20 percent increase to 10 percent increase?

Mr. ALTMAN. Right, you have the increase.

Mr. SCHEUER. You have the increase?

Mr. ALTMAN. Yes.

Mr. SCHEUER. Have you studied—can you give us a profile of the person who doesn't opt for the service and why they don't opt?

Mr. ALTMAN. Well, the profile—remember, I am talking about ambulatory care.

Mr. SCHEUER. Ambulatory care that they would have taken if there had been no coinsurance that they now not opt for?

Mr. ALTMAN. Well, the picture that I would paint would be far from complete and I might add that that question—a legitimate question—is one of the main reasons why the Department has funded the Rand Corp. to do a large 5-year study to look at the effect of out-of-pocket payment for health care on the way health services are utilized.

Mr. Scheuer. Here is the problem: What we are trying to do is move people away from the sophisticated and expensive national health care spectrum, from the tertiary hospital beds and scanners and all of that, to the preventive element and the educational elements of the system.

The funding meechanism right now pushes a guy with a sore thumb into a tertiary hospital bed because they don't reimburse him for the outpatient care; they don't reimburse the hospital for providing outpatient care. But they do reimburse him for the bed.

We are doing that at a tremendous cost. The financing mechanism should encourage them to go to things you have named here— outpatient clinics, outpatient department in hospitals, et cetera.

Mr. Altman. I agree.

Mr. Scheuer. If there is 25 percent coinsurance and $150 deductible, it deters people from using this end of the health care spectrum of services. They are sure as hell going to end up in the other end which are financed under medicare and medicaid, and it is going to cost us $150 a day instead of $25.

And I wonder if you have ever studied what treatment patients choose and what their motives are and what the health outcome was and what the utilization outcome was of other financing options.

Mr. Altman. First, let me say I agree with you and in the design——

Mr. Scheuer. I don't know what you are agreeing with because I am asking a lot of questions.

Mr. Altman. I understand what you are saying.

[Discussion off the record.]

Mr. Altman. With respect to the reason why I said I agree with you: I agree with you in the basic tenent of the entire question, which was the funding mechanism; what we make people pay; and what the system pays influences their movements. What I was trying to say was that the proposal—the CHIP proposal required cost sharing on hospital care; the same cost sharing on hospital care as it does on ambulatory care—so that an individual faced with two ways of getting the same services, one in a hospital, which for example, might cost $1,000, and the other in the outpatient unit which might cost $200; if they had to pay 25 percent of $1,000 it would be $250 as opposed to 25 percent of $200 which is $50.

Unfortunately, I recognize it is very difficult to convince people to impose cost sharing on hospital care. I know many good and valid reasons for it; nevertheless, when we get right down to it, where we wind up all the time in this country and most other countries, is that either we impose no cost sharing—then we have all induced effect and have the regulation following that—or we only impose it on the outpatient side. I don't want to necessarily discuss the President's proposed changes to the medicare program, but the intent underlying the 10 percent coinsurance feature on inpatient care was to offer at least a partial balance against the 20 percent coinsurance feature on outpatient care.

My understanding is that not everyone supports that proposal. There are a few.

Discussion of the Budget Issues ([23], pp. 1306–1307, 1309–1322)

The hearings of the Subcommittee on Health and the Environment, on the subject of national health insurance, continued with the participation of both Dr. Alice Rivlin of CBO and Dr. Stuart Altman of HEW. Testifying also was Bridger Mitchell, senior economist, of the Rand Corporation. Mr. Mitchell's prepared statement was presented to the sub-committee earlier and it is not reprinted here (see [23], pp. 1187–1212). Representatives also participating included James Scheuer, Tim Lee Carter, Paul Rogers, and Henry Waxman.

Mr. Scheuer. . . .

Dr. Rivlin, let me ask you one question. You really summed up the whole problem on page 16 of your testimony, where you said, in the fourth line: "This reduction in projected expenditures could only occur if very severe controls are imposed upon the health sector and adhered to over the 5-year period."

I think what you are saying—the only way we are going to get a handle on cost controls is if we are very tough and hard nosed in writing the legislation and if the health care system is very tough and hard nosed and hard nosed in making these cost controls a reality?

Ms. Rivlin. I think that is right. However, I think one has to have a certain amount of humility about what being hard nosed really means and what mechanism will work.

Mr. Scheuer. Tell us.

Ms. Rivlin. I can tell you what some of the options are.

One option is to try to change the incentives for individuals are providers so that hospitals will have more incentives to save money and individuals will have more incentives to seek lower cost care. That is difficult to structure, but it is one option.

The other extreme is to set price levels, fee schedules and other such ceilings. It is not obvious that that is more effective in the long run. There would be a form of collective bargaining between the medical profession and the Government, if the Government were paying the bill. The countries that have experienced this have not always found that it is easy to hold the cost down, even in that situation.

Mr. Scheuer. Well, at the very least you would give the consumer an incentive to enter into the health service system at the optimal point in terms of quality of services needed and the cost of services needed. We are doing the reverse of that now. We are making it difficult and expensive for them, for customers, for the constituency, to move into the system at the least expensive and least sophisticated end of the——

Ms. Rivlin. Yes, I think that is right. There is little disagreement about the fact, that the current system does push people toward the more expensive forms of care.

Mr. Scheuer. Both in terms of the incentives to the patient as well as the providers?

Ms. Rivlin. Exactly.

Mr. Scheuer. So both of those would have to be reversed.

Do you feel, also, that the patients ought to have some kind of an incentive to see not only their costs reduced but have an incentive to see that the public cost to the providers is kept to a reasonable minimum. That the payment structure should provide for them to have some kind of a role to play, some kind of informal oversight function, vis-a-vis the providers?

Do you understand what I am saying?

Ms. Rivlin. I understand the general objective. I think it is difficult to imagine an administrative mechanism that would work very well.

N5   Mr. Scheuer. In Australia and New Zealand they do. I was over there a month or so ago, and they emphasize that. They give the patient, no matter what they contribute themselves, give them a role in the payment system so the bill comes to them and the money flows back to them. If something outrageous is going on they can express some outrage and say something to the provider, say something to the payer; they can do something because they are taxpayers and citizens too.

Ms. RIVLIN. An interesting idea. Maximum information will certainly help. However, if patients are not paying the bill, they aren't likely to be very worried about the costs. . . .

Mr. CARTER. How should public financing responsibility be allocated among Federal, State, and local governments?

Mr. ALTMAN. Well, go ahead.

Ms. RIVLIN. That is a conversation stopper.

Mr. CARTER. Yes.

Ms. RIVLIN. Part of the answer is to examine what the various levels of government do well and what they do badly.

Sometimes decisions about the character of service delivery programs are probably best made at a local level. Other types of decisions are better made at a national level. I am not sure I have a general answer to that question at all, but at least I have given Stuart and Bridger time to think.

Mr. SCHEUER. Could I ask the witness a question?

You said that the type and design of the delivery systems are best decided at the local level?

Ms. RIVLIN. I said there are some kinds of service delivery questions that might better be carried out at the local level.

Mr. SCHEUER. How come a 1,000 out of 3,000 counties, a full 1,000, have no family planning services whatsoever? How come if the local community can best make those decisions we haven't had a preschool child development program in our school system?

Why do we need the Congress to legislate Head Start? I think that is a great myth that has been perpetrated on the American public.

Mr. CARTER. Mr. Chairman.

Mr. SCHEUER. I yield back my time.

Mr. CARTER. I thank the gentleman for yielding back my time.

Is there a difference in inflationary impact if Federal funds are spent?

Mr. ALTMAN. In my own view, Mr. Carter, there is not initially, but the longer term effect results in an inflationary impact. The Federal dollar, while it may be used to control spending, also, is often used to lever increases in spending.

The pressures on the Federal Government to do other things with those dollars are quite great, and our experience in many programs has been that when the Federal Government takes over the spending—and I might add my reason for discussing the renal program was not to be critical, but to show simply that at one time we had private health insurance for a lot of people with renal disease. However, simply by moving the dollars to the Federal Government it tends to take on the characteristic of being nobody's dollars, and I think the answer is, yes, spending increases.

Mr. CARTER. In your experience, what have you found to be barriers or limits of your ability to plan, allocate and control expenditures?

Mr. ALTMAN. Well, with respect to planning, the way the current Federal programs—most of the big ones, medicare and medicaid—we have very little planning associated with them. They are vendor payment programs with uncontrollable aspects, and if people use the care that providers think are necessary, we pay for it. So our capacity to plan efficiently or even plan at all for most of the Federal dollars is very, very small. We are trying, however, to do some planning for the entire health system, with hopes that it will impact positively on Federal programs.

Mr. CARTER. What mix of financing, if any, do you recommend to finance the plan, general revenue financing, Social Security tax or tax credit, or what else, for comprehensive health insurance—suppose we had it?

Mr. ALTMAN. My own personal view is that as much as possible of the payment should remain as a private premium and that the Federal Government should come in only to the extent of financing care for people that really can't afford it. Then I would favor the use of general revenue funds.

Now the other panelists may have quite different views.

Mr. CARTER. Would you like to express different views?

Ms. RIVLIN. I would not—simply because of my position as Director of the Congressional Budget Office. We don't take policy positions on matters that come before the Congress.

Mr. CARTER. Would you like to elucidate on it?

Mr. MITCHELL. I might amplify on the comment to one extent, to pick up your previous question about whether Federal expenditure is per se more or less inflationary than private expenditure in this sector.

I think that is in some ways a tough call, and certainly the history of Federal programs that Mr. Altman alluded to would justify his conclusion. But there is another issue, and that is the relative efficiency of the administraton of a health insurance program, whether it is located in the public sector as contrasted with being located in the private sector, which would be largely private insurance companies.

I think the evidence there is really quite uncertain at this point. One can point to some aspects of the operation of medicare and medicaid which give one hope that there are efficiencies to be had by public operations of a program. There are also some notable failures in that record, and there may be something to be said for having private insurance companies competing with one another to keep claim costs down.

So, I, myself, would not draw a conclusion one way or the other at this time as to whether a largely private or largely public mixture would be the preferred approach to financing.

Mr. CARTER. How can a financing system be designed to assure stability of funding?

Ms. RIVLIN. One way is to have an earmarked tax. Allocate a certain number of payroll tax points or income tax points which would give you a certain amount of stability of funding.

One problem of course is that those taxes go up and down with the national economy.

Mr. MITCHELL. Certainly private premiums accomplish the same goal if they are legally required. Employers will have to pay them in good years and bad.

Mr. CARTER. In bad years they might not be able to in some cases, I am afraid.

Is it possible to have an overall financing system which is progressive in nature?

Mr. MITCHELL. Well, the term "progressive" I think is really a technical term, and it means that the proportion of costs that would be paid by a taxpayer increased as his income increases.

Mr. CARTER. That is right.

Mr. MITCHELL. So perhaps on a $5,000 income the tax might be 5 percent, and on $25,000 it might be 7 or 10 percent. Unless we rely to a very great extent on income tax, all measures of financing will probably not be progressive, but I think what counts here is to actually look at the tax burden by level of income, as I tried to indicate in some of the examples in my testimony.

It is possible to accomplish quite a number of different patterns of distribution of that tax burden from, varying one that is nearly the same for everybody to one that is highly scaled with income. Whether it is technically progressive or regressive I think is not the point so much as what those burdens are.

Mr. CARTER. By the way, I was impressed by your testimony. I was called out several times, but I've reviewed it carefully and I have found it very good.

How can or should a budget take into account future advances in technology which could significantly redistribute costs for a particular service?

Mr. ALTMAN. I think, if you had a fixed budget—I assume you mean by that if we were to run it all through a fixed dollar amount and new technology would come along?

Mr. CARTER. Yes.

Mr. ALTMAN. Well, I guess there are two possible ways. One would be to allow some flexibility in the budget so that it was not completely fixed and built into it and expected increases in new services resulting from new technology. The other would be to require some unit, some unit even down to the local physicians or provider unit, the flexibility of making changes in allocations; so if a new, more expensive piece of machinery came along they might cut back on other things that were less useful.

Mr. CARTER. The funding would not have been allocated, I believe, in this case; this is new technology, and we have no funds for that. How would we obtain them? Do we have a breakthrough and we want to give the benefit of the breakthroughs to the people?

Mr. ALTMAN. Well, the point is, while breakthroughs are unpredictable at any particular moment in time, you can anticipate them somewhat by allowing funds to be built up in units for such breakthroughs. I think there are systems that have attempted to deal with that.

Mr. CARTER. Thank you.

Mr. ROGERS. I wanted to ask a few questions.

I must leave shortly and then Mr. Scheuer will Chair.

Dr. Mitchell, you said the Federal Government, in effect, subsidizes the sale of private health insurance. What effect does this have on its availability, nature, and growth?

Mr. MITCHELL. What effect do the subsidies have on growth of insurance?

The best evidence we have on this point is that the tax subsidies in effect make it possible for many taxpayers to purchase their health care at a lower cost by buying health insurance premiums and then getting the tax deduction.

Mr. ROGERS. We are giving them how much of a deduction; what does it amount to percentagewise?

Mr. MITCHELL. It is about one-third on the average of the premium. That will vary with the income level.

What that means is you can actually buy your hospital care or doctor visit more cheaply by first buying insurance, even though you have to pay the insurance company the administrative cost of 10 percent or so, than you can by paying the bill out of your own pocket. This has a substantial effect on encouraging more insurance.

Mr. ROGERS. Do you include the subsidization that we give through the tax in what the Government is now spending on? I presume you do. Is that part of the figure of what the government is now supplying for medical care? You don't count that?

Ms. RIVLIN. I wasn't including it in the figures I gave, but I think in principle it ought to be.

Mr. ROGERS. I would agree; shouldn't it be?

Mr. ALTMAN. Yes, but it is not, except it depends on how you count.

If you count on the spending side, yes, it is counted because the dollars come back and they are spent through some provider unit.

Mr. ROGERS. You don't count that as part of what the Government is contributing in public expenditures then?

Ms. RIVLIN. One of the features of the new Budget Act is that it does bring tax expenditures on to the books, so to speak. They have to be toted up every year, so at least the Congress knows the amount of the tax revenues foregone by these kinds of provisions.

Mr. WAXMAN. I just find it incredible that the $8 billion figure hasn't been taken into consideration.

Mr. ROGERS. Yes.

Mr. ALTMAN. When I say it is not——

Mr. ROGERS. You mean included as an expenditure?

Mr. ALTMAN. It is not officially included. I think it has been a subject of our discussions before the various committees for about—since I can remember—but it is the kind of expenditure which is not normally or has not in the past been included in the totaling up of health care expenditures. The movement toward including these expenditures at both the executive branch and Congress, I, personally, believe, is very welcome, because it is an indirect but nevertheless a way the Federal Government finances health care.

Mr. ROGERS. Fairly direct?

Mr. ALTMAN. Well——

Mr. ROGERS. Isn't it?

Mr. ALTMAN. It is indirect to the extent that they will provide you with a tax rebate or reduction. If you spend it it is not direct in the sense that the Federal Government goes out and spends the money for the care.

Mr. ROGERS. I understand that.

Mr. ALTMAN. It has the same effect.

Mr. ROGERS. Sure.

Should we use the tax system more to influence the health care system? Should we try to control costs through the tax system?

Mr. MITCHELL. I don't think it is my role here to advise the Congress what we ought or ought not to do, but I would like——

Mr. ROGERS. Is it feasible?

For instance, if someone says the reasonable cost of something is $50, you could use the tax system to take anything charged to the patient over that $50. Would that work, Mr. Altman?

Mr. ALTMAN. I guess my sense is not, in order to control health care spending, out-of-pocket costs ought to be closer to the time of use.

Mr. ROGERS. Is it easier to say directly that this financing mechanism pay only so much, or is it better to say for controlling costs that anything charged over that amount is subject to high taxation?

Mr. ALTMAN. Well, my feeling is that health care in and of itself is a complicated service to buy and to make decisions on. If you complicate the control mechanism and make it more circumspect, I think you lose some of its value, although it is quite an interesting idea. I am not sure I fully appreciate it. I have to think about it some more.

Mr. ROGERS. All of you think about that and let us have your comments for the record; you don't have to give it to us now. I think that would be helpful.

[The following statements were received for the record:]

USE OF EXCESS PROFITS TAX TO INFLUENCE HEALTH CARE COSTS—
RESPONSE OF ALICE M. RIVLIN, PH.D.

The use of an excess profits tax to discourage health care providers from charging more than a level determined as reasonable for a given service would be extremely difficult to administer, and probably ineffective, or perhaps counter-productive.

First, such a system would be extremely complex, expensive, and difficult to administer. For example, who would be responsible for setting the charges and reviewing the rates? Would the rates be uniform nationwide, state-wide?

As the process would work through the tax system, individual providers would be responsible for keeping track of their overpayments. This would create several problems. Providers would incur significant expense in keeping records itemized for each service component and later in preparing their tax returns. Also, the complexity and management of the system would invite widespread tax evasion because of the difficulty in monitoring compliance.

Secondly, such a system would probably be ineffective in achieving its goal, controlling costs. Unless the excess profits tax was set at 100 percent, physicians would simply increase fees to maintain the desired net income level. Even if "excess fees" were taxed at 100 percent, numerous other means could be used to achieve their income goals. These could easily result in cost increases as high or even higher than at present.

How the Tax System Might be Changed To Help Control Inflation of Health Care Prices—Response of Stuart Altman, HEW

The thrust of your question, Mr. Chairman, is whether and how those features of the tax system that subsidize purchase of health insurance and medical care might be utilized to impose some control on the health care system, in particular on inflation of health care prices.

Exemption of income received in the form of employer contributions to health insurance premiums, which Dr. Mitchell in his testimony has estimated to result in a $5.5 billion tax loss, holds some potential for imposition of conditions and specifications on the insurance package itself. There is evidence that this exemption has contributed to the widespread preference for first-dollar coverage of health care expenses. This suggests the possibility that the tax exemption be made more selective by continuing full exemption only for the cost of indepth insurance protection. That portion of premiums financing prepayment of budgetable, routine expenses would not be exempt.

The deduction of insurance premiums by individuals lends itself to the same line of argument. Only "qualifying" types of coverage would be deductible.

You have suggested that the medical expense deduction may provide a basis for some type of control over prices. For example, a ceiling on the amount of deductible could be specified for any given service. Having given the idea due consideration, I must report that there appear to be serious problems with this approach. Most importantly, only a minority of medical expenditures are claimed as deductions. In 1972, $8.0 billion was deducted, a large amount in absolute terms and in terms of the associated tax loss, but only 16.8 percent of the $47.7 billion of personal health expenditures in the private sector that year (40 percent was paid by insurance).

While a ceiling on the amount of deductible for a given service might have a marginal effect on overall demand, it would probably be insufficient to justify the costs and inconvenience incurred.

I would like to indicate general agreement with the thought that these tax subsidies should be examined from time to time to evaluate their effect on access to health care, on the equity of their redistributive impact, and on their contribution to demand and inflation.

Mr. MITCHELL. Fine.

There are potentially two types of cost controls we might think of here. One is a very detailed control of individual expense items, a particular hospital stay, a certain type of treatment, or a certain type of office visit. That sort of detailed control it seems to me is impossible through a tax system; it is not the right mechanism.

Mr. ROGERS. You have no more effective way to get quick results than a tax demand.

Mr. MITCHELL. The other one is the extent to which we encourage or discourage insurance through the tax system. This is something we can control to some extent. How much we subsidize premiums and whether we subsidize the system at all.

Mr. ROGERS. I am talking about controlling costs, not controlling purchase of insurance.

Mr. MITCHELL. I wanted to link that up with what Mr. Altman said earlier. To the extent we encourage policies that do have some degree of coinsurance and deductible requirements and that those cost sharing requirements encourage patients and doctors to economize on the use of medical resources, we are indirectly but, I think, in an important way exerting a control on medical expenditures.

Now, a tax policy which encourages people to buy policies that have some degree of cost sharing is getting at that control question albeit through the insurance premium route.

Mr. ROGERS. I can understand that. But it is very nebulous in a way, and people may still decide not to do it so it doesn't effect things overall. That is the point I was making.

Mr. MITCHELL. I think we have a fair amount of empirical evidence people do respond to the price of insurance in terms of determining how much they will buy and the tax is an important part of that decision.

Mr. ROGERS. I am sure it does have an effect.

Is there any evidence that people respond to tax law?

Mr. MITCHELL. Very much.

Mr. ROGERS. As far as expenditures are concerned?

Mr. MITCHELL. Yes.

Mr. ROGERS. If you have a heavy tax on something that usually discourages that course?

Mr. MITCHELL. Right.

Mr. SCHEUER. We have plant modernization tax incentives, whose only purpose is to get people to invest in order to get the tax base or whatever it is.

Mr. WAXMAN. Mr. Altman, I don't know if you were here for Congressman Adam's presentation.

Mr. ALTMAN. Yes, sir.

Mr. WAXMAN. I would be interested in your reaction to his statement regarding the need for some kind of cost controls and whether you think we need something along the lines of the economic stabilization program in order to hold down prices and costs.

Mr. ALTMAN. The economic stabilization program had its good and bad features. It worked well, reasonably well, during a period of time when we had a tremendous amount of voluntary compliance on the part of hospitals and on the part of the doctors.

I think during the first 2 or 3 years most of the savings came about not because of tight controls in the sense of a lot of the monitoring on the part of the Federal Government but rather in a willingness on the part of hospitals and doctors to live within the rules.

Towards the end of that program that began to break down in a fairly systematic and fundamental way, and quite frankly, Mr. Waxman, I am not sure we could have held that kind of program together with the strings and bailing wire with which it was put together. I have the sense that hundreds of Federal employees would have been needed and even then I am not sure we could have repeated the successes of the earlier period.

Nevertheless, I do believe that a control mechanism like that, if the country decided that it wanted it, is a possibility as something that could be effective.

Now, with respect to the present time, the situation is one where the President feels he does not want to use Federal powers over private spending but he did want to use them with respect to the programs for which he has responsibility.

I think that from his point of view and from his advisors, including myself, that was a legitimate call to make to see if by using the levers of the Federal Government we could bring a reduced rate of spending without having to exert Federal controls over all spending for health care, because controls are not a simple business.

I think people that come before you to tell you that just by imposing Phase IV, you are going to repeat all the successes of the past are being rather naive.

If you set a control mechanism—as I said in my testimony—and keep the reimbursement system the way it is, you still have the providers wanting more services, the patient wanting more services and the system ready to pay for more services. Under such a system, to ask a regulatory mechanism to superimpose itself will, in my opinion, eventually result in failure.

I think in the process of failing you are going to distort the system. I much prefer a change in the incentive structure. I don't think regulation can work without that change. Regulation can be helpful and may be considered necessary even if incentives are changed, but regulation alone would probably not work for any period of time.

Mr. WAXMAN. I was interested in your comments on cost sharing. You said cost sharing provides a measure of patient and provider involvement in the decisionmaking process.

I was interested in that comment because I wondered what kind of involvement it provides for a patient in deciding whether to allocate money for health that might be needed for other expenditures, personal expenditures, and how cost sharing allows the patient to make medical decisions affecting his own health problems.

Mr. ALTMAN. Let me go back to the answers that I gave to Mr. Scheuer before, and to the statement I made about regulators. Even if the patient at the time services are being prescribed goes along with what the provider says and make no choice, the fact that he or she is put in the position of recognizing enormous costs maybe not directly, but indirectly, whether that procedure was necessary, whether they were being overcharged, is a tremendous asset to a regulatory system, because if you don't have that, the regulator is there all by himself.

So, I think people who look at cost sharing simply as asking a befuddled and somewhat emotional patient in rather trying circumstances to make a rational choice, I think, are missing the point. The number of individuals that wrote us letters at the Cost of Living Council because their physicians' bills were going up 15 or 20 percent, when the rule said 2.5 was significant. On the other hand, we got very few letters from patients in hospitals. We did get a number of letters from the companies who were paying the insurance bills and self insurers saying "I am a company that is self insured, and one of my employees went into the hospital for two days and ran up a bill of $10,000. And here it is, is this reasonable?"

I think that is a critical component of any kind of a conscious, overall cost control, and if you do away with it and have no cost sharing on the part of the patient, what is likely is arbitrary controls with regulators who hide behind rule books for fear of being accused of being immoral or inhumane——

Mr. WAXMAN. Are you saying that you would have cost sharing not so much for control over utilization but for the purpose of generating some outrage at the runaway costs of health care?

Mr. ALTMAN. I would have it for both reasons.

I think Bridger has done some of the finest studies in the country with respect to the impact on utilization, but I was trying to emphasize another reason for it. It is not either/or, I think the both have an impact.

Mr. WAXMAN. Don't we have that feeling already instilled in us when we pay taxes, as opposed to asking sick people to come up with a certain sum of money when they need to see a doctor. What effect would that have on people who don't have the money?

Mr. ALTMAN. My own personal view is that for the average taxpayer the difference between the medical bill and his tax is so diffuse that he doesn't sense it at all.

Mr. WAXMAN. I want to ask you another question.

Some people maintain that in order to have a real impact on utilization, cost sharing has to be so high that it will have a real impact on decisions; and then the consequence of that may be that people will purchase supplemental insurance to cover cost-sharing requirements. This would do away with any impact of cost sharing.

How do you respond to that kind of argument?

Mr. ALTMAN. Let me turn the mike over the Bridger, because the Rand people, he and his colleagues, have done a number of studies to show how even modest cost sharing can impact on utilization. But I recognize what you say about insuring for the cost sharing, that tends to minimize it or eliminate its value, and I think here the comments that Bridger made with respect to taxing policies are relevant.

Mr. WAXMAN. Also, even if we acknowledge that cost sharing has an impact on utilization, is this, in terms of policy questions, equitable? Would we then be distributing the scarce benefits of health services, i.e., to those who can afford to come up with the cost sharing as opposed to those who can't?

Mr. ALTMAN. My own view is, yes, provided—with a big provided—provided that the cost sharing is scaled to income. We shouldn't make it so prohibitive for people based on their income so that for some it does make the difference.

Second is that we have limits so that the cost sharing is not unlimited. That is why in the CHIP proposal there was a $1,500 limit.

I understand that a number of insurance companies are writing policies which have a $1,000 limit. There is cost sharing, but it is not at such an amount that it would lead people to financial bankruptcy. It has its place in the arsenal of controlling costs. I don't believe that in and of itself it ought to be used as the sole method of trying to control cost, and it ought not to be so high people are denied care that really do need it.

Mr. MITCHELL. If I could just go back to a couple of your questions.

One, whether paying taxes doesn't induce a measure of cost consciousness and cost limitation of use of services on the part of the patient. If we think of people with automobile insurance policies we have a somewhat similar analogy.

We all pay our premiums for liability protection and perhaps for collision, but when we are unfortunate enough to get a dented fender, or the more serious dent, there is a natural tendency to be more careful about shopping for the lowest cost estimate for getting the best job when some part of the bill in coming out of our own pockets.

If we paid for it in premiums and the company reimbursed it in full it is up to the insurance company to figure out what is going to happen, but we really don't have a big incentive to keep those costs down. And I think it is quite similar with taxes or premiums, which are a long way in the past at the time one gets ill.

Now, the question about whether if we had a high degree of cost sharing or any degree of cost sharing that wouldn't be negated by purchase or voluntary policies in the private market.

I think perhaps Mr. Newhouse yesterday may have commented on this a bit as well. We have two considerations there.

One is that insuring the first dollar—the common office visit—expenses is intrinsically a costly business for an insurance company. Claims come in, they are small. Prescription drugs' claims are the best example of all. It costs a significant proportion of the dollar paid out just to send that paperwork through and audit and reimburse the provider, and it is in fact conceivable that a policy which insured the first $100 or $200 or expenses would actually cost more than $200 in premiums.

So in terms of a rational decision on the part of the patient, it could be preferable simply not to cover those expenses at all.

N6

But even if the premium were less than the actual maximum amount of cost, if we don't include the tax subsidy for these premiums, we basically put the decision on whether to buy supplementary insurance or whether to run the risk of a couple of hundred dollars out of pocket payments, on an even footing. We don't bias it in favor of buying more insurance. Under the present tax laws that bias exists, and it would certainly encourage patients to supplement their national plan.

Mr. WAXMAN. I am troubled about the cost sharing. It seems to me that the patient, due to lack of funds, might decide he or she ought not to see a doctor.

Mr. SCHEUER [presiding]. This is exactly the point I tried to make before. By having a small disincentive to use, on the part of the patient—to use the system at the early, preventive and ambulatory stages, you are going to end up with the patient in the institution in a tertiary hospital at far more cost to the public.

How do you create the right kind of incentives for patients using the best quality appropriate, but most cost-effective, care?

Mr. WAXMAN. I thank the gentleman for amplifying on my question.

Mr. ALTMAN. First, the amount of preventive activities that our medical system is capable of generating is unfortunately, from what I know—again, not being a physician I can't quote chapter and verse—what I have been told is not as great as either the medical community would like or we would hope.

Mr. SCHEUER. What isn't as great?

Mr. ALTMAN. The capacity of the system to prevent by early diagnosis costly medical interventions is rather limited. If someone feels fine but still goes through a series of annual or semiannual, or daily physicals little benefit is shown from early diagnosis.

Mr. SCHEUER. It may be early counseling, in terms of diet, exercise, drugs, alcohol, tobacco, proclivity to engage oneself in a violent situation which is a tremendous cause of morbidity and mortality. It is personal conduct and personal behavior which is by far the most important determinant of health outcomes. Surely you must be aware of that.

Mr. ALTMAN. But that is not coinsurance; that is not going to the doctor quicker.

I agree with you completely that in the area of health education for the individual I think we terribly undervalue and underinvest in that area.

Mr. SCHEUER. But that is counseling.

Mr. ALTMAN. That is counseling but it doesn't have to be. We don't have insurance that pays for it. We are not talking about coinsurance here—our whole mechanism.

Mr. SCHEUER. This is the whole point—we don't have incentives to get the person in the early stage of the system, we have disincentives and they end up in a tertiary hospital bed.

Mr. ALTMAN. It is not clear to me that we need the medical system, the highest priced provider units to provide that counseling.

Mr. SCHEUER. I am not talking about higher price provider units. I am talking about physician extenders, a neighborhood health nurse operating out of a neighborhood health clinic at a fraction of the cost of a health professional and especially a health professional in a tertiary hospital.

Mr. ALTMAN. I think you are right.

Ms. RIVLIN. Clearly the current system has the wrong incentives and we can improve them in several ways. However, ultimately, you really are back to the kind of discussion we were having earlier about expensive treatments for dying patients. You never are sure that the patient is really terminal. Some risk is taken that somebody's life might not be saved if you don't give them maximum care. The same kind of moral problem exists with regard to preventive care.

If you made all care free and very, very available at your corner, at everybody's corner, you would certainly save some lives. The question is at what cost?

Mr. SCHEUER. A perfectly legitimate question. If everything is free and very, very available, how do you prevent frivolous overuse and overstress of the system?

Ms. RIVLIN. That is the problem. We are looking to you for leadership. I think there are only two options.

One is cost sharing, which has all these problems. It may not be effective in getting people to use the care available. They will not get care when they need it.

Mr. SCHEUER. Supposing you had cost sharing at the more expensive element of the system, a tertiary hospital bed, but not when it comes to ambulatory outpatient care. Wouldn't that encourage people to think if I wait and really get sick it is going to cost me money. If I go in for a pill or a little stroking it is going to be free? Isn't that what we want them to do?

Ms. RIVLIN. Suppose he really is sick and he ought to be in a hospital and can't afford it. Then you have a problem.

Mr. SCHEUER. For the poor we would have to make other provisions.

Let me ask you the question I was asking for a few moments ago about the outrageous abuses to date in the medicaid and the medicare programs.

Is there some way we can create incentives to have either Government or the private medical profession or both exercise more adequate scrutiny and oversight than we have had in the last decade? How do we avoid that kind of disaster in the future if we put some more building blocks in place? We have put two building blocks in place and they have been abused in a systemic way. You can't describe it as haphazard. It has been systemic abuse.

Mr. ALTMAN. Mr. Chairman, if I could figure out a way to do something about it I would be the first to try to see an end to this abuse.

Mr. SCHEUER. Prosecute. The facts are known. They have been reported ad nauseum in the daily press over the years.

Mr. ALTMAN. Well, that is a State program. The medicaid program is what we are talking about.

Mr. SCHEUER. Aren't there Federal dollars? Couldn't the U.S. attorney in the southern district of New York indict these people?

Mr. ALTMAN. Again, just like I was a little fearful of practicing medicine without a license, I am out of my element here. I don't really know the ramifications of when a U.S. attorney can act.

Mr. SCHEUER. Is there some kind of incentive we could create?

Mr. ALTMAN. I think the example of New York City more than any other example I could cite demonstrates how budget controls and tight fee controls can lead to the worst effects. In New York City it is now well known that the medicaid program pays for physician services at less than 50 percent of what the physicians charge other members of the community. As a result, very few physicians—the estimates run anywhere between 10 and 25 percent of the practicing physicians—will treat medicaid patients.

In effect, the system lays itself open for the so-called medicaid mills and rip-off artists and everything you mentioned. The majority of the medical community in New York City does not treat medicaid patients. I have talked to high officials in the city of New York, and they know the problem. They are hard put to know what to do because the choice is either having medicaid patients go to the so-called medicaid mills or get no medical care at all.

I think the answer to your question is, yes, incentives can work and one of the incentives is to pay a rate which allows people whom you trust to provide good care to want to participate in the program. I don't think you save money in the long run by underpaying the medical community and that tough trade-off is between underpaying and overpaying.

Mr. SCHEUER. Doctors' salaries, the average doctor makes $55,000 a year in the country, which is a fine salary. Supposing you had him employed on an annual stipend, I would be happy to pay doctors $55,000, or start them at $40,000 and increase it incrementally. I would be willing to meet the market tests for young doctors if they would work in the underserved areas. That is not where the rip-off comes—from doctors' salaries.

One of the things I suppose we are going to have to experiment with is a variety of models of renumeration, not just in the HMO but in group practices and even individual practices. If a doctor wants to work in the ghetto I would be willing for the Government to pick up his rent and provide him with two service people—a nurse and a social worker—and give him an annual stipend. That is exactly what the British do, and it doesn't work that badly and they get doctors to work in what heretofore were underserved areas.

But what I am talking about is another kind of a rip-off. Do you know what I mean when I say family ganging and ping ponging?

Mr. ALTMAN. Yes, sir.

Mr. SCHEUER. The outrageous business of a kid comes in for his methadone and is sent for a variety of other tests on a weekly basis.

Mr. ALTMAN. Mr. Chairman, that is what I was referring to, where you pay $5 a procedure when the going rate is $15, the system lays itself open from this so-called gang family visits where you run them through, so I wind up with a bill of $75, although each procedure was only at the $5 rate.

I would argue that in cases like that it might be appropriate for the rates charged by the program to be increased.

Mr. SCHEUER. Now let me throw this at you: I asked some of our New York City DA's why they didn't prosecute these medicaid frauds and they said, we are so busy with violent personal crime, head-to-head crime, we don't have time for the white collar stuff.

Now, hundreds of millions of dollars of Government funds are going down the drain. Would it make sense for us to say in the law if any State division of health wants to set up a new division of medicaid fraud, a prosecuting arm to investigate and prepare cases and prosecute cases of medicaid and medicare fraud, that the Federal Government would pay 90 percent of the cost of funding that.

If the county DA, like Manhattan, New York County or Queens County or Brooklyn County would set up a division of medicaid fraud, in the DA's office, to ferret out these cases, prepare them and prosecute, the Federal Government will pay 90 percent of the cost of setting that up.

It might be that any recoveries that they got, any recoveries of funds they got might first go—or 50 percent or 75 percent of any reimbursement they got as a result of the prosecuting—would go to pay off the Federal assistance.

Would an approach like that make sense or do we tell the county medical society you have got to get to work to police your profession and we will give you thus and such assistance to do that job, which isn't being done? Is that an obligation that the medical profession itself ought to take on? Is it perhaps that they are not doing it because of the expense of policing their own profession? We have to have a whole new systemic approach to oversight here if we are going to put some more building blocks in place.

Mr. ALTMAN. Well, I can't and won't speak for the medical profession.

With respect to the 90 percent matching rates, such procedures have been tried in the past, not for activities like this one, and it is worthy of some thought.

My own feeling is New York and New York State and other States have very strong financial incentives to do it now but I can't tell you why——

Mr. SCHEUER. The moneys they recover aren't primarily their moneys, aren't they Federal money they are recovering?

Mr. ALTMAN. No, the medicaid program has a matching requirement right now where the costs in New York are shared 50–50. In some States the costs are 78 percent Federal money and 22 percent State money. So we already have in the medicaid program a substantial incentive for efficient State operation.

Mr. SCHEUER. It doesn't work. You may think you have the incentive but in practical terms it ain't there. They are not doing it.

Let me put it another way: Let me pose the same question I posed to Congressman Brock Adams.

If you were writing medicaid and medicare today, in the light of everything that we have learned and everything that you have learned in the decade that has passed, how would you do it differently in terms of the fraud and the ripoffs and the abuses? What would you factor in there that wasn't factored-in a decade ago?

Mr. ALTMAN. For one thing, I guess I would think seriously about even for reasonably low-income people some small amount of cost sharing so that they could let us know occasionally when they felt health care costs were out of line.

Second, I would change the reimbursement system so that in areas like New York City the rates were higher and that there was more accountability for services on the part of the general medical community rather than a small amount, but I think the question is much broader than that and I really don't feel qualified at this time to sort out all the answers. It is fairly broad and I can't tell you why New York City doesn't run a better fraud and abuse system.

Ms. RIVLIN. I think you put your finger on part of the problem. We have to do two things at once. We need an effective way of preventing fraud and abuse. But you have got to make sure you don't put all the potential providers out of business. This is part of the reason nursing home standards aren't better enforced.

Mr. SCHEUER. I didn't get that.

Ms. RIVLIN. I am agreeing with the basic point that Dr. Altman was making. When you have a good system to get rid of fraud you have to also be sure you don't put all of the potential providers out of business. You have to think about what the incentives are to the providers. This is the basic point Dr. Atlman was making.

Mr. SCHEUER. I agree with you and I agree that there ought to be legitimate professional and financial incentives for the whole broad range of the medical profession to be providers and to serve in those neighborhoods.

Well, you have all been extremely generous with your time and it has been very stimulating and very challenging, and we are delighted and grateful to you and, at this point, we will call the meeting adjourned.

[Whereupon, at 5:25 p.m. the subcommittee adjourned, to reconvene at 1:30 p.m. the following day, Thursday, February 26, 1976.]

A COMPARISON OF THE COSTS OF MAJOR NATIONAL HEALTH INSURANCE PROPOSALS ([1], pp. 1–50)

The following document is highly significant for understanding the debate on the budgetary impact of national health insurance proposals. Similar studies were conducted in prior years by the staff of HEW ([2]), but this one is more detailed and drew upon studies prepared by independent analysts. In examining the data presented, it should be noted that bills are identified by institutional sponsors, such as AMA, Health Insurance Association of America, rather than the authors (Fulton, Kennedy, etc.) The bills introduced in the 95th Congress and subsequent ones will, of course, vary in their supporters and perhaps in significant details. It is anticipated, however, that the general approach and overall cost involved will remain somewhat constant.

EXECUTIVE SUMMARY 1/

This paper summarizes the findings of a recent report on the comparative costs of major national health insurance proposals prepared for the DHEW by an independent actuary. Estimating health expenditures for national health insurance (NHI) is a difficult task because these estimates must often be based on limited information. In addition, the cost of a proposal may depend on how it is implemented. The DHEW has recognized these limitations and, to the extent possible, the report has applied uniform estimating methods and procedures to all the proposals with the objective of producing a consistent comparison of the likely expenditures under the various proposals considered. The actual expenditure levels of the proposals may differ from those forecast, but the relative magnitudes should remain in the same proportion.

Nature of the Proposals

The six national health insurance bills selected for this report include five bills introduced in the 94th Congress and one bill which was introduced in the 93rd Congress on behalf of the Administration, commonly known as the Comprehensive Health Insurance Plan (CHIP). The Administration did not introduce a national health insurance bill in the 94th Congress.

Table A provides detailed identifying information for each bill considered. The names by which these bills are commonly known, such as the names of their supporting organizations, are used to refer to them in this report. The bills which are described in further detail beginning on page 17 are shown below classified according to their general characteristics, into three groups. 2/

1/ Executive Summary prepared by Saul Waldman, Economist, Division of Health Insurance Studies, Office of Research and Statistics, Social Security Administration.

2/ For detailed analysis of the provisions of these bills, see Saul Waldman, National Health Insurance Proposals: Provisions of Bills Introduced in the 94th Congress as of February 1976, Office of Research and Statistics, Social Security Administration, HEW Publication No. (SSA) 76-11910.

TABLE A.--Listing of National Health Insurance Bills Included in Report 1/

Name of bill	First sponsor		Bill number		Supported by national organization	Short reference
	House	Senate	House	Senate		
Catastrophic Health Insurance and Medical Assistance Reform Act...............................	Waggonner......	Long-Ribicoff..	H.R. 10028..	S. 2470...	....	Long-Ribicoff
The Comprehensive Health Insurance Act of 1974 1/..	Mills-Schneebeli....	Packwood.......	H.R. 12687..	S. 2970...	Administration	CHIP
The National Health Care Act of 1975............	Burleson.......	McIntyre.......	H.R. 5990...	S. 1438...	Health Insurance Association of America.........	HIAA
Comprehensive Health Care Insurance Act of 1975..	Fulton.........	....	H.R. 6222...	....	American Medical Association.....	AMA
The National Health Care Services Reorganization and Financing Act......................	Ullman.........	....	H.R. 1......	....	American Hospital Association.....	AHA
The Health Security Act.........................	Corman........	Kennedy.......	H.R. 21.....	S. 3......	AFL-CIO, Committee for National Health Insurance	Health Security

1/ All bills listed were introduced in the 94th Congress, except the Comprehensive Health Insurance Act of 1974 which was introduced in the 93rd Congress on behalf of the Administration. The Administration has not introduced any national health insurance bill in the 94th Congress.

(1)   Catastrophic Protection: The Long-Ribicoff Bill--This bill
       provides a program for the general population whose benefits
       would be limited to persons who incur unusually long hospital
       stays or large health expenses. The program would be adminis-
       tered by the Federal government and financed by social security
       taxes. As an alternative to the government plan, employers and
       self-employed persons could purchase equivalent private health
       insurance. In addition, the proposal includes a Federal medical
       assistance plan which would replace and improve the present Medicaid
       program.

(2)   Mixed Private-Public Plans: The Proposals of the Administration
       (CHIP), The Health Insurance Association, The American Medical
       Association and the American Hospital Association--These proposals
       which have a broadly similar approach would all establish (a) an
       employer plan requiring or encouraging employers to offer specified
       private health insurance to their employees (b) a plan for low
       income persons administered and financed by Federal or State government,
       or a combination of both, and (c) continuation of the Medicare
       program or provision of other special coverage for the aged.
       Special arrangements or plans would also be provided under these
       proposals to assure coverage for self-employed and other persons.
       While coverage under a plan of the NHI programs would be available
       to the entire population, some persons would still find it advantageous
       to obtain private health coverage outside of the program.

(3)   Federal Program: Health Security--This bill would establish a
       program covering the entire population to be financed through a
       combination of social security taxes and general revenues, and
       to be administered by the Federal government.

Measuring the Cost of National Health Insurance

The question of "What is the cost of national health insurance" can be
answered in various ways. The findings of this report provide information
on the effects of each of the national health insurance proposals examined
on the following:

(1)   the increase in the Nation's total expenditures for health
       care,

(2)   the increase in Federal spending for health care,

(3)   the increase in Federal "tax expenditures" for health care,

(4)   the increase in the extent to which expenses for health care
       are covered by all types of insurance,

(5)   the extent to which health expenses are covered by the alterna-
       tive NHI programs,

(6)   the changes in the channels (sources) of payment through which
       health care expenses are   financed,

(7)   the changes in the channels (organizations) through which
       health care is administered,

(8)   the average premium cost of the health insurance, when financed
       by premiums,

(9)   the payroll tax rates for health insurance, when financed by
       this method,

(10) the extent of coverage of the population under the NHI program
and other health insurance plans, and

(11) the program costs for each proposed NHI program (by type of
plan for programs with more than one plan).

A fuller understanding of the findings of this report can be obtained by
first examining present arrangements for the financing of health care and
certain possible effects of any national health insurance program. The
costs of health care are currently paid from a variety of sources including
out-of-pocket spending by individuals, private health insurance plans
and a variety of Federal and State programs. Federal government programs
include health insurance plans such as Medicare, medical assistance
programs such as Medicaid, and VA, PHS and military medical facilities.
State and local health care activities also include medical assistance
programs and direct medical service facilities.

The aggregate amount spent on health care by or for all individuals from
all sources is known as total personal health care expenditures. 2/
Adoption of a national health insurance plan will cause changes in these
sources of payment for health expenses, for example, by shifting or
transferring costs previously paid out-of-pocket by individuals to
payment through a health insurance plan.

Induced Costs

Adoption of a national health insurance program may also result in
changing the Nation's total spending for health care, by encouraging
greater use of health services covered by the program, by adding insurance-
related administrative expenses and by paying for services formerly
provided through charity. Programs with provisions such as those which
impose controls on fees and charges may tend to reduce some costs, as
well. But the net effect of adopting any of the six proposals considered
in this report would be to increase total health care expenditures. While
this increase would be largely met and paid for through the program,
national health insurance may also affect health spending outside the
program, so that the costs induced under the program are shown in conjunction
with total health care expenditures rather than just as part of the NHI
program costs.

Total Health Insurance vs. National Health Insurance

The report shows the health expenditures that would be covered under all
private and public health insurance plans as well as by the national
health insurance program. The former represents a more complete measure
of health insurance coverage and protection than the latter. For example,
while some national health insurance proposals cover Federal employees
under the program and others do not, health coverage will no doubt
continue for this group. As indicated earlier, under certain conditions
some persons may prefer to obtain private health insurance coverage
outside of the NHI program. Also, none of the NHI proposals completely
cover all health care expenses, and some employers and individuals can
be expected to purchase private supplementary insurance to cover some

---

2/ The definition of personal health care expenditures used here excludes
spending for health research, construction, education, public health and
other personal activities not directly related to health care for people.
The expenditure figures used in this report are derived from the Social
Security Administration's national health expenditures series (See
Appendix C).

additional health services or to pay the costsharing (deductibles and coinsurance) of the NHI program, or both.

A national health insurance program is defined here to include the newly-established plan or plans of the proposal and the Medicare and residual Medicaid programs if these continue to operate. Some of the proposals studied eliminate the Medicare program and provide other special arrangements for its beneficiaries, while others continue it. All of the proposals establish new plans for health care for the poor, in place of the Medicaid program. Yet, most of them also retain a residual Medicaid program with services limited mostly to intermediate care facilities and other long-term services (types of services generally not considered as "insurable" under typical health insurance arrangements). In this report the figures for spending under the NHI program include those payments made by the plans defined as part of the NHI program, but do not include any payments made under private supplementary plans.

Assumptions in Making Estimates

In preparing these estimates, all the proposed programs are assumed to begin operation in mid-1977. The estimates of costs and expenditures themselves are shown for the period October 1979-September 1980 (referred to as fiscal year 1980). This lag is intended to allow time for the new programs to "shake down," and for some changes in health facilities and manpower and in methods of delivery of services. Information on the projection of health care expenditures to 1980 is given in Appendix C. For estimating purposes, the benefit and financing provisions for the proposals studied are assumed to be in full effect even though the bill may specify that they be phased in over a different period of time. The descriptions of the provisions of the proposals, given later, are also presented on this same basis. 3/

SUMMARY OF FINDINGS

A summary of some of the key measures of the cost of national health insurance in fiscal year 1980 is given in Table 1. Total U.S. health expenditures are projected to be $223 billion at that time assuming no national health insurance program is in effect, with $59 billion paid by the Federal government. Private and public health insurance plans are projected to cover $127 billion of the total.

Total U.S. health expenditures under the national health insurance proposals considered in the report would vary roughly in proportion to the increase in additional health insurance coverage resulting from adoption of the proposal. This would be expected because the increase in insurance coverage of health expenses, by encouraging greater use of health services, is the most significant factor in inducing greater demand for health services. Thus, the increased costs range widely from about $10 to $25 billion reflecting an increase in new insurance coverage of some $18 to $64 billion.

The differences in additional insurance largely reflect variation in the benefit provisions of the proposals, although all six proposals examined cover a broad range of diagnostic and treatment services (broader, for example, than the Medicare program). The Long-Ribicoff, CHIP, and HIAA

3/ The original report includes detailed information on the assumptions and methodology for the estimates including those applicable to specific proposals. In the original report all estimates refer to fiscal year 1980, but with some of these 1980 estimates expressed in 1976 dollars.

proposals tend to use a variety of cost-sharing mechanisms, limit preventive services to children, and concentrate most of their additional spending on the poor, while the AMA, AHA, and Health Security proposals tend to have little or no costsharing, provide preventive services to everyone, and increase insurance coverage broadly for the general population. Thus, the first group would induce some $10 to $11 billion in added health spending, while the second group would result in $20 to $25 billion in additional expenditures.

The rise in Federal expenditures for personal health care services reflect primarily the relative use of Federal vs. private financing under the various proposals. All six plans would add several billion to the Federal health care budget primarily to provide improved health services for the poor. But the range of some $8 billion to $130 billion in additional Federal spending reflects largely the extent to which health insurance funds for the general population are funnelled through a Federal health insurance mechanism or through private health insurance.

Channels of Payment

Table 2 shows the total amount of health care expenditures under each of the alternative proposals (including the increased cost induced by the proposal). It also summarizes for each proposal the changes in the channels of payment through which these expenditures would be financed. These changes in the channels of payment are sometimes described as the "transfer" or "redistribution" of payment for health expenses. Appendix tables A1 to A6 provide more detailed information on the transfer of expenditures among the channels of payment and on the induced costs associated with each of these transfers. 4/

As compared with no NHI program, all proposals would cause a reduction in out-of-pocket payments for individuals as these payments are shifted to the insurance coverage of the NHI proposal. Federal government spending would increase for all proposals partly to provide improved health services for the low income population. State and local expenditures would decline under all proposals, but the reduction would be relatively small for those proposals under which the States retain a significant role in financing the newly-created plans for the poor (the Long-Ribicoff, CHIP and HIAA proposals). This contrasts with the larger reductions for the other three proposals (the AMA, AHA, and Health Security proposals) under which the cost of health care for the poor is borne almost entirely by the Federal government.

With no NHI program the public sector would account for about 38 percent of total health care expenditures in fiscal 1980. The proportion would increase for all the proposals ranging from 43 percent under the Administration (CHIP) proposal to 46 percent for the American Hospital Association plan. However, for the Health Security proposal the public sector would account for 81 percent of total expenditures.

Table 2 (lower half) shows only those expenditures which flow through the NHI program, as the national health insurance program is defined above. The Health Security and Long-Ribicoff plans rely on little or no financing through the private sector. For the other proposals, the required employer health insurance plans would be financed largely through the private sector, while the plans for the poor and aged would be paid mainly by public funds.

4/ In these tables by channel of payment, a separate figure is given for government insurance premiums. These refer to premiums paid by enrollees in a government-administered program such as the premium for medical insurance (SMI) paid by Medicare beneficiaries.

Table 1   Cost Implications in 1980 of Alternative National Health Insurance Proposals   (in billions of dollars)

Personal Health Care Expenditures	No NHI Program	Alternative National Health Insurance Proposals					
		Long-Ribicoff	CHIP	Health Insurance Assoc.	American Medical Assoc.	American Hospital Assoc.	Health Security
Total U.S. health expenditures.............	$223.5	$233.3	$234.8	$234.5	$243.8	$248.5	$248.3
Additional expenditures resulting from adoption of proposal 1/..	---	+9.8	+11.3	+11.0	+20.3	+25.1	+24.8
Federal Government health expenditures 2/..................	59.3	74.9	68.7	67.0	82.0	95.8	189.4
Additional expenditure resulting from adoption of proposal......	---	+15.6	+9.4	+7.7	+22.7	+36.5	+130.1
Health expenditures covered by all insurance (private and public) 3/..........................	127.5	145.2	152.3	153.5	161.2	177.2	191.3
Covered by the National Health Insurance Program 3/..............	---	80.4	121.5	125.9	140.0	159.0	181.7
Additional insurance resulting from adoption of proposal......	---	+17.7	+24.8	+26.0	+33.7	+49.7	+63.8

1/ Represents the additional costs that would result from the national health insurance programs, for example, from increased use of health services.
2/ Represents total Federal expenditures for personal health care including health insurance programs and military, VA and PHS facilities.
3/ The national health insurance program is defined to include the plans established under the proposal, and the Medicare and residual Medicaid programs if these programs are retained under the proposal. The total for health insurance includes the NHI program and other coverage not required under some programs, for example, health coverage for Federal employees and additional insurance benefits, beyond those provided by law, purchased by employers and individuals.

Table 2 -- Total U.S. Health Care Expenditures, and Expenditures Covered by Alternative National Health Insurance Programs, by Channel of Payment, Fiscal Year 1980.

(In billions)

Channel of payment	No NHI program	Long-Ribicoff	Administration (CHIP)	Health Insurance Assoc. of America	American Medical Assoc.	American Hospital Assoc.	Health Security
				Total health care expenditures			
Total U.S. expenditures.....	$223.5	$233.3	$234.8	$234.5	$243.8	$248.5	$248.3
Private Sector..............	139.0	135.6	133.5	131.6	143.6	133.8	47.4
Out-of-pocket..............	70.1	66.0	60.5	57.9	59.5	50.1	38.2
Private insurance..........	66.3	67.1	70.6	71.2	81.7	81.7	7.6
Other private.............	2.6	2.5	2.4	2.5	2.4	2.0	1.6
Public Sector..............	84.5	97.7	101.3	102.9	100.2	114.7	200.9
Federal government.........	59.3	74.9	68.7	67.0	82.0	95.7	189.4
State and local government..	21.5	19.1	21.0	21.0	14.5	12.4	10.4
Government insurance premiums..	3.7	3.7	11.6	14.9	3.7	6.6	1.1
			Expenditures covered by National Health Insurance Program 1/				
Total expenditures..........	---	$80.4	$121.6	$125.9	$140.0	$159.0	$181.7
Private Sector: Private insurance........	---	6.8	44.0	47.8	64.7	67.7	0
Public Sector..............	---	73.6	77.6	78.1	75.3	91.3	181.7
Federal government.........	---	58.9	55.6	51.7	66.6	80.5	176.7
State and local government..	---	12.1	11.4	12.6	6.1	5.3	5.0
Government insurance premiums..	---	2.6	10.6	13.8	2.6	5.5	0

1/ The national health insurance program is defined to include the newly established plan or plans, and the Medicare and residual Medicaid program if these programs are retained under the proposal.

Table 3 -- Total U.S. Health Care Expenditures, and Expenditures Covered by Alternative National Health Insurance Programs, by Channel of Administration Payment, Fiscal Year 1980

(In billions)

Channel of administration	No NHI program	Long-Ribicoff	Administration (CHIP)	Health Insurance Assoc. of America	American Medical Assoc.	American Hospital Assoc.	Health Security
				Total health care expenditures			
Total U.S. expenditures.....	$223.5	$233.3	$234.8	$234.5	$243.8	$248.5	$248.3
Private Sector..............	139.0	135.6	133.5	131.0	168.3	138.0	47.4
Direct by individuals......	70.1	66.0	60.5	57.9	57.9	50.1	38.2
Private insurance..........	66.4	67.1	70.6	70.6	107.9	85.9	7.6
Other private.............	2.5	2.5	2.4	2.5	2.5	2.0	1.6
Public Sector..............	84.5	97.7	101.3	103.5	75.5	110.5	200.9
Federal government........	47.6	77.9	48.7	45.4	52.3	83.7	183.2
State and local government.	36.9	19.8	52.6	58.1	23.2	26.8	17.7
				Expenditures covered by National Health Insurance Program 1/			
Total expenditures..........	---	$80.4	$121.6	$125.9	$140.0	$159.0	$181.7
Private Sector: Private insurance..................	---	6.8	44.0	47.1	89.4	71.9	0
Public Sector..............	---	73.6	77.6	78.8	50.6	87.1	181.7
Federal government........	---	62.4	36.0	30.5	37.3	68.9	170.5
State and local...........	---	11.2	41.6	48.3	13.3	18.2	11.2

1/ The national health insurance program is defined to include the newly established plan or plans, and the Medicare and residual Medicaid program if these programs are retained under the proposal.

Channels of Administration

Table 3 shows the flow of funds by channel of administration--that is the
agency or organization with primary responsibility for administration
and underwriting of the insurance plan. For example, while the Medicare
program contracts with private organizations as agents to process claims
for benefits, the law places the responsibility for administration of
the program on the DHEW (SSA) and the program is included as Federally-
administered.

For several proposals, the agencies or organizations administering the
funds would differ from those which finance them. Under the Administration
(CHIP) and HIAA proposals, the State governments would administer the
newly-established plans for the poor, while the Federal government would
pay the larger share of the cost. Under the Long-Ribicoff medical
assistance plan, the States would contribute to this Federally-administered
plan. Under the employer plan of some proposals such as the AMA plan,
Federal subsidies would be paid toward the purchase of private health
insurance.

Federal Government Expenditures

Except for table 4, the data on Federal health care spending shown in
the report refers to direct outlays for health care. In table 4, however,
Federal "tax expenditures" for health care are estimated along with the
changes in tax expenditures which would result from adoption of the NHI
proposals studied here.

Tax expenditures refer to the loss of tax revenue from the allowable
deduction under Federal tax law, within certain limitations, of out-of-
pocket expenses for medical services and health insurance premiums.
Also the Federal tax law treats the cost of premiums for health insurance
paid by employers as an employee fringe benefit not taxable as income to
the employee.

In this report, employer contributions for health insurance premiums and
payroll taxes are considered as part of the total wage compensation
package of the employees. Thus, an increase in the amount of employer
premium payments from adoption of a NHI proposal is assumed to result in
a relative reduction in other employee compensation (so that there would
be no change in total business deductions for the wage package) but
would result in an increase in the amount of employee income excluded
from taxation.

Table 4 displays present Federal tax expenditures for health care expenses
and the increase in tax expenditures that would result from adoption of
the alternative NHI proposals. It also shows direct Federal outlays for
health care and the total impact of the proposals on the Federal budget.

The Health Insurance Association proposal would alter the present tax
provisions concerning deduction of health insurance premiums for employers
and individuals. As described later, this proposed change in tax law
is the major provision by which this proposal is intended to encourage
employers and individuals to participate in the proposed program. The
AHA proposal would liberalize the extent to which health insurance
premiums for individuals can be deducted from taxable income, while the
other four proposals would not change present tax laws.

Induced Costs

Previously, induced costs were defined as changes in health care spending
resulting from the provisions of a newly-adopted NHI proposal. Among
the six proposals considered here, the induced costs would raise total
health care expenditures by a range of 4.4 percent to 11.2 percent.
Table 5 indicates how eight major factors are estimated to induce changes

Table 4-- Federal Government Outlays and Tax Expenditures for Health Care Under
Alternative National Health Insurance Proposals, Fiscal Year 1980

(in billions)

Proposal	Total expenditures		Outlays		Tax expenditures 1/	
	Total	Increase	Total	Increase	Total	Increase
No NHI program...........	$77.5	---	$59.3	---	$18.2	---
Long-Ribicoff............	94.9	17.4	74.9	15.6	20.0	1.8
Administration (CHIP)....	89.0	11.5	68.7	9.4	20.3	2.1
Health Insurance Assoc...	90.3	12.8	67.0	7.7	23.3	5.1
American Medical Assoc...	104.2	26.7	82.0	22.7	22.2	4.0
American Hospital Assoc..	121.5	43.9	95.8	36.5	25.7	7.4
Health Security..........	208.1	130.6	189.4	130.1	18.7	0.5

1/ Tax expenditures refer to the loss of revenue under Federal tax laws, such as those
which result from individual and business deductions of medical expenses or health
insurance premiums.

Type of Services	Percent Increase (Applied to out-of-pocket expenses)
Institutional Services:	
Short-term hospital (inpatient care).............................	25%
Psychiatric and other long-term hospitals..........................	50
Skilled nursing and intermediate care facilities....................	75
Home health agency services.........	100
Preventive Services:	
Routine checkup and similar preventive services............................	67
Family planning services and supplies.	67
Diagnosis and treatment of illness:	
Physicians and other services..........	50

For prescription drugs, the increase factor is a composite of a greater
number of drugs prescribed due to increased use of physicians' services,
and an increase in the extent to which prescriptions are actually filled.

in health care expenditures.   The effect of each factor has been estimated independently and, in several cases, the interrelationship of the factors would tend to offset each other. 5/

(1)   Additional Health Services Rendered--Additional coverage by insurance of health care services, or reduction of present costsharing requirements generally encourages additional use of services (and also of relatively more expensive kinds of services). To estimate the induced costs of this type, a specified percent increase factor (shown below) was applied to the out-of-pocket spending for each type of health service. (No increase in use is calculated for services already covered by insurance or public programs but only for expenses now paid out-of-pocket).

(2)   Additional Administrative and Related Expenses--The induced costs for administrative expenses include (a) the added administrative costs of paying for health services through insurance (b) reductions in administrative expenses from replacement of private individual (nongroup) coverage by group insurance, government-administered plans or other less expensive mechanisms and (c) the costs of determining family income, operating a health credit card system and other special activities required under certain proposals. Administrative costs also include expenditures for regulation, planning and evaluation of a program by its administering agency.

(3)   Payment for Bad Debts, Unbilled Charges and Charity Services-- Additional insurance coverage will usually result in payment to hospitals and physicians for services previously not paid for because the patient did not pay the bill, the bill was reduced, or services were given on a charity basis.

(4)   Higher Rate of Payment for Services--The rates of payment to providers may increase under the new plans. For example, the new program may pay higher rates for services than are paid under the Medicaid programs of some States.

(5)   Maintenance of Government Appropriations and Philanthropic Donations-- Additional costs may result if the patient load of government hospitals or other direct service programs outside of the NHI program are reduced, without a proportionate decrease in the program's total budget. Similarly, if philanthropic funds used to pay for health care services are diverted to other health purposes, increased spending would be induced. In both cases, these induced costs occur outside the NHI program.

Unlike the five kinds of induced costs described above, the three types shown below are types which would tend to reduce costs.

(6) and (7) Controls on Reimbursement of Institutions and on Professional Fees--All the proposals considered set up some mechanism, administered by a State or Federal agency, or jointly, to set rates of payment to hospitals, physicians and other providers. These are mentioned in the description of the proposals, beginning on page 11.

(8)   Controls on Utilization--Similarly, all of the proposals include some kind of mechanism to review the necessity and quality of health services under the NHI program, either by incorporating the present Professional Standard Review Organization (PSRO) or establishing a new utilization review mechanism operating under State or Federal authority. These activities are also described later.

5/ For example, the "additional health services rendered" and the "controls on utilization," would in effect represent offsetting factors. Both these factors have been estimated independently.

TABLE 5.--Induced Expenditures 1/ Under Alternative National Health Insurance Proposals, by Source, Fiscal Year 1980.

(In billions)

Source of Induced Expenditures	Long-Ribicoff	Administration (CHIP)	Health Insurance Association	American Medical Association	American Hospital Association	Health Security
Total induced expenditures..........	$9.8	$11.3	$11.0	$20.3	$25.1	$24.8
Source of Increase:						
Additional health services rendered..........	3.6	6.0	7.6	9.2	15.3	21.0
Additional administrative and related expenses..........	2.0	4.6	4.3	4.1	5.6	2.3
Payment for bad debts, unbilled charges and charity services..........	2.6	4.5	3.6	4.3	6.0	6.0
Higher rate of payment for services..........	2.2	1.9	2.1	3.0	3.1	4.5
Maintenance of government appropriations and philanthropic donations..........	.4	1.0	1.1	1.0	1.6	2.0
Sources of Decrease:						
Controls on reimbursement of institutions..........	*	-4.5	-7.1	-.9	-1.0	-4.7
Controls on professional fees..........	-.4	-1.2	0	0	-4.5	-4.5
Controls on utilization..........	-.6	-1.0	-.6	-.4	-1.0	-1.8
Total induced expenditures, as percentage of total health care expenditures..........	4.4%	5.0%	4.9%	9.1%	11.2%	11.1%

* Less than .05 billion.

1/ Induced expenditures refer to changes in health care spending resulting from the adoption of a national health insurance program.

Premium Rates

Four of the proposals would establish employer plans financed mainly through private health insurance. Table 6 indicates the national average premium rate (combined employee-employer) for family and single enrollments and the average premium rate per employee. This latter rate approximates the average cost to the employer for each employee on his payroll because it represents a composite of the family and single rates and takes into account employees who would not enroll because they are covered under another family policy or have elected not to enroll.

The family premium rate for the four plans is distributed by type of health service and administrative costs in Table 7. The assessments by policy pools under certain plans (described later) are excluded from the percentage distribution. The proportion of the premium rate allocated for institutional services ranges from 42 percent to 46 percent. This is a smaller proportion than under many present health insurance policies, reflecting the relative emphasis of the NHI plans on noninstitutional services.

Comparative Payroll Tax Rates

For the two bills which would be financed in part by payroll and similar taxes, Table 8 compares the tax rates specified in the bills with the rates needed to finance their expenditures as estimated in this report. The earning base upon which these tax rates are calculated are taken from the financing provisions of the two bills described on [pp. 141 and 149].

Table **6.**-- Average Annual Premium Rates Under Employer Plans for Selected National Health Insurance Proposals, Fiscal Year 1980

Proposal	Premium rate		
	Employee and family	Single employee	Average per employee 1/
Administration (CHIP)..........	$1,042	$417	$558
Health Insurance Association...	1,209	465	649
American Medical Association...	1,501	562	794
American Hospital Association..	1,588	603	843

1/ Average premium rate per employee represents a composite of the family and single rates and takes into account those employees who would not enroll because they are the spouse of an employee who has enrolled for family coverage or for other reasons.

Table 7.--Average Annual Premium Rate for Family Policy Under Employer Plans for Selected National Health Insurance Proposals, by Type of Health Services, Fiscal Year 1980.

Type of Health Service	Administration (CHIP)	Health Insurance Association	American Medical Association	American Hospital Association
	Premium Rate			
Total............................	$1,042	$1,209	$1,501	$1,588 1/
Institutional Services...........	470	502	661	677
Ambulatory & Professional Services...	363	474	621	660
Prescriptions & Supplies.........	77	109	---	56
Administrative Cost..............	132	109	150	174
Assessments by Individual Plan Policy Pools........	---	15	68	14
	Percent Distribution 2/			
Total............................	100.0	100.0	100.0	100.0
Institutional Services...........	45.1	42.0	46.1	43.2
Ambulatory & Professional Services...	34.8	39.7	43.3	42.1
Prescriptions & Supplies.........	7.4	9.1	---	3.6
Administration..................	12.7	9.1	10.5	11.0

1/ Includes $7 for certain long-term care services not included under specified health services
2/ Distribution based on health services and administration (excludes assessments).

Table 8.--A Comparison of the Tax Rates on Earnings Specified in Selected NHI Proposals, and Tax Rates Needed to Finance Estimated Expenditures of the Proposal.

Type of tax on earnings	Tax Rate	
	Specified in proposal	Needed to finance estimated expenditures
Long-Ribicoff Catastrophic Plan:		
Employer payroll....................	1.0%	1.2%
Self-employment income............	1.0	1.2
Health Security Proposal:		
Combined employee-employer rate....	4.5	7.5
Employee payroll................	1.0	1.7
Employer payroll................	3.5	5.8
Self-employment income............	2.5	4.1
Unearned income....................	2.5	4.1

POPULATION AND EXPENDITURES UNDER THE PROPOSALS

This section of the report provides information for each of the six proposals, as follows:

(1) A description of the major provisions of the NHI proposals,

(2) the number of persons covered and the program expenditures of the NHI program, 1/

(3) the number of persons covered under other health insurance plans, including Federal civilian and Federal military personnel and persons voluntarily enrolling in private health insurance plans, and

(4) the number of persons not covered by any health insurance plan.

Definition of National Health Insurance (NHI) Program--As before, an NHI program is defined to include the newly-established plans or plans of the proposal and the Medicare and residual Medicaid programs, if these programs are retained under the proposal. The persons receiving residual Medicaid services (which are mainly long-term care services) would generally receive their basic health care under another plan of a program.

1/ Program expenditures refer to the payments for the specified benefits of the NHI proposal and do not include payments (for additional health service or costsharing) under supplementary insurance.

Therefore, no separate population figure is given for the residual
Medicaid program.

Private Health Insurance--As mentioned before, all NHI proposals make
coverage available under a plan to the entire population. However, some
self-employed persons and other individuals may find it advantageous to
obtain private health insurance outside the plans of the NHI proposals.
This decision will usually depend on the premium rate of the available
NHI plan (which reflects in part the extent to which the premium is
subsidized by government or by assessment against other insurance) as
well as on the age, health status and other characteristics of the
enrollee's family. The number selecting private health coverage varies
considerably among the proposals.

No Insurance--Where the program is voluntary, some persons will not
elect any health insurance coverage. This group is shown divided between
(a) employees and dependents who are eligible to elect a required employer
plan, and (b) other persons eligible under other plans of the proposal.
Some of these noninsured persons may be eligible for health care under
Federal programs for Indians, Alaskans, seamen and veterans or from
other programs.

Per Capita Costs--While the report gives figures for both population and
expenditures under the various plans of the programs, these data are
often not completely comparable and a valid per capita amount cannot be
calculated. This problem arises mainly because of the complex financial
interchanges among the plans of certain proposals.

Benefits--Generally, where an NHI program is composed of several plans,
each plan would provide essentially the same covered health services and
costsharing requirements. Usually, the standard costsharing is reduced
or eliminated for low income families, and sometimes special treatment
is given to the aged. In the descriptions below, there would be no limit
on the amount of service or number of visits under any proposal, unless
indicated.

Long-Ribicoff Proposal

The bill would establish (1) a catastrophic protection plan covering the
entire population and (2) a Federal medical assistance program for the
poor.

Catastrophic Plan

After a person has spent 60 days in the hospital, the program would
provide unlimited additional hospital care and a maximum of 100 days in
a skilled nursing facility. The program would also pay, after a family
has incurred $2,000 in medical expenses, insurance for physicians'
services, lab and X-ray, home health and other services. The patient
would pay no additional costsharing once he has reached the eligibility
limits.

The program would be financed by a tax of one percent on employers'
payroll and on self-employment income on the same earning base used for
the social security program. However, contributors could credit one-
half of their contributions against their Federal income taxes. Employers
and individuals could opt out of the government-administered plan by
establishing an approved private insurance plan providing equivalent
benefits.

Medical Assistance Plan

The medical assistance plan would cover families with incomes under
specified levels which would vary according to family size. The plan

also includes a "spend-down" provision under which families, whose income is above the eligibility limits, could become eligible when they have incurred a specified amount of health care expenses.

The program would cover the same services as in the catastrophic plan and in addition, well-baby care, maternity, family planning, physical checkups for children, and intermediate care facilities. The plan would be financed by Federal and State general revenues, with the State contribution being a fixed annual amount based on a formula designed to maintain, in part, their current spending for the Medicaid program. State contributions would be reduced, however, if the State provides its own assistance program to supplement the Federal plan.

Reimbursement and Other Provisions

Both plans of the proposal would be administered as part of the Medicare program and reimbursement would be based on Medicare principles. The Medicaid program would be abolished. The bill also includes provisions designed to encourage the expansion of basic private health insurance which would mesh with the benefits of the catastrophic plan.

Population and Expenditures

Table 9 indicates the population and program expenditures of the catastrophic plan including the alternative private plans established by employers and individuals. The population shown as covered under the medical assistance plan includes only persons qualifying under the specified income limits (theoretically, the entire population could

Table 9.--Long-Ribicoff Proposal: Covered Population and Expenditures Under the Proposed Program, Fiscal Year 1980.

Source of coverage	Population (in millions)	Expenditures (in billions)
Long-Ribicoff Proposal 1/.........	231.0	$80.4
Catastrophic Health Insurance.....	231.0	$13.6
Federally administered program..	95.7	6.8
Employer plans..................	127.7	6.4
Individual plans................	7.6	.4
Medical Assistance Plan...........	22.5 2/	30.4
Medicare.........................	26.9	32.0
Residual Medicaid.................	---	4.3

1/ In this report, the national health insurance program is defined to include the new plans established by the proposal and the Medicare and residual Medicaid programs if these programs are retained under the proposal.
2/ Represents the population with family income below the specified limits. Potentially, the entire population could become eligible under the "spend-down" provision (see text).

qualify under the "spend-down" provision). The expenditures, however, refer to total payments under the medical assistance program. As indicated, the bill abolishes the Medicaid program and the expenditures shown under the residual Medicare program represent the State supplementation of the Federal medical assistance program. (Information on persons covered under other health insurance plans is not available for the Long-Ribicoff proposal).

Administration (CHIP) Proposal

This proposal would establish (1) a plan requiring employers to offer specified health insurance to their employees, (2) a State-assisted plan for the low-income and high medical-risk population, and (3) an improved Federal Medicare program for the aged.

Under the employer plan, all employers, including State and local governments would have to offer the specified coverage to full-time employees and would have to pay at least 75 percent of the premium cost.

The State-administered assisted plan would be designed to make coverage available to (a) low-income families including low paid employees (b) self-employed and other individuals and (c) high-risk employment groups. The standard costsharing for benefits (described below) and the premiums required of enrollees would be reduced according to family income. The balance of the costs of the program would be financed by the Federal and State governments, with the State share (which would vary according to its per capita income) averaging somewhat less than one-quarter of the total.

The Federal plan for the aged would represent an improved Medicare program for the aged. Both costsharing and premiums for enrollees would be reduced according to their income. The present Medicare payroll tax would continue and Federal and State general revenues would finance the balance of the costs of the program.

Benefit Structure

Institutional Services: hospital, skilled nursing facility
(100 days).

Diagnosis and Treatment: physicians' services, lab and X-ray,
home health services (100 visits), prescription drugs,
medical supplies and appliances.

Preventive and Special Services: well-child care, maternity,
family planning, dental care (under age 13), vision care
including eyeglasses (under age 13), hearing care including
hearing aids (under age 13).

Costsharing: Standard costsharing under the employer and assisted
plans is an annual deductible of $150 per person and 25 percent
coinsurance, with an annual family maximum of $1,500 ($1,050
per single person) on total costsharing. For the Medicare
plan a $100 deductible and 20 percent coinsurance, with an
annual limit of $750 per person.

Reimbursement and Other Provisions

The States would set reimbursement rates in accordance with Federal procedures and criteria. These rates would have to be accepted as full payment by institutions, and by physicians for patients covered by the assisted plan and the Medicare program. Physicians could charge patients covered by the employee plan an additional fee, but the program includes incentives to encourage the physicians to accept the established fee as full payment.

Persons under all plans could elect to enroll in an approved prepaid plan (HMO) as an alternative to the regular plan. The States would regulate insurance carriers and approve their premium rates. They would also review and approve proposed capital expenditures of institutions. Professional Standards Review Organizations (PSRO's) would review all services under the program. The Medicaid program would be limited to providing intermediate care facilities and other specified long-term care services.

Population and Expenditures

Table 10 shows the population and expenditures of the CHIP proposal, for each of the plans included in the proposal. It also shows the estimated

Table 10.--Administration (CHIP) Proposal: Population and Expenditures Under the Proposed Program, and Population Under Other Health Insurance Plans, Fiscal Year 1980.

Source of coverage	Population (in millions)	Expenditures (in billions)
Total population..........	231.0	---
Administration (CHIP) proposal 1/..	204.8	$121.6
Employer plans.................	142.9	$ 44.0
State assisted plans...........	37.1	27.3
Federal plan for the aged (Medicare)....................	24.8	36.0
Residual Medicaid..............	---	14.3
Other Health Insurance Plans.....	21.4	---
Federal civilian employee plans........................	7.0	---
Federal military programs......	7.1	---
Private health insurance.......	7.3	---
No Insurance.....................	4.8	---
Employees and dependents.......	1.8	---
Others.........................	3.0	---

1/ In this report, the national health insurance program is defined to include the new plans established by the proposal and the Medicare and residual Medicaid programs if these programs are retained under the proposal.

number of persons who would be covered under health insurance plans outside of the proposal and the number with no health insurance coverage. Detailed data on the financial transactions of each of the three new plans is given in Appendix table B1, including data on income, disbursements, administrative costs and financial interchanges among the plans.

Health Insurance Association Proposal

The HIAA bill would establish (1) a plan encouraging employers to offer private health insurance to their employees, (2) a plan for self-employed and other individuals and (3) a State plan for the poor.

Under the first plan, employers must offer their employees a qualified health insurance plan as a condition for retaining the business tax deductions for health insurance premiums allowed under present tax law. (No business deduction would be allowed for unqualified plan.)   The sharing of the premium payments would be arranged between employers and employees, but the employee share would be limited, according to wage level, for low-paid workers. Employees could deduct their full premium contributions on their personal income tax return without regard to the limitations under present law.

The individual health care plan would make coverage available to self-employed persons and others through insurance pools arranged by the State, with losses of the pools assessed against participating insurance carriers. Like employees, persons under the individual plan could deduct their full premium contributions for tax purposes.

The States would establish plans for low-income families (not eligible for an employer plan). The standard costsharing requirement for benefits (described below) and the premiums payable under the plan would be reduced according to family income. The balance of the cost would be borne by the Federal and State governments, with the State share being 10 to 30 percent, according to its per capita income.

Benefit Structure

The benefits of the proposal would be phased-in over an eight year period. The description of this bill is based on first-stage benefits.

> Institutional Services: hospital care, skilled nursing facility (180 days).

> Diagnosis and Treatment: physicians' services, lab and X-ray, home health (270 days), prescription drugs, medical supplies and appliances.

> Preventive and Special Service: well-child care, maternity, family planning services, dental care (under age 13, one visit), vision care (under age 13, one visit).

> Costsharing: annual deductible of $100 per person, 20 percent coinsurance, with annual family limit of $1,000.

Reimbursement and Other Provisions

Each State would be required to establish a cost commission to review and approve prospective rates for institutions. The level of rates would be reviewed by the Federal government. Physicians would be paid according to reasonable, customary and prevailing charges. State planning agencies would review and approve proposed capital expenditures of institutions. Federal financial aid would be provided for the development of comprehensive ambulatory health care centers and for additional health manpower training.

Population and Expenditures

The population and expenditures under the plans of the HIAA proposal are shown in Table 11, together with estimates of the number of persons who would be covered under other health insurance plans. The detailed financial transactions of the three plans of the HIAA proposal are shown in Appendix table B2.

American Medical Association Proposal

The AMA proposal would establish (1) a plan requiring employers to offer health insurance to their employees including special provisions for the

Table 11.--Health Insurance Association Proposal: Population and Expenditures Under the Proposed Program, and Population Under Other Health Insurance Plans, Fiscal Year 1980

Source of coverage	Population (in millions)	Expenditures (in billions)
Total population.................	231.0	---
Health Insurance Association proposal 1/	196.6	$ 125.9
Employee plans.......................	118.6	$ 47.2
Individual plan pools................	15.8	8.7
State plan for the poor..............	35.3	26.1
Medicare	26.9	30.5
Residual Medicaid....................	---	13.4
Other Health Insurance Plans...........	28.0	---
Federal civilian employee plans......	7.2	---
Federal military programs............	7.1	---
Private health insurance plans.......	13.7	---
Not Insured...........................	6.4	---
Employees and dependents.............	4.0	---
Others...............................	2.4	---

1/ In this report, the national health insurance program is defined to include the new plans established by the proposal and the Medicare and residual Medicaid programs if these programs are retained under the proposal.

unemployed and (2) a plan for the nonemployed and self-employed. The employer plan would require all employers including Federal, State and local governments to offer specified health insurance to their employees, and pay at least 65 percent of the premium cost. Federal subsidies of premium costs would be provided for employers with relatively large increases in health premium costs, and for low-income workers. Coverage would be continued for workers receiving unemployment insurance with the Federal government paying the full employee-employer premium.

Under the plan for the nonemployed and self-employed, persons not eligible for an employer plan could purchase private insurance and the Federal government would pay from 10 to 100 percent of the premium cost, according to family income. This subsidy could be taken as a credit against

Table 12--American Medical Association Proposal: Population and Expenditures Under the Proposed Program, and Population Under Other Health Insurance Plans, Fiscal Year 1980.

Source of coverage	Population (in millions)	Expenditures (in billions)
Total population............	231.0	---
American Medical Association proposal 1/......................	212.9	$140.0 2/
Employer plans..................	148.8	$ 65.1
Individual policies	8.5	4.5
Individual policy pools.........	28.7	19.8
Medicare	26.9	36.3
Residual Medicaid	---	13.3
Other Health Insurance Plans......	14.6	---
Federal civilian employee plans.........................	7.2	---
Federal military program........	7.1	---
Private health insurance plans..	0.3	---
Not Insured......................	3.5	---
Employees and dependents........	2.3	---
Others.........................	1.2	---

1/ In this report, the national health insurance program is defined to in-include the new plans established by the proposal and the Medicare and residual Medicaid programs if these programs are retained under the proposal.
2/ Includes $1 billion not included in subtotals for administrative expenses of Federal Government for determining income under various plans.

Federal income tax, or by obtaining a certificate of entitlement which would be redeemed by insurance carriers. The States would arrange for the establishment of insurance pools of private carriers to assure coverage for everyone and the losses of the pool would be assessed against participating carriers.

Benefit Structure

Institutional Services: Hospital, skilled nursing facilities (100 days).

Diagnosis and Treatment: Physicians' services, lab and X-ray, home health services, medical supplies and equipment.

Preventive and Special Services: Physical checkups, well-child care, maternity, family planning, dental care (below age 18).

Costsharing: Coinsurance of 20 percent, with an annual maximim of $1,500 per individual and $2,000 per family. Costsharing would be reduced according to family income under both plans of the proposal.

Reimbursement and Other Provisions

Reimbursement for hospital services would be determined by State agencies based on prospective reimbursement methods, and payment for physicians' services would be on the basis of usual and customary or reasonable charges.

The population and expenditures under the various plans of the AMA proposal and coverage under other health insurance plans are shown in Table 12. 1/ The financial transactions of the AMA plans are given in Appendix table B3.

American Hospital Association

The proposal would establish (1) a plan requiring employers to offer specified health insurance for employees, (2) a plan for self-employed and other individuals, and (3) a plan for the poor and aged.

All employers including State and local governments would be required to offer specified coverage to their employees, and pay at least 75 percent of the premium. Federal subsidies would be provided toward the premiums for low-income employees, certain small employers, and enrollees of health care corporations. Self-employed and other persons could purchase health insurance through insurance pools arranged by the States. Losses of the pool would be assessed against participating carriers.

The Federal Government would contract with private carriers to provide coverage for low-income families and for all aged persons. Families would pay premiums according to their income with the balance of costs financed from the continued Medicare tax and from Federal general revenues.

Benefit Structure

Institutional Services: Hospital (90 days, $5 per day); skilled nursing facility (30 days, $2.50 per day); health-related custodial nursing home care (90 days, $2.50 per day).

1/ Although Federal civilian employees are covered under the AMA required employer plan, they are not included as such in this table or in the other data in this report.

Diagnosis and Treatment: Physicians service (10 visits, $2 per visit), lab and
X-ray (20 percent coinsurance); home health services (100 visits, $2 per
per visit), prescription drugs limited to specified conditions ($2 per
prescription), and medical supplies and appliances.

Preventive and Special Services: Physical checkups, well-child care, maternity,
dental care (under age 13), vision care and eyeglasses (under age 13)

Catastrophic Coverage: This provision would apply to persons under all three
plans of the proposal. When out-of-pocket expenses for the costsharing and
certain noncovered services reach a specified amount, varied by income and
age, the limits on the number of hospital days and physician's services would
be removed and all further costsharing would be waived.

Reimbursement and Other Provisions

State commissions would approve prospective charges of institutions and health
care corporations, based on standards specified in the bill. Reimbursement for
practitioners would be based on reasonable fees or compensation. The commissions would also review proposed capital expenditures of institutions. They
would also promote and regulate a system of health care corporations (a type of
HMO) approved to operate in designated geographical areas. Medicare would be
abolished and Medicaid limited to noncovered services. The population and
expenditures for the AHA proposal are shown in table 13 and the financial
transactions of the plans are given in appendix table B4.

Health Security Proposal

The proposal would establish a Federally-administered and financed program covering all U.S. residents. The program would be administered by a health security
board within the DHEW. No costsharing would be required for any health services.

Benefit Structure

Institutional Services: Hospital care, skilled nursing facilities (120 days).

Diagnosis and Treatment: Physicians services, lab and X-ray, home health
services, prescription drugs limited to specified chronic conditions, medical
supplies and appliances.

Preventive and Special Services: Physical checkups, well-child care, maternity,
family planning, dental care (up to age 25), vision care and eyeglasses, and
hearing care and hearing aids.

Financing

The program would be financed by special taxes as follows: 1 percent of
payroll for employees and 3.5 percent for employers, 2.5 percent for self-
employment income and 2.5 percent for unearned income. The employment taxes
would apply to all workers including Federal, State and local employees.
The unearned income tax would be levied on income included in Federal
adjusted gross income for tax purposes. The total amount of income subject
to these special taxes would be limited to an earnings base which is 1½
times the earnings base under social security (thus, the earning base for the
proposal would be $22,950 in 1976). The total amount received from special
taxes would be matched equally by payments from Federal general revenues.

Reimbursement and Other Provisions

A national health budget would be established and allocated to regions and
localities, by type of health care service. Hospitals and skilled nursing

facilities would receive an annual predetermined budget. Practitioners could select fee-for-service according to a fee schedule, capitation payments for persons enrolled with them or, by arrangement, a full or part-time salary.

A health resources development fund would be established. The fund, which would ultimately receive five percent of the total revenue of the program, would be used primarily for development of HMO's and for health manpower training.

The DHEW would review the necessity and quality of services. Institutional providers could be ordered to add or reduce services, or to relocate their place of service. The Medicare program would be abolished and Medicaid would be limited to noncovered services.

Table 13.--American Hospital Association Proposal: Population and Expenditures Under the Proposed Program, and Population Under Other Health Insurance Plans, Fiscal Year 1980.

Source of coverage	Population (in millions)	Expenditures (in billions)
Total population..............	231.0	--
American Hospital Association proposal 1/......................	209.6	$159.0
Employee plans...................	140.4	$ 72.0
Individual policy pools.........	10.5	7.4
Federal plan for poor and aged..	58.7	68.8
Residual Medicaid program.......	---	10.8
Other Health Insurance Plans......	18.0	
Federal civilian employee plans........................	7.0	---
Federal military program........	7.1	---
Private health insurance........	3.9	---
Not Insured......................	3.4	---
Employees and dependents........	1.9	---
Others..........................	1.4	---

1/ In this report, the national health insurance program is defined to include the new plans established by the proposal and the Medicare and residual Medicaid programs if these programs are retained under the proposal.

Population and Expenditures

Table 14 shows the covered population and expenditures of the proposed program on the same basis as for the other NHI bills. The proposal includes one newly-created plan which would cover the entire population of 231 million. The expenditures of this plan would total $170.6 billion, including $157.9 billion for health care benefits and $12.7 billion for administrative expenses. The total expenditures of the health security proposal including the residual Medicaid program is given below:

Table 14.--Health Security Proposal: Covered Population and Expenditures Under the Proposed Program, Fiscal Year 1980

Source of coverage	Population (in millions)	Expenditures (in billions)
Total population............	231.0	---
Health Security proposal 1/.........	231.0	$181.7
Health Security plan...............	231.0	$170.6
Residual Medicaid................	---	11.2

1/ In this report, the national health insurance program is defined to include the new plans established by the proposal and the Medicare and residual Medicaid programs if these programs are retained under the proposal.

The health security proposal is the only one examined which includes a health resources development fund. Since the expenditures of this fund would generally not be used to provide health care services, these expenditures are not included in any of the tables of this report (all of which refer to spending for personal health care). The total of the expenditures for health care services of $181.7 billion indicated in table 14 and the expenditures of $8.7 billion designated for the health resources development fund indicates total spending under the program of $190.4 billion.

TABLE A1.--A Comparison of Health Care Expenditures Under Present Law and the Long-Ribicoff
Proposal in 1980, Showing Transferred and Induced Expenditures by Channel of Payment

(In billions)

Channel of Payment	Health Care Expenditures		Change in Expenditures		
	No NHI Proposal	Long-Ribicoff Proposal	Total Change	Trans-ferred Expendi-tures	Induced Expendi-tures
TOTAL U.S.	223.5	233.3	9.8	0	9.8
PRIVATE SECTOR	139.0	135.6	-3.5	-4.1	.6
Out-of-pocket	70.1	66.0	-4.1	-3.7	-.4
Through insurance:					
Individual policies	9.6	9.0	-.5	-.5	*
Employee contributions	13.6	13.4	-.2	-.4	.1
Employer contributions	39.7	41.2	1.5	.9	.6
Workmen's compensation & TDI	3.5	3.5	0	.0	0
Other private	2.6	2.5	-.1	-.4	.2
PUBLIC SECTOR	84.5	97.7	13.3	4.1	9.2
Government insurance	3.7	3.7	*	*	*
Workmen's compensation & TDI	1.1	1.1	0	0	0
Medicare premiums	2.6	2.6	*	*	*
Federal taxpayers	59.3	74.9	15.6	6.4	9.2
Through third parties:					
Medicare	29.4	29.4	*	*	*
Medicaid contributions	13.6	0	13.6	-13.6	0
Catastrophic Health Insurance	0	6.8	6.8	4.6	2.2
Federal assistance	0	22.7	22.7	15.9	6.8
Other programs	3.1	3.0	-.1	-.1	0
Federal facilities & direct	13.2	13.0	-.1	-.2	.1
State and local taxpayers	21.5	19.1	-2.4	-2.4	*
Through third parties:					
Medicaid	10.8	4.3	-6.4	-6.4	*
Contributions to Federal Assistance	0	7.7	7.7	7.7	0
Other programs	.5	.5	*	*	*
Direct payments	10.2	6.6	-3.6	-3.6	0

* Less than $50 million.

TABLE A2.-- A Comparison of Health Care Expenditures Under Present Law and the Administration Proposal in 1980, Showing Transferred and Induced Expenditures by Channel of Payment

(In Billions)

Channel of Payment	Health Care Expenditures		Change in Expenditures		
	No NHI Proposal	Administration (CHIP)	Total Change	Transferred Expenditures	Induced Expenditures
TOTAL U.S.	223.5	234.8	11.3	0	11.3
PRIVATE SECTOR	139.0	133.5	-5.6	-10.0	4.5
Out-of-pocket	70.1	60.5	-9.6	-9.4	-.1
Through insurance:					
Individual policies	9.6	5.5	-4.1	-4.0	-.1
Employee contributions	13.6	14.0	.4	-.2	.6
Employer contributions	39.7	47.8	8.1	4.3	3.7
Workmen's Compensation & TDI	3.5	3.4	-.1	0	-.1
Other private	2.6	2.4	-.2	-.7	.5
PUBLIC SECTOR	84.5	101.3	16.9	10.0	6.8
Government Insurance	3.7	11.7	7.9	7.6	.4
Premiums for State Assisted Plans	0	9.4	9.3	9.0	.4
Premiums for Federal Plan for Aged	0	1.2	1.2	1.2	0
Workmen's Compensation & TDI	1.1	1.1	0	0	0
Medicare Premiums	2.6	0	-2.6	-2.6	0
Federal taxpayers	59.3	68.7	9.4	3.5	6.0
Through Third Parties:					
Federal Contribution to State Assisted Plans		13.9	13.9	9.9	4.0
Federal Health Plan for Aged		34.7	34.7	33.2	1.5
Medicare	29.4	0	-29.4	-29.4	0
Medicaid	13.6	7.0	-6.7	-6.7	*
Other Programs	3.1	2.7	-.4	-.4	*
Federal Facilities and Direct	13.2	10.4	-2.7	-3.2	.5
State and Local taxpayers	21.5	21.0	-.5	1.0	.5
Through Third Parties:					
State Assisted Plans		4.1	4.1	3.7	.4
Medicaid	10.8	7.3	-3.5	-3.6	.1
Other Programs	.5	.4	-.1	-.1	*
Direct Payments	10.2	9.2	-1.0	-1.0	*

* Less than $50 million.

TABLE A3.--A Comparison of Health Care Expenditures Under Present Law and the Health Insurance Association Proposal in 1980, Showing Transferred and Induced Expenditures by Channel of Payment.

(In billions)

Channel of Payment	Health Care Expenditures		Change in Expenditures		
	No NHI Proposal	Health Insurance Association	Total Change	Trans-ferred Expendi-tures	Induced Expendi-tures
TOTAL U.S.	223.5	234.5	11.0	0	11.0
PRIVATE SECTOR	139.0	131.6	-7.4	-10.0	2.6
Out-of-pocket	70.1	57.9	-12.2	-12.2	*
Through insurance:					
Individual policies	9.6	6.8	-2.7	-2.5	-.2
Employee contributions	13.6	16.4	2.7	1.9	.9
Employer contributions	39.7	44.6	5.0	3.4	1.6
Workmen's compensation & TDI	3.5	3.4	-.1	0	.1
Other private	2.6	2.5	-.1	-.6	.5
PUBLIC SECTOR	84.5	102.9	18.5	10.0	8.4
Government insurance premiums	3.7	14.9	11.2	8.7	2.5
State plans for poor and uninsurable		3.1	3.1	3.1	*
State individual plan pools		8.1	8.1	5.6	2.5
Workmen's compensation & TDI⁻	1.1	1.1	*	0	*
Medicare	2.6	2.6	*	*	*
Federal taxpayers	59.3	67.0	7.7	3.5	4.2
Through thrid parties:					
Federal contributions to state plans		17.4	17.4	12.3	5.1
Medicare	29.4	27.9	-1.5	.1	-1.6
Medicaid	13.6	6.4	-7.2	-7.2	*
Other programs	3.1	2.7	-.4	-.4	*
Federal facilities and direct	13.2	12.5	-.6	-1.4	.7
State and local taxpayers	21.5	21.0	-.4	-2.1	1.7
Through third parties:					
State plans for poor and uninsurable		5.6	5.6	3.8	1.7
Medicaid	10.8	7.1	-3.7	-3.7	*
Other programs	.5	.4	-.1	-.1	*
Direct payments	10.2	8.1	-2.1	-2.1	*

* Less than $50 million.

TABLE A4--A Comparison of Health Care Expenditures Under Present Law and the American Medical Association Proposal in 1980, Showing Transferred and Induced Expenditures by Channel of Payment

(In billions)

Channel of Payment	Health Care Expenditures		Change in Expenditures		
	No NHI Proposal	American Medical Association	Total Change	Trans-ferred Expenditures	Induced Expenditures
TOTAL U.S.	223.5	243.8	20.3	0	20.3
PRIVATE SECTOR	139.0	143.6	4.6	-5.7	10.3
Out-of-pocket	70.1	59.5	-10.5	-11.8	1.2
Through insurance					
Individual policies and pool	9.6	6.8	-2.7	-3.5	.7
Employee contributions	13.6	16.7	3.1	1.9	1.2
Employer contributions	39.7	54.7	15.0	8.3	6.7
Workmen's compensation & TDI	3.5	3.5	*	0	*
Other private	2.6	2.4	-.2	-.6	.4
PUBLIC SECTOR	84.5	100.2	15.8	5.7	10.0
Government insurance premiums	3.7	3.7	0	0	0
Workmen's compensation & TDI	1.1	1.1	*	0	*
Medicare	2.6	2.6	*	*	*
Federal taxpayers	59.3	82.0	22.7	12.6	10.0
Through thrid parties:					
Federal premium subsidies		18.6	18.6	12.4	6.2
Federal employer subsidies		5.0	5.0	3.7	1.2
Federal program for unemployed		2.1	2.1	1.5	.6
Medicare	29.4	33.7	4.3	3.1	1.2
Medicaid	13.6	7.2	-6.4	-6.4	*
Other programs	3.1	2.7	-.4	-.4	*
Federal facilities and direct	13.2	12.6	-.5	-1.2	.7
State and local taxpayers	21.5	14.5	-6.9	-7.0	0
Through third parties:					
Medicaid	10.8	6.1	-4.7	-4.7	*
Other programs	.5	.4	-.1	-.1	*
Direct payments	10.2	8.1	-2.1	-2.1	*

* Less than $50 million.

TABLE A5 --A comparison of Health Care Expenditures Under Present Law and the American Hospital
Association Proposal in 1980, Showing Transferred and Induced Expenditures by Channel
of Payment

(In billions)

Channel of Payment	Health Care Expenditures		Change in Expenditures		
	No NHI Proposal	American Hospital Association	Total Change	Trans- ferred Expendi- tures	Induced Expendi- tures
TOTAL U.S.	223.5	248.5	25.0	0	25.0
PRIVATE SECTOR	139.0	133.8	-5.2	-16.1	10.9
Out-of-pocket	70.1	50.1	-19.9	-20.7	.7
Through insurance:					
Individual policies	9.6	2.2	-7.3	-7.3	*
Employee contributions 1/	13.6	15.4	1.7	1.0	.7
Employer contributions 1/	39.7	60.8	21.1	12.4	8.7
Workmen's compensation & TDI	3.5	3.3	-.1	0	-.1
Other private	2.6	2.0	-.6	-1.5	.9
PUBLIC SECTOR	84.5	114.7	30.3	16.1	14.1
Government insurance	3.7	6.6	2.8	2.5	.4
Federal plan for poor and aged		2.1	2.1	2.1	0
State individual plan pools 2/		3.4	3.4	3.0	.4
Workmen's compensation & TDI	1.1	1.1	*	0	*
Medicare premiums	2.6	0	-2.6	-2.6	0
Federal taxpayers	59.3	95.8	36.5	22.7	13.8
Through third parties:					
Federal plan for poor & aged		66.4	66.4	56.4	9.9
Premium subsidies		7.1	7.1	4.5	2.6
Health care corporation sub- sidies		1.6	1.6	1.1	.5
Medicare	29.4	0	-29.4	-29.4	0
Medicaid	13.6	5.5	-8.2	-8.2	*
Other programs	3.1	2.7	-.4	-.4	*
Federal facilities and direct payments	13.2	12.5	-.6	-1.4	.7
State and local taxpayers	21.5	12.4	-9.0	-9.0	*
Through third parties:					
Medicaid	10.8	5.3	-5.5	-5.5	*
Other programs	.5	.4	-.1	-.1	*
Direct payments	10.2	6.7	-3.5	-3.5	*

1/ Includes assessments for state individual plan pools, and excludes Federal subsidies to low
income employee contributions, small employers, and health care corporations.
2/ Excludes assessments to private health insurers for pool losses.

* Less than $50 million.

TABLE A6--A Comparison of Health Care Expenditures Under Present Law and the Health Security
Proposal in 1980, Showing Transferred and Induced Expenditures by Channel of Payment

(In billions)

Channel of Payment	Health Care Expenditures		Change in Expenditures		
	No NHI Proposal	Health Security Proposal	Total Change	Trans-ferred Expendi-tures	Induced Expendi-tures
TOTAL U.S.	223.5	248.3	24.8	0	24.8
PRIVATE SECTOR	139.0	47.4	-91.7	-94.4	2.7
Out-of-pocket	70.1	38.2	-31.9	-33.4	1.5
Through insurance:					
Individual policies	9.6	1.2	-8.3	-8.3	*
Employee contributions	13.6	.5	-13.1	-13.2	*
Employer contributions	39.7	2.5	-37.2	-37.5	.2
Workmen's compensation & TDI	3.5	3.4	-.1	0	-.1
Other private	2.6	1.6	-1.0	-2.1	1.1
PUBLIC SECTOR	84.5	200.9	116.5	94.4	22.1
Government insurance	3.7	1.1	-2.6	-2.6	*
Workmen's compensation & TDI	1.1	1.1	*	0	*
Medicare premiums	2.6	0	-2.6	-2.6	0
Federal taxpayers	59.3	189.4	130.1	108.0	22.1
Through third parties:					
Health Security Program 1/		170.5	170.5	149.3	21.2
Medicare	29.4	0	-29.4	-29.4	0
Medicaid	13.6	6.2	-7.4	-7.4	*
Other programs	3.1	1.0	-2.1	-2.1	*
Federal facilities and direct	13.2	11.7	-1.5	-2.4	.9
State and local taxpayers	21.5	10.4	-11.0	-11.0	*
Through third parties:					
Medicaid	10.8	5.0	-5.8	-5.8	*
Other programs	.5	0	-.5	-.5	0
Direct payments	10.2	5.5	-4.7	-4.7	*

*Less than $50 million.
1/ Excludes $7.0 billion in spending for development of health resources.

Table B1--Income and Disbursement under the
Administration's Proposal, by Type of Plan, Fiscal Year 1980

A. Private Employer Plans   (In millions)

    Income:
        Employee contributions.. $9,200
        Employer contributions.. 38,200

        Total.. $47,400

    Disbursements:
        Benefits 1/... $38,400
        Administration.. 5,600
        Premiums paid to State Assisted Plans 2/...................... 3,400

        Total.. $47.400

B. Federal Program for the Aged

    Income:
        Premiums.. $1,200
        Payroll taxes... 22,300
        General revenue contributions................................. 12,400

        Total.. $36,000

    Disbursements:
        Benefits 1/... $33,100
        Administration.. 2,900

        Total.. $36,000

C. State Assisted Programs

    Income:
    Premium collections:
        Employers... $2,800
        Employees... 500
        Direct enrollees.. 6,000
        Federal government contributions.............................. 13,900
        State government contributions................................. 4,100

        Total.. $27,300

    Disbursements:
        Benefits 1/... $24,100
        Administration.. 3,200

        Total.. $27,300

1/ Includes uncollected amounts due under health credit card billings.
2/ Includes premiums paid by employers for low income employees electing
   coverage in an assisted plan and premiums paid by high cost groups.

Table   B2 --Income and Disbursement under the
Health Insurance Assoc. of America Proposal in Fiscal Year 1980

A. Employee Plans   (In millions)

Income:
     Employee contributions... $11,800
     Employer contributions... 36,000
        Total... $47,800

Disbursements:
     Benefits.. $42,800
     Administration.. 4,400
     Assessments by state pools.................................... 600
        Total... $47,800

B. State Plan for Poor and Uninsurable

Income:
     Premiums.. $3,100
     Federal contributions... 17,400
     State contributions... 5,600
        Total... $26,000

Disbursements:
     Benefits.. $22,300
     Administration.. 3,700
        Total... $26,000

C. State Individual Plan Pools

Income:
     Premiums.. $8,100
     Assessments to insurers....................................... 600
        Total... $8,700

Disbursements:
     Benefits.. $7,800
     Administration.. 900
        Total... $8,700

Table B3-- Income and Disbursement under the
American Medical Association Proposal in Fiscal Year 1980

A. **Employee Plans 1/**   (In millions)

Income:
Employee contributions... $12,900
Federal subsidy to low income employees 2/................... 1,400
Federal subsidy to premiums for unemployed.................. 1,900
Employer contributions.. 47,100
Federal subsidy to employers................................. 5,000
Total 3/.. $68,200

Disbursements:
Benefits... $58,300
Administration 3/.. 6,800
Assessments by individual qualified policy pools............ 3,100
Total 3/.. $68,200

B. **Private Qualified Policies 4/**

Income:
Premiums.. $4,100
Federal subsidy to premiums 2/............................... 600
Total 5/.. $4,700

Disbursements:
Benefits.. $3,800
Administration 5/.. 600
Assessments by individual qualified policy pools............ 200
Total 5/.. $4,700

C. **Individual Qualified Policy Pools 6/**

Income:
Premiums to enrollees.. $600
Federal subsidy to premiums for unemployed.................. 200
Federal subsidy to premiums for others 2/................... 15,600
Assessments to qualified carriers........................... 3,400
Total 7/.. $19,800

Disbursements:
Benefits.. $18,000
Administration 7/.. 1,900
Total 7/.. $19,800

D. **Federal Program for Unemployed**

Income (all Federal subsidies)................................ $2,100

Disbursements:
Payments to employee plans and carriers..................... $1,900
Payments to individual qualified policy pools............... 200
Total $2,100

1/ Includes groups underwritten as assigned risks and unemployed whose coverage
is continued through Federal subsidies.
2/ Includes certificates of entitlement and tax credits.
3/ Excludes an estimated $400 million of expense to Federal government to make
income determinations and issue certificates of entitlement.
4/ Includes qualified association group insurance policies.
5/ Excludes expenses of Federal government in connection with handling of certificates of entitlement and collection of data.
6/ Includes income and outlays related to persons eligible for Federal program
for uninsured.
7/ Excludes an estimated $600 million of expenses to Federal government to make
income determinations and issue certificates of entitlement.

Table B4-- Income and Disbursement under the
American Hospital Association Proposal in Fiscal Year 1980

A. Employer Plans   (In millions)

Income:
    Employee contributions (net of subsidies)................... $12,500
    Premium subsidies (low income employees).................... 600
    Health care corporation subsidies.......................... 1,100
    Employer contributions (net of subsidies).................. 55,200
    Tax credits to small employers............................. 3,100
        Total... $72,600

Disbursements:
    Benefits 1/.. $63,900
    Administration... 8,100
    Assessments by State individual plan pools................. 600
        Total... $72,600

B. Federal Plan for Poor and Aged

Income
    Premiums (net of subsidies)................................ $2,100
    Health care corporation subsidies.......................... 400
    Payroll taxes.. 22,300
    General revenue contributions.............................. 44,000
        Total... $68,800

Disbursements:
    Benefits for low income persons 1/......................... $23,800
    Benefits for aged persons 1/............................... 38,600
    Administration... 6,400
        Total... $68,800

C. State Individual Plan Pools

Income:
    Premiums (net of subsidies)................................ $3,400
    Premium subsidies.. 3,400
    Health care corporation subsidies.......................... 100
    Assessments to insurers.................................... 600
        Total... $7,400

Disbursements:
    Benefits 1/.. $6,600
    Administration... 900
        Total... $7,400

1/ Includes uncollected amounts due under health credit card billings.

APPENDIX C

ESTIMATES OF HEALTH CARE EXPENDITURES IN 1980

The basis for the projections made in this report is the national health expenditure series for fiscal year 1975 compiled by the Office of Research and Statistics (ORS) of the Social Security Administration 1/. Several modifications were made to the ORS data to obtain a data base more appropriate to estimating costs under national health insurance proposals. For example, certain items included in the ORS data which are not potentially insurable are excluded, such as expenditures in hospital gift shops and cafeterias.

In addition, there was concern that this report not understate the potential costs of the various proposals. While the ORS estimates are the best available, lack of adequate data for certain items suggest possible underreporting in these sources. To assure that all possible expenditures are accounted for, adjustments were made to increase the ORS estimates based sometimes on limited and incomplete data for physicians' services, drugs and drug sundries, eyeglasses, and certain other items.

To further conform to the needs of estimating potential costs of NHI proposals, several classification changes were made to the ORS categorization of expenditures by type of service and source of funds (referred to as "channel of payment" in this report). For example, separate estimates are given for short term hospital, long term hospital, psychiatric hospital, and so forth. Premium payments to government insurance programs are classified separately, and not included with government expenditures as in the ORS series. Complete information on the various adjustments to the ORS series are given in the full report.

The projections of expenditures to fiscal 1980 was based on an econometric model which took account of the anticipated increases in price and wage levels to 1980 and the historical differentials between rises in prices and wages and rises in various types of health care services 2/.

The projections of personal care spending by type of service and channels of payment are provided in the following tables.

1/ Mueller-Gibson: National Health Expenditures, Fiscal Year 1975, Research and Statistics Note No. 20-1975 (November 21, 1975).
2/ A detailed description of these procedures, including the types of equations used, are provided in the full report. In the full report, the data for 1980 in the body of the report are expressed in 1976 dollars; in Appendix D of the full report these data have been adjusted to 1980 price levels using the official inflation estimates of the Councial of Economic Advisors.

Table C1.-- PERSONAL HEALTH SPENDING AND PERCENTAGE DISTRIBUTION IN FISCAL 1976-80 BY TYPE OF SERVICE

	MILLIONS OF 1980 DOLLARS [1]					% of Personal Health Spending				
	1976	1977	1978	1979	1980	1976	1977	1978	1979	1980
TOTAL	140,385	162,610	182,080	202,740	223,460	100.0	100.0	100.0	100.0	100.0
INPATIENT INSTITUTIONAL SERVICES	59,660	69,700	78,570	88,340	98,290	42.5	42.9	43.2	43.6	44.0
General Hospital	35,840	42,270	47,820	54,050	60,380	25.5	26.0	26.2	26.7	27.0
General Hospital Psychiatric	1,840	2,170	2,450	2,770	3,090	1.3	1.3	1.4	1.4	1.4
Private Psychiatric	470	540	630	710	810	.3	.3	.4	.4	.4
State & Local Psychiatric	4,080	4,400	4,700	4,990	5,260	2.9	2.7	2.6	2.5	2.4
Long Term Hospital	1,150	1,250	1,330	1,410	1,490	.8	.8	.8	.7	.7
Federal Hospital	4,960	5,530	6,040	6,570	7,090	3.6	3.4	3.3	3.2	3.2
Skilled Nursing Facilities	7,820	9,160	10,450	11,950	13,500	5.6	5.7	5.7	5.9	6.0
Intermediate Care Facilities	3,500	4,380	5,150	5,890	6,670	2.5	2.7	2.8	2.8	2.9
PROFESSIONAL & OUTPATIENT SERVICES	55,100	64,280	72,190	80,300	88,360	39.2	39.5	39.6	39.6	39.5
Hospitals	5,460	6,800	8,090	9,510	11,020	3.9	4.2	4.4	4.7	4.9
Mental Health Facilities	2,830	3,160	3,450	3,780	4,090	2.0	1.9	1.9	1.9	1.8
Home Health Agencies	490	650	760	850	960	.3	.4	.4	.4	.4
Physicians	26,900	31,670	35,600	39,460	43,100	19.2	19.5	19.6	19.5	19.3
Dentists	8,740	9,990	11,120	12,320	13,540	6.2	6.1	6.1	6.1	6.1
Public Health	3,980	4,500	4,940	5,360	5,800	2.8	2.8	2.7	2.6	2.6
Other Professionals & Facilities	6,700	7,510	8,230	9,020	9,850	4.8	4.6	4.5	4.4	4.4
OTHER HEALTH SERVICES & SUPPLIES	17,630	19,340	20,900	22,480	24,010	12.6	11.9	11.5	11.1	10.8
Eyeglasses & Appliances	2,900	3,260	3,590	3,930	4,230	2.1	2.0	2.0	2.0	1.9
Prescriptions	9,520	10,400	11,200	11,990	12,760	6.8	6.4	6.1	5.9	5.7
OTC Drugs & Sundries	5,210	5,680	6,110	6,560	6,970	3.7	3.5	3.4	3.2	3.2
ADMINISTRATION & PLANNING	7,995	9,290	10,420	11,620	12,800	5.7	5.7	5.7	5.7	5.7

1/ Assumes rate of Increase in C.P.I. projected by the Council of Economic Advisors.

Table C2.--PERSONAL HEALTH SPENDING AND PERCENTAGE DISTRIBUTION IN FISCAL 1976-80 BY CHANNEL OF PAYMENT

	MILLIONS OF 1980 DOLLARS					% of Personal Health Spending				
	1976	1977	1978	1979	1980	1976	1977	1978	1979	1980
TOTAL U.S.	140,385	162,610	182,080	202,740	223,460	100.0	100.0	100.0	100.0	100.0
PRIVATE SECTOR	87,755	101,370	113,250	126,150	139,030	62.5	62.3	62.2	62.2	62.2
Out of pocket payments	46,660	52,870	58,250	64,200	70,060	33.2	32.5	32.0	31.6	31.3
Through insurance:										
Individual policies	5,750	6,770	7,650	8,620	9,590	4.1	4.2	4.2	4.2	4.2
Employee contributions	8,605	10,020	11,210	12,410	13,580	6.1	6.2	6.2	6.2	6.1
Employer contributions	22,680	27,080	31,030	35,320	39,700	16.2	16.6	17.0	17.4	17.8
Workmen's compensation & TDI	2,110	2,490	2,810	3,150	3,500	1.5	1.5	1.6	1.6	1.6
Philanthropy	1,170	1,260	1,340	1,420	1,500	.8	.8	.7	.7	.7
Employer health services	780	880	960	1,030	1,100	.6	.5	.5	.5	.5
PUBLIC SECTOR	52,630	61,240	68,830	76,590	84,430	37.5	37.7	37.8	37.8	37.8
Government insurance:	2,630	2,940	3,200	3,480	3,730	1.9	1.8	1.8	1.7	1.7
Workmen's compensation & TDI	710	820	930	1,060	1,170	.5	.5	.5	.5	.5
Medicare premiums	1,920	2,120	2,270	2,420	2,560	1.4	1.3	1.3	1.2	1.2
Federal taxpayers	35,130	41,580	47,330	53,230	59,270	25.0	25.6	26.0	26.3	26.6
Through third parties:										
Medicare	15,870	19,470	22,640	26,000	29,430	11.3	12.0	12.4	12.9	13.2
Medicaid	8,420	9,840	11,120	12,390	13,660	6.0	6.1	6.1	6.2	6.2
Maternal & child health	300	330	370	400	430	.2	.2	.2	.2	.2
Vocational rehabilitation	200	240	260	280	310	.1	.1	.1	.1	.1
Veterans Administration	240	280	320	350	380	.2	.2	.2	.2	.2
Defense Department	650	740	810	890	970	.5	.5	.4	.4	.4
Other	700	770	840	890	950	.5	.5	.5	.4	.4
Direct payments:										
Veterans Administration	3,450	3,830	4,200	4,570	4,940	2.4	2.3	2.3	2.2	2.2
Defense Department	2,490	2,770	3,020	3,290	3,560	1.8	1.7	1.7	1.6	1.6
Other	2,810	3,310	3,750	4,170	4,640	2.0	2.0	2.1	2.1	2.1
State & local taxpayers	14,870	16,720	18,300	19,880	21,430	10.6	10.3	10.0	9.8	9.5
Through third parties:										
Medicaid & vendor	6,710	7,770	8,750	9,740	10,740	4.8	4.8	4.8	4.8	4.7
Maternal & child health	290	330	360	390	420	.2	.2	.2	.2	.2
Vocational rehabilitation	40	50	60	60	60	*	*	*	*	*
Direct payments	7,830	8,570	9,130	9,690	10,210	5.6	5.3	5.0	4.8	4.6

NATIONAL HEALTH INSURANCE AND HEALTH POLICY OPTIONS, 1978–1982 ([16], pp. 141–155)

The Congressional Budget Office (CBO), created in 1974, is an oversight body having a congressional budget review process. Pursuant to its statutory mandate, CBO prepares an independent, nonpartisan annual report to the House and Senate Budget Committees on budget options available in the coming year and over a five-year period. The full report addresses such matters as defense spending, energy, housing, transportation. Reprinted here is the text of the 1977 report concerning health care. This report was prepared before the new national health insurance legislation was introduced in the 95th Congress and deals with general options and alternatives, based upon the approaches established in legislation then pending. New initiatives might vary in some detail, but the authors of the report were cognizant of that fact and confined their analyses to the general types of legislation which might be reasonably anticipated.

THE ISSUES

In the past decade national health expenditures, both public and private, have grown from $42 to $135 billion or from 5.9 to 8.4 percent of the GNP. 1/ The increase reflects both inflation -- medical care prices in the last decade have risen about a third faster than the Consumer Price Index (CPI) -- and significant increases in the use of health services, especially by the poor. Much of this increased use has been made possible by federal medicare and medicaid programs, which together will cost $32 billion in fiscal year 1977. Because so much health spending is now financed by the federal government, any future inflation in medical costs will have a substantial impact not only on the private costs of care but on the federal budget as well.

Despite massive increases in spending and trends toward more equal access to services, health care is still denied to some, either because they are poor or because they live in inner-city or rural areas where doctors are scarce. Approximately 40 million people with incomes under $10,000 have inadequate health insurance protection and are ineligible for medicaid.

While some people go without medical care, there is mounting evidence of inefficient use of existing resources. Some physicians provide services that could be handled by less-skilled health personnel; services that could be dealt with on a more economical outpatient or informal basis are provided in a hospital or nursing home. Furthermore, there have been indications of widespread provider and recipient fraud in two of the government's major health programs -- medicaid and medicare.

1/ For a more detailed treatment of the issues covered here, see Catastrophic Health Insurance, CBO Budget Issue Paper, January 1977, and a forthcoming CBO Budget Issue Paper on long-term care for the elderly and handicapped.

Federal health policy for the next few years depends heavily on two questions:

o What can be done to hold down increases in costs, especially for care financed by the federal government, without impairing quality?

o What can be done to improve access to medical care for those who still have difficulty obtaining it and paying for it?

These questions are related, since providing more health financing will only add to demand and exacerbate inflation unless ways are found to control costs. Hence, controlling costs in existing federal programs is sometimes seen as a prerequisite to broadening federal insurance protection. On the other hand, since it is difficult to devise ways of holding down costs in medicare and medicaid alone without adding to the burdens of the poor and the aged or providing them with second-class care, it is sometimes argued that medical care costs can only be controlled if the federal government pays an even larger share of the total -- and thus buys more leverage in the system.

CURRENT PROGRAMS

The federal government's complex array of health programs falls into four categories:

o Financing programs that help the poor and the aged pay for medical care.

o Tax expenditures designed to ease the burden of paying for care.

o Direct care programs for some special populations.

o Programs designed to increase the supply of medical resources.

Financing

Medicare for the aged and disabled, and medicaid for the poor, are the major federal health care financing programs. Together, they will cost an estimated $32.0 billion in fiscal year 1977, almost 83 percent of the federal health budget (excluding veterans' health programs). States, which administer medicaid, are expected to spend another $8.4 billion on that program. An estimated 23.6

million aged and 2.4 million disabled persons will be covered by medicare, while 24.4 million poor persons will receive benefits under the medicaid program.

Despite these large expenditures, serious coverage problems remain for both the aged and the poor. Because of medicare cost-sharing requirements and the exclusion of certain types of services -- particularly long-term care -- medicare pays only about 42 percent of the health expenditures of the aged. Approximately one-fifth of the aged receive medicaid benefits to supplement medicare. However, many low-income aged persons and other families with incomes below the poverty level are not eligible for benefits. In 1975, an estimated 8 to 10 million persons with incomes below the poverty level were excluded from the medicaid program.

Problems of provider and beneficiary fraud and program mismanagement in both medicare and medicaid have become a serious concern in recent years. It appears likely that legislation dealing with fraud and program management will be a high priority in this session of the Congress.

Tax Expenditures

The federal government also subsidizes medical care through the tax system. This is done by excluding from a person's taxable income the health insurance premiums paid on his behalf by his employer and by allowing large medical expenses as itemized deductions. In fiscal year 1977 an estimated $7.8 billion in federal tax revenue will be foregone as a result of these tax expenditures. The benefit of these expenditures, however, is not distributed evenly. While taxpayers with incomes in excess of $15,000 accounted for less than 30 percent of all tax returns in 1976, they received about 59 percent of the benefits of these tax expenditures.

Direct Care

Programs that provide services or comprehensive care to specific populations account for about 6 percent of the federal health budget, or $2.2 billion. The direct care programs operated by the federal government include the Indian Health Service, the National Health Service Corps, and the Public Health Service Hospitals. In addition, the Veterans Administration's health care system will spend an estimated $4.4 billion on direct care in fiscal year 1977.

Other federal programs provide local or state agencies with grants to establish community and migrant health centers, maternal and infant care programs, and children's and youth projects in low-income areas or in areas lacking in health resources. Comprehensive care programs serve an estimated 3.7 million persons. In addition, 1.4 million persons will receive hospital care through the Veterans Administration. Direct delivery systems can provide comprehensive care at lower costs per person than can financing programs, and they seem to be more effective at reaching persons in inner-city and isolated rural areas.

Resource Supply

Less than $1 billion of the $38.9 billion in federal health expenditures projected for fiscal year 1977 is devoted to such resource supply programs as health planning and manpower training assistance. Historically, resource development has been directed at increasing the number of hospitals, physicians, and other personnel on the assumption that this would not only improve access but lower the rate of increase of medical prices and expenditures. More recently, however, it appears that increasing the supply of health resources has little effect on prices or access. In fact, it may spur total expenditures by increasing the per capita consumption of physician services and physician-generated hospital services.

This problem -- one of excess capacity stimulating its own demand -- has been recognized by the Health Planning and Resource Development Act (Public Law 93-641), which makes federal planning assistance contingent upon state programs to control the supply of new health facilities. The importance of further action along these lines is underscored by projections that suggest that over the next quarter century the number of physicians per person in the nation will rise by 50 percent. If the amount of health care delivered continues to be determined by the supply of health resources, substantially higher per capita health expenditures could result.

CONGRESSIONAL DECISIONS

Several program authorizations expire in 1977: those for health planning and resource development programs, for the National Cancer Institute, for the National Heart and Lung Institute, and for community mental health and community health centers. A number of smaller programs will also expire. The fiscal year 1977 budgets for the two biomedical institutes were $1.0 billion. While the dollar expenditures for the nonbiomedical programs due to expire are small, some of these programs, such as the health facilities planning legislation, could significantly change total health expenditures. This is because the health facilities planning legislation includes provisions that control the number of facilities and supports state efforts to set hospital rates.

Far more direct budgetary importance attaches to current proposals to contain the rate of increase of medicare and medicaid expenditures. The 140 percent cost increase in these programs over the last five years has been caused largely by higher cost per unit of service rather than by either larger numbers of beneficiaries or higher rates of use. Many critics have concluded that the rapid increase in government health care spending is in itself a major cause of the cost increases. One reason may be that medicare and medicaid reimburse hospitals on a retrospective cost basis, which creates no incentives for efficiency or cost-consciousness.

In addition to considering methods of containing the cost of existing programs, the Congress may also make a preliminary decision on whether national health insurance is desirable. More than two dozen national health insurance bills were introduced in the 94th Congress; the new Administration has pledged to develop a national health insurance proposal within the next few years.

POLICY OPTIONS

Current Policy

If existing health programs are continued, federal health expenditures will be $45.2 billion in fiscal year 1978 and will grow to $75 billion by fiscal year 1982 (see Table 29). 2/ In addition, health-related tax expenditures will reduce federal revenues by $7 billion in fiscal year 1978 and by $15.1 billion in 1982. Although health planning, professional standards review organizations (PSROs), and recent health manpower legislation may marginally improve access and decrease costs over the next five years, it is doubtful that current trends in health care inflation or expenditure will greatly change.

Controlling the Costs of Current Programs

Proposals to reduce federal health costs usually focus on methods of controlling hospital charges, which account for 58 percent of federal medicaid and medicare costs. One approach is to increase cost-sharing by recipients. The Ford Administration's 1977 and 1978 budgets called for imposing 10 percent co-insurance for the first 60 days of hospitalization in the medicare program. Under the present statute, medicare completely covers the cost of the first 60 days of hospitalization after the recipient pays the deductible which is a fixed amount equal to the average cost of one hospital day.   The Administration estimated that the co-insurance plan would save the federal government $1.8 billion in fiscal year 1978. The savings could reach $3.2 billion by 1982.

One possible benefit of this approach would be a greater effort on the part of both physicians and patients to decrease the number of admissions and shorten hospital stays, which could cut costs considerably. The cost-sharing approach, however, would place a larger share of the burden on some people who could not afford it.

TABLE 29.   HEALTH CARE BUDGET OPTIONS, OUTLAYS IN BILLIONS OF DOLLARS, FISCAL YEARS a/

Option	1977	1978	1982
Current Policy	38.9	45.2	73.9
Changes From Current Policy			
Reimbursement Controls		- 0.7	- 5.9
Federalized Medicaid			
Federal/State Financed		17.1	24.3
Federal Financed		29.0	44.1
Long-Term Care			
Block Grant		1.0	2.0 to 4.0
Major Effort		6.0	16.2 to 22.2
Catastrophic Insurance			
Plan to Cover Unusual			
High Expenses		10.0 to 11.0	19.0 to 20.0
National Health Insurance			
Tax Financed		84.0 to 86.0	108.0 to 138.0
Premium Financed		18.0 to 21.0	14.0 to 27.0

a/ Includes function 550 but excludes Veterans Administration and Department of Defense health expenditures.

2/ Exclusive of Veterans Administration and Department of Defense programs.

Controlling hospital reimbursement rate increases is another approach frequently mentioned for limiting price rises. The permissible annual increase of hospital reimbursement rates could be held at a fixed percent (say, 10 or 12 percent) or could be tied to an index of general inflationary pressures (say, 3 percent more than the rise in the Consumer Price Index). Some flexibility would probably be required in such ceilings to allow hospitals to make needed capital purchases and major improvements.

The amount of savings that can be expected from such reimbursement schemes depends not only on the set rate, but also on whether that rate applies to all patients, to the public programs only, or to just certain public programs. 3/ If the rate of increase could be reduced by 3 percent per year from the expected pace, the medicaid and medicare programs would save approximately $700 million in fiscal year 1978 and $5.85 billion by 1982. A limit of 7 percent on the annual increases in medicare reimbursement alone, as was proposed in the Ford Administration's 1977 and 1978 budgets, would reduce medicare costs by $1.46 billion in fiscal year 1978 (see Table 30).

TABLE 30. MEDICARE COST SAVINGS FROM ALTERNATIVE PROSPECTIVE REIMBURSEMENT CEILINGS, FISCAL YEARS 1978 AND 1982, IN BILLIONS OF DOLLARS

Ceiling	1978	1982
7 percent	$1.46	$11.24
10 percent	1.00	8.07
12 percent	0.70	5.71
CPI plus 3 percent	1.33	10.14
CPI plus 5 percent	1.03	7.99
CPI plus 8 percent	0.57	4.45

A third approach is to limit some components that make up hospital costs. Three measures are frequently suggested:

o Limiting reimbursement to some set fraction of the average daily operating charges of similar hospitals

3/ While medicare reimbursements are set by the federal government, medicaid reimbursements are established by the states and under current statute are less amenable to federal policy.

in a region. For example, if the average routine cost were $100 per day, and the reimbursement ceiling were set at 20 percent above that, there would be no reimbursement for routine costs above $120 per day. Those hospitals with costs below the average could be given an incentive payment for their efficiencies. Senator Herman Talmadge of Georgia introduced a proposal similar to this in the 94th Congress (S. 3205).

o Limiting reimbursement for cost increases that come from nonlabor factors, such as the use of more technologically advanced equipment and more laboratory tests per patient. These intensity factors are projected to increase by approximately 10 percent during 1977 and to contribute more than 5 percentage points to the expected 16.6 percent increase in hospital costs. Limits could also be placed on costs related to increases in staff-to-patient ratios, which have been rising recently by 2 percent a year.

o Placing in an escrow account the portion of current hospital reimbursements that result from depreciation. These funds could later be used by hospitals for capital projects which have been approved by state health planning agencies. Such a proposal was incorporated in the Ford Administration's 1978 budget request and was estimated to save $440 million in 1978.

The savings that could result from applying some of these measures only to the medicare program are provided in Table 31. These measures could be imposed individually or collectively, but the savings from a combination of measures would not equal the sum of the savings of the individual measures. This is because hospitals would respond to different measures in a similar way. For example, efforts to hold down routine costs as well as limit cost increases attributable to higher staff-to-patient ratios result in a decrease in staffing; controls placed on the use of reimbursments for depreciation and limited reimbursments for cost increases related to nonlabor factors would both act to curb capital expenditures.

Controls applied only to reimbursements under public programs could create incentives for institutions to discriminate against public program beneficiaries, thus worsening the access problems. If public and private insurance programs maintained different reimbursement standards for a long time, medicare and medicaid beneficiaries might be given a lower standard of care than

TABLE 31. MEDICARE SAVINGS FROM LIMITING INCREASES IN SELECTED HOSPITAL COST COMPONENTS, FISCAL YEARS 1978 AND 1982, IN BILLIONS OF DOLLARS

	1978	1982
Limit on Routine Cost Reimbursement		
105 Percent Level	0.59	1.08
110 Percent Level	0.44	0.80
120 Percent Level	0.21	0.38
Limit Intensity Factors to 2 Percent per Year	0.58	4.50
Hold Intensity Factors to 60 Percent of Present Trend and No Increase Allowed in Staff per Patient	0.40	4.11
Hold Intensity Factors to 80 Percent and Limit Increases in the Staff per Patient Ratio to 1 Percent per Year	0.27	2.28

private patients.   In addition, some of the costs not reimbursed by medicare and medicaid might be shifted to private patients.   If this occurred, the net reduction in federal budget cost would be larger than the reduction in overall spending for health.

If reimbursement controls are applied to individual hospitals regardless of community needs and services, the controls may not curb the duplication of expensive treatment centers and surplus hospital beds.   These problems might be better addressed by such measures as guidelines or limits on the number of beds according to community size.   Alternatively, reimbursement programs could be linked more closely to planning and facility regulation so that rates would reflect the community's desires.

Increasing Access to Health Care

An estimated 25 million people (about 12 percent of the population) have neither private nor public coverage.   For

the most part, these persons are in families with incomes
below the national median. They are the self-employed, the
unemployed, the chronically ill, students, and employees of
small, low-wage businesses. Some 8 million of such uninsured persons may be able to obtain services from a source
such as the Veterans Administration; but this still leaves
17 million who must bear the full financial burden of their
health care.   An additional 19.4 million people from
families with incomes below the national median have very
poor private coverage -- that is, insurance in which out-of-
pocket expenditures can create a severe hardship.

Several proposals have been made for a limited expansion in current federal financing or delivery programs to
meet the most critical access problems. These include plans
to extend insurance coverage to all poor families (federalized medicaid) and plans to extend federal financing for
long-term care and catastrophic illnesses. These limited
expansion programs are sometimes thought of as steps in the
direction of comprehensive national health insurance.

Federalized Medicaid

A federalized medicaid program with uniform nationwide
eligibility and benefit standards could accomplish the first
objective and, via the spend-down provision, provide the
entire population with minimum protection from catastrophic
expenditures. 4/   Such a program was proposed in the 94th
Congress as part of the Catastrophic Health Program and
Medical Assistance Reform Act (S. 2470). The numbers of
persons aided and the cost would depend upon the choice of
eligibility levels and the benefit package. If a program
similar to the most generous state plans now underway were
chosen, an estimated 35 million persons would receive
benefits; about one-third of these would be people who at
present are uninsured.

The added cost of such a program would be $17 billion
in fiscal year 1978 and $24 billion in fiscal year 1982. If
states were required to maintain their current levels of
contributions, new federal costs would amount to $7.2
billion in fiscal year 1978.

4/   Spend-down eligibility under medicaid means that a
     family becomes eligible for medicaid benefits when its
     expenditures for medical services reduce its income to
     the level at which a family is normally entitled to join
     the program.

Long-Term Care

Federal, state, and local governments spent $5.1 billion in 1975 on long-term medical and social services for chronically disabled, mostly elderly, persons. While these expenditures are large and have risen threefold in the past five years, an estimated 0.8 to 1.4 million of the aged and disabled who need such long-term care do not receive it. They are kept from getting care not only by lack of finances but also because of the fragmented organization of long-term care.

One option for increasing federal aid in this area is through a consolidated long-term care block grant for nursing home and community services. Such a grant would funnel all long-term care funds through a single local agency which would be responsible for arranging for care in the community. The emphasis is on an improved organization of services, not necessarily on increased financing. While pressures to increase funding to meet demand would undoubtedly exist, federal expenditures could be controlled by the authorization and appropriation processes. If a grant equal to present long-term care spending plus roughly $1 billion were created, from 120,000 to 150,000 more people in need of long-term care services could get them.

Alternatively, a long-term care entitlement program that would include congregate housing and home health care would meet the potential demand for long-term care, but at a substantial cost. If such a program were phased in to permit the supply of housing and other services to grow, the incremental federal cost would be between $16 billion and $22 billion by 1982. Similar bills were introduced in the 94th Congress (S. 2702 and H.R. 2268).

Catastrophic Health Insurance

Catastrophic health costs are those that are either extremely large or are high relative to a family's resources. Such expenses usually arise from one of three causes: long-term care; moderate expenses incurred by low-income families; and the rare, extremely high-cost treatments that exceed the limits of an otherwise adequate insurance policy. There have been a number of recent proposals to protect all Americans against catastrophic expenditures. These include the Long-Ribicoff Bill (S. 2470) introduced in the 94th Congress, the Ford Administration's 1978 budget proposal for catastrophic benefits, and tax credit plans such as that proposed by Senator Brock (S. 1528) in the 94th Congress.

The cost of a catastrophic insurance plan depends upon the problem it tries to address. The long-term care and federalized medicaid proposals discussed earlier would provide protection against the first two sources of catastrophic expenditures. A plan for just the third problem -- unusually high expenses -- might involve payment of hospital care after the 150th day and nonhospital medical expenses that exceed $2,000 for the nonmedicare population. If such a plan were fully financed by the federal government, it would cost between $10 and $11 billion in fiscal year 1978.

A plan that met all health expenses over a certain percent of family income, say 15 percent, would cost about $16 billion in fiscal year 1978. Because such a plan would encourage a decrease in basic insurance coverage, it could decrease national health expenditures by $0.5 billion.

A catastrophic protection plan that covered long-term care, all expenses for low-income families, and unusually high expenditures would cost between $70 and $75 billion in fiscal year 1978. Such a plan would be similar to many of the national health insurance proposals and should be compared to other comprehensive alternatives.

Comprehensive National Health Insurance

While it is not realistic to envision passage of a national health insurance bill in time to affect the fiscal year 1978 budget, it is important to consider the possible impact of such a program if adopted in the next several years. A comprehensive national health insurance program could be wholly tax-financed and publicly administered; tax-financed but privately administered; or a voluntary or compulsory, mixed public and private system that covered the working population through employment-based insurance. N7 The federal budgetary impact of national health insurance depends on four factors: whether the plan is financed primarily through taxes or premiums, how broad a range of benefits is provided, how much of the costs beneficiaries would have to share, and the plan's cost control features.

A totally tax-financed plan with no cost-sharing for covered services could add from $168 to $200 billion to federal health expenditures by fiscal year 1982; in contrast, a compulsory employment-based, premium-financed plan with cost-sharing might increase federal spending by as little as $15 to $20 billion in 1982. The range of these cost estimates reflects the varying assumptions about the effectiveness of cost controls. While a tax-financed plan would lower revenues lost through health tax expenditures, a premium-financed plan would raise them.   Of course, private spending on health care would fall under all these plans but probably not as much as the rise in government outlays.

Because of the great costs of comprehensive insurance, the Congress may want to consider proposals that would slowly introduce national health insurance.   Among the plans that have been suggested for phasing in benefits are a catastrophic insurance plan, federalized medicaid, or a program for maternal and child health services (popularly known as kiddiecare).

CONCLUSION

In addition to options for phasing in national health insurance, the 95th Congress is likely to concentrate on cost control. The proportion of public and private expenditures now devoted to health is already great.   And the impact of increased health spending on inflation is likely to make cost controls the key criterion in evaluating any national health insurance proposal.

Control of health prices through insurance reimbursement is more difficult when there are multiple sources of funding. Purchasing power is now divided between public and private third-party reimbursement and consumer out-of-pocket spending.   This reduces and fragments the leverage that can be exerted on provider charges.   A single program covering the entire population could offer the greatest potential for controlling health costs.   It could do this by establishing hospital budgets and professional fee schedules in advance.   If that potential were not fully realized, however, a tax-financed public plan could be far more inflationary than the present mixed system.

NOTES AND REFERENCES

1. Three bills, similar to the prototype plans for national health insurance described in this section of the text by Dr. Alice Rivlin, were introduced in the 94th Congress. They were: (1) targeted approach: Long-Ribicoff/Waggonner; (2) comprehensive premium financed: Ullman; and (3) comprehensive tax financed: Kennedy-Corman. The statements of these legislative sponsors on their respective bills appear in Chapter 1, and further analyses of the three bills is provided in Appendix 2 of this volume.
2. The 1974 HEW report referred to by Dr. Stuart Altman is reprinted in [2].
3. The 1976 "new" estimates, referred to by Dr. Stuart Altman, were released in October 1976 in a report prepared for HEW by Gordon R. Trapnell Associates. An executive summary ([1]) of the Trapnell report appears later in this chapter.
4. The Nixon-Ford administrations' 1974 legislative proposal, (CHIP) the Comprehensive Health Insurance Program (S. 2970/H.R. 12684), was presented in the 93rd Congress on behalf of the Ford administration by Senator Bob Packwood and Repre-

sentative Herman Schneebeli. It was not reintroduced in the 94th Congress. Further information on CHIP is provided later in this chapter.

5. A review of the health care system of Australia and a summary chart of health care in New Zealand appears in Chapter 3.

6. Bridger Mitchell is referring to the February 24, 1976 testimony of Joseph Newhouse of the Rand Corporation (see [23], pp. 1100–1155). Mr. Newhouse discussed the relationship between cost sharing and cost containment.

7. For a description of proposals introduced in the 94th Congress, see *National Health Insurance Proposals: Provisions of the Bills Introduced in the 94th Congress,* prepared by the Social Security Administration in 1976. Descriptions of the major national health insurance proposals introduced in the 94th Congress appear in Appendix 2 of this volume.

Chapter 3
Health Insurance in Other Countries

Discussion and debate on the future of health care in the United States frequently includes reference to the relative position of this country with regard to infant mortality, longevity, or other indicators of the adequacy of the health care system. The success or failure of the systems of other countries serves to provide a useful guide in the shaping of a new American approach to health care. Most industrialized nations have some type of national health insurance program, and some have had many years of experience. The manner in which nine of those countries have organized the financing and delivery of health services is presented in Chapter 3. The text has been drawn from the House Committee on Ways and Means' *National Health Insurance Resource Book* ([34]) and an HEW publication, *National Health Systems in Eight Countries* ([11]).

INTRODUCTION ([34], p. 293)

In nearly every major industrialized country throughout the world, National Governments have assumed increasing responsibility for the provision and financing of health care to their citizenry. Many authorities in the health field have suggested that the experiences of these nations in the operation of their health care programs may reveal valuable insights for the United States. In the course of recent deliberations over national health insurance legislation, Members of Congress and the American public have expressed a growing interest in foreign health care systems and their possible relevance to this country.

Because the characteristics of each foreign system are largely a response to that country's unique social and political setting, no one system as a whole can be readily transferrable to another nation. Differences in social, economic, and governmental institutions, political philosophies, national priorities, modes of living, geographic and environmental conditions, inevitably limit to some extent the relevance and validity of any broad-scale international comparisons. In addition to these factors, there is a significant lack of sufficient comparable data on costs, utilization, conditions of practice, and public acceptability under the various systems.

Therefore, this report on the health care systems of selected foreign countries is intended only as a factual description of the main elements of each country's program—the people covered, the scope of benefits, the methods of financing and administration, and the mechanisms used to reimburse providers of health services. No attempt has been made to evaluate the relative success, effectiveness, or merits of the various programs, or to isolate aspects of each country's program which might be relevant to the United States. That process is up to the reader.

SUMMARY CHARTS ([11], pp. 1–8)

AUSTRALIA

Subject	Provisions
General concept and approach............	Voluntary nonprofit private hospital and medical insurance with Federal Government subsidies for medical benefits, hospital costs, and pharmaceuticals. Involves cost sharing by patient for medical services and prescription drugs.
Coverage of the population..............	All residents are eligible. Insurance fund membership necessary to obtain most Federal subsidies. At least 90 percent of population is covered by the program or other government arrangements.
Benefit structure......................	Comprehensive health benefits, drugs, and nursing-home care. Cost sharing required for most medical services. Most prescriptions filled for $1 fee. Basic hospital insurance generally covers all hospitalization charges. Low-income population eligible for subsidies toward insurance premiums.
Administration.........................	Insurance coverage administered by registered private carriers according to Federal regulations. Hospitals are administered by States through local semiautonomous boards.
Relationship to other government programs	The Pensioners Medical Service program provides free health care to about 90 percent of the pensioners. Health services in the Northern Territory and Australian Capital Territory are operated outside private insurance system by Federal Government. Cash sickness benefits are payable to gainfully employed persons earning less than $37 a week (about a third of the average wage).1/
Financing..............................	Medical and hospital insurance is financed through voluntary tax deductible premiums (about 2 percent of the average wage). Insurance benefits combined with government contributions from general revenue and with cost sharing to pay providers. Local and central government funds required to support hospitals and pharmaceutical programs.
Standards and controls.................	Standards for public hospitals are established by States. Voluntary fee schedule for medical services is determined by Federal negotiations with medical profession.
Reimbursement of providers of services...	Physicians: Usually paid directly by patient who then applies for partial reimbursement from his insurance fund. After reimbursement patient's residual cost cannot exceed $5 unless bill is more than schedule fee. Forty-four percent of typical fee paid by Federal grant, 37 percent by insurance, and 19 percent by patient. Specialists receive higher fees for identical services. Hospitals: Same procedure as for physicians to obtain insurance payment. $2 government subsidy also paid hospital on a per capita basis. Staff physicians are salaried employees. Half of hospitals' budgets funded by State revenues.
Costs..................................	State and Federal revenues cover more than one-half of total national health expenditures (including public health provisions) and along with insurance benefits leave less than a third to be paid by out-of-pocket payments of the patient.

1/ 1 Australian dollar equals U.S. $1.32.

Note: The Government has announced a new universal health care delivery system to be introduced in July 1975 which would provide free hospitalization and more of the cost of medical services. As of April 1975, many of the details were still not determined.

CANADA

Subject	Provisions
General concept and approach............	Provincial hospitalization and medical care programs which vary somewhat according to Province. The national government sets minimum requirements for the plans and provides grants to the Provinces for approximately 50 percent of the costs.
Coverage of the population..............	All residents are eligible. Coverage must be portable while temporarily out of the Province or country. 99 percent of population is covered.
Benefit structure......................	Physicians: All medically required services rendered by a physician without dollar limit or exclusions. Some cost sharing may be involved. Hospital: All usual inpatient services and extensive outpatient services in a few Provinces. Nursing home and home care, dental and drugs: Optional at expense of Province, generally not provided
Administration.........................	Provincial public health departments or medical care insurance commissions and hospital commissions. Federal Department of National Health and Welfare administers grants to Provinces and offers consultative services.
Relationship to other government programs	Special national programs for needy persons, seamen, Indians, and Eskimos for services not otherwise covered. Unemployment benefits available if unable to work due to sickness, injury, or maternity.
Financing..............................	Medical care: Federal Government contributes 50 percent of the national per capita cost of insured medical care services, multiplied by the average number of insured persons in the Province. Provinces finance the remaining 50 percent principally by general revenues, but a few also impose premiums. In Quebec, an income tax surcharge is used on employees with a matching levy on employers. Hospital care: Federal grants to Provinces for approximately 50 percent of cost of operation (25 percent based on national per capita cost of covered services and 25 percent based on that Province's per capital cost). Provinces finance the remaining 50 percent mainly through general revenues with some Provinces raising a portion of needed funds through premiums.
Standards and controls.................	Set by Provinces. Federal Health and Welfare Ministry provides consultative services on request by the Province.
Reimbursement of providers of services...	Physicians: Direct billing to the provincial plans which usually have fee schedules. There are variations by Province. A doctor may bill the patient directly and the patient must then seek reimbursement. Provincial payments usually cover 85-90 percent of fee for service as stipulated in schedule. Any charges by physician exceeding this level must be paid by patient. Hospitals: Based on annual budgets for individual institutions negotiated with provincial boards. Semimonthly lump-sum payments to cover fixed costs plus a slight margin of excess. Additional payments, based on per diem rates, for slightly less than the variable costs. Capital expenditures or service on capital debt is not compensated.
Costs..................................	Health planning and research: The Provinces have active groups, and the ability to control hospital operating budgets and professional fee reimbursement. Construction: Federal and Provincial grants cover about 20 percent of cost of approved projects. Several Provinces have made provisions to assume the financial burden of new and old construction totally. Local communities must finance the balance. Manpower training: Federal Government will pay up to 50 percent of approved projects to construct teaching and research facilities. Public funds account for nearly three-fourths of total national health expenditures.

FEDERAL REPUBLIC OF GERMANY

Subject	Provisions
General concept and approach.............	Decentralized health insurance system under government regulation which covers virtually all medical expenses of covered population, as well as extensive income replacement during illness.
Coverage of the population...............	About 90 percent of population is covered. Membership is obligatory for all manual workers and for self-employed and white collar workers earning below a stipulated ceiling (DM 22,500 per year).1/
Benefit structure........................	Comprehensive medical and dental services including hospital care and drugs. Nominal cost-sharing element principally for prescriptions and dental work. Cash benefits amount to 75–85 percent of wages if illness extends beyond 6 weeks; before that time employer must pay full wages.
Administration...........................	General supervision by Ministry of Health. Administration of contributions and benefits by 1,900 sickness funds. Funds organized mainly on a geographical basis, managed by elected representatives of insured persons and employers, and united into State and national federations.
Relationship to other government programs.	No other significant program other than government arrangements for welfare recipients and war victims. Under regular program, old-age pensioners are assessed reduced premiums which are paid by the pension funds. Miners also receive special benefits.
Financing................................	Both medical care and cash benefits under the system are financed by payroll contributions averaging about 9 percent of wages (half is paid by employer and half by employee).
Standards and controls...................	Ministry of health sets standards for physicians and hospitals. Regional Physicians' Associations monitor their members for overcharging or overprescribing.
Reimbursement of providers of service.....	Physicians: Physicians' payments derived from lump-sum fund negotiated on a quarterly basis between Regional Physicians' Associations and Sickness Funds. Each physician receives a varying share of lump sum, depending on services provided members, weighted according to national standard fee schedule guidelines. Hospitals: Hospitals are paid directly by Sickness Funds on flat rate per patient-day basis negotiated according to government guidelines. Hospital physicians are normally salaried employees.
Costs....................................	In addition to cash benefits, the governmental health insurance system pays for virtually all of the real cost of members' medical care, or about 60 percent of the total national health bill. In addition, the Government, mainly through its public health efforts and hospital subsidies, pays for about a fourth of total national health expenditures.

1/ 1 mark equals U.S. 40 cents.

FRANCE

Subject	Provisions
General concept and approach.............	A national health insurance system, supervised by the Ministry of Public Health and Social Security and administered through local sickness funds.
Coverage of the population..............	Over 98 percent of the population is covered under the national health insurance system or other specialized governmental systems.
Benefit structure.......................	Medical and hospital benefits provide the individual with partial reimbursement of ordinary expenses (physicians' fees, hospital costs, dental care, and prescription drugs) and full coverage for the expenses of costly or prolonged illness. Cash sickness benefits are paid for up to 3 years and cash maternity benefits for up to 14 weeks. Some additional income maintenance comes from family allowances.
Administration..........................	Registration of insured, payment of cash benefits, and reimbursement of medical expenses are primarily administered by 122 Primary (local) Sickness Insurance Funds, coordinated by 16 Regional Funds under a National Sickness Insurance Fund. Each level subject to governing boards with representatives appointed from labor and management. Entire health care delivery is under the general supervision of the Ministry of Social Affairs.
Relationship to other government programs	Sizable special systems for agricultural employees, miners, and others with somewhat different financing and benefit levels. Additional income maintenance from family allowances which continue during illness.
Financing..............................	Costs are basically met through payroll contributions, which for the average worker total 3.5 percent of his earnings and an additional 12.45 percent from his employer. These funds not only support medical care and cash benefits but also disability benefits. In addition, social security covers health care expenses of pensioners who are exempt from contributions. System has often required transfers from other revenue sources to bring its operations into balance.
Standards and controls..................	Physicians are subject to standards established by professional associations. Private hospitals and pharmaceutical must meet prescribed standards set by the Government and insurance mechanisms to qualify for reimbursement of fees.
Reimbursement of providers of services...	Physicians: Both generalists and specialists, as well as dentists and pharmacists, are generally paid by the patient who then receives partial reimbursement from the insurance system according to a fee-for-service schedule or pharmaceutical reimbursement lists. Hospitals: Fees are usually composed of a basic daily rate approved by local authorities plus the charge for physicians' services as set down in the fee-for-service schedule. These fees are usually paid directly by the insurance system to the hospital, except for the deductible which is paid in most cases by the patient. Most hospitals are public institutions but a number of privately owned hospitals also adhere to the agreed rate structure. Public hospital physicians are salaried. Those attached to private hospitals ordinarily receive payment directly on a fee-for-service basis.
Costs...................................	The social security health insurance programs pay about 60 percent of the nation's total personal health care costs and the private individual pays about a third through cost sharing directly and through premiums to mutual societies.

NETHERLANDS

Subject	Provisions
General concept and approach............	A governmental insurance plan designed to cover most of the population, except for higher income brackets. Parallel systems cover the whole population for catastrophic illness and all workers for cash sickness benefits.
Coverage of the population..............	70 percent of population is covered for ordinary medical care. On a compulsory basis membership includes workers earning below a stipulated ceiling and their families. Voluntary membership is open to self-employed and pensioners with income below the ceiling. Entire population covered for catastrophic costs and special medical care. Whole working population also covered for cash sickness and maternity benefits.
Benefit structure......................	Insured receives comprehensive medical and dental services including hospital care, nursing home care, and drugs. Whole population, in cases of catastrophic illness, is generally entitled to full cost of medical care after 1 year of illness and for certain types of institutional care before that time. Cash benefits amount to 80 percent replacement of earnings for an unlimited time.
Administration.........................	Administered by about 90 private insurance funds under supervision of Government's Sickness Funds Council.
Relationship to other government programs	Special system for miners, railway employees, seamen, and public employees. Cash sickness pays for every incapacity during first year, including work-connected illness and those which elsewhere would be covered by disability pensions. Some additional income maintenance comes from family allowances.
Financing..............................	Employers and the insured each contribute 4.75 percent of earnings. An additional 2.6 percent is paid by employer for catastrophic coverage. These funds are essentially adequate to finance all medical care extended to the insured. Minor subsidies are paid by the Government to help defray the cost of medical care for pensioners and low-income groups. Cash benefits are financed by payroll contributions of 1 percent by employee and 6.4 percent by employer on earnings up to a stipulated ceiling.
Standards and controls.................	The sickness funds keep statistics on prescription practices by the physicians and on referrals of patients to specialists. In cases where significantly above-average frequencies or cost in either category can be attributed to a physician's practice the funds' medical adviser may ask the practitioner for an explanation and, in some instances, funds may impose fines or suspensions. Medical complaints against physicians may be lodged with the Netherlands Medical Association. Although most hospitals are private their operations are subject to review by a variety of governmental authorities; expansion is controlled by the central government.
Reimbursement of providers of services...	Reimbursement procedures for physicians cover a wide spectrum of methods: General practitioners are paid on a capitation basis, while specialists are reimbursed by methods utilizing salary, fee-for-service, or case-payment approaches. Some of these procedures have been devised in an effort to discourage prolonged and unnecessary treatment of the patient.. The typical hospital is a private institution paid directly by a sickness fund primarily utilizing a schedule of fees set by the Union of Hospital Associations under government guidelines, but also taking into account annual budget considerations of the specific hospital. Some hospitals bill separately for hospital physicians' services.
Costs..................................	Virtually all of the nation's total medical costs are covered by health insurance expenditures, except for routine medical expenses of 30 percent of population not covered by system and small cost-sharing element. Government subsidies total about 13 percent of insurance expenditures and remainder comes from payroll contributions. In combination, public insurance and other public funds pay for more than two-thirds of the nation's total health bill. Cash benefits are financed entirely from payroll contributions.

NEW ZEALAND

Subject	Provisions
General concept and approach.............	The national health care system of New Zealand is based on a public hospital service and subsidized treatment by private medical practitioners.
Coverage of the population...............	All residents and their dependents are covered.
Benefit structure........................	Medical benefits include physician care, hospital care, most prescription drugs, laboratory and X-ray work, and prosthetic devices. Dental care is provided to children under age 16. The patient, however, normally pays a significant part of the cost particularly for treatment by physicians who in most cases are private practitioners. Employed workers with limited income are eligible for cash sickness benefits which are administered by the Department of Social Welfare. A cash maternity benefit, which is also income-tested, is payable to employed women 3 months before and after confinement.
Administration...........................	The system is administered by the Department of Health and 30 elected hospital boards.
Relationship to other government programs	A nominal amount of hospital care covering work-connected illness is financed by the Workmen's Compensation Board.
Financing................................	The government's health program is financed entirely out of general revenue. The total cost of those medical services paid directly by the patient is equal to slightly more than a fourth of the total amount spent by the nation on health.
Standards and controls...................	Department of Health carries out 1 percent postal check on physician claims. Medical health officers review physicians' practices to determine whether there are excessive consultations and overprescribing.
Reimbursement of providers of services...	Physicians' fees are not controlled, but the flat-rate government payment toward each patient consultation is fixed. The general practitioner normally bills the Department of Health directly for this amount and the patient pays the difference. Most private specialists are paid in full by their patients who then seek the fixed-government payment from the Department of Health. Physicians employed by public hospitals are paid on a salaried basis. Over 80 percent of the hospital beds are in publicly owned institutions where both inpatient and outpatient care are provided free. Such hospitals receive budgetary allotments for current expenses and large capital expenses are met by government-guaranteed public loans. Private hospitals receive various forms of public financial support, most notably a subsidy for each occupied bed, thereby reducing the amount that must be charged to the patient.
Costs....................................	Estimated government expenditures pay for slightly less than three-fourths of the nation's total health costs.

SWEDEN

Subject	Provisions
General concept and approach............	A modified health insurance system relying heavily upon facilities funded and operated by various levels of government. The system provides nearly all necessary and medical services to the whole population, but involves a significant degree of cost sharing by the patient for ambulatory care.
Coverage of the population..............	Health insurance is compulsory for all residents. Coverage for cash sickness benefits includes virtually all gainfully employed and, on a voluntary basis, most housewives and students.
Benefit structure......................	All necessary medical and hospital services with a newly expanded dental care program. Includes nursing home coverage and a well-developed system of home nursing and home help arrangements. Cash sickness benefits of unlimited duration generally pay about 90 percent of earnings to the typical worker.
Administration..........................	Much of the administrative work connected with benefits and contributions is performed by about 600 government-operated local funds which are also active in other areas of social insurance. The local funds are supervised by 26 regional offices under a National Social Insurance Board and the Ministry of Health and Social Affairs. Operation and fiscal management of health facilities are mainly by local county governments with planning shared with the central government.
Relationship to other government programs	Health insurance is administered as part of overall social insurance. Local governments are directly responsible for providing most health services.
Financing..............................	Compulsory contributions to health insurance by insured are paid along with income tax. (Approximately 2 percent of earnings from average worker and an additional 3.8 percent of earnings paid by his employer.) However, health insurance funds pay for only about 10 percent of the total national health bill. The rest comes primarily from general revenues and cost sharing. About 70 percent of health insurance funds are utilized to pay for cash benefits.
Standards and controls.................	Standards for health services provided by local governments regulated by national statutes. National planning provides for norms and standards of new and expanded facilities. Patients may lodge complaints with Ombudsmen who act as watchdog committee for Parliament.
Reimbursement of providers of services...	Physicians: Most physicians are salaried as public employees either in district medical offices principally in rural areas or as hospital staff. Patient pays 12 kronor for each visit and health insurance pays local government 48 kronor.[1] About a fourth of ambulatory care is provided by private physicians who are paid directly by patient who in turn receives partial reimbursement from the insurance system. Hospitals: Hospitals are financed by the county budgets. Inpatient hospital services are essentially free to the patient but the health insurance system pays 15 kronor per day on his behalf.
Costs..................................	Health insurance funds play a relatively small role in meeting total national health costs. Local and central government funds pay for most of the remainder. Somewhat less than a fifth of the total is met by patient fees.

[1] 1 krona equals U.S. 23 cents.

UNITED KINGDOM

Subject	Provisions
General concept and approach..............	Universal health care delivery system through a national health service.
Coverage of the population...............	All residents are eligible. Visitors are also eligible in most instances.
Benefit structure........................	Comprehensive medical care including drugs and dental care. Small amount of cost sharing for prescriptions and dental treatment. Extended-care facilities under expansion. Home nursing care services provided under public health features of program.
Administration...........................	Overall supervision by Department of Health and Social Security. On April 1, 1974, a unified scheme replaced three separate jurisdictions for (1) physician and allied services, (2) hospital services (including specialist treatment), and (3) public health programs.
Relationship to other government programs	None for medical care. Public health features are more important than in most countries particularly with respect to home nursing. Cash benefit program is administered separately as part of overall pension branch of social security. (A typical worker making the average wage is entitled to a benefit corresponding to about 70 percent of his wages.)
Financing................................	System is financed mainly by general revenue. Approximately 15 percent is financed by cost-sharing features and weekly payroll contributions. The small compulsory flat-rate contributions amount to 0.18 pound weekly for a male worker and about 0.08 pound from his employer (totaling less than 1 percent of the typical worker's wage).1/
Standards and controls...................	The Department of Health and Social Security supervises hospitals through Area Health Authorities. Physicians' standards are supervised by the Area Authorities and Family Practitioner Committees. Their prescribing procedures are subject to special scrutiny by Regional Medical Officers.
Reimbursement of providers of services....	Physician receives payment on capitation basis with supplements. Specialists are normally salaried hospital employees. Hospitals are governmental institutions with budgets funded from government appropriations.
Costs....................................	The National Health Service finances, including receipts from cost sharing, account for at least 90 percent of total national health care costs. There is still a small private medical sector which accounts for a large part of the remainder.

1/ 1 pound equals U.S. $2.32.

NATIONAL HEALTH SYSTEMS

Canada ([34], pp. 295–321)

INTRODUCTION

Canada's national health insurance program consists of two distinct parts—a hospital and outpatient diagnostic services plan and a medical care plan covering primarily physicians' services. The two parts of the program were developed and enacted separately almost 10 years apart. Separate and different arrangements between the Federal Government in Ottawa and the various Provinces govern the operation of each plan.

Prior to development of its hospital and medical insurance plans, Canada had embarked on several programs which were to prove to be precursors of a nationwide system of health insurance. In 1948, the Federal Government had introduced a program of National Health Grants, offering support for a wide range of Provincial health services, including health planning, public health measures, hospital construction, and professional medical training. The activities supported by these grants-in-aid to the Provinces were regarded as fundamental prerequisites to a national health insurance program.

At about the same time, several Provinces began to establish government sponsored hospital and medical insurance plans. By the time the Federal hospital insurance program was enacted in 1957, four Provinces had instituted Provincial hospital programs, a factor which "undoubtedly . . . helped to pave the way for development of a national health insurance program and (contributed to) its being placed on a Federal-Provincial basis." [1]

During the post-World War II period, Canada had also experienced a rapid growth of voluntary health insurance plans, a development which may have temporarily decreased interest in a government-sponsored national health insurance program. By the end of 1954, an estimated 3.6 million Canadians were covered for hospital insurance under various nonprofit plans and 3.2 million under insurance company plans. An additional 2.7 million people were covered by nonprofit medical care plans (typically "physician-sponsored" plans somewhat similar to Blue Shield plans in the United States), with about 1.3 million of those insured having comprehensive coverage. Another 2.9 million were covered by insurance companies for surgical benefits and 1.5 million for medical (nonsurgical) benefits. All in all, about 9 million people, or somewhat over half of the total population, had some form of private health insurance coverage.

In the years preceding passage of the Federal Medical Care Act in 1966, a number of Provinces introduced government-sponsored medical care insurance plans. In 1962, Saskatchewan established a universal, compulsory, publicly operated medical insurance plan. Over the next four years, three other Provinces (Alberta, British Columbia, and Ontario) began operating voluntary subsidized medical insurance schemes.[2] By the end of 1966, an estimated 80.1 percent (16.2 million) of the Canadian population was covered for medical expenses under a combination of voluntary health insurance plans (insurance company

---

[1] Louis Reed, "The Canadian Hospital Insurance Program." Public Health Reports, Feb. 1962: 93.

[2] For an overview of the development of these Provincial medical insurance plans, see "Medical Services Insurance: The Next Phase in Canada's National Health Program," by Frederick D. Mott, M.D., Medical Care Review, July and August, 1967.

plans, physician-sponsored plans, employer or union-sponsored plans, cooperative plans, and plans offered through government agencies) and miscellaneous plans (including the compulsory Saskatchewan medical care plan, social assistance plans, and plans for the Armed Forces, Indians, and Eskimos).[3]

Hospital Insurance Program [4]

In 1957, the Canadian Government enacted the Hospital Insurance and Diagnostic Services Act, under which the Federal Government agreed to bear approximately half the cost of Provincial programs for the provision of general hospital care to their populations. The act came into effect on July 1, 1958, with five Provinces having signed participating agreements. By January 1, 1961, the last of the Provinces had programs underway. Under the terms of the Federal legislation, each participating Province is required to make insured services available to all its residents on uniform terms and conditions, without exclusion on grounds of age, income, or preexisting conditions. Residents of the Province are defined as those persons legally entitled to remain in Canada who make their homes and are ordinarily present in the Province.

COVERAGE

By the end of 1974, all or virtually all of the net population of each Canadian Province was entitled to receive insured hospital services. The "net population" of Canada reached almost 22 million in 1974; this figure excludes members of the Armed Forces, the Royal Canadian Mounted Police, and inmates of penitentiaries, who are not entitled to receive insured services, their medical care being otherwise provided for.

Coverage is automatic or compulsory in most Provinces. In the case of Ontario, coverage is mandatory for employee groups of 15 or more, and it remains voluntary for the rest of the population. Persons living in Alberta may "opt-out" on a yearly basis, but such choice affects coverage under both the hospital and medical insurance plans.

Provisions governing the coverage of immigrants vary from Province to Province. Some provide coverage from the day of arrival, while others may require a 3-month waiting period. Canadian residents who move to another Province are covered for at least 2 months (subsequently the individual qualifies for benefits in the new Province).

BENEFITS

Federal law requires that certain specified benefits be covered under any Provincial plan participating in the hospital insurance program. All 10 Provinces and the Northwest and Yukon Territories provide the following as insured patient benefits:

---

[3] C. Howard Shillington, "The Road to Medicare in Canada." Del Graphics Publishing Dept., Toronto, 1972: 200.

[4] Due to the fact that the hospital and medical care insurance programs were enacted almost 10 years apart, and that, at the present time, the two programs are still administered and financed through separate and different arrangements, this report is subdivided into two main sections—the first section dealing with the hospital program, the second with the Federal-Provincial medical care plans.

(1) Accommodation and meals at the standard ward level.
(2) Necessary nursing service.
(3) Laboratory and diagnostic services.
(4) Drugs and biologicals.
(5) Use of operating and case room and anesthetic facilities.
(6) Routine surgical supplies.
(7) Use of radiotherapy and physiotherapy facilities where available.

Excluded from coverage are services provided in tuberculosis and mental hospitals and custodial institutions. Most Provinces cover directly, or under their hospital insurance programs at their own expense, benefits for tuberculosis and mental hospital care, and home care; such services are not presently eligible for cost-sharing with the Federal Government. Nursing home care is also not ordinarily a benefit. Ontario is an exception in this regard, since it does extend such benefits when medically necessary, subject to a daily copayment levied on the patient. Alberta covers services provided in "auxiliary hospitals" where the patient's stay exceeds 120 days, subject to a $3 a day copayment after the 120th day; such extended care is presumably closer to that provided in skilled nursing homes than in active treatment hospitals.

To the required benefits may be added, by separate agreements between the Federal and Provincial Governments, specified outpatient and emergency services. Provinces are free to choose which, if any, outpatient services they will provide as insured services. All Provinces include emergency services and
N2 outpatient followup and a varying list of other outpatient benefits. . . .

Federal law does not prohibit Provinces from imposing authorized charges on patients for insured services, so long as such cost-sharing does not deter patients, particularly low-income persons, from obtaining needed care. As of 1974, however, only three plans (those operating in British Columbia, Alberta, and the Northwest Territories) utilized patient cost-sharing—in these cases, in the form of nominal daily copayments for inpatient hospital care.

Although participation has been extremely reduced as a result of the government health insurance plans, private health insurance organizations continue to offer coverage for a variety of services supplemental to, or not insured under, the government plans. The extent of participation and the nature of the benefits provided under these private plans is described in the section of this report dealing with benefits under the Federal-Provincial Medical Care Plans.

ADMINISTRATION

The Federal law allowed the Provinces to make their own determinations with regard to the method to be used for administration of the hospital plan. Each Province was required, however, to designate a Provincial authority charged with direct administrative responsibility for the plan. In no case did a Province utilize private health insurance carriers for any type of intermediary administrative function (in contrast, several Provinces were later to make use, at least on a temporary basis, of private carriers for various functions under the medical insurance plans). By the end of fiscal year 1974, six Provinces and two Territories were using departmental administration (either directly through the Provincial ministry of health or through a divison of the Provincial department of health) and four (Alberta, Manitoba, Nova Scotia, and Prince Edward Island) were administering the plan through separate public commissions.

The Federal Government does not share with the Provinces any administrative costs incurred under the Provincial plans. In 1966, the administrative expenses of the 10 Provinces totaled $12,200,000, equal to 1.1 percent of the total expenditures for hospital care under their programs. Administrative expenses as a percentage of benefit expense ranged from 0.37 percent in Alberta to 3.49 percent in Manitoba. In general, the administrative expense ratios were higher in those Provinces that raised some of the funds for their programs through premiums. In these Provinces, administrative expenses include the cost of collecting premiums. The following table for fiscal 1966 shows for each Province the total expenditures for hospital care, the administrative expense, the ratio of administrative to hospitalization expense, and administrative expense per capita of the Provincial population.

Canada: Administrative expense of hospital insurance, 1966 [1]

Fiscal year ending—	Province	Total hospitalization expense	Administrative expense	Ratio administrative to hospital expense (percent)	Net population 1966	Per capita administrative expense
Mar. 31	British Columbia	$76,207,739	$635,608	0.83	1,862,000	$0.34
Do	Alberta	77,503,057	286,826	.37	1,447,000	.20
Dec. 31	Saskatchewan	57,405,592	1,045,369	1.82	950,000	1.10
Do	Manitoba	53,352,178	1,859,764	3.49	952,000	1.95
Do	Ontario	392,592,994	6,015,426	1.53	6,783,000	.88
Mar. 31	Quebec	351,209,381	1,576,200	.45	5,744,000	.27
Do	New Brunswick	28,996,680	270,724	.93	620,000	.44
Do	Nova Scotia	33,720,157	239,497	.71	742,000	.32
Dec. 31	Prince Edward Island	4,251,047	131,707	3.10	107,000	1.23
Mar. 31	Newfoundland	23,562,380	160,000	.68	504,000	.32
Total, all Provinces		1,098,801,205	12,221,121	1.11	19,801,000	.62
Federal Government			470,000			
Total Federal Provincial Programs		1,098,801,205	12,691,121	1.15	19,801,600	.64

[1] Annual Report 1973–74, Hospital Insurance and Diagnostic Services, for fiscal year ended Mar. 31, 1974. Department of National Health and Welfare, Ottawa, Canada, 1974: 41.

Source: Prepared by Office of Research and Statistics, Social Security Administration, U.S. Department of Health, Education, and Welfare, Nov. 7, 1968, Research and Statistics note No. 21–1968.

FINANCING

The Government of Canada contributes out of consolidated revenues approximately 50 percent of the net operating costs of each Provincial hospital insurance plan, based on a formula which gives special help to the poorer Provinces. Federal contributions are calculated on the basis of the following formula: the sum of 25 percent of the per capita cost of inpatient services in Canada as a whole, and 25 percent of the per capita cost of inpatient services in the Province, multiplied by the average number of insured persons in that Province. In addition, the Federal Government contributes with respect to outpatient services an amount that is in the same proportion to the cost of these services (less any authorized charges) as the amount contributed for inpatient services is to the cost of inpatient services. As one authority has noted:

> The effect of the formula is that high-cost Provinces receive a lower percentage of their costs from the Federal Government than do the low-cost Provinces. The inclusion in the formula of the national per capita cost acts as a deterrent to the high-cost Provinces, since

the more that Provincial costs exceed the national costs, the lower will be the percentage of the Federal contributions.[5]

The following tables indicate the cost of inpatient services for 1971, for Canada as a whole and by individual Province, and the contributions by the Federal Government for insured inpatient services based on the formula explained above.

Cost of inpatient services, 1971, net population, June 1, 1971; total and 25 percent per capita cost, 1971, by Province [1]

Province	Cost of inpatient services, 1971	Net population June 1, 1971	Per capita cost, 1971	
			Total	25 percent
Newfoundland	$37, 921, 239	521, 040	$72. 7799	$18. 1950
Prince Edward Island	7, 909, 800	110, 357	71. 6747	17. 9187
Nova Scotia	66, 674, 542	774, 018	86. 1408	21. 5352
New Brunswick	56, 889, 281	628, 334	90. 5399	22. 6350
Quebec	671, 829, 017	6, 012, 446	111. 7397	27. 9349
Ontario	804, 768, 804	7, 670, 746	104. 9140	26. 2285
Manitoba	90, 529, 069	981, 365	92. 2481	23. 0620
Saskatchewan	84, 736, 939	922, 322	91. 8735	22. 9684
Alberta	163, 067, 437	1, 617, 198	100. 8333	25. 2083
British Columbia	188, 086, 958	2, 171, 668	86. 6094	21. 6524
Yukon	1, 093, 742	18, 333	59. 6597	14. 9149
Northwest Territories	3, 201, 911	34, 464	92. 9060	23. 2265
Canada	2, 176, 708, 739	21, 462, 291	101. 4201	25. 3550

[1] Annual Report 1973–74, Hospital Insurance and Diagnostic Services, for fiscal year ended Mar. 31, 1974. Department of National Health and Welfare, Ottawa, Canada, 1974: 41.

Source: Prepared by Office of Research and Statistics, Social Security Administrations U.S. Department of Health, Education, and Welfare, Nov. 7, 1968. Research and Statistic, note No. 21–1968.

Contribution by Canada with respect to inpatient services, 1971 [1]

Province	25 percent of national per capita	25 percent of provincial per capita	Less 25 percent per capita authorized charges	Aggregate per capita cost	Average number of insured persons	Inpatient contribution by Canada
Newfoundland	$25. 3550	$18. 1950		$43. 5500	521, 040	$22, 691, 292
Prince Edward Island	25. 3550	17, 9187		43. 2737	110, 357	4, 775, 556
Nova Scotia	25. 3550	21. 5352		46. 8902	774, 018	36, 293, 859
New Brunswick	25. 3550	22. 6350		47. 9900	628, 334	30, 153, 749
Quebec	25. 3550	27. 9349		53. 2899	6, 012, 446	
Ontario	25. 3550	26. 2285		51. 5835	7, 661, 888	395, 227, 000
Manitoba	25. 3550	23. 0620		48. 4170	1, 009, 578	48, 880, 738
Saskatchewan	25. 3550	22. 9684	$0. 7133	47. 6101	929, 367	44, 247, 256
Alberta	25. 3550	25. 2083	. 5771	49. 9862	1, 617, 198	80, 837, 583
British Columbia	25. 3550	21. 6524	. 4658	46. 5416	2, 171, 668	101, 072, 903
Yukon	25. 3550	14. 9149		40. 2699	18, 333	738, 268
Northwest Territories	25. 3550	23. 2265	. 5310	48. 0505	34, 464	1, 656, 012
Total contributions by Canada for inpatient services, 1971						766, 574, 216

[1] Annual Report 1973–74, Hospital Insurance and Diagnostic Services, for fiscal year ended Mar. 31, 1974. Department of National Health and Welfare, Ottawa, Canada, 1974: 41.

Source: Prepared by Office of Research and Statistics, Social Security Administration, U.S. Department of Health, Education, and Welfare, Nov. 7, 1968. Research and Statistics note No. 21–1968.

---

[5] Lloyd Detwiller, "The History and Philosophy of Health Care in Canada and British Columbia," in National Health Care: the British Experience, Office of Comprehensive Health Planning, Olympia, Wash., 1971: 16.

Provincial costs versus Federal contributions under the hospital insurance and medical care programs 1973–74 [1]

Province	Hospital insurance program					Medical care program			
	Estimated Provincial costs (thousands)	Estimated Federal contributions (thousands)	Contributions of Provincial costs (thousands)	Balance of Provincial costs (percent)		Estimated Provincial costs (thousands)	Estimated Federal contributions (thousands)	Contributions cf Provincial costs (percent)	Balance of provincial costs (percent)
Newfoundland	$58,824	$33,866	$57.6	42.4		$20,434	$16,657	81.5	18.5
Prince Edward Island	11,388	6,807	59.8	40.2		4,752	3,529	74.3	25.7
Nova Scotia	97,085	53,049	54.6	45.4		38,948	24,552	63.0	37.0
New Brunswick	85,108	43,631	51.3	48.7		26,539	20,093	75.7	24.3
Quebec	912,822	438,750	48.1	51.9		370,835	188,332	50.8	49.2
Ontario	1,072,851	530,230	49.4	50.6		550,442	246,351	44.8	55.2
Manitoba	133,608	70,944	53.1	46.9		54,030	31,703	58.7	41.3
Saskatchewan	115,481	61,280	53.1	46.9		46,997	28,189	60.0	40.0
Alberta	241,858	121,106	50.1	49.9		94,389	53,159	56.3	43.7
British Columbia	268,734	142,225	52.9	47.1		162,758	72,137	44.3	55.7
Yukon Territory	1,878	1,142	60.8	39.2		1,144	619	54.1	45.9
Northwest Territories	5,099	2,476	48.6	51.4		1,667	1,146	68.7	31.3
Canada	3,004,736	1,505,506	50.1	49.9		1,372,935	686,467	50.0	50.0

[1] Maurice LeClair, "The Canadian Health Care System," in "National Health Insurance: Can We Learn from Canada?" ed. by Spyros Andreopoulos. John Wiley & Sons, New York, 1975: 39.

Notes: The Federal contribution for the Province of Quebec, under the hospital insurance program is paid through tax rebate under the established programs (interim arrangement) acts, effective 1965–66.
The Provincial costs under the hospital insurance program are calculated on a "calendar year" basis, but have been "fiscalized" for comparison purpose with the medical care program. The last years for which actual audited costs are available is calendar year 1971 for hospital insurance and fiscal year 1972–73 for medical care.

The data in two preceding tables indicate that the Federal contribution for inpatient hospital services in 1971 ranged from 60 percent of Provincial costs for Newfoundland and Prince Edward Island to 49 percent of Ontario's costs. The table below shows Provincial costs versus Federal contributions under both the hospital and medical insurance programs for 1973–74. Note that these data, more recent than that used in the preceding tables, include cost-sharing expenditures under the hospital program for both inpatient care and the outpatient diagnostic services also insured under the program.

The actual costs of Provincial hospital plans which are shared by the Federal Government are, in general, the operating costs of hospitals determined in accordance with recognized and generally accepted accounting principles and procedures, and approved by the Provincial authority administering the plan. The Federal law specifically excluded from shared costs any amounts spent on the capital cost of land, buildings, or physical plant; payment of any capital debt or interest on debt incurred before effective date of the agreement; or any provision for depreciation on land value, buildings, or physical plant. However, cost or depreciation of items of furniture and equipment is shared.

In addition to financial aid, the Federal Government provides technical assistance to the Provinces, endeavors to assure coordination among the Provincial programs, and holds Federal-Provincial conferences for discussion of problems relating to the program.

The Provinces finance their share of program costs from a variety of sources—general revenues, premiums, and special taxes. Additionally, British Columbia, Alberta, and the Northwest Territories use copayment amounts, although these amounts are deducted from overall program costs before the Federal share is computed. In Ontario and Alberta, a joint monthly premium is charged for both the hospital and medical insurance programs (in Ontario,

$11 for single persons, $22 for families; in Alberta, $5.75 for single subscribers, $11.50 for family coverage). Premium assistance is available both in Ontario and Alberta for certain categories of residents with limited incomes, and premium exemption is provided for residents over age 65. Nova Scotia relies on a provincial health services tax. British Columbia and the remaining Provinces finance the Provincial share of costs out of general Provincial revenue. Prior to 1974, Manitoba and Saskatchewan had utilized premiums for partial financing of the Provincial costs, but both Provinces have since abandoned this method. (In the case of Saskatchewan, fines could previously be incurred for nonpayment of the compulsory premium.)

Over the past few years, the Government of Canada has been actively recommending to the Provinces that measures be taken to control the rate of cost increase under both the hospital and medical programs. Ottawa has given the required 5-years notice of its intention to renegotiate with the Provinces the basis of Federal participation in the Hospital Insurance and Diagnostic Services Act. The proposed formula for future Federal contributions and other issues surrounding the problems of rising health costs in Canada are discussed at the end of the section of this report dealing with the medical insurance program.

REIMBURSEMENT METHODS

All Provinces have instituted a system of annual prior budget review of hospital expenses insured under Provincial hospital plans. Each hospital is required to submit a detailed budget before the beginning of the year, giving data on volume of services provided in the last complete year, an estimate of volume of services to be provided in the current year, and an estimate of services in the year being budgeted for. These budgets are reviewed by a rate board consisting of senior members of the staff of the Provincial agency, as well as by persons familiar with the operation of that hospital and other hospitals. From the hospitals' total expenses are deducted, in accordance with the Federal definition of shareable hospital costs, generally: (1) At least 50 percent (some Provinces require deduction of 60 or 100 percent) of estimated income from charges for semiprivate and private accommodations, and (2) income from other sources, such as patient income from workmen's compensation cases, and noncovered persons, outpatient services if not covered by the hospital insurance program, cafeteria services, and so forth. The hospital receives its approved costs for the year, with slight increments or decrements for days of service in excess of or below the original estimates.

The Provincial authority sets all per diem hospital rates—for ward, semiprivate, and private accommodations. Provinces have adopted different policies with regard to what percentage of the differential between ward and semiprivate or private accommodation may be retained by the hospital and what percentage must be returned to the government. In Newfoundland, Nova Scotia, and Saskatchewan, for example, hospitals may retain 50 percent of the room differential. In Prince Edward Island, on the other hand, the hospital is not permitted to retain any portion of the differential.

Initial implementation of prospective budgeting for hospitals apparently did not produce any significant strain. According to government sources in Ontario, for example, hospitals operated under prospective budgeting for 1-year's time as a "dry run" and in the following year implemented the procedure on a regular basis without noticeable difficulties. The following remarks by

Donald M. Cox, former Deputy Minister of Hospital Insurance, Victoria, British Columbia, illustrate how the prospective budgeting process operates in one Province:

> Hospitals are expected to present to our service before the end of each calendar year detailed estimates of their operating costs and occupancy for the coming year. In practice it has been impossible in most years for hospitals to send in estimates that soon because their staffs are almost all unionized, and bargaining often extends well into the new year. Estimates are of little value if salary costs are not known.
>
> Upon receipt of estimates by our service, they are tabulated and are then reviewed in detail by the consultants who pay particular attention to staffing patterns, staffing requirements, service developments, diagnostic and treatment programs, and by the accountants who are responsible for development of cost comparisons and particular examination of supply and other nonsalary costs. The recommendations of the reviewing staffs are considered by the rate board of our service, composed of four senior personnel under the chairmanship of the Assistant Deputy Minister. The board must, of course, reconcile recommendations with the overall money voted by the legislature for the operation of the service.
>
> Firm budgets are then established and all-inclusive per diem rates set.
>
> As a simplified example, a hospital may have an acceptable estimate of 100,000 adult and child inpatient days of care with an approved budget setting a gross expenditure of $5,600,000 and estimated sundry revenue of $600,000 from outpatient charges, newborn days at a fixed rate, semiprivate and private room charges, and so forth. After deducting the sundry revenue, there remains $5 million to be recovered from inpatient charges. On a basis of 100,000 days' care, this works out to an inclusive rate of $50 per day.
>
> This rate is used for billing purposes, but it is recognized that no hospital will achieve its exact estimate of days of care, and this is why we use the term "firm" rather than "fixed" budget. If the hospital in question during the year is 500 days short of its estimate, the only saving is in supplies calculated at $4 per day. That hospital would be paid $500 less $4 or $46 per day for its readiness to serve, or overhead, cost for the 500 days short of the approved estimate. If the hospital had 500 days over estimates, it would be paid only the $4 supply cost for the extra 500 days.
>
> Our principal medical teaching hospital has an inclusive standard ward per diem rate of $58.90 a day; the next hospital in size, $56.40 a day; and a typical community hospital of 125 beds, a rate of $43 a day.
>
> The cost of inpatient hospital care for this year will average approximately $81.60 per person resident in the Province.
>
> In notifying hospitals of approved budgets, we outline the broad areas of reductions and, in some cases, increases recommended by our rate board. However, once a budget has been set, a hospital is free to spend its income as it sees fit. It can spend more on salaries and less on other costs or make any other variations that it wishes.
>
> Finally, after such year-end adjustments are approved, if a hospital has sustained a deficit it must find funds to meet the deficit and if it has a surplus it retains the surplus to use as it sees fit, and hospitals have assurance that they are not going to be penalized by having accumulated a surplus. We don't take the money away from them the next year and cut them down.
>
> Over the years, a good many of the hospitals have had surpluses and a good many others have had deficits. I recently met with the board and the administration of a 500-bed hospital at their request. They were concerned about a projected deficit for this year. Over the

past 10 years that hospital had surpluses totaling $188,000 and deficits totaling $111,000.[6]

As noted earlier, the Federal Government does not contribute to capital costs under the Provincial hospital insurance plans. Between 1948 and 1970, a separate national grants program was in operation at the Federal level to assist Provinces in financing hospital construction. Since 1970, however, allocation of Federal health resources funds has been limited to teaching hospitals. The Federal Government no longer shares with the Provinces costs of capital construction or modernization of nonteaching facilities. At the Provincial level, there is considerable variation with regard to capital financing of hospitals:

> One Province pays charges for depreciation (but requires that it be funded), notwithstanding the lack of Federal reimbursement. Several have set up special capital cost funds from which payments are made to hospitals which they may use for new construction or for interest on or repayment of debt. Alberta took over the existing debts of all hospitals when it instituted its program and provides 100 percent of the cost of all new approved construction.[7]

In Ontario, the Provincial government provides two-thirds of the cost of basic construction of community hospitals and guarantees 100 percent of the cost of constructing teaching hospitals (the Federal Government shares in the cost of the latter facilities). In all Provinces, there can be no hospital construction without approval of the Provincial agency. "The reason for this is obvious. Under the programs, the Provinical government is meeting 100 percent of the cost of operation of all hospitals in the Province; it must, therefore, be able to approve of any new plant." [8]

For example, in Ontario, the government recently declared a moratorium on all community hospital construction and even took steps to reduce what was considered an unnecessarily high bed/population ratio (approximately 5/1,000 in 1971). For fiscal year 1973, hospital budgets were to be based on a 4.5 ratio of beds per 1,000 population. If a hospital exceeded the 4.5 ratio, the Province was not to provide financing for operating costs of additional beds.

For additional information on various aspects of the Provincial hospital plans, their financing, and reimbursement procedures, see Appendix I to this section.

MEDICAL CARE INSURANCE PROGRAM

In December 1966, Canada entered the second phase of its national health insurance program with passage of the Medical Care Act, which became effective July 1, 1968, and committed the Federal Government to contributing to participating Provinces approximately half the costs of insured services under Provincial medical care plans that satisfied the following criteria:

(1) Comprehensive coverage for all medically required services rendered by a physician or surgeon. There can be no dollar limit or exclusions except on the grounds that the services were not medically required. The benefit coverage must be administered in such a way that there will be no financial impediment or preclusion to an insured person receiving necessary medical

---

[6] Donald Cox, "Development of the British Columbia Hospital Insurance Service," in National Health Care: The British Columbia Experience, Office of Comprehensive Health Planning, Olympia, Wash., 1971: 34-37.

[7] Louis S. Reed, "The Canadian Hospital Insurance Program." Public Health Reports Feburary 1962: 100.

[8] Ibid., p. 101.

care. Certain surgical-dental services rendered by dental surgeons in hospitals have been included as benefits from July 1, 1968.

(2) Universal availability to all eligible residents of a participating Province on equal terms and conditions and covering, in addition, at least 90 percent of the total eligible population (and 95 percent during the year commencing April 1, 1971). This insures access to coverage by all residents and prevents premium discrimination on account of previous health, age, nonmembership in a group or other consideration. At the same time, subsidization in whole or in part for low-income groups is permitted if a plan is financed by means of a premium system.

(3) Portability of benefits when the beneficiary is temporarily absent from his own Province and when he is moving from one participating Province to another. It is not related to employment insurance groups and, consequently, coverage is not lost when an individual changes job or residence.

(4) Administration on a nonprofit basis by a public authority which is accountable to the Provincial government for its financial transactions.[9]

Two Provinces, British Columbia and Saskatchewan, entered the Federal program on the effective date. By January 1, 1971, all 10 Provinces had signed participating agreements with the Yukon and Northwest Territories entering the program by April of 1972.

The act also allows Provincial authorities to designate nongovernmental organizations as agencies permitted to undertake restricted functions in connection with premium-collection or claims-payment administration of the Provincial plan. Such agencies must be nonprofit and the payment of claims must be subject to assessment and approval by the Provincial authority.

Some of the main differences between the hospital insurance and medical care insurance programs were summarized by one author as follows:

> 1. The chief objections of Provincial governments to hospital insurance were both the concept of the Province having to sign an "agreement," with the Federal intervention that the the agreement entailed, and the requirement of a Federal audit. These requirements were eliminated in the medical care program.
> 2. The implicit assumption in 1956 that Provincial hospital plans would be administered by a public agency was made explicit in the medical plan. This led to the withdrawal of commercial insurance coverage for these benefits in all Provinces, the use of voluntary plans as "agents" of the government in some Provinces, and the winding up of the voluntary plans in other Provinces.
> 3. The financial formula ignores Provincial variations in per capita costs and pays to each Province one-half of the national per capita cost in respect of each member of its insured population. Thus the equalization factor is greater than in the hospital financing formula (80 percent of the cost in Newfoundland, but only 45 percent in Ontario).[10]

COVERAGE

Of an estimated 22.2 million Canadian residents eligible for coverage under Provinical medical care plans in fiscal year 1973–74, very few currently remain uninsured. One hundred percent of the eligible population are now

---

[9] Taken from the Annual Report of the Minister of National Health and Welfare, respecting operations of the Medical Care Act for the fiscal year ending March 31, 1974. Ottawa: Information Canada, 1974: 2.

[10] Malcolm Taylor, "The Canadian Health Insurance Program." Public Administration Review, Jan.–Feb. 1973: 36.

insured in Newfoundland, Prince Edward Island, Nova Scotia, New Brunswick, Quebec, Manitoba, Saskatchewan, the Northwest Territories, and the Yukon Territory. Virtually 100 percent of the eligible population in Alberta, British Columbia, and Ontario are covered.

The methods for determining the number of insured persons in a Province differ, since the method used by a Province to finance the Provincial share of costs has a direct bearing on the availability of an actual count of insured persons. Thus, in some Provinces the number of insured persons is estimated from the Provincial population as defined in the Medical Care Act and in other cases the number of insured persons is based on a more precise determination.

The Medical Care Act defines "population" to mean the population of the Province on the first day of October in that fiscal year as certified by the Chief Statistician of Canada, after excluding members of the Canadian Armed Forces, Royal Canadian Mounted Police, and persons serving a term of imprisonment in a penitentiary as defined in the Penitentiary Act. The exclusions amount to some 0.5 percent of the total population.

Insurable residents of a participating Province who are eligible and entitled to receive insured services under any other act of the Parliament of Canada or under any law of a Province relating to workmen's compensation are not entitled to benefits under the Medical Care Act. For example, war veterans entitled to medical care under other Federal legislation are excluded from the benefit coverage of the Medical Care Act insofar as their compensable disability is concerned.[11]

BENEFITS

For a participating Province to benefit from the Federal program, its own plan must provide for the financing of comprehensive physicians' services for all insurable residents without regard to their age, ability to pay, or other circumstances. In addition, the Medical Care Act empowers the Federal Government to include additional health care services provided by nonphysician professional personnel, under terms and conditions specified by the Governor-in-Council. Six Provinces presently cover the services of optometrists. Ontario, Alberta, and British Columbia also cover services performed by osteopaths, chiropractors, podiatrists, and certain other health personnel. Routine dental care is generally not a covered service, although there are exceptions—(1) in September 1974, Saskatchewan began phasing in an insured dental service plan for children up to 12 years of age, (2) Quebec has passed legislation for dental services, but the program has not yet been implemented, and (3) since January 1974, Alberta has extended routine dental care and optical care to residents over age 65 and their dependents. For a complete description of the differences among the various Provincial plans, see Appendix II.[12]

All Provinces now prohibit the sale of any private insurance duplicating in any way the benefits covered under the Federal-Provincial plans. However, most Provinces do allow nonprofit organizations and commercial insurers to supplement the government coverage; that is, for such typically noncovered items or services as dental care, drugs, ambulance service, et cetera. In some cases the Provincial government authority itself markets a separate supplemental package or licenses (as in the case of British Columbia) its nonprofit carriers

---

[11] Annual Report of the Minister of National Health and Welfare, respecting operations of the Medical Care Act for the fiscal year ending Mar. 31, 1974, Ottawa, Canada: 28.

acting as administrative agents for the government plan to sell supplemental benefits.

Precise figures are not available on the extent of supplemental health insurance coverage from all combined sources—government agencies, nonprofit organizations, and commercial insurers—throughout the Provinces. The table below presents data obtained from the Canadian Association of Accident and Sickness Insurers (formerly, the Canadian Health Insurance Association) from its 1971 survey of health insurance benefits in Canada. Data reported in this 1971 survey were submitted by a total of 44 member insurers of the CAASI. The figures do not, therefore, reflect the extent of coverage under Provincial government-sponsored supplemental plans or plans sold through non-profit organizations. Judging from the data presented in this table, it would appear that disability income insurance has become an attractive area for private insurers.

---

[12] Joseph G. Simanis, "National Health Systems in Eight Countries." U.S. Department of Health, Education, and Welfare, Social Security Administration, Office of Research and Statistics. DHEW Publication No. (SSA) 75–11924, U.S. Govt. Print. Off., Wash., DC, January 1975: 28.

Group and individual coverage in force (as of Dec. 31, 1971), direct premiums written and direct claims paid during 1971

	Group					Individual			
	Contracts in force	Persons covered		Direct premiums written	Direct claims paid	Persons covered		Direct premiums written	Direct claims paid
		Employees	Dependents			Principals	Dependents		
Accidental death and dismemberment	16,750	1,757,007	(1)	$14,695,761	$8,008,669	(1)	(1)	(1)	(1)
Loss of income:									
Short term	21,034	1,760,999	(1)	125,702,795	111,562,049	60,654	(1)	$4,567,156	$2,632,395
Long term	5,684	1,023,107	(1)	48,059,173	18,716,806	287,207	(1)	34,965,423	18,501,626
Creditors	35	387,794	(1)	12,495,979	7,483,781	(1)	(1)	(1)	(1)
Extended health care [2]	16,131	1,995,840	3,929,146	62,300,057	43,563,839	23,021	47,110	2,436,298	1,273,631
Drug expense [2]	1,662	105,191	222,688	2,762,727	2,413,567	7	18	2,119	19
Supplementary hospital [2]	4,758	497,198	976,751	8,107,639	4,410,980	5,855	6,370	170,606	107,207
Dental	642	59,862	125,241	4,769,334	3,542,220	(1)	(1)	(1)	(1)
Miscellaneous	287	(1)	(1)	1,829,396	1,280,410	(1)	(1)	21,854,718	9,090,350
Not allotted by type of coverage	(1)	(1)	(1)	16,044,574	13,011,417	(1)	(1)	5,689,949	4,430,802
Total	(1)	(1)	(1)	296,767,435	213,993,738	(1)	(1)	69,686,269	36,036,030

[1] The drug expense and supplementary hospital coverage reported was provided under contracts set up principally to provide those benefits only.

[2] Coverage providing payments to cover a wide range of health care expenses such as ambulance services; crutches, braces and other medical appliances; private-duty nursing; services of nonmedical practitioners and, in the majority of cases, prescribed drugs and hospital expenses. Coverage frequently extends to include most health care expenses not paid by Provincial government plans.

Source: Canadian Association of Accident and Sickness Insurers, Toronto, Canada, 1971.

It has been reported by other sources that more than six million Canadians are presently insured under a wide variety of private health insurance plans, mainly through group enrollment. Such plans reportedly utilize deductibles (generally $25 per person per year or $50 per family) or coinsurance limiting amount of claims paid to 80 percent of total cost. It is common for such plans to have a life-time maximum of $5,000 to $50,000. Coverage for the cost of prescription drugs is reported to be one of the most important elements of group health plans, with about 85 percent of all claims for drugs.[13]

FINANCING

Provinces can finance services in any manner they wish, but the act contains a provision the intent of which is that no insured person shall be impeded or precluded from reasonable access to insured services as a consequence of direct charges associated with the services received. A Province may adopt any method it wishes for the reimbursement of providers of services, subject only to the proviso that the fee schedule for authorized payments is on a basis that assures reasonable compensation for the services rendered.

The formula for calculating Federal contributions to the cost of Provincial plans is such that Provinces with relatively low per capita costs would be assisted by something more than half their Provincial costs. In general terms, the Federal contribution to a participating Province is an amount equal to (a) 50 percent of the average per capita cost for the year of all insured services in all participating Provinces, and (b) multiplied by the number of insured persons in each Province respectively. As under the hospital program, the Federal Government makes no contribution to administrative costs incurred by the Province. A two-percent income surtax (maximum $100), referred to as the social development tax, is used by the Federal Government to finance its share of the medical insurance program.[14]

The Provinces finance their share in the medical program from a variety of sources—general revenues in four Provinces, premium payments in five Provinces, et cetera. In Quebec, the program is financed through a 0.8 percent payroll tax on employers and personal income tax of an equal amount (up to a maximum contribution of $125). In some Provinces which utilize premium financing, persons over 65 or persons receiving some form of social assistance income pay no premiums. The Federal Government assumes payment of any required premiums for low-income Indians and Eskimos.[15]

The Federal contribution is paid to Provinces on the basis of regular monthly advance payments in order to allow the Provinces to reimburse physicians and other providers on a continuing basis:

> In order to expedite the payment of advances and, at the same time, to forestall the likelihood of a major financial adjustment after the end of each fiscal year, the formula which is used for the calculation of the advance payments provides for a holdback of up to 10 percent of the amount due to the Province. The formula for the advance payments, therefore, differs from the formula for the annual contribution, in that 45 percent of estimated national per capita cost is paid to the Provinces as advances on account of contributions.

---

[13] "Canada: Private Health Insurance," Medical Care Review, May 1974: 623.
[14] Taylor, p. 36.
[15] Ibid.

The remaining 5 percent of the national per capita cost multiplied by the average number of insured persons in a Province, plus or minus adjustment to actual costs, is paid to Provinces following receipt of final cost reports from all participating Provinces * * * [16]

In 1975, the Government of Canada announced its intention to establish a ceiling on the amount of annual increase in the contributions the Federal Government would make to the Provinces under the terms of the Medical Care Act. The ceiling was to be effective for 1976 and subsequent years with regard to the per capita growth rate in Federal contributions to the Provinces. For 1976–77, the ceiling was to be 13 percent over the amount of Federal contributions in the preceding year, 10.5 percent for 1977–78, and 8.5 percent for 1978–79 and subsequent years. The reasons for this action are more fully described in the section of this report dealing with rising health costs in Canada.

ADMINISTRATION

The Federal Medical Care Act of 1966 specified that Provincial "medicare" [17] programs be operated on a "nonprofit basis by a public authority subject to Provincial audit." Beyond these broad guidelines, the Provincial governments were free to make their own determinations with regard to the administration of the program at the Provincial level. The Federal law contained a provision which allowed Provincial authorities to designate certain nongovernmental organizations as agencies permitted to undertake restricted functions in connection with the day-to-day premium collection and claims payment administration of the Provincial plan. Thus, existing voluntary insurance carriers who so wished might apply for an agency arrangement under the Provincial authority. However, it would be necessary to handle this agency aspect of their business on a nonprofit basis and the actual payment of claims would, in accordance with the Federal act, be subject to assessment and approval by the Provincial authority.

The Federal medicare plan was considerably more flexible with regard to a potential role for private insurance carriers than was its predecessor, the hospital insurance and diagnostic services plan. The act which established the hospital insurance program has stipulated that Provincial plans be operated directly by a "public agency," thus effectively eliminating any possible role for nongovernmental organizations.

In 1967 a Federal-Provincial conference of health ministers was held in Ottawa to explore the ability of the Provinces to meet the Federal conditions and to interpret and clarify provisions of the Medical Care Act (which was to become operative on July 1, 1968). One of the major issues discussed at this conference centered around interpretation of "administration on a nonprofit basis by a public authority responsible to the Province and subject to public audit." According to press accounts, Federal Health and Welfare Minister Allan MacEachen stated on several occasions that:

A Province could integrate a doctor-sponsored plan into its program or even designate a private insurance company to be its agent, to collect premiums and make payments, but that the assessment of claims and the determinations of payments represent a

---

[16] Annual Report of the Minister of National Health and Welfare, respecting operations of the Medical Care Act, for the fiscal year ending Mar. 31, 1974:5.

[17] The term "medicare" is used in this report to denote the Federal medical care program, enacted in 1966.

crucial function that should be undertaken by a public authority; and that the claim of insurance people, that with respect to health insurance, they represent a nonprofit organization, is a matter that could be verified in a Province proposing to use a private carrier.

Costs incurred in the administration of the medicare plan at the Provincial level were not shareable with the Federal Government. Provincial governments were presented, therefore, with a strong incentive to develop the least expensive type of administrative mechanism, presumably a single public agency rather than a mixture of public authority and multiple private agencies.

Seven Provinces are presently using public commissions for administration of the Provincial plan. The remaining Provinces and Territories have vested administrative responsibility either directly in the Provincial Department of Health or in an agency of the Provincial government. Initially, some Provinces did utilize private insurance carriers for various administrative functions under the medical care plan. Such carriers were obligated under the terms of the Federal law to participate on a nonprofit basis as "designated agents" of the Provincial health authority. They were not allowed to assess or approve claims or to determine the amount of money to be paid with respect to claims. With the exception of Ontario and British Columbia, the Provinces generally opted for direct administration through a single public authority.

In Saskatchewan, approved nonprofit health agencies perform limited "post office" functions, receiving claims from medical members and passing on claims payments from the Provincial commission to physicians. In Nova Scotia, the medical insurance plan is operated by a conjoint public authority, consisting of the Provincial commission and Maritime Medical Care In., a doctor-sponsored prepayment agency authorized to act on a nonprofit basis as the fiscal agent of the public authority.

The British Columbia plan is marketed through two preexisting nonprofit plans (which are licensed to sell additional benefits over and above the basic Provincial plan, either separately or as a package connected with the governmental contract) and through the British Columbia Medical Plan, a governmental agency. The two nongovernment carriers limit their services under the plan to group coverage. Premiums collected by them on behalf of the governmental contract must be remitted to the Province and cannot be held in reserve. Carriers are responsible for enrolling residents, collecting premiums, and paying claims, but they do not assess or approve claims or determine amounts to be paid.

The situation in Ontario was somewhat unique. When the Province entered the medicare program on October 1, 1969, a majority of the residents were insured through more than 200 separate insuring agencies, each with its own administration and premium collection system. The Ontario government entered into an agreement with a consortium composed of 30 of the largest carriers, who were employed by the Provincial government as "designated agents." Private insurance firms which chose to participate in the Provincial plan were allowed to enroll their premedicare subscribers and to collect premiums on behalf of the Provincial plan. A government agency absorbed the subscribers of those carriers who were not interested in remaining in the field, as well as continuing to make coverage available to those who had been covered by the previous Provincial governmental plan, together with new pay-direct subscribers. Designated agents were responsible for enrollment, billing, and, in some cases, claims payment after certification by a Provincial official.

This operation continued for approximately two and one-half years and was phased out by April 1, 1972, at which time the Ontario Health Insurance Commission assumed responsibility for administration of both the hospital and medical insurance plans. The consortium arrangement had not proved effective in terms of economy of operation, uniformity of data collection, or continuity of coverage for enrollees changing from one to another carrier.

REIMBURSEMENT METHODS

Since the fee-for-service method of payment had been the almost universal mode of physician-reimbursement prior to medicare, it was regarded as a logical arrangement for the new program. The Government of Canada acknowledged certain distinct advantages to this system, as noted below:

> * * * it enables governments to obtain, collate and analyze information about virtually every medical act rendered to a resident of Canada indicating what service was rendered, to whom, by whom, when, where and why, as a byproduct of the fee-for-service mechanism. The resulting data can be put to use in a variety of ways. For example, defects in the health system and deficiencies or surpluses in the availability of medical manpower are being identified, studied, and solutions sought. Many of these problems might otherwise have been ignored or remained ill-defined in the absence of data on medical care utilization being collected on a universal basis in each Province.[18]

An estimated 96 percent of total expenditures under the medical insurance program are currently made on the basis of fee-for-service, the remainder being paid to salaried physicians in organized clinic settings.[19] Generally, the bases for payments are the authorized fee schedules negotiated between the Provincial governmental authority and the Provincial medical association. In general, a physician has a choice 1) of dealing directly with the Provincial plan or its agents and accepting the plan's payment for his service (typically 85 to 90 percent of the fee schedule; Alberta and Quebec pay 100 percent of the fee schedule amount) as payment in full, or 2) "opting out" and dealing directly with his patient, who is then reimbursed by the Provincial agency only for the authorized amount and must make up from his own pocket any additional amount the "opted out" physician may charge. In one Province (Quebec), the physician who "extra-bills" is considered to be a "nonparticipating" physician, and the patient receives no reimbursement whatsoever for any services this category of physician may provide.

When the Province of Ontario first entered the Federal medicare program, it initially allowed physicians and other providers either to participate directly with the government for all insured patients, to participate on a patient-by-patient basis, or not to participate at all. Under these arrangements, the physician was allowed the following options with regard to reimbursement: (1) bill the government (or one of the approved private agents Ontario was using at that time for administration of the Provincial plan) directly for 90 percent of the amount set forth in the fee schedule negotiated between the Ontario Medical Association and the Provincial government, (2) bill the patient for the full amount of the physician's charge, in which case the government

---

[18] "Questions and Answers: the Federal Medical Care Program." Minister of National Health and Welfare, Health Insurance Directorate, Health Programs Branch, Ottawa, 1974: 11.

[19] Taylor, pp. 36–37.

reimbursed the patient 90 percent of the approved fee schedule and the patient made up the difference, or (3) bill both the plan for its 90 percent of the fee schedule and the patient for any remaining charge the physician wished to impose.

Beginning on January 1, 1972, however, the Provincial government required the physician to participate fully for all his insured patients or not at all. Under these circumstances, the provider is now required to accept 90 percent of the fee schedule from the government plan as full payment, with no "extra-billing" of the patient allowed, or he must bill all his patients directly. Estimates indicate that only about 9 to 10 percent of Ontario's physicians are currently not participating. It has been suggested that it is more in the physician's interest to be assured of 90 percent fee schedule reimbursement from the government than to rely upon reimbursement from the patient after the patient has received payment from the government agency. Another source has noted that:

> Obviously it is much simpler for each physician to send one statement to the government for all patients seen during the treatment period rather than to try to collect from hundreds of individual patients. Each physician participating in the Provincial plan regularly receives a lump sum payment, seldom has a bad debt, and is paid for virtually everybody he sees, and does not have the added expense of collecting his fees from individual patients.[20]

The following table presents the current situation regarding Canadian physicians who have opted-out of the medical insurance plans in the various Provinces.

Current situation regarding opted-out physicians [1]

Province	Situation
Newfoundland	Four opted-out out of total of 500.
Nova Scotia	Extra-billing amounts to only 2.8 percent of plan payments.
New Brunswick	Four opted-out.
Prince Edward Island	None opted-out. Extra-billing less than one-half of 1 percent.
Quebec	Seven specialists opted-out. Three general practitioners opted-out (out of nearly 7,000 physicians).
Ontario	Nine percent opted-out.
Manitoba	Five percent opted-out.
Saskatchewan	Approximately 3 to 4 percent opted-out.
Alberta	None opted-out—can extra-bill under certain circumstances.
British Columbia	None opted-out.

[1] LeClair, p. 55.

The following excerpt from a paper presented by the executive director of the British Columbia Medical Association provides an example of how one Province developed its methods of reimbursement and professional peer review over utilization of services:

> In our discussions in 1964 and 1965 prior to the introduction of the British Columbia medical plan, the association representatives tried to clarify certain points that were important in maintaining a healthy attitude of physicians toward whatever system developed because by and large physicians are suspicious and at times resentful of what appears to them to be government interference with their freedom to practice a high quality of medical care. There were two

---

[20] LeClair, p. 55.

or three points that had to be made very clear and which took a lot of discussion in the early stages. One of these was opting out. It was felt that the physicians would not easily accept the idea that they must all be in the plan without any opportunity of maintaining their professional freedoms and working outside the plan if they so wished. The government, of course, wanted all physicians in because they felt that they were taking citizens' money, and if all doctors opted out in one town or in one speciality, then they would be accepting money for a service which they could not provide. They were most anxious to have no "opting out clause" in the agreement. The physicians were equally adamant that it was most important to allow physicians to opt out if they wished to. Otherwise a lot of good doctors would leave the Province. The association representatives said that the right to opt out was a very important right that should not be denied the physician. He should be able to practice inside the plan or outside the plan (if he could survive), as he so desired. It was also equally important that the patient should be able to go to a participating doctor or to a doctor who was outside the plan if the patient so desired. It was finally agreed that doctors could opt out without loss of benefits to insured persons. It might be interesting here to know that in the first two years of the plan, not one single doctor in British Columbia opted out. There is a recent example of a doctor who opted out on a Friday. When his patients came into his office on Saturday, he told them this and they said they would go to another physician. By Monday, he was back in the plan. Three plastic surgeons in Victoria have recently opted out, and it will be interesting to see what results

N4 from this action.

Another important facet of the plan was how fee schedules would be arranged. It was agreed that the writing of the fee schedule and the determination of the amounts to be paid for certain procedures was the association's business. It was also agreed that the overall cost was a matter of interest to both the profession and the government. It was therefore agreed that at periodic intervals the profession and the government would discuss the overall cost and then the details of the fee schedule would be worked out by the profession within the range of the agreed upon increase—or change in the overall cost. At this time, for the first time anywhere, indexes were used as a guide, and the profession tied itself to two indexes to be used in the amount of change in the overall cost of the plan. After lengthy discussion regarding disposable income index—cost of living, wages and salaries indexes, and so forth—the cost of living index for the city of Vancouver and the wages and salaries index for the Province of British Columbia were used with equal weighting in the determination of a joint index that was used to provide the overall cost of changes in the fee schedule. At the time that this was discussed, some five years ago, the average of the two indexes together was running about 2½ to 3 percent per year, and it was finally agreed that 2.75 percent per annum would be taken as an automatic increase providing the indexes rose that much, and if they went more than that then we would negotiate and take into account any other factors in the economy which might be playing a part in doctors' costs and incomes. We also agreed that if the joint indexes rose to more than eight percent, that either side could ask for compulsory arbitration. We have had two negotiations under this formula, which have worked very well. The signed agreement was for a five-year term, which runs out at the end of this year. It is very obvious that some arrangement with regard to changing fees must be made because the profession cannot be put in the position of going with their hat in their hand and asking for more money at regular intervals, and the government always has some other areas that need available money. This is why a written agreement covering these points is essential. Our agreement is what makes these points clear and makes the cooperation possible.

Another point that was felt necessary for the profession to be content with the scheme was the point of "extra-billing." After much discussion it was agreed that there were times when extra-billing should be allowed—if the patient demands Cadillac care instead of the regular model Ford that is being offered this year, he should be prepared to pay a little more. It was agreed that extra-billing could be allowed provided the doctor made an arrangement with the patient before he started care, and it was agreed that this arrangement with the patient would be in writing so that there would be no misunderstanding. So that we all understand what we are talking about, we should realize that extra-billing means a charge over and above the current agreed minimum fee schedule. The plan does not pay for this as they pay the current fee schedule on a 90 percent basis only.

Another point clarified was discipline of physicians. It was also agreed that the public purse must be protected against those few members of the profession who sometimes appear to abuse it. At the same time, we agreed that the government should not be the body to discipline the profession as they cannot do it nearly as well as the profession itself, if they are willing to do it. Therefore, it was decided that any abuses by the profession should be referred to the British Columbia Medical Association for appropriate action. This is a most important point, and it is essential for the government to obtain the cooperation of the profession in matters of this kind. It is equally essential for the profession to maintain its own internal discipline. In British Columbia every patient receives a copy of every bill submitted by the doctor for his care, and of every payment made to the doctor for this care. This is the stage at which most of the few irregularities are spotted, and it is easy to do with modern computer and the techniques employed by the plans in administering accounts. By the computer it is possible to produce patterns of practice of doctors involving their utilization of services and the amounts of money and the numbers of times the patients are recalled, laboratory services, etc.

There is a pattern of practice profile kept on every doctor, to compare him with his fellows in the same type of community and carrying on the same type of practice. You can get a pretty good idea of what the norm is and should be. If there is a variation of more than two standard deviations a committee of the association looks at the profiles and may interview the doctors concerned, and the appropriate action is recommended. We also have other committees which really do what is commonly referred to as a "peer review," such as Reference Committee, Cost Quality Study Committee, and so forth.[21]

Prior to implementation of the medical insurance program, opponents of medicare had warned that Canadian doctors were likely to find practice more attractive and lucrative in other countries, particularly the United States, and that the country's less than optimum physician-per-population ratio of 1 per 763 in 1966 would suffer as a result of a massive physician-emigration. Statistics from the Canadian Department of National Health and Welfare appear to dispel this fear—in 1973, the ratio had improved to 1 doctor for every 633 Canadians, partly through a marked reduction in the number of Canadian-born physicians emigrating to the United States and partly through a doubling of the number of physicians and surgeons immigrating to Canada since enactment of medicare.

---

[21] E. C. McCoy, M.D., Executive Director, British Columbia Medical Association, "History of the Development of the Health Care Program in British Columbia, Particularly Related to Physicians' Services." In "National Health Care: the British Columbia Experience," Office of Comprehensive Health Planning, Olympia, Wash., 1971.

Canada has experienced, however, a chronic problem with maldistribution of medical personnel, particularly in its sparsely populated rural and northern regions. Over one-third of Canada's active physicians are located in Ontario, which had a ratio of one doctor for every 616 persons in 1971; by way of contrast, Prince Edward Island had 1 doctor per 1,143 persons. Maldistribution has been eased scmewhat in recent years, due in part to special financial incentives offered by some Provinces to persuade doctors to locate in underserved areas and partly through equalization of the economic differential between less or more wealthy Provinces through elimination of bad debts. Newfoundland, for example, has experienced a 250 percent improvement in its physician: population ratio from 1:1,467 in 1968 to 1:1,090 in 1971.[22]

There have been reports that increasing numbers of doctors in several Provinces have been threatening to opt-out of Medicare if their fee schedules are not raised. Yet doctors still rank as Canada's highest paid category of workers and reportedly make only slightly less than five times the amount of the average Canadian wage earner.

In the 10-year period between 1959 and 1969, Canadian doctors more than doubled their gross and net earnings from fees, while holding their expenses to a lesser increase. Average gross earnings for physicians in 1969 climbed to $46,328, up from $22,910 in 1959. Average net earnings rose to $30,861 in 1969, compared with $14,590 ten years earlier. The 10-year average increase in average net and average gross earnings was 7.8 percent and 7.3 percent, respectively. According to an analysis of 1973 Federal income tax returns, the average self-employed doctor earned $42,730 in that year, substantially more than the next highest contender—lawyers at $36,598 a year. Between 1968 and 1973, the average doctor's income is reported to have climbed by 46 percent, while his average tax payment increased by only 20 percent.[23] The following table gives the average net earnings of fee-for-service physicians in Canada from 1963 through 1974 (preliminary estimates only):

---

[22] "Questions and Answers: the Federal Medical Care Act," p. 12.
[23] "Canada: Physician Income." Medical Care Review, January 1976: 59–60.

Average net professional earnings [1] of active fee practice physicians, Canada, by Province, 1963 to 1974

Province	1963	1964	1965	1966	1967	1968	1969	1970 [2]	1971 [2]	1972 [2]	Preliminary estimate [3]	
											1973	1974
Newfoundland	$19,455	$21,523	$23,028	$23,304	$25,578	$30,488	$37,817	$41,562	$38,846	$38,282	$42,800	$45,300
Prince Edward Island	15,777	16,478	17,835	18,910	20,716	22,636	22,760	26,892	38,822	37,687	37,500	42,500
Nova Scotia	14,839	17,851	19,146	20,395	21,480	24,642	29,880	35,776	35,351	37,715	37,600	40,100
New Brunswick	17,701	19,255	20,251	20,807	24,662	27,544	29,678	33,083	39,944	43,012	41,100	42,500
Quebec	16,696	18,534	20,532	21,231	23,133	25,112	27,233	27,402	41,131	43,401	44,400	45,200
Ontario	20,492	22,247	24,188	23,456	29,354	32,098	33,903	38,993	41,363	40,968	39,400	42,500
Manitoba	18,178	18,720	19,681	21,565	23,229	26,108	31,678	38,657	38,803	35,545	34,400	35,000
Saskatchewan	21,625	23,879	23,530	24,274	24,697	25,175	27,657	31,288	32,314	34,889	34,300	35,700
Alberta	19,111	21,117	22,681	24,356	27,591	33,221	33,165	39,678	40,357	39,687	36,500	35,900
British Columbia	17,464	19,560	20,121	22,209	25,169	26,239	28,829	31,006	31,138	32,991	35,200	35,900
Yukon and Northwest Territories [4]	16,480	13,601	15,731	13,039	13,220	18,000	15,807	17,262	21,610	25,691	NA	NA
Canada	18,688	20,484	22,064	23,262	26,093	28,615	30,861	34,360	39,203	39,978	39,600	42,200

[1] Includes net professional fees (i.e., gross receipts minus expenses of practice), and earnings received in the form of wages and salaries incidental to professional practice.

[2] Excludes earnings of some salaried physicians in active practice.

[3] Estimates largely based upon changes in fee payments made by Provincial medical care insurance programs and, upon estimated changes in expenses of practice, taking into account recent increases in relevant price and wage levels.

[4] Data to 1968 for the Yukon and Northwest Territories are posetd for record only.

NOTE.—Preliminary review of data for 1973 just received from Revenue Canada suggests that expenses of practice increased less than estimated, and that net income in 1973 tended to be slightly higher than is shown in the table. The data indicate that for Canada as a whole net incomes in 1973 were about 2 to 3 percent higher than in 1972.

Source: Revenue Canada, unpublished statistics.

RISING COSTS

Over the decade of the 1960s, Canadian expenditures for all types of health care more than tripled. Year-to-year percentage increases from 1960 to 1970 were never below 8 percent. National health expenditures as a proportion of the GNP rose from 3.8 percent in 1960 to 7.1 percent by 1971. The Federal share in total national health expenditures rose from 27.1 percent in 1966 to 33.0 percent in 1971. Per capita spending on health care reached $306.11 in 1971, representing 9 percent of disposable net personal income. It has been estimated that by 1980, health care expenditures in Canada will represent 9.1 percent of the GNP, or 13.3 percent of disposable net personal income.[24]

Until fiscal year 1974–75, actual combined costs—both Federal and Provincial—for the insured services of the hospital and medical insurance programs were lower than estimated costs. Since 1974, however, estimates have been outstripped by actual cost experience. For fiscal year 1975–76, it is estimated that combined Federal/Provincial expenditures for both the hospital and medical insurance plans will exceed $6 billion. In fiscal year 1974–75, Federal costs alone ran over $2.7 billion, up 19.8 percent from the previous year.[25]

Year to year increases in hospital costs have been far more of a problem than annual increases in medical costs. In fiscal year 1974–75, the costs of insured hospital services went up 25.5 percent over the previous year, as compared with a 6.5 percent increase in the costs for insured medical services for the same year. Per capita costs for insured hospital services reached $175.10 in fiscal year 1974–75, with medical services costing $64.98 per person. In fiscal year 1974–75, British Columbia and Ontario registered the greatest percentage increase in Provincial hospital costs over the previous year (39.2 percent and 31.6 percent, respectively), while the Northwest Territories and Prince Edward Island led the Provinces in increased costs of insured medical services (50.3 percent and 20.5 percent, respectively).[26]

Per capita hospital operating expenditures in Canada rose from $38.14 in 1961, to $105.64 in 1970 and $127.78 in 1972. Hospital operating costs per patient day rose from $23.01 in 1961 to $56.27 in 1970 and $68.74 in 1972.[27] In an attempt to deal with the problem of ever-inflating hospital costs, many Provinces have imposed ceilings on the percentage of increased allowed to hospitals over their previous year's net base operating expense—5 percent being the most common percentage increase allowed by most Provincial hospital authorities. Some Provinces are actually decommissioning many active-treatment beds and some small rural hospitals in an attempt to reach a lower bed-per-population ratio (the desired goal reported to be 4 to 4.5 beds per 1,000). Such efforts have met with resistance in certain areas where alternative facilities are remote from the local area or where the decommissioned facility has provided a substantial source of employment and economic support for the community.

Ninety-three percent of the Canadian hospital beds are in public hospitals most of which are privately operated but dependent on public sources for most

---

[24] Andreopoulos, p. 2.

[25] Unpublished Canadian Government data from June 1975 budget excerpt regarding health care services.

[26] Ibid., financial and statistical tables.

[27] Annual Report 1973–74 on Hospital Insurance and Diagnostic Services Act, pp. 64–65.

of their operating revenues. In 1972, Canada had 1,276 hospitals with a total of 150,043 beds. (These figures include only hospitals listed under agreements for purposes of the Hospital Insurance and Diagnostic Services Act, and exclude facilities which are mental hospitals, tuberculosis sanatoria, or custodial or domiciliary institutions.) The short-term hospital bed-per-population ratio in 1972 was 5.5 per 1,000 population; if long-term beds in listed hospitals are included, the ratio was 6.9 per 1,000 population.[28]

Not only does Canada have far more hospital beds per population than the United States (which registered about 5 beds per 1,000 population for the comparable time period), but it also makes greater use of those beds as indicated in comparative hospital utilization statistics for the two countries. In 1972, hospitals in Canada registered an admissions rate of 168.9 per 1,000 population, up from 157.7 in 1961; data for the United States in 1972 showed an admissions rate of 148.3 per 1,000 population. In 1972, Canada experienced the shortest average length of stay—11.7 days—of any year since 1961; in the United States, average length of hospital stay has never, in any year since 1961, exceeded 9.1 days with the average for 1972 set at 8.4 days. Canada has traditionally reported a higher overall hospital occupancy rate than in the United States—in 1972, Canada's rate of 80 percent reflected an actual decrease of 1.8 percent from the 1971 rate, whereas the current U.S. rate is about 75 percent.[29]

While the rate of increase in medical expenditures has not equaled that associated with hospital care, there is concern nonetheless that total expenditures on insured physicians' services under medicare have continued to rise steadily throughout Canada regardless of whether physicians' fees have actually risen. The connection between fee increases and total program expenditures is obvious, but various studies on the Canadian program have shown that the absence of such fee increases has not inhibited overall growth rates. Elimination of bad debts and greater adherence to fee schedule amounts (rather than reduction or waiver of such amounts for poor patients) are assumed to have had an initial impact on increasing program expenditures for physicians' services. Yet, relative price increases in the medical care industry have actually slowed down since medicare went into effect and program expenditures for physicians' services have nonetheless continued to climb. On an annual per capita basis, the rate of increase in medical costs is currently almost one-third less than it was in the several years leading up to medicare.[30]

Nor can increased expenditures be directly attributed to significant increases in patient utilization of services. As one author has observed:

> The before-and-after medicare study of physician utilization in Montreal reports that aggregate visit rates did not rise in response to insurance and that physician hours of work did not increase. Instead, physicians reorganized their practice patterns and generated more income from a given number of initial patient contacts. This is supported by data from Trans-Canada Medical Plans showing that in insured populations, rates of physician-generated services per capita tend to rise faster over time and to be more closely associated with physician availability than are rates of patient-generated services * * * Rather than having physician expense driven by independent shifts in demand, we seem to be observing a linkage between supply

---

[28] Annual Report 1973–74 on Hospital Insurance and Diagnostic Services Act, pp. 19–22.
[29] Ibid, pp. 22–25.
[30] LeClair, p. 48.

of physicians and the quantity of services they choose to perform to total expense.[31]

The author concludes that "efforts to modify patterns of expenditures by incentives directed at the consumer of care cannot hope to influence overall cost trends," and that official attention will probably be directed at approaches which will alter the existing structure of medical practice, e.g., through such vehicles as restriction of physician immigration, public ownership and operation of facilities, employment of physician-personnel in networks of Community Health Centers, unilateral government determination of fee schedules or absolute limits on physician earnings, more intensive scrutiny and utilization of the physician profiles described in the reimbursement section, etc.[32]

In its June 1975 budget message, the Canadian Government announced the introduction of two measures designed to restrain future program cost increases at the Federal level and to spur initiative at the Provincial level to formulate more effective cost control mechanisms. With regard to the hospital insurance program, Ottawa gave formal notification of its intention to re-negotiate in 5-years time the basis of Federal financial participation with the Provinces. Secondly, it announced the imposition of a ceiling on the annual percentage increase which would be allowed with regard to the amount of Federal contributions to the Provinces for insured medical services. For fiscal year 1976–77, the ceiling would initially be set at 13 percent (apart from those expenditures attributable to population growth), with a 10.5 percent maximum increase allowed for fiscal year 1977–78, and 8.5 percent for fiscal 1978–79 and thereafter.

France ([34], pp. 351–358)

In 1945, the French Government passed the Ordinances of October, providing for a unification of the voluntary social insurance funds which had previously insured a large portion of the population for both benefits during periods of illness and medical care services (the combination is referred to as "sickness insurance"). Approximately 98.5 percent of the French population is now covered for sickness insurance, the majority (70 percent) through a compulsory general system covering nonagricultural workers and salaried employees. Benefits under the program include a daily sickness cash benefit, maternity and disability cash payments, and at least 75 percent reimbursement of ordinary medical expenses (physicians' fees, hospital costs, and costs of dental care and prescription drugs) and full reimbursement of medical expenses for a costly or prolonged illness.

The costs of sickness insurance are met through employer contributions of about 12.5 percent of payroll, employee contributions of 3.5 percent of earnings, and certain earmarked taxes. Deficits are covered by general revenues and transfers from other social security funds.[1] The Ministry of Health and Social Security supervises the program at the national level, with Regional Sickness Insurance Funds and Primary (local) Sickness Insurance Funds assuming

---

[31] Robert G. Evans, "Beyond the Medical Marketplace: Expenditure, Utilization, and Pricing of Insured Health in Canada," in National Health Insurance: Can We Learn from Canada? ed. by Spyros Andreopoulos. John Wiley and Sons, New York, 1975: 159–162.

[32] Ibid.

[1] "Main Features of Selected National Health Care Systems," Research and Statistics Note No. 9–197. U.S. Department of Health, Education, and Welfare, Social Security Administration, Office of Research and Statistics, May 18, 1973: 3.

responsibilities for coordination of funds, registration of the insured, payment of cash benefits, and refunds of medical expenses.[2]

COVERAGE

Approximately 15.2 million workers are covered for sickness insurance under the general system ("general regime") and its affiliated groups. An additional 5.2 million workers are insured under other Government programs.[3]

The general regime covers salaried persons working in industry, trade, and administration. Salaried persons attached to special sectors are covered by "special regimes." These are principally for agricultural workers, electricity and gas workers (nationalized industries), seamen, miners, workers in State industries (explosives, gun factories, military force plants), and civil servants of local authorities. While the different regimes are run independently of each other, the covered benefits are the same for all kinds of salaried workers, including agricultural workers.[4]

Certain nonsalaried workers are covered by special funds. This coverage has been extended to students, newspapermen, writers, artists, and civil war victims. This category of coverage has been gradually extended to certain other nonsalaried groups—in 1961, self-employed farmers were brought into the program, and in 1966, self-employed persons in nonagricultural occupations.[5]

Private voluntary funds continue to offer coverage to persons not under the compulsory scheme and also offer benefits which supplement those provided under the Government program.

Under certain conditions, coverage is also extended to foreign workers employed in France (there are special arrangements for citizens of the Common Market Countries) and to French people working abroad and overseas (especially in the former French colonies).[6]

BENEFITS [7]

The sickness insurance program in France generally provides cash refunds to the insured for part of the cost of medical care. The insured normally pays for services out of pocket and is then reimbursed by his local sickness fund in amounts ranging from 70 to 100 percent of the costs for services, in accordance with negotiated and approved fee schedules. Minor medical treatment is not fully reimbursed. The social insurance program does, however, have a form of catastrophic coverage in that it reimburses the full cost of prolonged or unusually expensive treatment or treatment provided in the following cases:

When the patient belongs to certain categories, such as the retired, invalids, and veterans.

When the medical or surgical procedures are over a certain cost level, which is that of the normal appendectomy (all major surgery is reimbursed at 100 percent).

[2] Jozef Van Langendonck, "The European Experience in Social Health Insurance," Social Security Bulletin, July 1973: 23.

[3] Robert W. Weise, "Social Security Abroad: Medical Care Agreement With French Doctors." Social Security Bulletin, July 1972: 32.

[4] R. F. Bridgman, "Medical Care Under Social Security in France." International Journal of Health Services, November 1971: 334.

[5] "Social Security and National Health Insurance in France." Embassy of France, Press and Information Service, New York, 1971: 6.

[6] Bridgman, p. 334.

[7] Ibid., pp. 335–336.

Provision of blood, plasma, or human milk.

Provision of important prosthetics and appliances.

Care of premature newborns.

Especially expensive treatment (e.g., cobalt therapy, artificial kidneys) and hospital stays over 30 days.

Long-term diseases (e.g., tuberculosis, cardiopathies, cancer, mental disturbances, infantile diabetes).[8]

For minor medical treatment—that is, when the catastrophic type situation does not apply—the program reimburses the following amounts:

Expensive and essential drugs—90 percent.

Physician and paramedical fees and laboratory procedures in public or private nonprofit hospitals, or in hospital outpatient departments—80 percent.

Hospitalization costs up to 30 days in public or nonprofit private hospitals, or proprietary institutions under an agreement with the Government—80 percent.

Physician fees for home or office consultations and visits—75 percent.

Laboratory tests, drugs other than essential ones, dental care outside the hospital, eyeglasses and small appliances, cure in spas—70 percent.

FINANCING

Health insurance is financed mainly by payments from employers and employees in proportion to their salaries as follows:

For salaries up to a 1975 ceiling of 2,750 francs a month, the employer pays 10.45 percent and the employee 2.5 percent of the salary.[9] For monthly salaries higher than 2,750 francs, the employer pays an additional 2 percent and the employee 1 percent, calculated on the entire remaining salary, not subject to any ceiling. The combined employer-employee contributions for the average worker total about 16 percent of his earnings; this amount, however, includes contributions not only for health care but also for cash sickness and maternity benefits and for disability and death benefits. Only about four-fifths of total expenditures are actually spent on medical care; the remainder is used for the various cash benefits. Prorating the combined employer-employee contributions according to funds expended would thus alot four-fifths of the full 16 percent to health care, or about 12.8 percent.[10]

In health plans for nonagricultural self-employed workers, the size of the contribution is determined, subject to certain arrangements, on the basis of the earned income declared to the income tax administration. As a rule, the insured are divided into categories of contributions within given income brackets.

Unlike most other European systems in which the role of Government subsidies has expanded, the French program is financed almost entirely through the employer-employee contributions noted above. Partial Government sub-

---

[8] The July 1972 Social Security Bulletin (p. 32) reports that, for costs of treatment for 21 "scheduled diseases," the amount payable "can be waived and the social security system may absorb the entire cost of care."

[9] As of December 31, 1975, one French franc was equivalent to about 21¢ in U.S. currency.

[10] Joseph G. Simanis, "National Health Systems in Eight Countries." U.S. Department of Health, Education, and Welfare, Social Security Administration Office of Research and Statistics. DHEW Publication No. (SSA) 75–11924, January 1975: 51.

sidies from general revenues are provided only for the care of specific groups, such as pensioners, welfare recipients, students, unemployed workers, and farmers, who have little or no earnings on which to pay taxes, or in the case of serious deficits in the social insurance funds.[11] In the past, such deficits have been made up by drawing on funds from other areas of social security income (such as those for family allowances), from a surtax on automobile insurance premiums, and from an alcohol tax.

It has been estimated that approximately 66 percent of health insurance funds are derived from employers' contributions, 28 percent from insured persons' contributions, and 6 percent from Government subsidies.[12]

ADMINISTRATION

The health insurance program in France has decentralized administration. Autonomous, semipublic funds operate at local, regional, and national levels. These primary funds are administered by boards composed of representatives of employers and the insured. All people who reside or work in a given district must be registered with the local fund serving that district.

There are 122 of these primary social insurance funds whose districts usually cover a "department," the term used for an administrative and geographic political subdivision within France, corresponding somewhat to a State in the United States. Primary funds are responsible for registering the insured and for paying out sickness, maternity, death, temporary disability, and industrial injury benefits. In addition, the funds carry out certain health and social policies on behalf of the insured within the district.

Sixteen regional social insurance funds coordinate the activities of the primary funds within their jurisdictions. In particular, they develop and coordinate industrial injury prevention measures, guarantee the uniformity of charges, and pursue health and social policies.[13]

At the national level, the responsible branch of government is the Ministry of Public Health and Social Security, which is in charge of supervising the "general regime" administered through the primary and regional funds. The "special regimes" (for seamen, miners, railroad employees, etc.) are administered, wholly or in part, by the occupations concerned. Other funds covering businessmen, artisans, self-employed farmers and members of the professions are administered in a similar manner.[14]

A feature of the French system seldom observed in other countries permits social insurance funds to participate in capital expenditures for health facilities and in governmental preventive health care programs. Prior to World War II, the funds could spend their savings on the operation or subsidization of health institutions. Following the Ordinance of October 1945, which provided for the unification of the former voluntary mutual aid societies or funds, a broad health and social policy fund was created with a national center and regional branches. This central fund is no longer derived from savings but comes from a percentage of the total budget of each main social insurance branch, the proportion being determined each year by a ministerial regulation.[15]

---

[11] Van Langendonck, p. 25.

[12] Gabriel Pallez, "Urban Problems: Social Security and the Teaching Hospital [in France]." Journal of Medical Education, Dec. 1973, pt. 2: 111.

[13] Bridgman, p. 338.

[14] "Social Security and National Health Insurance in France," p. 19.

[15] Bridgman, p. 338.

Social insurance organizations do not have complete freedom to create or subsidize any health or social institution. They must follow a plan determined by the Ministry of Public Health and Social Security, and endorsed by the National Planning Board. Over the last 30 years, the resources of the health and social policy funds have supported about 30 percent of the capital expenditures for hospital construction and equipment, a large share of the cost of maternal and child health, tuberculosis and mental health programs, and an important part of the development of private group practice and public health centers.

The social insurance funds were also required by the Ordinances of October 1945 to offer free health examinations to their insured groups and dependents "at certain periods of their lifetime." This provision of the law has not, however, been implemented on a broad scale, with only 20 primary funds having initiated such projects by 1969.[16]

REIMBURSEMENT METHODS

The French system utilizes both indirect and direct payment methods for health care providers. The indirect system applies mainly to institutional care. When an insured person is hospitalized, he is responsible only for payment of the deductible (if any) when discharged; the hospital submits the remainder of the bill to the patient's social insurance fund for reimbursement. Reimbursement rates are fixed at a certain percentage of a ceiling value determined by a central government decision in the case of hospital care. These rates are based primarily on the cost of operating the hospital per patient per day and are also applicable to participating proprietary hospitals and nursing homes, because their cost per patient day cannot exceed that of the nearest public hospital.

In 1974, there were about 240,000 beds in public hospitals and 123,000 beds in private hospitals. About half of the private beds were in voluntary nonprofit institutions and the remainder in private, for-profit hospitals.[17] The overall bed per population ratio was about 7 beds per 1,000 population.

Forty-five percent of surgical and maternity beds were in private, rather than public, hospitals. Private hospitals registered both a shorter average length of stay and a higher rate of surgical admissions than public institutions. In 1969 the average length of stay for all public hospitals in France was 19.1 days. For private hospitals, the average length of stay in short-term acute hospitals in 1969 was 12.0 days.[18] Private hospitals registered 31 surgical admissions per year per 1,000 per 1,000 population as against 24.2 surgical admissions in public hospitals.[19]

Approval of the central government must be obtained before a private hospital can be opened. In this way, the Government tries to prevent uncontrolled competition.

Eighty percent of private, for-profit hospitals and clinics are owned totally or partially by doctors. These private, profitmaking hospitals have been discribed as "financially prosperous, because they select 'good cases,' they have a high turnover of patients, and they collect physicians' and surgeons' fees." [20]

---

[16] Ibid, p. 339.

[17] Simanis, p. 48.

[18] Richard Johnson, "Statistics Make U.S. Hospitals Look Healthy." Modern Hospital, February 1972: 102.

[19] Bridgman, p. 341.

[20] Ibid., p. 337.

Physicians' services and other medical care rendered to a hospital inpatient are paid for on a fee-for-service basis according to a fee schedule. In private hospitals, these fees are passed on to the hospital physician; in public hospitals, they usually are not, since the doctor is paid either a full-time or part-time salary, depending on the hours per week spent on hospital care. In addition to salaries, the medical staff of public hospitals receive a portion of their income by sharing a part of receipts from fees. In dividing these funds, some weight is given to the rank of the individual doctor.[21]

For outpatient medical care, the triangular relationship among the patient, his physician, and his social insurance fund has remained basically unchanged. The principle of direct payment of full medical fees by the patient to the physician, with partial reimbursement to the patient by his social insurance fund, is the general pattern; but in the case of care given by hospital physicians, the patient may delegate his rights to be reimbursed to a third party and pay only the deductible to his physician.

Until recently, reimbursement rates for medical services were fixed at a certain percentage of a ceiling value which was determined by agreement between the medical profession (medical unions) and the social insurance funds, or by agreement between the funds and individual physicians, or by Government decision in the absence of any agreement, after a hearing by an interministerial committee.

This system was less than satisfactory, however, from the point of view of both the medical profession and the Government:

> This situation has been unstable and has led to periodic denunciation of agreements because of the constant tendency of physicians to increase their fees, along with the rising cost of living, while the sickness funds tend to freeze the fees and adopt anti-inflationary measures. During the negotiations, fees have run wild and the reimbursement rates have fallen to a low percentage. Patients have been very dissatisfied, and political tension has risen. A law was recently enacted which established a national matrix for ceiling fees and guaranteed for the next 4 years a fixed percentage of reimbursement. The medical profession protested, but it is most unlikely that the doctors will go on strike. At this time one should recall the high value the population has set on social insurance. On several occasions groups of workers, such as miners, were covered by special funds which gave them better protection than the general system. It happened that some mines, being exhausted, were closed by Government decision and the miners were resettled in industry. But, falling under the general social security regime, they lost some of their privileges. This was a very serious affair, despite the fact that their salaries were increased. These people preferred receiving less money in cash, but being better protected against social and sickness hazards.[22]

On November 1, 1971, a new agreement between the Government and the medical profession became effective for a period lasting until May 1, 1975. Unlike previous agreements which were applicable for only a single year and binding only within the limits of a specific geographic area, the new agreement was applicable nationwide to all practitioners except those doctors who individually elected to be excluded. Under the terms of the new agreement, participating doctors were authorized to charge the prevailing rates shown below:

---

[21] Simanis, p. 54.
[22] Bridgman, p. 336.

Types of care	Prevailing rates (francs)	
	Doctors adhering to agreement	Doctors not adhering to agreement
Office consultation:		
General practitioner_____	20	4. 00
Specialists_____	32	8. 00
Home visits:		
General practitioner_____	27	5. 20
Specialists_____	40	10. 40

Seventy-five percent of the official fee schedule amounts are reimbursable by social insurance funds, the remaining 25 percent by the patient. Charges exceeding the schedule are not to be reimbursed. Fees above the standard amounts may, however, be charged by specialists or other outstanding doctors who are so designated by the regional (departmental) medical association. Doctors who choose not to participate must inform the social insurance funds of their decision. As of March 1972, approximately 49,000 or 95.7 percent of all registered physicians were reported to be participating under the new agreement, an increase over the number of participating physicians (88 percent) in the previous year.

Patients who use nonparticipating physicians are reimbursed for home and office visits only at the maximum rates established in the fee schedule. Special medical care and retirement benefits, now available to the medical profession, are not provided to nonparticipating doctors. In addition, nonparticipating physicians are not allowed to benefit from the improved income tax provisions which permit affiliated doctors to make substantial deductions for professional expenses.[23] These provisions, when taken together would seem to explain the very high participation rate.

The 1971 agreement also introduced the concept of self-discipline by the medical profession with regard to the cost of medical care. Medical profiles showing the average cost of medical care are now published quarterly by the medical agencies. These profiles are compared with the charges made by each doctor. A medico-social commission within each department, or region, composed equally of representatives of the social insurance funds and the regional medical association is responsible for reviewing the cost profiles of any doctor whose charges substantially exceed those of his colleagues. Doctors with unjustifiable excess charges are asked to refund the amount of overcharge. Continuing abuses are considered grounds for exclusion from the program, upon the recommendation of the regional commission. It is expected that this monitoring of doctors' fees will result in an annual savings of 1 billion francs.[24]

In 1973, there were approximately 77,000 qualified doctors in France, with about 55,000 in private practice and the rest occupied in industrial pursuits, social security, hospital services, and miscellaneous activities. Less than half of those in private practice were general practitioners. About 40 percent of the private practitioners, most of them specialists, also work part-time in hospitals, clinics, or dispensaries. About 43 percent of French physicians are designated as specialists on a registry under the control of the local doctors' associations. The growth in specialty practice in recent years is explained in large part by the

---

[23] Weise, p. 34.
[24] Ibid.

fact that specialists are allowed to charge usually twice the fee allotted to the general practitioner for the same service and that general practitioners normally cannot follow their patients into the hospital—even for routine X-rays or for laboratory services, the general practitioner must refer his patient to a specialist.[25]

Rising Costs

Escalating health costs have placed a considerable burden on the social insurance programs in France, particularly because they are designed in principle to be self-supporting. Deficits in the health insurance funds reached an estimated 1.9 billion francs in 1970. Between 1966 and 1970, the projected 7.3 percent annual rate of growth in health insurance benefits was exceeded and reached an actual rate of 8.9 percent.[26]

For the period from 1960 to 1969, the total cost for the delivery of health services increased from 11.9 billion francs to 39.1 billion francs, or at an average annual rate of 14.5 percent. After taking into account factors such as population increases and inflation, medical costs still doubled during this period. Expressed in terms of the gross national product, health care expenditures rose from 4 percent in 1960 to 6.25 percent in 1969.[27]

In order to cover deficits in the health insurance funds, the Government has had to provide general revenue subsidies and also transfer a portion of the family allowance contribution rate (a separate social insurance program) to the health insurance fund. Since 1970, other economy measures have included the lowering of the fixed prices of several hundred most-often prescribed medications and the elimination from the list of reimbursable prescriptions of more than 2,000 other medications no longer considered important for modern therapy. Fixed prices of pharmaceuticals are revised at 2-year intervals on the basis of real production costs and volume of sales. Other steps taken by the Government in an attempt to contain costs have included the introduction of the multiyear fixed fee schedule and medical "cost profiles" on physicians, as described earlier.

Japan ([34], pp. 359–367)

With the passage of a 1922 act dealing with workers' health insurance, Japan became the first Asian country to introduce a social insurance law. The entire Japanese population is now covered by either a government-administered or a government-supervised health insurance program. There are two main programs: (1) the national health insurance program (NHI), which covers residents not insured through their employment, and (2) the employees' health insurance program (EHI), compulsory for persons employed in manufacturing, mining, and retail establishments employing five or more persons, and voluntary for workers in businesses with fewer than five employees. In addition to these two programs, there are separate, government-administered health insurance plans for seamen and day laborers. Government employees, workers in public corporations, and teachers are covered under yet another scheme, administered through mutual aid associations.

---

[25] Simanis, pp. 47–48.
[26] Palmer D. Hoskins, "Recent Social Security Reforms in France." Social Security Bulletin, January 1971; p. 35.
[27] Weise, p. 23.

In principle, all of the health insurance programs cover the same range of benefits, including physicians' services, hospitalization, nursing, transportation, drugs, dental care, etc. However, there are variations among the plans with regard to duration of benefits, amount of patient cost-sharing, provision (or absence of provision) for cash sickness benefits in times of illness.

Under NHI, a special tax on insured persons covers 25 percent of the cost, with the remainder financed through the national treasury. For the EHI program and the separate programs for day laborers and civil servants, the employee and the employer each pay contributions, generally in equal amounts, based on earnings, but the contribution rates vary among the different plans, as do the income ceilings to which the rates are subject. All of the employee plans received a partial government subsidy.

The national health insurance program and the programs for seamen and day laborers are government-administered. The plan for civil servants is handled through mutual aid associations under the direction of the responsible government department. The employee health insurance program is managed either by approved health insurance societies (for firms employing 300 or more employees) or directly by the Government (for firms with fewer than 300 employees).

Private institutions play a major role in the Japanese health care system. More than half the hospital beds and 90 percent of general medical clinics are under private management. Reimbursement to these facilities is based on a government-approved fee schedule. Physicians and dentists are also paid in accordance with a government-approved fee schedule consisting of over 700 items of service.

Coverage

Virtually the entire Japanese population is covered under one of the following programs:

(1) Employee health insurance (EHI) program, which is compulsory for any person employed by a firm, factory, hospital, or other working place which regularly has five or more employees. Exceptions are persons employed in restaurants, hotels, fishing, forestry, and agriculture who may, however, elect to become insured voluntarily. For purposes of voluntary coverage, over half the employees in the business must consent, and the action must have the approval of the prefectural governor.

The EHI program is administered either directly by the national government or by a health insurance society especially established for this purpose. Under the government-managed part of the program, there were a total of 13.3 million insured persons (or about 25 percent of the total insured) in 1975. There were 10.9 million insured persons (or about 22 percent of the total) under the health insurance society programs in that same year.

The total number of insured persons under both parts of the EHI program was 24.2 million in 1975. With dependents included, total coverage was 53.2 million. (See section of this chapter dealing with administration for explanation of conditions applying to government-managed versus health-insurance-society-managed programs.)

(2) National health insurance program (NHI), a nationwide scheme for all Japanese residents not covered by EHI or one of the special programs listed below. This program was set up primarily for the self-employed, farmers, and fishermen. Essentially a community-based program, it is now compulsory for all local community residents not covered under some other health insurance scheme. This program covers a substantial number of pensioners and other

older persons who have not been drawn into industry and who have remained in rural areas (nearly 60 percent of the population over age 60 are under the NHI program). In 1975, NHI insured 43.8 million persons, including dependents (or about 41 percent of total number of insured).

(3) Day laborers' health insurance program, for persons employed by the day, together with seasonal and other temporary workers. In 1975, the total number of insured plus dependents covered under this program was 752,000.

(4) Seamen's insurance, under which coverage has been fairly static from year to year, with about 734,000 persons and dependents presently covered.

(5) Mutual aid associations, set up to cover national and local government employees, workers in public corporations, and teachers. Coverage is about 12 million persons, including both the insured and their dependents.

It should be noted that the term "dependents," when used in the Japanese system, may include ascendants, grandchildren, and younger siblings, as well as spouse and children and any other dependent relative living in the household.

BENEFITS

It has been said that "the sick person as a rule fares best under a society-managed EHI plan, slightly less well under the government-managed EHI program, and not as well under NHI."[1] Although in principle the range of medical care benefits is basically the same under all the plans described in the preceding section, there are important differences with regard to amount of patient cost-sharing, duration of benefits, provision (or absence of provision) for cash sickness allowances, waiting periods, etc.

A. SERVICE BENEFITS

Service benefits under all the plans consist of:
(1) Physicians' services, in or out of hospital.
(2) All drugs (from a list of more than 7,000 items approved by the Ministry of Health and Welfare).
(3) All approved appliances (except eyeglasses).
(4) Inpatient care in hospitals and clinics.
(5) Nursing care, exclusive of private-duty nursing.
(6) Laboratory services, therapy, and treatment.
(7) Transportation.
(8) Dental care, including most dentures.

Illnesses resulting from the following are not covered: criminal acts of the insured, self-induced disorders, fighting, intoxication, or extreme "profligacy." In cases where an insured person disobeys the instructions of physicians without proper cause, part of the benefits is not given.[2]

B. EXTRA BENEFITS

In addition to the above, insurers may, at their option, provide other services for the purpose of health promotion and prevention, such as periodic health exams, home visiting services, nutrition clinic services and guidance, and provision of rest homes. Such additional benefits are commonly provided through some of the more financially well-off health insurance societies established by larger industries.

---

[1] Paul Fisher, "Major Social Security Issues: Japan, 1972." Social Security Bulletin, March 1973: 34.
[2] Kenzo Kiikuni, "Health Insurance Programs in Japan." Inquiry, March 1972: 19.

C. WAITING PERIODS AND DURATION OF BENEFITS

The day laborers' health insurance scheme is the only one of the plans which applies a waiting period to benefits. Eligibility for medical care under this program depends upon the payment of contributions for more than 28 days within the preceding 2 months, or for more than 78 days within the preceding 6 months. The day laborers' program is also unique in its limitation on the duration of benefits—5 years from the first day of treatment. None of the other schemes applies a durational limit on benefits, although certain plans (with the exception of the NHI program) may apply rules governing the period of free coverage after termination of insurance.[3]

D. CASH SICKNESS ALLOWANCE

Some of the plans also provide cash benefits, including disability allowances for insured persons, funeral grants, delivery grants, and infant nursing allowances for both the insured and their dependents. Under EHI, cash sickness allowances amount to 60 percent (in cases of hospitalization, 40 percent if the insured person has no dependents) of the respective standard renumeration. Cash benefits are subject to a 4-day waiting period and are payable for 6 months (in tubercular cases, 18 months). Under NHI, there is no cash sickness benefit.[4]

E. COST SHARING

Under the national health insurance plan, there is general cost-sharing by the patient of 30 percent of the cost of services. The 30-percent patient share is paid directly by the patient to the medical facility.

Under the employee health insurance plan, cost-sharing by the insured patient is limited to a fee of 200 yen (about 66 cents) for the first consultation and about 60 yen (about 20 cents) for each day of the first month's hospitalization.[5] Dependents of the insured pay 30 percent of the cost of services, up to a maximum of 30,000 yen (about $100) per dependent "per case" (defined as a complete course of medical treatment, including any hospitalization).[6] This ceiling on dependents' cost-sharing also applies to dependents under the NHI scheme.

Since 1973, persons over age 70 and bedridden persons over age 65 have been eligible for exemption from cost-sharing if their annual income (or that of the family that supports them) is less than certain amounts (in 1973, about 600,000 yen or roughly $2,000).[7]

FINANCING

Each of the Japanese health insurance programs is financed through separate and different arrangements, as noted below:

A. EMPLOYEE HEALTH INSURANCE

The government-managed part of the EHI plan is financed through equal contributions from employer and employee. As of October 1973, the combined

---

[3] Derick H. Fulcher, "A Study of Some Aspects of Medical Care Systems in Industrialized Countries." International Labour Office, Geneva, 1973: 52–53.

[4] Fisher, p. 34.

[5] As of December 1974, there were approxmately 301 yen in U.S. $1.

[6] Fulcher, p. 53.

[7] Fisher, p. 35.

contribution rate was fixed at 7.6 percent of the employee's total standard remuneration up to a ceiling of 200,000 yen (about $670) a month. The Ministry of Health and Welfare is empowered to increase the contribution rate up to a maximum of 8 percent, with a corresponding increase in the percentage of government subsidy. Total remuneration includes wages, salary, allowances, bonuses, and other income earned by the insured person.[8] There is a national government subsidy of 10 percent of benefit expenditure, plus payment of administrative costs.

Under the plans managed by health insurance societies, the society may charge a contribution rate of between 3 and 9 percent of remuneration within the ceiling applicable to the government-managed program. The employees share cannot, however, exceed 4 percent. The national government subsidizes the program only to a very small extent (in 1974, the subsidy amounted to less than 0.2 percent of total income).

B. NATIONAL HEALTH INSURANCE

Thirty percent of the cost of this program is borne directly by the insured through the cost-sharing mechanism applied to benefits. The remaining 70 percent of the cost of the program is financed through the national treasury (45 percent) and through a national health insurance tax collected from the insured (25 percent). The NHI tax is set according to the financial ability of each household and is collected and accounted for by the local communities.[9] Forty percent of the tax is in proportion to income, 10 percent to property valuation, 35 percent to the number of the insured in the household, and 15 percent on a flat rate. The annual rate is limited to a maximum of 120,000 yen per household (about $400). In 1974, the NHI tax represented 2.8 percent of the taxable income of the households concerned. In addition to the 45-percent subsidy of medical care expenditures, the national government also pays full administrative costs of the program and provides additional grants for poorer local communities and for hospital construction, nursing, and midwife care.

C. DAY LABORERS' HEALTH INSURANCE

Contributions are shared, in principle, equally between employer and employee and are fixed at a flat rate which ranges from 20 yen to 660 yen per day in accordance with the wage class. The national government funds the administrative expenses and 35 percent of all benefit costs for the plan.

D. SEAMEN'S HEALTH INSURANCE

This program is part of a total insurance scheme for seamen; thus, the contribution rate covers far more than health insurance. For the total scheme, a ceiling of 200,000 yen a month applies with 33 income grades below it. Government funds meet administrative costs and subsidize part of the expenses for medical benefits.

E. MUTUAL AID ASSOCIATIONS

Contributions are shared equally by the employee and the employer, which in this case is a public body. Rates are determined by each association and range from 5.4 to 8.8 percent of earnings. Administrative costs are subsidized by the government.

---

[8] Kiikuni, p. 20.

[9] Kiikuni, p. 20.

ADMINISTRATION

The employee health insurance program is administered either directly by the national government through the Ministry of Health and Welfare or by a legally authorized health insurance society. Approval to operate the EHI program through a health insurance society has traditionally been granted only to firms having 300 or more employees; in recent years, only those firms with 1,000 or more employees have been granted such approval.[10] Such a society may be set up by a single employer or by a group of employers acting together. At least one-half of the employees concerned must agree to the establishment of a society, and approval must be received from the Ministry of Health and Welfare.

There are about 1,616 health insurance societies administering the EHI program, under the general supervision of the Ministry of Health and Welfare. Collectively, these societies represent 45 percent of the workers covered under EHI. Most societies serve an individual enterprise, but 257 are general societies organized by the employers and employees of more than one firm. Policy matters are handled by a "conference" consisting of equal numbers of employees and employers, with a board of directors, again with equally representative membership, responsible for executive functions.

In addition to direct administration of the day laborers' and seamen's health insurance programs, the national government is responsible for that part of the EHI program not handled through health insurance societies. The Government Social Insurance Administration, through its network of branch offices, operates the program on behalf of some 55 percent of workers covered under EHI.

The national health insurance program is operated through more than 3,200 local authorities (cities, towns, villages, and wards in the city of Tokyo), with central control being vested in the local prefectural government, and ultimately in the Ministry of Health and Welfare. As a parallel to local authority administration, nearly 200 national health insurance associations have been authorized to administer the program on behalf of local residents with occupational or trade affinities. These associations must have at least 300 members and the approval of the prefectural governor. Such organizations include only about 2.6 million of the 44.3 million people covered by national health insurance.[11]

The Japanese system includes various advisory and appeals councils at the national and local levels. A Social Security Advisory Council, whose membership includes vice-ministers, members of the Diet, representatives of employers, employees, medical care providers, and others with experience in the field, advises the Prime Minister on legislation in the area of social security and health insurance. A Social Insurance Council directly advises the Minister of Health and Welfare and the director of the Social Insurance Agency on planning and operation of the health insurance scheme. Citizens' advisory councils are set up at the local level to advise local authorities on the management and operation of the NHI program. Social insurance referees and social insurance appeals committees handle questions and complaints arising under the health insurance (and other State insurance) schemes submitted by insured persons

---

[10] Fulcher, p. 46.

[11] "Outline of Social Insurance in Japan." Japanese Government Social Insurance Agency, Tokyo, 1973:33.

and employers. Final appeal on a decision rendered by a social appeals committee may be made to the courts.

Various reports have noted the unequal performance record between the two parts of the EHI program. Particular concern has been expressed over the need for increasing government subsidization of the government-managed employee system:

> The * * * health insurance societies apparently offer the employee-and particularly his dependents-superior and additional services, are better managed than the other plans, and (probably with the aid of substantial employer subsidies) are able to stay within their budget. About 84 percent of the health insurance societies received in contribution the same or a smaller percentage of payroll as those for the government-managed system. The remainder of these societies obtained from one-half of 1 percent to 1 percent more than the * * * payroll tax * * * that applies to EHI. In contrast, the government-managed employee system requires each year sizable and growing subsidies from general revenues.

> One reason for the unequal performance of the two parts of EHI may lie in the unequal distribution or risks. The government-managed program, which covers the great number of relatively small enterprises (with less than 300 employees), insures relatively more employees past age 55 with higher morbidity and utilization rates than those insured under the society-managed programs, where persons over age 55 are likely to have been eliminated from the payroll. * * * Insured employees in the government-managed program have a lower average income, and thus pay a lower average contribution. Because their health care needs are greater, however, health care expenditures for this group, particularly for medical care, are higher than for employees in the society-managed plans.[12]

It appears that pressures from large companies, the labor unions, and the National Federation of Health Insurance Societies have thwarted efforts of the government to eliminate the "dual-tract" EHI system. Proposals to unify the EHI and NHI programs have met with even stronger opposition, mainly because such a move would reduce benefits (by eliminating provision for cash sickness payments) and would free the employer from his present obligation to pay one-half the payroll tax under EHI.

In 1972, the society-managed EHI system ended the year with a comparatively sound balance of contributions to expenditures. Of the more than 1,500 approved societies participating in that year, only 284 showed a deficit of funds, amounting to a total for all societies of 53 million yen (about $142,500). In contrast, the government-managed EHI program ended the year with a one-year deficit of 60 billion yen; when added to the accumulated deficit from previous years, the result was a total deficit of 270.6 billion yen by the end of March 1973.[13]

As a nation, Japan has been rapidly increasing its expenditures for medical care in recent years. In 1972, gross national expenditures for medical care totaled 34 trillion yen, a 25 percent increase over the previous year, and representing 4.46 percent of the gross national product in 1972. Of the total expenditures for health, 35.3 percent was spent for hospitalization, 54.9 percent for office and domiciliary care, and 10 percent for dental care. Forty-two percent of the medical care expenditure is spent for medicine, showing that the consump-

12 Fisher, p. 34.
13 "Outline of Social Insurance in Japan," p. 3.

tion of medicine in Japan is quite high when compared with countries such as Sweden—15 percent, West Germany—13.5 percent, etc.[14]

REIMBURSEMENT METHODS

Medical services covered under Japanese health insurance are available from registered health insurance doctors at "designated health insurance medical facilities," which are hospitals or clinics approved by the governor for participation in the program. Almost all hospitals and clinics in Japan are designated facilities, and nearly all medical doctors are registered with the system. Thus, freedom of choice of physician and institutional provider is virtually guaranteed under the Japanese system.

More than three-fourths of the hospitals and almost all clinics in Japan are privately owned. Private physicians are generally not permitted to practice in hospitals. (Hospitals have salaried physicians who care for patients in the hospital.) Most physicians have, therefore, set up their own private clinics, many of which have inpatient beds, extensive medical equipment such as X-ray apparatus and laboratories, and ancillary personnel such as nurses and nurse assistants.

Private practitioners usually do not refer their patients to hospitals unless the patient urges them to do so. The patient, however, has freedom of choice in selecting a hospital or clinic for his point of entry into the health system. Practitioners in private clinics commonly perform even minor surgery on the premises.

Several health insurance societies own and operate their own hospitals and clinics. The income from these institutions and that from contributions is often invested in convalescent homes and sanatoria, as well as in rest and vacation centers for the healthy insured.[15]

The general pattern of reimbursement under the Japanese system is that of fee-for-service. Mechanisms such as all-inclusive per diem rates or annual prospective budgets have not been employed for institutional providers in Japan. Hospital income under the health insurance system is governed by a system of "point values" assigned to different services performed in the hospital. The point system establishes a hierarchy of prices for individual services. The value of each point is negotiated in the national Social Insurance Medical Council. In addition to the amount reimbursed through the health insurance system the provider receives directly from the patient the fixed amount of individual cost-sharing applicable under the different plans.

At the end of 1973, the total number of beds in hospitals and clinics was approximately 1.4 million, or about 13 hospital and clinic beds per 1,000 population. The average length of hospital stay is about 34 days excluding psychiatric and tuberculosis cases. [16]

Japan has about 130,000 doctors, or about one physician per 860 people. Even without hospital privileges, private practitioners generally earn higher incomes than hospital staff physicians who are paid according to a full-time fixed salary base. No house staff physician in Japan is permitted to have private beds in the hospital.

Reimbursement for the private practitioner is also on the basis of the point system. Each act of medical care is given a point score, which is deter-

[14] Mikio Yamamoto and Junshiro Ohmura, "The Health and Medical System in Japan." Inquiry, June 1975: 48.

[15] Fisher, p. 36.

[16] Yamamoto, p. 45.

mined after due consideration is given to the degree of technical difficulty of the medical service, as well as to economy.

After the patient has directly paid his share of the bill, the remainder is submitted to the Social Insurance Medical Care Fee Payment Fund, in the case of employee health insurance, or to the Federation of National Health Insurance Organizations, in the case of NHI. Both organizations pool the money from each program; and a review is made by a medical consultant before the bill is paid. Unnecessary treatment is sometimes cut off. Payment is generally made within 45 days after submission of the bill. [17]

The Minister of Health and Welfare, through the prefectural governors, has the responsibility for overall supervision of the various health insurance payment agencies. The ultimate sanction in cases of serious and deliberate abuse is revocation of the practitioner's or institution's status as a participating provider under the program.

Dentists are paid and evaluated under the same system that applies to physicians. Drug prices are controlled to some extent by the industry and by government price schedules. Most drugs prescribed by a physician are supplied to the patient directly by the doctor himself, and the doctor's daily point score reflects a component for drug prescribing and supplying.[18]

Sweden ([34], pp. 368–376)

The Swedish Parliament first passed legislation providing for a compulsory national health insurance program in 1947. However, the effective date for implementation of this legislation was postponed for several years. During this time, studies were conducted to investigate alternative forms of compulsory basic health insurance possibly to be combined with voluntary supplemental group health insurance. Once again in 1953, Parliament approved the creation of a national health insurance program, but delayed the effective date until January 1, 1955.[1]

Since 1955, the entire Swedish population has been covered for a broad array of medical benefits combined with cash payments during periods of working incapacity due to illness or injury. Medical benefits include physician care (small flat-rate fee paid by the patient), hospitalization, and partial reimbursement for prescription drugs and dental care.

About 8 percent of Sweden's gross national product is used for public health and medical care. Costs of the overall health system are financed approximately as follows: (1) combined national and local (county council) government funds, mainly through county council taxation—75 percent, (2) compulsory health insurance contributions from employers and employees—10 percent, and (3) cost-sharing by patients for noncovered or partially covered services—15 percent.[2]

---

[17] Kiikuni, p. 20.

[18] Fulcher, p. 56–57.

[1] Odin Anderson in "Health Care: Can There be Equity?" (John Wiley and Sons, New York, 1972) explains the delay as follow: "According to Swedish political protocol . . . a law is not put into effect until the government decides to do so . . . The 8 years were used to iron out administrative and relationship problems with the medical profession." (p. 77)

[2] Joseph G. Simanis. "National Health Systems in Eight Countries." U.S. Department of Health, Education, and Welfare, Social Security Administration, Office of Research and Statistics. DHEW Publication No. (SS) 75–11924. Washington, U.S. Govt. Print. Off., January 1975: 87.

Coverage

All resident Swedish citizens and registered aliens are entitled to medical benefits. Coverage is compulsory—at age 16, all citizens must register with one of the more than 600 local social insurance offices in Sweden responsible for administering the program. Children up to age 16 are covered by their parents' insurance. Foreign nationals are also included—immediately where there are reciprocal arrangements between their country and Sweden (for example, foreigners from other Nordic countries, Italy, the United Kingdom), or after census registration which can take a few months to become effective.[3]

In addition to coverage of medical benefits, all gainfully employed persons earning more than a specified minimum amount, and all homes spouses, are covered for a sickness cash benefit during a period of working incapacity.

Benefits

1. *Inpatient hospital care.*—Unlimited period of maintenance and treatment, nursing care, drugs, auxiliary services, etc., for an individual in a public ward of a public hospital (there are very few private hospitals in Sweden). For hospital inpatients who are receiving a sickness cash benefit (described below), 10 kronor a day are deducted from the sickness benefit.[4] For persons age 67 or over, or those who are drawing on old age pension or full early retirement pension under the National Pension Scheme, hospitalization is payable in full for 365 days in a spell of illness, after which time the patient is liable for a fee of 15 kronor per day of hospitalization.[5]

Reimbursement is also made for related travel expenses and for expenses of an attendant or companion if required. Ambulance service is free; other travel reimbursement is limited to expenses in excess of 8 kronor for the cheapest form of conveyance medically advisable in terms of the patient's health.

2. *Physicians' services.*—The patient who consults a publicly salaried physician pays a flat fee of 15 kronor per office visit. This fee also includes any X-ray exams, laboratory tests, X-ray and radium treatment, and the first visit after referral to another publicly salaried doctor. For a home visit, the patient pays 20 kronor, and for a telephone consultation 2 kronor.

Since January 1, 1975, the patient who consults a private physician is charged a uniform fee similar to that within the public medical care system. In most cases the patient himself pays 20 kronor at the time of his visit, while the local insurance fund office pays the rest of the fee directly to the doctor.[6] Prior to 1975, patients choosing private physicians were required to pay directly the full amount of the physician's fee and be reimbursed by the local social insurance office for 75 percent of an amount stipulated in the Government fee schedule for physicians' services.

When hospitalized in a publicly owned facility, the patient is assigned to a publicly salaried physician or specialist (private physicians do not have hospital privileges) and all costs of physician treatment are covered in full.

---

[3] Derick H. Fulcher, "A Study of Some Aspects of Medical Care Systems in Industrialized Countries." International Labour Office, Geneva, 1973. Contained in "Medical Care Systems in Industrialized Countries," committee print, 93rd Congress, 2nd Session, Subcommittee on Health, Senate Committee on Labor and Public Welfare, May 1974: 147.

[4] A Swedish kronor is equivalent to approximately 23 cents in U.S. currency.

[5] Fulcher, p. 149.

[6] "Social Insurance in Sweden." The Swedish Institute, Stockholm, November 1975: 1–2.

For persons seeking outpatient medical treatment, a certain portion of travel expenses (and expenses of a companion when necessary) is also refunded.

3. *Drugs.*—Free of charge when provided as part of inpatient treatment or for treatment of certain specified chronic or serious diseases, whether on an inpatient or outpatient basis. For all other prescribed drugs, the patient pays 50 percent of the cost up to a maximum of 20 kronor per prescription, regardless of the price of the drug.

4. *Dental care.*—Free treatment for children under age 17. In January 1974, a national dental insurance program was initiated, covering all citizens over age 17 for 50 percent reimbursement of dental care expenses; for expenses in excess of 1,000 kronor, the patient is reimbursed for 75 percent of the total amount. Pregnant women can receive reimbursement for up to 75 percent of the actual dental expenditure. Travel expenses incurred for dental treatment are reimbursed if they exceed 15 kronor per visit.

5. *Other institutional care.*—Free care in public mental hospitals and nursing homes on the same basis as care provided in public hospitals (60-day limit in convalescent homes).

6. *Maternity care.*—Medical care, hospital treatment, and travel in connection with pregnancy and childbirth are reimbursed on the same terms applying to other conditions. Public maternity clinics also offer free prenatal and postnatal care.

7. *Medical treatment abroad.*—Costs of medical and hospital care of an insured person who becomes sick while temporarily outside Sweden are reimbursed to a certain extent in accordance with regulations.

8. *Home nursing grants.*—Chronic patients cared for at home by relatives can be compensated for the costs of such care, if it is of the same standard as that offered by a nursing home and is certified by a county medical officer.

9. *Physiotherapy, speech therapy, and prostheses therapy.*—Patient pays a flat charge of 7 kronor for such services.[7]

10. *Sickness cash benefit.*—Generally, the social insurance program reimburses about 90 percent of the income loss in the most common income brackets up to a ceiling of about 70,000 kronor a year. The amount is calculated according to estimated annual income. The lowest sickness benefit paid is 8 kronor per day, which is the basic sickness benefit generally paid to home spouses earning no income from gainful employment. Home spouses and students can also self-insure on a voluntary basis and for a low premium become entitled to receive a maximum total sickness benefit of up to 20 kronor per day.[8]

ADMINISTRATION

At the national level, the Ministry of Health and Social Affairs gives general supervision to the insurance program. Within the Ministry, the National Board of Health and Welfare is the principal governmental institution for supervising and promoting health and medical care throughout the country. The Board is responsible for the scope and direction of national health policies and for supervision and planning for training of medical personnel, location and construction of hospitals.

However, the bulk of the administrative work for the national insurance system is handled through about 600 local social insurance offices (at one time

---

[7] Ibid. ("Social Insurance in Sweden," p. 1).
[8] Ibid.

called "sickness funds") supervised by 26 regional insurance offices with geographical jurisdiction corresponding to those of the county councils. The regional offices are independent, self-governing bodies, centrally managed and inspected by a State body the National Social Insurance Board. Each regional office is administered by a managing committee consisting of representatives appointed by various levels of government.

The 600 local insurance offices manage health insurance contributions and benefits on the local level and are also responsible for administering the national pension insurance (both basic and supplementary pensions) and industrial injury insurance. Prior to the advent of the compulsory national scheme, more than 1,000 government sponsored voluntary sickness funds had insured a large portion of the population (according to one source, about 70 percent of the population in the early 1950s).[9] When the compulsory program was adopted, many of these voluntary funds were converted and their funds absorbed into the national system.

Local (county council) government in Sweden plays a major part in the actual delivery of medical care. County councils operate the hospitals and other medical facilities within their jurisdictions and employ the physicians and other health personnel who work in these facilities or as district medical officers. Plans for construction and alteration of medical facilities must meet with approval of the National Board of Health and Welfare. The Board also has the right to control the number of physicians who are given posts in publicly funded health facilities. Only those physicians who work strictly in private practice are not submitted to this control in terms of total numbers.

FINANCING

Costs of the health system are financed through the following resources: (1) combined national and local (county council) government funds, mainly through county council taxation—75 percent, (2) compulsory health insurance contributions from employers and employees—10 percent, and (3) cost-sharing by patients for noncovered or partially covered services—15 percent.[10]

In 1971, Swedish county councils spent 78 percent of their total budget (approximately $2 billion, or about $250 per person) on medical care, an eightfold increase compared to expenses in 1960.[11] In order to meet the increasing costs of their health responsibilities, county councils have steadily increased their proportional county income tax rate—from 3 percent on taxable income in 1951 to 10.2 percent in 1975.[12] These taxes are combined with communal taxes into a total local income tax payable with the national income taxes once a year.

Health insurance contributions from employers and employees have historically provided only a small part of the total funds expended for the Swedish health system. Combined with national government subsidies (paid out of general revenues) which presently meet about one-third of the costs for the health insurance program itself, health insurance contributions finance only about 10 percent of the overall health system. While health insurance contributions cover both health care and cash benefits, the latter category absorbs the greater share—about 70 percent—of total health insurance expenditures.[13]

---

[9] Simanis, p. 80.

[10] Simanis, p. 87.

[11] Joseph L. Andrews, Jr., MD. "Medical Care in Sweden." Journal of the American Medical Association, Mar. 19, 1973: 1370.

[12] "The Organization of Medical Care in Sweden," The Swedish Institute, Stockholm, July 1975: 2.

[13] Simanis, p. 87.

Employer contributions are currently set at 3.8 percent of each worker's earnings up to a ceiling of 60,750 a year, an amount which is adjusted periodically to reflect certain economic indicators. Employees and the self-employed pay a flat 300 kronor per year, plus 1.3 percent of income below the same stipulated ceiling applying to employer contributions. This contribution by employees is roughly equivalent to 2 percent of the average industrial wage and is usually collected along with the national income taxes through payroll deductions made by employers on behalf of their employees.[14] Certain insured individuals (for example, pensioners, people over age 65, children under age 16, home spouses, and persons without taxable income) are completely exempt from required health insurance contributions.

Current annual expenditures by the health system amount to about 12 billion kronor (about $2.6 billion). The rate of average annual increase in total costs for health services for the period from 1968 to 1975 was an estimated 6.2 percent.[15] Between 1970 and 1974, the total overall increase in medical care prices was 40.0 percent as compared with 33.6 percent for all goods and services.[16]

REIMBURSEMENT METHODS/ORGANIZATION OF CARE

The organization of Swedish health care is highly decentralized. By law, the various county council areas are responsible for providing all country residents with both outpatient and inpatient care for illness, injury, deformity, and childbirth.

For over a hundred years, hospital care in Sweden has been provided almost entirely in public hospitals, which are owned and operated by the counties and municipalities and supported from tax revenues—primarily county taxes with a small grant from the State government. Within each county, a hospital board, consisting of publicly elected members, is responsible for supervising one or more hospitals. In 1963, the county councils took over the national system of district medical officers, who until then had been employed by the national Government. In 1967, the counties assumed similar responsibility for mental health care, thereby gaining uniform authority over the bulk of Swedish medical care.

As noted below, the national Government plays a relatively minor role with regard to the operations and funding of hospital services:

> The central government contributes relatively little to either capital funding or the daily operations of the county and municipally owned hospitals. The leverage the central government has, however, on the hospitals is in its allocation of medical staff throughout the country. The National Medical Board determines staffing ratios and quality criteria. Hence, while a county can actually build or expand a hospital, it better not do so unless it is assured of medical staff by the National Board.[17]

Sweden has one of the highest bed per population ratios in the world—18 beds per 1,000 population in 1974 (in 1970, the ratio was 16 beds per 1,000):

> Of every 16 beds in Swedish hospitals, 8 are in general hospitals, 3 are in medical hospitals, and 5 are in hospitals for the chronically ill.

---

[14] Ibid., p. 88.

[15] S. Ake Lindgren, "Sweden," reprinted from Health Service Prospects, an international survey, published jointly by the Lancet and the Nuffield Provincial Hospitals Trust, London, 1973: 106.

[16] "Statistical Abstract of the United States, 1974," U.S. Department of Commerce, Bureau of the Census, July 1974: 847. U.S. Govt. Print. Off., Washington.

[17] Anderson, p. 112.

Nationwide planning for the locations, sizes, and types of new hospitals is accomplished by cooperation between the National Board of Health and Welfare in Stockholm, which sets national planning priorities in cooperation with the Ministry of Health and Sweden's 23 county councils and 3 municipalities, which are directly responsible for financing and running the hospitals within each area. Under the leadership of the National Board of Health, a systems approach evolved to provide adequate health care facilities to meet expanding health needs. With the use of current data for area populations, illness rates, medical facilities, and personnel, and projecting figures for future needs, hospitals are planned according to principles of regionalization, centralization, rationalization, and integration.[18]

For hospitalized patients, reimbursement is based on the number of hospital days for each patient. The total cost per bed per day in most counties varies from about $15 (in chronic disease hospitals or wards) to more than $100 (in neurosurgery, plastic surgery, acute coronary care, renal dialysis). For this, the patient pays nothing, and the local insurance office pays the county council 20 kronor (as of 1/1/76) on behalf of each patient day, regardless of what type of service the patient gets.[19] The remainder of the hospital's cost is borne by the county government.

A recent study of comparative utilization data for 1968 showed that Sweden experienced a higher rate of general hospital admissions per 1,000 population, a longer average length of hospital stay, and considerably more general hospital days per 1,000 population than either the United States or Great Britain. Sweden experienced 137.7 admissions to general hospitals per 1,000 population, whereas the figures for the United States and England were 136.9 and 98.2, respectively. Average length of stay in short-term general hospitals in Sweden was 11.9 days in 1968; for the United States, it was 8.4 days and for England, 11.6 days. In terms of general hospital days per 1,000 population, Sweden far outstripped both the United States and England in 1968—1,569 days versus 1,154 for the United States and 1,132 for England.[20]

Salaries account for 70 to 80 percent of expenditures under the average hospital budget. In 1965, hospital care accounted for 46.9 percent of expenditures for the Swedish health care system, in contrast to 34 percent for the United States and 38.9 percent for England.[21]

Medical services for ambulatory patients are provided through hospital outpatient departments, by district medical officers employed by the counties, and to a lesser extent, by hospital-based doctors practicing outside the hospital for part of the day or week, and by private practitioners. Outpatient services in general practice and specialized care amount to about 20 million visits to the doctor, or about 2.5 visits per person per year. About 50 percent of these visits are outpatient consultations in hospitals, 25 percent are outpatient visits with publicly salaried doctors outside the hospitals (such as the district medical officers), and 25 percent are with private practitioners.[22]

Of the approximately 12,000 active physicians in Sweden, an estimated 10 percent are in strictly private practice. Of these, about 25 percent are over age 65 and many work only part time. As older physicians retire, the number of private practitioners continues to dwindle, as few new doctors appear to

[18] Andrews, p. 1374.

[19] Lars Werko, M.D., "Swedish Medical Care in Transition." New England Journal of Medicine, Feb. 18, 1971: 362.

[20] Anderson, oo. 130–132.

[21] Ibid., p. 121.

[22] Bror Rexed, M.D., "The Role of Medical Education in Planning the Development of a National Health Care System." Journal of Medical Education, Jan. 1974: 29.

be taking their place. Of the 1,200 general practitioners in Sweden in 1969, 400 were in private practice, while 800 were government employed district medical officers. During 1970, in Goteborg, which then had 196 private practitioners, not one new physician entered private practice.[23] The fact that private practitioners do not have hospital privileges in Sweden may contribute to the declining interest in private practice among specialists who normally rely upon hospital facilities for patient care.

Physicians in private practice are under no contractural agreement with the government or the local insurance offices which administer the program. Until 1975, such physicians collected their fee directly from the patient, who was then reimbursed by the local insurance office for 75 percent of the fee, if that fee did not exceed a rate stipulated in the official Government-determined fee schedule. Generally, however, fees of private physicians did exceed the Government scale, in some cases by 30 to 40 percent. In 1970, the average charge of private practitioners was 40 kronor.[24]

Since January 1975, payment which the Swedish patient must meet out of his own pocket when visiting a private physician was set at 20 kronor per visit. This charge was coupled with a fixed fee schedule—then set at 48 kroner and scheduled to go up as high as 70 kronor—designed to cover the rest of the physician's charges under the compulsory health insurance system.[25] Payment of this fee schedule amount is made directly to the doctor by the local insurance office.

Physicians who are employed by the government—as district medical officers, hospital-based physicians, etc.—are allowed to supplement their government salary with private practice and, until the introduction the "7-kroner reform," discussed below, were reportedly earning at least half their annual income from such part-time private practice. Under the provisions of the "7-kroner reform," effective January 1970, the Swedish patient who visited a publicly salaried doctor was to pay a maximum fee of 7 kroner, regardless of the type of consultation (that fee has now been raised to 15 kroner, as noted in the section of this report dealing with benefits). The 7-kroner reform expressly prohibited all doctors employed by the government from receiving any fees directly from patients, whether hospitalized or seen on an outpatient basis in the hospital during the specified hours when the physician is working for the government; thus, the patient now pays the fee directly to the institution or clinic where he receives his care and the government-employed physician is on a regular direct salary. In addition to the 15 kroner patient fee the provider of service (in effect, the institution or other health facility) is reimbursed by the local insurance office 48 kroner for each outpatient visit.

Prior to January 1970, government-employed hospital doctors received a base salary (representing usually about half of their local income) from their employers (the state, county, and local governments) and had as duties to take care of both inpatients and outpatients. For treatment of outpatients, however, physicians were reimbursed directly by patients in accordance with a government-approved fee schedule. Arrangements for the district medical officers were on the same salary-plus-fees basis.

Under the new system, publicly employed physicians were placed on a regular salary, and all doctors with equal positions and equal length of service

---

[23] Andrews, p. 1372.

[24] Alan Wilson, "Outcome of the Standard Medical Fee Reform in Sweden." Royal Swedish Ministry for Foreign Affairs, Information Service, Dec. 1972: 4.

[25] Ragnar Berfenstam and Ray H. Elling, "Regional Planning in Sweden: A Social and Medical Problem." Scandinavian Review, Sept. 1975: 46–47.

were to be paid the same salary for the same number of working hours, regardless of speciality. The fixed salary scale was increased to compensate for loss of outpatient fees. The work week was also fixed at 40 hours, with agreement reached between the doctor and his employer if local shortages and demands warranted additional overtime. In actuality, most hospital physicians work between 45 and 48 hours per week. Government doctors are still free to practice privately beyond these fixed working hours and be reimbursed on the same basis as full-time private practitioners; however, few government-employed physicians are reported to be doing so.

While it has no part in the day-to-day formal operating authority of the health system, it should be noted that the Swedish Medical Association does participate in reaching central agreements on salary and working conditions through bargaining with the Federation of County Councils on behalf of physicians employed by the county councils in hospitals and as district medical officers.[26]

The Swedish system has developed a form of professional peer review in order to control misuse of the insurance system by fee-for-service physicians;

> The Swedish sick funds employ control doctors to police abuse. If any doctor performs medically unnecessary or excessively repeated medical procedures for money over the statistical norms calculated by the National Insurance Office, the control doctor could ask him to desist. * * * The control doctor can file charges with the Swedish Medical Association, but this action is unusual. The control system is hardly used in Sweden since the economics and ethics of Swedish medicine produces little unnecessary work; because of the severe shortage of doctors, the profession is kept busy doing what is clinically necessary.[27]

The Swedish system has indeed been operating for many years with a considerably lower physician/population ratio than is found in many other industrialized nations. Sweden's physician/population ratio is currently about 1 per 680 population, representing a substantial improvement over the 1 per 1,450 physician population ratio in 1950. National policy is aimed at reducing the physician shortage even further to reach goal of 1 physician for every 450 Swedes by 1980. Medical school enrollment has been so vastly expanded that among 20-year old Swedes one in every 115 is now becoming a doctor. Despite such efforts, however, more than 12 percent of existing public positions remain unfilled, without even a substitute.

About 70 to 75 percent of Swedish physicians are based full time in hospitals, an indication, according to one commentator, of the emphasis that Sweden has placed on institutional care. Apparently, in training greater numbers of physicians, attempts are being made by the central government to increase the supply of physicians without hospital appointments by maintaining a constant number of hospital positions.[28]

Under the new dental insurance scheme, a fee schedule has been established for all dental work provided through public dental clinics and dentists in private practice who join the public program and agree to adhere to the fee schedule. Participation is obligatory for dentists in public dental clinics, but voluntary for private dental practitioners. Private dentists who remain outside the scheme are not reimbursed through the plan, so the patient in this situation

---

[26] Berfenstam, p. 47.

[27] William A. Glaser, "Paying the Doctor, Systems of Remuneration and Their Effect." The Johns Hopkins Press, Baltimore, 1972: 189–190.

[28] Anderson, pp. 123–124.

pays the full fee himself. The patient who visits a participating dentist will pay the dentist directly, or through billing, one-half of the fee, and the local social insurance office is billed for the remaining one-half.

United Kingdom ([34], pp. 377–387)

The British National Health Service came into being on July 5, 1948. The purpose of the program was to "promote the establishment in England and Wales of a comprehensive health service designed to secure improvement in the physical and mental health of the people of England and Wales and the prevention, diagnosis, and treatment of illness, and for that purpose to provide or secure the effective provision of services." With the establishment of the NHS, virtually all medical and health services became available to people normally resident in Britain without regard to any insurance qualifications. Although all services were originally free to users, small charges for certain services, such as dental treatment, drugs, and eyeglasses, have since been introduced. The structure of the NHS established in 1948 was substantially reorganized in 1974.

Practically all of Britain's hospitals, clinics, and asylums were nationalized by the NHS and are now owned or controlled by the government. This ownership and control is exercised indirectly through a variety of legally independent bodies; for example, the Regional Health Authorities, which are, however, financially entirely dependent on the central government.

Hospital doctors and personnel are salaried employees. General practitioners are independent contractors who are paid on a per capita basis for all patients who are registered with them; dentists are paid partly on a fee-per-item-of-service basis. General practitioners and part-time hospital consultants can also conduct private practice. Only a small minority of specialists, about 2 percent of general practitioners, and a negligible number of dentists, retail pharmacists, ophthalmologists, and opticians take no part whatsoever in the National Health Service.

The Service is financed mainly through funds from the Exchequer raised through general taxation. Other income is derived from NHS contributions and from charges paid by patients using certain services.[1]

COVERAGE

All people normally resident in Britain may receive services through the National Health Service without regard to any insurance qualification or prior history of contributions to the Service. Foreign visitors to Britain can be given free emergency treatment, but visitors who come to Britain specifically for medical treatment are expected to pay for it. Certain countries have reciprocal arrangements with Great Britain whereby services are furnished to foreign nationals residing in Britain on the same basis that services are provided to British nationals residing abroad.

BENEFITS

The National Health Service pays for virtually the entire range of health and medical care as provided through Regional Area Health Authorities and Family Practitioner Committees. The following services are included, subject in some cases to limited patient cost-sharing as noted below:

---

[1] "Health Services in Britain." Issued by Central Office of Information, London, 1974.

I. PRACTITIONER SERVICE

The Practitioner Service includes the family doctor service, the dental service, the ophthalmic service, and the pharmaceutical service. In the case of the family doctor (or general practitioner) service, patients are required to register with a particular physician and receive most primary services through him. However, the patient is not required to register with a particular dentist, ophthalmologist, optician, or pharmacist. Patients have free choice of these practitioners, and practitioners are also free to accept or reject a particular patient. However, a family doctor must give any necessary treatment to any person who applies to him for treatment when the patient is not on the list of another physician or when treatment is needed in an emergency and the patient's regular doctor is not available.

(a) Through the family doctor service, the professional attention of a general practitioner is made available free of charge to everyone. In order to receive services, each person must register with a particular physician. About 97 percent of the population is registered with family doctors throughout the country. Each general practitioner is allowed a list of 3,500 patients, but the size of the average practice in England and Wales is about 2,400 patients. No charge is made to the patient for either home or office visits. In general the family doctor does not have hospital privileges and must refer any patient in need of inpatient care or treatment to a hospital-based specialist. Patients are free to change doctors, but unless certain conditions apply (change of patient address or location of physician's office, for example) the transfer can be effected immediately or may take up to 14 days.

(b) The general dental service provides all forms of treatment deemed necessary for dental fitness. Unlike the system of open office hours maintained by the general practitioner, the dentist generally sees a patient only by appointment. Unless exempted, patients must pay the full cost of each item of treatment, not including dentures, or £3.50, whichever is the less. There are separate charges for dentures, but a course of treatment including the supply of a denture cannot cost more than £12.00.[2]

No charges are made, however, for clinical examinations, arrest of bleeding, or repairs to dentures. Certain dental procedures require prior approval by the Dental Estimates Board. The following persons are exempt from all dental charges—expectant mothers or those who have borne a child in the preceding 12 months; children under 16; persons under 21 and still in full-time schooling; persons (and their dependents) in receipt of supplementary pension or allowance, family income supplement; and free prescriptions, free milk and vitamins because of low income. Persons over 16 and under 21 who are not in full-time attendance at school are entitled to exemption from charges for any treatment other than the supply or modification of dentures.

(c) The general ophthalmic service provides only for the testing of vision and the supply of eyeglasses; treatment beyond this point is performed at an eye hospital or hospital eye clinic. Vision tests are free of charge. The patient pays the cost of prescription eyeglasses. There is a charge of up to £5.00 for each lens, and a charge for a standard pattern frame. For children up to age 16, and older children if they are still at school, lenses are supplied free, provided they are fitted to one of the NHS frames designated as suitable for

---

[2] As of December 1975, one pound (£) English sterling was the equivalent of about $2.34 in U.S. currency. One pound consist of 100 pence (p). Ten pence would, therefore, equal about 23 cents, and 50p equals about $1.17.

children. If some other NHS frame is chosen, the usual charge for it must be paid, and if the child is under age 10, the usual charge for the lenses must also be paid. Exemption from such cost-sharing amounts is allowed for certain individuals, e.g. persons with low income, in receipt of certain pensions, allowances, etc., as under the dental service.

(d) Through the pharmaceutical service, everyone receiving treatment under the family doctor service is entitled to medicines and certain appliances prescribed by a doctor as part of that treatment. Patients pay a charge usually amounting to 20 pence for each such prescription item. The following categories are exempt from these charges—children under age 16; men aged 65 or over and women aged 60 or over; expectant mothers and mothers of children under age 1; people suffering from certain medical conditions; persons exempted because of low income; and certain war or service pensioners.

II. HOSPITAL SERVICES

All forms of hospital care and treatment in general and special hospitals for inpatients, outpatients, and day patients are provided by the Health Authorities. Hospital consultants also provide specialist opinion and treatment, either in hospitals and clinics, or when advisable, at the patient's home. A blood transfusion service, pathological laboratory service, and X-ray service are at the disposal of every hospital. Other hospital services include screening for cervical cancer, prenatal and postnatal clinics, and treatment and supervision of drug addiction. All services are available free of charge to every member of the public, whether or not they use the family doctor service and irrespective of nationality and national insurance qualifications. As a general rule, patients are referred by their family doctors, who make arrangements for specialist advice and the specialist in turn for hospital admission or treatment on an outpatient basis.

Charges for medicines or appliances are made on the same principles and rates as when provided out of hospital. Unless medically required, accommodations above the general ward level are subject to a fixed charge of £ 3.00 a day for a single room and £ 1.50 a day for beds in small wards. At some hospitals, a limited number of "pay beds" are set aside for privately paying patients treated by those NHS consultants who are entitled to engage in private practice. Patients using these beds pay the full cost of the accommodation and services provided and the fees of the consultant.

Treatment for mental disorders is also provided as part of the NHS. Patients can consult their family doctor and receive specialist advice at hospital outpatient clinics, or can enter the hosptial for inpatient treatment without formalities.

Special rehabilitation facilities are provided in the department of physical medicine and occupational therapy at main hospitals and at some special rehabilitation centers not attached to a hospital.

III. COMMUNITY HEALTH SERVICES

Health Authorities also provide a wide variety of other services, including maternity and child health services, such as family planning, midwifery, and baby care; home nursing; health visitors; vaccination and immunization; services for the prevention of illness and the care and aftercare of illness, including mental disorders; ambulance services; health education of the public; and standard setting and registration of nursing homes. Area health authorities are also empowered to build health centers, which are available for the provision of general medical, dental, and pharmaceutical services, and consultant and other hospital outpatient services. Between 1948 and 1964, the development of health centers progressed slowly with only 21 centers opened in England and Wales. Since that time, however, there has been a marked increase in the number of centers; 468 were in operation as of December 1973, and about 10 percent of general practitioners were working in them.

Despite the broad array of services provided under the National Health Service either free of charge or at a nominal cost, an estimated 2.1 million persons in Great Britain are insured with private health insurance societies. Benefits offered by these societies include such items as care at convalescent homes operated by the societies, small cash benefits during hospitalization, assistance toward meeting the cost of home help, and contributions toward the expense of eyeglasses.

Aside from these benefits, the private plans supplement services paid for under the NHS in several important areas: (1) the private plans allow members to select their own specialist for in-hospital care, whereas the NHS patient generally has no such choice and is assigned to a particular specialist upon hospitalization; (2) the private plans will pay for one of the 4,500 private "pay beds" available in NHS hospitals for persons willing to pay the full cost of their hospital and medical services; the privately insured patient may, therefore, more readily gain admission to the hospital for elective surgery, whereas NHS patients may commonly incur a waiting period of up to 1 year for elective procedures; (3) privately insured patients may also use 1 of the 14 private nursing homes affiliated with private insurance organizations; (4) the private plans will also pay the cost-sharing for "amenity beds" (private beds which may be made available to patients for a small fee, when not needed for medical cases requiring privacy); and (5) private plans may also reimburse for services received from the small number of British physicians who operate a full-time or part-time private practice.[3]

It has been noted, however, that in spite of the existence of private insurance in Britain, private expenditures on medical care represent only a minor portion of total outlays for health care services:

> Overall total expenditure on private medicine is now probably running at the rate of about £30 million (about $75 million) a year; the current cost of the National Health Service is £2 billion (about $5 billion) a year. The contrast between these two figures (a ratio of almost 70 to 1) not only puts the size of the private sector into perspective; it also confirms the verdict of the public opinion polls which invariably record overwhelming satisfaction with the NHS.[4]

FINANCING

The National Health Service is financed from the following sources: (1) 88 percent from general taxation (Exchequer funds), (2) 9 percent from NHS weekly contributions, (3) 2.5 percent from copayments by patients for certain services such as drugs, eyeglasses, et cetera, and (4) 0.5 percent from miscellaneous sources. The fact that general taxation supports such a substantial part of the NHS has been described as both "the strength and weakness of the political economy model as established in Britain":

---

[3] Joseph G. Simanis, "Private Health Insurance in West Germany and Great Britain." Social Security Bulletin, October 1970: 40–41.

[4] Rudolf Klein, "The Political Economy of National Health." Public Interest, No. 26, Winter 1972: 115.

It opens the public purse to the NHS and removes the economic obstacles to the use of medical services, but it does so in a way which also means that health has to battle with a number of other services in a competitive scramble for money * * *. The theoretical advantage of the political economy model health service is, of course, that it allows the central government to allocate resources in what is (hopefully) the most rational, the most effective, and the most democratic way * * *. Thus, the British system allows the government to decide its priorities first between public and private consumption (do we raise more taxes to finance greater government spending, or do we leave more money in people's pockets?); then between different forms of welfare or social spending (do we build more hospitals or more schools?); and finally, between different sectors in the same service (do we concentrate extra resources on accident departments or geriatric beds?). Further, the British system of central government budgeting has now developed a fairly sophisticated 5-year forward projection which provides a framework for deciding priorities between different programs.[5]

The NHS weekly contribution is collected with the social security contribution for cash benefits and is shared between employer and employee; the contribution is earnings related, the employee paying 0.4 percent and the employer 0.6 percent.

A recent study estimates that Great Britain devoted 5.6 percent of its gross national income to health care in 1970, up from 4.4 percent in 1950.[6] Total public expenditures on health and personal social services reached £3.8 billion in fiscal year 1973–74 and are expected to reach £5.2 billion by fiscal year 1975–76. About 20 percent of the health budget goes for payments to the family doctor, general dental, ophthalmic, and pharmaceutical services. Hospital and specialist services account for the largest share—about 75 percent of the total health budget. The remaining amount is absorbed by the area health authorities providing a wide range of health and health-related activities.[7]

During the period from 1962 to 1969, the average annual rate of increase in health expenditures in Britain, adjusted by the average of the Consumer Price Index and wage index changes, reflected an annual growth rate of 5.1 percent.[8] In 1967, 16.6 percent of the total government budget was devoted to health expenditures.[9]

ADMINISTRATION

Administrative authority for the National Health Service in England is vested in the Secretary of State for Social Services in the Department of Health and Social Security. Corresponding ministerial responsibility for health services varies somewhat in other parts of Great Britain. The Secretaries of State for Scotland, Wales, and Northern Ireland have the responsibility in those jurisdictions. Although there are separate systems for Scotland and Northern Ireland, the general organization and function of the health services are broadly similar throughout Great Britain.

The Secretary of State for Social Services is advised by a Central Health Services Council comprised of nominated members who are office-holders of

[5] Klein, pp. 115–116.

[6] Odin W. Anderson, "Health Care; Can There be Equity? The United States, Sweden, and England." John Wiley and Sons, New York, 1972: 138.

[7] Health Services in Britain, p. 55.

[8] Joseph G. Simanis, "Medical Care Expenditures in Seven Countries." Social Security Bulletin, March 1973: 40.

[9] Ibid, p. 42.

the principal medical and other professional bodies and selected members representing the various health service professions and the public viewpoint. The Secretary has direct responsibility for the provision on a national basis of all hospital and specialist services, facilities for the prevention of illness, the care of persons suffering from illness and the aftercare of such persons, the conduct of health research, a Public Health Laboratory Service, and a Blood Transfusion Service. He has indirect responsibility for the family practitioner services; five Standing Advisory Committees (on medicine, dentistry, nursing, midwifery, etc.) are under the jurisdiction of the Central Health Services Council.

Decisions regarding allocation of funds and physical resources to regions are made at the central level. Facilities are distributed according to a national plan, thereby allowing for control over the location of expensive units, such as those for cardiac surgery or hemodialysis. The distribution of specialists' posts (hospital consultants) is also made on the advice of the standing advisory committees.

Prior to April 1, 1974, the National Health Service had been divided into three functional branches which covered (1) hospital and specialist services, (2) local authority services (i.e. public health, school health, etc.), and (3) general practitioner services. A massive reorganization of the NHS became effective April 1, 1974, and resulted in the elimination of many of the institutions previously active in administering the service, including regional hospital boards, hospital management committees, executive councils, and boards of governors of teaching hospitals. A single structure now encompasses hospital and specialist services, general practitioner services, and those community health services which were formerly provided by the local authorities. Most of the functions of the 119 executive councils, which formerly administered all problems concerning general practitioner services and other forms of primary care, have been assumed by newly designated bodies called Family Practitioner Committees (described below). Boards of governors at certain specialized postgraduate teaching hospitals will be temporarily maintained. Local authorities have also surrendered their National Health Service and school health responsibilities.[10]

In England, 14 Regional Health Authorities have now been assigned responsibility for determining area plans, allocating resources to subsidiary authorities, and monitoring their performance—including the design and construction of new buildings. Members of each Regional Health Authority are appointed by the Secretary of State after consultant with universities, local authorities, the medical profession, and other interested groups, such as the voluntary associations, employers, and trade unions. The Regional Health Authorities are subdivided into 90 Area Health Authorities. The larger areas have been subdivided into 2 or more Districts for a total of about 205 Districts. Area Health Authorities are responsible for assessing needs in the area and for planning, organizing, and administering health services to meet them. All levels will have responsibilities in planning, but day-to-day operations will be supervised primarily on the District level.[11]

---

[10] Joseph G. Simanis, "National Health Systems in Eight Countries." U.S. Department of Health, Education, and Welfare, Social Security Administration, Office of Research and Statistics. DHEW Publication No. (SSA) 75–11924, Washington, D.C., U.S. Govt. Print. Office, Jan. 1975: 93–94.

[11] Simanis, pp. 93–94.

Administration of the Family Practitioner Service is the responsibility of 98 Family Practitioner Committees (including 8 in Wales). There is a separate Committee for the area of each Area Health Authority. Fifteen members of each Committee are appointed by local committees of doctors (8 members), dentists (3 members), pharmacists (2 members), and opticians (2 members). Four members are appointed by the local authority and 11 by the Area Health Authority. Among the responsibilities of the Family Practitioner Committees are the following: (1) consideration of application by practitioners to practice in the area, (2) publication of a list of general practitioners in the area, and (3) investigations of complaints against any of these practitioners.

Community Health Councils (numbering about 207) have been established for each District to provide representation of the consumer's viewpoint regarding the structure and effectiveness of the NHS. At least half the Council members are appointed by the relevant local government authorities, and at least a third by voluntary bodies with a strong interest in the health services of the District. The remainder are appointed by the Regional Health Authority after consultation with the local government authorities and others. Councils have the right to secure information, to visit hospitals and other institutions, to bring to the attention of the Area Health Authority local complaints, to send an observer to AHA meetings, and to take other action in consultation with the AHA.[12]

Reimbursement Methods

National Health Service doctors in general practice are reimbursed according to the number of patients served. A physician may maintain a list of up to 3,500 patients and receive a capitation amount for each patient. In addition to the ordinary capitation fee, there is a higher fee for treating patients age 65 or over. Additional payments are made for practicing in doctor-shortage areas, for accepting responsibility out of normal hours, for night visits to patients, and for expenses associated with a rural practice. A basic fee is provided for each patient receiving complete maternity service through the general practitioner; an extra "out-of-hours" capitation fee is paid for each patient in excess of 1,000 on the GP's list.[13]

A special allowance is made for doctors practicing in groups. About one-half of all general practitioners now qualify for this allowance. Allowances are made for seniority and for vocational training. Additional fees are paid for services encouraged as a matter of public health, such as vaccination and cervical smears. Reimbursment is also made for the general practitioner's office rent and taxes and for employment of ancillary personnel. Exchequer grants are available for the improving of practice premises and a finance corporation has been set up to make loans for the purchase, construction, and improvement of premises.[14]

Complaints about services received from a general practitioner are investigated by the Family Practitioner Committee. (Before April 1974, a local Executive Council with similar functions investigated complaints.) According to one report, 50 complaints were investigated in the inner London area in 1972 In its findings, the local body decided against physicians in 12 cases (failure or unreasonable delay in making house calls) and in a 13th case, the Committee Executive Council (as it then was) agreed with a government complaint that

---

[12] Simanis, p. 94.

[13] "Health Services in Britain," p. 16–18.

[14] "Health Services in Britain," p. 16–18.

a physician had falsified a certificate of illness for a worker absent from his job.[15] Dr. Dennis Cook, secretary of the Inner London Medical Committee, does not consider the problem of complaints to be serious or extensive:

> Fifty formal complaints a year in an urban area with 2,000 doctors and 3 million patients is a comfortable figure. I myself practiced for 13 years without even knowing the terms of service in my contract. In all of that time there was one complaint against me and that was dismissed.
>
> * * * The extent of the problem can be seen by the size of the insurance premium to the Medical Defense Union: a general practitioner in Great Britain gets unlimited indemnity for £21 a year ($52).[16]

The local Family Practitioner Committee and the National Medical Practices Committee (appointed by the Secretary of State for Social Services) must approve all applications for location of new general practices. Applications are reviewed on the basis of whether there is need for an additional doctor in the given area. In addition to their NHS practice, general practitioners are allowed to practice privately. The fact that, under the terms of the NHS, the GP or a personally appointed deputy is responsible for the care of patients on his list for 24 hours a day, 7 days a week, 52 weeks a year, somewhat limits the amount of time which can be devoted to handling privately paying patients.

Hospital medical staff are full-time, part-time, or honorary. Paid part-time staff are usually remunerated on a sessional basis at a proportion of the appropriate full-time salary and they are free to accept private patients. Senior hospital consultants (specialists appointed to their positions) earn salaries ranging from £7,536 to £10,689 a year (about $17,600 to $25,000 U.S. currency as of December 1975). Junior hospital staff earn substantially less than these amounts. House officers or interns reportedly earn about £2,200 per year in their first post, with second or third year residents earning from £3,198 to £3,879.[17]

In addition to their salary, consultants are eligible for a limited number of merit awards for exceptional contributions to medicine, the actual amount of the award ranging from £1,506 to £7,947 per year. The basis for determining the awards, and the names of the winners, is not formally announced, but there were reportedly only 124 physicians throughout England and Wales who received the highest award (A+) in 1974. [18]

In 1973, there were about 71,000 active physicians in Great Britain. Some worked part-time in more than one branch of medicine, but, in general, there were 25,000 in general practice and 35,000 in full-time or part-time hospital work. The remainder were employed in university, industrial, military or public health work. About 16,000 were junior hospital staff (the equivalent of residents and interns) and 12,500 were specialists at the consultant grade. The doctor-population ratio in Great Britain was 1 per 1,010 in 1950 but by 1973 this ratio had improved to 1 per 766.[19]

The British Medical Association estimated that as of April 1973, the average net income of the general practitioner was $14,300 annually. For top specialists, net earnings averaged $19,000. These figures include only earnings

---

[15] Nathan Horwitz, "Britain's NHS at 25." Medical Tribune, Nov. 14, 1973:28.

[16] Horwitz, p. 28.

[17] Unpublished government data made available through the Information Division, Department of Health and Social Security, London, August 1974.

[18] Ibid.

[19] Ibid.

from fixed government salaries or contracts for NHS work. As noted earlier, part-time consultants are permitted to have private patients, bringing in anywhere from $5,000 to $20,000 more per year, and many general practitioners make extra money by contracting to serve as insurance, school, or hotel physicians.[20]

As indicated in the section of this report dealing with the administration of the NHS, the medical profession is well represented at most levels of decision-making. Commenting on the influence of the medical profession on public policy, one author makes the following points:

> The influence of the medical profession on public policy has, if anything, been increased by the NHS. Indeed it is tempting to diagnose a kind of tacit agreement. On the one hand, under the British NHS the doctor in effect administers the rationing system. It is up to him to decide who should use the scarce resources available—who should be treated in the hospital, who should go on the waiting list, and so on. In short, the British system is one of rationing by medical discretion (though obviously the scope for this discretion is affected by the availability of resources). The fact that the British doctor has no personal financial incentive in offering treatment may help to explain the ability of the NHS to contain costs; conversely, though, the system doesn't offer the doctor any monetary incentive to improve efficiency. * * * Even more important is the medical profession's ability to dominate the execution of national policy and so to make the administrators dependent on its good will. Paradoxically, the medical profession is most independent and powerful where its position appears least so. Hospital consultants are salaried employees, yet dispose of their beds with complete freedom from any control; there is nothing in Britain which resembles a medical audit or any form of quality or efficiency control. General practitioners, who bitterly fought salaried status and are independent contractors, are subject to rather more, though still slight, supervision over such matters as the amount of drugs prescribed. Finally, dentists, who in theory ought to have the greatest freedom since they work on a fee-for-service basis, are in fact subject to the most detailed checks on the quality and amount of work performed. In other words, the British experience suggests that doctors can achieve most power when they infiltrate the health service system itself; by insisting on "independence," general practitioners have remained on the periphery of the NHS in every sense, isolated from the hospital service and from power.[21]

Other practitioners under the NHS are reimbursed in a variety of ways. Dentists practicing in their own offices are reimbursed on a free-per-item-of-service basis according to a prescribed scale of fees, which is only partially covered by direct charges to patients. Most dental treatment, including fillings and root treatment, extractions not requiring replacement by dentures, and ordinary denture repairs, may be given without approval of any outside authority' extensive and prolonged gum treatment, some dentures, crown and inlays, and special appliances and oral surgery require prior approval by the Dental Estimates Board, consisting preponderantly of dental practitioners. Dentists are free to accept private patients if they wish.

Ophthalmic practitioners and opticians are paid prescribed fees for vision tests; opticians who dispense eyeglasses are paid according to the number and types of eyeglasses supplied, including a dispensing fee for professional service, together with the cost of the eyeglasses and some addition to cover the risk of breakages. Pharmacists dispensing on their own premises are paid on the basis

---

[20] Horwitz, p. 28.
[21] Klein, pp. 122–123.

of the prescriptions they dispense. Almost all pharmacies in England and Wales take part in the NHS. In addition to the direct charge to the patient for each prescription, pharmacies are paid for each prescription the cost of the ingredients, a percentage on cost, a container allowance, and a professional fee.[22]

The Regional Health Authorities are responsible for reviewing the distribution, delivery, and costs of services, and for the improvement and construction of facilities. Based on its review, each Authority submits an annual estimate of expenditure to the central government for approval. Within the overall budget allocated to each regional or area authority, it may decide upon the number and kind of personnel, but it has no control over salary ranges, which are established nationally and are, with few exceptions, uniform throughout England and Wales. The day-to-day operation and fiscal management of individual hospitals are under the Area Health Authorities, which control staffing, facilities, and equipment, and report to and are monitored by the Regional Health Authorities.

In England in 1973, the average length of hospital stay for non-psychiatric cases was 13.5 days. The hospital bed occupancy rate for non-psychiatric cases in England for the same period was 76.7 percent.[23] In 1972, there were 9.02 available hospital beds per 1,000 population in England, a slight decrease over previous years coincident with both an elimination of obsolete installations and a more intensive use of inpatient facilities. The number of inpatient cases treated per available bed rose from 9.42 in 1962 to 12.51 in 1972, an increase of some 33 percent.[24]

Union of Soviet Socialist Republics ([34], pp. 388–387)

Public health and medical services in the Soviet Union are considered a responsibility of the State and a function of government, and as such, are provided as a public service. Soviet socialized medicine is a nationalized health service and not a health insurance scheme. Personal medical services are available to the entire population at no direct costs (with a few minor exceptions) at the time of use. The system is financed entirely by and through the State from taxation, and costs are represented as part of the different national, Republic and local budgets.

The origins of the present structure of the Soviet health system can be traced to 1918, when a Commissariat of Health Protection was established by decree of the new Bolshevik government. The Commissariat was charged with responsibility for administration of the nation's health system. In the U.S.S.R., socialized medicine is officially defined as a socialist system of governmental and community measures having as their main purpose the prevention and treatment of illness, the provision of healthy working and living conditions, and the achievement of a high level of work capacity and long life expectancy.

Responsibility for administration of the health system rests with the Ministry of Health and its counterpart ministries in the constituent Republics

---

[22] Health Services in Britain, pp. 19–20.

[23] "Health and Personal Social Services Statistics, 1974." Her Majesty's Stationery Office, London, p. 72.

[24] Derick Fulcher, "Medical Care Systems in Industrialized Countries." Contained in a committee print, Senate Labor and Public Welfare Committee, Subcommittee on Health, 93rd Congress, 2nd Session. U.S. Govt. Print. Office, May 1974, p. 90.

and the health departments at the different administrative levels, down to the localities. Health services are organized in a series of tiers of increasingly sophisticated medical treatment as one moves from local facilities to those that serve larger areas.

According to one source, total direct expenditures by the Soviet Government on health care represent an estimated 3.5 percent of the gross national product.[1] Between 1969 and 1976, the Soviet Union's health budget rose by about 32.5 percent (from 8.6 billion to 11.4 billion rubles). It should be noted that the total amount allocated by the Government for health purposes does not include moneys expended for scientific research, medical education, social security payments, or rest homes or sanitoria. Nor does it include amounts expended by collective farms, factories, plants, and other organizations which are required to provide their employees with health services in their own health facilities. The amount budgeted for such purposes in 1976 is 2.7 billion rubles.

COVERAGE

The entire population is provided with comprehensive health services.

BENEFITS

The Soviet health system is designed to make virtually every kind of health and medical care available and accessible to all. All medical care is free of charge, except for some nominal payment required for drugs, dentures, eyeglasses and certain surgical appliances—but almost one-half the population are exempt from these charges (i.e., children, invalids, people afflicted with certain medical conditions, war veterans, etc.)

Great emphasis is placed on preventive care and health education of the public. It has been estimated that 80 percent of Soviet citizens attend their local polyclinic (comprehensive outpatient facility) at least once every year, and that the average annual attendance rate is between 7 and 10 attendances per person at risk.[2] Immunizations and other prophylactic measures, physical exams and screenings, rehabilitation and physiotherapy are provided through the system.

There is generally no free choice of physician. People within a given geographical neighborhood (or "uchastok") are allocated to the physician who has been assigned for the particular locality.

In terms of health facilities, the U.S.S.R. has 91 medical schools, 26,000 hospitals, 38,000 establishments providing medical ambulatory-polyclinical aid, 3,000 emergency aid stations, and 5,200 sanatoria. In 1975, the Soviet Union had close to 12 hospital beds per 1,000 population; the official policy is in favor of increasing this ratio still further. In 1972 the average general hospital stay was about 16 days, twice the U.S. average.[3] Excluding hospitalization for pregnancy, labor, and related conditions, the hospitalization rates were 148.4 per 1,000 population.[4]

---

[1] James E. Muller, M.D., et al., "The Soviet Health System—Aspects of Relevance for Medicine in the United States." New England Journal of Medicine, Mar. 30, 1972: 698. The authors note that this figure for percentage of GNP spent on health care should be considered in light of the fact that different methods are used by other countries in calculating the GNP, that there is some uncertainty over the magnitude of health activities supported by sources outside the Soviet health budget, and that the system is notable for the low pay of health personnel in relation to other Soviet professionals.

[2] John Fry, Medicine in Three Societies; a Comparison of Medical Care in the USSR, USA and UK. American Elsevier Publishing Co., Inc., New York, 1970: 67.

[3] "Medical News Around the World," Medical World News, Feb. 4, 1972: 12 M.

[4] T. M. Ryan, "Primary Medical Care in the Soviet Union," International Journal of Health Services, May 1972: 250.

Financing

The Soviet health system is financed entirely by the State through taxation. Taxes are channeled into the State treasury and reallocated to the health sector, as well as to other sectors of the economy, through three main sources: (1) Payments made by industrial organizations from their profits, or the difference between the cost of production (including salaries) and the value of the output; (2) the income tax, which is a minor source of revenue; and (3) the turnover tax, a major source of revenue which is essentially a sales or excise tax applied to all consumer goods in the Soviet Union. Costs of the health system are represented as part of the national, Republic, and local budgets.[5] In 1971, health services accounted for 7.5 percent of the total Soviet budget.

Organization and Administration of Health Services

The administration and organization of the Soviet health services corresponds exactly to the general structure of the central and local government because they are integral parts of central and local government services. Starting with the Ministry of Health and extending down to the smallest units, the pattern is similar in form and shape. The following is an outline of the administrative structure of the Soviet health system.

1. THE MINISTRY OF HEALTH

At the highest level of government, the central administrative unit is the Council of Ministers of the Union of Soviet Socialist Republics and the Minister of Health is a member of the Presidium or Cabinet. The Ministry of Health is located in Moscow and is under the direction of the Minister of Health, who is always an eminent practicing physician.

The Ministry of Health of the U.S.S.R. is responsible for long term planning and policy decisions on health services for the entire population, including the calculation and publication of norms and standards for resources and qualitative standards for medical care throughout the country. The Ministry of Health is also responsible for the nation's health budget, and for defining priorities in keeping with the overall goals and objectives; in that responsibility, it collaborates closely with the Central Planning Council.

The Ministry is also responsible for 10 of the 85 Soviet medical schools and for 13 postgraduate institutes. The others are under the direction of local Republics.

The staff of the Ministry of Health is about 900, of which two-thirds are physicians. Although this would seem a small staff for an organization responsible for directing the health care of a nation of 250 million, it is appropriate because the U.S.S.R. Ministry of Health is essentially a policy-formulating body and is not concerned directly with local administration which is the responsibility of the local Republics. It should be noted, however, that although the various Republics have some autonomy in administering health services within their boundaries, the Health Ministry of the U.S.S.R., through its power of health legislation, can invalidate any health legislation enacted at the Republic level if such legislation is found to be inconsistent with or contradictory to legislation adopted at the national level.

---

[5] Mark G. Field, Soviet Socialized Medicine. The Free Press, New York, 1967: 190.

2. MINISTRY OF HEALTH OF THE SOVIET REPUBLICS

The U.S.S.R. is divided into 15 Republics, each having its own ministry of health, headed by a minister who is appointed by the Central Soviet of the Republic on the approval of the Minister of Health of the U.S.S.R. The Republics vary in size and in population and in the nature of their geographical and medical problems, extending as they do from Western Europe to the Arctic.

The Republican ministries have more departments than the Health Ministry U.S.S.R., and their administrative structures are more complex, reflecting greater direct responsibility for the administration of health services. For example, the administrative structure of the Health Ministry of the Russian Soviet Federated Republic (RSFSR) includes the following departments: Administration for Medical Preventive Assistance; Administration for Preventive Assistance for Children and Mothers; Administration for Medical Schools; Administration for Capital Construction; Administration for Specialized Sanitoria; Pharmaceutical Administration; Sanitary-Epidemic-Control Administration, Administration for Scientific Research Institutes of Epidemiology, Microbiology, and the Production of Vaccines and Sera, as well as the usual administrative and housekeeping departments such as personnel and financial administration.

Despite this apparent operating autonomy, the budgets of each individual Republic are derived from central government funds and are not based on any local taxation.

3. REGIONAL HEALTH DEPARTMENT

The detailed administration of the Soviet health system is carried out at the regional level through regional health departments (oblasts). The size of a region may vary from 1 to 5 million persons and large cities such as Leningrad with a population of more than 4 million function as a single region.

Each region has an executive council composed of members elected by the population. The chief medical officer of the region is an elected member of that council with the responsibility for all the health services and institutions in the regions, including all polyclinics and dispensaries, hospitals, and public health services. The chief medical officer is assisted by a number of physicians called chief specialists who head the various speciality sections. These speciality sections in most instances include: therapy, surgery, gynecology, obstetrics, epidemic diseases; and the chief specialists are responsible for the level and quality of the services rendered in their speciality areas. For example, the chief specialist in surgery is responsible for the organization and quality of surgical work in the region. In discharging that responsibility he maintains contact with and supervision of all surgeons and is responsible for insuring adequate postgraduate training.[6]

4. DISTRICT HEALTH SERVICES

Although the region has the responsibility for the direct administration of the delivery of health services, it is much too large for effective day-to-day management of the various health services. Regions are, therefore, divided into districts (rayons) serving populations of 40,000 to 150,000. The district may have a single central hospital, but there are frequently several hospital

---

[6] Fry, pp. 29–33.

units, a number of polyclinics, and at least one public health unit. All of these health facilities are under the direction of the chief physician of the district, who is usually the senior physician of the central district hospital.

5. MICRODISTRICTS

The whole system of Soviet health care rests ultimately on the concept of neighborhood areas (microdistricts) where personal care of the people is provided by small teams of medical and paramedical workers.

Microdistricts (uchastoks) in an urban area usually consist of about 4,000 adults and children; the boundaries of microdistricts must be periodically reexamined and redrawn to reflect changes in population. Under the microdistrict system, a person is assigned to a health territorial unit on the basis of his residence; should he move to another area, he is assigned to a corresponding microdistrict. As might be expected, in the countryside, microdistricts are generally much larger, geographically, than in the cities. In addition, many rural microdistricts have their own small hospitals to insure inpatient services for the people, particularly when distances are great and there are transportation difficulties. On the other hand, urban microdistricts, characteristically, have no medical facilities of their own; such facilities are usually placed at the district level.

There are usually 10 microdistricts in each district. The ideal district is one with a population of 40,000 divided into 10 microdistricts with a population of 4,000 each.

6. ORGANIZATION OF HEALTH CARE IN THE INDUSTRIAL SETTING

The majority of the Russian population receive their basic health care services in the territorial network of districts and microdistricts. In addition, however, there are networks based, not so much on geographical location, as on occupation. Industrial plants and organizations are required to build and maintain health facilities out of their own budgetary resources. In the factories, the shop plays a role equivalent to the microdistrict. The workers in a single shop constitute a panel of potential patients, with each panel consisting of from 1,000 to 1,500 workers. The health personnel who service these workers are appointed, paid, and supervised by the local health departments to provide a degree of uniformity in the delivery and standards of health care.

7. OTHER RESIDUAL HEALTH SYSTEMS

In addition to the industrial health care system, the U.S.S.R. has a number of other closed panels of patients related to status. There are a number of health facilities which are designated for the use of the members of the Soviet political elite, including the Kremlin clinics and hospitals. These facilities are also often those to which prominent Communist party members from outside the U.S.S.R. are treated when they come to Russia for medical care. Similarly, members of the Soviet Academy of Science, which is composed of the top Soviet cultural elite, along with their families, have access to health facilities outside the regular health system.[7]

8. DISTRICT POLYCLINICS

No description of the organization of the Soviet health system would be complete without a discussion of the nature and function of the district poly-

---

[7] Field, pp. 87–95.

clinic. Essentially, the district polyclinic is a comprehensive outpatient facility and health center designed to provide a broad range of health services with the exception of inpatient hospital care. Patients whose conditions require hospitalization are directed to the appropriate facility by the personnel of the polyclinic. (In those districts where there is a district hospital, the polyclinic is designated as an administrative subdivision of that hospital.) The personnel in the polyclinic are appointed and paid by the municipal health department in the cities, and by the rural health department or the district hospitals in the countryside.

The polyclinic may be housed in a building of its own or it may share space in a building used for nonmedical purposes—for example, an apartment building. It usually consists of a reception hall where the patients report for appointments. To facilitate continuity of care, the polyclinic maintains the records for patients in the service area, classified by microdistrict and by address. Additional space in the polyclinic is devoted to treatment rooms, procedure rooms with diagnostic and medical equipment, and laboratories for diagnostic tests.[8]

The size of polyclinics and the services they provide vary with the size and geography of the area they serve. In large cities such as Moscow and Leningrad, there are specialized clinics for children, adults, and for disease entities such as women's diseases, tuberculosis, dental surgery, and skin and venereal disease. In smaller cities, there is generally an all-purpose polyclinic that provides care for the entire population; even in these facilities, the treatment of children, adults and various disease categories is divided among separate physicians. There is no evidence of a form of family practice which would provide for the treatment of an entire family in the polyclinic setting; despite the existence of the polyclinic, the delivery of basic health services can be so fragmented that an individual may be under the care of three or more physicians who are located in different buildings.

In large cities an adult polyclinic may serve a population of from 40,000 to 60,000. Polyclinics devoted to the treatment of children in cities of comparable size may provide care for a patient population of from 15,000 to 20,000 children under the age of 15. In addition, a polyclinic specializing in the treatment of women may include the service areas of a number of adult polyclinics and draw from a patient population of as many as 250,000 women.[9]

In general, all urban polyclinics are built and organized along the same lines. A description of one polyclinic in Moscow, serving a patient population of about 41,000 indicates that the facility has a staff of 90 physicians, 133 paramedical workers, 20 clerical assistants and 15 cleaners. The range of specialities housed at that facility include urologists, pathologists, radiologists, gynecologists (for diagnostic work only), ophthalmologists, and dental surgeons, along with a complement of surgeons, specialists, therapists, and other health professions.

Office hours at the Moscow polyclinic, as is the case with all other counterpart facilities, are from 8 a.m. to 8 p.m. In addition, the polyclinic has two emergency units on call during the entire day, with a small emergency room for minor traumas. The workload of the polyclinic is between 1,000 to 1,500 visits a day, and 20 to 25 evening and night visits.[10] Also characteristic of urban polyclinics, the facility has the responsibility for a number of local factories, each with an industrial health unit, and each staffed by the polyclinic with a

---

[8] Field, pp. 88–90.
[9] Fry, pp. 105–108.
[10] Ibid.

physician and four feldshers (paramedical workers under the supervision of a physician).

REIMBURSEMENT METHODS/CONDITIONS OF PRACTICE

The physician is trained at State expense and works as a salaried State employee in a State-owned facility. The State establishes conditions of work, norms of patients to be seen, and salary levels. While private practice still exists, it is frowned upon ideologically, and it is slated eventually to disappear. Even the few doctors who have a private practice (mainly stomatologists, venereologists, and a small number of other physicians acting in a "consultant" capacity) must have at least one full-time job with the State. There are also a few paying polyclinics, somewhere between private and State-owned facilities, where for a relatively modest fee a patient can avail himself of a consultant or specialist. There are no private medical facilities, such as hospitals, clinics, or sanatoria.

As is the case with all other employed persons in the U.S.S.R., doctors are paid salaries drawn from the general revenue of the Government. Each economic sector has its own wage scale and Soviet doctors are paid according to the scale for all employees in health. Positions on all Soviet pay scales are based on the characteristics of the job and of the individual—"arduousness," education, skill, and other personal qualifications, managerial or other responsibilities, length of service of the incumbent, importance of the industry in the entire economy, and geographical location of the medical facility. The categorical wage decrees embodying the pay scales for all Soviet workers are issued by the Council of Ministers and are binding on all Government agencies, trade unions, and employing organizations.

Under the present salary scale, directors of hospitals and other medical facilities receive higher rates on the average:

> For example, the chief physician of an urban hospital with a staff of 200 physicians receives a base pay of 225 rubles per month, whereas a physician practicing in the hospital for less than 5 years receives a base pay of 90 rubles per month. With 30 years of professional service the chief physician's base pay would increase only to 230 rubles, whereas the practicing physician's base pay would increase to 165 rubles per month.[11]

Chiefs-of-service in hospitals and in polyclinics receive supplements to their base-pay rates according to the size of their departments, size in this case being determined by the number of physicians working in that department. Supplements to the base pay of all physicians are also provided on the basis of level of professional achievement, the difficulties or hazards of working conditions, and territorial location:

> Physicians who are certified to be in the "higher-qualification" category on the basis of their continuing education progress receive an additional 30 rubles per month. A "Doctor of Medicine" receives a 20-ruble supplement, whereas an "Honored Physician of the Republic" receives a 10-ruble supplement. Base pays are increased by 20 percent for night work and 15 percent to 30 percent for work with radiologic equipment or patients with tuberculosis. Physicians who work in isolated rural areas or the far North receive 30 percent to 100 percent increases in their base pay.[12]

[11] Muller et al., p. 697. A rubble is worth about $1.32.
[12] Ibid.

A major exception to the customary pay scale for Soviet physicians has been made for professors in medical institutes and clinical scientists who have traditionally been paid on the basis of a separate salary scale. In the past, these differentials were the source of considerable disparities in salary between the academicians and scientists on the one hand and the practitioners on the other. For example, in 1962, the 103 members of the Academy of Sciences held 1,037 jobs, and received a salary from each job. A number of reforms, including reductions in the pay of medical school professors and a prohibition against a physician receiving more than one salary, have reduced the differentials in pay. However, members of medical faculties can still supplement their income by clinical practice and writing.

According to most commentaries on the conditions of the medical profession in the Soviet Union, physicians are not highly paid in relation to other professionals in the Soviet Union:

> The urban hospital physician with less than 5 years' service and a base pay of 90 rubles per month receives the same compensation as a librarian with a college education but less than 5 years' service, a secondary school instructor with between 5 and 10 years of service, or the principal of a secondary school with less than 280 students and less than 5 years' experience. The dean of a university with more than 3,500 students who is a professor receives 600 rubles per month as base pay.[13]

In return for his salary, the Soviet physician is expected to work 6 hours a day, 6 days a week, which has always been the work schedule for the Russian urban professional. Some urban doctors and all rural doctors must be available for emergency duty, but most polyclinics and hospitals have their own separate emergency staffs. The volume of work per primary physician per week (the weekly number of physician/patient consultations) averages 120 visits, including polyclinic consultations and home visits.[14]

Roughly 70 percent of the Soviet Union's 830,000 doctors are women. The USSR has one of the highest ratios of doctors per population in the world—in 1975, there was 1 physician for every 308 persons (comparable figures for the U.S. in 1973 were 1 per 641 persons). Dentistry, or "stomatology," is considered a medical specialty, rather than a distinct profession; thus, the physician total does include doctors of dentistry. "Middle medical workers," (i.e. nurses, feldshers, etc.) whose responsibilities and authorities are below the level of a physician's training, numbered about 2.5 million in 1975, or a ratio of about three auxiliary workers to every doctor (the comparable ratio in the U.S. is about 8 to 1).

Upon graduation from medical school, four out of five physicians practice in places assigned by the Ministry of Health. The remaining 20 percent go on for further academic specialization. Practicing physicians are encouraged to have some form of advanced training every 3 years if they practice in rural areas, and every 5 years if they work in urban areas. Some advanced training is not obligatory by law, but incentives are provided in the form of increased salaries and more desirable work assignments after training. And there is substantial physician participation; for example, in 1973, nearly 70,000 physicians took part in some form of advanced training.

In addition to programs for advanced study, Soviet health authorities

---

[13] Muller et al., p. 697.

[14] John Fry, "Structure of medical care services in the USSR." International Journal of Health Services, May 1972: 242.

have instituted a program ot continuing postgraduate education and training. Under such programs, formal course and practical instruction are available to physicians who have been practicing for a number of years. The purpose of the continuing education program is to provide physicians in community practice, particularly in rural areas, with knowledge of advances in modern medical practice.

There are substantial variations in the distribution of physicians among the various constituent Republics and particularly between rural areas and the large urban centers. For example, the ratio of physicians to population ranges from 34.6 per 10,000 in the Georgian Soviet Socialist Republic to 14.9 in the Tadzhik Soviet Socialist Republic.[15]

Similarly, Moscow and Leningrad, the two largest Soviet cities and the most important administrative, medical and research centers, have the highest physician to population ratio in the country. The most recent statistics indicate that Moscow has 62.5 physicians per 10,000 people. The supply of physicians falls off substantially in the provincial centers, the outlying districts, and particularly in the countryside. The ratio of physicians working full-time in rural areas to the population they serve has been indicated by Soviet health authorities to be as low as 5.4 physicians per 10,000 population.

Efforts to increase the number of physicians available to rural inhabitants have not proved very successful. Most Soviet physicians, upon completion of their medical education, are assigned to serve in medically underserved areas for from 3 to 5 years. Attempts to provide financial incentives to physicians to remain in practice in underserved rural areas through differentials in pay and more generous retirement provisions have not been sufficient to motivate many physicians to practice in the countryside.

It has been suggested that adequate pay differentials cannot be introduced into the Soviet system because the salary structure is based on the administrative clinical hierarchy. A pay differential sufficient to encourage rural practice could conceivably result in a rural physician with no administrative responsibilities being paid a salary at least equal to that paid to a service chief in a hospital. To date, however, the Soviet salary scale has not permitted such a major deviation from the rank hierarchy.[16]

Because of the demand for medical personnel and particularly the shortage of doctors in rural areas, the role of the feldsher is an important one in the Soviet health system. The feldsher has been a part of the Russian health care system for several centuries. Feldshers (from the German feldshere, meaning field barber or company surgeon) were originally introduced into Russia by Peter the Great in the 17th century to serve the military. In the 19th century, many retired military feldshers began practice in the countryside where they became the major source of medical care for the peasantry.[17]

The present feldsher is a qualified paramedical worker who has undergone a special 2- to 3-year training course and who works as part of a health team under the supervision of a physician. Although feldshers are still chiefly found in rural areas, they also work in urban communities in such specialized areas as emergency care, mental illness, and occupational health and preventive care.

In theory, the feldsher is only a doctor's assistant, not entrusted with medical functions and medical decisions:

---

[15] John D. Cooper, M.D., "Education for the Health Professions in the Soviet Union." Journal of Medical Education, May 1971: 412–415.

[16] William Glaser, "Paying the Doctor." Johns Hopkins Press, Baltimore, 1970: 232–234.

[17] Field, pp. 127–128.

The fact of the matter, however, is that under conditions where there is no physician around, or when no physician is available, the feldsher will fulfill many medical functions, except perhaps for routine surgery * * * In some respects the feldsher's functions in rural districts resemble those of the public health nurse in the more isolated districts of the United States.[18]

Feldshers in rural areas have fewer people under their care than do microdistrict (uchastok) doctors, usually less than 1,000 persons. Their work consists primarily of simple and straightforward medical and minor surgical matters, preventive care and immunization, and aftercare supervision of chronic illness. Soviet health authorities indicate that 20 to 30 percent of all medical students are former feldshers and that every year 2 to 5 percent of the feldshers enter medical school to become physicians.[19]

Federal Republic of Germany ([34], pp. 398–404)

Germany's system of social health insurance was established in 1883, at which time about 15 percent of the population (primarily low-income workers) was first legally required to obtain membership in sickness insurance funds. Today the system encompasses almost 90 percent of the population. More than 1,800 semiautonomous sickness funds administer the decentralized program, under the general supervision of the Ministry of Health.

The statutory health insurance program provides a wide range of designated benefits, including service benefits for medical and dental treatment and drugs, and sickness cash benefits during periods of unemployment due to illness. In addition to the required benefits, sickness funds may at their own option provide supplementary benefits.

In general, employers and employees make equal contributions to the program in fixed amounts ranging from 4 to 5.5 percent on both worker and employer of total insurable wages up to DM 22,500 per year.[1] The actual contribution rate varies from fund to fund with the average combined rate reaching 9.4 percent by January 1974. The Social Pensions Insurance Funds pay contributions on behalf of retired and disabled pensioners and the Federal Institute for Labor makes contributions on behalf of persons receiving unemployment benefits or assistance and maintenance allowances.

Coverage

Approximately 17.8 million employees and 7.9 million pensioners are compulsorily insured under the German program. About 4.6 million persons are voluntarily insured. Along with 24 million dependents of these people, the total number of insured persons represents almost 90 percent of the total population. Included among the 90 percent of the population covered by health insurance are the following recipients of social benefits who receive their medical treatment through statutory health insurance (acting on behalf of other branches of the government):

War victims and their dependents, war survivors.
Recipients of social aid, based on local arrangements.

---

[18] Ibid., p. 127.
[19] Cooper, pp. 412–415.
    [1] As of December 1975, one DM (Deutsche Mark) equaled about 40 cents in U.S. currency.

Victims of industrial injuries and diseases.
Recipients of reparations benefits.
Returnees.

About 4.6 million persons are privately insured. Persons with no insurance coverage total about 1.4 percent of the population.[2] All wage and salary workers and self-employed persons whose earnings are below a stipulated ceiling (DM 22,500 a year as of January 1974) are compulsorily insured. All blue-collar workers (manual workers in specified job classifications) are compulsorily covered regardless of whether their income exceeds the stipulated ceiling. Unemployed persons receiving unemployment benefits and pensioners are also insured on a compulsory basis.

Prior to 1971, salaried white-collar workers and the self-employed who earned more than the stipulated ceiling were not eligible to participate in the program. In January 1971, new regulations allowed all workers earning above the ceiling to obtain membership on a voluntary basis during a 3-month open season. Since that time, persons entering the work force with earnings above the ceiling have been allowed a similar 3-month grace period to join the public system on a voluntary basis.

Benefits

Federal law requires all sick funds to cover the following items without patient cost-sharing, except as noted:

Physicians' services, in home, office, or elsewhere.

Prescription drugs, subject to 20 percent coinsurance up to a maximum of DM 2.50; pensioners, persons on cash assistance, and partially employed persons are exempt from such cost-sharing.

Hospitalization up to a maximum of 78 weeks per illness over a 3-year period; includes medical and related treatment, room and board in ward or semiprivate accommodations, nursing services, drugs, use of medical aids and apparatus, etc.

Prenatal care, delivery, and cash benefits for the period of maternity nursing.

Screening for prostatic, rectal, and cervical cancer, as well as a number of infant diseases.

Routine dental care, with partial payment for orthodontics and dental prostheses; treatment is covered only when provided by authorized insurance fund dental surgeons on basis of a special certificate presented by the patient; for dentures and other prosthetic devices, patient generally pays at least one-third of the cost.

Prosthetic equipment, e.g. eyeglasses, trusses, artificial limbs, orthopedic shoes; for minor medical appliances, 20 percent of the charges are paid by the patient; for major appliances the patient is generally required to pay one-third of the cost.

Home care when used as a substitute for hospitalization.

Cash payment in the event of death.

Cash sickness allowance fixed by law, payable after the employer has paid the full wage or salary for 6 weeks from the beginning of a disability; amounts range from 75 percent of the customary wage for persons without dependents to 85 percent of the customary wage for persons with dependents, for up to 78 weeks in a 3-year period.

The insured persons have free choice of so-called insurance fund doctor (defined later in this section). Upon receipt of services from a physician, the patient must present the doctor with a "sick certificate," which acts as proof of membership in an insurance fund and also serves as the basis for payment for services received. Sick certificates are issued free of charge to each person once

---

[2] Survey of Social Security in the Federal Republic of Germany. Federal Minister for Labor and Social Affairs, Bonn, 1972: 125–129.

every calendar quarter and entitle the patient to unlimited physician visits within that quarter.

For the physician, sick certificates act as a money substitute; the doctor turns in the sick certificates to the Insurance Fund Doctor's Association for cash reimbursement of the services he has rendered to the insured patient.

Beginning in 1970, insured persons who did not use their sick certificates were repaid up to DM 30 per year, or DM 10 for as many as three of the four books of certificates each insured person is entitled to receive each year. As a utilization control, redemption of unused sick certificates for cash proved to be of questionable merit:

> Some doctors believe that this measure may inhibit patients from seeking medical advice although they are in need of it. Others believe that the amount of DM 10 is too low to serve as an incentive to pay for services privately.[3]

This "no claim" bonus system cost the insurance funds more than DM 300 million in the first year of its operation, without providing any offset savings; on October 1, 1973, the scheme was abolished.

Only a few funds pay for convalescent home treatment and home nursing care on a standard basis, but treatment provided at West German health spas is part of standard coverage.

FINANCING

Health insurance is financed primarily by equal contributions from employers and employees. For very low wage earners the employer pays the full contribution. Each insurance fund fixes its contribution rates for members according to its own needs. In general, however, the range is between 4 and 5.5 percent of insurable earnings up to DM 22,500 per year on both the worker and employer. The ceiling placed on wages is automatically adjusted on an annual basis, in accordance with a formula taking into account changes in national wage levels.

Contributions on behalf of compulsorily insured pensioners (all persons employed for remuneration are compulsorily insurable for pension insurance without regard to the nature of work or amount of their income) are paid by the social insurance pension funds. Voluntarily insured pensioners (persons whose employment was exempted from compulsory pension insurance—for example, part-time or intermittent workers, government employees, workers not previously insurable due to the pre-1967 wage ceiling, etc.) make direct contributions which are refunded by the pension funds. The Federal Institute for Labor makes contributions for persons receiving unemployment compensation and maintenance allowances.

The amount an individual pays to his sick fund is related only to the amount of his wages and is independent of the medical or social risks he may present to the fund. In addition, the amount of the wage earner's contribution to the fund is also unrelated to whether he is an individual enrollee or whether he has dependents who are also legally eligible to receive medical services through the fund.

Until January 1971, employers had been required to make health insurance contributions only for those employees who were compulsorily insured (all blue-collar workers and those white-collar workers with earnings below the ceiling). Thus, for white-collar workers whose earnings were above the ceiling,

---

[3] M. Pflanz, "German Health Insurance: The Evolution and Current Problems of the Pioneer System." International Journal of Health Services, Nov. 1971: 319.

employer participation in health insurance contributions was entirely voluntary. Since 1971, however, employers must make a payment for all insured workers regardless of how high the earnings. If an employee does not join the public system, he can apply his employer's contribution toward private health insurance premiums. For high-income white-collar workers, the employer's contribution equals the maximum he would have to pay if their earnings were at the ceiling.[4]

Government subsidies play only a small role in financing the public health insurance system and are mainly for refunds to the sickness funds of DM 400 for every cash maternity allowance payment. Sizable government contributions to the health care delivery system are, however, provided through payments to the hospitals and for public health programs. Government expenditures account for about one-fourth of total national health care costs, with public insurance expenditures accounting for about three-fifths.

ADMINISTRATION

More than 1,800 semiautonomous health insurance funds and mutual benefit insurance funds administer the program, under the general supervision of the Ministry of Health. Each fund is financially and organizationally autonomous and responsible for balancing its own income and expenditures. They are organized as follows:

A total of 401 local health insurance funds (general scheme funds), 107 land health insurance funds for agriculture, 1,133 works health insurance funds operating in the larger enterprises, 178 trade association health insurance funds for small-scale artisan firms, 1 seaman's health insurance fund for seagoing employment, the miners' special scheme, 7 mutual benefit funds for nonmanual workers, 8 mutual benefit funds for manual workers. At the beginning of 1970, the insurance funds employed about 77,000 persons.

The insurance funds are self-governing bodies * * * with an executive committee and a delegates' assembly, comprised of equal numbers of representatives of workers and employers. Exceptions are the organs of the mutual benefit funds, which are comprised solely of representatives of the insured persons, and the organs of the miners' special scheme fund, which are comprised of two-thirds of workers' representatives, and one-third of employers' representatives. The delegates' assembly resolves on the statutes of the funds, in which contribution rates and additional benefits are laid down.

For the purpose of safeguarding supralocal and common interest, the insurance funds are organized in insurance fund associations:

Federal Association of Local Health Insurance Funds in Bad Godesberg.

Federal Association of Land Insurance Funds in Hannover.

Federal Association of Works Health Insurance Funds in Essen.

Federal Association of Trade Association Health Insurance Funds in Cologne.

Association of Manual Workers Mutual Benefit Funds in Hamburg.

Association of Nonmanual Health Funds in Hamburg.

Miner's Special Scheme in Bochum.

Working Community for Common Problems of Health Insurance in Frankfort.

Federal Association of Insurance Fund Doctors in Cologne.

Federal Association of Insurance Dental Surgeons in Cologne.[5]

---

[4] Joseph G. Simanis, "Health Insurance Legislation in West Germany." Social Security Bulletin, June 1971: 20–21.

[5] Taken from "Survey of Social Security in the Federal Republic of Germany," p. 144.

The government establishes broad legislative guidelines with respect to the operation of the insurance system. Contract and payment agreements and benefit packages of the various sick funds may not violate those guidelines. However, in all other matters, the government may not interfere in the negotiated decisions of the sick funds and the associations of insurance doctors, since the funds are legally autonomous bodies and are not government agents or subdivisions.

As self-governing, autonomous organizations, the sick funds are subject to direct governmental supervision only in cases of violation of the law. They are administered by an executive committee composed of an equal number of representatives of the insured members and of their employers.

For blue-collar workers, membership in a particular sick fund is generally determined by the locality of type of firm by which the individual is employed. White-collar workers, on the other hand, have been allowed to join so-called substitute funds (Ersatzkassen) in lieu of those funds they would have had to join if they were grouped together with blue-collar workers according to place of work. Traditionally, about 85 percent of eligible white-collar workers have belonged to substitute funds, which have frequently offered more generous benefits because of higher contribution rates on the higher salaries of their white-collar members.

Since the capacity of funds is influenced considerably by the number of members and their financial contributions, insurance funds are in mutual competition to enlarge their membership. Questions have been raised about the relative advantages of a multiplicity of sick funds in competition with one another:

> With respect to this, there are, of course, endeavors toward a centralized and unified insurance system. This may possibly be contrary to the interest of the insured, who receive more individual protection under present conditions. Certainly it is not favored by many of the sick funds officials, who may presently pursue their particular interest and initiatives; and such a centralization would not be viewed favorably by the doctors, since the multiplicity of funds allows a certain latitude in negotiating on fees.
>
> There must be raised, however, the questions of whether a relative unification (if not a total centralization) of the dispersed parts of the system of funds should be realized * * * in order to achieve a better balance of risks connected with very expensive treatment, and in order to rationalize by computer the many administrative processes. Until now, computers are used by many funds only for keeping books on contributions and for calculating fee-for-service rates. Most of the funds and the associations of insurance doctors have only small computers. Moreover, data are not related to the individual rendered service, but only to the worker primarily insured, with the exclusion of his dependents. For this reason, a genuine calculation of risk, within defined categories of the population, is as difficult as a continuous control of efficiency. Better electronic data processing will be possible, however, when a unified system of identify numbers is introduced, which is planned for 1973.[6]

REIMBURSEMENT METHODS

Hospitals in West Germany are predominantly public or voluntary (charity) institutions. Proprietary hospitals are few and play little part in providing medical care to publicly insured patients. Within limits set by the Federal Government, hospitals negotiate with the sick funds a prospective per diem

---

[6] Pflanz, p. 321.

rate for hospitalization. Sick fund payments do not, however, cover the real costs of hospital care. Community tax income and charitable contributions subsidize the nonreimbursed costs of care. The average per diem rate paid by sick funds in 1970 for hospital care was DM 40.

Hospital physicians (about a third of the country's qualified physicians) are generally salaried employees and, as such, do not qualify for fee-for-service reimbursement by the sick funds. Their services are included in the hospital's bill.

West Germany currently has about 11 hospital beds per 1,000 population. Comparative international statistics for 1969 showed that West Germany had a higher rate of hospital admissions per inhabitant (143 per 1,000 inhabitants) than any other country in the Western World. The average length of stay in an acute care hospital in 1969 was 18.6 days, more than double the 1969 rate of 8.5 days for the United States. Because the official per diem hospital rate approved by the government for reimbursement by sick funds is considered inadequate to cover real costs, it has been suggested that hospitals in West Germany attempt to solve this problem by keeping patients longer than necessary:

> To one outside the medical fraternity, this might not make sense, but it does because a hospital loses money during the initial days of a patient's stay when costly tests and procedures are being done and makes money later on when the patient is virtually nothing more than a hotel guest * * *.
> Another shortcoming is the peculiar prohibition that tradition and nonhospital doctors have forced onto the system, preventing hospitals from having outpatient clinics. (The only exceptions are the teaching hospitals that may have clinics for educational purposes.) As a result of this ban, patients who require more care than a nonhospital physician can provide must be hospitalized in costly facilities even though they could be treated on a more economical outpatient basis.[7]

For physicians, reimbursement is based on the number of sick certificates (or krankenschein) received from insured patients each quarter and forwarded to an association of insurance doctors for reimbursement. Individual services rendered to each patient are recorded on the certificate and the doctor receives points for each task. The average number of points, or services rendered, is calculated for all doctors at the end of each quarter. If the physician's average number of services is at or below the national average for all doctors, he receives full payment, but if his average is above this, he may receive a cutback.

Fee schedules are determined by a commission representing the doctors, sickness insurance funds, government, and other interested parties. The schedules include over 1,500 different procedures, ranging from such items as the amount a doctor can charge for mileage on a house call to the cost of an injection. Doctors are permitted to charge private patients higher fees than those set forth in the negotiated fee schedules for publicly insured patients. Although private patients compose only 12 percent of all patients, about 20 percent of the physician's average office income comes from the treatment of such patients.

In 1973, West Germany had more than 100,000 doctors (a physician-per-population ratio of 1 per 600, one of the most favorable in the world). About 55 percent of qualified physicians are engaged in independent practice, about one-third employed in hospitals, and about one-tenth involved in administration or research activities. Almost all physicians engaged in independent practice

---

[7] Donald Drake, "Health Care—The European Way: Germany Uses Dual System." Philadelphia Inquirer, Dec. 19, 1969. Reprinted in the Congressional Record, Dec. 19, 1969; S17340.

participate in the public health insurance scheme as "insurance doctors." Insurance doctors are organized in regional associations, which are self-governing and headed by elected physician members. It is the association, not the individual doctor, which negotiates fee-for-service contracts with particular sick funds. The association then distributes sick-fund contributions in proportion to the services rendered by each member physician. Treatment provided by dentists is remunerated on generally the same basis as that for physicians.

Review of physicians' services provided to insured sick-fund members is utilized primarily as an economic control, rather than a control over the quality of care:

> Although they would be authorized by legislation, there are no quality controls, while economical behavior of doctors is relatively often submitted to scrutiny. The initative for scrutiny may be taken by the sick fund or by the association of insurance doctors. But in any case, disciplining a doctor is a matter for doctors who are elected members of a committee of the association of insurance doctors. * * *
> * * * The average, to which every control is oriented, is calculated from the sum of costs referrable to the different specialty groups of doctors (including, of course, general practitioners). There are two categories of doctors who are responsible for lowering this crucial average and so, in fact, handicap their colleagues who order more expensive therapeutic prescriptions: (a) older doctors who fall behind in acquiring new knowledge and thereby do not participate in medical progress which necessarily requires more expensive measures; (b) doctors who to a large extent get free specimens from pharmaceutical firms in order to distribute them to their patients.[8]

HEALTH EXPENDITURES

In 1969, West Germany expended 5.7 percent of its gross national product on health care. Between 1961 and 1969, health expenditures rose at an average annual rate of 10.3 percent. During this period, the average annual rate of growth in the Consumer Price Index was 2.6 percent; the average annual rate of increase in health expenditures, adjusted by the average of the CPI and wage index changes, registered 4.7 percent. Government health expenditures, as a percent of the total government budget, reflected a decrease in 1969 to 3.5 percent, down from 3.7 percent in the previous year.[9]

It has been reported that the financial situation of the public health insurance scheme has tended to deteriorate in recent years. Until 1967, insurance fund income exceeded expenditure, but beginning in 1968, annual expenditure has exceeded income by about 1 percent. This ratio of income-to-expenditure has apparently been stabilized, with estimated health insurance fund expenditures for 1973 exceeding income by DM 305 million, or slightly less than 1 percent of total income.

Netherlands ([11], pp. 57–68)

Health care delivery in the Netherlands is based on an insurance system administered by private sickness funds under the supervision of the Government.

Seventy percent of the population is covered for general medical care. About half of the total population is covered on a compulsory basis.

---

[8] Pflanz, p. 320.

[9] Joseph G. Simanis, "Medical Care Expenditures in Seven Countries." Social Security Bulletin, March 1973: 39–42.

Another 15 percent of the population has voluntary coverage. There is a third coverage group, about 5 percent of the population, made up primarily of pensioners. Although the higher income groups are excluded from the government scheme for general sickness, the entire population is covered under a special program for catastrophic illness. And the whole working population is covered under still another program for cash sickness and maternity benefits.

Medical benefits include complete coverage of necessary medical care and basic hospital care (including nursing-home services) with elements of cost sharing for a few types of medical services. The whole population, in cases of catastrophic illness, is generally entitled to the full cost of medical care after 1 year of illness and to certain types of institutional care before that time. Cash sickness benefits for the wage earner continue for an unlimited time and are normally set at 80 percent of earnings before the onset of illness. Cash maternity benefits are paid under the same program that provides cash sickness benefits.

Under compulsory membership the employer and the insured each pay 4.75 percent of earnings up to the ceiling. The employer pays an additional 2.6 percent for catastrophic illness. Minor subsidies are paid to the sickness insurance system by the Government to help defray the cost of medical care for pensioners and low-income groups.

Reimbursement procedures for physicians cover a wide spectrum of methods: General practitioners are paid on a capitation basis, while specialists are reimbursed through salary, fee-for-service, or case-payment approaches.

The typical hospital is a private institution paid directly by a sick fund primarily utilizing a schedule of fees set by the Union of Hospital Associations under government guidelines, but also taking into account annual budget considerations of the specific hospital. Some hospitals bill separately for hospital physicians' services.

BACKGROUND

National health insurance came to the Netherlands at a later date than to most other West European countries. Although a number of national cash sickness plans were formulated in the early 20th century and a bill was actually passed to this effect by Parliament in 1913, the legislation was never implemented because of a change in governments. In 1929 another program was approved by Parliament which went into effect in 1930, introducing compulsory coverage for cash sickness benefits. This legislation also gave impetus to expansion of private insurance coverage for health care since it stipulated that a worker, to be eligible for cash benefits, had to demonstrate that he had provided for coverage of medical care costs in case of illness.

By 1941 when compulsory health care insurance went into effect, approximately 4 million people, or about 50 percent of the population, were covered for medical care under private insurance arrangements. The 1941 scheme provided general practitioner care, surgical and specialist treatment, and 42 days of hospitalization along with limited dental care and partial payment for care in tuberculosis sanitariums.

Generally, those workers earning above a stated figure were ineligible to join either program, for cash sickness benefits or health care. Such ineligibility based on earnings considerations has remained a feature of health insurance to the present time.

In 1967 another law was passed introducing a program to meet special sickness costs and expenses incurred by extended illness. This catastrophic illness program covers the whole population, including the 30 percent excluded under the general sickness insurance program.

ORGANIZATION OF HEALTH CARE DELIVERY

The Ministry of Social Affairs and Public Health is the central authority responsible for health services. It not only exercises general supervision and control but also operates a few hospitals under its own jurisdiction. At a lower level, the municipalities also exercise certain controls over the health care delivery system. However, voluntary organizations play a much larger part in this respect, particularly in the operation of hospitals and in the provision of such services as home nursing.

Presently, about 90 sickness funds administer health care insurance for the insured population. Most of them are organized along geographical lines and are managed by delegates chosen by the members. Some also have directors chosen by medical professions. The insured persons usually are free to choose any fund which operates in their area unless they are employed by a firm which has its own fund. Any ordinary sickness fund may refuse to accept an insured person who is eligible for an enterprise fund or one of the other funds organized to appeal to special groups.

The sickness funds are grouped into several national associations of which the largest is the Federation of Sickness Funds. The associations in turn are grouped together in a Joint Association of Sickness Fund Organizations which negotiates physicians' fees with the Netherlands Medical Association.

General supervision over operation of the sickness fund system is exercised by the Sickness Fund Council, which is responsible to the Minister of Social Affairs and Public Health. The Council includes representatives of the sickness funds, the government, the medical profession, and employers and employees. It can regulate the administration of sickness insurance and also distributes the contributions for compulsory insurance to the individual sickness funds. It also advises the Minister on all problems concerning sickness insurance.

The Sickness Funds Council also exercises supervision over the castastrophic insurance program and the relevant finances from which the sickness funds and private insurance companies obtain reimbursement for expenditures under that program. Cash payments during incapacity for work are administered by occupational associations which also dispense family and unemployment benefits.

Physicians

General practitioners.--Of approximately 11,000 qualified physicians practicing in 1970 in the Netherlands, 40 percent were general practitioners. The general practitioner is usually self-employed, operating from his own office. He ordinarily does not work in the hospital and has admitting privileges only for maternity cases, although he can visit his patients who have been admitted by specialists.

The sickness funds keep statistics on prescription practices by the physicians and on referrals of patients to specialists. When higher-than-average referrals or cost can be attributed to a physician's practice, the funds' medical adviser may ask the practitioner for an explanation. Some of the large funds utilize special committees to impose fines and suspend practitioners for insurance practices which the funds find objectionable.

Specialists.--Slightly under 6,500 practicing physicians in the Netherlands, or approximately 60 percent of the total, are specialists. Like the general practitioner the specialist is usually self-employed. However, he invariably has an affiliation with a hospital. He receives remuneration from the hospital or through the sickness fund for inpatient care. At the same time, he usually uses hospital facilities for outpatient care which he administers on a free-agent basis and is reimbursed through channels that are entirely separate from those of the hospital. Normally the specialist chooses to operate through hospital facilities because of the small charge for utilizing these facilities and the excellent range of equipment provided.

Hospitals

Most hospitals in the Netherlands are private institutions run by religious communities or charitable organizations, but about 20 percent are public institutions controlled by local authorities.

Virtually all hospitals allow only specialists to treat inpatients, except in the case of obstetrics, and most hospitals exclude any physician who is not a member of the staff. Institutions which exclude outside specialists are called "closed" hospitals while those without such restrictions are "open" hospitals. Many hospitals also have a number of trainee specialists who come under the direction of chief specialists; these trainees are usually reimbursed on a salary basis by the hospital.

In recent years, nursing homes for prolonged care have become more and more important in the overall structure of health care in the country. As of 1970, there were approximately 23,000 beds in nursing homes compared to 66,000 beds in general hospitals (as opposed to psychiatric and other special-purpose institutions).

Each nursing home ordinarily has a full-time physician, usually a general practitioner. Nursing care is provided by the approximate equivalent of practical nurses under the jurisdiction of one or more registered nurses. There are usually facilities for physiotherapy and occupational therapy . A social worker is also usually assigned to the nursing home.

COVERAGE

In discussing coverage of population for the government-sponsored health insurance in the Netherlands, it is necessary to distinguish between general insurance for routine health care and the National Exceptional Medical Expenses Insurance Program designed to meet the cost involved in catastrophic illness or long-term institutional care. Exceptional Medical Insurance covers the entire population. However, only 70 percent of the population is covered by the general sickness insurance program for ordinary medical care, broken down as follows.

Compulsory

All wage and salary workers with earnings below a stipulated ceiling (17,680 florins in 1973 or slightly less than 1-1/2 times the average wage in manufacturing) must join the system.1/ About 50 percent of the population including dependents is in this category.

Voluntary

Approximately 15 percent of the population is covered by this category that includes primarily the self-employed earning below the ceiling of 17,680 florins per year and their dependents.

Pensioners

Slightly over 5 percent of the population is covered in this group which is open to people over age 65 who have incomes of less than 13,821 florins per year.

BENEFITS

Medical

Under the general sickness insurance scheme an insured person generally receives free care for any medical service needed. Dental treatment is also provided free of charge, except for fillings required by those who have failed to have a checkup in the previous 6 months. There is also a provision for cost sharing with regard to dentures and in a few other situations.

Most childbirth confinements take place at home with the services of a midwife covered by health insurance. If complications necessitate a physician's services or hospitalization, such treatment is also covered. Hospitalization for routine childbirth is covered but involves some cost sharing.

The provisions of the Exceptional Sickness Insurance Program usually apply when a person is hospitalized for more than 1 year, in which case the program pays for his institutional expenses beyond that point. It also pays for nursing-home care as well as confinement in homes for the handicapped or the mentally retarded--even when required before the lapse of 1 year. As a result, many health care services are provided under this program which in most other countries would be provided by governmental institutions funded by general revenue, in many instances, as a form of public assistance.

Cash Benefits

A worker who is incapacitated receives a benefit equal to 80 percent of his average earnings over the 3 months preceding commencement of the incapacity. No benefit is paid for the first 2 days of incapacity and also no benefit is paid on that portion of the wages which are not insured (above 132 florins per day as of January 1, 1973).

The benefit is paid for 1 year at which time it is normally replaced by a disability pension--also equal to 80 percent of prior earnings. Cash sickness benefits are funded and administered separately from medical

---

1/ 1 florin equals U.S. 39 cents.

care insurance. In 1973 they were financed by payroll contributions of
1 percent of the employee's wages and 6.4 percent by his employer on
wages up to 17,680 florins per year. The whole working population is
covered for cash sickness benefits, regardless of income. All workers
with children are also entitled to sizable family allowances which continue during illness.

Maternity

Maternity benefits are payable to an expectant mother who has been an
active member of the labor force. The allowance is normally paid for
12 weeks and begins 6 weeks before the expected date of delivery. The
benefit corresponds to 100 percent of the mother's daily wage up to a
maximum of 132 florins per day as of January 1, 1973. If the insured
woman remains incapacitated because of the confinement after this 12-
week period, she can continue to receive benefits equal to 100 percent
of her daily wage, up to a maximum of 52 weeks.

PROCEDURES FOR OBTAINING CARE

To be eligible for medical treatment by a general practitioner, the
insured person and his family must be registered with a physician who
has signed a contract with the sickness fund to which they belong. The
same procedure applies in obtaining pharmacist and dentist services.
The insured person may change general practitioners at frequent intervals.

If the general practitioner decides that the services of a specialist
are necessary, he issues a referral card to his patient. The patient
may not consult a specialist directly. Admission to a hospital·normally
depends on the decision of the specialist that such care is necessary
and takes place after he has prepared the necessary papers. The hospitalization decision is subject to review and final approval by a controlling doctor of the relevant sickness fund.

ROLE OF PRIVATE INSURANCE

Private insurance in the Netherlands plays a rather important role in
financing overall health care. Perhaps as much as 95 percent of the
population covered by governmental health insurance also contracts for
supplemental insurance. The original reason for such widespread insurance under private auspices was to assure financial help in case of
prolonged hospitalization, an important consideration before 1965 when
governmental health insurance only covered hospitalization for 70 days.
However, since then, even with virtually unlimited hospitalization provided by the governmental scheme, private insurance of this type has not
receded significantly. Most of the population continues to contract for
such coverage, ostensibly to provide for better accommodations than are
provided under the regular scheme.

Most hospitals have at least three different classes of accommodations
for patients and many subdivide the second-class into two subcategories,
thus in effect creating four classes. Social insurance covers expenses
only in the lowest, or third class. Not only do room rates rise for
higher class accommodations but physicians' fees are also usually increased.

Nearly all of the population not covered by the governmental scheme depend on private health insurance for their primary coverage of health care. Approximately 140 insurance companies are involved in private health insurance. Essentially, there are three types of insurance companies which participate--commercial insurance companies, cooperative insurance associations, and associations involved only in the coverage of hospital care expenses.

The private insurance companies have played a role in administering the Exceptional Sickness Insurance Program since its inception in 1968. For those individuals who have their primary insurance with a private company rather than a sickness fund, the private company is responsible for initiating action for transfer of payment from one source to the other.

Physicians--particularly specialists--derive a large share of their income from their private patients. The fees permitted for physician care of private patients in third-class hospital accommodations are three times those for sickness fund cases. In certain types of second-class accommodations they are six times as high, and medical treatment for first-class patients is probably even higher.

FINANCING

Contributions

Compulsory.--Persons who earn a wage of no more than 17,680 florins per year are compulsorily insured. The contribution for sickness fund insurance is in the form of a payroll tax and totals 9-1/2 percent of the worker's wage up to 68 florins per day. The employer and the employee each pay half.

Voluntary.--The contributions paid by voluntarily insured persons vary from fund to fund and must be paid for each adult covered. Children under age 16 are automatically covered without extra charge. In 1971, the contributions averaged 48 florins a month for each adult or 96 florins for a family of two adults. (Under compulsory insurance the family with one working adult making the average wage in manufacturing would have paid about 82 florins a month.)

Old peoples' insurance.--People over age 65 whose income does not exceed 13,821 florins per year can join the governmental health insurance scheme on a voluntary basis. Weekly contributions as of January 1973 ranged from 6.30 florins on annual incomes below 9,996 florins up to 22.05 florins on annual incomes between 11,964 and 13,821 florins. For the upper ranges of this salary scale the contributions correspond to about 9.5 percent of income or the combined employer-employee payment for worker coverage under compulsory insurance. However, rates are lower for the pensioner on a percentage basis where incomes are smaller. The payments are family contributons; the wife and children (below age 16) are also covered.

Exceptional Medical Expenses Program.--The whole population is compulsorily insured under the Exceptional Medical Expenses Act. Contributions are payable entirely by the employer (or the self-employed) and amount to 2.6 percent of earnings up to a maximum of 24,300 florins a year. Pensioners are exempt from paying a contribution for this type of coverage.

Role of Government

Total government contributions to the cost of health care in the Netherlands are modest. The Government takes no part in the routine financing
of compulsory sickness insurance, which is basically supported by contributions and some cost sharing. There are some minor exceptions. The
Government subsidizes sickness insurance for students, disabled children,
and other groups that pay small premiums. The elderly have part of their
sickness insurance premium paid from a special fund which the Government
and the compulsory insurance system jointly support. In 1972, the Government contributed 303 million florins or about 7.5 percent of total expenditures of the Sickness Fund system for general medical care.

As of 1972 the National Insurance Scheme for Exceptional Medical Care
received a contribution from the Government of 583 million florins a
year. This contribution, stipulated by law, corresponded to nearly 30
percent of total expenditures under the program in 1972.

In 1967, the Government's share of total sickness insurance expenditures
was still only about 5 percent. It has been rising slowly each year since
and reached about 13 percent in 1972 for both schemes.

Cost Sharing

Medical care in Holland is virtually free of charge to the patient with
the following exceptions:

(a) The patient usually must pay part of the cost of dental
care if he has not undergone a regular checkup in the previous 6 months.

(b) A stay in a tuberculosis sanitarium involves payment
of 25 percent of the costs by the patient.

(c) After 6 months in a hospital or other medical institutions,
an unmarried patient must pay part of the costs involved if his
monthly income exceeds 162 florins (324 florins for a married
couple if both are hospitalized). This means that pensioners
often must also forfeit part of their old-age pension if they
are hospitalized for an extended period and there is no spouse
maintaining a separate household.

REIMBURSEMENT PROCEDURES

General Practitioners

The general practitioner is paid on a capitation basis. For the first
1,800 patients registered with the family doctor, the payment by the
sickness fund in 1971 was 42.27 florins per person registered. Above
1,800 patients, the payment dropped to 29.22 florins for each registered
patient. The size of a general practice in the Netherlands averages
about 3,000 patients, of which approximately 2,100 are members of government-sponsored insurance.

For the 30 percent of the population not covered by governmental insurance,
payment is usually made by the patient himself or by private insurance
companies. Such patients are billed on the basis of a fee for each consultation subject to government price control. The average doctor re-

ceives about 40 percent of his total receipts for patient care from his private practice.

Specialists

Specialists are paid for their services in a number of different ways, depending on the context in which treatment is rendered.

Hospital specialists (inpatient care).--Many specialists in hospitals are paid on a salary basis particularly in so-called "all-in" hospitals. (See discussion on Hospitals, p. 67.) The same is true even in the "all-out" hospitals where the lower ranking staff physicians are paid on a salary basis while the higher ranking specialists are paid directly on a fee-for-service basis and then reimburse the hospital for part of the services used of the lower ranking staff. The fee-for-service approach is used mainly for surgical specialties, and the actual level of the fees is based largely on the time assumed to be involved in each procedure. The case-payment approach is also widely used and is employed in those cases where specialists must continue, on a relatively long-term basis, to check patients on a daily basis or more frequently. In such situations the doctor is paid on a per-day basis according to the type of illness but the daily rate drops sharply after the first few days. When negotiating committees fix the ratios and the monetary values, they take into account what a typical practice will return to the physician financially and assure that the income derived is adequate. As a result, surgeons are paid according to an elaborate schedule of fees for the specific operation performed unless, of course, they are attached to hospitals which reimburse on a salary basis. If the patient receives care under an all-out situation the sickness fund pays the case-payment directly to the specialist but also pays laboratory doctors on a fee-for-service basis according to the schedule.

Hospital specialists (outpatient care).--Specialists in this category are usually the same doctors who also provide treatment to inpatients. However, there are slight variations in the reimbursement procedures. Those working in all-in hospitals are paid on a salary basis like the doctors treating inpatients. A fee-for-service approach is used mainly for technical specialists while the case-payment method is often utilized in other instances. The doctor is paid according to a schedule of fees on a monthly basis and the fee varies according to the illness and the specialty. If renewal cards become too numerous in any specialty, the rate decreases or rises more slowly for that specialty in the following year. Fee-for-service payments are at a higher rate for private patients and apply not only to uninsured patients but also to those who ask for higher than third-class accommodations.

Specialists (freelance).--Freelance specialists are paid either on a fee-for-service basis according to a schedule or on a case-payment basis, usually on a monthly scale, just as in the case of hospital specialists doing outpatient work. Freelance specialists are also entitled to fee-for-service payments at a higher rate for private patients than for others.

Although the patient must have a referral card from a general practitioner to inititate consultation with a specialist, the specialist himself can issue renewal certificates for additional visits. Subsequent treatments of the same patient, however, are reimbursed at a lower rate. The assumption behind this approach is that the specialist will try to complete his diagnosis and treatment as quickly as possible so that he will have time to accept other patients on a first-time basis and receive a greater proportion of higher rates in his overall schedule.

Hospitals

Hospitals in the Netherlands use several different approaches toward billing for physician's care and for other medical care such as the cost of nursing. Approximately 30 percent of the hospital days accounted for in the Netherlands are subject to billing practices which include costs of both physician and other medical care in the daily charges, which in such cases are called "all-in" rates. Most of the hospital days are covered by hospitals which bill only for hospital costs other than medical care, a practice which is called "all-out." In all-out hospitals, the higher ranking specialist receives direct payment for his services; he then reimburses the hospital for about 80 percent of the salary of the staff needed to assist him in the treatment.

Hospitals base their charges on a schedule negotiated with the Council for Hospital Tariffs. The Council is an official body composed of representatives of the sickness funds and insurance companies on the one hand and representatives of the national hospital council on the other. The costs which hospitals are allowed to charge are largely based on each institution's annual budget. The more modern hospitals are usually more expensive to operate and are accordingly permitted to charge higher rates.

Hospitals that bill on an all-out basis receive some income by charging rent to doctors who treat patients, both private and insured, on an out-patient basis.

The charges that hospitals are permitted to make do not allow for profit but are aimed at adequately covering all costs, including depreciation.

Pharmaceuticals

An insured person must have prescriptions filled at a pharmacy with which he is registered. There is no charge for the drug prescription that he presents to his pharmacist. Each pharmacist is paid on an average capitation fee per year. Fees are negotiated annually. The pharmacist is reimbursed for the cost of the drug plus a service charge for each item.

Approximately a third of the prescriptions in the country are dispensed by doctors themselves, usually in rural areas where pharmacists are scarce. Such dispensing doctors receive an additional capitation fee for each patient and roughly the same payment the pharmacist would receive per prescription.

Dentists

Most dental work is free of charge to the patient provided he has consulted his dentist in the previous 6 months and has a valid treatment certificate, obtainable every 6 months from his sickness fund at a cost of 5.75 florins. Children under age 4 receive all types of treatment free. Patients ordinarily must pay about 60 percent of the cost of dentures. There are also cost-sharing fees for other items.

The dentist is entitled to payment for the treatment he gives according to a tariff of fees drawn up between the dental association and the sickness fund. With regard to private patients, dentists apply tariffs which are similar to those applied by specialists.

Australia ([11], pp. 9–21)

Australia's health care system relies on voluntary insurance plans that are administered primarily by nonprofit carriers but heavily subsidized by government funds. All residents are eligible to enroll with a specific carrier for either medical or hospital insurance or both and pay premiums according to the coverage they elect. At least 90 percent of the population is covered by the system or other government arrangements for health care delivery, such as a special free medical care program for pensioners.

For the typical insured patient, medical benefits include the services of physicians, hospitals, and nursing homes but exclude normal dental care.

The physician is usually paid directly by the patient' who in turn receives partial reimbursement in the form of combined payments from his insurance and from the Federal Government through his medical benefit fund. These payments are based on schedules drawn up in each State according to the "most common fee." If the physician's charge does not exceed the schedule, the patient's net out-of-pocket payment averages less than 20 percent of the total fee and is subject to a ceiling of $5.1/ Settlement of hospital charges follows the same pattern as that for physicians, except that the patient normally receives full reimbursement for his expenses according to contracted coverage. The Federal Government pays a separate subsidy per patient directly to the hospital.

The whole cost of a means-tested cash sickness benefit program is borne by the Federal Government. The Federal Government also pays the insurance premiums of low-income groups. Hospitals and physicians providing services to the elderly under the special pensioners program receive reimbursement entirely from the Government, but at rates lower than those they receive for treating other patients. All Australian residents, whether or not insured, benefit from the subsidized pharmaceutical program under which prescriptions generally cost only $1.

The Government has announced a new program to supplant the present scheme effective July 1975. In essence, the changes aim at providing free hospitalization and more of the cost of physician care. The new system depends on general revenue to provide more of the overall financing and Federal-State cost sharing to finance the hospitals.

BACKGROUND

In the 1930's and early 1940's, expansion of the public role in the health care delivery system was impeded by constitutional limitations on Federal powers and the traditional resistance of medical practitioners to Government controls. As a result, until after World War 11, Federal involvement in health care was limited to such public health services as quarantine programs and the prevention of disease. In 1946, however, a constitutional amendment gave the Federal Government authority to legislate expenditures for social welfare and health care programs.

The first subsequent legislative effort to provide comprehensive medical care on a national basis came under the 1948 National Health Services

---

1/ 1 Australian dollar equals U.S. $1.32.

Bill. As enacted, the Bill gave the Federal Government authority to provide residents with medical services, to maintain and manage hospitals and other health facilities, and to subsidize a portion of physicians' fees. Most of these provisions were not implemented, largely because of resistance by a majority of physicians. Later, another significant program did obtain the support of the medical profession; this was the Pensioner Medical Service Plan implemented in 1951, which provides free medical services to pensioners whose income does not exceed a prescribed amount.

To surmount opposition, the Government replaced the 1948 health plan with a series of substitute programs which it introduced gradually and then consolidated under the National Health Act of 1953. This legislation remains the country's basic health program despite a number of amendments. The 1953 Act reaffirmed the voluntary insurance approach to health care protection but extended the scope and duration of government financing by establishing a program of subsidization for insurance funds and hospitals. Under this approach, the Government paid a fixed amount for each medical service according to a fee schedule, benefit funds made a minimal matching payment, and the patient paid the residual, which was intended to be at least 10 percent of the total. The program also established a list of free "lifesaving" drugs (a 50-cent charge was introduced in 1960, raised to $1 in 1971). In 1963 a government subsidy was made available for patients in approved nursing homes.

A number of important changes were made when the National Health Act was amended by the Health Benefits Plan of 1970. A new concept, the most common fee, was introduced as the basis for a revised fee schedule. Once again, however, the fee schedule was made voluntary and depended on the cooperation of the medical profession to make it workable. The new schedule provided for a fixed patient fee-for-service copayment. It was hoped that cost to the patient would be lowered as a result. Under the previous arrangement, the out-of-pocket payment by the patient was averaging about a third of the total fee. The amendments also introduced a government program--the Subsidized Health Benefit Plan--to pay the insurance premiums for certain low-income families. Additional government regulations relating to more rigid registration were instituted under the plan to limit the expenditures for operating the health benefit funds.

ORGANIZATION OF HEALTH CARE DELIVERY

The delivery of institutional health care is primarily the administrative responsibility of each State. Functional operations of community health facilities and public hospitals are generally administered by State Ministries of Health, usually through a local board of directors. At the Federal level, the Department of Health has direct administrative responsibility for health care delivery in the sparsely populated Northern Territory. This department also administers the quarantine programs and health care delivery in the small Australian Capital Territory and in veterans' institutions. Before 1973, the Department of Health also administered the subsidy programs for medical and hospital benefits. It still retains jurisdiction over the pharmaceutical benefits program.

Since 1973, the Federal program of subsidization has been the responsibility of the Department of Social Security. Under this Department, the Health Insurance and Benefits Division establishes national standards for the State public health care facilities and the benefit funds; it also negotiates with representatives of the medical profession and Department of the Treasury to set the common fee for most medical services in each State. In negotiations with the voluntary insurance benefit funds, the Government establishes standards for health insurance plans applicable to each State. A benefit fund is required to register separately for each State in which it operates; and as part of the registration requirements, each benefit fund must prove that it is financially sound and set premiums in accordance with its financial status.

Administrative problems in the delivery of health care in Australia are alleviated by the unusual concentration of the population in urban areas, where about 85 percent of the population and medical practitioners live. Over 40 percent of the total population of 12.7 million live in the Sydney and Melbourne areas alone. Remote rural areas are served by a network of medical practitioners who travel by air transport when emergencies arise.

Physicians

Australia had 16,000 medical practitioners in 1972, or about 1 for every 800 people. General practitioners make up about 44 percent of this total, specialists 27 percent, and medical service officers 29 percent. Slightly more than two-thirds of the medical practitioners practice on a freelance basis; these include almost all general practitioners and about 80 percent of the specialists. Most of the salaried physicians are medical service officers, general practitioners, and specialists employed by public hospitals, veterans' facilities, local community health centers, and health-related facilities such as public parks and recreational areas.

General Practitioners.--The percentage of physicians who are general practitioners declined from 79 percent in 1947 to 44 percent in 1965, largely because of the emphasis on specialization in medical schools and the higher earnings available to specialists. The generalist provides most of the initial health care and performs all normal duties required for general medical treatment, including surgery. However, only a small percentage of younger doctors perform major surgery. In 1965, 70 percent of all subsidized medical services were still performed by general practitioners; but this proportion had declined to 58 percent by 1973.

About 80 percent of generalists work in groups of three or four, and about 1,000 generalists practice in health centers which have been informally modeled after those in the United Kingdom, Canada, and Finland. These health centers provide the general practitioner with support from social workers, psychiatrists, and nurses. By 1975, the proportion of physicians affiliated with such health centers is expected to increase to 28 percent of all general practitioners. Growth of health centers reflects government and Australian Medical Association policies favoring medical facilities which provide social and nursing services, to relieve the physician of work that does not require his skill. The health centers also meet with the approval of many physicians because they emphasize preventive health care at lower costs, provide more effective health care in rural areas, and present a possible alternative to any compulsory national health insurance system.

Specialists.--The relative decline in general practitioners has been paralleled by an increase in specialists as the specialized needs of public hospitals have grown. Although a patient may consult a specialist without first seeing a general practitioner, in such cases he must ordinarily pay a larger share of the specialist's fee himself. Without evidence of a formal referral, the government subsidy is limited to the level paid to general practitioners rather than that set under the higher specialist fee schedule.

Hospital physicians.--Physicians practicing in large hospitals are either specialists who are full-time, salaried medical service officers employed by the hospital or private practitioners who charge a fee-for-service for treatment they give to patients. Although all patients admitted to a public hospital must be under the supervisory care of a specialist, the patient may choose to be attended by his family doctor, who is normally a general practitioner.

Hospitals

As of 1971, about 70 percent of the 1,100 approved hospital facilities in Australia and over 80 percent of the 78,000 beds were public. Public hospitals are administered and regulated by State governments through a semiautonomous local board of directors. Public hospital facilities normally include ward, semiprivate, and private accommodations. Some States have combined wards and semiprivate accommodations under a single "standard ward." The overall ratio of hospital beds to population is 6.1 beds per 1,000 people. Of these, public hospitals provide 5.1 beds per 1,000.

Nonprofit voluntary and private facilities, which make up the remaining 30 percent of hospitals, tend to be smaller than public hospitals. There are only 5 private hospitals with more than 200 beds compared to 77 public facilities of that size. Recently, many private hospitals have concentrated on treating the less seriously ill or have converted to nursing homes.

Nursing Homes

Nursing homes assume care of chronically ill and sick aged persons who do not need the intensive care provided by hospitals. Patients must be referred by a medical practitioner for admittance. About 80 percent of these patients are aged pensioners entitled under the Pensioner Medical Service. The number of public and private nursing-home beds in Australia increased from 16,500 in 1959 to over 51,000 by 1972. Fifty-four percent of the nursing homes are private, 27 percent are run by religious and charitable institutions, and 19 percent are operated by State governments.

COVERAGE

Official estimates place the percentage of population covered by health insurance at 80 percent for medical benefits and at 79 percent for hospital benefits. Excluding Queensland, the scope of medical and hospital insurance coverage is nearly uniform among the States with a range of 81 to 87 percent of the population covered. Since hospital treatment in public wards and outpatient clinics is free for all residents of Queensland, the proportion of its population which has contracted for insurance is low, only 55 percent for hospitalization and 57 percent for medical benefits. Thus, hospital insurance coverage there generally applies only to private accommodations.

If the portion of the population outside Queensland with insurance is added to those pensioners covered under a special program, far less than 10 percent of the population is left without coverage. However, these people are generally assumed to be the poor who cannot afford to meet medical care out of their savings.

Although membership in hospital and medical benefit funds is voluntary for all residents in Australia, coverage is a prerequisite for receiving a government subsidy toward payment for medical service charges. An individual can insure with only one hospital and one medical benefit fund.

Usually a single organization is registered to handle both types of insurance. A resident may enroll in any fund regardless of his history. Persons with a pre-existing, chronic, or long-term illness can obtain coverage under a government-subsidized program.

Pensioners

Persons receiving an old-age, invalidity, or widow's pension and meeting a means test are entitled to free medical treatment under the Pensioner Medical Service. Dependents of such pensioners are also covered under the program. Over 90 percent of pensioners are enrolled and with their dependents they comprise 10.3 percent of the total population. Expenditures for this program represent about 5 percent of the total national health expenditures, which include government subsidies for medical, hospital, nursing home, and pharmaceutical benefits.

Low-Income Families

The Subsidized Health Benefits Plan provides low-income families and social security beneficiaries receiving unemployment or sickness benefits with hospital and medical insurance coverage through a private benefit fund. The Government pays the full insurance premium for nonpensioner families whose income is below $60.50 a week (about two-thirds of the average industrial wage in 1973).

Partial premium payments were made on a graduated scale for families with incomes up to $69.50 a week. In late 1972, about 29,000 families or about 2.7 percent of the total population received total or partial payments under this program. An estimated 250,000 families (about 23 percent of the population) would be entitled under the program if they applied. A wide-scale campaign has been launched to inform noninsured and underinsured families of their potential eligibility.

BENEFITS

Medical

Medical benefits for insured persons include physician services, all surgical procedures, and some types of oral surgery. All services by general practitioners and specialists are covered. All Australian residents, whether or not they are insured, can obtain pharmaceuticals which are on the approved list for a small cost-sharing fee. Generally all drugs regarded as essential for medical treatment are included on the list.

There is no general provision for medical appliances, but pensioners, widows, and disabled persons usually receive assistance under special government arrangements.

There has been a notable expansion of home care services since 1969 when State programs in this regard became eligible for financial assistance from the Commonwealth on a matching basis.

Under a separate program, the Pensioner Medical Service, comprehensive medical treatment is provided without charge to qualified pensioners and their dependents by general practitioners under contract. Private specialist services are not included in the Pensioner Medical Service program but are available without charge on an inpatient basis in public hospitals.

Free medical care is also provided to certain long-term or chronically ill patients. If the insurance liability ends because of a costly or prolonged illness, the Federal Government assumes responsibility for continued payment of the contracted benefits.

Hospital

Minimum hospital insurance coverage provides for comprehensive protection in public ward accommodations. However, patients can contract for private or semiprivate accommodations by paying a higher premium. Daily rates for public wards range from $15 in New South Wales and Victoria to $20 for a standard ward in Western Australia. Services performed by staff physicians for public ward patients are provided without charge. In New South Wales and Victoria--the two most populous States--public wards are restricted to persons who meet a means test. Insured patients who do not meet this test are generally covered for semiprivate or private accommodations by their hospital insurance. In Queensland, public wards and related services are free for all residents of the State. In all States, pensioners entitled to the Pensioner Medical Service are treated in public wards without charge.

Nursing Home

All patients of an approved nursing home are entitled to a Federal subsidy of $3.50 a day for ordinary care and $6.50 a day for intensive care. Under the Pensioner Medical Service, elderly persons receive a Federal subsidy which pays the difference between a fixed copayment of $2.55 a day for both ordinary and intensive care and a set standard nursing-home fee established by the Government. The amount of the subsidy varies according to the level of fees applicable in each State. Since March 1973, a $2-a-day subsidy is also paid to persons who care for aged relatives in their own homes.

Rehabilitative treatment is provided for certain disabled persons who are receiving unemployment or sickness benefits, tuberculosis allowances, invalid benefits, or widows' pensions. The treatment may include the full cost of medical, dental, psychiatric, and hospital care, physiotherapy and occupational therapy, as well as vocational training.

Cash Payments

Cash sickness benefits are payable on a means-tested basis under the Social Services Act to gainfully employed breadwinners earning less than $37 a week (about one-third the average industrial wage in 1974). Lower earnings levels apply to single adults, workers over age 16, and families in which the wife works. Benefits in 1974, payable after a 7-day waiting period, were $31 as a maximum plus supplements for dependents and rental allowances.

Maternity

A woman who permanently resides in Australia receives a lump-sum grant of $30 upon giving birth to a child, if there are no other children under age 16 in the family. The grant rises to $32 when there are one or two other children, and to $35 when there are three or more children. The grant is increased by $10 for each additional newborn child in case of multiple birth.

Expectant or nursing mothers are entitled to free day-care services at infant welfare centers and baby clinics. A mother enrolled in a hospital insurance fund will normally be covered for private accommodations in a public hospital or a public outpatient clinic for her delivery. If she chooses a private hospital facility, she must pay for any cost of care above the normal hospital coverage for public accommodations in that State. The lump-sum maternity grant is not affected by her choice of accommodations.

PROCEDURES FOR OBTAINING CARE

To receive government-subsidized medical and hospital care for himself and family, a person must be a member of a registered benefit fund. Any adult resident can apply for membership in an insurance fund of his choice. Once enrolled, the patient can make an unlimited number of visits to a physician of his choice. No registration is required for any one medical practitioner. A patient can also visit a self-employed specialist without a formal referral from a generalist but, in this case, additional subsidies for the higher specialist rates are not paid.

Admission to a public hospital (including outpatient clinics) is usually based on a referral by a medical practitioner. Generally, patients referred to a hospital are those suffering from acute conditions or are maternity cases. Persons with less serious illnesses are referred to nursing homes.

Immigrants are considered as residents for purposes of hospitalization and are eligible for membership in a benefit fund. They are entitled to retroactive coverage for the period immediately after their arrival as long as they apply for membership within the first 2 months.

ROLE OF PRIVATE INSURANCE

Basically all health insurance in Australia is private. The nonprofit funds which operate in this field, however, must meet certain national standards and be registered with the Government. Federal regulations also control the amount of a benefit fund's financial reserves and operating expenses. The funds offer limited competition in the range of services and premium rates.

Of the 90 registered benefit funds, all provide hospitalization coverage and 81 provide medical insurance. More than two-thirds of the total membership is enrolled in five funds which provide both types of insurance. Although membership is generally nonrestrictive, 26 funds provide coverage only for persons employed in particular industries, trades, or professions. Thirty-six of the medical benefit funds and 34 hospital benefit funds provide coverage for persons eligible under the Subsidized Health Benefits Program. Eighty-five medical benefit funds and 70 hospital funds maintain government-subsidized plans for long-term and chronic illnesses.

FINANCING

Contributions

Medical or hospital insurance coverage is financed through tax deductible premiums made on a voluntary basis to one of the benefit funds. Payroll deductions for coverage with a benefit fund can be made if requested, or an individual may choose to make payments directly to a fund or pay the premium through a fund agent (often a pharmacist). Premiums are payable in advance on a monthly or quarterly basis. The combined premiums for family coverage under medical and hospital insurance are about 2 percent of the average industrial wage. For families in 1973, the insurance premiums for medical benefits ranged from a flat rate of 50 to 84 cents a week and for minimum hospitalization coverage from 70 cents to $1.05 a week. As a rule, premiums for single persons are about half the family rates. In addition to marital status, the variation in premiums is often due to the scope of coverage and the State in which the coverage applies.

The Role of Government

The latest available data show that in 1970 about 55 percent of the funding for national health expenditures (excluding public health activities, research, and education) was met by public funds: Federal (30 percent), State (24 percent), and local government (1 percent). The remaining 45 percent of health care costs were funded by patients' fees (31 percent), insurance benefits (13 percent), and charity (1 percent). Preliminary data indicate that the combined public portion rose to nearly 60 percent in 1972. The increased share of government expenditures has been due primarily to the new program and procedures initiated under the 1970 amendments.

As of 1974, the Federal Government provided 43.8 percent of the total cost of physician services, prepaid insurance benefits provided 36.7 percent, and insured patients' payments provided 19.5 percent (plus any portion which exceeds the most-common-fee schedule). By contrast, back in 1954, the first year of operation under the Health Benefits Plan, the payments were 31.4 percent by Federal subsidies, 31.7 percent by benefit funds, and 36.9 percent by patients.

Federal.--Federal subsidization payments, designed to help provide low-cost health protection on a voluntary basis, are directed toward physician services, hospital treatment, and pharmaceuticals. For physicians' services, the subsidies are made to the medical benefit fund for payment to the patient. Subsidies for hospitalization are paid to the hospital on a per capita basis of $2 a day (80 cents a day for uninsured persons and $5 a day for pensioners entitled under the Pensioner Medical Service).

Pharmaceutical benefits constitute 33 percent of the Commonwealth's health services expenditures. This is the most expensive category in the subsidization program and covers 80 to 90 percent of all prescribed drugs. Oral contraceptives are the main exclusion from a national list of approved pharmaceutical items.

State.--About 50 percent of all public hospital expenditures are funded by State revenues. (Federal subsidies comprise about 20 percent of the total costs, insurance benefits 21 percent, and patients' fees 8 percent.)

Cost Sharing

Out-of-pocket payments made by insured patients for medical treatment average slightly less than 20 percent of the fee-for-service up to $40 but never more than $5 for any charge made within the common fee guidelines. The insured patient pays for any excess amount charged by the physician over the common fee. In 1973 the proportion of fees which exceeded common fee guidelines ranged from a high of 42 percent in Victoria to a low of 30 percent in Western Australia.

There is also a nominal copayment of $1 per item for approved prescription drugs. Low-income persons eligible under the Subsidized Health Benefits Plan pay only 50 cents for each pharmaceutical item.

Normally, insured hospital patients are either covered in full for hospitalization or are entitled to free public accommodations. If the insurance does not cover special accommodations where free facilities are not available, a patient must make an out-of-pocket payment for such services.

A fixed copayment of $2.55 a day is also made by insured persons and qualified pensioners admitted to nursing homes where rates are charged in compliance with a government-determined standard fee.

REIMBURSEMENT PROCEDURES

General Practitioners

General practitioners usually receive payment for services directly from the patient. The patient in turn files a claim for reimbursement from his insurance fund. The amount of benefits awarded by the carrier is determined by a schedule based on the most common fee charge for the State where the service was rendered. All carriers within the same State pay an equal amount of reimbursement for identical medical services but there are slight variations from State to State. The payment made by the fund to the patient includes a government subsidy which is determined by a separate Commonwealth-wide schedule. If the patient is unable to pay the physician the full amount immediately, he may file a claim with the fund, which will forward a check in the physician's name to the patient for delivery.

General practitioners and other providers of medical services who are under contract with the Government to treat members of the Pensioner Medical Service receive remuneration at a somewhat lower rate than is customary for other patients. For the general practitioners, until recently, the fee was $2.50 for each consultation and $3.60 for a home visit. In July of 1974, these rates were raised to $3.75 and $5.70, respectively.

Specialists

Specialists in private practice receive fee-for-service payments based on a schedule of the most common fee for services performed in a hospital or at their office. For approximately 300 services that could be performed either by a generalist or a specialist, the official schedules prescribe a higher fee to the specialist even though the actual treatment may be identical.

Hospitals

Public hospitals are paid directly by the patient in 70 percent of the cases. The patient then files for reimbursement or requests the benefit fund to pay the hospital. The benefits paid by the fund vary with the amount of contracted insurance. Insurance payments generally meet total costs but cannot exceed actual charges made by the hospital.

Payments for medical services in outpatient clinics are made the same way as for hospital inpatients. In Queensland and Tasmania outpatient services are free. The charges for any type of accommodation are standardized for all hospitals within each State and include physician services, unless a patient is attended by a private physician. The Federal subsidy is not a part of the insurance payment, but is paid directly to the hospital per patient per day. Federal subsidies paid to nursing homes are made in a similar manner.

Pharmaceuticals

When purchasing prescription drugs the patient pays a flat rate of $1 per listed item to the pharmacist who receives payment for the remainder from the Federal Government. Reimbursement to the pharmacist includes his full costs together with markups for his services. The drug must be on the national list of approved drugs but the purchaser need not be a member of a benefit fund.

APPENDIX

A new national health scheme, designated as Medibank, has been drawn up by the current Labor Government and on August 8, 1974 received Parliment-tary approval as the Health Insurance Act of 1973. As announced by the Government, the legislation was to be implemented in July 1975. Follow-ing is a brief outline of major provisions which are subject to revision as a result of discussions which continue with factions desiring changes from the ranks of Parliament, the State Governments, and the health insurance industry.

The new program provides (1) coverage for all residents, (2) a minimum of 85 percent of the average cost for medical services to be paid by the Government (with a $5 maximum cost to the patient for any service charge of $33 or more), and (3) free comprehensive hospitalization in standard ward accommodations, financed by Federal-State cost sharing.

The principal administrative change in the new proposal is the replace-ment of the voluntary benefit funds by a single organization under the direct supervision of the Department of Social Security. Private health insurers may offer supplemental coverage of health services for such items as more expensive accommodations in public and private hospitals than provided under standard ward care and such services as physiotherapy and home-nursing care on a fee-for-service basis.

Under the provision for sharing hospital costs between State and Federal governments, Federal subsidies are to be determined by negotiations with the States, and Federal payments are made on a per diem basis for up to 50 percent of the total cost. Currently, all States finance more than half the hospital costs.

Hospital patients are entitled to free standard ward accommodations under the care of a staff physician. If they prefer, they may engage private specialists on a fee-for-service basis. Those who wish to have private accommodations may either pay the extra charge directly or insure with a private benefit fund.

Medical care continues on a fee-for-service basis by a private physician of the patient's choice, but greater adherence to a new schedule of fees is expected than prevails under the old system.

NOTES AND REFERENCES

1. During the February 1976 hearings before the House Committee on Interstate and Foreign Commerce, Subcommittee on Health and the Environment, Walter McNerney, president of the Blue Cross Association, presented an assessment of the problems of national health insurance in England, Canada, West Germany, Scan-dinavia, Australia, and New Zealand. Note [23], p. 1435 ff. for McNerney's statement.

2. Details on each Canadian province's hospital insurance plan appears in Appendix I of [34], p. 322 ff.

3. Peter Fisher, a California businessman, has taken an active interest in the national health insurance debate and offers some ideas and insights on British Columbia's health care experience. Refer to [41], p. 332–355.

4. Bette Stephenson, a physician from Toronto, Canada, appeared before the Subcommittee on Health of the House Ways and Means Committee on September 12, 1975 and offered her views on Canada's comprehensive medical care insurance program. Refer to [35], p. 380 ff.

5. Additional information on medical care in Sweden is provided in the transcript of the September 1975 hearings of the Subcommittee on Health of the House Ways and Means Committee. Refer to [35], p. 392 ff.

6. Annette Lynch, a physician and the director of the School Health Program, Pennsylvania Department of Health, appeared before the Subcommittee on Health of the House Ways and Means Committee in November 1975. Dr. Lynch, a U.S. citizen, who practiced medicine in England from 1965 to 1967, stressed the importance of government involvement in insuring citizens' rights to health services. Refer to [36], Part 2, pp. 694–703.

7. Reginald Murley, a physician from London, England, testified before the Subcommittee on Health of the House Ways and Means Committee on September 12, 1975. He presented additional perspectives on the British National Health Service, particularly as it relates to hospital and specialist care. Refer to [35], p. 368 ff.

PART II
U. S. HEALTH CARE INDUSTRY: KEY FACTS ON COMPONENTS AND COSTS

Introduction

Part II of this volume addresses health care as an "industry." In order to understand what is occurring in American health care, where it is going, and what factors are at play, it is useful to set aside idealized conceptions of the family physician, the cheerful nurse, and the sparkling clean hospital and examine the manner in which the industry is structured. Health care in the United States has many features in common with a service industry. There is a recurring demand, an organized marketplace, a pricing system, "industry association," and continuing controversy about the desirability of self-regulation over government control. The health industry performs a significant role in the nation's economy and, as public sector involvement increases, occupies a sizeable portion of the federal budget. The ethical codes, the commitments to humanitarian service, the mystique of the "healer" are not at issue in the national health insurance deliberations. What is at issue is the manner in which health delivery systems are organized, how service is delivered, how it is paid for, how the practitioner is compensated, and how the government's role is to be defined. As such, the national health insurance debate concerns health care as an industry.

The chapters in Part II are intended to serve as reference resources on the contemporary American health care industry. In following the course of the sometimes emotional debate on the need for and the structure of a national health insurance system, it is useful to examine a variety of factual data—to lend perspective and to verify facts. To that end, the House Committee on Ways and Means published a *National Health Insurance Resource Book* in 1974 and an updated edition in 1976 ([33] and [34]). It provides a documentation of the arguments and counterarguments of the debate on national health insurance. A substantial portion of the 1976 edition is incorporated in the chapters that follow. The material is presented in the same order as in the original text: health care institutions, health manpower, private health insurance, and the patients. Chapters on public programs (Medicare/Medicaid), as well as on health care costs, have been added by the editors. Some tables and charts have been deleted to conserve space; what has been deleted and where items can be located appear in Notes and References at the end of Chapters 4 and 5.

OVERVIEW OF THE INDUSTRY ([34], pp. 1–13)

The material that follows presents in chart and brief narrative form the major characteristics of the American health industry. It should be especially useful for the reader who wishes to gain a quick overview of this complex industry. . . .

Chart 1a. Health is the third largest industry in the United States, employing 4.7 million people

The health care industry encompasses a wide variety of institutions, organizations, and personnel that provide the full gamut of medical, therapeutic, and related services to the 200-plus million persons in the United States. More specifically, these services include prevention, detection, treatment, rehabilitation, research, training, and capital investment in medical facilities. They are financed through a mixture of private and Federal, State, and local government funds.

The health care field in 1960 was the third largest U.S. industry, employing 2.5 million persons. By 1974, the number employed in that field rose to an estimated 4.7 million persons an increase of 88 percent or over 2 million persons above the 1960 level.

Since the turn of the century, the supply of health manpower has increased about twelvefold. The most noticeable trend has been the development of new health occupations resulting from increased demand for health services, improved medical technology, and other advances. There has been a sharp decline in the ratio of physicians to all health personnel because of relatively small numerical increases in physicians so far in this century. Steadily increasing numbers of registered nurses and other medical-related personnel have largely accounted for the overall growth of the health labor force to its present size.

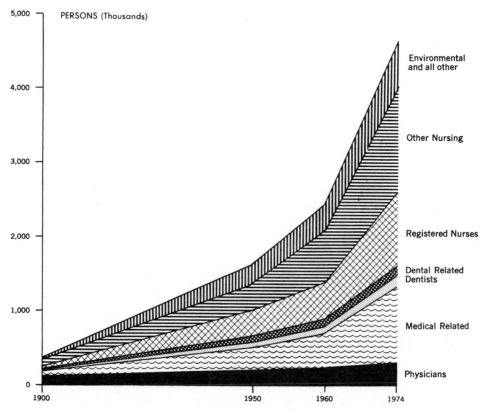

Source: Pennell, Maryland Y., and Hoover, David B., *Health Manpower Source Book*, Sec. 21, Public Health Service Publication No. 263, U.S. Department of Health, Education, and Welfare, 1970.

Health Resources Statistics, 1975. Public Health Service, U.S. Department of Health, Education, and Welfare.

Chart 1b. Half of all health care personnel provide nursing-related services

The more than 2.3 million nurses, aides, and orderlies made up 50 percent of the Nation's health manpower in 1974—by far its largest component. Physicians and dentists (including dental assistants) comprised about 14 percent of the total. The remaining 36 percent were employed in over 30 other skilled and unskilled health-related occupations. Altogether, about three-fifths of the health personnel were employed by hospitals.

The health care industry figures used here, though broad in scope, exclude millions of workers in occupations associated directly or indirectly with the health care field, such as the manufacture of drugs. The following list includes the 14 major health occupations, the number of persons employed in each in 1974, and the proportion of total health manpower each represents:

Occupation	Number	Percent of total
1. Nursing and related services..........	2,319,000	50
2. Medicine and osteopathy..............	362,700	8
3. Secretarial and office services........	275,000– 300,000	6
4. Dentistry and allied services...........	279.800	6
5. Clinical laboratory.....................	172,500	4
6. Pharmacy.............................	132,900	3
7. Radiologic technology.................	100,000	2
8. Dietetic and nutritional service........	72,200	2
9. Medical records.......................	60,000	1
10. Administration of health services.....	48,200	1
11. Medical social work..................	38,600	1
12. Optometry, opticianry, and ocular services............................	37,100 37,300	1
13. Psychology..........................	35,000	1
14. Veterinary medicine..................	33,500	1

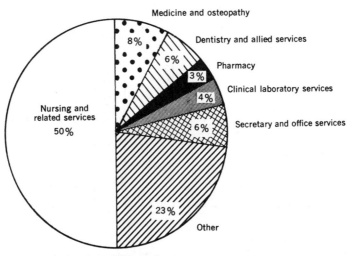

Total: 4.7 million workers

Chart 1c. Health spending today—$118.5 billion—is 10 times the spending of 25 years

The past few years have witnessed sharp increases in the amounts spent for medical care. In fiscal 1975, this Nation spent $118.5 billion for health and medical care—4.6 times the amount spent in 1960 and nearly 10 times the amount spent in 1950. Growth in medical care spending has outdistanced that of the economy in general. In fiscal year 1950, medical care expenditures totaled $12.0 billion and represented 4.6 percent of the gross national product (the total market value of the Nation's annual output of goods and services). By fiscal 1960 their share of the gross national product (GNP) had reached 5.2 percent. The acceleration in health spending in 1975 coupled with a slowed growth in the GNP resulted in a significant increase its share of the GNP—from 7.7 in 1974 to 8.3 percent in 1975.

Part of the increasing share of GNP attributable to health is due to the higher prices for medical care compared with other items. There has also been an increased demand for health services resulting from population growth generally, rising per capita incomes, and growth of private health insurance and prepayment plans. Additional contributing factors include a rising proportion of elderly in the population, higher educational levels, a shift from acute illnesses to more expensive long-term illnesses, introduction of new medical techniques and procedures to treat conditions that formerly could not be treated at all, and finally, the growing awareness of the benefits of medical care.

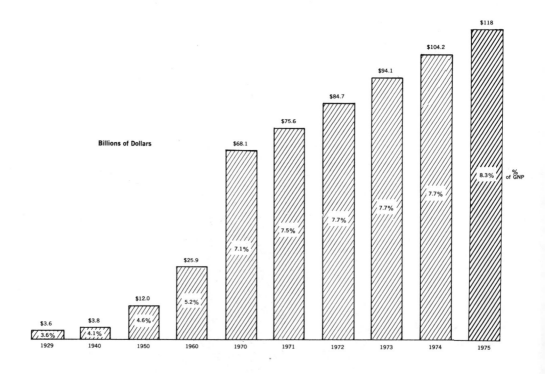

Source: Mueller, Marjorie Smith and Robert M. Gibson. "National Health Expenditures, Fiscal Year 1975." *Social Security Bulletin,* February 1976, U.S. Department of Health, Education, and Welfare.

Chart 1d. In the past two decades, each person's average health bill has grown from $78 to $547

In fiscal 1975, the average health bill for each American was $547. In 1960, the average health bill was about a fourth that amount—$142—and in 1950, it was less than one-seventh the 1975 amount. This growth, from $78 in 1950 to $547 in 1975, represents about a 600-percent increase over the 25-year period.

Included in the total personal health bill are payments for health care services under government programs, private health insurance payments, voluntary health giving, and direct payments for health care by individuals.

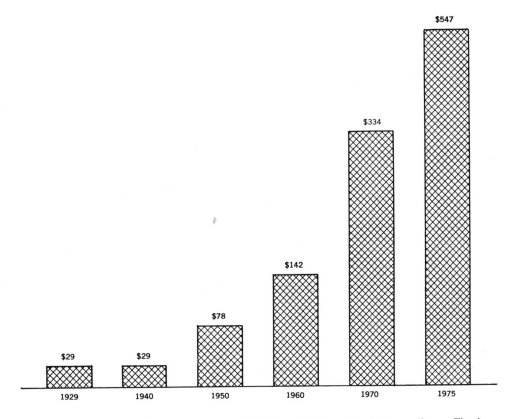

Source: Mueller, Marjorie Smith and Robert M. Gibson. "National Health Expenditures, Fiscal Year 1975." *Social Security Bulletin,* February 1976, U.S. Department of Health, Education, and Welfare.

Chart 1e. Higher prices caused over half the 10-year growth in personal health care expenditures

During the period 1965–1975, personal health care expenditures (those for the direct benefit of the individual, e.g., hospital care, physicians' services) rose by $70 billion. The spiraling increases in such expenditures during that period resulted from three major factors:

• Fifty-three percent, or $36.9 billion, can be attributed to price increases.

• Another 9 percent, or $6.1 billion, results from population growth.

• The remaining 38 percent, or $26.7 billion, is due to increased use of services and the introduction of new medical techniques.

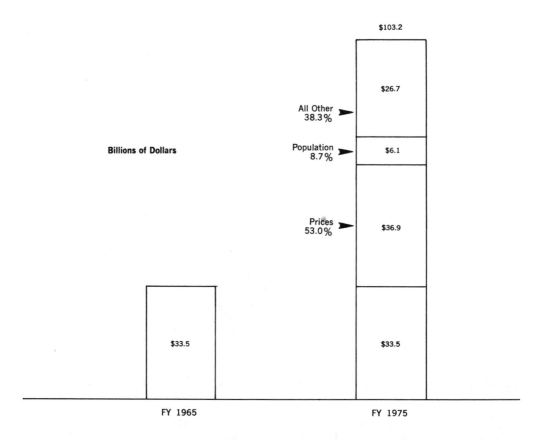

Source: Mueller, Marjorie Smith and Robert M. Gibson. "National Health Expenditures, Fiscal Year 1975." *Social Security Bulletin*, February 1976, U.S. Department of Health, Education, and Welfare.

Chart 1f. Medical care prices have accelerated rapidly since the economic Stabilization Act expired

Recent inflationary trends in the economy in general, and for medical care in particular, are a major concern today. The following table compares annual rates of change for selected components of the Consumer Price Index during 3 periods: (a) the 2 years preceding the Economic Stabilization Program (FY 1969–71), (b) the ESP period (August 1971 through April 1974), and (c) the cumulative post-ESP period (April 1974–February 1976). Mandatory controls were in effect for the health industry throughout the ESP period, but were not continuously in effect for the rest of the economy.

A slowdown in medicare care prices was recorded under the ESP compared to the FY 1969–71 period. During the post-ESP period, medical prices accelerated rapidly, rising faster than the overall CPI.

Item	Annual rate of change during—		
	Prefreeze period fiscal years 1969–71	Economic stabilization program, August 1971– April 1974	Post–ESP period, April 1974– February 1976
CPI, all items..........................	5.6	6.4	8.5
Less medical care...................	5.5	6.5	8.3
CPI, all services......................	7.4	5.1	10.0
Less medical care...................	7.4	5.2	9.5
Medical care, total....................	6.7	4.3	11.9
Hospital service charges [1]..........	NA	[2] 4.6	15.5
Physicians' fees.....................	7.4	4.0	12.8
Dentists' fees.......................	6.4	4.2	9.3
Drugs and prescriptions..............	2.0	.7	7.7

1. January 1972=100.

2. Annualized rate of change based on change from January 1972 rather than November 1971.

Source: Consumer Price Index, Bureau of Labor Statistics.

Chapter 4
Health Care Institutions

The institutional setting in which health services are provided is a complex mixture of public, private, long- and short-term facilities whose financial arrangements, operating costs, and charges for use are confusing and highly variable. Particularly noticeable is regional variation in costs and quality of patient care. There is a growing awareness that much patient care, especially for older people, can be provided outside the confines of hospitals. The costs of operating hospitals continue to rise and to consume a significant portion of the nation's health budget. One element in the national health insurance debate is the need to put some order into the institutional structure used to provide patient care. The issue of how a national health insurance system would handle the proliferation of private and public care facilities can better be understood by examining how these institutions are currently operating. Chapter 4 offers basic data on types of hospitals, their operating costs, use, and charges. It also includes a section on nursing homes, both public and private, operating under Medicare. Finally, there is material on home health care services, a subject which is receiving increasing attention as the costs and efficiency of hospital services are questioned more and more.

HOSPITALS ([34], pp. 87–99)

A. KEY FACTS ABOUT HOSPITALS (1974)

- There were 7,174 hospitals with 1,512,684 beds.
- Of these, 5,875 were short-term community hospitals, 589 were psychiatric or tuberculosis, 387 were Federal, 221 were other long-term or special hospitals, and 102 were hospital units of other institutions.
- Admissions to community hospitals totaled 32,865,867, or about 1 admission for each 6 residents of the United States (up 16 percent since 1969).
- Community hospitals employed 2.28 million full-time equivalent personnel.
- Community hospital employees per 100 adjusted patient census was 290 (up from 226 in 1960).
- Average salary of employees in community hospitals was $7,787 (up 44.8 percent over the $5,379 average for 1969).
- Expense per adjusted patient day in community hospitals reached $113.55 (up 76.7 percent over the $64.26 figure for 1969).
- 775 community hospitals with 69,600 beds (out of 925,996 beds in all community hospitals) were organized for profit.

The 7,174 domestic hospitals constituted one of the Nation's largest industries in 1974, with a total capacity of 1.51 million beds and overall assets approximating $51.7 billion. As a rough measure of this industry's output, hospitals handled some 35.5 million admissions and more than 250 million outpatient visits at a total expense of more than $41.4 billion. They employed 2.92 million full-time equivalent employees with a total payroll of more than $23.8 billion.

The hospital industry represents a mix of both the public and private sectors. Thirty-eight percent of all hospitals are publicly owned; they supply 50.2 percent of the bed capacity in the Nation's domestic hospitals. State hospitals are the largest in terms of average bed size, followed in ranking by Federal, voluntary nonprofit, local government, and for-profit hospitals.

N1

Public hospitals receive their operating revenue from different sources. Federal hospitals and, to a lesser extent, State and local government hospitals, operate largely on funds budgeted by Government agencies. Private hospitals generally receive their revenue directly from the patient or from third-party payers (including private insurance carriers) and public programs such as medicare and medicaid

Hospitals can be classified into four groups representing a special type of care: psychiatric, tuberculosis, short-term general and other special, and long-term general and other special. Short-term general and other special hospitals, which contain 61.1 percent of all beds (67.7 percent of the beds in the case of non-Federal institutions), provide highly intensive care for a wide range of acute disorders. Consequently, they require relatively large numbers of employees and an array of highly sophisticated equipment. Long-term care hospitals, on the other hand, are bigger units, providing much less intensive care for chronic conditions which cannot be corrected quickly. As a result, they use fewer employees and usually do not have as much of the sophisticated diagnostic and therapeutic services and equipment likely to be found in short-term hospitals.

COMMUNITY HOSPITALS

In order to consider that segment of the hospital industry which provides general medical care to the public as a whole, it is necessary to focus on the short-term general and other special hospitals, and to exclude psychiatric hospitals, tuberculosis hospitals, long-term general and other special hospitals, and Federal hospitals. In addition, a small component of the short-term general and other special hospitals grouping—hospital units of other institutions (such as prison and college infirmaries)—must be excluded. The remaining hospitals referred to as community hospitals, are defined as all non-Federal short-term general and other special hospitals, excluding hospital units of institutions, whose facilities and services are available to the public. Community hospitals represent about 82 percent of all hospitals, handle over 92 percent of all admissions and 75 percent of all outpatient visits, employ 78 percent of the industry's total labor force and account for 79 percent of the total cost of hospital care.

Bed capacity of community hospitals totaled about 926,000 in 1974—45 percent above the 1960 level. In terms of beds per 1,000 population, community hospital beds during the same period have increased from 3.59 to 4.41. Admissions and patient days per 1,000 population in 1974 were 156.7 and 1,217, respectively. Outpatient visits were 901.0 per thousand population.

NONCOMMUNITY HOSPITALS

On the other hand, noncommunity hospital beds have decreased markedly—from 1,019,000 in 1960 to 586,688 in 1974. This decrease is a reflection of changes in medical technology. Significant discoveries were made which shortened the treatment of many conditions previously requiring long-term care—particularly in psychiatric and tuberculosis hospitals.

HOSPITAL PRICE AND COST INFLATION

Hospital price and cost inflation can be measured in various ways. Rates of change in hospital *prices* can be measured by the Bureau of Labor Standards semiprivate room charge index. This index, a component of the Consumer Price Index, refers to the average daily charge for room and board and routine nursing care in semiprivate accommodations. All special services, such as drugs, tests, blood, and use of the operating room intensive and care units, are excluded. Since the semiprivate room charge index reflects only charges for a portion of hospital services, it will accurately reflect changes in overall prices only if the weighted average of all other prices increases at the same rate. As yet no comprehensive hospital price index exists for which historical data are available.

Comprehensive measures of hospital *cost* inflation, on the other hand, are available; the American Hospital Association's average expenses per patient day and per admission. The average expense per patient day is an estimate of the total cost of a day of hospital care. It is an aggregate figure derived by dividing total expenses (including outpatient and other expenses not attributable to inpatient care) by the number of adult and pediatric (not newborn) patient days. Expenses incurred by inpatients but not billed by the hospital, such as physicians' fees for treatment, are also excluded.

The problem of dividing by an output figure (i.e., inpatient days) which excludes outpatient care can be alleviated by a variant of this measure called average expense per adjusted patient day. For this measure total expenses are divided by adjusted patient days in which patient days are added together with the patient-day equivalents of outpatient visits. For example, if the value of an inpatient day is four times the value of an outpatient visit, then four visits will be equal (in terms of effort required) to 1 inpatient day. Adjusted patient days would then equal patient days plus one-fourth of the number of outpatient visits.

Another measure of cost inflation is the average expense per admission derived by dividing total expense by the number of admissions. This represents the cost per case. A similar correction for the exclusion of outpatient visits is required to get the average expense per adjusted admission—if the value of one admission is 30 times the value of one outpatient visit, then adjusted admissions are derived by adding admissions and one-thirteith of the number of outpatient visits.

The following table shows the values of the various measures since 1950 and the rates of increase for several periods. The difference between the rate of change in expense per day and expense per admission results from changes in length of stay. Because length of stay has been falling since 1969, the rate of change of expense per admission is somewhat lower than the rate for expense per day.

Year	Hospital semiprivate room charges	Total expense per patient day	Expense per adjusted patient day	Expense per admission	Expense per adjusted admission
			Index or amount		
1950	30. 3	$15. 62	(¹)	$127. 23	(¹)
1955	42. 3	23. 12	(¹)	179. 79	(¹)
1960	57. 3	32. 23	(¹)	244. 54	(¹)
1961	61. 1	34. 98	(¹)	267. 38	(¹)
1962	65. 3	36. 83	(¹)	281. 44	(¹)
1963	68. 6	38. 91	$35. 11	298. 10	$269. 15
1964	71. 9	41. 58	37. 58	321. 28	285. 97
1965	75. 9	44. 48	40. 56	345. 65	310. 79
1966	83. 5	48. 15	43. 66	382. 05	337. 54
1967	100. 0	54. 08	49. 46	447. 64	409. 04
1968	113. 6	61. 38	55. 80	519. 21	471. 30
1969	128. 8	70. 03	64. 26	587. 99	539. 25
1970	145. 4	81. 01	73. 73	668. 67	610. 10
1971	163. 1	92. 31	83. 43	743. 15	675. 01
1972	173. 9	105. 21	94. 87	830. 13	749. 47
1973	182. 1	114. 49	102. 44	895. 83	799. 03
1974	201. 5	127. 81	113. 55	992. 42	885. 69
			Average annual percentage increase		
1950–74	8. 2	9. 2	(¹)	8. 9	(¹)
1950–60	6. 6	7. 5	(¹)	6. 8	(¹)
1960–65	5. 8	6. 7	² 7. 5	7. 2	² 7. 5
1965–70	13. 9	12. 7	12. 7	14. 1	14. 4
1965–67	14. 8	10. 3	10. 4	13. 8	14. 7
1967–69	13. 5	13. 8	14. 0	14. 6	14. 8
1969–71	12. 5	14. 8	13. 9	12. 4	11. 9
1971–73	5. 7	11. 4	10. 8	9. 8	8. 8
1973–74	10. 7	11. 6	13. 2	10. 8	10. 8

¹ Not available.
² Average annual percentage increase from 1963 to 1965.

Source: Charges data are from the "*Consumer Price Index*," Bureau of Labor Statistics. Expenses data are from *Hospital Statistics 1974*, American Hospital Association, 1975.

In addition, costs are higher where occupancy rates are low. If a hospital is used more intensively, then fixed costs can be distributed over more patients, thus reducing the average cost. Finally, costs may be higher where hospitals are larger. Bigger hospitals tend to provide more specialized services and facilities than smaller hospitals. They also tend to treat more difficult cases, thus raising the average cost.

ECONOMIC STABILIZATION PROGRAM

In August 1971, the President ordered a 90-day freeze on prices, wages, salaries, and rents and the creation of a Cost of Living Council to administer the freeze and to advise on further economic stabilization policies. Three months later, phase II of the economic stabilization Program (ESP) began. The ESP goal was to reduce the rate of inflation to about one-half of the pre-freeze rate. Because of the special problems of inflation in the health care industry, a special advisory panel was established to assist the Council in the health area. In December 1971, specific mandatory phase II rules were promulgated for the health care industry, rules which were continued for the industry when the phase III, or voluntary control program, began in January

1973. Modified controls (phase IV) were imposed on the health industry in June 1973. Price controls over the health industry (and certain other segments of the economy) ended in April 1974.

The prices of all goods and services in the economy, including medical care prices, have jumped appreciably since the lifting of price controls in April 1974. On an annualized basis, all consumer prices, less medical care, rose by 9.3 percent for the postcontrol period ending in September 1975. Medical care prices rose at an annualized rate of 12.6 percent.

Annualized rate of increase in medical care prices (pre-ESP, total ESP, and post-ESP periods)

Index	Pre-ESP, fiscal years 1966–71	Total ESP, (August 1971– April 1974	Post-ESP, April 1974– September 1975
CPI (less medical care)_____	4. 3	6. 5	9. 3
Medical care_____	6. 5	4. 3	12. 6
Hospital charges (semiprivate room)_	14. 6	5. 7	18. 2
Physician fees_____	6. 9	4. 0	12. 8
Dentist fees_____	5. 7	4. 2	10. 3

HOSPITAL USE

Like most other characteristics of the hospital industry, average length of stay varies by area, from a low 6.5 days in Mountain and Pacific census divisions to 9.3 days in the Middle Atlantic census division. Patterns of medical practice differ from State to State regarding admission and discharge policies and utilization review practices. The incidence of different kinds of disease differs from one area to another as does the age distribution of the population. In sparsely populated areas where people must travel far for medical care, minor cases may be hospitalized to avoid repeat visits, resulting in shorter stays. Economic characteristics such as income levels and insurance coverage also have important impact. Hospitals with high occupancy rates may postpone elective admissions, yielding a case-mix composition with relatively longer stays.

Length of stay also differs according to the type of hospital. Average length of stay was 7.7 days in State and local short-term hospitals, 7.9 days in non-profit hospitals and 6.7 days in for-profit hospitals during 1974.

FINANCIAL POSITION OF HOSPITALS

Annual net incomes of nonprofit and for-profit hospitals increased from $29 million in 1950 to $547 million in 1971 (the latest year for which comparable data are available). On a patient-day basis, net income for all nongovernmental community hospitals during that period rose from 29 cents to nearly $3. These trends are a result of several factors. Private hospitals have been used more intensively since 1965 than during earlier periods. Both the extent and level of insurance coverage have increased, resulting in more stable incomes for hospitals and lower losses due to bad debts and charity. Medicare and medicaid apparently contributed significantly to these improvements.

Considerable differences have continually existed between for-profit hospitals, which earned $6.43 per patient day in 1971, and nonprofit hospitals, which earned $2.63 (as shown below). This differential results mainly from the fact that nonprofit hospitals are larger, provide more specialized and expensive services and facilities, and probably serve a slightly different patient population than for-profit hospitals.

Year	Net income per patient day		
	Total	Nonprofit	For profit
	Amount		
1950	$0. 29	$0. 17	$1. 36
1955	. 50	. 37	2. 25
1960	1. 01	. 93	2. 11
1965	1. 70	1. 55	3. 57
1967	2. 31	2. 12	4. 74
1969	2. 55	2. 34	5. 27
1970	2. 55	2. 24	6. 36
1971	2. 91	2. 63	6. 43
	Average annual percentage increase		
Period:			
1950–71	11. 6	13. 9	7. 7
1950–60	13. 3	18. 5	4. 5
1960–65	11. 0	10. 8	11. 1
1965–70	8. 4	7. 6	12. 2
1965–67	16. 6	17. 0	15. 2
1967–69	5. 1	5. 1	5. 4
1969–71	6. 8	6. 0	10. 5

Source: Hospitals, guide issues, Aug. 1, various years.

Plant assets of community hospitals totaled nearly $27.9 billion in 1974 an 1,000-percent increase over the value in 1950. When converted to plant assets per average daily census or assets required per unit of output, the rate of growth is reduced to 532 percent. This percentage increase, however, overstates the growth of real assets required per unit of output.

SOURCE OF FINANCING

While hospital care expenditures have been rapidly increasing, the source of financing for this care has been changing. Medicare and medicaid have been taking over more and more of the private burden of paying for hospital care.

In fiscal 1966, the year before medicare, the private sector contributed 64 percent of the $14.2 billion bill for hospital care. The Federal Government had a 13-percent share, and State-local governments paid the remaining 23 percent.

Preliminary estimates for fiscal year 1975 indicate that the private sector's share declined to 44.9 percent. Some of the State and local share had been shifted to the Federal Government so that by fiscal 1975, 39.2 percent came from Federal funds and 15.8 percent from State and local spending.

The proportion of hospital care expenditures paid by private insurance declined from 42 percent in fiscal 1966 to 35.4 percent in fiscal 1974.

B. SELECTED CHARACTERISTICS OF FOR-PROFIT HOSPITALS—1974 *

1. NUMBER AND BEDS

The number of for-profit hospitals which serve as community hospitals has decreased over the period 1946 to 1974 from 1,076 to 775. Over that same

---

*Compiled from American Hospital Association data.

period, however, the number of beds in such hospitals increased from 39,000 to 70,000. The number of voluntary nonprofit community hospitals increased from 2,584 to 3,355, with an increase in beds from 301,000 to 649,000 over the same period.

The range in size of for-profit hospitals serving as community hospitals compared with all community hospitals was as follows:

Bed size	For-profit community hospitals		All community hospitals	
	Number	Percent	Number	Percent
Total	775	100. 0	5, 775	100. 0
Under 25 beds	64	8. 3	308	5. 2
25 to 49 beds	216	27. 9	1, 176	20. 0
50 to 99 beds	239	30. 1	1, 504	25. 6
100 to 199 beds	194	25. 0	1, 346	22. 9
200 to 299 beds	47	6. 1	658	11. 2
300 and over	15	1. 9	883	15. 0

Of the 775 non-profit community hospitals in 1974, 490 (64.0 percent) were accredited by the Joint Commission on Hospital Accreditation.

2. GEOGRAPHIC LOCATIONS

For-profit hospitals are concentrated in three areas in the United States, New York City and western Long Island, the Los Angeles area, and the rural South (see table 1 for regional breakdown).

A further analysis shows that of the 7,173 beds in short-term for-profit hospitals in New York State, the majority were in institutions in New York City and Nassau County and Suffolk County. Most of the remainder were located in other areas near New York City.

Of the 17,881 beds in California for-profit community hospitals, most were in institutions in Los Angeles and neighboring Orange County.

3. FINANCES AND PERSONNEL

The ratio of personnel to patients in for-profit hospitals has increased from 137 per 100 patients in 1946 to 283 per 100 patients in 1974. The comparable figures for nonprofit community hospitals ranged from 156 per 100 patients in 1946 to 323 in 1974. Thus, while there has been an increase in this ratio over the period 1946 to 1974 for-profit hospitals still lag behind the nonprofits.

Total expenses of community for-profit hospitals have increased over the period 1946 to 1974 from $94 million to $2,046 million. Assets have also increased—the total assets for community for-profit hospitals in 1947 were $129,119,000; by 1974 the figure had reached $2,288 million.

The sources of capital formation for for-profit hospitals are roughly similar to other businesses: the savings of the entrepreneur, sale of stock, and borrowing. For-profit hospitals are not eligible for Government funds which can be used for capital development (other than as part of the reimbursement under medicare or medicaid). Nor do for-profit hospitals obtain funds through public subscription—hospital fund raising drives.

4. CHARACTERISTICS OF PATIENT LOAD

The occupancy rates for for-profit hospitals are lower than for nonprofit hospitals. Occupancy rates for for-profit hospitals ranged from 64.1 percent in 1946 to 67.5 percent in 1974; for nonprofits the rate ranged from 76.7 percent in 1946 to 77.9 percent in 1974. Not only are there more empty beds in for-profit hospitals but patients stay there for a shorter time. The average length of stay for for-profit community hospitals has shown very little change from 1946 to the present—6.6 days in 1946 and 6.7 days in 1974. The average stay in nonprofit hospitals in 1946 was 8.8 days and 7.9 days in 1974.

The shorter stays in for-profit hospitals may be accounted for by several factors. In some areas of the country, particularly in rural areas, a doctor may set up a "hospital" in connection with his office as a place where he can keep a closer watch on the patient, and provide nursing services more economically than if he had to visit the patient at home. However, in all likelihood he will still send his more seriously ill patients to a larger hospital in a nearby city or town. In such cases, the patients in the for-profit hospitals would not, as a group, be as seriously ill as those in the nonprofit hospitals. There is also evidence that some for-profit hospitals restrict their admissions to patients with certain types of disorders or who need rather simple forms of surgery, tending to avoid the complicated cases with their longer stays.

In addition, it is likely that physicians in some areas who cannot, or do not wish to, gain staff privileges in a local nonprofit hospital have organized their own hospitals in which to care for their patients.

5. SERVICES OFFERED

On almost every count for-profit short-term hospitals offer a narrower range of services than do nonprofit hospitals. For example 61.0 percent of the nonprofit hospitals have pathology laboratories but only 43.2 percent of the for-profit hospitals have them. Similarly, 86.7 percent of the nonprofit hospitals have a postoperative recovery room; 80.5 percent of the for-profit hospitals have such facilities. More than 74 percent of the nonprofit hospitals have intensive care units while only about 57 percent of the for-profit hospitals have them.

6. PER PATIENT DAY COSTS

The per patient day cost for for-profit hospitals increased from $10.13 in 1946 to $119.81 in 1974. Such costs in nonprofit hospitals increased from $10.04 in 1946 to $127.24 in 1974. A number of factors which were discussed earlier contribute to the difference in per diem costs between the nonprofit and for-profit hospitals: The smaller range of services offered in the for-profit hospitals; the tendency in some for-profit hospitals to avoid admitting the more seriously ill patient; and the lower ratio of personnel to patients. These factors offset the effect on costs of the lower occupancy rates and shorter stays for the for-profit hospitals—which by themselves would produce higher per patient day costs. It should also be noted that the for-profit hospitals have been subject to the same economic conditions—population changes, increase in utilization, inflation, and increases in payroll and nonpayroll expenses which have produced the large increases in hospital costs in the past 20 years.

7. CONTROL

Table 2 details the for-profit hospitals in each State and indicates other pertinent data about the for-profit hospitals in each State.

TABLE 1.—*Regional distribution of for-profit hospitals and beds, 1974*

Region	Hospitals	Beds
Total	775	69, 600
New England	7	829
Middle Atlantic	73	9, 769
South Atlantic	121	12, 494
East North Central	14	832
East South Central	75	7, 240
West North Central	22	1, 400
West South Central	230	15, 863
Mountain	23	2, 157
Pacific	210	19, 016

TABLE 2.—*For profit short-term general and other special hospitals, 1974*

State	Hos-pitals	Beds	Occu-pancy rate (percent)	Average stay (days)	Total assets (thou-sands)
Alabama	21	2, 603	70. 0	7. 4	$99, 140
Alaska	0	0	NA	NA	NA
Arizona	9	706	64. 7	6. 7	23, 031
Arkansas	13	700	70. 1	5. 9	14, 230
California	192	17, 881	60. 9	6. 1	673, 858
Colorado	1	240	72. 1	5. 8	9, 747
Connecticut	0	0	NA	NA	NA
Delaware	0	0	NA	NA	NA
District of Columbia	1	284	66. 5	7. 8	10, 834
Florida	43	5, 150	67. 4	7. 4	222, 630
Georgia	21	1, 900	63. 6	5. 7	61, 416
Hawaii	1	30	60. 0	5. 8	610
Idaho	2	191	64. 9	5. 5	4, 229
Illinois	10	699	60. 1	6. 6	17, 665
Indiana	1	76	73. 7	5. 4	2, 216
Iowa	3	87	64. 4	6. 7	591
Kansas	4	115	66. 1	5. 9	3, 306
Kentucky	9	1, 433	73. 6	6. 7	34, 490
Louisiana	36	2, 267	65. 1	6. 0	67, 487
Maine	0	0	NA	NA	NA
Maryland	1	33	81. 8	5. 8	489
Massachusetts	7	829	63. 4	8. 7	21, 209
Michigan	1	18	55. 6	4. 6	560
Minnesota	0	0	NA	NA	NA
Mississippi	4	243	64. 2	5. 3	5, 654
Missouri	13	1, 127	69. 0	6. 8	27, 844
Montana	3	65	60. 0	5. 5	1, 534
Nebraska	1	43	32. 6	7. 1	289
Nevada	6	852	65. 6	5. 8	52, 455
New Hampshire	0	0	NA	NA	NA
New Jersey	5	857	75. 0	8. 2	41, 425
New Mexico	0	0	NA	NA	NA
New York	51	7, 173	80. 0	8. 1	205, 229
North Carolina	8	578	67. 8	5. 6	20, 749
North Dakota	1	28	39. 3	5. 4	569
Ohio	1	6	33. 3	1. 0	122
Oklahoma	13	698	66. 3	6. 9	16, 145
Oregon	10	666	55. 9	5. 5	22, 081
Pennsylvania	17	1, 739	75. 3	8. 0	50, 277
Rhode Island	0	0	NA	NA	NA
South Carolina	5	224	82. 1	5. 8	6, 244
South Dakota	0	0	NA	NA	NA
Tennessee	41	2, 961	69. 6	7. 0	90, 542
Texas	168	12, 198	66. 2	6. 4	335, 537

Table 2.—*For profit short-term general and other special hospitals, 1974*—Con.

State	Hos-pitals	Beds	Occu-pancy rate (percent)	Average stay (days)	Total assets (thou-sands)
Utah	2	103	68. 9	4. 6	3, 268
Vermont	0	0	NA	NA	NA
Virginia	24	2, 769	79. 1	7. 5	81, 329
Washington	7	439	56. 3	4. 5	12, 836
West Virginia	18	1, 556	71. 7	6. 5	45, 049
Wisconsin	1	33	75. 8	9. 5	671
Wyoming	0	0	NA	NA	NA
Total	775	69, 600	67. 5	6. 7	2, 287, 587

NA = Not available.

C. Expense Per Adjusted Patient Day in Community Hospitals, by State

Nationally, average expense per adjusted patient day in 1974 ranged from a low $62 in nonmetropolitan Minnesota to $190 in metropolitan Alaska. The cost level of hospital care is related to various factors. Costs tend to be higher where personal income is above average because hospitals must compete for labor in the local market. Costs also tend to be higher where length of stay is relatively short. Many of the expensive diagnostic tests used in present-day medical care are administered in the first day or two of a hospital stay; after that, ancillary costs decline. Thus the longer the patient stays, the lower his average cost per day.

In addition, costs are higher where occupancy rates are low. If a hospital is used more intensively, fixed costs can be distributed over more patients, thus reducing the average cost. Also, costs may be higher in large hospitals, since they usually provide more specialized services and facilities and tend to treat more difficult cases. Finally, costs will be higher where the number of outpatient visits is relatively low.

These factors help to explain differences in expense per adjusted patient day between and within States. Wide cost differences often exist between a State's metropolitan and nonmetropolitan areas. Urban hospitals incur higher costs because they are generally larger and provide more specialized services. In addition, they must pay higher wages to compete in the local labor market.

Differences in cost levels between regions of the country are similarly explained to some extent by these factors. Cost per day ranged from a low of $87.37 in the East South Central States to a high of $148.50 in the Pacific States with New England close behind at $138.14.

Table 3.—*Expense per adjusted patient-day by region and State, including metropolitan and nonmetropolitan areas, 1974*

	Total	Metropolitan	Nonmetro-politan
United States	$113. 55	$123. 61	$81. 86
New England	138. 14	149. 44	103. 77
Connecticut	141. 56	141. 98	138. 12
Maine	96. 54	117. 16	87. 56
Massachusetts	152. 33	157. 67	115. 42
New Hampshire	95. 12	98. 12	94. 43
Rhode Island	133. 61	135. 72	113. 52
Vermont	99. 49	N/A	99. 49

Footnote at end of table.

TABLE 3.—*Expense per adjusted patient-day by region and State, including metropolitan and nonmetropolitan areas, 1974*—Continued

	Total	Metropolitan	Nonmetro-politan
Middle Atlantic_____	123. 69	128. 78	85. 56
New Jersey_____	109. 58	110. 16	98. 89
New York_____	140. 02	146. 85	84. 63
Pennsylvania_____	104. 36	108. 36	83. 24
South Atlantic_____	103. 49	114. 02	80. 00
Delaware_____	113. 15	120. 72	94. 25
District of Columbia_____	146. 38	146. 38	(1)
Florida_____	113. 13	115. 42	97. 12
Georgia_____	102. 57	115. 50	81. 38
Maryland_____	130. 44	136. 01	100. 65
North Carolina_____	88. 18	102. 82	73. 06
South Carolina_____	86. 45	101. 92	71. 78
Virginia_____	91. 81	99. 10	77. 72
West Virginia_____	82. 08	85. 52	78. 98
East North Central_____	111. 99	119. 96	81. 77
Illinois_____	121. 01	128. 36	84. 55
Indiana_____	95. 43	100. 35	83. 07
Michigan_____	122. 46	129. 82	86. 90
Ohio_____	107. 36	112. 15	82. 68
Wisconsin_____	98. 20	115. 18	73. 03
East South Central_____	87. 37	97. 12	73. 43
Alabama_____	91. 58	99. 14	75. 34
Kentucky_____	85. 26	93. 31	74. 93
Mississippi_____	80. 36	102. 18	74. 34
Tennessee_____	88. 88	96. 99	69. 00
West North Central_____	92. 20	106. 24	75. 57
Iowa_____	85. 52	92. 85	79. 69
Kansas_____	87. 02	107. 45	71. 18
Minnesota_____	98. 06	114. 16	62. 33
Missouri_____	97. 96	104. 01	79. 36
Nebraska_____	90. 93	110. 96	64. 96
North Dakota_____	78. 40	104. 92	72. 31
South Dakota_____	77. 86	89. 02	74. 64
West South Central_____	96. 83	103. 39	78. 18
Arkansas_____	82. 27	91. 79	72. 26
Louisiana_____	103. 03	108. 69	85. 59
Oklahoma_____	98. 22	109. 90	81. 55
Texas_____	97. 17	102. 21	76. 48
Mountain_____	111. 16	127. 03	84. 12
Arizona_____	129. 45	137. 25	94. 56
Colorado_____	111. 74	121. 38	83. 82
Idaho_____	88. 40	121. 88	80. 90
Montana_____	82. 56	86. 13	81. 03
Nevada_____	142. 41	150. 47	97. 59
New Mexico_____	103. 23	131. 83	83. 13
Utah_____	110. 27	116. 23	78. 69
Wyoming_____	84. 55	(1)	84. 55
Pacific_____	148. 50	153. 49	109. 57
Alaska_____	163. 04	189. 90	130. 78
California_____	155. 78	158. 15	120. 05
Hawaii_____	118. 19	124. 69	101. 66
Oregon_____	116. 82	127. 46	96. 61
Washington_____	125. 83	133. 17	104. 34

[1] Not available.
Source: Hospital Statistics, 1974.

D. PSYCHIATRIC HOSPITALS

Between 1946 and 1962, the number of non-Federal psychiatric hospital beds in the United States steadily increased. Since then, however, the number of beds has declined from a peak of 717,000 to 383,000 in 1974. These beds are located in some 543 institutions throughout the country. Occupancy rates between 1946 and 1974 in psychiatric hospitals have declined—from 91.0 percent to 80.0 percent. New drugs, new therapy techniques, and alternatives to institutional care have contributed to this decline.

Though the demand for inpatient services in psychiatric hospitals has declined markedly over the last decade or so, the demand for outpatient services has dramatically increased. In 1962, outpatient visits to psychiatric hospitals amounted to 892,000; in 1974, the number of visits had reached 5,240,000.

TABLE 4.—*Non-Federal psychiatric hospitals, 1974*

Hospital classification	Number	Beds	Occupancy (percent)	Outpatient visits
Total	543	383, 480	80. 0	5, 240, 106
Short-term, total	137	11, 569	69. 3	1, 399, 618
Nongovernmental, nonprofit	44	2, 967	75. 8	434, 384
For profit	66	4, 169	65. 2	137, 669
Local governmental	4	667	55. 8	154, 309
State governmental	23	3, 766	71. 1	673, 256
Long-term total	406	371, 911	80. 3	3, 840, 488
Nongovernmental, nonprofit	44	5, 574	81. 3	335, 810
For profit	49	4, 615	76. 9	154, 637
Local governmental	16	9, 648	77. 5	178, 039
State governmental	297	352, 074	80. 4	3, 172, 002

Source: Hospital Statistics, 1974.

TABLE 5.—*Teaching hospitals*

Hospital classification	Number	Medical and dental interns and residents	Other trainees	Total trainees
Total	662	47, 250	14, 476	61, 726
Nongovernmental	519	28, 396	9, 959	38, 355
Under 300 beds	136	2, 459	516	2, 975
300 to 399 beds	117	4, 167	1, 671	5, 838
400 to 499 beds	96	4, 707	1, 338	6, 045
500 and over	170	17, 063	6, 434	23, 497
State and local government	143	18, 854	4, 517	23, 371
Under 300 beds	39	1, 506	351	1, 857
300 to 399 beds	24	1, 817	520	2, 337
400 to 499 beds	23	2, 516	276	2, 792
500 and over	57	13, 015	3, 370	16, 385

Source: Hospital Statistics, 1974.

E. TEACHING HOSPITALS

In 1974 there were 662 community hospitals in the United States which had affiliations with medical schools and which conducted approved education programs for medical and dental interns and residents. The majority of these hospitals—78.4 percent—were nongovernmental facilities employing 672,138 personnel, including more than 10,700 physicians and dentists. The remaining institutions were owned or controlled by State and local governments, utilizing 239,473 persons of whom more than 8,770 were physicians and dentists. Nearly a quarter of all community teaching hospitals are located in the Middle Atlantic States of New Jersey, New York, and Pennsylvania.

During 1974, the teaching hospitals were training 47,250 medical and dental interns and residents and 14,746 other persons in trainee status.

NURSING HOMES ([34], pp. 100–106, 109)

INTRODUCTION

The term "nursing home" is a generic term covering a wide variety of institutions providing health care of various levels to people with health problems ranging from minimal to very serious [1] Nursing homes typically provide one or more of the following groupings of services:

(1) *Nursing care and related medical services.*—Nursing care provided or supervised by registered nurses and licensed practical nurses. Related medical services include physical therapy, occupational or speech therapy, dental services, medical social services, dietary consultation, laboratory and radiation services, and pharmaceutical services.

(2) *Personal care.*—Personal services and unskilled nursing services including assistance in walking, getting in and out of bed, bathing, dressing, eating, and preparation of special diets.

(3) *Residential care.*—Room, board, social programs, laundry facilities, and help with shopping, obtaining transportation and letter writing.

The medicare and medicaid programs cover a variety of nursing homes for several classes of people and patients as follows:

Medicare.—Medicare permits participation in that program of those nursing homes which meet the definition of "skilled nursing facility" under title XVIII of the Social Security Act. In addition, medicare has a set of requirements relating to prior hospitalization and levels of required care which result in coverage only for relatively short periods of time following hospitalization.

Medicaid.—All medicaid programs must cover services in "skilled nursing facilities" with the same definitions as that used in medicare. States can add to the minimum Federal requirements. States also set the eligibility conditions

---

[1] The generic term "nursing home" is defined by the American College of Nursing Home Administrators as follows:

"A 'nursing home or its equivalent' is a facility, institution, or an identifiable unit of an acute hospital or other care service facility or institution licensed for:

"1. Care for persons who because of physical or mental conditions, or both, require or desire living accommodations and care which as a practical matter, can best be made available to them through institutional facilities, other than acute care units of hospitals, providing a protective and/or supervised environment, and

"2. Care of persons and patients who require a combination of health care services and personal care services which are in addition to the avove and may include, but are not necessarily restricted to, one or more of the following care services:

"(a) Therapeutic diets,

"(b) Regular observation of the patient's physical and mental condition,

"(c) Personal assistance including bathing, dressing, grooming, ambulation, transportation, housekeeping (such as bedmaking, dusting, etc.) of living quarters,

"(d) A program of social and recreational activities,

"(e) Assistance with self-administered medications,

"(f) Emergency-medical care including bedside nursing during temporary periods of illness,

"(g) Professional nursing supervision,

"(h) Skilled nursing care,

"(i) Medical care and services by a licensed practitioner,

"(j) Other special medical and social care services for diagnostic and treatment purposes of rehabilitative, restorative, or maintenance nature, designed to restore and/or maintain the person in the most normal physical and social condition attainable."

and any limits on the number of days covered. The average length of stay in a skilled nursing facility under medicaid is generally much longer than the average length of stay in a skilled nursing facility under medicare. Medicaid skilled nursing facility benefits are, of course, available only to the poor or medically needy.

State medicaid programs can also cover care in "intermediate care facilities" (ICF's) a term defined in title XIX of the Social Security Act.

The care provided in intermediate care facilities is for patients who may need a broad spectrum of services ranging from those just above room and board up to the skilled nursing facility level.

The classification of various institutions described or named as nursing homes can become very confusing. For example, many institutions with the word "hospital" in their names are not hospitals but may be skilled nursing facilities or intermediate care facilities. Similarly, many nursing homes do not use the words in their names. A few general guidelines to the term are:

(1) Nursing homes are usually licensed as such by the States. (The States are required, under the medicaid program, to license administrators of nursing homes, but not administrators of hospitals. This difference may facilitate distinguishing between the two general types of institutions.)

(2) Skilled nursing facilities and intermediate care facilities are terms in specific government programs and include the concept of participation in those programs. A single institution may meet one or all of the definitions.

(3) In addition to facilities which provide some amount of nursing care there are facilities which provide only personal care or which provide residential services where nursing care in infrequent and intermittent or absent altogether.

(4) Categories of homes may vary markedly from one geographical area to another.

NUMBERS OF NURSING CARE FACILITIES

There has been a substantial growth over the last 10 years in the numbers of nursing care facilities and beds in the United States. In 1963, for example it was estimated that nursing care facilities numbered 8,128 with a capacity of 319,224 beds. By 1973–74, facilities had increased by 93.2 percent to 15,700, while capacity grew by 268 percent to 1,174,800 beds.

TABLE 6.—*Nursing care facilities, 1963–74*

Year or period	Facilities	Beds
	Number	
1963	8, 128	319, 224
1967	10, 636	584, 052
1969	11, 484	704, 217
1971	12, 871	917, 707
1973–74	15, 700	1, 174, 800
	Percentage increase	
1963–1973–1974	93. 2	268. 0
1963–67	30. 9	83. 0
1967–69	8. 0	20. 6
1969–71	12. 1	30. 3
1971–73–74	22. 0	28. 0

Source: "Health Resources Statistics," Department of Health, Education, and Welfare, National Center for Health Statistics, selected years; and, "Selected Operating and Financial Characteristics of Nursing Homes, United States: 1973–74 National Nursing Home Survey." U.S. Department of Health, Education, and Welfare, Public Health Service; Vital and Health Statistics series 13–No. 22.

TABLE 7.—*Selected operating characteristics of nursing homes, 1973–1974*

Operating characteristics	All facilities
Number of homes	15, 700
Number of beds	1, 174, 800
Average bed size	75
Average total FTE employees per 100 beds	63. 9
Nursing FTE employees per 100 beds	38. 7
RN FTE employees per 100 beds	4. 4
LPN FTE employees per 100 beds	5. 7
Nurses' aide FTE employees per 100 beds	28. 6
Administrative, medical, and therapeutic FTE employees per 100 beds	4. 6
All other FTE employees per 100 beds	20. 6
Number of residents	1, 075, 800
Number of resident days of care (1972)	368, 906, 000
Average occupancy rate (1972)	88. 2

Source: "Selected Operating and Financial Characteristics of Nursing Homes, United States: data from the 1973–74 National Nursing Home Survey," U.S. Department of Health, Education, and Welfare, Public Health Service, Vital and Health Statistics Series 13–Number 22.

In 1973–74, the average total monthly charge in nursing homes equalled $479. The average total cost per resident day was $15.63. Labor costs accounted for about three-fifths of a facility's average total costs, or $9.17 per resident day.

TABLE 8.—*Selected financial characteristics of U.S. nursing homes*

1973–1974 resident charges:	
Average total monthly charge per resident	$479
Percent of homes by average total monthly charge per resident:	
Less than $299	17. 8
$300 to $399	28. 1
$400 to $499	25. 3
$500 to $599	14. 9
$600 or more	13. 9
1972 facility costs:	
Average total costs per resident day	$15. 63
Labor costs per resident day	9. 17
Fringe benefit cost per resident day	0. 67
Wage costs per resident day	8. 50
Nursing staff costs per resident day	5. 36
Other staff costs per resident day	3. 14
Fixed costs per resident day	2. 37
Operating costs per resident day	3. 41
Food and drug costs per resident day	1. 60
All other costs per resident day	1. 81
Miscellaneous costs per resident day	0. 68
Percent of homes by average total costs per resident day:	
Less than $10	23. 0
$10 to $14.99	36. 3
$15 to $19.99	22. 9
$20 or more	17. 8
Percent of homes by average labor costs per resident day:	
Less than $4	8. 5
$4 to $7.99	41. 8
$8 to $11.99	32. 0
$12 or more	17. 7
Percent of homes by average fixed costs per resident day:	
Less than $1	19. 6
$1 to $1.99	32. 4
$2 to $2.99	22. 4
$3 or more	25. 6
Percent of homes by average operating costs per resident day:	
Less than $2	20. 0
$2 to $2.99	39. 7
$3 to $3.99	18. 8
$4 or more	21. 5
Percent of homes by average miscellaneous costs per resident day:	
Less than $0.50	55. 5
$0.50 to $0.99	26. 8
$1 to $1.99	12. 7
$2 or more	5. 0

NOTE: Figures may not add to totals due to rounding.

SOURCE: "Selected Operating and Financial Characteristics of Nursing Homes, United States: 1973–74 National Nursing Home Survey." U.S. Department of Health, Education, and Welfare, Public Health Service, Vital and Health Statistics Series 13–Number 22.

A substantial majority of nursing homes are proprietary. In 1973–74, about 75 percent of all homes were operated on a for-profit basis. Proprietary homes had the greatest proportion, almost 71 percent, of all nursing home beds and served about 70 percent of all nursing home residents during that period.

TABLE 9.—*Selected operating characteristics of nursing homes by ownership classification, 1973–74*

Operating characteristics	Proprietary	Nonprofit
Number of homes	11, 900	3, 900
Number of beds	830, 700	344, 300
Average bed size	70	88
Average total FTE employees per 100 beds	57. 4	83. 5
Nursing FTE employees per 100 beds	36. 7	44. 1
Administrative, medical, and therapeutic FTE employees per 100 beds	4. 9	3. 8
All other FTE employees per 100 beds	15. 6	35. 5
Number of residents	756, 200	319, 700
Number of resident days of care (1972)	260, 449, 600	108, 456, 400
Average occupancy rate (1972)	88. 8	86. 5

Note: Figures may not add due to rounding.

Source: "Selected Operating and Financial Characteristics of Nursing Homes, United States: 1973–74 National Nursing Home Survey." U.S. Department of Health, Education, and Welfare, Public Health Service Vital and Health Statistics Series 13, No. 22.

In 1972, nonprofit nursing homes incurred greater costs than proprietary homes. Average total costs per resident day were about 20 percent more for non-profit homes, reflecting substantially higher costs for labor and nursing staff.

Resident charges were lower in nonprofit homes. In 1973–74, nonprofit nursing homes had an average monthly resident charge of $456 or 7.2 percent less than proprietary homes.

TABLE 10.—*Selected financial characteristics of nursing homes by ownership classification*

	Proprietary	Nonprofit
1973–74 resident charges:		
Average total monthly charge per resident_____	$489	$456
Percent of homes by average total monthly charge per resident:		
Less than $299_____	16. 2	22. 4
$300 to $399_____	27. 4	30. 2
$400 to $499_____	26. 1	22. 9
$500 to $599_____	16. 5	10. 0
$600 or more_____	13. 8	14. 4
1972 facility costs:		
Average total costs per resident day_____	$14. 86	$17. 71
Labor costs per resident day_____	8. 53	10. 90
Nursing staff costs per resident day_____	5. 10	6. 06
Operating, fixed, and miscellaneous costs per resident day_____	6. 33	6. 81
Percent of homes by average total cost per resident day:		
Less than $10_____	24. 7	17. 6
$10 to $14.99_____	36. 9	34. 4
$15 to $19.99_____	24. 3	18. 5
$20 or more_____	14. 1	29. 5
Percent of homes by average labor costs per resident day:		
Less than $4_____	9. 5	5. 6
$4 to $7.99_____	43. 4	36. 7
$8 to $11.99_____	34. 1	25. 4
$12 or more_____	13. 0	32. 3
Percent of homes by average fixed costs per resident day:		
Less than $1_____	13. 2	39. 5
$1 to $1.99_____	33. 4	29. 6
$2 to $2.99_____	24. 6	15. 5
$3 or more_____	28. 8	15. 4
Percent of homes by average operating costs per resident day:		
Less than $2_____	21. 1	16. 8
$2 to $2.99_____	43. 6	27. 7
$3 to $3.99_____	18. 7	19. 3
$4 or more_____	16. 7	36. 2
Percent of homes by average miscellaneous costs per resident day:		
Less than $0.50_____	53. 8	60. 9
$0.50 to $0.99_____	29. 4	18. 9
$1 to $1.99_____	12. 4	13. 4
$2 or more_____	4. 5	6. 8

Note: Figures may not add to totals due to rounding.

Source: "Selected Operating and Financial Characteristics of Nursing Homes, United States: 1973–74 National Nursing Home Survey." U.S. Department of Health, Education, and Welfare, Public Health Service. Vital and Health Statistics Series 13, No. 22.

Included in the total numbers of nursing homes are skilled nursing facilities which are homes certified to provide skilled nursing care and related services under the medicare or medicaid programs, and in some cases, both programs. In July 1975, there were 3,932 skilled nursing facilities approved for medicare beneficiaries. These participating institutions accounted for 287,479 beds, or 13.3 beds per 1,000 medicare enrollees. The availability of medicare skilled nursing beds, however, is uneven through the country, ranging from 2.6 beds per 1,000 enrollees in the West South Central States to 33.1 beds per 1,000 enrollees in the Pacific States.

TABLE 11.—*Medicare participating skilled nursing facilities, as of July 1975*

Division and State	Facilities	Beds [1]	Beds per 1,000 enrollees [2]
All areas	3, 932	287, 479	13. 3
United States	3, 926	287, 087	13. 4
New England	304	21, 206	15. 8
Maine	17	687	5. 4
New Hampshire	20	1, 006	11. 4
Vermont	21	820	15. 6
Massachusetts	95	5, 880	9. 0
Rhode Island	21	1, 133	10. 3
Connecticut	130	11, 680	37. 9
Middle Atlantic	654	67, 508	16. 6
New York	357	45, 690	22. 9
New Jersey	125	9, 249	12. 6
Pennsylvania	172	12, 569	9. 4
East North Central	664	42, 362	10. 6
Ohio	183	14, 229	13. 7
Indiana	108	5, 189	10. 0
Illinois	173	7, 919	7. 0
Michigan	144	11, 906	14. 8
Wisconsin	56	3, 119	6. 2
West North Central	227	10, 813	5. 4
Minnesota	83	4, 301	10. 0
Iowa	32	915	2. 5
Missouri	55	2, 855	4. 9
North Dakota	3	46	. 6
South Dakota	10	326	3. 9
Nebraska	15	806	4. 2
Kansas	29	1, 564	5. 6
South Atlantic	500	32, 770	10. 1
Delaware	11	632	12. 9
Maryland	67	5, 490	17. 3
District of Columbia	5	641	9. 8
Virginia	36	1, 498	3. 8
West Virginia	28	1, 718	8. 3
North Carolina	89	6, 086	13. 2
South Carolina	71	4, 738	12. 0
Georgia	47	2, 787	7. 0
Florida	146	9, 185	8. 1
East South Central	230	12, 799	9. 3
Kentucky	84	5, 289	14. 8
Tennessee	38	1, 383	3. 3
Alabama	89	5, 372	15. 1
Mississippi	19	755	3. 1
West South Central	76	5, 158	2. 6
Arkansas	10	557	2. 2
Louisiana	11	1, 127	3. 4
Oklahoma	7	434	1. 4
Texas	48	3, 040	2. 8
Mountain	177	8, 741	11. 0
Montana	26	870	11. 9
Idaho	28	1, 588	20. 8
Wyoming	2	128	3. 9
Colorado	62	3, 772	18. 7
New Mexico	7	323	3. 8
Arizona	19	1, 000	5. 1
Utah	14	431	5. 0
Nevada	19	629	15. 9
Pacific	1, 094	85, 730	33. 1
Washington	90	3, 106	8. 9
Oregon	51	2, 150	8. 7
California	933	78, 895	40. 8
Alaska	4	166	21. 5
Hawaii	16	1, 413	27. 1

Footnotes at end of table.

TABLE 11.—*Medicare participating skilled nursing facilities, as of July 1975*—Continued

Division and State	Facilities	Beds [1]	Beds per 1,000 enrollees [2]
Outlying areas	6	392	1. 9
Guam	1	33	21. 8
Puerto Rico	5	359	1. 8
Virgin Islands			
American Samoa			

[1] Includes skilled nursing beds only.

[2] Based on number of enrollees in hospital insurance program as of Jan. 1, 1974, reflected in SSA records as of Oct. 1, 1973.

Source: Social Security Administration, Office of Research and Statistics, Health Insurance Studies Division.

In November 1975, some 7,100 skilled nursing facilities with about 537,000 certified beds were providing services under State-administered medical assistance (medicaid) programs. During that period, about 8,600 intermediate care facilities with more than 493,000 certified beds were also providing care to medicaid recipients.[1] California, by far, had the greatest number of skilled nursing facilities and certified skilled nursing beds (25.2 percent and 21.7 percent, respectively); while, Texas had the largest number of intermediate care facilities and certified intermediate care beds (9.2 percent and 12.7 percent, respectively).

---

[1] It should be cautioned that a certain percentage of beds certified as intermediate care facility at the same time, may be certified as skilled nursing facility beds due to current State medicaid policies known as the "swing bed" concept. Under these policies, a State may define a certified bed as an intermediate care or skilled nursing care bed based on the medical diagnosis of the patient currently occupying that bed.

EXPENDITURES FOR NURSING HOME CARE

During fiscal year 1975, nursing home care expenditures in the United States reached $9.0 billion or 7.6 percent of total expenditures for health services and supplies. Nearly 58 percent of all nursing home care is financed from public funds, particularly the medicaid program. The Federal Government provides 57.3 percent of all public moneys used to purchase nursing home care.

TABLE 13.—*Expenditures for nursing home care, fiscal year 1975*

Total	$9, 000, 300, 000
Private sources, total	3, 799, 000, 000
Consumers	3, 767, 000, 000
Other	32, 000, 000
Public sources, total	5, 201, 300, 000
Public assistance payments, total	4, 782, 400, 000
Federal	2, 562, 900, 000
State and local	2, 219, 500, 000
Medicare	257, 000, 000
Veterans' Administration	161, 900, 000

Source: "National Health Expenditures." Social Security Bulletin; February 1976.

TABLE 14.—*Expenditures for nursing home care, fiscal years 1950–75*

[In millions]

	Total expenditures	Source of funds		Public expenditures as percent of total expenditures
		Private	Public	
1950	$178	$167	$11	6. 2
1960	480	353	127	26. 5
1965	1, 271	822	449	35. 3
1966	1, 407	(1)	(1)	(1)
1967	1, 751	844	907	51. 8
1968	2, 360	894	1, 466	62. 1
1969	3, 057	1, 354	1, 703	55. 7
1970	3, 818	2, 145	1, 673	43. 8
1971	4, 890	2, 919	1, 971	40. 3
1972	5, 860	3, 395	2, 465	42. 1
1973	6, 650	3, 477	3, 173	47. 7
1974	7, 450	3, 574	3, 876	52. 0
1975	9, 000	3, 799	5, 201	57. 8

[1] Not available.

Source: "National Health Expenditures." Social Security Bulletin; February 1975 and February 1976.

HOME HEALTH CARE ([34], pp. 110–111)

The term "home health care" is generally used to describe therapeutic and preventive health services provided to patients in their place of residence because of acute or chronic illness or disability. The Department of Health, Education, and Welfare describes the varying levels of home health care in this way:

> Home health services are provided singly or in combinations of varying intensity that are defined as "levels" of care as follows: (1) concentrated or intensive services for those individuals who otherwise would need to be hospitalized but who can benefit from multiple professional, diagnostic, therapeutic, and supportive services under professional supervision and coordination on an intermittent basis; (2) intermediate services—a less concentrated array of home health services for individuals who need convalescent care from acute illness or have a temporary disability related to chronic illness; and (3) basic services—a simple combination of health supervision and maintenance designed to maintain individuals who have long-term care needs in their own homes, thus preventing or postponing the need of institutionalization.[1]

Both medicare and medicaid pay for home health services. Medicare provides up to 200 home health visits to a beneficiary who has been certified by a physician as requiring part-time skilled nursing care or physical or speech therapy. A maximum of 100 home health visits is authorized under the Hospital Insurance Program (part A) as a posthospital benefit during the 12 months following hospitalization; and a maximum of 100 visits is provided under the Supplementary Medical Insurance Program (part B) without prior hospitalization during any calendar year. Medicare pays the full cost of a home health visit under part A and the full cost under part B after the patient has satisfied a $60 yearly deductible for all part B services.

Home health services are defined by the medicare statute as part-time or intermittent nursing care provided by or under the supervision of a registered professional nurse; physical, occupational, or speech therapy; medical social services, medical supplies and equipment; and, to the extent permitted by regulation, home health aide services.

Coverage of home health services is a mandatory requirement under the medicaid program for all medicaid recipients who are eligible to receive skilled nursing facility services. Unlike medicare, medicaid places no restrictions on the number of visits provided to a recipient if he is eligible to receive them. However, as with all services provided under medicaid, a State may place limits on the amount and scope of any service offered under its medical assistance program.

The medicaid statute does not define the term "home health services." However, regulations permit the inclusion of any of the following services in a State's home health care plan when provided on the recommendation of a licensed physician to a patient in his place of residence:

> (1) Intermittent or part-time nursing services furnished by a home health agency;
> (2) Intermittent or part-time nursing services furnished by a registered nurse or licensed practical nurse under the direction of the patient's physician, when no home health agency is available;

---

[1] Department of Health, Education, and Welfare. Public Health Service. "Health Resources Statistics, 1974".

(3) Medical supplies, equipment, and appliances authorized by the physician;

(4) Services of a home health aide, assigned to give personal care services to a patient in accordance with the physician's plan of treatment, and supervised by the home health agency.

HOME HEALTH AGENCIES

Medicare statute defines a home health agency as a public or private organization which is primarily engaged in providing skilled nursing and other therapeutic services. Proprietary organizations are permitted to participate in the program if they are licensed by State law. Currently, fourteen States license home health agencies. In addition to the statutory language, medicare regulations specify that the agency must provide part-time or intermittent skilled nursing services and at least one other therapeutic service, on a visiting basis, in the patient's place of residence. A public or nonprofit private agency must provide one service directly through its own employees, but is permitted to contract for the provision of additional services. Proprietary agencies must provide all services directly.

Although the medicaid statute does not define a home health agency, medicaid regulations define it as a public or private organization which is qualified to participate as a home health agency under medicare, or is determined currently to meet the requirements for medicare participation.

In fiscal year 1975, medicare expenditures for home health care totaled $183 million ($132 million under Part A and $51 million under Part B). In fiscal year 1974 (latest available data), medicaid expenditures for home health care equaled $31 million. In both years, home health care accounted for less than 1 percent of total expenditures under each program.

NOTES AND REFERENCES

1. An HEW document, prepared by the Cambridge Research Institute in October 1975, provides additional information on proprietary, speciality, and teaching hospitals; hospital utilization, personnel, and affiliated doctors; and governance of hospitals. See [5], p. 295 ff.

2. The following table, deleted by the editors because of space limitations, appears in the original document ([34], pp. 107–108) as "Table 12: Survey of skilled nursing homes and intermediate care facilities, as of November 1975."

3. The following tables, deleted by the editors because of space limitations, appear in the original document ([34], pp. 112–113) as "Table 15: Medicare participating home health agencies, by region and state, December 1975," and "Table 16: Medicaid participating home health agencies, by state, November 1975."

Chapter 5
Health Manpower

In this chapter, statistical information on the supply and education of health manpower is set forth in narrative and tables drawn from the *National Health Insurance Resource Book* ([34]). The manner in which almost five million health personnel work and are compensated will be affected by national health insurance. The establishment of any national health insurance program will require its creators and administrators to think in national terms in setting up a nationwide health manpower program. Under the present manpower development and allocation system, medical and paramedical personnel have tended to locate in areas of greater professional and financial opportunity, namely the more populous, more affluent communities. A wide variation exists between regions and types of cities as to the availability of health manpower. The medical education field, effectively controlled by existing professional interests, has not been increasing the supply of trained personnel available to the nation at the rate many feel is needed, and policymakers will inevitably have to come to terms with that aspect of health manpower. The statistical profile of health professionals and paraprofessionals which follows provides a resource for understanding the dimensions of the problems to be faced in developing a national health manpower policy.

INTRODUCTION

The health industry employes about 4.7 million professional and non-professional workers. There are, of course, . . . many different kinds of workers in the health care field. This chapter deals with almost all of the health professions whose members deal directly with patients in providing health care services.

The educational data for physicians is more comprehensive than that for other professions, first because the field is complex, and second because the supply and distribution of physicians is a key element in developing health policy.

N1

PHYSICIAN MANPOWER ([34], pp. 115–132, 140–172, 181, 186)

A. NUMBERS, SPECIALTIES, AND GEOGRAPHIC DISTRIBUTION OF DOCTORS OF MEDICINE

There were 330,266 professionally active physicians [1] in the United States and its possessions as of December 31, 1974. In addition, 21,614 physicians were

---

[1] Unless otherwise noted all data presented in this section on physician manpower are provided by the American Medical Association's Center for Health Services Research and Development in "Distribution of Physicians in the United States, 1972," vol. 1.
Information on doctors of osteopathy (D.O.) is presented later in this chapter. . . .

considered inactive; the activity status of 20,343 was uncertain; and 7,525 could not be located.

Of the active physicians in the United States, the vast majority (91.2 percent) were engaged in patient care activities. The remaining were involved in medical teaching, administration, research, or other activities.

Of the total number of physicians engaged in patient care activities, 52,932 (17.5 percent) were in general practice; 80,526 (26.7 percent) were in medical specialties; and 89,821 (29.8 percent) were in surgical specialties. Table 1 presents this data in more detail.

TABLE 1.—*Federal and non-Federal physicians by activity and specialty group, Dec. 31, 1974*

Activity: Specialty group	Total [1] (100 percent)
Total physicians	330, 266
Total patient care	301, 238
General practice	52, 932
Medical specialities	80, 526
Surgical specialities	89, 821
Other specialities	77, 959
Medical teaching	6, 464
Administration	11, 739
Research	8, 159
Other	2, 666

[1] Excludes 21,614 inactive, 20,343 not classified, and 7,525 address unknown.

Source: "Physician Distribution and Medical Licensure in the U.S., 1974" Center for Health Services Research and Development, AMA, 1975.

TABLE 2.—*Non-Federal physicians in United States and possessions, by specialty and activity, Dec. 31, 1974*

Specialty	Total physicians	Major professional activity								
		Patient care					Medical teaching	Administration	Research	Other
		Total	Hospital based practice							
			Office based practice	Interns	Residents	Full-time physicians staff				
Total physicians	345, 607	278, 517	203, 943	10, 777	43, 733	20, 064	5, 863	9, 918	7, 051	2, 301
General practice	51, 861	50, 935	46, 808	--------	2, 280	1, 847	144	507	89	186
Medical specialties	81, 411	73, 289	49, 795	4, 131	14, 493	4, 870	2, 187	2, 378	3, 173	384
Allergy	1, 571	1, 452	1, 423	--------		29	22	19	75	3
Cardiovascular diseases	5, 758	4, 900	4, 404	--------		496	260	194	358	46
Dermatology	4, 090	3, 868	3, 288	--------	510	70	76	42	90	14
Gastroenterology	1, 819	1, 495	1, 392	--------		103	108	45	165	6
Internal medicine	46, 158	41, 874	25, 993	3, 243	10, 174	2, 464	956	1, 298	1, 821	209
Pediatrics	19, 302	17, 577	11, 827	888	3, 674	1, 188	558	625	450	92
Pediatric allergy	412	371	296	--------	55	20	13	6	22	--------
Pediatric cardiology	516	386	215	--------	80	91	63	18	46	3
Pulmonary diseases	1, 785	1, 366	957	--------		409	131	131	146	11
Surgical specialties	87, 322	84, 282	64, 987	1, 705	14, 772	2, 818	1, 044	939	826	231
General surgery	28, 902	27, 906	19, 325	1, 351	6, 024	1, 206	289	383	245	79
Neurological surgery	2, 688	2, 559	1, 893	--------	542	124	51	21	45	12
Obstetrics and gynecology	19, 892	19, 008	15, 116	354	2, 915	623	287	317	232	48
Ophthalmology	10, 211	9, 901	8, 450	--------	1, 280	171	99	57	136	18
Orthopedic surgery	10, 102	9, 850	7, 759	--------	1, 839	252	121	48	50	33
Otolaryngology	5, 122	4, 961	4, 146	--------	715	100	63	34	47	17
Plastic surgery	1, 977	1, 914	1, 566	--------	299	49	31	12	13	7
Colon and rectal surgery	649	637	607	--------	20	10	1	5	4	2
Thoracic surgery	1, 759	1, 668	1, 316	--------	241	111	36	26	26	3
Urology	6, 020	5, 878	4, 809	--------	897	172	66	36	28	12
Other specialties	83, 056	70, 011	42, 353	4, 941	12, 188	10, 529	2, 488	6, 094	2, 963	1, 500
Aerospace medicine	182	123	91	--------	23	9	6	23	17	13
Anesthesiology	11, 782	11, 080	8, 460	--------	1, 681	939	434	150	91	27
Child psychiatry	2, 303	1, 899	1, 337	--------	278	284	132	199	45	28
Diagnostic radiology	2, 728	2, 526	1, 675	--------	499	352	95	31	16	60
Forensic pathology	184	95	76	--------	7	12	9	30	5	45
Neurology	3, 334	2, 766	1, 695	--------	831	240	180	71	296	21
Occupational medicine	2, 138	1, 554	1, 506	--------	3	45	3	478	25	78
Psychiatry	21, 073	18, 508	11, 731	--------	3, 484	3, 293	438	1, 619	392	116
Pathology	10, 215	8, 255	3, 834	145	2, 180	2, 096	426	454	543	537
Physical medicine and rehabilitation	1, 332	1, 208	586	--------	256	366	22	72	14	16
General preventive medicine	591	242	200	--------	25	17	43	228	58	20
Public health	2, 237	568	481	--------	37	50	91	1, 391	81	106
Radiology	10, 588	9, 934	6, 713	--------	1, 777	1, 444	219	123	98	214
Therapeutic radiology	988	945	575	--------	206	164	23	7	13	--------
Other specialty	5, 845	3, 104	2, 150	--------		954	333	1, 052	1, 190	166
Unspecified	7, 536	7, 204	1, 243	4, 796	901	264	34	166	79	53
Not classified	20, 343									
Inactive	21, 614									

Source: "Physician Distribution and Medical Licensure in the U.S., 1974," Center for Health Services Research and Development, AMA, 1975.

The distribution of active non-Federal physicians by region is outlined in table 3. The northeast census region (New England and Middle Atlantic States) has the largest number of active non-Federal physicians. This region has the largest percentage of physicians in patient care activities, administration, and research. Almost 40 percent of all physicians engaged in research are located in this census region.

TABLE 3.—*Non-Federal physicians by census region division, and activity, Dec. 31, 1974*

Census Region Division	Total physicians [1]		Patient care		Medical teaching		Administration		Research		Other	
	Number	Percent	Number	Percent	Number	Percent	Number	Percent	Number	Percent	Number	Percent
Total, Non-Federal	303,650	100.0	278,517	100.0	5,863	100.0	9,918	100.0	7,051	100.0	2,301	100.0
Northeast	89,969	29.6	81,327	29.2	1,656	28.2	3,468	35.0	2,800	39.7	718	31.2
New England	22,006	7.2	19,703	7.1	372	6.3	847	8.5	907	12.9	177	7.7
Middle Atlantic	67,963	22.4	61,624	22.1	1,284	21.9	2,621	26.4	1,893	26.8	541	23.5
North Central	71,241	23.5	65,990	23.7	1,394	23.8	1,992	20.1	1,351	19.2	514	22.3
East North Central	51,211	16.9	47,561	17.1	932	15.9	1,457	14.7	880	12.5	381	16.6
West North Central	20,030	6.6	18,429	6.6	462	7.9	535	5.4	471	6.7	133	5.8
South	79,525	26.2	73,328	26.3	1,681	28.7	2,405	24.2	1,555	22.1	556	24.2
South Atlantic	43,539	14.3	39,872	14.3	919	15.7	1,501	15.1	923	13.1	324	14.1
East South Central	13,471	4.4	12,509	4.5	270	4.6	359	3.6	244	3.5	89	3.9
West South Central	22,515	7.4	20,947	7.5	492	8.4	545	5.5	388	5.5	143	6.2
West	60,262	19.8	55,425	19.9	1,068	18.2	1,948	19.6	1,317	18.7	504	21.9
Mountain	12,272	4.0	11,396	4.1	203	3.5	359	3.6	216	3.1	98	4.3
Pacific	47,990	15.8	44,029	15.8	865	14.8	1,589	16.0	1,101	15.6	406	17.6
Possessions	2,653	.9	2,447	.9	64	1.1	105	1.1	28	.4	9	.4

[1] Excludes 21,614 inactive, 20,343 not classified, and 7,525 address unknown.

NOTE.—Percentages may not add due to rounding.

TABLE 4.—*Distribution of non-Federal physicians, by State and major professional activity, Dec. 31, 1974*

State	Total physi-cians	Patient care	Medical teaching	Adminis-tration	Research	Other	Not classified	Inactive
Alabama	3,509	2,967	49	71	75	22	149	176
Alaska	302	245	5	12	4	1	21	14
Arizona	3,772	2,876	59	92	34	21	178	512
Arkansas	2,039	1,699	34	40	20	16	83	147
California	44,093	35,001	677	1,266	885	348	2,349	3,567
Canal Zone	43	36	--------	2	--------	--------	4	1
Colorado	4,488	3,645	71	134	110	31	224	273
Connecticut	6,646	5,282	105	272	189	46	336	416
Delaware	850	709	8	31	7	1	38	56
District of Columbia	3,249	2,408	106	157	76	24	332	146
Florida	14,275	10,368	185	266	162	97	711	2,486
Georgia	5,916	4,928	112	158	62	31	361	264
Hawaii	1,412	1,131	30	56	17	8	68	102
Idaho	802	683	5	10	4	7	29	64
Illinois	17,594	14,409	285	506	324	134	1,177	759
Indiana	5,919	4,962	92	149	81	35	267	333
Iowa	3,122	2,614	71	59	50	20	128	180
Kansas	2,969	2,441	52	73	40	19	173	171
Kentucky	3,879	3,253	89	96	48	25	187	181
Louisiana	4,806	4,007	120	95	68	31	275	210
Maine	1,342	1,071	15	39	17	7	52	141
Maryland	8,567	6,517	178	331	300	52	752	437
Massachusetts	13,226	10,228	204	430	610	91	983	680
Michigan	12,608	10,184	214	354	179	75	981	621
Minnesota	6,522	5,294	132	137	166	38	399	356
Mississippi	2,112	1,818	19	30	20	12	108	105
Missouri	6,741	5,433	132	195	188	46	414	333
Montana	814	719	2	10	4	6	26	47
Nebraska	1,971	1,613	67	53	22	7	78	131
Nevada	695	587	7	16	3	4	26	52
New Hampshire	1,247	1,014	15	35	30	10	31	112
New Jersey	12,102	9,884	126	405	208	89	736	654
New Mexico	1,401	1,090	21	42	22	17	88	121
New York	45,026	35,874	811	1,634	1,276	308	2,927	2,196
North Carolina	6,614	5,286	126	220	176	40	392	374
North Dakota	632	538	6	14	5	2	35	32
Ohio	15,383	12,938	244	323	205	84	839	750
Oklahoma	2,892	2,430	51	66	29	17	135	164
Oregon	3,736	3,038	67	94	47	27	185	278
Pennsylvania	19,349	15,866	347	582	409	144	999	1,002
Puerto Rico	2,826	2,298	64	101	28	8	246	81
Rhode Island	1,733	1,411	12	34	24	15	114	123
South Carolina	2,981	2,449	51	90	20	14	179	178
South Dakota	566	496	2	4	--------	1	26	37
Tennessee	5,480	4,471	113	162	101	30	367	236
Texas	15,440	12,811	287	344	271	79	824	824
Utah	1,789	1,481	36	47	39	7	87	92
Vermont	931	697	21	37	37	8	39	92
Virginia	6,846	5,467	127	203	103	47	479	420
Virgin Islands	72	60	--------	1	--------	--------	1	10
Washington	5,694	4,614	86	161	148	22	264	399
West Virginia	2,128	1,740	26	45	17	18	145	137
Wisconsin	6,026	5,068	97	125	91	53	279	313
Wyoming	375	315	2	8	--------	5	17	28
Pacific Islands	55	53	--------	1	--------	--------	--------	1

Source: "Physician Distribution and Medical Licensure in the U.S., 1974," Center for Health Services Research and Development, AMA, 1975.

The demographic county classification system, as developed by the American Medical Association, is a way of classifying counties in the United States in order to relate the distribution of physicians to the distribution of resident civilian population. Nine classifications are used, ranging from non-metropolitan counties with 0 to 9,999 inhabitants to counties in standard metropolitan statistical areas (SMSA's) with 5 million or more inhabitants. The distribution of propulation under this system is shown in table 5.

TABLE 5.—*Demographic county classification, Dec. 31, 1974*

Demographic county classification and definition	Number of SMSA's	Number of counties	Resident population, Dec. 31, 1973
Total 50 States and District of Columbia_	300	3, 084	210, 908, 300
9. Counties in SMSA's with 5,000,000 or more inhabitants_____	3	16	23, 919, 100
8. Counties in SMSA's with 1,000,000 to 4,999,999 inhabitants_____	32	163	62, 959, 000
7. Counties in SMSA's with 500,000 to 999,999 inhabitants_____	39	130	27, 690, 700
6. Counties in SMSA's with 50 000 to 499,999 inhabitants_____	179	320	39, 419, 400
5. Counties considered potential SMSA's_____	47	59	4, 849, 400
4. Nonmetropolitan counties with 50,000 or more inhabitants_____		219	16, 104, 700
3. Nonmetropolitan counties with 25,000 to 49,999 inhabitants_____		466	16, 254, 800
2. Nonmetropolitan counties with 10,000 to 24,999 inhabitants_____		929	15, 176, 700
1. Nonmetropolitan counties with 0 to 9,999 inhabitants_____		782	4, 534, 500

NOTE.—Cities defined as independent are included in "number of counties" column.

Source: "Physician Distribution and Medical Licensure in the U.S., 1974," Center for Health Services Research and Development, AMA, 1975.

An uneven distribution of physicians and other health resources is illustrated by the application of the demographic classification system. Table 6 indicates that 54.6 percent of the Nation's physicians are located in the most densely populated metropolitan areas and serve the needs of 40.4 percent of the resident population. In contrast, only 7.3 percent of the physicians are located in nonmetropolitan areas to serve 17 percent of the population.

Table 6 also indicates that physicians in general practice are more evenly distributed, nationwide, than specialists. A greater percentage of physicians in medical and surgical specialties, in proportion to population, are located in highly urban areas.

Table 6 also shows an uneven distribution of hospitals, and at the same time outlines a rather even distribution of hospital beds. A larger percentage of hospitals are located in rural areas to serve the needs of a relatively smaller population.

TABLE 6.—*Percentage distribution of non-Federal physicians, hospitals, hospital beds, and population by county classification*

Demographic county classification	Total physicians (percent)	Office based practice					Hospital based practice	Other professional activity [1]	Inactive	Not classified	Hospitals (Dec. 1, 1974)	Hospital beds (Dec. 1, 1974)	Resident population (Dec. 31, 1973)
		Patient care	General practice	Medical specialty	Surgical specialty	Other specialty							
Total	100.0	100.0	100.0	100.0	100.0	100.0	100.0	100.0	100.0	100.0	100.0	100.0	100.0
Possessions	0.9	0.9	1.0	0.7	0.6	0.6	1.3	0.8	0.4	1.2	0.9	0.8	(2)
1	.6	.6	2.9	.2	.3	.2	0.1	.2	1.2	0.4	8.1	2.0	2.1
2	2.6	2.7	9.8	1.2	2.0	1.4	.7	.7	3.9	1.6	16.6	6.4	7.2
3	4.1	4.2	9.4	3.3	4.7	3.4	1.5	2.1	5.9	2.7	12.5	7.7	7.7
4	4.8	4.9	8.1	4.8	6.3	4.8	1.9	2.5	6.8	3.6	8.7	7.2	7.6
5	1.8	1.9	2.2	1.9	2.4	1.9	1.2	1.6	2.1	1.4	2.2	2.5	2.3
6	17.1	17.3	16.9	17.6	20.4	18.6	13.9	15.1	18.9	14.2	15.7	19.9	18.7
7	13.6	13.6	11.0	14.3	14.4	13.2	14.4	14.0	13.0	12.9	8.1	12.4	13.1
8	37.4	36.7	26.6	38.2	35.3	38.4	42.4	43.0	35.3	41.7	20.1	29.0	29.9
9	17.2	17.1	12.2	17.8	13.7	17.3	22.6	20.1	12.6	20.3	7.3	12.2	11.3

[1] Includes Medical Teaching, Administration, Research, and other.
[2] Not available.

NOTE.—Percentages may not add due to rounding.

Table 7 lists 145 counties in the United States which had no active physician in patient care, as of December 31, 1974. This represents an increase of 5 counties since 1972, and 13 since 1970. The 145 counties cover approximately 153,592 square miles, or about 4.3 percent of the total U.S. land area. Over one-half million people, or 0.3 percent of the total population, reside in these counties.

The vast majority of the counties (202) are located in the Western portion of the country. Thirty-nine are adjacent to standard metropolitan statistical areas.

TABLE 7.—*Counties without an active physician in patient care, land area, resident population, and population per square mile*

State and county, Dec. 31, 1974	Square miles	Resident population, Dec. 31, 1973	Population per square mile
Total, 50 States and District of Columbia	3,084	3,536,855	210,908,300	60
Percent	(100.0)	(100.0)	(100.0)	
Total counties without a physician	145	153,592	537,700	4
Percent	(4.7)	(4.3)	(.3)	
California		156,361	20,705,100	132
Alpine		727	500	1
Colorado		103,766	2,472,800	24
Dolores		1,026	1,200	1
Hinsdale		1,054	300	(1)
Washington		2,526	5,400	2
Florida		54,090	7,841,600	145
Glades		753	4,500	6
Lafayette		549	3,200	6
Georgia		58,073	4,816,200	83
Baker		355	3,500	10
Brantley		447	7,000	15
Bryan		443	8,000	18
Dawson		211	4,200	20
Glascock		143	2,300	16
McIntosh		426	8,800	21
Quitman		156	2,000	13
Schley		162	3,000	19
Taliaferro		195	2,500	13
Warren		284	7,400	26
Webster		195	2,100	11
Wheeler		306	4,800	16
Idaho		82,677	77,700	9
Adams		1,371	2,900	2
Boise		1,910	2,100	1
Clark		1,751	800	1
Owyhee		7,641	7,300	1
Kansas		81,787	2,297,200	28
Elk		647	3,700	6
Gray		872	4,700	5
Haskell		580	4,300	7
Kearney		855	3,400	4
Stanton		676	2,500	4
Wichita		724	3,200	4
Kentucky		39,650	3,363,600	85
Carlisle		195	6,000	31
Lee		210	6,800	32
Menifee		210	4,000	19
Robertson		101	2,400	24
Michigan		56,817	9,092,800	160
Keeweenaw		538	1,900	4
Montmorency		555	6,100	11

Footnote at end of table.

TABLE 7.—*Counties without an active physician in patient care, land area, resident population, and population per square mile*—Continued

State and county, Dec. 31, 1974	Square miles	Resident population, Dec. 31, 1973	Population per square mile
Mississippi	47, 296	2, 292, 900	48
Issaquena	414	2, 800	7
Missouri	68, 995	4, 772, 000	69
Bollinger	621	9, 300	15
Carter	506	4, 200	8
Clark	506	8, 500	17
Dallas	537	10, 800	20
DeKalb	423	7, 300	17
Hickory	377	5, 000	13
Maries	525	6, 800	13
McDonald	540	14, 100	26
Mercer	455	5, 000	11
Osage	608	11, 400	19
Ozark	732	7, 400	10
Putnam	518	6, 100	12
Reynolds	817	6, 100	7
Schuyler	306	5, 300	17
Scotland	441	5, 800	13
Wayne	766	9, 900	13
Montana	145, 587	727, 500	5
Golden Valley	1, 176	1, 000	1
Judith Basin	1, 880	2, 500	1
Meagher	2, 354	2, 300	1
Petroleum	1, 655	800	(1)
Treasure	985	1, 100	1
Wibaux	890	1, 300	1
Nebraska	76, 483	1, 548, 200	20
Arthur	704	600	1
Banner	738	1, 300	2
Blaine	710	700	1
Deuel	436	3, 000	7
Gosper	464	2, 400	5
Greeley	570	4, 000	7
Hayes	711	1, 800	3
Hitchcock	712	4, 500	6
Keya Paha	768	1, 100	1
Logan	570	1, 000	2
Loup	574	1, 000	2
McPherson	856	900	1
Sioux	2, 063	2, 100	1
Thomas	716	1, 100	2
Wheeler	576	1, 000	2
Nevada	109, 889	555, 400	5
Esmeralda	3, 570	500	(1)
Eureka	4, 182	1, 200	(1)
Lander	5, 621	2, 000	(1)
Storey	262	700	3
New Mexico	121, 412	1, 120, 800	9
Guadalupe	2, 998	5, 100	2
Harding	2, 134	1, 000	1
North Dakota	69, 273	642, 900	9
Billings	1, 139	1, 200	1
Dunn	1, 992	3, 700	2
Oliver	721	1, 900	3
Sargent	853	5, 200	6
Sheridan	989	3, 000	3
Slope	1, 225	1, 100	1
Ohio	40, 975	10, 759, 700	263
Vinton	411	10, 400	25
Oklahoma	68, 782	2, 678, 100	39
Dewey	1, 018	5, 800	6
Oregon	96, 184	2, 247, 500	23
Sherman	830	1, 700	2
Wheeler	1, 707	1, 500	1

Footnote at end of table.

TABLE 7.—*Counties without an active physician in patient care, land area, resident population, and population per square mile*—Continued

State and county, Dec. 31, 1974	Square miles	Resident population, Dec. 31, 1973	Population per square mile
South Dakota	75, 955	687, 600	9
Aurora	709	4, 700	7
Buffalo	482	2, 100	4
Campbell	732	3, 700	5
Clark	964	4, 700	5
Corson	2, 470	4, 900	2
Dewey	2, 351	5, 600	2
Edmunds	1, 154	4, 700	4
Hanson	430	3, 300	8
Harding	2, 682	2, 000	1
Hyde	863	2, 100	2
Jones	973	1, 500	2
Mellette	1, 306	2, 400	2
Miner	570	4, 200	7
Perkins	2, 860	4, 500	2
Sanborn	570	3, 200	6
Stanley	1, 414	1, 800	1
Sully	1, 004	2, 900	3
Union	452	9, 200	18
Washabaugh	1, 061	1, 900	2
Ziebach	1, 981	3, 000	2
Tennessee	41, 328	4, 126, 200	100
Meigs	191	5, 100	27
Union	212	10, 000	47
Texas	262, 134	11, 896, 100	45
Borden	907	900	1
Briscoe	874	2, 300	3
Carson	900	6, 900	8
Concho	1, 004	2, 100	2
Glasscock	863	1, 000	1
Hartley	1, 488	2, 400	2
Hood	426	6, 800	9
Hudspeth	4, 554	2, 000	[1]
Irion	1, 073	1, 100	1
Jeff Davis	2, 259	1, 500	1
Kenedy	1, 394	700	1
Kent	880	1, 300	1
King	944	500	1
Kinney	1, 393	2, 000	1
Lipcomb	934	3, 400	4
Loving	648	300	[1]
McMullen	1, 159	1, 500	1
Rains	210	4, 200	20
Real	622	2, 400	4
Roberts	899	1, 400	2
San Jacinto	624	6, 300	10
Stonewall	926	2, 400	3
Terrell	2, 391	1, 100	[1]
Utah	82, 096	1, 166, 900	14
Emery	4, 439	5, 000	1
Piute	754	1, 200	2
Rich	1, 023	2, 000	2
Wayne	2, 486	1, 700	1
Vermont	9, 267	468, 200	51
Grand Isle	83	3, 600	43
Virginia	39, 780	4, 833, 300	122
Bland	369	5, 900	16
Charles City	181	6, 800	38
King and Queen	318	5, 300	17
West Virgina	24, 070	1, 793, 800	75
Clay	343	10, 200	30
Doddridge	319	6, 800	21

Footnote at end of table.

TABLE 7.—*Counties without an active physician in patient care, land area, resident population, and population per square mile*—Continued

State and county, Dec. 31, 1974	Square miles	Resident population, Dec. 31, 1973	Population per square mile
Wisconsin_____	54, 464	4, 593, 000	84
Florence_____	487	3, 200	7
Wyoming_____	97, 203	356, 600	4
Crook_____	2, 882	3, 900	1

[1] Less than 0.5.

Sources: U.S. Bureau of the Census, "County and City Data Book, 1972" (A Statistical Abstract Supplement). Washington, D.C.: U.S. Government Printing Office; 1973."1974 Survey of Buying Power," Annual Statistical Issue, Sales Management Inc. Vol. 113, No. 1 July 8, 1974.

In 1972, 52,968 non-Federal physicians in general practice were professionally active in the United States and its possessions. By 1974, that figure had decreased to 51,861. Although total figures for this 3-year span reflect a 9.2-percent decrease in the number of general practitioners nationwide, the actual number of physicians in general practice increased in fifteen States. The number of general practitioners decreased in 29 States during this same period. Hawaii, Kentucky, and New Hampshire showed no change. The changes in eight States were too minute to compute.

Table 8 outlines the distribution of professionally active general practitioners, State by State, for 1968 and 1972.

TABLE 8.—*Distribution of non-Federal physicians in general practice, 1972 and 1974*

State	1972	1974	Percent change between 1972 and 1974
Alabama	698	679	−3
Alaska	71	73	+3
Arizona	517	584	+13
Arkansas	557	582	+5
California	6,735	6,624	−2
Canal Zone	6	3	−50
Colorado	601	632	+5
Connecticut	636	592	−7
Delaware	133	135	+2
District of Columbia	189	178	−6
Florida	1,578	1,754	+11
Georgia	875	881	+1
Hawaii	195	195	------------
Idaho	255	245	−4
Illinois	2,849	2,820	−1
Indiana	1,586	1,592	+3
Iowa	869	862	−1
Kansas	639	644	+1
Kentucky	859	859	------------
Louisiana	801	785	−2
Maine	251	247	−2
Maryland	778	773	−1
Massachusetts	1,345	1,183	−12
Michigan	1,709	1,652	−3
Minnesota	1,220	1,260	+3
Mississippi	541	535	−1
Missouri	843	808	−4
Montana	230	223	−3
Nebraska	517	540	+4
Nevada	138	145	+5
New Hampshire	220	220	------------
New Jersey	1,648	1,508	−9
New Mexico	185	208	+12
New York	4,757	4,253	−11
North Carolina	1,063	1,074	+1
North Dakota	169	176	+4
Ohio	2,586	2,470	−5
Oklahoma	604	580	−4
Oregon	624	638	+2
Pennsylvania	3,187	3,064	−4
Puerto Rico	598	570	−5
Rhode Island	191	170	−11
South Carolina	680	747	+10
South Dakota	193	184	−5
Tennessee	834	802	−4
Texas	2,837	2,831	−2
Utah	280	282	+1
Vermont	144	127	−12
Virginia	1,110	1,091	−2
Virgin Islands	9	6	−33
Washington	1,081	1,092	+1
West Virginia	424	380	−10
Wisconsin	1,189	1,173	−1
Wyoming	124	119	−4
Pacific Islands	10	11	+10
Total	52,968	51,861	−2

Source: "Physician Distribution and Medical Licensure in the United States, 1974," AMA, 1975.

Table 9 shows the physician/population ratios for selected years beginning in 1950. Table 10 shows physician/population ratios by State.

TABLE 9.—*Physicians, population and physician/population ratios, selected years, 1950–73*

Year	Total physicians [1]	Total population [2] (thousands)	Physicians per 100,000 total population	Total population per 1 physician	Non-Federal physician in patient care [3]	Civilian resident population [3][4] (thousands)	Non-Federal physicians in patient care per 100,000 civilian resident population	Civilian resident population per 1 non-Federal physician in patient care
1950	219,997	156,472	141	711	(5)	151,238	(5)	(5)
1955	241,711	170,499	142	705	(5)	164,597	(5)	(5)
1960	260,484	185,370	141	712	(5)	179,742	(5)	(5)
1965	292,088	199,278	147	682	237,482	192,633	123	811
1966	300,375	201,585	149	671	241,730	194,355	124	804
1967	308,630	203,704	152	660	247,256	196,359	126	794
1968	317,032	205,758	154	649	236,460	198,287	[6]119	839
1969	324,942	207,863	156	640	245,368	200,466	122	817
1970	334,028	209,539	159	627	252,778	203,106	124	803
1971	344,814	211,578	163	614	261,335	205,497	127	786
1972	356,534	213,046	167	598	269,095	207,313	130	770
1973 (estimate)	366,379	214,524	171	586	272,850	208,958	131	766

[1] Includes inactive and address unknown as of December 31.
[2] Includes Armed Forces and their dependents in the United States and abroad, civilians in the 50 States, District of Columbia, and U.S. outlying areas; and U.S. Government and civilian employees and their dependents abroad.
[3] Excludes U.S. outlying areas (Canal Zone, Pacific Islands, Puerto Rico, and Virgin Islands).
[4] As of January 1 of following year.
[5] Not available.
[6] In 1968 approximately 21,564 physicians were reclassified by AMA from patient care activities into other activities.

Source: "1974 Socioeconomic Issues of Health," AMA, 1973.

TABLE 10.—*Non-Federal physicians, civilian population, physician-population ratios and rank by State*

State	Civilian population (July 1, 1974)	Non-Federal physicians (Dec. 31, 1974)		Physicians per 100,000 population		Rank of physician-population ratio by State	
		Total	Patient care	Total	Patient care	Total	Patient care
Total (50 States and District of Columbia [1]	209,689,000	342,611	276,070	163	132		
Alabama	3,551,000	3,509	2,967	99	84	49	47
Alaska	311,000	302	245	97	77	49	50
Arizona	2,126,000	3,772	2,876	177	135	11	12
Arkansas	2,052,000	2,039	1,699	99	83	47	48
California	20,610,000	44,093	35,001	214	170	5	5
Colorado	2,448,000	4,488	3,645	183	149	21	8
Connecticut	3,076,000	6,646	5,282	216	172	4	4
Delaware	567,000	850	709	150	125	20	21
District of Columbia	714,000	3,249	2,408	455	337	1	1
Florida	8,002,000	14,275	10,368	178	130	8	18
Georgia	4,832,000	5,916	4,928	122	102	36	34
Hawaii	6,792,000	1,412	1,131	178	143	10	10
Idaho	793,000	802	683	101	86	46	46
Illinois	11,096,000	17,594	14,409	159	130	17	17
Indiana	5,319,000	5,919	4,962	111	93	40	40
Iowa	2,854,000	3,122	2,614	109	92	42	41
Kansas	2,240,000	2,969	2,441	133	109	27	27
Kentucky	3,321,000	3,879	3,253	117	98	38	38
Louisiana	3,733,000	4,806	4,007	129	107	31	30
Maine	1,036,000	1,342	1,071	130	103	30	33
Maryland	4,041,000	8,567	6,517	212	161	6	6
Massachusetts	5,785,000	13,226	10,228	229	177	3	3
Michigan	9,084,000	12,608	10,184	139	112	25	25
Minnesota	3,915,000	6,522	5,294	167	135	12	13
Mississippi	2,302,000	2,112	1,818	92	79	50	49
Missouri	4,752,000	6,741	5,433	142	114	24	24
Montana	729,000	814	719	112	99	39	36
Nebraska	1,531,000	1,971	1,613	129	105	32	31
Nevada	564,000	695	587	123	104	35	32
New Hampshire	803,000	1,247	1,014	155	126	18	20
New Jersey	7,300,000	12,102	9,884	166	135	14	11
New Mexico	1,107,000	1,401	1,090	127	98	33	37
New York	18,083,000	45,026	35,874	249	198	2	2
North Carolina	5,265,000	6,614	5,286	126	100	34	35
North Dakota	624,000	632	538	101	86	45	45
Ohio	10,723,000	15,383	12,938	143	121	23	22
Oklahoma	2,680,000	2,892	130	108	91	43	42
Oregon	2,263,000	3,736	3,038	165	134	15	15
Pennsylvania	11,824,000	19,349	15,866	164	134	16	16
Rhode Island	930,000	1,733	1,411	186	152	8	7
South Carolina	2,711,000	2,981	2,449	110	90	41	43
South Dakota	676,000	566	496	84	73	51	50
Tennessee	4,108,000	5,480	4,471	133	109	26	28
Texas	11,890,000	15,440	12,811	130	108	29	29
Utah	1,169,000	1,789	1,481	153	127	19	19
Vermont	470,000	931	697	198	148	7	9
Virginia	4,751000	6,846	5,467	144	115	22	23
Washington	3,427,000	5,694	4,614	166	135	13	14
West Virginia	1,790,000	2,128	1,740	119	97	37	39
Wisconsin	4,565,000	6,026	5,068	132	111	28	26
Wyoming	356,000	375	315	105	88	44	44

[1] Excludes physicians (2,996 total non-Federal and 2,447 patient care and population in possessions Canal Zone, Pacific Islands, Puerto Rico, and Virgin Islands. Population total does not add due to rounding.

Source: Estimates of the Population of States: July 1, 1973 and 1974 (Advance Report. *"Current Population Reports"* Series P-25, No. 533, October 1974.

The data presented in the preceding pages relates to doctors of medicine (M.D.). Table 11 outlines the numbers and distribution of doctors of osteopathy, by State, for 1975. Doctors of osteopathy (D.O.) are licensed in most States to practice medicine and surgery on the same basis as M.D.'s. D.O.'s tend to be concentrated in four States—Michigan, Missouri, Ohio, and Pennsylvania. These States account for over 44 percent of the total number of osteopaths in the United States.

TABLE 11.—*Distribution of osteopathic physicians, 1975*

Location	Number	Location	Number
Alabama	5	Nevada	28
Alaska	5	New Hampshire	19
Arizona	413	New Jersey	898
Arkansas	16	New Mexico	138
California	232	New York	622
Colorado	273	North Carolina	28
Connecticut	44	North Dakota	8
Delaware	45	Ohio	1,245
District of Columbia	7	Oklahoma	458
Florida	883	Oregon	183
Georgia	121	Pennsylvania	1,825
Hawaii	21	Rhode Island	86
Idaho	26	South Carolina	10
Illinois	337	South Dakota	29
Indiana	182	Tennessee	59
Iowa	414	Texas	885
Kansas	203	Utah	17
Kentucky	39	Vermont	40
Louisiana	19	Virginia	44
Maine	205	Washington	204
Maryland	32	West Virginia	87
Massachusetts	182	Wisconsin	182
Michigan	2,447	Wyoming	10
Minnesota	66	Canada	76
Mississippi	3	Foreign	70
Missouri	1,144	In military service	253
Montana	29		
Nebraska	32	Total	14,929

Source: "1975 American Osteopathic Association Yearbook and Directory of Osteopathic Physicians." Figures include only osteopaths with a directory listing. Members and nonmembers of AOA are included.

B. FOREIGN MEDICAL GRADUATES

As of Dec. 31, 1973, there were 71,335 graduates of foreign medical schools (FMG's) in the United States (excluding Canadian graduates). The greatest number graduated from schools in the Philippines (13.4 percent), and India (10.2 percent). Table 12 presents data on FMG's in the United States by country of graduation.

TABLE 12.—*Foreign medical graduates by country of graduation, Dec. 31, 1973*

Country	Total physicians Number	Total physicians Percent	Country	Total physicians Number	Total physicians Percent
Total physicians_	71, 335	100. 0	Jamaica_____	91	. 1
			Japan_____	871	1. 2
Afghanistan_____	27	(¹)	Lebanon_____	719	1. 0
Algeria_____	1	(¹)	Malaysia_____	6	(¹)
Argentina_____	1, 663	2. 3	Malta_____	6	(¹)
Australia_____	375	. 5	Mexico_____	2, 223	3. 1
Austria_____	1, 619	2. 3	Netherlands_____	741	1. 0
Bangladesh_____	43	. 1	New Zealand_____	100	0. 1
Belgium_____	611	. 9	Nicaragua_____	103	0. 1
Bolivia_____	212	. 3	Nigeria_____	73	0. 1
Brazil_____	580	. 8	North Korea_____	2	(¹)
Bulgaria_____	67	. 1	North Vietnam_____	3	(¹)
Burma_____	182	. 3	Norway_____	52	0. 1
Cambodia_____	3	(¹)	Pakistan_____	1, 249	1. 8
Ceylon_____	307	. 4	Panama_____	36	0. 1
Chile_____	323	. 5	Paraguay_____	117	0. 2
China_____	646	. 9	Peru_____	785	1. 1
Colombia_____	1, 214	1. 7	Philippines_____	9, 533	13. 4
Congo (Kinshasa)_____	1	(¹)	Poland_____	773	1. 1
Costa Rica_____	36	. 1	Portugal_____	108	0. 2
Cuba_____	3, 112	4. 4	Rumania_____	406	0. 6
Czechoslovakia_____	702	1. 0	Senegal_____	1	(¹)
Denmark_____	83	. 1	Singapore_____	40	0. 1
Dominican Republic___	763	1. 1	South Africa_____	411	0. 6
East Germany_____	660	. 9	South Korea_____	3, 132	4. 4
Ecuador_____	197	. 3	South Vietnam_____	21	(¹)
El Salvador_____	145	. 2	Spain_____	2, 231	3. 1
Ethiopia_____	2	(¹)	Sudan_____	2	(¹)
Finland_____	37	. 1	Surinam_____	3	(¹)
France_____	727	1. 0	Sweden_____	76	0. 1
Greece_____	950	1. 3	Switzerland_____	2, 511	3. 5
Guatemala_____	154	. 2	Syria_____	370	0. 5
Haiti_____	405	. 6	Taiwan (Formosa)_____	1, 711	2. 4
Honduras_____	69	. 1	Thailand_____	1, 308	1. 8
Hong Kong_____	139	. 2	Turkey_____	995	1. 4
Hungary_____	854	1. 2	Uganda_____	42	0. 1
Iceland_____	43	. 1	U.S.S.R._____	759	1. 1
India_____	7, 244	10. 2	United Arab Republic		
Indonesia_____	156	. 2	(Egypt)_____	1, 103	1. 6
Iran_____	2, 229	3. 1	United Kingdom_____	2, 742	3. 8
Iraq_____	245	. 3	Uruguay_____	70	0. 1
Ireland_____	1, 032	1. 5	Venezuela_____	254	0. 4
Israel_____	303	. 4	West Germany_____	3, 383	4. 7
Italy_____	3, 502	4. 9	Yugoslavia_____	510	0. 7

¹ Less than 0.05 percent.

Source: Martin, Beverly, C., "Medical School Alumni," Center for Health Services Research and Development, American Medical Association, 1975.

In the 11-year span between 1962 and 1973, approximately 101,000 foreign physicians were admitted to the United States. During that same period, U.S. medical school graduated almost 98,000 medical students. Table 13 indicates that in 1962. U.S. medical schools graduated 24 percent more physicians than were admitted from foreign nations. Eleven years later, however, 18 percent more FMG's were entering the United States than were graduated from U.S. medical schools. The number of foreign physicians admitted to the United States with immigrant status grew remarkably between 1962 and 1973—from 1,297 to 7,119. Table 13 also outlines the entry status of FMG's during this period.

Table 14 shows physicians and surgeons admitted as immigrants to the United States by country of last permanent residence for the fiscal years 1966, 1969, and 1972. The vast majority of FMG's admitted as immigrants in 1972 were from Asian countries. India led the list with over 1,500 physicians admitted with immigrant status from that country in fiscal year 1972.

TABLE 13.—*Foreign physicians and surgeons admitted to the United States in comparison with number of U.S. medical graduates: 1962–73*

| Fiscal year | U.S. medical graduates | Foreign physicians [1] | | Nonimmigrants | |
		Total	Immigrants	Exchange visitors	Other
Total____	97, 809	101, 066	43, 089	55, 360	2, 617
1962_____	7, 168	5, 767	1, 797	3, 970	NA
1963_____	7, 264	6, 730	2, 093	4, 637	NA
1964_____	7, 336	6, 767	2, 249	4, 518	NA
1965_____	7, 409	6, 172	2, 012	4, 160	NA
1966_____	7, 574	6, 922	2, 552	4, 370	NA
1967_____	7, 743	8, 897	3, 326	5, 204	367
1968_____	7, 973	9, 125	3, 128	5, 701	296
1969_____	8, 059	7, 515	2, 756	4, 460	299
1970_____	8, 367	8, 523	3, 158	5, 008	357
1971_____	8, 974	10, 947	5, 756	4, 784	407
1972_____	9, 551	11, 416	7, 143	3, 935	338
1973_____	10, 391	12, 285	7, 119	4, 613	553

[1] Including Canadians.

Source: Reference 22. Unpublished data from the U.S. Department of Justice Immigration and Naturalization Service.

TABLE 14.—*Physicians and surgeons admitted as immigrants by country of last permanent residence*

| | Selected fiscal years | | |
	1966	1969	1972
Europe:			
Austria_____	16	49	15
Belgium_____	17	6	14
Czechoslovakia_____	5	10	24
Germany_____	81	52	72
Greece_____	38	36	64
Ireland_____	22	18	26
Italy_____	43	51	32
Poland_____	22	21	25
Spain_____	53	51	58
Sweden_____	20	8	17
Switzerland_____	27	12	25
Turkey_____	57	42	50
United Kingdom_____	187	140	364
Yugoslavia_____	12	36	33
Other_____	67	47	78
Total_____	667	579	911

TABLE 14.—*Physicians and surgeons admitted as immigrants by country of last permanent residence*—Continued

	Selected fiscal years		
	1966	1969	1972
Americas:			
Argentina	115	42	45
Bolivia	19	13	23
Brazil	33	7	12
Canada	393	236	439
Chile	11	8	13
Colombia	80	47	82
Cuba	150	54	55
Dominican Republic		21	40
Ecuador	23	29	23
Guatemala	8	8	13
Haiti	29	27	21
Jamaica	15	14	18
Peru	46	14	36
Other	288	67	139
Total	1, 210	587	959
Asia:			
Burma	5	24	28
China (Mainland)	5	13	68
Hong Kong	26	39	45
India	40	129	1, 513
Indonesia		28	27
Iran	78	99	459
Iraq	5	3	33
Israel	31	30	62
Japan	31	28	61
Korea	35	128	768
Lebanon	14	30	53
Pakistan	11	22	201
Philippines	259	785	782
Syria	9	8	19
Thailand	11	12	268
Taiwan	11	27	470
Other	17	2	139
Total	588	1, 435	4, 996
Africa:			
Egypt	23	96	63
Kenya	1	6	13
Libya	1	3	18
Nigeria	2	2	21
South Africa	15	8	36
Tanzania		2	19
Uganda			24
Other	18	22	31
Total	60	137	222
Oceania:			
Australia	21	14	43
New Zealand	2	4	12
Other	1		
Total	24	18	55
Other	3		
Grand total	2, 552	2, 756	7, 143

Source: "The Foreign Medical Graduate and Physicians Manpower in the United States," DHEW, August 1973. "Scientists, Engineers, and Physicians from Abroad," fiscal years 1966 and 1967, NSF 69–10, p. 12, Washington, Government Printing Office, 1969; National Science Foundation, Immigration, tables D1 and D2.

Like U.S. physicians, the great majority of FMG's are specialists. Only 10 percent of the FMG's in the United States, as of December 31, 1973, were in general practice. The data also indicates that more FMG's treat patients in a hospital-based, rather than office-based, setting. Table 15 outlines the number of FMG's in the United States and possessions by specialty group. Table 16 outlines the number of FMG's in the United States and possessions by major professional activity.

TABLE 15.—*Foreign medical graduates by specialty, Dec. 31, 1973*

Specialty group	Foreign schools
Total physicians [1]	71, 335
General practice	7, 287
Internal medicine [2]	11, 720
Surgery [3]	11, 078
Obstetrics-gynecology	3, 799
Pediatrics [4]	4, 593
Psychiatry [5]	6, 086
Radiology [6]	2, 589
Anesthesiology	4, 251
Pathology [7]	3, 880
Other [8]	7, 226

[1] Includes inactive, not classified and physicians classified as address unknown who are not distributed throughout table.
[2] Includes internal medicine, allergy, cardiovascular diseases, gastroenterology and pulmonary diseases.
[3] Includes general surgery, neurological surgery, ophthalmology, orthopedic surgery, otolaryngology, plastic surgery, colon and rectal surgery, thoracic surgery and urology.
[4] Includes pediatrics, pediatric allergy and pediatric cardiology.
[5] Includes psychiatry and child psychiatry.
[6] Includes radiology, diagnostic radiology, and therapeutic radiology.
[7] Includes pathology and forensic pathology.
[8] Includes dermatology, aerospace medicine, neurology, occupational medicine, physical medicine and rehabilitation, general preventive medicine, public health, as well as other or unspecified specialties.

Source: Martin, Beverly, C., Medical School Alumni, Center for Health Services Research and Development, American Medical Association 1975.

TABLE 16.—*Foreign medical graduates by major professional activity*

Activity	Foreign schools
Physicians	71, 335
Patient care	57, 337
Office based	27, 270
Hospital based	30, 067
Interns	3, 556
Residents	15, 637
Physician staff	20, 874
Other professional activity	5, 172
Not classified	4, 922
Inactive	2, 115
Address unknown	1, 789

Source: Martin, Beverly, C., Medical School alumni, Center for Health Services Research and Development, American Medical Association, 1975.

C. UNDERGRADUATE MEDICAL EDUCATION

By the fall of 1974, there were 114 medical schools in the United States. Ninety-eight were fully accredited 4-year schools of medicine; three were accredited schools of basic medical sciences; and four were developing medical schools, with students enrolled and provisional approval but not yet eligible for full approval. . . .

In addition to the 114 U.S. schools with students enrolled, there are several schools in various stages of planning and development.

Table 24 outlines proposed medical schools (no students enrolled), fall of 1975.

TABLE 24.—*Proposed medical schools (no students enrolled), fall 1975*

School	Tentative starting date	Maximum 1st-year enrollment planned
East Carolina Universiry School of Medicine, Greenville, N.C.	January 1977 _ _ _ _ _ _ _	40
East Tennessee State University School of Medicine, Johnson City, Tenn.	Fall 1978 _ _ _ _ _ _ _ _ _ _ _	72
Marshall University School of Medicine, Huntington, W. Va.	Fall 1977 _ _ _ _ _ _ _ _ _ _ _	72
Mercer University School of Medicine, Macon, Ga_ _ _	[1]	60
Morehouse College Medical Education Program, Atlanta.	Fall 1977 _ _ _ _ _ _ _ _ _ _ _	100
American Indian School, Northern Arizona University, Ariz.	[1]	[1]
Northeastern Ohio Universities College of Medicine, Kent, Ohio.	Fall 1977 _ _ _ _ _ _ _ _ _ _ _	100
University of South Carolina Medical School, Columbia, S.C. [2]	Fall 1976 _ _ _ _ _ _ _ _ _ _ _	112
Texas A. & M. University/Baylor College of Medicine, College Station, Tex.	Fall 1977 _ _ _ _ _ _ _ _ _ _ _	96
Medical School of the University of Health Sciences of the Uniformed Services, Bethesda, Md _ _ _ _	[1]	125
Wright State University, School of Medicine, Dayton, Ohio [2]	Fall 1976 _ _ _ _ _ _ _ _ _ _ _	96

[1] As yet unknown.
[2] These schools have letters of assurance from the LCME.

Source: Journal of the American Medical Association. Dec. 29, 1975, vol. 234, No. 13.

There were 36,336 full-time faculty members reported teaching in medical schools during the 1974–75 academic year. This represents less than a 10-percent increase over the number of faculty reported for 1972–73.

The medical student-faculty ratio had decreased from 1.6 in 1967–68 to 1.4 in 1972–73 but rose to 1.5 for the past two years.

Table 25 compares faculty data for the past 8 academic years—with respect to the number of medical students and the total number of students for which medical faculty is responsible.

TABLE 25.—*Number of full-time faculty, medical students, and total student equivalents in U.S. medical schools*

	1967–68	1968–69	1969–70	1970–71	1971–72	1972–73	1973–74 [1]	1974–75 [2]
Full-time faculty_ _ _ _ _ _ _ _	22,163.0	23,014.0	24,706.0	[3] 26,504.0	[3] 29,469.0	[3] 33,550.0	33,172.0	36,336.0
Medical students_ _ _ _ _ _ _ _	34,538.0	35,833.0	37,669.0	40,487.0	43,650.0	47,546.0	49,808.0	53,143.0
Medical student-faculty ratio_ _ _ _ _ _ _ _ _ _ _ _ _	1.6	1.6	1.5	1.5	1.5	1.4	1.5	1.5
Total student equivalents_ _ _ _ _ _ _ _ _ _ _ _ _	86,319.0	91,046.0	92,678.0	98,012.0	109,984.0	118,587.0	119,568.0	142,238.0
Total students-equivalents-faculty ratio_ _ _ _ _	3.9	4.0	3.7	3.7	3.7	3.5	3.6	3.9

[1] Yale did not report faculty, Harvard did not report students; both schools are excluded.
[2] Arkansas and Cincinnati did not report faculty; both schools are excluded.
[3] Harvard did not provide figures for 1970–71; Missouri-Kansas City and Nevada did not provide figures in 1972–73.

Source: Journal of the American Medical Association, Dec. 29, 1975, vol. 234, No. 13.

Of the 36,336 faculty members in the 1974–75 academic year, 9,047 were professors, 7,925 were associate professors, 12,445 were assistant professors, and 6,144 were instructors. The number of budgeted but vacant full-time faculty positions reported was 2,173, or 5.6 percent of the total budgeted positions.

Table 26 presents data on budgeted but unfilled full-time faculty positions for academic years 1966–67 through 1974–75, while table 27 shows actual figures for budgeted (filled and unfilled) positions by department for academic year 1974–75.

TABLE 26.—*Budgeted unfilled full-time faculty positions in medical schools, 1966–67 to 1974–75*

Department	1966–67	1967–68	1968–69	1969–70 [1]	1970–71	1971–72 [2]	1972–73	1973–74	1974–75
Basic sciences anatomy	76	79	93	80	76	81	95	98	112
Biochemistry	90	92	92	73	64	58	66	52	46
Microbiology	82	82	77	70	71	50	75	87	83
Pathology	108	129	124	113	125	141	135	172	159
Pharmacology	58	79	57	70	56	53	65	77	83
Physiology	73	96	87	83	82	66	75	93	72
Other	33	13	49	52	34	47	63	22	49
Subtotal	520	570	579	541	508	496	575	601	609
Clinical anesthesiology	60	60	70	81	98	99	96	125	107
Dermatology	8	8	7	8	7	11	15	15	15
Family medicine							71	102	108
Medicine	138	164	233	228	184	219	259	288	346
Neurology	37	43	45	34	25	42	41	55	62
Obstetrics-gynecology	67	71	82	98	67	83	87	100	118
Ophthalmology	17	22	18	25	23	35	37	34	29
Orthopedics	20	23	25	30	31	30	28	37	34
Otolaryngology	19	12	21	18	14	28	23	24	28
Pediatrics	83	100	102	76	78	114	114	136	142
Physical medicine	21	30	33	29	19	20	26	31	29
Psychiatry	95	128	131	104	89	103	97	121	133
Public health and preventive medicine	65	90	73	67	55	44	44	69	51
Radiology	78	110	94	105	114	117	85	110	135
Surgery	87	95	118	132	104	160	147	182	169
Urology	17	15	12	17	14	12	35	48	27
Other	42	40	48	41	60	124	66	15	31
Subtotal	854	1,015	1,112	1,093	982	1,241	1,271	1,492	1,504
Total	1,374	1,585	1,691	1,584	1,490	1,737	1,846	2,093	2,113

[1] Minnesota did not provide information.
[2] Missouri-KC and Nevada did not provide information.

Source: Journal of the American Medical Association, Dec. 29, 1975, vol. 234, No. 13.

TABLE 27.—*Percentage of budget (filled and unfilled) positions vacant, by department, in medical schools* [1]

Department	Full-time faculty, number	Positions unfilled, number	Total budgeted positions, number	Positions unfilled, percent
Basic science:				
Anatomy	1, 522	111	1, 633	6. 7
Biochemistry	1, 440	46	1, 486	3. 1
Microbiology	1, 224	83	1, 307	6. 4
Pathology	2, 456	159	2, 615	6. 1
Pharmacology	1, 194	88	1, 282	6. 9
Physiology	1, 359	72	1, 431	5. 0
Other basic sciences	861	49	910	5. 4
Subtotal	10, 056	608	10, 664	5. 7
Clinical science:				
Anesthesiology	1, 376	107	1, 483	7. 2
Dermatology	262	15	277	5. 4
Family medicine	550	108	658	16. 4
Medicine	6, 630	346	9, 976	5. 0
Neurology	1, 022	62	1, 084	5. 7
Obstetrics-gynecology	1, 305	118	1, 423	8. 3
Opthalmology	531	29	560	5. 2
Orthopedics	373	34	407	8. 3
Otolaryngology	430	28	458	6. 1
Pediatrics	2, 970	142	3, 112	4. 6
Physical medicine	459	29	488	5. 9
Psychiatry	3, 580	133	3, 713	3. 6
Public health and preventive medicine	1, 103	51	1, 154	4. 4
Radiology	2, 275	135	2, 410	5. 6
Surgery	2, 579	169	2, 748	6. 2
Urology	235	27	262	10. 3
Other clinical departments	600	31	631	4. 9
Subtotal	26, 280	1, 564	27, 844	5. 6
Total	36, 336	2, 172	38, 508	5. 6

[1] Arkansas and Cincinnati did not report faculty; Columbia University did not break-out total by ranks.

Source: Journal of the American Medical Association. Dec. 29, 1975, vol. 234, No. 13.

The medical student population can be characterized by the number of applicants, enrollment, student attrition, and utilization of student financial resources.

Applicants to medical schools totaled 42,624 for academic year 1974–75. The number of applicants accepted was 15,066 or 35 percent of the total number of applicants to medical schools. The number of students applying for admission into medical schools in the United States has increased 122 percent in the past 10 years. The number of applicants for the 1964–65 entering class was 19,168. The applicants/acceptance ratio has steadily increased since the 1960–61 academic year—from 1.7 in that year to 2.8 in 1974–75—indicating that the number of individuals applying to medical schools is growing at a faster rate than the number of individuals accepted for enrollment in medical schools.

Table 28 summarizes medical school application activities for the past 22 academic years.

TABLE 28.—*Summary of application activity during the past 22 years*

1st-year class	Applicants [1]	Total number of applications [1]	Applications per individual [1]	Accepted applicants [1]	Applicants/acceptance ratio [1]	1st-year enrollment
1953–54	14,678	48,586	3.3	7,756	1.9	7,449
1954–55	14,538	46,568	3.3	7,878	1.8	7,576
1955–56	14,937	54,161	3.6	7,969	1.9	7,686
1956–57	15,917	59,798	3.8	8,263	1.9	8,014
1957–58	15,791	60,951	3.9	8,302	1.9	8,030
1958–59	15,170	59,102	2.9	8,366	1.8	8,128
1959–60	14,952	57,888	2.9	8,512	1.8	8,173
1960–61	14,397	54,662	3.8	8,550	1.7	8,298
1961–62	14,381	53,834	3.7	8,682	1.7	8,483
1962–63	15,847	59,054	3.7	8,959	1.8	8,642
1963–64	17,668	70,063	4.0	9,063	1.9	8,772
1964–65	19,168	84,578	4.4	9,043	2.1	8,856
1965–66	18,703	87,111	4.7	9,012	2.1	8,759
1966–67	18,250	87,627	4.8	9,123	2.0	8,964
1967–68	18,724	93,332	5.0	9,702	1.9	9,479
1968–69	21,117	112,195	5.3	10,092	2.1	9,863
1969–70	24,465	134,557	5.5	10,514	2.3	10,401
1970–71	24,985	148,797	6.0	11,500	2.2	11,348
1971–72	29,172	210,943	7.2	12,335	2.4	12,361
1972–73	36,135	267,306	7.4	13,757	2.6	13,726
1973–74	40,506	328,275	8.1	14,335	2.8	14,185
1974–75	42,624	362,376	8.5	15,066	2.8	14,963

[1] From the study of applicants, Association of American Medical Colleges.

Source: Journal of the American Medical Association, Dec. 29, 1975, vol. 234, No. 13.

In 1930–31, there were 76 medical schools; by 1972–73, there were 112; today there are 114. Total enrollments grew from 21,982 in 1931–32 to 54,074 in 1974–75. The number of graduates increased from 4,735 to 12,714.

Table 29 presents data on the number of medical schools, students, and graduates, 1930–31 through 1974–75.

TABLE 29.—*Students and graduates in the medical and basic science schools, 1930–75*

Year	Number of schools [1]	Total en-rollment	1st year	Intermedi-ate years	Graduates
1930–31	76	21,982	6,456	10,791	4,735
1935–36	77	22,564	6,605	10,776	5,183
1940–41	77	21,379	5,837	10,267	5,275
1945–46	77	23,216	6,060	11,330	5,826
1950–51	79	26,186	7,177	12,874	6,135
1955–56	82	28,639	6,686	14,108	6,845
1956–57	85	29,130	8,014	14,320	6,796
1957–58	85	29,476	8,030	14,582	6,861
1958–59	85	28,614	8,128	14,626	6,860
1959–60	85	30,084	8,173	14,830	7,081
1960–61	86	30,288	8,298	14,996	6,994
1961–62	87	31,078	8,483	15,427	7,163
1962–63	87	31,491	8,642	15,595	7,264
1963–64	87	32,001	8,772	15,893	7,386
1964–65	88	32,428	8,856	16,163	7,409
1965–66	88	32,835	8,759	16,562	7,574
1966–67	89	33,423	8,964	16,716	7,743
1967–68	94	34,536	9,479	17,086	7,973
1968–69	99	35,833	9,863	17,911	8,059
1969–70	101	37,669	10,401	18,901	8,367
1970–71	103	40,487	11,348	20,165	8,974
1971–72	108	46,650	12,361	21,733	9,551
1972–73	112	47,546	13,726	23,429	10,391
1973–74	114	50,886	14,185	25,088	11,613
1974–75	114	54,074	14,963	26,397	12,714

[1] Prior to 1956–57, schools in development were not included.

Source: Journal of the American Medical Association Dec. 29, 1975, vol. 234, No. 13.

Table 30 outlines the number of new first-year students and number of M.D. graduates projected by 114 medical schools, spring 1975. The number of students accepted with advanced standing from other graduate programs or from foreign medical schools was not taken into account by these projections.

TABLE 30.—*Number of new first-year students and number of M.D. graduates projected by 114 medical schools (spring 1975)*

Year	1st-year class	M.D. graduates
1975–76	14,874	13,505
1976–77	15,262	13,818
1977–78	15,516	14,452
1978–79	15,821	14,849
1979–80	15,946	14,999

Source: Journal of the American Medical Association, Dec. 29, 1975, vol. 234, No. 13.

In 1974–75, 984 medical students (or 1.83 percent of total medical school enrollments) were not promoted with their class. This figure includes students who withdrew or were dismissed for academic reasons, those who withdrew to pursue advanced study, and those who withdrew or were dismissed for other reasons. When the 984 total is reduced by the number of students withdrawing to pursue advanced studies, the attrition drops to 1.50 percent.

The net attrition rate, which is defined as the percentage of students withdrawing entirely from the pursuit of an M.D. degree, is only 1.31 percent of the total enrollment for 1974–75. Academic reasons were given in less than half of these dropout cases.

Tables 31 and 32 present data on student attrition rates in medical schools for academic year 1974–75.

TABLE 31.—*Net attrition rate in medical schools, 1974–75* [1]

| Class year | Enroll-ment | Attrition [2] | |
		Number	Percent
1st	14, 870	314	2. 11
Intermediate	26, 216	337	1. 28
Final	12, 625	52	. 41
Total	53, 711	703	1. 31

[1] Does not include Medical College of Pennsylvania.
[2] Excluded are students who transferred to another medical school or who withdrew to pursue advanced studies.

Source: Journal of the American Medical Association. Dec. 29, 1975, Vol. 234, No. 13.

TABLE 32.—*Number of students who withdrew or were dismissed, 1974–75* [1]

| Class year | Total enroll-ment | Reason for withdrawal | | | Total with-drawals |
		Poor academic record	Ad-vanced study	Other	
1st	14, 870	133	2	199	334
Intermediate	26, 216	100	156	322	578
Final	12, 625	11	19	42	72
Total	53, 711	244	177	563	984

[1] Medical College of Pennsylvania, which did not report medical student attrition is not included.

Enrollments and graduations of minority students in U.S. medical schools have increased in recent years. In 1972–73, blacks, Mexican Americans, American Indians, and mainland Puerto Ricans comprised about 6.6 percent of total medical school enrollments. In 1974–75, the percentage increased to 8.1. First-year enrollments increased from 8 percent in 1972–73 to 8.8 percent in 1974–75. Graduates in these categories increased from 3.9 to 6.3 percent. . . .

In 1974–75, women represented almost 18.1 percent of total enrollments in medical schools, 37.5 percent of the first-year class, and 13.4 percent of the graduates. The number of women entering medical school represents a 360 percent increase over the number entering just four years ago. Table 35 summarizes application activities enrollments and graduations of women in U.S. medical schools for the past 35 years.

TABLE 35.—*Women in U.S. medical schools (selected years from 1939 to 1975)*

Academic year	Women applicants [1]		Women in entering class		Total women enrolled		Women graduates	
	Num-ber	Per-cent	Num-ber	Per-cent	Num-ber	Per-cent	Num-ber	Per-cent
1939–40	632	5. 4	[2] 296	5. 0	1, 145	5. 4	253	5. 0
1949–50	1, 390	5. 7	387	5. 5	1, 806	7. 2	595	10. 7
1959–60	1, 026	6. 9	494	6. 0	1, 710	5. 7	405	5. 7
1964–65	1, 731	9. 0	786	8. 9	2, 503	7. 7	503	6. 8
1969–70	2, 289	9. 4	952	9. 2	3, 390	9. 0	700	8. 4
1970–71	2, 734	10. 9	1, 256	11. 1	3, 894	9. 6	827	9. 2
1971–72	3, 737	12. 8	1, 693	13. 7	4, 755	10. 9	860	9. 0
1972–73	5, 480	15. 2	2, 315	16. 9	6, 099	12. 8	924	8. 9
1973–74	7, 202	17. 8	2, 743	19. 6	[3] 7, 731	[3] 15. 4	1, 264	11. 1
1974–75	8, 712	20. 4	3, 260	22. 3	9, 786	18. 1	1, 706	13. 4

[1] From the study of applicants, Association of American Medical Colleges.
[2] Potthoff, E. F.: "The Future Supply of Medical Students in the U.S." (table 1). 35:224, 1960.
[3] Harvard did not provide enrollment figures.

Source: Journal of the American Medical Association, Dec. 29, 1975. Vol. 234, No. 13.

During the 1974–75 academic year, an estimated 110 foreign students were enrolled in first-year classes in 45 U.S. medical schools. Table 36 outlines data on foreign students in U.S. medical schools, 1951 through 1975.

TABLE 36.—*Number of foreign students in U.S. medical schools*

Academic year	Number of foreign students	Number of U.S. medical schools accepting foreign students
1951–52 through 1962–63 (total)	1, 231	80
1st-year classes only:		
1963–64	108	43
1964–65	86	40
1965–66	123	38
1966–67	136	38
1967–68	151	48
1968–69	121	38
1969–70	170	40
1970–71	230	71
1971–72	239	67
1972–73	241	68
1973–74	217	72
1974–75	[1] 110	[1] 45

[1] Estimate.

Source: "Medical School Admissions Requirements, 1975–76," Association of American Medical College, 1974.

First-year expenses for medical students have increased considerably in recent years. In 1970–71, estimated first-year expenses for tuition and fees ranged from $1,068.50 to $2,620 at private medical schools. Tuition and fees at public schools ranged from $200 to $1,000 for residents and from $200 to $2,140 for nonresidents.

By 1975–76 the schools estimate that the same expenses will range from

$1,200–$4,000 in private schools. In public schools such expenses will range from $300–$3,500 for residents and from $570–$4,500 for nonresidents.

Tables 37 and 38 compare estimated minimum expenses for first-year students at U.S. medical schools for the academic years 1970–71 and 1975–76.

TABLE 37.—*School estimates of minimum expenses for 1st-year students, 1970–71*

| Item | Private schools (N=46) | | Public schools (N=56) | | | |
| | | | Resident | | Nonresident | |
	Range	Median	Range	Median	Range	Median
Tuition and fees [1]	$1, 068. 50–$2, 620	$2, 000	$200–$1, 000	$682. 80	$200–$2, 140	$1, 300
Room and board	900. 00– 3, 000	1, 350	810– 2, 400	1, 200. 00	810– 2, 400	1, 200
Books and supplies (not including microscopes)	100. 00– 400	250	100– 480	250. 00	100– 480	250

[1] 3 private schools cite a lower tuition for residents. Some schools have a higher tuition for upper years. Note that some schools have additional fees.

Source: "Medical School Admission Requirements, 1969–70." Association of American Medical Colleges, 1969.

TABLE 38.—*Estimated minimum expenses for 1st year students at U.S. medical schools (1975–76)*[1]

| 1st-year expense item | Private schools [2] | | | Public schools | | |
	Range	Median	Average	Range	Median	Average
Tuition and fees:						
Resident	} $1, 200–$4, 000	$3, 075	$3, 139	{ $300–$3, 500	$960	$1, 031
Nonresident				{ 570– 4, 500	2, 060	2, 129
Room and board (minimum)	1, 080– 3, 500	2, 000	2, 086	940– 4, 000	1, 800	1, 898
Books and supplies (not including microscope)	180– 700	315	344	150– 1, 100	350	370

[1] Figures based on data provided fall 1973 by 45 private schools and 69 public schools.
[2] 4 private schools—Baylor, Mayo, Pittsburgh, and Rush—report lower tuition fees for residents than for nonresidents. The higher fees for these schools are used in the table.

Source: "Medical School Admission Requirements, 1975–76, "Association of American Medical Colleges, 1974.

During 1972–73, 36.0 percent of students enrolled in U.S. medical schools received a loan, while 28.6 percent received some financial support from scholarships. The average value of a loan was $1,695. The average value of a scholarship was $1,440. The amount of funds expended for loans and scholarships to medical students in academic year 1974–1975 totaled $52,879,604.

TABLE 39.—*Scholarships and loans administered by U.S. medical schools, 1973–74 and 1974–75* [1]

| | 1973–74 | | 1974–75 | |
	Scholarships	Loans	Scholarships	Loans
Funds expended	$18, 927, 233	$29, 772, 970	$21, 321, 805	$31, 557, 799
Number of students	15, 059	19, 251	14, 806	18, 615
Average amount awarded	$1, 256	$1, 546	$1, 440	$1, 695
Percent of enrollment receiving awards	[2] 31. 0	[2] 39. 7	[2] 28. 6	[2] 36. 0

[1] Data provided by 109 schools each year.
[2] Represents percentage of enrollment of the 109 reporting schools.

Source: Journal of the American Medical Association, Dec. 29, 1975, vol. 234, No. 13.

In the 1974–75 academic year, funds administered by the schools for scholarships and loans increased over the previous year. The average value of the scholarships and of the loans increased, although the number of students benefiting decreased. In 1973–74, 31 percent of the students enrolled in 109 reporting schools received scholarship funds, and 39.7 percent received loans.

In the 1974–75 academic year these percentages were down, with 28.6 percent of the enrollment receiving scholarships and 36 percent of the enrollment receiving loans.

During the 1974–75 year, bank guaranteed loans represented the major source of student financial aid, other than that disbursed by the school. 13,627 students (enrolled in the 109 reporting schools) received $28.3 million from this source during that year. The Armed Forces Health Professions Scholarships (HPS) ranked as the second largest source of aid not disbursed by the school with 2,549 students (enrolled in the 109 reporting schools) receiving $14.5 million aid from that source. . . .

TABLE 46.—*Number of M.D. degree-granting accredited medical schools by amount of regular support for general operations*

Magnitude of general operating support	1972–73		1973–74	
	Number of schools	Percent	Number of schools	Percent
Under $2,000,000			2	2
Over $2,000,000 and under $4,000,000	7	8	9	9
Over $4,000,000 and under $6,000,000	13	15	12	12
Over $6,000,000 and under $8,000,000	14	16	13	13
Over $8,000,000 and under $10,000,000	16	18	15	14
Over $10,000,000 and under $15,000,000	21	23	25	25
$15,000,000 and over	18	20	25	25
Total	89	100	101	100
Support range:				
Minimum support	$2,753,992		$1,691,893	
Maximum support	25,275,709		24,929,904	
Median support	9,218,428		9,784,764	
Average support	10,182,922		11,081,006	

Source: Journal of the American Medical Association, Dec. 29, 1975, vol. 234, No. 13.

Table 47 summarizes data on expenditures by medical schools 1973–74. Schools reported total expenditures of $2,417,219,000.

TABLE 47.—*Summary of medical school financial support, 1973–74* [1]

	Colleges using source (number)	Amount (thousands)
Sources of sponsored support:		
1. Federal contracts and grants for teaching and training	104	$250, 181
2. Non-Federal contracts and grants for teaching and training	97	66, 525
3. Total of sponsored teaching and training contracts and grants (1 and 2)	104	(316, 706)
4. Federal contracts and grants for research	103	498, 310
5. State, city, and county contracts, gifts and grants for research	75	12, 725
6. Nongovernment contracts, gifts, and grants for research	102	107, 151
7. Endowment income restricted for research	37	6, 770
8. Total non-Federal support for sponsored research (5 through 7)	102	(126, 646)
9. Total support for sponsored and endowed research (4 plus 8)	104	(624, 956)
10. Other Federal sponsored multipurpose and service	86	95, 946
11. Other non-Federal sponsored multipurpose and service	83	232, 242
12. Total support for sponsored multipurpose and service (10 plus 11)	94	(328, 188)
13. Total sponsored support (3 plus 9 plus 12)	104	(1, 269, 850)
B. Sources of operating support:		
14. Tuition and fees	100	105, 878
15. Recovery of indirect costs on Federal contracts and grants	96	136, 960
16. Recovery of indirect costs on nonfederal contracts and grants	84	16, 937
17. Total indirect cost recovery on contracts and grants (15 plus 16)	96	(153, 897)
18. Endowment income	64	41, 249
19. Gifts	69	26, 474
20. State, city, and county grants-in-aid or subsidies to private schools or payments via interstate compacts such as WICHE	35	32, 408
21. State appropriations	66	449, 597
22. Professional fee (medical service plan) income	69	194, 414
23. Income from college services	62	63, 112
24. Other income	77	68, 835
25. Total miscellaneous income (23 plus 24)	90	(131, 947)
26. Total regular support	104	(1, 135, 864)
27. Funding of net excess of expenditures over revenues [2]	90	11, 505
28. Total operating support	104	(1, 147, 369)
29. Total support (13 plus 28)	104	(2, 417, 219)

[1] Data as reported by 104 fully accredited schools of medicine and basic medical sciences in response to the 1973–74 LCME Financial Questionnaire. The following fully accredited institutions did not return a completed questionnaire in time to be included in the JAMA report: 1973–74—Baylor, Harvard, Hawaii, Howard, and Medical College of Virginia.

[2] A combination of general university funds, principal, or funds functioning as endowment, prior-year balances and/or reserves.

D. Osteopathic Undergraduate Education

There were 1,032 first-year students in the colleges of osteopathic medicine in 1975. The 1975–76 enrollment in the nine osteopathic colleges reached 3,439. Of that number, 363 were women students. In 1975, osteopathic colleges graduated 695 doctors, 45, of which, were women. Based on the current enrollment in the nine osteopathic colleges, the projected number of graduates for 1976 is 827. Tables 48 through 50 present data on undergraduate osteopathic education.

Table 48.—*Enrollment, 1975–76*

	1st year students	2d year students	3d year students	4th year students	Total
Total	1,032	959	878	570	3,439

Source: Department of Educational Services, American Association of Colleges of Osteopathic Medicine, 1976.

Table 49.—*Enrollment, 1975–76*

College	Total enrollment		
	Men	Women	Total
Chicago College of Osteopathic Medicine	349	31	380
College of Osteopathic Medicine and Surgery [1]	478	44	522
Kansas City College of Osteopathic Medicine	533	46	579
Kirksville College of Osteopathic Medicine	438	55	493
Michigan State University College of Osteopathic Medicine [1]	194	70	264
Oklahoma College of Osteopathic Medicine and Surgery [1]	85	7	92
Philadelphia College of Osteopathic Medicine	713	85	798
Texas College of Osteopathic Medicine	217	17	234
West Virginia School of Osteopathic Medicine	69	8	77
Grand total	3,076	363	3,439

[1] Denotes 3-year academic program.

Source: Department of Educational Services, American Association of Colleges of Osteopathic Medicine, 1976.

Table 50.—*Size of graduating classes, 1975*

College	Graduates		
	Men	Women	Total
Chicago College of Osteopathic Medicine	82	3	85
College of Osteopathic Medicine and Surgery [1]	133	11	144
Kansas City College of Osteopathic Medicine	113	5	118
Kirksville College of Osteopathic Medicine	95	7	102
Michigan State University College of Osteopathic Medicine [1]	53	12	65
Oklahoma College of Osteopathic Medicine and Surgery [1]			
Philadelphia College of Osteopathic Medicine	150	6	156
Texas College of Osteopathic Medicine	24	1	25
West Virginia School of Osteopathic Medicine			
Grand total	650	45	695

[1] Denotes 3-year academic program.

Source: Department of Educational Services, American Association of Colleges of Osteopathic Medicine, 1976.

E. Graduate Medical Education

For academic year 1973–74, the number of hospitals offering internships decreased from the prior year as did the number of positions offered and filled.

The drop in the number of intership positions offered represented the second consecutive year of decline for those figures. The percentage of positions filled in 1973–74 increased, but the number of positions filled declined over 1972–73. The number of positions offered declined by 1,485 as compared with 1972–73; the number of positions filled declined by 132.

Tables 51 through 57 present data on internship programs—including the number of internships, number of internships by medical school affiliation and bed capacity, and salaries offered interns.

TABLE 51.—*Number of internships, 1964–73*

	Number of hospitals	Number of internship positions offered	Number of internship positions filled	Percentage of positions filled
1964–65	757	12,728	10,097	79
1965–66	772	12,954	9,670	75
1966–67	816	13,569	10,366	76
1967–68	853	13,761	10,419	76
1968–69	821	14,112	10,464	75
1969–70	900	15,003	10,808	72
1970–71	896	15,354	11,552	75
1971–72	797	15,422	12,066	78
1972–73	883	13,650	11,163	82
1973–74	741	12,165	11,031	91

Source: "Directory of Approved Internships and Residencies, 1974–75." AMA, 1975.

TABLE 52.—*Types of internship programs offered, 1964–73*

Academic Year	Types of programs								Total
	Rotating—no major emphasis		Rotating with Emphasis on a specialty [1]		Straight		Family and general practice		
	Number	Percent	Number	Percent	Number	Percent	Number	Percent	
1964–65	658	50	189	14	467	35	14	1	1,328
1965–66	641	45	251	17	531	37	17.	1	1,440
1966–67	568	24	1,211	51	582	24	17	5	2,378
1967–68	563	20	1,502	54	687	25	16		2,768
1968–69	581	21	1,504	54	703	25			2,788
1969–70	504	17	1,675	57	714	25	29	1	2,922
1970–71	523	17	1,665	53	963	30			3,151
1971–72	499	15	1,737	53	1,018	31			3,254
1972–73	459	15	1,562	54	892	31			2,912
1973–74	421	19	948	43	835	38			2,204

[1] Listed in tables previous to 1966–67 as "mixed" internships.

Source: "Directory of Approved Internships and Residencies, 1974–75," AMA, 1975.

TABLE 53.—*Number of internships by medical school affiliation and bed capacity*

Classification	Number of hospitals	Number of approved programs	Number of internships				Number of interns on duty			
			Total positions offered Sept. 1, 1973	Total positions filled Sept. 1, 1973	Positions vacant Sept. 1, 1973	Percentage filled	Graduates, United States, Canada Sept. 1, 1973	Foreign graduates Sept. 1, 1973	Percentage foreign graduates in filled positions	Total flexible positions offered, 1975-76
Affiliated:										
Combined hospitals	86	239	2,052	1,964	88	96	1,729	235	12	283
Less than 200 beds	47	109	625	547	78	88	459	88	16	146
200 to 299	50	79	420	373	47	89	180	193	52	94
300 to 499	206	1,172	2,632	2,322	310	88	1,481	841	36	606
500 over	228	845	4,760	4,363	397	92	3,377	986	23	1,033
Total	617	1,858	10,489	9,569	920	91	7,226	2,343	24	2,162
Nonaffiliated:										
Combined hospitals	4	12	89	83	6	93	41	42	51	23
Less than 200 beds	8	20	130	123	7	95	16	107	87	---
200 to 299	35	74	329	282	44	87	20	262	93	78
300 to 499	60	310	772	658	114	85	145	513	78	177
500 over	17	85	359	316	43	88	158	158	50	93
Total	124	346	1,676	1,462	214	87	380	1,082	74	371
Grand total	741	2,204	12,165	11,031	1,134	91	7,606	3,425	31	2,533

Source: "Directory of Approved Internships and Residencies, 1974-75," AMA, 1975.

TABLE 54.—*Annual salaries offered interns* [1]

Annual salary offered	Programs in affiliated hospitals	Programs in nonaffiliated hospitals	Total programs
$5,001 to $5,500	7		7
$6,001 to $6,500	1		1
$6,501 to $7,000	56	4	60
$7,001 to $7,500	39	2	41
$7,501 to $8,000	65	25	90
$8,001 to $8,500	124	59	183
$8,501 to $9,000	272	46	318
$9,001 to $9,500	331	47	378
$9,501 to $10,000	502	103	605
$10,001 to $10,500	312	51	363
$10,501 to $11,000	218	71	289
$11,001 to $11,500	72	9	81
$11,501 to $12,000	39	14	53
$12,001 to $12,500	95	27	122
$12,501 to $13,000	34	20	54
$13,001 to $13,500	7		7
$13,501 to $14,000	13	11	24
$14,001 to $14,500	1	13	14
$14,501 to $15,000	6		6
Over $15,000			
Total programs reporting	2,194	502	2,696
Data not available	187	30	217
Total programs	2,381	532	2,913
Mean—Annual salary	$9,827	$10,140	$9,886
Median—Annual salary	9,501–10,000	9,501–10,000	9,501–10,000
Mode—Annual salary	9,501–10,000	9,501–10,000	9,501–10,000

[1] Data collected prior to July 1, 1973. Data on internship salaries not collected in 1974.
Source: "Directory of Approved Internship and Residencies, 1973–74." AMA, 1973.

Tables 55 through 57 show number of residencies by specialty, number of residencies by medical school affiliation and bed capacity, and annual salaries offered residents.

TABLE 55.—*Number of residencies, by specialty*

Specialty	Number of residency positions					Number of residents on duty			Total residency positions offered 1975-76
	Number of approved programs	Total positions offered Sept. 1, 1973	Total positions filled Sept. 1, 1973	Positions vacant Sept. 1, 1973	Per-centage filled	Graduates United States, Canada Sept. 1, 1973	Foreign graduates Sept. 1, 1973	Percentage foreign graduates in filled positions	
Anesthesiology	170	2,211	2,008	203	91	896	1,112	55	2,624
Child psychiatry	138	754	588	166	78	429	159	27	800
Diagnostic radiology	175	2,147	2,009	138	94	1,766	243	12	2,292
Dermatology	92	713	688	25	96	628	60	9	766
Family practice	206	2,412	1,765	647	73	1,606	159	9	3,832
General practice	51	343	260	83	76	53	207	80	527
Surgery	482	7,616	7,131	485	94	4,600	2,531	35	9,121
Internal medicine	433	9,816	9,427	389	96	6,601	2,826	30	14,709
Neurological surgery	100	641	609	32	95	490	119	20	643
Neurology	117	1,088	981	107	90	716	265	27	1,227
Nuclear medicine	26	46	41	5	89	22	19	46	83
Obstetrics and gynecology	347	3,413	3,183	230	93	2,044	1,139	36	3,988
Opthalmology	177	1,515	1,500	15	99	1,385	115	8	1,577
Orthopedic surgery	207	2,353	2,268	85	96	2,037	231	10	2,568
Otolaryngology	113	1,033	995	38	96	835	160	16	1,071
Pathology	502	3,509	2,846	663	81	1,327	1,519	53	3,753
Forensic pathology	30	54	31	23	57	24	7	23	68
Neuropathology	29	78	57	21	73	39	18	32	74
Pediatrics	274	4,409	4,231	178	96	2,848	1,383	33	5,180
Pediatric allergy	46	110	99	11	90	75	24	24	131
Pediatric cardiology	56	152	120	32	79	73	47	39	159
Physical medicine	69	478	368	110	77	152	216	59	546
Plastic surgery	117	391	359	32	92	281	78	22	435
Do	1	3	3	---	100	2	1	33	3
Colon and rectal surgery	20	33	30	3	91	18	12	40	39
Psychiatry	270	4,992	4,315	677	86	3,008	1,307	30	5,413
Radiology	211	1,415	1,205	210	85	755	450	37	1,617
Therapeutic radiology	97	480	348	132	73	206	142	41	526
Thoracic surgery	96	314	282	32	90	169	113	40	321
Urology	188	1,169	1,122	47	96	876	246	22	1,264
Total	4,840	53,688	48,869	4,819	91	33,961	14,908	31	65,357
Other than hospitals:									
General preventive medicine	4	63	44	19	70	42	2	5	4
Aerospace medicine	28	214	122	92	57	116	6	5	28
Occupational medicine (academic)	4	23	4	15	35	5	3	38	4
Occupational medicine (in-plant)	19	26	4	22	15	4	0	-----	19
Public health	23	123	35	88	28	31	4	11	23
Totals—Other than hospitals	78	449	209	236	47	198	15	7	78
Grand total	4,918	54,137	49,078	5,055	91	34,159	14,923	30	65,435

Source: "Directory of Approved Internships and Residencies, 1974-75." AMA, 1975.

TABLE 56.—*Number of residencies, by medical school affiliates and bed capacity*

Classification	Number of hospitals	Number of approved programs	Number of residencies				Number of residents on duty			
			Total positions offered, Sept. 1, 1973	Total positions filled, Sept. 1, 1973	Positions vacant, Sept. 1, 1973	Percentage filled	Graduates United States, Canada, Sept. 1, 1973	Foreign graduates Sept. 1, 1973	Percentage foreign graduates in filled positions	Total residency positions offered, 1975-76
Affiliated:										
Combined hospitals	161	1,202	19,645	18,524	1,121	94	14,824	3,700	20	23,150
Less than 200 beds	217	250	2,704	2,402	302	89	1,842	560	23	3,099
200-299	109	187	1,378	1,229	149	89	878	351	29	1,746
300 to 499	304	971	7,693	6,760	933	88	4,216	2,544	38	9,800
500 or over	309	1,600	17,283	15,764	1,519	91	10,470	5,294	34	21,223
Totals	1,100	4,210	48,703	44,679	4,024	92	32,230	12,449	28	59,018
Nonaffiliated:										
Combined hospitals	28	49	634	581	53	92	308	273	47	858
Less than 200 beds	184	135	931	723	208	336	325	398	55	1,092
200 to 299	79	79	480	379	101	79	85	294	78	673
300 to 499	109	211	1,382	1,175	207	85	422	753	64	1,914
500 or over	77	156	1,558	1,332	226	85	591	741	56	1,802
Totals	477	630	4,985	4,190	795	84	1,731	2,459	59	6,339
Grand totals	1,577	4,840	53,688	48,869	4,819	91	33,961	14,908	31	65,357

Source: "Directory of Approved Internships and Residencies, 1974–75." AMA, 1975.

TABLE 57.—*Annual salaries offered residents*

Annual salary offered	Programs in affiliated hospitals	Programs in nonaffiliated hospitals	Total programs
0 to $3,500	1		1
$5,501 to $6,000	2	2	4
$6,501 to $7,000	10		10
$7,001 to $7,500	7	1	8
$7,501 to $8,000	14	1	15
$8,001 to $8,500	30	8	38
$8,501 to $9,000	84	13	97
$9,001 to $9,500	197	15	212
$9,501 to $10,000	374	39	413
$10,001 to $10,500	424	68	492
$10,501 to $11,000	436	70	506
$11,001 to $11,500	356	26	382
$11,501 to $12,000	323	38	361
$12,001 to $12,500	123	12	135
$12,501 to $13,000	70	25	95
$13,001 to $13,500	112	69	181
$13,501 to $14,000	66	6	72
$14,001 to $14,500	33	19	52
$14,501 to $15,000	132	41	173
$15,001 to $15,500	48	10	58
$15,501 to $16,000	16	7	23
$16,001 to $16,500	19	1	20
$16,501 to $17,000	16	1	17
$17,001 to $17,500	6	2	8
$17,501 to $18,000	1	2	3
$18,001 to $18,500		1	1
$18,501 to $19,000	3	3	6
$19,501 to $20,000	1		1
Over $20,000		4	4
Total programs reporting	2,904	484	3,388
Data not available	1,306	146	1,452
Total programs	4,210	630	4,840
Mean annual salary	$11,249	$12,015	$11,359
Median annual salary	$10,501–$11,000	$11,001–$11,500	$10,501–$11,000
Mode annual salary	$10,501–$11,000	$10,501–$11,000	$10,501–$11,000

NOTE: Data collected prior to July 1, 1974.

Source: "Directory of Approved Internships and Residences 1974–75." AMA, 1975.

N6

TABLE 67.—*Male and female graduates as of June 30, 1974*

	Men	Percent of total class	Women	Percent of total class	Total class
Graduates of medical schools in:					
United States	10,101	88.9	1,264	11.1	11,365
Canada	1,253	80.2	309	19.8	1,562
Total graduates	11,354	87.8	1,573	12.2	12,927

Source: Journal of the American Medical Association, Dec. 29, 1975, vol. 234, No. 13.

N7

TABLE 72.—*Physicians certified by specialty boards, as of Dec. 31, 1974* [1]

	Graduates			Total certified	Percent foreign
	U.S. schools	Canadian schools	Foreign schools		
American Board of—					
Allergy and Immunology	944	11	100	1, 055	9. 5
Anesthesiology	4, 753	178	1, 289	6, 220	20. 7
Colon and Rectal Surgery	344	16	57	417	13. 7
Dermatology	2, 867	55	202	3, 121	6. 5
Family Practice	5, 618	78	380	[2] 7, 018	5. 1
Internal Medicine	27, 404	330	2, 282	[3] 30, 016	7. 6
Neurological Surgery	1, 430	51	154	1, 635	9. 4
Nuclear Medicine	1, 310	32	247	1, 589	15. 5
Obstetrics Gynecology	11, 106	234	1, 143	12, 483	9. 1
Ophthalmology	6, 766	156	441	7, 363	5. 9
Orthopaedic Surgery	7, 327	188	529	8, 044	6. 6
Otolaryngology	4, 508	127	376	5, 011	7. 5
Pathology	6, 236	209	2, 091	8, 586	24. 5
Pediatrics	12, 441	236	2, 297	14, 976	15. 3
Physical Medicine and Rehabilitation	643	19	256	918	27. 9
Plastic Surgery	1, 132	29	122	1, 283	9. 5
Preventive Medicine	2, 231	51	104	2, 386	4. 3
Psychiatry and Neurology	9, 779	350	1, 486	11, 615	12. 8
Radiology	10, 081	197	1, 270	11, 498	11. 0
Surgery	16, 332	298	1, 863	18, 493	10. 1
Thoracic Surgery	2, 318	46	378	2, 742	13. 8
Urology	3, 703	66	318	4, 087	7. 8
Total	139, 223	2, 959	17, 365	160, 509	10. 8

[1] Compiled from the physicians records of the American Medical Association, and prepared by the department of graduate medical education.
[2] Includes net increase of 1,288 by end of 1974 on certifications not reported until 1975.
[3] Includes net increase of 2,797 by end of 1974 on certifications not reported until 1975.

Source: Journal of the American Medical Association, Dec. 29, 1975, Vol. 234, No. 13.

NURSING PROFESSIONS ([34], pp. 186-190, 193-194, 198)

A. DATA ON REGISTERED NURSES

TABLE 73.—*Registered nurses in relation to population, selected years, 1960–74*

Year [1]	Resident population (thousands) [1]	Number of nurses in practice Total	Number of nurses in practice Full time	Number of nurses in practice Part time	Nurses per 100,000 population
1974 [2]	210, 674	857, 000	608, 000	249, 000	407
1973 [3]	209, 118	815, 000	578, 000	237, 000	390
1972 [3]	207, 364	780, 000	548, 000	232, 000	376
1971 [3]	205, 056	750, 000	534, 000	216, 000	366
1970 [3]	202, 617	722, 000	519, 000	203, 000	356
1969 [3]	200, 985	694, 000	503, 000	191, 000	345
1968 [3]	199, 017	667, 000	489, 000	178, 000	335
1967 [3]	196, 858	643, 000	476, 000	167, 900	327
1966	194, 899	621, 000	466, 000	155, 000	319
1964	190, 169	582, 000	450, 000	132, 000	306
1962	184, 598	550, 000	433, 000	117, 000	298
1960	178, 729	504, 000	414, 000	90, 000	282

[1] As of Jan. 1.
[2] Preliminary.
[3] Revised estimates.

Sources: Interagency Conference on Nursing Statistics. U.S. Bureau of the Census, Population estimates, "Current Population Reports," Series P-25, No. 525. Also, prior reports.

TABLE 74.—*Estimated number of employed registered nurses, by educational preparation, selected years 1964–74, and projected need 1980*

Year	Total	Diploma Number	Diploma Percent	Associate degree Number	Associate degree Percent	Baccalaureate Number	Baccalaureate Percent	Master's or above Number	Master's or above Percent
1980 need	1, 100, 000	660, 000	60. 0	([1])	([1])	308, 000	28. 0	132, 000	12. 0
1974	857, 000	647, 000	75. 5	51, 600	6. 0	130, 400	15. 2	28, 000	3. 3
1973	815, 000	627, 500	77. 0	43, 200	5. 3	118, 200	14. 5	26, 100	3. 2
1972	780, 000	613, 400	78. 6	35, 200	4. 5	107, 200	13. 8	24, 200	3. 1
1971	750, 000	603, 100	80. 4	27, 800	3. 7	96, 600	12. 9	22, 500	3. 0
1970 [2]	722, 000	593, 400	82. 2	21, 400	3. 0	87, 000	12. 0	20, 300	2. 8
1969 [2]	694, 000	579, 900	83. 6	17, 000	2. 4	78, 400	11. 3	18, 700	2. 7
1968 [2]	667, 000	566, 000	84. 9	12, 000	1. 8	72, 000	10. 8	17, 000	2. 5
1967 [2]	643, 000	548, 700	85. 3	10, 000	1. 6	68, 200	10. 6	16, 100	2. 5
1966	621, 000	533, 200	85. 8	8, 000	1. 3	64, 500	10. 4	15, 300	2. 5
1964	582, 000	516, 600	88. 8	([1])	([1])	52, 100	8. 9	13, 300	2. 3

[1] For 1980 and 1964 nurses with associate degrees as their highest educational preparation are included with diploma.
[2] Estimates revised 1974.

Source: U.S. Department of Health, Education, and Welfare, Public Health Service, Division of Nursing, Source Book of Nursing Personnel, DHEW Publication No. (HRA) 75-43, revised 1974, p. 69; Interagency Conference on Nursing Statistics for total estimates, 1964-74.

TABLE 75.—*Educational preparation of registered nurses in various fields of employment—1970 (includes 50 States and District of Columbia)*

Field of employment	Total	Master's or doctoral degree	Bacca-laureate	Associate degree	Nursing diploma
NUMBER					
Total	700, 000	19, 000	80, 000	22, 000	579, 000
Hospitals	446, 000	3, 800	40, 000	14, 000	388, 200
Nursing homes	40, 000	500	3, 500	3, 100	32, 900
Public health and school	51, 000	3, 100	17, 500	400	30, 000
Nursing education	31, 000	11, 000	13, 000	300	6, 700
Occupational health	20, 000	200	1, 400	500	17, 900
Private duty, office nurse, and other	112, 000	400	4, 600	3, 700	103, 300
PERCENT					
Total	100. 0	2. 7	11. 4	3. 2	82. 7
Hospitals	100. 0	. 9	9. 0	3. 1	87. 0
Nursing homes	100. 0	1. 2	8. 8	7. 8	82. 2
Public health and school	100. 0	6. 1	34. 3	. 8	58. 8
Nursing education	100. 0	35. 5	41. 9	1. 0	21. 6
Occupational health	100. 0	1. 0	7. 0	2. 5	89. 5
Private duty, office nurse, and other	100. 0	. 4	4. 1	3. 3	92. 2

Source: Total numbers and field of employment estimated by Interagency Conference on Nursing Statistics; educational preparation by Division of Nursing, U.S. Department of Health, Education, and Welfare, Public Health Service, Bureau of Health, Manpower, Education.

TABLE 76.—*Field of employment of registered nurses, Jan. 1, 1972*

Field of employment	Number of nurses	Percent of total
Total	[1] 748, 000	100. 0
Hospitals and nursing homes	526, 000	70. 3
Public health and school	54, 000	7. 2
Nursing education	35, 000	4. 7
Occupational health	20, 000	2. 7
Private duty, doctor's office, and other fields	113, 000	15. 1

[1] Preliminary estimate.

Source: Division of Nursing, Bureau of Health Manpower Education, National Institutes of Health. In: "Health Resources Statistics, 1972–73." DHEW, 1973.

TABLE 77.—*Location of full-time registered nurses employed in hospitals in relation to hospital beds, 1973*

Location	Hospital beds	Registered nurses (full time)	Registered nurses per 1,000 beds
United States	1, 449, 062	379, 749	262
Alabama	24, 937	5, 021	201
Alaska	1, 608	537	334
Arizona	10, 891	4, 342	399
Arkansas	11, 875	2, 462	207
California	111, 887	38, 316	342
Colorado	15, 004	4, 967	331
Connecticut	19, 147	5, 644	295
Delaware	4, 315	1, 119	259
District of Columbia	11, 666	3, 109	267
Florida	50, 629	14, 324	283
Georgia	33, 188	7, 046	212
Hawaii	4, 519	1, 678	371
Idaho	3, 718	1, 064	286
Illinois	75, 883	22, 073	291
Indiana	33, 140	7, 268	219
Iowa	19, 986	4, 999	250
Kansas	17, 201	3, 899	227
Kentucky	20, 087	4, 804	239
Louisiana	25, 327	5, 017	198
Maine	7, 350	1, 888	257
Maryland	26, 166	6, 835	261
Massachusetts	51, 344	15, 805	308
Michigan	53, 916	14, 569	270
Minnesota	29, 613	7, 699	260
Mississippi	17, 838	2, 795	157
Missouri	36, 453	8, 183	224
Montana	5, 707	1, 186	208
Nebraska	11, 301	2, 972	263
Nevada	3, 256	934	287
New Hampshire	5, 604	1, 319	235
New Jersey	49, 012	12, 268	250
New Mexico	6, 225	1, 630	262
New York	158, 600	45, 288	286
North Carolina	32, 974	8, 420	255
North Dakota	5, 501	1, 264	230
Ohio	70, 900	17, 516	247
Oklahoma	17, 141	3, 379	197
Oregon	12, 114	4, 028	333
Pennsylvania	97, 827	26, 504	271
Rhode Island	7, 997	1, 922	240
South Carolina	18, 885	3, 570	189
South Dakota	6, 315	1, 400	222
Tennessee	30, 975	6, 192	200
Texas	75, 886	16, 855	222
Utah	4, 811	1, 475	307
Vermont	3, 613	1, 012	280
Virginia	33, 522	7, 973	238
Washington	17, 554	6, 035	344
West Virginia	16, 424	3, 286	200
Wisconsin	36, 444	7, 251	199
Wyoming	2, 786	607	218

Source: Unpublished data from the National Center for Health Statistics master facility census.

TABLE 78.—*Location of full-time registered nurses in nursing and related homes, 1973*

Location	Beds in nursing and related homes	Registered nurses	Registered nurses per 1,000 beds
United States	1, 327, 704	41, 181	31
Alabama	14, 844	298	20
Alaska	606	40	66
Arizona	6, 430	299	47
Arkansas	17, 952	301	17
California	150, 956	4, 400	29
Colorado	16, 670	725	44
Connecticut	23, 294	1, 336	57
Delaware	2, 213	107	48
District of Columbia	3, 147	91	29
Florida	34, 956	1, 372	39
Georgia	25, 936	573	22
Hawaii	2, 726	157	58
Idaho	4, 190	153	37
Illinois	80, 151	2, 046	25
Indiana	34, 247	955	28
Iowa	35, 152	709	20
Kansas	22, 889	407	18
Kentucky	18, 177	308	17
Louisiana	17, 004	340	20
Maine	9, 227	319	35
Maryland	17, 755	367	37
Massachusetts	53, 858	2, 327	42
Michigan	48, 567	1, 373	28
Minnesota	44, 661	1, 178	27
Mississippi	7, 886	196	25
Missouri	33, 644	736	22
Montana	4, 759	209	44
Nebraska	17, 396	338	20
Nevada	1, 482	75	51
New Hampshire	5, 873	350	60
New Jersey	34, 430	1, 822	53
New Mexico	3, 345	96	30
New York	92, 888	4, 697	51
North Carolina	22, 145	564	25
North Dakota	6, 631	178	27
Ohio	65, 134	1, 879	29
Oklahoma	29, 512	427	15
Oregon	18, 306	587	32
Pennsylvania	65, 963	3, 156	48
Rhode Island	6, 493	232	36
South Carolina	8, 131	289	36
South Dakota	7, 795	203	26
Tennessee	14, 827	251	17
Texas	80, 510	957	12
Utah	4, 556	103	23
Vermont	3, 902	228	58
Virginia	16, 732	493	30
Washington	31, 147	1, 143	37
West Virginia	4, 753	151	31
Wisconsin	51, 960	1, 304	25
Wyoming	1, 896	66	35

Source: National Center for Health Statistics, Division of Health Manpower and Facilities Statistics, data collected in the 1973 master facility inventory survey of inpatient health facilities.

B. Data on Practical Nurses

TABLE 81.—*Practical nurses in relation to population, selected years, 1950–74*

Year [1]	Resident population in thousands	Number of nurses in practice		Nurses per 100,000 population
		Total	In AHA registered hospitals	
1974	210, 674	492, 000	------------	234
1973	209, 118	459, 000	------------	219
1972	207, 361	427, 000	237, 346	195
1971	205, 050	400, 000	------------	182
1970	203, 145	370, 000	221, 935	172
1968	199, 017	320, 000	185, 391	161
1966	194, 899	282, 000	151, 000	145
1964	190, 169	250, 000	128, 800	131
1962	184, 598	225, 000	126, 825	122
1960	179, 323	206, 000	------------	115
1950	151, 326	137, 500	49, 800	91

[1] As of Jan. 1.

Source: U.S. Public Health Service, Division of Nursing's estimates of practical nurses employed 1962, U.S. Bureau of the Census data for 1950 and 1960. U.S. Bureau of the Census, population estimates, "Current Population Reports." Series P–25, No. 525. Also, prior reports.

TABLE 82.—*Location of licensed practical nurses according to activity status and ratio to population: 1967*

Location	Number of nurses					Employed nurses per 100,000 popula- tion (ad- justed)
	Total	Employed in nursing	Not employed in nursing	Activity status not reported	Employed in nursing (adjusted) [1]	
United States	343,635	252,522	69,189	21,924	269,523	135
Alabama	5,271	4,263	805	203	4,437	125
Alaska	285	198	86	1	199	73
Arizona	2,221	1,709	478	34	1,737	104
Arkansas	4,128	3,360	664	104	3,448	176
California	26,203	18,479	5,626	2,098	20,091	103
Colorado	4,510	3,657	809	44	3,696	181
Connecticut	4,386	3,549	683	154	3,677	125
Delaware	803	640	149	14	650	125
District of Columbia	2,431	2,090	259	82	2,162	267
Florida	11,625	8,753	1,674	1,198	9,747	158
Georgia	4,987	3,801	1,046	140	3,912	88
Hawaii	1,588	1,203	244	141	1,319	176
Idaho	1,957	1,439	510	8	1,445	205
Illinois	14,571	11,150	2,231	1,190	12,146	111
Indiana	3,885	2,997	620	268	3,222	64
Iowa	3,335	2,373	876	86	2,440	87
Kansas	2,422	1,801	503	118	1,897	83
Kentucky	3,621	2,787	666	168	2,924	92
Louisiana	6,322	5,032	1,248	42	5,067	138
Maine	1,037	655	327	55	691	70
Maryland	3,990	3,025	912	53	3,005	82
Massachusetts	16,633	9,532	3,176	3,925	12,409	228
Michigan	16,122	10,781	3,778	1,563	11,948	140
Minnesota	6,226	4,964	1,158	104	5,053	139
Mississippi	3,579	2,912	533	134	3,029	130
Missouri	7,901	6,490	1,032	379	6,819	149
Montana	812	587	221	4	591	82
Nebraska	1,528	1,144	348	36	1,172	79
Nevada	802	544	246	12	552	116
New Hampshire	1,436	932	388	116	1,011	151
New Jersey	11,086	7,464	2,776	846	8,081	115
New Mexico	1,515	1,116	307	92	1,188	112
New York	34,850	24,961	9,436	453	25,293	139
North Carolina	6,593	5,229	1,153	211	5,407	108
North Dakota	766	603	160	3	606	94
Ohio	18,368	14,683	3,307	378	14,998	141
Oklahoma	4,195	2,973	713	509	3,387	136
Oregon	3,001	2,164	818	19	2,179	109
Pennsylvania	31,747	23,940	6,878	929	24,652	210
Rhode Island	2,153	1,585	505	63	1,632	181
South Carolina	2,676	2,183	428	65	2,239	85
South Dakota	817	614	159	44	651	92
Tennessee	6,969	5,669	1,155	145	5,793	149
Texas	30,814	20,237	5,270	5,307	24,440	222
Utah	1,551	1,191	339	21	1,207	116
Vermont	1,279	935	316	28	956	236
Virginia	5,859	4,808	959	92	4,884	107
Washington	7,014	4,757	2,143	114	4,835	155
West Virginia	2,821	2,317	406	98	2,402	136
Wisconsin	4,570	3,969	573	28	3,996	94
Wyoming	374	277	92	5	281	80

[1] Adjusted for activity status not reported.

Sources: Marshall, E., and Moses, E.: "L.P.N.'s 1967: An Inventory of Licensed Practical Nurses." Division of Nursing, Bureau of Health Manpower Education, Public Health Service. U.S. Department of Health, Education, and Welfare. Washington, U.S. Government Printing Office, January 1971. In: "Health Resources Statistics, 1972–73." DHEW, 1973.

TABLE 86.—*Programs of practical nurse training and number of admissions and graduates, selected years, 1961–62 through 1973–74*

Academic year [1]	Approved programs [2]	Admissions	Graduates
1973–74	1, 314	60, 249	45, 863
1972–73	1, 306	60, 475	46, 456
1971–72	1, 310	61, 680	44, 446
1970–71	1, 291	60, 057	38, 556
1969–70	1, 253	55, 635	37, 128
1968–69	1, 252	49, 107	34, 864
1967–68	1, 191	45, 076	30, 833
1966–67	1, 149	41, 269	27, 644
1965–66	1, 081	38, 755	25, 688
1964–65	984	36, 489	24, 331
1963–64	913	34, 131	22, 761
1961–62	739	26, 660	18, 106

[1] Includes American Samoa and the Virgin Islands for 1961–62 and succeeding years. Includes Puerto Rico for all years.

[2] Number of programs is as of Oct. 15; admissions and graduates are based on academic year and include those in programs that closed during the year.

Sources: American Nurses' Association: "Facts about Nursing: A Statistical Summary." New York, 1969. Also, prior issues. National League for Nursing: "State-Approved Schools of Nursing—L.P.N./L.V.N." New York, 1975. Also, prior issues.

DENTAL MANPOWER ([34], pp. 201–202)

TABLE 89.—*Dentists in relation to population, selected years, Dec. 31, 1950, through 1973*

	1950	1960	1970	1973
Active civilian dentists	75, 310	84, 500	95, 680	100, 780
Resident civilian population (thousands)	151, 240	179, 740	203, 110	208, 094
Active civilian dentists per 100,000 civilians	49. 8	47. 0	47. 1	48

[1] State figures do not add to total due to rounding. Civilian populations as of July 1, 1973.

Sources: Division of Dentistry, Bureau of Health Manpower, Health Resources Administration, Department of Health, Education, and Welfare. U.S. Bureau of the Census: Population Estimates: "Current Population Reports," Series P–25, No. 508, November 1973.

TABLE 90.—*Distribution of dentists by State, region, and Federal dental service, 1972*

Region and State	Total number of dentists, 1972	Population per dentist	Number of 1972 graduates	Estimated population
New England	7, 633	1, 584	170	12, 093, 100
Connecticut	2, 060	1, 505	24	3, 101, 000
Maine	469	2, 147	3	1, 006, 800
Massachusetts	4, 005	1, 445	122	5, 786, 000
New Hampshire	384	2, 010	5	771, 900
Rhode Island	484	1, 992	8	964, 000
Vermont	231	2, 006	8	463, 400
Mideast	29, 494	1, 519	636	44, 808, 400
Delaware	255	2, 204	9	562, 000
District of Columbia	646	1, 137	15	734, 600
Maryland	2, 039	1, 978	83	4, 032, 300
New Jersey	4, 488	1, 638	78	7, 353, 700
New York	14, 735	1, 252	284	18, 452, 200
Pennsylvania	6, 656	1, 791	148	11, 918, 600
West Virginia	675	2, 600	19	1, 755, 000
Southeast	17, 577	2, 452	436	43, 091, 300
Alabama	1, 173	2, 978	31	3, 493, 200
Arkansas	679	2, 881	9	1, 956, 500
Florida	4, 189	1, 705	35	7, 143, 600
Georgia	1, 690	2, 778	31	4, 694, 800
Kentucky	1, 279	2, 586	34	3, 307, 300
Louisiana	1, 451	2, 547	11	3, 696, 400
Mississippi	647	3, 446	13	2, 229, 500
North Carolina	1, 791	2, 887	64	5, 171, 400
South Carolina	808	3, 269	21	2, 641, 600
Tennessee	1, 813	2, 216	126	4, 016, 800
Virginia	2, 057	2, 304	61	4, 740, 200
Southwest	7, 261	2, 357	196	17, 112, 200
Arizona	951	1, 977	18	1, 880, 100
New Mexico	383	2, 704	11	1, 035, 500
Oklahoma	1, 063	2, 475	19	2, 630, 800
Texas	4, 864	2, 378	148	11, 565, 800

TABLE 90.—*Distribution of dentists by State, region, and Federal dental service, 1972*—Continued

Region and State	Total number of dentists, 1972	Population per dentist	Number of 1972 graduates	Estimated population
Central	27, 705	1, 894	666	52, 460, 900
Illinois	6, 259	1, 794	156	11, 227, 800
Indiana	2, 341	2, 266	57	5, 305, 800
Iowa	1, 477	1, 938	31	2, 863, 000
Michigan	4, 741	1, 908	119	9, 045, 400
Minnesota	2, 686	1, 456	67	3, 911, 100
Missouri	2, 389	2, 000	86	4, 777, 600
Ohio	5, 210	2, 079	91	10, 830, 600
Wisconsin	2, 602	1, 729	59	4, 499, 600
Northwest	5, 689	1, 813	138	10, 311, 700
Colorado	1, 405	1, 647	29	2, 313, 900
Idaho	387	1, 911	7	739, 600
Kansas	1, 093	2, 069	32	2, 261, 500
Montana	393	1, 816	2	713, 600
Nebraska	967	1, 575	32	1, 523, 200
North Dakota	281	2, 234	5	627, 800
South Dakota	293	2, 299	10	673, 600
Utah	701	1, 591	18	1, 115, 300
Wyoming	169	2, 031	3	343, 200
Far West	18, 892	1, 461	467	27, 608, 700
Alaska [1]	125	2, 540	6	317, 500
California	14, 077	1, 444	372	20, 329, 900
Hawaii	534	1, 492	10	796, 600
Nevada	271	1, 898	6	514, 400
Oregon	1, 524	1, 434	26	2, 185, 400
Washington	2, 361	1, 468	47	3, 464, 900
Total listed by State	114, 251	------------	2, 709	------------
Federal dental services	9, 098	------------	1, 116	------------
Air Force	1, 996	------------	253	------------
Army	3, 094	------------	332	------------
Navy	2, 305	------------	408	------------
Public Health Service	783	------------	88	------------
Veterans' Administration	920	------------	35	------------
United States total	123, 349	1, 682	3, 825	207, 486, 300
Outlying areas:				
American Samoa	1	27, 000	0	27, 000
Guam	15	5, 667	2	85, 000
Mariana Islands	1	10, 000	0	10, 000
Panama Canal Zone	16	2, 750	0	44, 000
Puerto Rico	610	4, 446	27	2, 712, 000
Virgin Islands	26	2, 385	0	62, 000

[1] A relatively high proportion of the Alaska population receives dental care from dentists counted in the "Federal dental services." Approximately 100 Federal dentists are located in Alaska. If they were included in the Alaska count, the Alaska population per dentist would be about 1,411.

Source: "Distribution of Dentists in the United States by State, Region, District, and County." ADA, 1973.

OPTOMETRIC MANPOWER ([34], pp. 208-209)

TABLE 97.—*Optometrists in relation to population: selected years 1950 through 1973*

Year	Population in thousands [1]	Optometrists [2]	Optometrists per 100,000 population
1973	210, 557	21, 798	10
1971	207, 336	20, 736	10
1969	203, 145	20, 611	10
1968	201, 005	20, 301	10
1967	199, 017	20, 565	10
1966	196, 967	20, 610	11
1964	191, 372	20, 818	11
1960	179, 992	21, 824	12
1950	151, 234	20, 792	14

[1] Includes civilians and members of armed forces in 50 States and the District of Columbia for 1960–67. Excludes Hawaii and Alaska for 1950. As of December for 1967–73. As of March for 1966. As of July 1 for 1950–64.
[2] Active and inactive optometrists.

Sources: The Blue Book of Optometrists. Chicago. Professional Press, Inc., 1972. Also, prior biennial editions of this directory. National Center for Health Statistics, Division of Health Manpower and Facilities Statistics—data collected in the 1968 vision and eye care manpower survey of optometrists, September to December 1968. Data collected from Optometric resources project conducted under contract with the Bureau of Health Manpower, 1973. U.S. Bureau of the Census: Population estimates. Current Population Reports, Series P–25, Nos. 229, 422, 442, 478 and 533.

TABLE 98.—*Location of optometrists: December 1973*

Location	Total [1]	Active [1]	Location	Total [1]	Active [1]
All locations	21, 798	19, 356	Nebraska	164	149
			Nevada	57	48
United States	21, 701	19, 268	New Hampshire	82	72
			New Jersey	753	675
Alabama	193	181	New Mexico	86	80
Alaska	18	18	New York	1, 836	1, 590
Arizona	179	148	North Carolina	358	337
Arkansas	178	163	North Dakota	80	74
California	2, 820	2, 421	Ohio	1, 060	974
Colorado	220	208	Oklahoma	293	273
Connecticut	303	267	Oregon	338	305
Delaware	47	39	Pennsylvania	1, 285	1, 128
District of Columbia	75	68	Rhode Island	140	127
Florida	799	621	South Carolina	195	179
Georgia	306	290	South Dakota	95	87
Hawaii	88	74	Tennessee	400	363
Idaho	90	86	Texas	911	828
Illinois	1, 825	1, 569	Utah	87	75
Indiana	592	538	Vermont	47	44
Iowa	335	314	Virginia	350	325
Kansas	262	247	Washington	435	385
Kentucky	243	225	West Virginia	149	136
Louisiana	243	225	Wisconsin	473	436
Maine	138	123	Wyoming	40	40
Maryland	245	210	Canal Zone	3	2
Massachusetts	849	749	Guam	3	3
Michigan	825	745	Puerto Rico	7	6
Minnesota	391	361	Virgin Islands	2	2
Mississippi	137	124	Foreign	65	60
Missouri	480	422	Not reported	17	15
Montana	108	101			

[1] Figures may not add to totals due to rounding.

Source: Data collected from optometric manpower resources project conducted under contract with the Bureau of Health Manpower.

TABLE 99.—*Principal form of employment of optometrists: 1973*

Type of practice	Optometrists	
	Number	Percent
All active optometrists_____	[1] 19, 356	100. 0
Total self-employed_____	14, 913	77. 0
Solo practice_____	11, 905	61. 5
Partnership practice_____	2, 518	13. 0
Group practice_____	490	2. 5
Total employees_____	3, 636	18. 8
Employed by:		
Government_____	538	2. 8
Optometrist(s)_____	1, 066	5. 5
Ophthalmologist(s)_____	158	. 8
Physician(s) other than ophthalmologist(s)_____	17	. 1
Firm or corporation (proprietary)_____	1, 229	6. 3
Nonprofit organization or institution_____	371	1. 9
Other forms of employment_____	256	1. 3
Not reported_____	807	4. 2

[1] Subtotals may not add to totals due to rounding.

Source: Data collected from optometric manpower resources project conducted under contract with the Bureau of Health Manpower.

TABLE 100.—*Schools of optometry, students and graduates: selected years, 1964–65 through 1973–74*

Academic year	Schools	Students [1]		Graduates
		Total	1st year	
1973–74_____	12	3, 529	988	684
1972–73_____	12	3, 328	984	691
1971–72_____	12	3, 094	906	683
1970–71_____	11	2, 831	884	528
1969–70_____	11	2, 488	786	445
1968–69_____	10	2, 203	771	441
1967–68_____	10	1, 962	646	477
1966–67_____	10	1, 882	669	481
1965–66_____	10	1, 745	643	413
1964–65_____	10	1, 547	593	377

[1] Fall enrollment of undergraduate students.

Source: American Optometric Association.

PHARMACIST MANPOWER ([34], p. 210)

TABLE 101.—*Pharmacist registrations according to residence and activity status and ratio of pharmacists to population: Jan. 1, 1973*

Location	Total regis- trations	Pharmacists resident in State			Pharma- cists out of State	Resident pharma- cists in practice per 100,000 popu- lation [1]
		Total	In practice	Not in practice		
Total	191, 247	145, 374	132, 899	12, 475	45, 876	62. 0
Alabama	[2] 2, 674	2, 477	2, 301	176	197	66. 7
Alaska	188	121	96	25	67	29. 5
Arizona	2, 881	1, 393	1, 171	222	1, 488	60. 2
Arkansas	1, 821	1, 311	1, 098	213	510	55. 5
California	14, 626	13, 639	12, 485	1, 154	987	61. 0
Colorado	3, 412	1, 953	1, 631	322	1, 459	69. 2
Connecticut	[2] 2, 507	2, 235	2, 105	130	272	68. 3
Delaware	537	282	259	23	255	45. 8
District of Columbia	1, 555	625	570	55	930	76. 2
Florida	6, 310	4, 750	4, 370	380	1, 560	60. 2
Georgia	4, 572	3, 730	3, 280	450	842	69. 5
Hawaii	343	268	268	---------	75	33. 1
Idaho	1, 429	583	510	73	846	67. 5
Illinois	[2] 9, 720	6, 634	6, 163	471	3, 086	54. 8
Indiana	5, 573	3, 732	3, 276	456	1, 841	61. 9
Iowa	3, 076	1, 821	1, 635	186	1, 255	56. 7
Kansas	2, 347	1, 739	1, 482	257	608	65. 6
Kentucky	2, 527	2, 047	1, 789	258	480	54. 2
Louisiana	3, 186	2, 471	2, 411	60	715	64. 8
Maine	789	526	520	6	263	50. 5
Maryland	3, 210	2, 585	2, 372	213	625	58. 5
Massachusetts	7, 083	5, 511	5, 021	490	1, 572	36. 6
Michigan	6, 549	5, 965	5, 585	380	584	61. 5
Minnesota	3, 413	2, 553	2, 367	186	860	60. 8
Mississippi	1, 609	1, 249	1, 186	63	360	52. 4
Missouri	4, 610	3, 288	2, 682	606	1, 322	56. 4
Montana	[2] 846	531	447	84	315	62. 2
Nebraska	2, 196	1, 259	1, 012	247	937	66. 4
Nevada	3, 311	345	330	15	2, 966	62. 6
New Hampshire	674	415	355	60	259	46. 0
New Jersey	5, 890	4, 763	4, 024	739	1, 127	54. 6
New Mexico	1, 181	640	607	33	541	57. 0
New York	18, 325	14, 420	14, 076	344	3, 905	76. 6
North Carolina	2, 967	2, 464	2, 204	260	503	42. 3
North Dakota	1, 355	489	447	42	866	70. 7
Ohio	8, 524	7, 648	[3] 7, 274	374	876	67. 5
Oklahoma	3, 131	2, 253	2, 173	80	878	82. 5
Oregon	2, 267	1, 540	1, 368	172	727	62. 7
Pennsylvania	[2] 12, 081	11, 404	10, 559	845	677	88. 5
Puerto Rico	1, 133	1, 133	1, 066	67	---------	[4] 39. 6
Rhode Island	1, 257	710	549	161	547	56. 7
South Carolina	1, 932	1, 545	1, 509	36	387	56. 6
South Dakota	901	480	463	17	421	68. 2
Tennessee	3, 541	2, 609	2, 477	132	932	61. 4
Texas	8, 759	7, 144	6, 418	726	1, 615	55. 1
Utah	1, 366	812	769	43	554	68. 3
Vermont	869	232	225	7	637	48. 7
Virginia	[2] 2, 968	2, 335	2, 065	270	633	43. 3
Virgin Islands						
Washington	3, 738	2, 838	2, 507	331	900	72. 8
West Virginia	1, 227	793	743	50	434	41. 7
Wisconsin	3, 477	2, 789	2, 394	395	688	53. 0
Wyoming	784	295	205	90	489	59. 4

[1] Total Civilian Resident Population, "Current Population Reports," U.S. Bureau of Census, series P-25, No. 500.

[2] As of Jan. 1, 1972.

[3] Estimated.

[4] Total Civilian Resident Population, estimated by U.S. Bureau of Census for Puerto Rico, July 1, 1972, series P-25.

Source: "Licensure Statistics, Census." National Associations of Boards of Pharmacy, 1974.

NOTES AND REFERENCES

1. An econometric study of the effect of various hypothetical national health insurance plans on demand for health care and manpower requirements was prepared for the National Institutes of Health in 1974 under contract by Robert Nathan Associates ([6]).

2. Recent statistical trends regarding the number and distribution of doctors and nurses appear in [4], p. 103 ff. and [5], pp. 342–405.

3. The following tables, deleted by the editors because of space limitations, appear in the original document ([34], pp. 133–145) as:

   Table 17: Foreign medical graduates in the United States, by speciality and activity (excludes Canadian graduates), December 31, 1970

   Table 18: Physicians by age and country of medical school, December 31, 1973

   Table 19: Physicians in the United States by country of graduation and sex, December 31, 1973

   Table 20: Physicians in the United States by State of practice and country of graduation, December 31, 1970

   Table 21: Foreign medical graduates in the United States by State of practice and major professional activity, December 31, 1970

   Table 22: Foreign medical graduates in the United States by State of practice and licensure, December 31, 1970

   Table 23: Approved medical schools and schools of basic medical science

4. The following tables, deleted by the editors because of space limitations, appear in the original document ([34], pp. 152–155) as:

   Table 33: Percentage minority enrollment in United States medical schools, 1972–73 and 1974–75

   Table 34: Minority student information by individual United States medical schools

5. The following tables, deleted by the editors because of space limitations, appear in the original document ([34], pp. 159–163) as:

   Table 40: Sources of loan funds received by medical students, 1974–75

   Table 41: Sources of scholarship funds received by medical students, 1974–75

   Table 42: Medical financial support by source

   Table 43: Number of M.D. degree-granting accredited medical schools by size of total support

   Table 44: Changing pattern of sponsored and total support in medical colleges, 1964–65 through 1973–74

   Table 45: Number of M.D. degree-granting accredited medical schools by size of sponsored support

6. The following tables, deleted by the editors because of space limitations, appear in the original document ([34], pp. 173–180) as:

   Table 58: Number of foreign graduates in United States graduate training programs, by origin of medical education, as of December 31, 1974 and December 31, 1973

   Table 59: Foreign countries contributing greatest number of graduates to United States graduate programs as of December 31, 1974

   Table 60: Foreign medical graduates in training programs

   Table 61: Distribution of trainees in graduate programs, September 1, 1973

   Table 62: Status of internship and residency programs in the United States

   Table 63: Number of foreign graduate trainees in the United States, by origin of medical education, as of December 31, 1973 and 1972

   Table 64: 12 foreign medical schools contributing the largest number of graduates to United States graduate medical education programs, December 31, 1974

   Table 65: Women in internship positions, as of September 1, 1974

   Table 66: Women physicians serving in residencies, by speciality and hospital affiliation, as of September 1, 1974

7. The following tables, deleted by the editors because of space limitations, appear in the original ([34], pp. 182–185) as:

> Table 68: Black United States citizens serving in internship and residency programs, as of September 1, 1974

> Table 69: Black United States citizens serving in residencies, by speciality and hospital affiliation, as of September 1, 1974

> Table 70: Twelve United States medical schools contributing the largest number of graduates to United States graduate medical education programs, December 31, 1974

> Table 71: Interns and residents by State location of school of medical education, as of December 1974

8. The following tables, deleted by the editors because of space limitations, appear in the original document ([34], pp. 191–192) as:

> Table 79: Schools of nursing—registered nurses and number of students and graduates by type of program: selected years, 1960–61 through 1974–75

> Table 80: Locations of schools of nursing—registered nurses and number of students and graduates, 1974

9. The following tables, deleted by the editors because of space limitations, appear in the original document ([34], pp. 195–197) as:

> Table 83: Location of full-time licensed practical nurses employed in hospitals in relation to hospital beds, 1973

> Table 84: Location of full-time licensed practical nurses in nursing and related homes, 1973

> Table 85: Licensed practical nurses, employed in nursing, by field of employment, 1967

10. The following tables, deleted by the editors because of space limitations, appear in the original document ([34], pp. 199–200) as:

> Table 87: Location of programs of practical nursing and number of admissions and graduates, 1973–74

> Table 88: Location of nursing aides, orderlies, and attendants employed in AHA hospitals in relation to hospital beds, 1970

11. The following tables, deleted by the editors because of space limitations, appear in the original document ([34], pp. 203–207) as:

> Table 91: Number of dental specialists, selected years, 1955 through 1972

> Table 92: Dental schools, students, and graduates, selected years 1949–50 through 1973–74

> Table 93: Undergraduate enrollment in the dental schools of the United States, as of October 15, 1975

> Table 94: United States dental schools—women enrollment by class, 1974–75 and 1975–76

> Table 95: United States dental schools—minority enrollment and graduates, 1975–76

> Table 96: Dental school graduates, 1975

12. The following tables, deleted by the editors because of space limitations, appear in the original document ([34], pp. 211–217) as:

> Table 102: Type of practice of pharmacists by States, January 1, 1973

> Table 103: Schools of pharmacy, students, and graduates, 1960–61 through 1973–74

> Table 104: Location of total and active podiatrists in relation to population, 1974

> Table 105: Type of practice of active podiatrists, 1974

> Table 106: Podiatry colleges, students, and graduates: selected years, 1960–61 through 1974–75

Chapter 6
Private Health Insurance

Private health insurance represents a large industry, having considerable experience in financing health care and significant influence within government as a political interest group. Between 75 and 80 percent of the American people are covered by some type of private health insurance. Over 900 companies operate as health insurance carriers and disburse over $30 billion in claims each year—about a quarter of the total national health care cost. These companies vary greatly in size, structure, and in services offered, and they are regulated at the state level. Their performance in meeting the promises offered in promotions has been criticized and their administrative efficiency is a subject of controversy. A central issue in the debate over national health insurance is the role to be played, if any, by private carriers. Some proposals would utilize them as administrative agents; others would phase them out or drop them altogether. Whatever the outcome of the national health insurance debate, it is certain that the future of the private health insurance industry will be profoundly affected.

INCOME, EXPENSE, AND COVERAGE ([34], pp. 218–220)

MEDICAL CARE OUTLAYS, FISCAL YEAR 1975

The total personal health care bill for all Americans was $103 billion. Of this total, $33.6 billion (32.6 percent) was paid by direct payments of private funds; $40.9 billion (39.7 percent) was paid by public programs (Federal, State, and local); $27.3 billion (26.5 percent) was paid by private health insurance; and $1.3 billion (1.3 percent) was paid by philanthropy and other sources.

PRIVATE HEALTH INSURANCE COVERAGE OF INDIVIDUAL HEALTH EXPENDITURES

(a) In fiscal year 1975, the average medical bill for a person (per capita personal health care expenditures) amounted to $476.40, of which 26.5 percent was paid by private health insurance. The person himself paid 32.6 percent, largely for uninsured items such as drugs, long-term institutional care, and dental care. The rest was paid primarily by Government programs (39.7 percent) and by philanthropic or other sources (1.3 percent).

(b) Private health insurance paid 35.8 percent of patient's expenditures for hospital care, 39 percent of the cost of physicians' services, 9.8 percent of dentists' services, 6.5 percent of drugs and drug sundries, and 3.8 percent of all other services.

Percentage of under age 65 civilian population with private health insurance coverage, as of Dec. 31, 1974

	Percent
Hospital care	79. 9
Surgery	78. 3
Physicians' in-hospital visits	77. 5
X-ray and laboratory examinations	77. 5
Visiting nurse service	70. 1
Private duty nursing	72. 9
Out-of-hospital prescribed drugs	73. 2
Physicans' home and office visits	62. 3
Nursing home care	35. 2
Dental care	17. 4

Number of persons under age 65 covered by private health insurance, by type of plan

	Millions
Blue Cross and Blue Shield	76
Commerical insurance companies	108
Other (independent) plans	9

Income and expenses of all private health insurance organizations, 1974

	Billions
Premium income	$28. 4
Benefits paid (87 percent of premium income)	24. 8
Operating expense (14 percent of premium income)	3. 9

Income and expenses of Blue Cross-Blue Shield plans, 1974

	Billions
Premium income	$12. 3
Benefits paid (94 percent)	11. 6
Operating expense (7 percent)	. 9

Income and expenses of commercial health insurance companies, 1974

Total premium income (billions of dollars)	[1] 13. 8
Group insurance benefits paid (percent of premium income)	90. 6
Individual insurance benefits paid (percent of premium income)	46. 3
Group insurance operating expense (billions of dollars)	1. 4
Individual insurance operating expense (billions of dollars)	1. 5

[1] Of this amount, 24 percent came from individual policies and 76 percent came from group business.

For all commercial insurance policies, operating expense amounted to 21 percent of premium income. Individual business had a net underwriting gain of 6.7 percent of premium income, and group business showed a net underwriting loss of 3.6 percent.

Income and expenses of other plans

Total premium income (billions)	$2. 1
Benefits paid (percent)	93. 2
Operating expense (percent)	7. 6

Public Programs (fiscal year 1975)

	Billions
All public programs	$45. 6
Federal programs	31. 0
Medicare (includes administrative costs of $660.6 million)	15. 0
Medicaid (Federal funds only; includes administrative costs)	7. 0
Defense Department hospital and medical care (including military dependents)	3. 0
Veterans' hospital and medical care	3. 2
State and local programs (including State share of medicaid program)	15. 0

Financial experience of private health insurance organizations, 1974

[Amounts in millions]

| | Pre-mium income | Benefits paid | | Operating expenses | | Net under-writing loss or gain |
		Amount	Percent of income	Amount	Percent of pre-mium income	
Total_____	28. 4	24. 8	87. 2	3. 9	14. 1	−0. 3
Blue Cross_____	8. 6	8. 3	96. 1	. 4	5. 4	−. 2
Blue Shield _____	3. 7	3. 3	89. 5	. 4	11. 8	−. 04
Commercial group ____	10. 6	9. 6	90. 6	1. 3	13. 0	−. 3
Commercial individual_	3. 2	1. 5	46. 3	1. 5	47. 0	6. 7
All other plans _____	2. 2	2. 0	93. 2	. 1	7. 6	−. 08

MAJOR MEDICAL INSURANCE

COMMERCIAL INSURANCE COMPANIES

Major medical plans

Major medical plans offered by commercial insurance companies are of two types: (a) Supplementary, which supplement plans of basic benefits, and (b) comprehensive, which have no basic coverages and furnish a complete and integrated coverage in one package. The first type covers more people than the second by a ratio of nearly 3 to 1.

Supplementary plans

Supplementary plans typically pay 80 percent of covered expenses over and above the expenses covered under a basic plan, and after the payment of a deductible, up to a specified maximum benefit computed on an illness basis, or dollar limit per year or lifetime.

BLUE CROSS-BLUE SHIELD

Major medical plans

Major medical plans offered by Blue Cross-Blue Shield are of the supplementary type. Supplementary "major medical" contracts are similar to those sold by insurance companies. They provide coverage of hospital care and physicians' services in the office, home, and hospital (in addition to benefits under the basic Blue Cross-Blue Shield contract), drugs, appliances, private-duty and visiting-nurse service, and sometimes nursing home care—all on a deductible and coinsurance basis (that is, payment after an initial deductible of 75 percent or 80 percent of covered expenses).

"Extended benefit" contracts generally provide additional hospital coverage for days beyond the basic contract and coverage of physicians' services and, possibly, drugs after hospitalization. In many cases they also provide some coverage of outpatient diagnostic X-ray and laboratory service, visiting-nurse service, and, in lesser degree, nursing home care.

Blue Cross-Blue Shield developed these policies in a competitive response to the commercial health insurance industry, which were the first to develop such policies.

REGULATION OF PRIVATE HEALTH INSURANCE[1]
([34], pp. 221–249)

A. BASIS FOR STATE REGULATION

Health insurance, like other kinds of private insurance, historically has been regulated by State, not Federal law. In 1944, the Supreme Court reversed its traditional position toward the business of insurance by declaring, in *U.S.* v. *South Eastern Underwriters Association*, 322 U.S. 533, that insurance transactions across State lines are in interstate commerce. This decision led to action by the Congress to maintain State regulation. Public Law 15, 59 Stat. 33, enacted on March 9, 1945, states "That the continued regulation and taxation by the several states of the business of insurance is in the public interest, and that silence on the part of the Congress shall not be construed to impose any barrier to the regulation or taxation of such business by the several States * * * The business of insurance, and every person engaged therein, shall be subject to the laws of the several States which relate to the regulation or taxation of such business." The act also provided, however, that, effective in 1948, Federal antitrust laws "shall be applicable to the business of insurance to the extent that such business is not regulated by State law."

In order to avoid possible Federal action to regulate the industry the National Association of Insurance Commissioners and the industry collaborated in writing new or stronger State laws, including some suggested uniform State insurance acts. Considerable variation among the States in their regulation of the insurance industry still exists, however, with respect to basic State law and to characteristics of administration by State insurance departments. Some of these differences are described in the remainder of this section.

B. HEALTH INSURANCE CARRIERS

Most State insurance laws refer only to life or casualty insurance companies, either of which may write health insurance. A company wishing to carry health insurance only usually incorporates either as a life or a casualty insurance company and must meet the statutory requirements for that category of company. In 1970, there were 916 companies in the health insurance field, with 327 companies doing about 96 percent of the health insurance business.[2]

Each commercial company is required to incorporate in its State of domicile and meet initial minimum solvency standards before transacting business. The specific requirements, usually involving specified amounts of paid-in capital, or initial free surplus, or both, vary widely depending on a variety of factors such as the kind of company involved (whether it is a stock or mutual company), how the company is organized (is it a domestic, foreign or alien insurer), the number and/or combination of insurance lines that the company will or does offer, and the length of time during which the insurer has had actual experience in a particular insurance line or in the business of insurance generally. Each insurer must satisfy comparable requirements in each State in which it desires to do business. Its financial statements, reserves and investments are subject to control by the State of domicile and by the States in which policies are issued. Policy forms must also be submitted for approval in the States in which they are issued and policy language must conform to the requirements of State law.

---

[1] Based on Library of Congress, Congressional Research Service study, "State Regulation of Private Health Insurance," May 1, 1972.

[2] Of these, 701 are life companies and 215 are casualty insurers.

C. REGULATION OF POLICY FORMS

Use of a single standardized health insurance form by all companies in the business has never been required by law or achieved through industry practice, as has occurred in fire and automobile insurance. Every State requires that individual policy forms must be filed with and reviewed by the insurance commissioner before being used, and 45 jurisdictions require filing of group forms. Insurance codes generally authorize the commissioner to disapprove a policy if it contains one or more provisions which are "unjust, unfair, inequitable, misleading, deceptive or encourage misrepresentation * * *" In the case of individual contracts the codes also require inclusion in substance of 12 required and 11 optional policy provisions which have been adopted by every State, after being approved in 1950 by the National Association of Insurance Commissioners.

The 12 uniform provisions required to be included in every individual health insurance policy deal with such matters as the method of giving notice of claim and proof of loss, cancellation and reinstatement rights, the grace period for paying premiums and making changes of beneficiary, and the time and method of paying claims. The 11 optional provisions pertain to prorating benefits in the event of a change of occupation, results of misstatement of age, or the existence of other insurance covering the same loss, and also include an optional 5-day cancellation provision. Two of the optional provisions touch on policy exclusions, since they permit the insurer to exclude losses attributed to the insured's engaging in an illegal occupation, committing a felony, or being intoxicated or under the influence of narcotics.

Except for these two optional provisions, the uniform policy provisions required by law do not affect coverage, exclusions or benefit levels. An insurer may (1) combine coverages in any way; (2) include or exclude inhospital surgical or medical care, ambulance, anesthesia or other services with hospital insurance; (3) use any relationship between the hospital room and board benefit and the allowance for miscellaneous services, or make them independent; and (4) offer any level of hospital daily benefit, any maximum period of coverage, and any schedule of surgical or ancillary benefits.

In group health insurance 32 jurisdictions prescribe some requirements. These usually include such items as (1) provision for issuing certificates to employees; (2) provision that statements are representations and not warranties; (3) rules concerning remittance of premiums; (4) provisions for adding new employees; and (5) provisions for dealing with proofs of loss and payment of claims.

D. PREMIUM RATES

Health insurance premium rates are not regulated by State insurance departments, although many jurisdictions require the filing of such rates. The reason usually given for the lack of premium rate regulation in the health insurance field is that such regulation is neither needed nor justified because of the highly competitive market in which health insurance, and particularly group health insurance, is sold; the argument is that the market itself serves to keep rates and benefits competitive. (The basic reason why States are active in rate regulation in property and casualty insurance areas is that these companies sought and received exemption from antitrust laws, and, in view of the practice of rate-making in concert, regulation of rates by State insurance departments was needed to prevent monopolistic practices.)

Under their authority to disapprove health insurance policy forms, however, about half of the States permit their insurance commissioners to disapprove a policy form, usually on grounds that the benefits provided are unreasonable in relation to the premium charged, or the policy contains a provision or provisions which are unjust, unfair, inequitable, misleading, deceptive, or encourage misrepresentation.

An insurer must submit to any State insurance department requesting the information the loss ratio [3] of each health insurance policy form. This information provides data which can be used to determine whether benefits are reasonable in relation to premiums, that is, whether premium rates are so high as to result in very low loss ratios. The National Association of Insurance Commissioners, in an effort to establish guidelines for applying this provision, has adopted a general benchmark of a 50-percent loss ratio. By implication, any policy form which, over a substantial period of time, pays out in benefits less than 50 percent of premiums collected offers "benefits unreasonable in relation to the premium charged." This standard is difficult to enforce, since experience over several years is generally needed to determine whether a policy form really has a loss ratio of less than 50 percent and it is obviously of limited usefulness in the case of new policy forms.

E. BENEFIT LEVELS IN INDIVIDUAL HEALTH INSURANCE POLICIES

State laws are almost completely silent on the question of the adequacy of the benefits offered by individual health insurance policies to the needs of the policyholder. A committee of the National Association of Insurance Commissioners studied the question of whether minimum benefit legislation should be recommended, but was discharged in 1952 without proposing any model legislation. Only California, with its 1949 minimum benefits law, attempts to require that health insurance policies provide benefit levels which meet certain minimum standards. New Jersey has through administrative action ruled out one-disease-only and similar contracts.

The absence of such standards has resulted in issuance by some insurers of policies providing clearly inadequate amounts of coverage for the risks of daily hospital costs, fragmentation of protection into unrealistically low itemization of costs for specific services such as X-rays, laboratory tests, oxygen, et cetera, and medical expense benefits that cover a small fraction of the cost of physicians and other services. In addition, there has been increased promotion of one-disease-only, or accident-and-one-disease policies. The number of different health insurance policies written in the United States today probably approaches 10,000. The combinations are infinite.

As a result of the great number of different possible combinations of benefit amount, length of stay, ancillary benefits and surgical schedules, often combined with a great variety of income coverage for loss of time because of accident or sickness, health insurance has become the most heterogeneous and confusing type of insurance. It is extremely difficult, if not impossible, for the purchaser of an individual health insurance policy to compare benefits and costs and to shop intelligently among those available. The task is further complicated by the existence of different classifications of policies such as guaranteed renewable, conditionally renewable, and cancellable, with different levels of cost, and with specific maeanings of these terms as used in the industry not necessarily clear to the potential purchaser....

---

[3] Loss ratio here means the ratio of benefits paid out to premiums collected.

F. GROUP INSURANCE ELIGIBILITY REQUIREMENTS

State laws defining group health insurance and the minimum size of a group follow generally the model group accident and health insurance bill recommended by the National Association of Insurance Commissioners, but many vary in form. The New York law, as an example, defines six different kinds of groups, each with different requirements as to minimum size and participation requirements. New York differentiates among group health insurance policies issued to an employer, a trade association, a labor union or other employee association, a multiemployer or joint union-employer welfare fund, a creditor group, and a public welfare district. Each of these six classes, which are the only types of groups to which group insurance may be issued must meet certain specified requirements, such as: (1) the group must have been formed for a purpose other than obtaining insurance; (2) the minimum number of covered persons in a group varies from two for an employer-employee group to 100 for the employees or members of a trade association, the number increasing as the group becomes less homogeneous and more likely to include persons who joined just to get the insurance; (3) the amount of coverage must usually be based on a plan which precludes individual selection; and (4) if the employer contributes to the cost of the insurance, at least 75 percent of the employees must agree to purchase it, while an employer who pays the entire cost must insure all of his employees, or all those belonging to the class (for example, white collar or clerical employees) covered by the policy.

On the one hand, it has been held by some that liberalization of State laws defining a group to make group health insurance more widely available might result in broader and less expensive coverage for many people, since the 90-percent loss ratio common in group hospital and medical insurance shrinks to between 50 and 60 percent in individual policies. On the other hand, the fact that, in the 16 or so States without statutory definitions of group health insurance, the types of groups written do not differ greatly from those in the States with legal restrictions, indicates that the underwriting rules in laws like New York's are safeguards which any prudent insurer is likely to adopt. Moreover, the lower loss ratios on group health insurance are probably accounted for, in part, by the amount of administrative and claims work done in large groups by the employer, rather than the carrier. This helps account for the fact that large group contracts are relatively inexpensive for the carrier to administer with premiums only 5 to 10 percent higher than the cost of the claims incurred. This would not, of course, be true in very small groups, or in nonemployer employee groups in which the insurer had higher administrative costs in collecting premiums and processing claims.

G. REGULATION OF MAIL-ORDER INSURERS AND HEALTH INSURANCE ADVERTISING

Mail-order selling of health insurance is more widespread than in other forms of insurance, almost all of it for individually written health insurance policies. Until 1950 mail-order insurers could incorporate in one State and then operate, free of regulation, in all the others. If the State of incorporation was one with lax insurance statutes, a mail-order company could escape effective regulation of any kind and, in addition, avoid taxation by all States other than the State of domicile. This situation has changed somewhat since 1950, when the U.S. Supreme Court upheld Virginia's right to assert jurisdiction over a

Nebraska mail-order company by ordering it to cease and desist from solicitation or sale of policies to Virginia residents unless it obtained authority in accordance with Virginia law (*Travelers Health Association* v. *Virginia*, 339 U.S. 643).

Most States have also adopted the Unauthorized Insurers Service of Process Act, recommended by the National Association of Insurance Commissioners, which provides that any insurer doing business in a State, by mail or otherwise, automatically designates the State insurance commissioner as his agent for service of process, and that service of process on the commissioner gives the State courts jurisdiction over the mail-order insurer.

Some State insurance departments have tried to eliminate mail-order insurers by asking local news media to refuse advertising from unauthorized insurers and by issuing periodic press releases warning the public to check with the insurance department before buying insurance by mail.

Wisconsin has levied a special premium tax on unauthorized insurers at a higher rate than on authorized insurers and the courts have upheld its constitutionality. In California, too, mail-order insurance has been held by the courts to be subject to regulation, based on a suit by the California insurance commissioner to prevent three companies from doing business in the State without obtaining a certificate of authority.

In 1954, the Federal Trade Commission cited a number of insurance companies for false and misleading advertising of health insurance policies. The States responded to the Federal Trade Commission's initiative by adopting a set of rules governing insurance advertising drafted by an all industry committee of representatives of the companies and State insurance departments. The U.S. Supreme Court held, when the first of these Federal Trade Commission cases reached it in 1957, that the McCarran Act of 1945 "withdrew from the Federal Trade Commission the authority to regulate respondents' advertising practices in those States which are regulating those practices under their own laws." (*F.T.C.* v. *National Casualty Company*, 337 U.S. 560.)

The U.S. Supreme Court subsequently ruled, however, in 1960 that the existence of State laws regulating advertising did not nullify the FTC's jurisdiction over mail-order insurance, on the grounds that the State in which policies are sold has no effective way of regulating the activities of out-of-State mail-order companies. In 1964, the FTC issued its Guides for the Mail Order Insurance Industry.

The legal authority of the States to regulate insurer advertising is based on the Uniform Trades Practices Act, adopted by every State soon after enactment of the McCarran Act in 1945. These acts, intended to "regulate trade practices in the business of insurance" define and prohibit practices "which constitute unfair methods of competition or unfair or deceptive acts or practices." Among other unfair trade practices, "misrepresenting the terms of any policy issued or the benefits or advantages promised thereby," and "publishing * * * an advertisement, announcement or statement containing any assertion, representation or statement with respect to the business of insurance * * * which is untrue, deceptive or misleading" are prohibited. This same Uniform Trades Practices Act contains an antidiscrimination section pertaining to health insurance which prohibits "permitting any unfair discrimination between individuals of the same class and of essentially the same hazard in the amount of premium * * * or rates charged."

H. DUPLICATION OF COVERAGE AND SUBROGATION

Duplication of benefits can occur when a person covered under more than one health or accident insurance policy collects payments for the same hospital or medical expenses from more than one insurer. State laws recognize this situation in the area of possible duplication between individual health insurance contracts by providing, in four of the optional uniform provisions which may be included in individual health insurance policies, against overinsurance due to two similar policies issued by the same insurer; loss-of-time coverage in excess of the insured's monthly earnings; and duplicate coverage with other insurers.

Antiduplication clauses appear also in some group insurance policies, primarily major medical, but there remains the problem of duplication between Blue Cross and group health insurance, or between either group insurance or Blue Cross and individual policies.

In addition to the duplication between different types of hospital and medical expense coverage, there is also overlap between health insurance policies and automobile liability insurance and medical payments coverage enabling injured persons in many cases to collect the same medical expense costs from more than one insurance carrier.

It is of interest in this regard that the proposed Federal Uniform Motor Vehicle Insurance Act (S. 945, 92d Congress, 1st sess.) provides that an individual's reimbursement for his economic loss due to automobile accident injury would be reduced by the amount of any benefits or payments to which he is entitled for the same injury "under any private or public insurance or plan or other source of benefits." This provision would make insurance carriers and public programs other than automobile insurance companies the primary sources of payment for motor vehicle injuries, with the automobile insurance carrier responsible only for the "net economic loss" remaining after the other benefits are paid.

The Civil Service Commission and the Department of HEW have expressed reservations about this aspect of the proposed Uniform Motor Vehicle Insurance Act, insofar as it would make the Federal employees health benefits program and medicare, rather than the no-fault insurance, the primary source of payments for motor vehicle injuries. They recommended that there be subrogation among insurance carriers to insure prompt payment of medical expenses without duplication of benefits. Their position is that when a motor vehicle accident results in injury, the motor vehicle insurance should bear the expenses, with the Federal employees health benefits program and medicare paying any medical costs not paid for by the motor vehicle insurance.

It is considered desirable by some insurance experts that private health insurance, including Blue Cross or group hospital insurance, should have subrogation rights similar to those in most automobile, fire, and other types of property insurance policies. The health insurance company or plan, having paid a policyholder's hospital bill, could then assume his right to sue, if the accident causing his hospitalization were due to someone's negligence, and be reimbursed for its outlay. (The Michigan Supreme Court has ruled that common law and equitable principles of subrogation did not permit the Michigan Blue Cross to exercise subrogation rights, even if its policyholder collected, in a liability suit, for the hospital bills Blue Cross had paid (*Michigan Hospital Service* v. *Sharpe*, 339 Mich. 357, 63 N.W.2d, 638, 1954). However, Michigan

Blue Shield was permitted to recoup the amount it had paid for medical expenses for the same individual because Blue Shield, unlike Blue Cross, had a subrogation clause in its contract.)

Cancellation

One of the optional provisions which may be included in individual health insurance policies, at the insurer's option, is a clause permitting the insurer to cancel the policy on 5 days' notice. Cancellation would not affect a benefit that had already been furnished, but would protect the carrier from having to pay future claims for an individual whose past claims history indicates that he may be a substandard risk. Some States have enacted legislation prohibiting cancellation of health insurance contracts between policy anniversaries, in order to prevent cancellation at a time when the person may most need the coverage.

Even though most insurers do not exercise the right to put a cancellation provision in individual health insurance policies, most health insurance policies are annual contracts so that absence of a cancellation clause merely guarantees protection for 1 year. An insurer may refuse to renew the policy after its expiration date in the case of a person whose health has deteriorated since the policy was purchased or who has chronic ailments that might require future expensive medical care, in the absence of a statute or policy provision limiting this right. Or as an alternative, the carrier may offer to renew the policy but only with a rider excluding the condition most likely to require medical care.

New York State has a statutory safeguard against the right of insurers to refuse renewal which prohibits an insurer from refusing to renew, after 2 years from the date of issuance, any hospital or medical expense insurance policy "because of a change in the physical or mental condition or the health of any person covered thereunder"; restrictive riders are also prohibited.

Some 10 other States do not permit an insurer to write policies cancelable on 5 (or 10 or 30) days' notice, while some require that any right by the insurer to cancel or refuse renewal be stated prominently on the face of the policy.

Categorized according to increasing policyholder security as to renewability, there are currently five types of hospital and medical expense contracts sold in the United States:

(a) Cancelable policies, giving the insured or the insurer the right to cancel at any time, on 5 days' written notice. This type, formerly prevalent, is now relatively rare, due primarily to competition rather than statute.

(b) Renewable at the option of the company. These cannot be canceled between anniversary dates, but the insurer has the right to renew or not, at its option, on any anniversary. (The insured can also exercise this right by neglecting to pay the next year's premium.)

These two types, characterized by relatively modest short-term benefits, have made up the bulk of commercial policies, but the trend has been in the direction of contracts providing broader and longer term benefits, with restrictions on the carrier's right to refuse renewal.

(c) Conditionally renewable policies, which restrict the company's right to cancel or refuse to renew an individual policy, but permit it to refuse renewal of an entire class of policies. This type of "renewal guarantee" clause usually defines what is meant by refusal to renew a class of policies; for example, the right to refuse renewal of all policies issued on the same policy form to persons residing in the same State, or enumerating certain reasons, such as the health of an individual, which the insurer cannot use as grounds for refusal to renew.

This type of policy protects only against nonrenewal at the same premium, but does not prevent the insurer from raising the premium rate—but only for the whole class of insureds, not for any individual policyholder.

(d) Guaranteed renewable. These policies, usually written by life insurance companies, provide broad long-term benefits and completely eliminate the insurer's right to cancel or refuse renewal. Most such policies terminate at age 65 especially since the advent of medicare; and the insurer has the right to increase premiums for all policies in a class, but not for any individuals in the class.

(e) Noncancelable. This term, in industry usage, is reserved for policies that guarantee not only the right to renew, but the right to renew at a specific premium. Few such policies include hospital or medical care coverage, because of their rising costs from year to year.

I. REGULATION OF BLUE CROSS AND BLUE SHIELD PLANS

Number of Plans

There are 75 Blue Cross and 71 Blue Shield plans in the United States.

Regional and State Variation in Enrollment

Blue Cross-Blue Shield plans are strongest in the New England and Middle Atlantic States, where these plans cover about half of the population under hospital and surgical-medical benefits.

The plans are weakest in the West South Central States, where only about 20 percent of the population is enrolled for hospital and surgical-medical benefits.

In the Pacific, Mountain, and South Atlantic States, the plans cover about 25 percent of the population.

Organization

The 75 separate Blue Cross plans in the United States are each individual organizations, providing hospital insurance in a specific geographical area, usually a State or part of a State. The plans are interconnected, however, through the national Blue Cross Association, which represents them in national affairs and provides certain marketing, research, and professional and public relations services, and operates both an interplan bank that arranges coverage for subscribers who use hospital services outside the area of their own plan, and an interplan transfer agreement to facilitate transfer of coverage for subscribers who move permanently from one area to another.

The Blue Cross Association also operates a stock insurance company, Health Service, Inc., which offers a uniform contract for groups whose employees and activities are located in areas served by more than one plan. The capital to organize Health Service, Inc.—initially $200,000 with $282,000 surplus—was contributed in 1949 by certain Blue Cross plans, and the directors of the company are selected largely by these plans with a minority chosen by the Blue Cross Association. Earnings go to the association.

Blue Shield plans are also organized on a geographical basis, usually in the same areas as Blue Cross. Blue Cross and Blue Shield share common administrative arrangements in many plan areas. They are similarly linked by the National Association of Blue Shield Plans, which serves them in somewhat the same way that the Blue Cross Association serves its constituent plans, and also operates its own stock insurance company, Medical Indemnity of America, Inc., for national accounts.

Administrative Organization

Blue Cross and Blue Shield plans are governed by boards of directors chosen from among representatives of hospitals, the medical profession, and the public. Boards of directors are not elected by subscribers; they are either self-perpetuating or, in the case of many Blue Cross plans, chosen by a special "corporation" comprised of individuals from various businesses and professions, particularly hospitals and local medical societies. In Blue Shield plans, physicians commonly are appointed to the boards directly by State or county medical societies.

The boards of directors have general policymaking authority, elect the plan's officers, and control appointment of the managing director and major committees.

The managing director, usually called the executive director, oversees the plan's operations in enrollment, ratemaking and underwriting, accounting, service to subscribers, hospital and professional relations, and public relations.

Over the years, much discussion and controversy have occurred with regard to the proper makeup of boards of directors of the Blue plans. State laws are not consistent in providing for representation of the public on these boards, nor in specifying what form such representation should take. While hospital representatives have tended to dominate Blue Cross boards, and physicians those of Blue Shield, some public representation is provided for. However, the manner of selection of these public representatives leaves room for some question as to the extent to which they represent the plans' subscribers, or other community interests. Questions have also been raised as the propriety of large insurance enterprises like Blue Cross and Blue Shield being controlled by the organizations and individuals that sell services to them—that is, hospitals and physicians—rather than directly by those who pay for and use those services—that is, the plan's subscribers, both employers and employee groups (as well as individuals not in groups). For example, only recently has the Blue Cross Association and the American Hospital Association taken steps to reduce duplication on the two boards of directors and for ownership of the Blue Cross symbol to be transferred from the American Hospital Association to the Blue Cross Association.

Regulation

Blue Cross and Blue Shield plans are established in most States under special enabling acts which exempt them from the usual capital reserve requirements to which commercial insurance companies are subject, as well as from State and local taxation on income or assets, but not from regulation. Some 44 States have laws regulating Blue Cross plans—in 41 of them by the State insurance department. The great majority of Blue Shield plans are also regulated by State insurance commissioners; a notable exception is the California Physicians' Service (Blue Shield of California) which is under the sole jurisdiction of the State attorney general (as the result of a court ruling which held it to be a nonprofit organization outside the scope of the insurance laws, leaving it essentially unregulated).

The regulatory areas in which Blue Cross and Blue Shield plans are treated very much like other types of health insurance companies include permits to commence operations, approval of benefit structures, investment limitations, advertising procedures, and reporting and examination requirements. Blue Cross and Blue Shield associations are generally regulated less stringently than insurance companies in the areas of taxation, capital and surplus requirements, reserve standards, and licensing of sales representatives. The subscriber rates of the plans are supervised more closely than are commercial health insurance companies, which generally do not have their premiums reviewed by insurance commissioners. Other features which characterize Blue plans, but generally not insurance companies, are public hearings on rate changes, benefit modifications, reimbursement, and fee schedules. In most cases, also, they must confine their operations within specified territorial boundaries and conform to certain expense limits.

In addition to meeting State statutory and administrative requirements, Blue Cross and Blue Shield organizations must comply with the provisions of approval programs administered by their national associations, which may be stricter than those imposed by State law and regulation.

The laws of many States establish some form of ratemaking machinery for Blue Cross and Blue Shield. The statutory language used in State laws is usually quite general, and rarely if ever, includes any detailed criteria for determining how rates are to be approved. Connecticut's hospital service corporation contains language typical of that found in many State laws regarding rates:[4]

> No such corporation shall enter into any contract with subscribers unless and until it has filed with the insurance commissioner a full schedule of the rates to be paid by the subscribers and has obtained said commissioner's approval thereof. The commissioner may refuse such approval if he finds such rates to be excessive, inadequate, or discriminatory.

At the same time, many of the States also require that the rates of payment to participating hospitals and physicians are to be "fair and reasonable" or "adequate and reasonable" [5] The list following indicates which of the States have premium rate approval requirements for the Blue plans.[6]

---

[4] General Statutes of Connecticut, section 33–166.

[5] Alaska Insurance Statutes, section 21.87.190.

[6] From data supplied by the National Association of Insurance Commissioners as modified by information obtained from individual States.

RATE APPROVAL REQUIREMENTS OF BLUE CROSS AND BLUE SHIELD PLANS

STATE AND REQUIREMENT

Alabama—Yes
Alaska—Yes
Arizona—No
Arkansas—No
Colorado—Yes
Connecticut—Yes
District of Columbia—No regulation
Florida—Yes
Hawaii—No
Idaho—Yes
Illinois—Yes
Indiana—Regulated under insurance laws
Iowa—Yes
Kansas—Yes
Kentucky—Yes
Maryland—Yes
Massachusetts—Yes
Michigan—Yes
Minnesota—Yes

Missouri—No regulation
Montana—No
Nevada—No
New Hampshire—Yes
New Jersey—Yes
New Mexico—Yes
New York—Yes
Ohio—No
Oregon—No
Rhode Island—Yes
South Carolina—Regulated under insurance laws
South Dakota—Yes
Texas—Yes
Utah—No
Vermont—No
Virginia—No
Wisconsin—No
Wyoming—Regulated under insurance laws

TABLE 1.—*Estimates of net number of different persons under private health insurance plans and percent of population covered, by age and specified type of care, as of Dec. 31, 1974*

Type of service	All ages		Under age 65		Aged 65 and over	
	Number (in thousands)	Percent of civilian population [1]	Number (in thousands)	Percent of civilian population [2]	Number (in thousands)	Percent of civilian population [3]
Hospital care	163, 396	77. 6	150, 585	79. 9	12, 811	57. 9
Physicians services:						
Surgical services	159, 518	75. 7	147, 570	78. 3	11, 948	54. 0
In-hospital visits	155, 022	73. 6	146, 110	77. 5	8, 912	40. 3
X-ray and laboratory examinations	153, 017	72. 7	146, 006	77. 5	7, 011	31. 7
Office and home visits	125, 183	59. 4	117, 321	62. 3	7, 862	35. 5
Dental care	33, 297	15. 8	32, 887	17. 4	410	1. 9
Prescribed drugs (out-of-hospital)	141, 755	67. 3	138, 023	73. 2	3, 732	16. 9
Private-duty nursing	141, 167	67. 0	137, 446	72. 9	3, 721	16. 8
Visiting-nurse service	136, 687	64. 9	132, 044	70. 1	4, 643	21. 0
Nursing-home care	69, 840	33. 2	66, 343	35. 2	3, 497	15. 8
HIAA estimates:						
Hospital care	171, 760	81. 6	160, 483	85. 2	11, 277	51. 0
Surgical services	162, 571	77. 2	153, 346	81. 4	9, 225	41. 7

[1] Based on Bureau of the Census estimate of 210,593,000 as of Jan. 1, 1975.
[2] Based on Bureau of the Census estimate of 188,467,000 as of Jan. 1, 1975.
[3] Based on Bureau of the Census estimate of 22,126,000 as of Jan. 1, 1975.

TABLE 2.—*Gross enrollment under private health insurance plans for persons of all ages, by type of plan and specified type of care, as of Dec. 31, 1974*

[In thousands]

Type of plan	Hospital care	Physicians' services				Dental care	Pre-scribed drugs (out-of-hospital)	Private duty nursing	Visiting-nurse service	Nursing-home care	Vision care
		Surgical services	In-hospital visits	X-ray and lab-oratory examina-tions	Office and home visits						
Total enrollment	207,895	194,576	191,429	181,634	150,612	33,297	148,731	148,113	148,382	71,202	(¹)
Blue Cross-Blue Shield	83,845	76,878	74,847	64,240	34,854	3,790	40,329	38,785	31,297	38,108	1,446
Blue Cross	81,399	4,289	3,785	(¹)	1,261	(¹)	(¹)	(¹)	(¹)	(¹)	(¹)
Blue Shield	2,446	72,634	71,062	(¹)	33,598	(¹)	(¹)	(¹)	(¹)	(¹)	(¹)
Insurance companies	114,566	105,164	104,898	105,142	103,804	16,842	103,095	103,075	103,075	29,025	(¹)
Group policies	85,759	86,630	97,317	97,894	96,593	16,756	95,840	95,840	95,840	23,960	(¹)
Individual policies	28,807	18,534	7,581	7,248	7,211	86	7,235	7,235	7,235	5,065	(¹)
Independent plans	9,484	12,539	11,684	12,252	11,954	12,665	5,327	8,253	9,010	4,069	6,636
Community	3,638	6,110	6,110	6,010	6,020	1,211	1,796	4,830	5,400	1,600	4,200
Employer-employee-union	5,695	6,275	5,420	6,088	5,760	1,900	3,500	3,403	3,600	2,363	2,294
Private group clinic	151	154	154	154	154	54	31	20	10	106	142
Dental service corporation						9,500					

¹ Data not available.

TABLE 3.—*Gross enrollment under private health insurance plans for persons under age 65, by type of plan and specified type of care, as of Dec. 31, 1974*

[In thousands]

Type of plan	Hospital care	Physicians' services				Dental care	Pre-scribed drugs (out-of-hospital)	Private duty nursing	Visiting-nurse service	Nursing-home care	Vision care
		Surgical services	In-hospital visits	X-ray and lab-oratory examina-tions	Office and home visits						
Total enrollment	192,467	182,960	181,324	173,747	140,785	32,887	144,924	144,318	138,646	67,670	(1)
Blue Cross-Blue Shield	75,992	69,838	68,012	60,127	28,238	3,699	38,880	35,433	29,129	35,468	1,157
Blue Cross	73,798	3,830	3,492	(1)	1,187	(1)	(1)	(1)	(1)	(1)	(1)
Blue Shield	2,194	66,008	64,520	27,051	27,051	(1)	(1)	(1)	(1)	(1)	(1)
Insurance companies	107,602	101,288	102,340	102,080	101,272	16,578	101,065	101,065	101,065	28,425	(1)
Group policies	84,234	85,170	95,222	95,023	94,237	16,492	94,047	94,047	94,047	23,512	(1)
Individual policies	23,368	16,118	7,118	7,057	7,035	86	7,018	7,018	7,018	4,913	(1)
Independent plans	8,873	11,834	10,972	11,540	11,275	12,610	4,979	7,820	8,452	3,777	6,182
Community	3,442	5,838	5,838	5,738	5,748	1,187	1,713	4,638	5,146	1,502	3,946
Employer-employee-union	5,299	5,863	5,001	5,669	5,394	1,871	3,255	3,165	3,296	2,178	2,107
Private group clinic	132	133	133	133	133	52	11	17	10	97	129
Dental service corporation						9,500					

1 Data not available.

TABLE 4.—*Gross enrollment under private health insurance plans for persons aged 65 and over, by type of plan and specified type of care, as of Dec. 31, 1974*

[In thousands]

Type of plan	Hospital care	Physicians' services				Dental care	Pre-scribed drugs (out-of-hospital)	Private duty nursing	Visiting-nurse service	Nursing-home care	Vision care
		Surgical services	In-hospital visits	X-ray and laboratory examinations	Office and home visits						
Total enrollment	15,428	11,616	10,105	7,887	9,827	410	3,807	3,795	4,736	3,532	(¹)
Blue Cross-Blue Shield ²	7,853	7,035	6,835	³4,113	6,616	91	1,449	1,352	2,168	³2,640	28
Blue Cross	7,601	409	293	(¹)	74	(¹)	(¹)	(¹)	(¹)	(¹)	(¹)
Blue Shield	252	6,626	6,542	(¹)	6,542	(¹)	(¹)	(¹)	(¹)	(¹)	(¹)
Insurance companies	6,964	3,876	2,558	3,062	2,532	264	2,010	2,010	2,010	600	(¹)
Group policies	1,525	1,460	2,095	2,871	2,356	264	1,793	1,793	1,793	448	(¹)
Individual policies	5,439	2,416	463	191	176	------	217	217	217	152	(¹)
Independent plans	611	705	712	712	679	55	348	433	558	292	45
Community	196	272	272	272	272	24	83	192	254	98	25
Employer-employee-union	396	412	419	419	386	29	245	238	304	185	18
Private group clinic	19	21	21	21	21	2	20	3	------	9	1
Dental service corporation	------	------	------	------	------	0	------	------	------	------	------

¹ Data not available.
² Includes disabled persons under age 65.
³ Mainly coverage of medicare deductibles.

TABLE 5.—*Percentage distribution of total gross enrollment under private health insurance plans, by age, type of plan, and specified type of care, as of Dec. 31, 1974*

| Age group and type of plan | Hospital care | Physicians' services | | | | Dental care | Prescribed drugs (out-of-hospital) | Private-duty nursing | Visiting-nurse service | Nursing-home care |
		Surgical services	In-hospital visits	X-ray and laboratory examinations	Office and home visits					
Total, all ages	100.0	100.0	100.0	100.0	100.0	100.0	100.0	100.0	100.0	100.0
Blue Cross-Blue Shield	40.3	39.5	39.1	35.4	23.1	11.4	27.1	24.8	21.8	53.5
Insurance companies	55.1	54.0	54.8	57.9	68.9	50.6	69.3	69.6	71.9	40.8
Group policies	41.2	44.5	50.8	53.9	64.1	50.3	64.4	61.7	66.8	33.7
Individual policies	13.9	9.5	4.0	4.0	4.8	.3	4.9	4.9	5.0	7.1
Independent plans	4.6	6.4	6.1	6.7	7.9	38.0	3.6	5.6	6.3	5.7
Under age 65	100.0	100.0	100.0	100.0	100.0	100.0	100.0	100.0	100.0	100.0
Blue Cross-Blue Shield	39.5	38.2	37.5	34.6	20.1	11.2	26.8	24.6	21.0	52.4
Insurance companies	55.9	55.4	56.4	58.8	71.9	50.4	69.7	70.0	72.9	42.0
Group policies	43.8	46.6	52.5	54.7	66.9	50.1	64.9	65.2	67.8	34.7
Individual policies	12.1	8.8	3.9	4.1	5.0	.3	4.8	4.8	5.1	7.3
Independent plans	4.6	6.5	6.0	6.6	8.0	38.3	3.4	5.4	6.1	5.6
Aged 65 and over	100.0	100.0	100.0	100.0	100.0	100.0	100.0	100.0	100.0	100.0
Blue Cross-Blue Shield	50.9	60.6	67.6	52.1	67.3	22.2	38.1	35.6	45.8	74.7
Insurance companies	45.1	33.4	25.3	38.8	25.8	64.4	52.8	53.0	42.4	17.0
Group policies	9.9	12.6	20.7	36.4	24.0	64.4	47.1	47.2	37.9	12.7
Individual policies	35.2	20.8	4.6	2.4	1.8	------	5.7	5.7	4.6	4.3
Independent plans	4.0	6.1	7.0	9.0	6.9	13.4	9.1	11.4	11.8	8.3

TABLE 6.—*Hospital benefits: gross enrollment under private health insurance plans for persons of all ages and estimates of the net number of different persons covered, by type of plan, 1950–74*

[In thousands]

End of year	Gross enrollments												Net number of different persons covered, as estimated by—			
	Total	Blue Cross-Blue Shield			Insurance companies			Independent plans					Household surveys		HIAA	
		Total	Blue Cross	Blue Shield	Total	Group policies	Individual policies	Total	Community	Employer-employee-union	Medical society	Private group clinic	Number[1]	Percent of civilian population	Number	Percent of civilian population
1950	81,691	37,645	37,435	210	39,601	22,305	17,296	4,445	1,445	2,280	500	220				
1955	113,976	48,924	47,719	1,205	58,507	38,620	19,887	6,545	2,920	3,220	360	45				
1960	140,055	57,464	55,938	1,526	76,597	54,416	22,181	5,994	1,604	4,000	340	50				
1965	160,485	63,662	61,651	2,012	89,839	65,415	24,424	6,984	1,954	4,971	8	51			138,671	71.9
1966	164,958	65,638	63,408	2,230	92,687	67,799	24,888	6,633	1,964	4,618		51			142,369	73.2
1967	170,636	67,513	65,188	2,325	96,073	71,544	24,619	7,050	2,300	4,700		50	145,454	73.9	146,409	74.4
1968	177,138	70,510	67,958	2,552	99,351	74,073	25,278	7,277	2,507	4,749		20	150,888	75.9	151,947	76.4
1969	184,808	73,211	70,620	2,591	103,895	77,973	25,922	7,702	2,672	5,000		30			155,025	77.2
1970	190,758	75,464	72,942	2,522	107,163	80,505	26,658	8,131	2,900	5,200		31	154,063	75.9	158,847	78.2
1971	193,308	76,349	74,383	1,966	108,414	80,641	27,773	8,545	3,100	5,400		45			161,849	78.8
1972	198,132	78,605	76,322	2,283	110,537	81,526	29,011	8,990	3,370	5,560		60	155,253	74.9	164,098	79.2
1973	201,684	81,345	79,199	2,146	111,170	83,626	27,544	9,169	3,538	5,491		140			167,147	80.0
1974	207,895	83,845	81,399	2,446	114,566	85,759	28,807	9,484	3,638	5,695		151	163,396	77.6	171,760	81.6

[1] Estimated by applying percentages to total civilian population.

TABLE 7.—*Surgical benefits: gross enrollment under private health insurance plans for persons of all ages and estimates of the net number of different persons covered, by type of plan, 1950–74*

[In thousands]

End of year	Total	Blue Cross-Blue Shield			Insurance companies			Independent plans					Net number of different persons covered, as estimated by—			
													Household surveys		HIAA	
		Total	Blue Cross	Blue Shield	Total	Group policies	Individual policies	Total	Community	Employer-employee-union	Medical society	Private group clinic	Number[1]	Percent of civilian population	Number	Percent of civilian population
1950	55,950	17,253	1,151	16,102	34,937	21,219	13,718	3,760	940	1,950	600	270				
1955	98,000	37,395	3,194	34,201	54,675	39,703	14,972	5,930	2,130	3,200	430	170				
1960	127,091	48,266	3,773	44,493	71,489	55,464	16,025	7,336	2,760	4,020	346	210				
1965	148,236	56,236	3,660	52,669	83,222	65,487	17,735	8,684	3,400	5,068	10	206			130,530	67.7
1966	152,106	57,916	3,417	54,499	85,865	68,114	17,751	8,325	3,526	4,601		198			133,995	68.9
1967	158,654	60,433	3,416	57,017	89,641	72,038	17,603	8,580	3,900	4,500		180	142,082	72.2	138,898	70.6
1968	164,540	63,279	3,464	59,815	92,509	75,038	17,471	8,752	4,132	4,476		143	148,082	74.5	143,625	72.2
1969	173,108	66,595	3,629	62,966	96,563	78,864	17,699	9,950	4,500	5,300		150			147,774	73.6
1970	179,152	69,110	3,874	65,236	99,510	81,549	17,961	10,532	4,900	5,500		132	150,001	73.9	151,440	74.6
1971	181,191	70,395	3,831	66,564	99,936	81,802	18,134	10,860	5,100	5,630		130			153,093	74.5
1972	185,153	72,433	4,020	68,413	101,230	82,670	18,560	11,490	5,350	6,000		140	152,651	73.6	154,687	74.6
1973	190,359	75,136	4,098	71,038	103,091	84,483	18,608	12,132	5,930	6,057		145			158,624	75.9
1974	194,576	76,873	4,239	72,634	105,164	86,630	18,534	12,539	6,110	6,275		154	159,518	75.7	162,571	77.2

[1] Estimated by applying percentages to total civilian population.

TABLE 8.—*Hospital benefits: Gross enrollment under private health insurance plans and estimates of the net number of different persons covered, by age and type of plan, 1960–72*

[In thousands]

End of year	Gross enrollments					Net number of different persons covered, as estimated by—				Gross enrollment as percent of net, estimated by—	
	Total	Blue Cross-Blue Shield	Insurance companies		Independent plans	Household surveys		HIAA		Household surveys	HIAA
			Group policies	Individual policies		Number	Percent of civilian population	Number	Percent of civilian population		
Under age 65											
1960	139,855	53,070	53,718	27,487	5,580	------	------	120,772	74.1	------	115.8
1961	142,576	52,750	55,263	27,951	6,612	------	------	124,595	75.4	------	114.4
1962	146,626	54,194	56,853	29,121	6,458	120,220	72.3	128,877	76.8	122.0	114.0
1963	152,822	55,072	60,417	30,662	6,671	------	------	133,267	78.2	------	114.7
1964	157,083	56,663	62,006	32,057	6,357	------	------	(1)	(1)	------	------
1965	162,461	57,884	64,504	33,572	6,501	------	------	140,219	80.3	------	115.9
1966	170,053	60,575	67,546	35,729	6,203	------	------	146,507	83.3	------	116.1
1967	²75,672	62,103	71,279	35,670	6,620	136,907	77.0	151,628	85.3	128.3	115.9
1968	182,440	65,086	74,128	36,451	6,775	141,572	78.9	157,128	87.6	128.9	116.1
1969	190,320	67,251	78,194	37,621	7,254	------	------	160,189	88.3	------	118.8
1970	197,038	69,128	80,685	39,595	7,630	143,611	78.6	164,210	88.9	137.2	120.0
1971	201,365	69,704	81,047	42,589	8,025	²146,565	79.4	167,588	90.7	137.4	120.2
1972	207,451	71,677	82,261	45,073	8,440	³148,285	79.7	169,555	91.1	140.0	122.4
Aged 65 and over											
1960	9,008	4,394	1,500	2,700	414	------	------	9,235	54.8	------	97.5
1961	10,450	5,210	1,750	3,000	490	------	------	9,822	57.2	------	106.4
1962	12,003	5,424	2,300	3,800	479	9,125	54.1	10,299	59.1	131.5	116.5
1963	12,320	5,626	2,400	3,800	494	------	------	11,308	63.8	------	108.9
1964	12,538	5,766	2,500	3,800	472	------	------	(1)	(1)	------	------
1965	12,661	5,778	2,600	3,800	483	------	------	11,264	61.5	------	112.4
1966	10,439	5,073	2,024	2,912	430	------	------	9,357	50.1	------	111.6
1967	10,150	5,410	2,072	2,238	430	8,547	45.0	9,021	47.5	118.8	112.5
1968	11,115	5,424	1,931	3,258	502	⁴9,316	48.2	10,081	52.2	119.3	110.3
1969	12,155	5,960	1,899	3,848	448	------	------	10,666	54.3	------	114.0
1970	12,749	6,336	2,027	3,885	501	10,452	51.4	11,172	54.9	122.0	114.1
1971	12,909	6,645	1,806	3,938	520	⁵10,618	51.1	11,350	54.6	121.6	113.7
1972	13,821	6,928	1,507	4,836	550	⁶11,270	⁶53.2	12,047	56.9	122.6	114.7

¹ Data not available.

² Estimated by applying HIAA percentage increase in net enrollment from 1970 to 1971 to the NCHS figures for 1970.

³ Estimated by applying HIAA percentage increase in net enrollment from 1971 to 1972 to the 1971 estimate.

⁴ Estimated on basis of percentage increase in gross enrollment from the preceding year.

⁵ Estimated on basis of HIAA percentage increase in net enrollment from the preceding year.

⁶ In the Current Medicare Survey of the Social Security Administration, 57.6 percent of those enrolled for supplementary medical insurance were reported as having private hospital insurance as of Jan. 1, 1973.

TABLE 9.—*Surgical benefits: Gross enrollment under private health insurance plans and estimates of the net number of different persons covered, by age and type of plan, 1960–74*

[In thousands]

End of year	Gross enrollments					Net number of different persons covered, as estimated by—				Gross enrollment as percent of net, estimated by—	
	Total	Blue Cross-Blue Shield	Insurance companies		Independent plans	Household surveys		HIAA		Household surveys	HIAA
			Group policies	Individual policies		Number	Percent of civilian population	Number	Percent of civilian population		
Under age 65											
1960	127,386	45,226	54,104	21,212	6,844	-----	-----	109,452	67.2	-----	116.4
1961	132,209	45,649	55,673	22,962	7,925	-----	-----	114,645	69.3	-----	115.3
1962	134,609	46,599	57,487	22,791	7,732	113,569	68.3	(¹)	(¹)	118.5	(¹)
1963	139,278	46,086	60,888	24,273	8,031	-----	-----	122,112	71.6	-----	114.1
1964	144,811	49,825	62,439	24,806	7,741	-----	-----	(¹)	(¹)	-----	(¹)
1965	150,946	51,348	64,957	26,539	8,102	-----	-----	129,514	74.2	-----	116.5
1966	157,504	53,613	68,574	27,479	7,838	-----	-----	136,062	77.4	-----	115.8
1967	163,643	56,020	72,583	26,965	8,075	133,706	75.2	141,208	79.4	122.4	115.9
1968	168,588	58,390	75,619	26,300	8,279	139,061	77.5	145,553	81.1	121.2	115.8
1969	176,716	60,499	79,571	27,196	9,450	-----	-----	149,847	82.6	-----	117.9
1970	183,587	63,066	82,201	28,347	9,973	140,505	76.9	153,352	83.9	130.7	119.7
1971	185,865	63,891	82,548	29,144	10,282	² 141,944	76.9	154,923	83.9	130.9	120.0
1972	191,023	65,642	83,786	30,725	10,870	³ 143,523	77.1	156,646	84.2	133.1	122.0
1973	196,110	67,798	82,861	33,989	11,462	145,352	77.6	159,462	85.1	-----	123.0
1974	182,960	69,838	85,170	16,118	11,834	147,570	78.3	153,346	81.4	-----	-----
Aged 65 and over											
1960	6,732	3,040	1,400	1,800	492	-----	-----	7,852	46.6	-----	85.7
1961	7,894	3,725	1,700	1,900	569	-----	-----	8,306	48.4	-----	95.0
1962	9,832	4,277	2,300	2,700	555	7,792	46.2	(¹)	(¹)	126.2	(¹)
1963	9,962	4,285	2,400	2,700	577	-----	-----	9,842	55.6	-----	101.2
1964	10,404	4,648	2,500	2,700	556	-----	-----	(¹)	(¹)	-----	(¹)
1965	10,864	4,982	2,600	2,700	582	-----	-----	9,923	54.2	-----	109.5
1966	8,307	4,304	1,694	822	487	-----	-----	7,222	38.7	-----	115.0
1967	8,407	4,413	1,735	1,754	505	8,376	44.1	7,521	39.6	100.4	111.8
1968	9,059	4,889	1,796	1,901	473	⁴ 9,021	46.7	8,424	43.6	100.4	107.5
1969	10,289	6,096	1,792	1,901	500	-----	-----	8,737	44.5	-----	117.8
1970	10,316	6,044	1,932	1,781	559	9,496	46.7	9,303	45.8	108.6	110.9
1971	10,594	6,504	1,846	1,666	578	⁵ 9,766	47.0	9,568	46.0	108.5	110.7
1972	10,679	6,791	1,504	1,764	620	⁶ 9,813	46.3	9,615	45.4	108.8	111.1
1973	11,014	7,338	1,165	1,841	670	11,561	53.6	9,954	46.1	-----	110.6
1974	11,616	7,035	1,460	2,416	705	11,948	54.0	9,225	41.7	-----	-----

¹ Data not available.
² See footnote 2, table 8.
³ See footnote 3, table 8.
⁴ See footnote 4, table 8.
⁵ See footnote 5, table 8.
⁶ In the Current Medicare Survey of the Social Security Administration, 46.7 percent of those enrolled for supplementary medical insurance were reported as having private surgical insurance as of Jan. 1, 1973.

TABLE 10.—*Estimates of the net number of different persons under private health insurance plans and percent of population covered by specified type of care, 1962–74*

End of year	Hospital care	Physicians' services				Dental care	Prescribed drugs (out-of-hospital)	Private-duty nursing	Visiting-nurse service	Nursing-home care
		Surgical services	In-hospital visits	X-ray and laboratory examinations	Office and home visits					
Number (in thousands):										
1962	129,800.0	120,528.0	(1)	65,671.0	(1)	1,006.0	47,907.0	46,143.0	43,203.0	4,975.0
1965	(1)	(1)	(1)	79,500.0	(1)	3,100.0	53,200.0	56,000.0	60,100.0	9,900.0
1966	(1)	(1)	(1)	90,000.0	(1)	4,227.0	65,544.0	68,722.0	79,004.0	17,814.0
1967	145,454.0	142,082.0	(1)	92,480.0	(1)	4,679.0	71,201.0	76,080.0	81,771.0	18,754.0
1968	(1)	(1)	128,174.0	97,703.0	(1)	5,821.0	79,280.0	83,485.0	90,523.0	19,046.0
1969	(1)	(1)	133,914.0	125,002.0	(1)	8,510.0	89,805.0	91,211.0	100,343.0	28,044.0
1970	154,263.0	150,001.0	145,589.0	142,441.0	101,970.0	12,210.0	100,966.0	100,235.0	106,882.0	32,392.0
1971	(1)	(1)	148,514.0	145,207.0	(1)	15,348.0	106,985.0	104,730.0	110,215.0	38,636.0
1972	155,253.0	152,651.0	149,734.0	149,444.0	(1)	17,904.0	111,374.0	108,959.0	115,904.0	45,460.0
1973	(1)	(1)	153,461.0	152,797.0	(1)	21,626.0	124,971.0	118,805.0	122,688.0	69,152.0
1974	163,396.0	159,518.0	155,022.0	153,017.0	125,183.0	33,297.0	141,755.0	141,167.0	136,687.0	69,840.0
Percent of civilian population:										
1962	70.0	65.0	(1)	35.0	(1)	.5	26.0	25.0	23.0	3.0
1965	(1)	(1)	(1)	41.2	(1)	1.6	27.6	29.0	31.2	5.1
1966	(1)	(1)	(1)	48.0	(1)	2.2	33.7	35.5	40.6	9.2
1967	75.9	72.2	(1)	47.0	(1)	2.4	36.2	38.7	41.6	9.2
1968	(1)	(1)	64.5	49.2	(1)	2.9	39.9	42.0	45.5	9.6
1969	(1)	(1)	66.6	62.2	(1)	4.2	44.7	45.4	49.9	14.0
1970	75.9	73.9	71.7	70.2	50.2	6.0	49.7	49.4	52.6	16.0
1971	(1)	(1)	72.3	70.7	(1)	7.5	52.1	51.0	53.6	18.8
1972	74.9	73.6	72.2	72.1	(1)	8.6	53.7	52.6	55.9	21.9
1973	(1)	(1)	73.4	73.1	(1)	10.4	59.8	56.9	58.7	33.1
1974	77.6	75.7	73.6	72.7	59.4	15.8	67.3	67.0	64.9	33.2

¹ Data not available.

TABLE 11.—*Number of persons covered under major medical policies of insurance companies and under supplementary major-medical and comprehensive extended-benefit contracts of Blue Cross, Blue-Shield plans, 1960–74*

[In thousands]

End of year	Insurance companies					Blue Cross-Blue Shield [1]		
		Group policies						Compre-hensive extended-benefit
	Total	Net total	Supple-mentary	Compre-hensive	Individual policies	Total	Supplemen-tary major-medical	
1960	25, 371	24, 429	17, 991	8, 463	1, 607	3, 713	3, 020	693
1961	32, 334	30, 729	24, 488	9, 851	2, 372	5, 059	4, 015	1, 044
1962	37, 130	35, 002	28, 445	10, 636	2, 949	7, 501	5, 068	1, 735
1963	42, 003	39, 446	32, 307	11, 699	3, 459	(2)	(2)	(2)
1964	47, 338	44, 087	36, 925	12, 241	4, 185	(2)	(2)	(2)
1965	53, 020	49, 700	42, 450	12, 962	4, 456	[3] 14, 600	(2)	(2)
1966	57, 881	54, 732	46, 830	14, 154	4, 516	14, 352	10, 409	3, 943
1967	63, 248	60, 517	51, 824	15, 570	4, 552	16, 279	12, 408	3, 871
1968	68, 171	65, 076	55, 422	17, 014	4, 873	17, 807	14, 078	3, 729
1969	73, 752	70, 272	58, 905	19, 260	5, 377	20, 328	16, 666	3, 662
1970	77, 061	73, 702	61, 718	20, 244	5, 414	24, 905	21, 658	3, 247
1971	80, 252	76, 971	63, 442	22, 111	5, 479	26, 780	23, 429	3, 351
1972	83, 668	79, 025	64, 443	23, 363	6, 630	30, 082	26, 879	3, 203
1973	87, 839	82, 724	66, 225	25, 690	7, 310	37, 328	33, 947	3, 381
1974	91, 321	86, 256	68, 122	27, 718	7, 235	40, 862	37, 239	3, 623

[1] Comparable data not available for earlier years; before 1965 data shown are for Blue Cross plans only; beginning 1965, data are jointly developed by Blue Cross Association and National Association of Blue Shield Plans on un-duplicated number of persons covered.

[2] Data not available.
[3] Data for Blue Cross plans plus an estimated 1,600,000 in Blue Shield plans not affiliated with Blue Cross.

TABLE 12.—*Private health insurance enrollment under independent group practice prepayment plans, by specified type of care, 1953–74*

[In thousands]

Year		Physicians' services			Dental care	Drugs
	Hospital care	Surgical services	In-hospital visits	Office, clinic, or health center		
1953	1, 802	2, 410	2, 507	2, 853	452	(1)
1956	2, 428	3, 177	3, 399	3, 395	248	(1)
1959	2, 526	3, 280	3, 400	3, 694	318	(1)
1961	2, 586	3, 484	3, 643	3, 613	398	518
1964	2, 695	3, 504	3, 176	3, 844	438	889
1966	2, 771	3, 763	3, 430	4, 158	(1)	(1)
1967	3, 060	4, 130	3, 760	4, 480	(1)	(1)
1968	3, 043	4, 051	3, 730	4, 404	518	1, 382
1969	3, 730	4, 750	4, 210	5, 050	800	1, 720
1970	4, 131	5, 032	4, 532	5, 432	910	2, 121
1971	4, 415	5, 230	4, 880	5, 630	965	2, 321
1972	4, 679	5, 473	5, 123	5, 865	977	2, 543
1973	4, 905	5, 671	5, 288	6, 066	1, 000	[2] 1, 741
1974	4, 976	5, 779	5, 424	6, 174	997	[2] 1, 821

[1] Data not available.
[2] Excludes those enrolled under plans that sell drugs to members at reduced rates.

TABLE 13.—*Financial experience of private health insurance organizations, 1974*

[Amounts in millions]

Type of plan	Total income	Subscription or premium income	Claims expense		Operating expense		Net underwriting gain		Net income	
			Amount	Percent of premium income	Amount	Percent of premium income	Amount	Percent of premium income	Amount	Percent of total income
Total	(1)	$28,399.9	$24,766.8	87.2	$3,992.8	14.1	$359.7	-1.3	(1)	(1)
Blue Cross-Blue Shield	$12,611.8	12,367.0	11,639.5	94.1	911.0	7.4	-183.5	-1.5	$61.3	0.5
Blue Cross	8,757.7	8,647.6	8,311.1	96.1	470.2	5.4	-133.7	-1.5	-23.6	-.3
Blue Shield	3,854.1	3,719.4	3,328.4	89.5	440.8	11.8	-49.8	-1.3	84.9	2.2
Insurance companies	(1)	13,867.0	11,109.3	80.1	2,916.9	21.0	-159.2	-1.1	(1)	(1)
Group policies	(1)	10,590.0	9,592.2	90.6	1,376.7	13.0	-378.9	-3.6	(1)	(1)
Individual policies	(1)	3,277.0	1,517.1	46.3	1,540.2	47.0	219.7	6.7	(1)	(1)
Independent plans	2,221.0	2,165.9	2,018.0	93.2	164.9	7.6	-17.0	-.8	38.1	1.7
Community	855.4	847.5	798.1	94.2	57.2	6.7	-7.8	-.9	.1	.1
Employer-employee-union	938.0	897.0	853.4	95.1	62.7	7.0	-19.1	-2.1	21.9	2.3
Private group clinic	34.8	33.4	26.5	79.3	5.0	15.0	1.9	5.7	3.3	9.5
Dental service corporation	392.8	388.0	340.0	87.6	40.0	10.3	8.0	2.1	12.8	3.3

[1] Data not available.
[2] Less than 0.05 percent.

TABLE 14.—*Percentage distribution of subscription or premium income and claims expense, by type of private health insurance organization, 1948–73*

Year	Total	Blue Cross-Blue Shield plans			Insurance companies			Independent plans				
		Total	Blue Cross	Blue Shield	Total	Group policies	Individual policies	Total	Community	Employer-employee-union	Private group clinic	Dental service corporation
					Subscription or premium income							
1948	100.0	42.3	36.5	5.8	48.8	24.6	24.2	8.8	(1)	(1)	(1)	(1)
1950	100.0	44.4	33.8	10.6	46.8	25.8	21.1	8.7	(1)	(1)	(1)	(1)
1955	100.0	41.0	28.9	12.1	51.7	32.5	19.2	7.3	(1)	(1)	(1)	(1)
1960	100.0	42.5	30.4	12.1	51.8	36.0	15.8	5.7	2.3	3.2	0.2	(2)
1961	100.0	42.0	30.0	12.0	51.4	36.2	15.2	6.6	2.2	3.8	.2	0.1
1962	100.0	42.1	29.9	12.2	51.4	36.5	14.9	6.5	2.2	3.8	.1	(2)
1963	100.0	42.2	30.3	11.9	51.4	36.2	15.2	6.4	2.3	3.6	.2	.1
1964	100.0	42.1	30.0	12.1	51.8	36.7	15.1	6.1	2.2	3.7	.1	.1
1965	100.0	41.7	29.9	11.8	52.2	36.6	15.6	6.1	2.2	3.7	.1	.1
1966	100.0	41.0	29.2	11.8	52.9	37.7	15.2	6.1	2.3	3.5	.1	.2
1967	100.0	41.0	29.1	11.9	52.8	38.5	14.3	6.2	2.5	3.3	.1	.3
1968	100.0	40.2	28.4	11.8	53.7	40.0	13.7	6.1	2.5	3.2	.1	.3
1969	100.0	42.0	29.8	12.2	51.6	38.8	12.8	6.4	2.6	3.3	.1	.4
1970	100.0	42.9	30.0	12.9	50.9	39.4	11.5	6.2	2.6	3.1	.1	.4
1971	100.0	44.7	31.7	13.0	48.8	36.8	12.0	6.5	2.7	3.3	.1	.4
1972	100.0	44.4	31.6	12.8	48.8	37.2	11.6	6.8	2.8	3.2	.1	.7
1973	100.0	45.1	32.1	13.0	47.7	36.6	11.1	7.2	2.9	3.3	.1	.9
					Claims expense							
1948	100.0	50.8	44.4	6.4	37.6	24.4	13.2	11.6	(1)	(1)	(1)	(1)
1950	100.0	49.5	38.6	10.9	40.3	25.9	14.4	10.2	(1)	(1)	(1)	(1)
1955	100.0	45.2	32.8	12.4	46.5	33.8	12.7	8.3	(1)	(1)	(1)	(1)
1960	100.0	45.8	32.9	12.8	47.8	38.0	9.8	6.4	(1)	(1)	(1)	(1)
1961	100.0	45.4	32.8	12.6	47.5	38.1	9.4	7.1	(1)	(1)	(1)	(1)
1962	100.0	45.6	32.5	13.1	47.5	38.7	8.8	6.9	(1)	(1)	(1)	(1)
1963	100.0	45.6	33.2	12.4	47.7	38.3	9.5	6.7	(1)	(1)	(1)	(1)
1964	100.0	45.6	33.1	12.5	48.0	38.6	9.4	6.3	(1)	(1)	(1)	(1)
1965	100.0	44.8	32.7	12.1	48.9	39.1	9.8	6.3	2.3	3.8	.1	.1
1966	100.0	43.5	31.5	12.0	50.2	40.6	9.6	6.4	2.4	3.6	.1	.2
1967	100.0	42.8	31.0	11.7	50.7	41.9	8.8	6.5	2.6	3.5	.1	.3
1968	100.0	42.7	31.1	11.6	51.0	42.7	8.3	6.3	2.6	3.3	.1	.3
1969	100.0	45.2	32.7	12.5	48.2	40.9	7.3	6.6	2.7	3.4	.1	.4
1970	100.0	44.9	31.9	13.0	48.6	41.3	7.3	6.5	2.7	3.4	.1	.3
1971	100.0	46.2	33.4	12.8	47.1	39.9	7.2	6.7	2.9	3.4	.1	.3
1972	100.0	46.1	33.3	12.8	46.7	39.7	7.0	7.2	2.9	3.5	.1	.7
1973	100.0	46.3	33.3	13.0	45.9	38.5	7.4	7.8	3.2	3.6	.1	.9

[1] Data not available.
[2] Less than 0.05 percent.

TABLE 15.—*Benefit expenditures of private health insurance organizations, by specified type of care, 1974*

[In millions]

Type of plan	Total	Hospital care	Physi- cians' services	Dental care	Pre- scribed drugs (out-of hospital)	Private- duty nursing	Visiting- nurse service	Nursing- home care	Vision care	Other types of care
Total	$24,766.8	$15,005.6	$7,795.3	$778.4	$619.3	$211.6	$8.4	$27.9	$13.2	$307.1
Blue Cross-Blue Shield	11,639.5	7,841.3	3,304.0	53.5	183.3	14.6	7.0	25.9	2.8	207.1
Blue Cross	8,311.1	7,670.0	322.2	31.5	89.8	11.1	6.2	25.2	1.6	153.5
Blue Shield	3,328.4	171.3	2,981.8	22.0	93.5	3.5	.8	.7	1.2	53.6
Insurance companies	11,109.3	6,458.0	3,705.0	332.2	344.9	194.1	(1)	(1)	(1)	75.1
Group policies	9,592.2	5,398.6	3,315.1	332.2	342.6	129.6	(1)	(1)	(1)	74.1
Individual policies	1,517.1	1,059.4	389.9		2.3	64.5	(1)	(1)	(1)	1.0
Independent plans	2,018.0	706.3	786.3	392.7	91.1	2.9	1.4	2.0	10.4	24.9
Community	798.1	242.6	480.9	28.0	27.0	1.4	.1	.2	6.0	11.9
Employer-employee-union	853.4	455.7	291.5	22.4	63.5	1.4	1.3	.8	4.2	12.5
Private group clinic	26.5	8.0	13.9	2.3	.6	.1	--------	1.0	.2	.4
Dental service corporation	340.0			340.0						

[1] Included in "other types of care."

TABLE 16.—*Subscription or premium income and benefit expenditures of private health organizations, 1950–74*

[In millions]

Year	Total	Blue Cross-Blue Shield			Insurance companies			Independent plans
		Total	Blue Cross	Blue Shield	Total	Group policies	Individual policies	
Income:								
1950	$1,291.5	$574.0	$436.7	$137.3	$605.0	$333.0	$272.0	$112.5
1955	3,149.6	1,292.4	910.7	381.7	1,626.9	1,022.5	604.4	230.3
1960	5,841.0	2,482.0	1,773.0	709.1	3,027.0	2,104.0	923.0	331.9
1965	10,001.3	4,169.0	2,993.7	1,175.3	5,224.0	3,665.0	1,559.0	608.3
1966	10,564.1	4,327.8	3,085.9	1,241.9	5,595.0	3,987.0	1,608.0	641.3
1967	11,105.3	4,555.3	3,230.0	1,325.3	5,858.0	4,270.0	1,588.0	692.0
1968	12,898.7	5,187.1	3,665.0	1,522.1	6,933.0	5,159.0	1,774.0	778.6
1969	14,657.7	6,155.6	4,365.2	1,790.4	7,569.0	5,685.0	1,884.0	933.1
1970	17,184.8	7,370.9	5,147.1	2,223.8	8,746.0	6,774.0	1,972.0	1,067.9
1971	19,659.1	8,790.2	6,239.6	2,550.6	9,601.0	7,231.0	2,370.0	1,267.9
1972	22,806.8	9,923.3	7,066.9	2,856.4	11,342.0	8,614.0	2,728.0	1,541.5
1973	25,294.2	11,059.1	7,862.1	3,197.0	12,386.0	9,393.0	2,993.0	1,849.1
1974	28,399.9	12,367.0	8,647.6	3,719.4	13,867.0	10,590.0	3,277.0	2,165.9
Benefit expenditures:								
1950	$991.9	$490.6	$382.9	$107.7	$400.0	$257.0	$143.0	$101.3
1955	2,535.7	1,146.7	832.3	314.5	1,179.0	858.0	321.0	210.0
1960	4,996.3	2,287.1	1,646.2	640.9	2,389.0	1,901.0	488.0	320.2
1965	8,728.9	3,912.9	2,853.4	1,059.5	4,265.0	3,413.0	852.0	551.0
1966	9,141.8	3,975.4	2,882.2	1,093.2	4,585.0	3,711.0	874.0	581.4
1967	9,544.8	4,082.8	2,963.1	1,119.7	4,837.0	3,998.0	839.0	625.0
1968	11,343.6	4,840.6	3,529.2	1,311.4	5,791.0	4,841.0	950.0	712.0
1969	13,068.5	5,903.1	4,271.4	1,631.7	6,306.0	5,349.0	957.0	859.4
1970	15,743.5	7,060.2	5,009.3	2,050.9	7,656.0	6,510.0	1,146.0	1,027.4
1971	17,713.1	8,178.7	5,906.9	2,271.8	8,341.0	7,067.0	1,274.0	1,193.4
1972	19,532.3	8,990.9	6,501.3	2,489.6	9,120.0	7,754.0	1,366.0	1,421.4
1973	21,334.7	10,004.2	7,187.3	2,816.9	9,647.7	8,185.3	1,462.4	1,682.8
1974	24,766.8	11,639.5	8,311.1	3,328.4	11,109.3	9,592.2	1,517.1	2,018.0

TABLE 17.—*Financial experience of Blue Cross plans, 1950–74* [1]

[Dollar amounts in thousands]

Year	Reserves	Earned subscription income	Total earned income	Claims expense	Operating expense	Total net income	As percent of subscription income			Net income as percent of total income
							Claims expense	Operating expense	Underwriting gain	
1950	$116,531	$433,770	$436,984	$383,331	$36,281	$17,371	88.4	8.4	3.3	4.0
1955	254,407	916,690	925,197	836,546	58,368	30,283	91.3	6.4	2.4	3.3
1960	363,253	1,783,172	1,802,789	1,654,951	90,821	57,017	92.8	5.1	2.1	3.2
1965 [2]	561,906	3,031,470	3,074,551	2,887,187	134,559	52,805	95.2	4.5	.3	1.7
1966	649,633	3,121,111	3,168,187	2,912,733	154,132	101,322	93.3	4.9	.7	3.2
1967	797,575	3,270,022	3,327,677	2,996,779	177,632	153,266	91.6	5.4	3.0	4.6
1968	801,389	3,711,798	3,776,487	3,571,797	211,698	-7,008	96.2	5.7	-1.9	-.2
1969	711,274	4,419,296	4,489,266	4,322,341	256,227	-89,302	97.8	5.8	-3.6	-2.0
1970	651,655	5,385,835	5,467,512	5,220,662	302,463	-55,613	96.9	5.6	-2.5	-1.0
1971	747,230	6,390,127	6,477,615	6,053,537	338,910	85,168	94.7	5.3	(3)	1.3
1972	1,053,428	7,280,243	7,386,914	6,681,619	385,029	320,266	91.8	5.3	2.9	4.3
1973	1,464,418	8,091,784	8,248,680	7,374,871	436,210	437,600	91.1	5.4	3.5	5.3
1974	1,606,507	8,736,512	8,932,360	8,283,503	505,798	143,059	94.8	5.8	-.6	1.6

[1] Data in all years exclude Health Services, Inc., and Medical Indemnity of America, and are not adjusted for duplication between Blue Cross and Blue Shield.

[2] Includes Puerto Rico.

[3] Less than 0.05 percent.

TABLE 18.—*Financial experience of Blue Shield plans, 1950–74* [1]

[Dollar amounts in thousands]

Year	Reserves	Earned subscription income	Total earned income	Claims expense	Operating expense	Total net income	As percent of subscription income			Net income as percent of total income
							Claims expense	Operating expense	Underwriting gain	
1950	$34,954	$140,817	$141,594	$111,039	$18,653	$11,902	78.8	13.2	7.9	8.4
1955	164,705	399,781	404,294	331,068	43,610	29,616	82.8	10.9	6.3	7.3
1960	228,634	741,164	761,529	670,776	76,245	14,508	90.5	10.3	-.8	1.9
1965 [2]	347,266	1,318,915	1,338,907	1,190,486	115,940	32,481	90.3	8.8	.9	2.4
1966	398,374	1,399,890	1,413,185	1,226,383	129,864	56,938	88.2	9.3	2.5	4.0
1967	509,094	1,489,640	1,519,309	1,261,650	148,750	108,909	84.7	10.0	5.3	7.2
1968	578,390	1,709,548	1,747,867	1,481,070	180,154	86,643	86.6	10.5	2.8	5.0
1969	555,079	2,007,970	2,054,571	1,834,495	222,519	-2,438	91.4	11.1	-2.5	-.1
1970	491,066	2,320,877	2,369,600	2,165,572	254,726	-50,698	93.3	11.0	-4.3	-2.1
1971	528,202	2,814,696	2,868,368	2,530,826	295,282	-42,260	89.9	10.5	-.4	-1.5
1972	691,445	3,282,927	3,342,589	2,864,633	346,861	131,095	87.3	10.6	2.2	3.9
1973	791,147	3,761,845	3,841,613	3,339,650	396,965	104,998	88.8	10.6	2.7	2.7
1974 [3]	802,957	5,197,629	5,285,098	4,827,006	523,635	-65,513	92.9	10.1	-2.9	-1.2

[1] Data in all years exclude Health Services, Inc., and Medical Indemnity of American and are not adjusted for duplication between Blue Cross and Blue Shield.

[2] Includes Puerto Rico but excludes Jamaica.

[3] Data for 1974 are not directly comparable with earlier years because of the corporate merger of New York City Blue Cross and Blue Shield.

TABLE 19.—*Benefit expenditures of all private health insurance organizations, by specified type of care, 1950–74*

[Dollar amounts in millions]

Year	Total	Hospital care	Physicians' services	Other types of care
Amount:				
1950	$992	$680	$312	[1]
1955	2, 536	1, 679	857	[1]
1960	4, 996	3, 304	1, 593	$99
1965	8, 729	5, 790	2, 680	259
1966	9, 142	5, 993	2, 831	318
1967	9, 545	6, 134	2, 964	447
1968	11, 344	7, 329	3, 477	538
1969	13, 069	8, 356	4, 029	684
1970	15, 744	10, 008	4, 908	828
1971	17, 713	11, 279	5, 430	1, 004
1972	19, 532	12, 242	6, 092	1, 198
1973	21, 335	13, 154	6, 683	1, 498
1974	24, 767	15, 006	7, 795	1, 966
Percentage distribution:				
1950	100. 0	68. 5	31. 5	[1]
1955	100. 0	66. 2	33. 8	[1]
1960	100. 0	66. 1	31. 9	2. 0
1965	100. 0	66. 3	30. 7	3. 0
1966	100. 0	65. 5	31. 0	3. 5
1967	100. 0	64. 3	31. 0	4. 7
1968	100. 0	64. 6	30. 7	4. 7
1969	100. 0	63. 9	30. 8	5. 3
1970	100. 0	63. 6	31. 2	5. 2
1971	100. 0	63. 7	30. 6	5. 7
1972	100. 0	62. 7	31. 2	6. 1
1973	100. 0	61. 7	31. 3	7. 0
1974	100. 0	60. 6	31. 5	7. 9

[1] Included in "physicians' services."

TABLE 20.—*Retentions* [1] *of private health insurance organizations as a percent of subscription or premium income, 1950–74* [2]

Year	Total	Blue Cross-Blue Shield			Insurance companies			Independent plans [3]				
		Total	Blue Cross	Blue Shield	Total	Group policies	Individual policies	Total	Community	Employer-employee union	Private group clinic	Dental service corporation
1950	23.2	14.5	12.3	21.6	33.9	22.8	47.4	10.0	(3)	(3)	(3)	(3)
1955	19.5	11.3	8.6	17.6	27.5	16.1	46.9	8.8	(3)	(3)	(3)	(3)
1960	14.5	7.9	7.2	9.6	21.1	9.6	47.1	3.5	(3)	(3)	(3)	(3)
1965	12.7	6.1	4.7	9.9	18.4	6.9	45.3	9.4	8.2	10.2	10.7	6.9
1966	13.5	8.1	6.6	12.0	18.1	6.9	45.6	9.3	8.0	10.2	11.8	6.5
1967	14.0	10.4	8.3	15.5	17.4	6.4	47.2	9.7	8.4	10.8	13.3	6.2
1968	12.1	6.7	3.7	13.8	16.5	6.2	46.4	8.6	6.2	9.7	5.8	17.2
1969	10.8	4.1	2.2	8.9	16.7	5.9	49.2	7.9	6.9	8.2	12.9	10.8
1970	8.4	4.2	2.7	7.8	12.5	.9	41.9	3.8	4.5	1.6	18.0	14.7
1971	9.9	7.0	5.3	10.9	13.1	2.3	46.2	5.9	5.3	4.3	19.1	20.0
1972	14.4	9.4	8.0	12.8	19.6	10.0	49.9	7.8	6.9	6.3	21.0	13.3
1973	15.7	9.5	8.6	11.9	22.1	12.9	51.1	9.0	6.3	9.9	19.8	13.0
1974	12.8	5.9	3.9	10.5	19.9	9.4	53.7	6.8	5.8	4.9	20.7	12.4

[1] Amounts retained by the organizations for operating expenses, additions to reserves, and profits.

[2] Derived from table 16.
[3] Data by type of plan before 1965 not available.

Chapter 7
The Patients

The "interest" group with the greatest stake in the outcome of the national health insurance debate is the public itself. Just how well served is the American public by the current health care system and how much improvement, if any, might be expected under the various programs set forth? This chapter does not attempt to answer these questions, but it does set forth some facts and statistical trends which are useful in evaluating the assertions of both advocates and opponents of national health. Included are documents which provide recent facts on longevity, incidence of disease, and utilization of services. These data are broken down to show, for instance, differences in longevity, indicating variations within the United States by region, age, and race. Additional summary information on the status of health in the United States and the use of health services appears in [4], pp. 147 ff., and recent demographic and morbidity trends are set forth in Chapter one of [5].

HEALTH STATUS OF THE AMERICAN PUBLIC ([34], pp. 250-263)

Marked improvements in two key indicators of Americans' health status— average life expectancy and death rates—have been noted since the early 1900's; changes over recent years have been less pronounced. Significant declines in two other key indicators—infant and maternal mortality rates— have been registered since 1950. However, provisional figures for the maternal mortality rates for 1974 show a sharp rise over the rate recorded in 1973.

TABLE 1.—*Key indicators of Americans' health status, selected years*

	1920	1950	1973	1974 [1]
Birth rates (per 1,000 population)	27. 7	24. 4	14. 9	15. 0
Death rates (per 1,000 population)	13. 0	9. 6	9. 4	9. 1
Life expectancy (in years)	54. 1	68. 2	71. 3	72. 0
Infant mortality (per 1,000 live births)	([2])	29. 2	17. 7	16. 5
Maternal mortality (per 100,000 live births)	([2])	83. 2	15. 2	20. 8

[1] Provisional data.
[2] Not available.

Source: U.S. Department of Health, Education, and Welfare, Public Health Service, National Center for Health Statistics. Summary report—Final Mortality Statistics, 1973. Monthly Vital Statistics Report (HRA) 75–1120, vol. 23 No. 11, supplement (2), February 10, 1975; and Annual Summary for the United States, 1974, Provisional Statistics. Monthly Vital Statistics Report, vol. 23, No. 13, May 30, 1975.

The statistics on the major causes of death are not as encouraging. During the period from 1950 to 1974, significant increases occurred in the death rates for malignant neoplasms and cirrhosis of the liver, with somewhat smaller increases for diabetes mellitus and suicide. The most notable decreases were for death rates for certain diseases of mortality for early infancy and accidents.

The incidence of acute conditions has declined considerably since 1971. However, the rates for days of disability and activity limitations associated with chronic conditions have generally increased over the period.

The following sections contain summaries of the key indicators of Americans' health status:

  A. Life expectancy.
  B. Death rates.
  C. Infant and maternal mortality.
  D. Acute conditions.
  E. Chronic conditions.
  F. Disability.
  G. Communicable diseases.
  H. Individual health assessment.

A. Life Expectancy [1]

Based on the most recent period available for each reporting country, the United States ranks 7th for female and 19th for male life expectancy at birth among the 35 sovereign countries with the highest life expectancy and populations of at least 1 million.

The estimated average length of life in the United States has increased from 54.1 years in 1920 to 72.0 years in 1974. In 1974, white males had an estimated average length of life of 68.9 years, while nonwhite males had a life expectancy of 62.9 years. White females had an estimated average of 76.7 years to live while nonwhite females had an average expectancy of 71.3 years. There is also considerable variation in average lifetime among the 50 States and the District of Columbia. For the period 1969–71, the latest period for which such comparisons are available, Hawaii led the States with a life expectancy of 73.6 years while Washington, D.C., ranked the lowest with 65.7 years.

B. Death Rates

An estimated 1,933,000 deaths occurred in the United States during 1974, compared with 1,973,003 in 1973. The estimated death rate for 1974 was 9.1 per 1,000 population, a decrease of 0.3 percent compared with the 9.4 rate for 1973. Paralleling the overall decrease was the slight decline in the estimated death rates for most of the leading causes of death. Approximately 73 percent of all deaths occurring in this country in 1974 were attributable to four major causes— heart disease, malignant neoplasms, cerebrovascular diseases, and accidents.

---

[1] Source: Health—United States, 1975, Public Health Service, U.S. Department of Health, Education, and Welfare, 1975.

TABLE 2.—*Death rates from 15 leading causes of death: United States, selected years*

Rank and cause of death	Death rates		
	1950	1973	1974 [1]
All causes	963. 8	940. 2	914. 4
1 Diseases of heart	356. 8	360. 8	353. 1
2 Malignant neoplasms, including neoplasms of lymphatic and hematopoietic tissues	139. 8	167. 3	169. 5
3 Cerebrovascular diseases	104. 0	102. 1	97. 2
4 Accidents	60. 6	55. 2	48. 9
5 Influenza and pneumonia	[2] 31. 3	29. 8	25. 7
6 Diabetes mellitus	16. 2	18. 2	17. 4
7 Cirrhosis of liver	9. 2	15. 9	16. 0
8 Arteriosclerosis	20. 4	15. 5	15. 2
9 Certain causes of mortality in early infancy	40. 5	14. 5	13. 2
10 Suicide	11. 4	12. 0	12. 5
11 Bronchitis, emphysema, and asthma	([3])	14. 2	12. 4
12 Homicide	5. 3	9. 8	9. 8
13 Congenital anomalies	12. 2	6. 7	6. 5
14 Nephritis and nephrosis	18. 7	4. 0	3. 8
15 Peptic ulcer	5. 5	3. 7	3. 3
All other causes	131. 9	110. 5	109. 8

[1] Preliminary data.
[2] Excludes pneumonia of newborn.
[3] Data not available separately.

Source: U.S. Department of Health, Education, and Welfare, National Center for Health Statistics, Monthly Vital Statistics Report, Summary Report Final Morality Statistics (HRA) 75-1120, vol. 23, No. 11, supplement (2), February 10, 1975. (2) U.S. Department of Health, Education, and Welfare, National Center for Health Statistics, Monthly Vital Statistics Report, Provisional Statistics—Annual Summary for the United States, 1974, vol. 23, No. 13, May 30, 1975. (3) U.S. Department of Commerce, Bureau of the Census, Statistical Abstract of the United States, 1975.

C. Infant and Maternal Mortality

The 1974 estimated infant mortality rate for the entire U.S. population was 16.5 per 1,000 live births—a 7-percent decrease from the 17.7 rate recorded in 1973. This was the lowest annual rate ever recorded in the United States. Both neonatal (under 28 days) and postneonatal (28 days to 11 mos) mortality rates declined in 1974 with the postneonatal rate showing a proportionately greater decline. Certain gastroentestinal diseases was the only case of infant deaths to show an increase in 1974.

The 1974 estimated infant mortality rate for the United States was 16.5 per 1,000 live births. The figures by race continued to show a higher mortality rate for the nonwhite population—24.6 per 1,000 live births as compared to the white population rate of 14.7. Over the 10-year period 1961–71, the rate for the entire country decreased by 33 percent; this represents a decrease of 31 percent for whites and 40 percent for nonwhites over the period. In 1973 the United States ranked 15th in the world with an infant mortality rate of 17.7.

TABLE 3.—*Infant mortality rates, 1970–74*

[Rates per 1,000 live births]

	1970	1971	1972	1973	1974 [1]
Total	20. 0	19. 1	18. 5	17. 7	16. 5
White	17. 8	17. 1	16. 4	15. 8	14. 7
All other	31. 9	28. 5	27. 2	26. 2	24. 6

[1] Estimated.

Source: Monthly Vital Statistics Report, Provisional Statistics, Annual Summary for the United States, 1974. U.S. Department of Health Deduction, and Welfare, National Center for Health Statistics, May 30, 1975.

Between 1940 and 1973, the maternal mortality rate decreased from 376 to 15.2 deaths per 100,000 live births. However, in 1974 the estimated rate increased to 20.8 deaths per 100,000 live births.

D. ACUTE CONDITIONS

During 1974, an estimated 364.3 million acute illnesses or injuries occurred among the civilian noninstitutional population of the United States. The incidence rate of 175.7 per 100 persons per year was roughly the same as the 1973 rate of 175.1, but was considerably less than the rates recorded in 1971 and 1972. Some of this reduction is, however, attributable to the different reporting method used for the National Health Interview Survey beginning in 1973.

Acute illnesses and injuries caused an average of 9.4 days of restricted activity and 4.1 days in bed in 1974. The rate of restricted activity increased from the 8.8-day rate recorded in 1971. There were an estimated 286 million days lost from work attributable to acute illness. The per person work-loss rate declined from 3.8 in 1973 to 3.4 in 1974, while days lost from school per child for those aged 6 to 16 remained at 4.9 over the period.

During 1974, there were an estimated 28.5 persons injured per 100 population, a decrease from the 30.9 figure recorded in 1971. Males continued to have higher rates of injury than did females, and persons under 17 had higher rates than older age groups. About 3 days of restricted activity per person were associated with injury with about 1 day spent in bed.

TABLE 4.—*Incidence of acute conditions, 1971–74*

[Estimated data for civilian noninstitutional population]

	Number per 100 persons per year			
	1971	1972	1973	1974
All acute conditions	218. 5	219. 7	175. 1	175. 7
Infective and parasitic diseases	27. 2	22. 9	19. 4	19. 5
Respiratory conditions	116. 6	120. 8	91. 7	94. 4
Digestive system conditions	11. 1	11. 2	8. 4	7. 8
Injuries	32. 7	33. 2	30. 7	30. 4
All other acute conditions	30. 9	31. 6	24. 9	23. 5

Source: "Current Estimates From the Health Interview Survey, United States, 1974." U.S. Department of Health, Education, and Welfare, National Center for Health Statistics, DHEW publication No. (HRA) 76–1527, September 1975.

TABLE 5.—*Incidence of acute conditions per 100 persons of all ages by selected demographic characteristic: United States, 1973*

[Rate per 100 persons of all ages]

Demographic characteristic	All acute conditions	Selected acute conditions		
		Infective and parasitic	Respiratory	Injuries
Total	175. 1	19. 4	91. 7	30. 7
Sex:				
Male	171. 3	18. 9	87. 5	36. 8
Female	178. 7	19. 9	95. 7	25. 0
Region:				
Northeast	153. 3	24. 7	72. 2	28. 7
North Central	185. 4	14. 1	105. 6	30. 0
South	171. 7	24. 7	81. 7	30. 6
West	192. 3	11. 0	115. 0	34. 9
Residence:				
Metropolitan	177. 4	20. 4	91. 6	31. 2
Nonmetropolitan	170. 1	17. 2	92. 0	29. 7

NOTE.—Excluded from these statistics are all conditions involving neither restricted activity nor medical attention.

Source: Health: United States, 1975, Public Health Service, U.S. Department of Health, Education, and Welfare, 1975.

TABLE 6.—*Days of disability associated with acute conditions, 1971–74*

[Estimated data for civilian noninstitutional population]

	Rate per person per year			
	1971	1972	1973	1974
Restricted activity days	8. 8	9. 5	9. 1	9. 4
Red-days	3. 9	4. 1	4. 0	4. 1
Work-loss days (ages 17 and over) [1]	3. 4	3. 7	3. 8	3. 4
School-loss days (ages 6 to 16)	5. 0	4. 7	4. 4	4. 9

[1] For currently employed population.

Source: "Current Estimates From the Health Interview Survey, United States, 1974." U.S. Department of Health, Education, and Welfare, National Center for Health Statistics, DHEW publication No. (HRA) 76–1527, September 1975.

TABLE 7.—*Number of persons injured per 100 persons per year, 1971–74*

[Estimated data for civilian noninstitutional population]

	1971	1972	1973	1974
All accidents	30. 9	31. 5	29. 1	28. 5
Moving motor vehicle	2. 3	2. 3	1. 9	2. 1
At work	4. 8	3. 9	4. 4	4. 5
Home	11. 9	11. 8	11. 0	10. 3
Other	12. 9	14. 5	13. 0	12. 7

Source: "Current Estimates From the Health Interview Survey, United States, 1974." U.S. Department of Health, Education, and Welfare, National Center for Health Statistics, DHEW publication No. (HRA) 76–1527; September 1975.

E. Chronic Conditions

Approximately 14.1 percent of the population experienced some degree of limitation in their activities in 1974 due to chronic conditions; three-fourths of these persons were limited in a major activity. Four percent of the persons under 17 reported some limitation in their activities while 46 percent of the persons over 65 were limited in their activities by one or more chronic conditions.

In 1972, an estimated 6.5 million persons or 3.2 percent of the civilian non-institutionalized population had some degree of limitation of mobility due to chronic illness; limitations ranged from being confined to the house to having trouble getting around by themselves. The majority of persons experiencing the mobility limitations were age 65 or over.

TABLE 8.—*Limitation of activity due to chronic conditions, 1971–74*

[Estimated data for civilian noninstitutional population]

	Percent of total population			
	1971	1972	1973	1974
Limited in all activity	12.3	12.7	13.5	14.1
Limited in major activity	9.3	9.6	10.2	10.6
No limitation of activity	87.7	87.3	86.5	85.9

Source: "Current Estimates From the Health Interview Survey, United States, 1974," U.S. Department of Health, Education, and Welfare, National Center for Health Statistics, DHEW publication No. (HRA) 76–1527, September 1975.

TABLE 9.—*Persons with limitation of activity due to chronic conditions, by degree of limitation according to sex and age: United States, 1974*

[Estimated data for civilian noninstitutionalized population]

	Percent distribution			
Sex and age	Total population	With activity limitation	With limitation in major activity	With no activity limitation
Both sexes:				
All ages	100.0	14.1	10.6	85.9
Under 17 yr	100.0	3.7	1.9	96.3
17 to 44 yr	100.0	8.8	5.6	91.2
45 to 64 yr	100.0	24.1	18.9	75.9
65 yr and over	100.0	45.9	39.3	54.1
Male:				
All ages	100.0	14.3	10.7	85.7
Under 17 yr	100.0	4.0	2.1	96.0
17 to 44 yr	100.0	9.2	5.5	90.8
45 to 64 yr	100.0	25.3	19.8	74.7
65 yr and over	100.0	49.7	44.8	50.3
Female:				
All ages	100.0	14.0	10.5	86.0
Under 17 yr	100.0	3.3	1.7	96.7
17 to 44 yr	100.0	8.6	5.8	91.4
45 to 64 yr	100.0	23.0	18.1	77.0
65 yr and over	100.0	43.1	35.3	56.9

Source: "Current Estimates From the Health Interview Survey, United States, 1974," U.S. Department of Health, Education, and Welfare, National Center for Health Statistics, DHEW publication No. (HRA) 76–1527, September 1975.

TABLE 10.—*Percent of persons all ages with limitation of mobility by selected demographic characteristics: United States, 1972*

Demographic characteristic	Population all ages (thousands)	Percent of population of all ages with limitation of mobility			
		Total	Confined to the house	Needs help in getting around	Has trouble getting around alone
Total [1]	204, 148	3. 2	0. 9	1. 0	1. 3
Sex:					
Male	98, 445	2. 9	. 8	. 9	1. 2
Female	105, 704	3. 4	1. 0	1. 1	1. 3
Color:					
White	178, 727	3. 1	. 8	1. 0	1. 2
All other	25, 421	3. 7	1. 2	1. 0	1. 6
Region:					
Northeast	48, 011	3. 1	1. 0	1. 0	1. 1
North Central	55, 974	2. 7	. 6	1. 0	1. 1
South	64, 128	3. 9	1. 1	1. 1	1. 6
West	36, 036	2. 7	. 7	. 9	1. 1
Residence:					
Metropolitan	131, 100	2. 9	. 8	. 9	1. 1
Nonmetropolitan	73, 049	3. 7	. 9	1. 2	1. 6
Family income:					
Under $5,000	40, 835	8. 6	2. 6	2. 7	3. 2
$5,000 to $9,999	59, 134	2. 5	. 6	. 8	1. 1
$10,000 to $14,999	51, 074	1. 3	. 3	. 4	. 6
$15,000 and over	40, 983	1. 1	. 2	. 4	. 5

[1] Includes unknown income.

Source: Health—United States, 1975, Public Health Service, U.S. Department of Health, Education, and Welfare.

Among reported chronic conditions, arthritis and hearing impairments rank 1st and 2d, respectively. However, heart conditions cause more limitation of activity than any other condition.

TABLE 11.—*Prevalence of selected chronic conditions reported in health interviews and selected measures of impact: all ages, United States*

Prevalence and impact of conditions	Arthritis (1969)	Asthma (1970)	Chronic bronchitis (1970)	Diabetes (1973)	Heart conditions (1972)	Hypertensive disease[1] (1972)	Visual impairments (1972)	Hearing impairments (1971)
Number of conditions (thousands)	18,339.0	6,031.0	6,526.0	4,191.0	10,291.0	12,271.0	9,596.0	14,491.0
Number per 1,000 persons	92.9	30.2	32.7	20.4	50.4	60.1	47.4	71.6
Percent of conditions—								
Causing activity limitation	17.6	17.1	4.0	29.7	41.6	8.9	12.5	4.0
With doctor visit in past year	41.6	60.3	71.5	82.6	75.2	80.7	36.2	21.0
Ever hospitalized	7.6	19.1	14.3	29.4	41.0	7.1	(2)	(2)
Under medical treatment	36.4	51.4	19.9	73.6	58.6	59.5	(3)	(3)
With 1 or more bed days in past year	8.1	31.7	47.1	13.6	21.6	6.9	2.3	1.6
With 15 or more bed days in past year	3.1	5.2	5.8	4.4	10.5	1.4	.4	.1

[1] Without heart involvement.
[2] Not available.

Source: Health—United States, 1975, Public Health Service, U.S. Department of Health, Education, and Welfare, 1975.

F. Disability

There were an estimated 17.2 days of restricted activity per person in 1974 as a result of chronic and acute illnesses or injuries; this represents an increase of 0.7 days from the previous year and 1.5 days since 1971. The number of restricted activity days per person ranged from about 10.7 days for children under age 17 to 38.0 days for persons 65 years and over. The average number of bed days remained relatively constant from 1971 to 1974; 6.7 days per person was recorded in 1974.

There were an estimated 414 million days lost from work due to illness or injury in 1974, or an average of 4.9 days per currently employed person over age 17. The number of days lost from school for children age 6 to 16 years was 5.6 days per person for the same period. Females generally reported more restricted activity, and bed and work-loss days than did males.

TABLE 12.—*Days of disability and limitation of activity: United States, 1971–74*

[Estimated data for civilian noninstitutional population]

	Days of disability per person per year			
	1971	1972	1973	1974
Restricted activity days	15. 7	16. 7	16. 5	17. 2
Bed days	6. 1	6. 5	6. 4	6. 7
Work-loss days (ages 17 and over) [1]	5. 1	5. 3	5. 4	4. 9
School-loss days (ages 6 to 16)	5. 5	5. 3	5. 1	5. 6

[1] For currently employed population.

Source: "Current Estimates From the Health Interview Survey, United States, 1974 " U.S. Department of Health, Education, and Welfare, National Center for Health Statistics, DHEW publication No. (HRA) 76–1527, September 1975.

TABLE 13.—*Days of disability per person per year by sex and age, 1974*

[Estimated data for civilian noninstitutional population]

Sex and age	Restricted activity	Bed-disability days	Work-lost days [1]	Days lost from school [2]
Total population, all ages	17. 2	6. 7	4. 9	
Under 17 yr	10. 7	4. 8		5. 6
17 to 24 yr	11. 2	4. 6	4. 4	
25 to 44 yr	14. 8	5. 8	4. 6	
45 to 64 yr	23. 6	8. 4	5. 8	
65 yr and over	38. 0	14. 3	4. 4	
Males, all ages	15. 6	5. 8	4. 8	
Under 17 yr	11. 1	4. 8		5. 7
17 to 24 yr	9. 4	3. 3	3. 9	
25 to 44 yr	12. 5	4. 5	4. 3	
45 to 64 yr	22. 0	7. 4	5. 9	
65 yr and over	36. 8	14. 2	5. 6	
Females, all ages	18. 7	7. 5	5. 1	
Under 17 yr	10. 3	4. 8		5. 5
17 to 24 yr	12. 8	5. 8	5. 0	
25 to 44 yr	17. 0	7. 0	5. 2	
45 to 64 yr	25. 1	9. 4	5. 5	
65 yr and over	38. 8	14. 4	(3)	

[1] Work loss reported for currently employed persons aged 17 yr and over.
[2] School days lost reported for children ages 6 to 16 yr.
[3] Less than 0.1 percent.

Source: "Current Estimates From the Health Interview Survey, United States, 1974," U.S. Department of Health, Education, and Welfare, National Center for Health Statistics, DHEW publication No. (HRA) 76–1527, September 1975.

TABLE 14.—*Number of disability days per person per year, by selected demographic characteristics: United States, 1973*

[Days per person]

Demographic characteristic	Restricted activity days	Bed disability days	Work loss days
Total	16. 5	6. 4	5. 4
Sex:			
Male	14. 7	5. 3	5. 2
Female	18. 1	7. 3	5. 8
Color:			
White	16. 1	6. 1	5. 3
All other	18. 8	8. 0	6. 7
Region:			
Northeast	13. 9	5. 5	5. 2
North Central	15. 5	5. 8	5. 2
South	18. 4	7. 4	5. 9
West	18. 1	6. 6	5. 2
Residence:			
Metropolitan	16. 3	6. 4	5. 6
Nonmetropolitan	16. 9	6. 2	5. 0
Family income:			
Under $5,000	28. 8	10. 7	6. 8
$5,000 to $9,999	16. 5	6. 5	6. 3
$10,000 to $14,999	13. 0	5. 2	5. 1
$15,000 and over	12. 2	4. 5	4. 9

Source: Health: United States, 1975, Public Health Service, U.S. Department of Health, Education, and Welfare, 1975.

G. COMMUNICABLE DISEASES

There were 1,390,955 reported cases of communicable disease in the United States in 1973. Gonorrhea ranked first, chickenpox second, and syphilis third. When underreporting and undetected cases are considered, it is estimated that 2.7 million cases of gonorrhea occur each year. The following table shows by illness the number of instances of specified notifiable diseases in 1973.

TABLE 15.—*Communicable diseases—Number of reported cases, United States, calendar year 1973*

GONORRHEA (842,621)

CHICKENPOX

SYPHILIS (87,469)

MUMPS

HEPATITIS

TUBERCULOSIS

RUBELLA

MEASLES

SALMONELLOSIS (excluding typhoid fever)

SHIGELLOSIS

ASEPTIC MENINGITIS

RHEUMATIC (acute)

WHOOPING COUGH

MALARIA

ALL OTHERS

Total Number of Reported Cases of Specified Notifiable Diseases — 1,390,955

Disease Cases in Thousands

100   200   300   400   900

Source: Health—United States, 1975, Public Health Service, U.S. Department of Health, Education, and Welfare, 1975.

H. Individual Health Assessment

In general, the American people think of themselves as being in good health. As part of the National Health Interview Survey, persons were asked to compare their health with other persons their own age. Eighty-seven percent regarded their health as excellent or good, 9 percent as fair, and only 3 percent as poor. Males were more likely than females, and whites more likely than nonwhites to report excellent health.

Table 16.—*Assessment of health status as reported in health interviews for persons of all ages, according to selected demographic characteristics: United States, 1973*

[Percent distribution]

Demographic characteristic	Health status, all ages				
	Total	Excellent	Good	Fair	Poor
Total [1]_____	100. 0	48. 7	38. 4	9. 4	2. 8
Sex:					
Male_____	100. 0	51. 9	36. 5	8. 3	2. 7
Female_____	100. 0	45. 7	40. 2	10. 6	2. 9
Color:					
White_____	100. 0	50. 4	37. 6	8. 8	2. 6
All other_____	100. 0	36. 7	44. 2	14. 1	4. 2
Region:					
Northeast_____	100. 0	48. 6	40. 3	8. 2	2. 2
North central_____	100. 0	50. 3	38. 1	8. 8	2. 3
South_____	100. 0	44. 4	39. 6	11. 4	3. 9
West_____	100. 0	54. 1	34. 3	8. 6	2. 5
Residence:					
Metropolitan_____	100. 0	50. 4	37. 8	8. 7	2. 4
Nonmetropolitan____	100. 0	44. 8	39. 9	11. 1	3. 7
Family income:					
Under $5,000_____	100. 0	32. 4	41. 3	17. 9	7. 7
$5,000 to $9,999_____	100. 0	44. 5	41. 4	10. 9	2. 6
$10,000 to $14,999___	100. 0	53. 0	38. 1	6. 7	1. 6
$15,000 and over_____	100. 0	60. 7	33. 2	4. 7	. 8

[1] Includes unknown income.

Source: Health: United States, 1975, Public Health Service, U.S. Department of Health, Education, and Welfare, 1975.

HEALTH SERVICES UTILIZATION PATTERNS OF THE AMERICAN PUBLIC ([34], pp. 263–291

The following sections contain an analysis of the utilization patterns of health care services by the American population.

A. Hospital utilization.
B. Physician visits.
C. Dental visits.
D. Utilization of preventive care services.
E. Utilization of mental health care and mental retardation facilities.
F. Long-term care utilization.

A. HOSPITAL UTILIZATION

In 1974 there were 35.5 million admissions to over 7,000 hospitals in the United States. Approximately 426 million inpatient days and 250 million outpatient visits were recorded during this period.

The most commonly used data on hospital utilization are based on figures obtained for community hospitals, i.e., short-term general and other special hospitals (excluding Federal hospitals which are not generally available to the public). Community hospitals represent about 82 percent of all hospitals, handle over 93 percent of all admissions and 75 percent of all outpatient visits, employ 78 percent of the industry's total labor force, and account for 79 percent of the total cost of hospital care.

In 1974 there were approximately 32.9 million admissions to community hospitals, 255 million patient days and 189 million outpatient visits. The average length of stay was 7.8 days; this included an average stay of 7.9 days in nonprofit hospitals, 7.7 days in State and local government hospitals, and 6.7 days in for-profit hospitals. The larger hospitals tend to have longer lengths of stay than smaller community hospitals. This reflects the fact that such hospitals, generally located in urban areas, tend to offer a broader range of services and serve a population consisting of relatively more aged and poor persons.

The Health Interview Survey conducted by the National Center for Health Statistics (which is based on sampling data that includes some Federal hospitals) showed that approximately 10.7 percent of the population was hospitalized at least once in 1974; this figure represented at least one hospital episode for 8.8 percent of the male population and 12.5 percent of the female population. While only 5.7 percent of the persons under 17 had been hospitalized, 16.8 percent of the population 65 and over had received such care.

TABLE 17.—*Hospital utilization: Admissions, inpatient days, outpatient visits, percent occupancy, average stay, and surgical operations, 1974*

	Admissions (thousands)	Inpatient days (thousands)	Outpatient visits (thousands)	Occupancy (percent)	Average stay (days)	Surgical operation (thousands)
United States, total	35, 506	425, 878	250, 481	77. 2	(1)	16, 937
Federal	1, 841	39, 936	48, 682	80. 7	(1)	658
Non-Federal	33, 666	385, 942	201, 799	76. 8	(1)	16, 279
Psychiatric	595	111, 962	5, 240	80. 0	(1)	25
Tuberculosis	21	1, 884	91	63. 2	(1)	7
Long-term general and other special	106	16, 335	1, 630	82. 5	(1)	31
Short-term general and other special	32, 943	255, 762	194, 838	75. 3	(1)	16, 217
Hospital units of institutions	77	568	5, 899	30. 4		23
Community hospitals	32, 866	255, 193	188, 940	75. 6	7. 8	16, 193
Nongovernment nonprofit	23, 359	184, 467	130, 438	77. 9	7. 9	12, 270
Investor-owned (for profit)	2, 553	17, 078	8, 667	67. 5	6. 7	1, 233
State and local governmental	6, 953	53, 649	49, 835	71. 0	7. 7	2, 690

1 Not available.

Note.—Totals may not add due to rounding.

Source: "Hospital Statistics, 1974," American Hospital Association, 1975.

TABLE 18.—*Selected measures of hospital utilization in all U.S. hospitals, 1964, 1973, 1974*

Measure	All U.S. hospitals					Community hospitals				
	1964	1973	1974	Percent change		1964	1973	1974	Percent change	
				1964-74	1973-74				1964-74	1973-74
Hospitals	7,127.0	7,123.0	7,174.0	0.7	0.7	5,712.0	5,789.0	5,875.0	2.9	1.5
Beds (thousands)	1,696.0	1,535.0	1,513.0	-10.8	-1.4	721.0	898.0	926.0	28.4	3.1
Beds per thousand population[1]	8.9	7.3	7.2	-18.0	-1.4	3.8	4.3	4.4	13.1	2.3
Admissions (thousands)	28,266.0	34,352.0	35,506.0	25.6	3.4	25,987.0	31,671.0	32,866.0	26.5	3.8
Admissions per thousand population[1]	148.0	164.0	168.0	10.8	2.4	138.0	152.0	157.0	10.1	3.3
Average daily census	1,421.0	1,189.0	1,167.0	-17.9	-1.9	550.0	680.0	700.0	27.3	2.9
Average length of stay, days	(2)	(2)	(2)	---	---	7.7	7.8	7.8	1.3	---
Occupancy, percent	83.8	77.5	77.2	-7.9	-0.4	76.3	75.7	75.6	-.9	-.1
Outpatient visits (thousands)	[3]125,123.0	233,555.0	250,481.0	100.2	7.2	[3]91,430.0	173,068.0	188,940.0	106.6	9.2
Outpatient visits per thousand population[1]	(2)	1,112.9	1,184.9	---	6.5	(2)	831.7	901	---	8.3

[1] Population figures used are total resident population for all U.S. hospitals and total civilian resident population for community hospitals.
[2] Comparable data not available.
[3] Based only on hospitals reporting outpatient visits.

Source: "Hospital Statistics, 1974," American Hospital Association, 1975.

TABLE 19.—*Average length of stay in community hospitals by bed sizes, 1974*

Hospital bed size	Average length of stay
All sizes	7. 8
6 to 24	5. 8
25 to 49	6. 1
50 to 99	6. 9
100 to 199	7. 2
200 to 299	7. 5
300 to 399	7. 9
400 to 499	8. 2
500 or more	9. 2

Source: "Hospital Statistics, 1974," American Hospital Association, 1975.

TABLE 20.—*Percent distribution of persons with short-stay hospital episodes during the past year by number of episodes, according to sex and age: United States, 1974. Data are based on household interviews of the civilian, noninstitutionalized population*

Sex and age	Popula-tion	Number of hospital episodes			
		None	1	2	3 plus
Both sexes, all ages	100. 0	89. 3	8. 9	1. 3	0. 5
Under 17 years	100. 0	94. 3	5. 0	. 5	. 1
17 to 24 years	100. 0	88. 7	9. 9	1. 1	. 3
25 to 34 years	100. 0	86. 7	11. 5	1. 4	. 4
35 to 44 years	100. 0	88. 8	9. 2	1. 4	. 6
45 to 64 years	100. 0	87. 3	10. 1	1. 9	. 7
65 years and over	100. 0	83. 2	12. 7	2. 9	1. 2
Male, all ages	100. 0	91. 2	7. 2	1. 2	. 4
Under 17 years	100. 0	94. 1	5. 2	. 6	. 2
17 to 24 years	100. 0	93. 8	5. 4	. 6	*
25 to 34 years	100. 0	92. 9	6. 0	. 8	. 3
35 to 44 years	100. 0	91. 9	6. 6	1. 0	. 5
45 to 64 years	100. 0	87. 1	10. 1	2. 0	. 8
65 years and over	100. 0	82. 0	13. 2	3. 5	1. 3
Female, all ages	100. 0	87. 5	10. 5	1. 5	. 5
Under 17 years	100. 0	94. 6	4. 9	. 4	. 1
17 to 24 years	100. 0	83. 9	14. 2	1. 5	. 4
25 to 34 years	100. 0	80. 9	16. 6	2. 1	. 4
35 to 44 years	100. 0	86. 0	11. 5	1. 7	. 7
45 to 64 years	100. 0	87. 4	10. 2	1. 9	. 6
65 years and over	100. 0	84. 0	12. 3	2. 5	1. 1

Source: "Current Estimates from the Health Interview Survey, United States—1974." U.S. Department of Health, Education and Welfare, National Center for Health Statistics, DHEW Publication No. (HRA) 76–1527.

The rate of hospitalization, the number of days of care per 1,000 population, and the average length of stay increase with age and decrease as income rises.

TABLE 21.—*Discharges from short-stay hospitals per 1,000 population, days of hospital care per 1,000 population, and average length of stay by sex, age, geographic region and family income: United States, 1973*

Sex, age, region, and income	Population (thousands)	Discharges per 1,000 population	Days of care per 1,000 population	Average length of stay in days
Total	205, 836	160	1, 238	7. 8
Male	99, 307	132	1, 090	8. 3
Female	106, 529	185	1, 375	7. 4
Age:				
0 to 14 years	55, 559	72	329	4. 6
15 to 44 years	87, 342	158	898	5. 7
45 to 64 years	42, 641	186	1, 698	9. 1
65 years and over	20, 294	350	4, 228	12. 1
Region:				
Northeast	48, 940	148	1, 334	9. 0
North-central	56, 772	178	1, 426	8. 0
South	64, 499	160	1, 169	7. 3
West	35, 625	146	930	6. 4
Family income:				
Under $5,000	34, 931	236	2, 297	9. 6
$5,000 to $9,999	51, 628	172	1, 349	7. 9
$10,000 to $14,999	50, 924	133	873	6. 5
$15,000 and over	53, 549	126	800	6. 4

B. PHYSICIAN VISITS

In 1974, there were approximately 1 billion visits to medical doctors (excluding visits to patients in hospitals) for the civilian noninstitutional population, or an average of 4.9 visits per person per year. This figure is about equal to the rates which were recorded in the preceding 3 years (4.9 visits in 1971 and 5.0 visits in 1972 and 1973). The number of visits per person ranged from 4.1 visits for children to 6.5 visits for persons 75 years old and over. In 1974, females continued to have more doctor visits than did males in all age groups for those under age 17.

Almost 75 percent of the civilian noninstitutional population saw a medical doctor at least once during the preceding 12 months. This figure was highest for those persons over age 65; however, 6.7 percent of this population group had not seen a physician in the past 5 years. Females of child bearing age had more visits during the preceding 12 months than did females in the remaining age groups.

TABLE 22.—*Physician visits for civilian noninstitutional population, 1971–74*

	1971	1972	1973	1974
Number per person per year	4. 9	5. 0	5. 0	4. 9
Percent of persons with visits in past year	72. 4	72. 6	74. 5	75. 3

Source: "Current Estimates From the Health Interview Survey, United States, 1974." U.S. Department of Health, Education, and Welfare, National Center for Health Statistics. DHEW publication No. (11HRA) 76–1527, September 1973.

TABLE 23.—*Number of physician visits per person per year, by age and sex, United States, 1974 (for civilian noninstitutional population)*

Sex	All ages	Under 17 yr	17–24 yr	25–44 yr	45–64 yr	65–74 yr	75 yr and over
Both sexes_____	4. 9	4. 1	4. 5	5. 0	5. 5	6. 9	6. 5
Male_____	4. 3	4. 3	3. 2	3. 5	4. 9	6. 8	6. 3
Female_____	5. 6	4. 0	5. 8	6. 3	6. 1	6. 9	6. 6

Source: "Current Estimates From the Health Interview Survey, United States, 1974," U.S. Department of Health, Education, and Welfare, National Center for Health Statistics, DHEW publication No. (HRA) 76–1527.

TABLE 24.—*Number and percent distribution of persons by time interval since last physician visit, according to sex and age: United States, 1974*

[Data are based on household interviews of the civilian, noninstitutionalized population]

Sex and age	Total population	Time interval since last physician visit (percent distribution)			
		Under 1 yr	1 to 4 yr	5 yr and over	Other [1]
Both sexes:					
All ages_____	100. 0	75. 3	20. 1	3. 8	0. 8
Under 17 yr_____	100. 0	74. 3	22. 1	2. 5	1. 2
17 to 24 yr_____	100. 0	77. 0	19. 9	2. 2	. 9
25 to 44 yr_____	100. 0	76. 2	19. 7	3. 4	. 4
45 to 64 yr_____	100. 0	73. 9	19. 8	5. 7	. 6
65 yr and over_____	100. 0	77. 2	15. 6	6. 7	. 5
Male:					
All ages_____	100. 0	71. 2	23. 4	4. 5	1. 0
Under 17 yr_____	100. 0	75. 0	21. 6	2. 4	1. 0
17 to 24 yr_____	100. 0	69. 1	26. 9	2. 9	1. 2
25 to 44 yr_____	100. 0	67. 8	26. 2	5. 1	. 7
45 to 64 yr_____	100. 0	69. 4	23. 1	6. 8	. 7
65 yr and over_____	100. 0	74. 6	17. 4	7. 5	([2])
Female:					
All ages_____	100. 0	79. 3	16. 9	3. 1	. 7
Under 17 yr_____	100. 0	73. 5	22. 6	2. 6	1. 3
17 to 24 yr_____	100. 0	84. 4	13. 4	1. 5	. 5
25 to 44 yr_____	100. 0	83. 9	13. 8	1. 9	. 3
45 to 64 yr_____	100. 0	77. 9	16. 8	4. 8	. 3
65 yr and over_____	100. 0	79. 2	14. 3	6. 1	. 4

[1] "Other" includes "never" and "unknown".
[2] Less than 0.1 percent.

Note: Numbers may not add due to rounding.

Source: "Current Estimates From the Health Interview Survey United States 1974", U.S. Department of Health, Education, and Welfare, National Center for Health Statistics, DHFW publication No. (HRA) 76–1527, September 1975.

Utilization of physician services varies considerably among different segments of the population. Females see a physician more frequently than males, and white persons more frequently than nonwhite persons. Over the decade 1964–73 there was an appreciable increase in the number of physician visits per poor person per year, and a notable decrease in the number of poor who had no physician visits in the preceding 2 years. Over two-thirds of all outpatient physician contacts occur at the physician's office, with the poor and minorities using hospital outpatient clinics more frequently than other segments of the population. The following tables highlight the significant demographic variables in physician visit patterns.

TABLE 25.—*Number of physician visits per person per year and percent of the population with no physician visits in the past 2 years by poor and not poor status, and color for all ages: 1964 and 1973*

Age and year	Total		White		All other	
	Poor	Not poor	Poor	Not poor	Poor	Not poor
All ages—Number of physician visits per person per year:						
1964	4. 3	4. 6	4. 7	4. 7	3. 1	3. 6
1973	5. 6	4. 9	5. 7	5. 0	5. 0	4. 3
All ages—Percent with no physician visits in past 2 yr:						
1964	27. 7	17. 7	25. 7	17. 1	33. 2	24. 7
1973	17. 2	13. 4	16. 8	13. 2	18. 5	15. 3

NOTE.—Definition of poor is based on family income: Under $3,000 in 1964; under $6,000 in 1973. In each case, this included about 1/5 of the population.

Source: Health—United States, 1975, Public Health Service, U.S. Department of Health, Education, and Welfare, 1975.

TABLE 26.—*Number of physician visits per person per year and percent of population with one or more visits in past year by selected demographic characteristic: Persons of all ages, United States, 1973*

Demographic characteristic	Number of visits per person per year	Percent with physician visit in past year
Total [1]	5. 0	74. 5
Sex:		
Male	4. 3	70. 4
Female	5. 6	78. 3
Color:		
White	5. 1	75. 1
All other	4. 5	70. 7
Region:		
Northeast	4. 9	75. 5
North Central	5. 0	74. 3
South	4. 0	73. 7
West	5. 4	74. 9
Residence:		
Metropolitan	5. 2	75. 7
Nonmetropolitan	4. 5	71. 8
Family income:		
Under $5,000	5. 7	73. 8
$5,000 to $9,999	4. 8	72. 9
$10,000 to $14,999	4. 9	75. 3
$15,000 and over	5. 1	77. 4

[1] Includes unknown income.

Source: Health—United States, 1975, Public Health Service, U.S. Department of Health, Education, and Welfare, 1975.

TABLE 27.—*Physician visits by place of visit by selected demographic characteristic: Persons of all ages, United States, 1973*

[Percent distribution]

Demographic characteristic	Total visits [1] (thousands)	Office	Hospital out-patient clinic	Hospital emergency room	Tele-phone	Home
Total [2]	1,031,010	69.1	6.8	3.9	12.7	1.4
Sex:						
Male	429,734	67.8	6.8	4.7	11.5	1.5
Female	601,276	70.0	6.8	3.3	13.6	1.3
Color:						
White	914,208	70.2	5.6	3.5	13.6	1.5
All other	116,802	60.1	16.4	7.0	5.9	.9
Region:						
Northeast	241,030	65.7	7.9	4.7	12.6	2.8
North Central	284,012	70.1	6.0	3.4	14.3	1.2
South	314,792	68.9	7.1	3.8	12.0	1.0
West	191,155	72.0	6.0	3.6	11.6	.4
Residence:						
Metropolitan	742,845	67.1	7.5	4.1	13.5	1.5
Nonmetropolitan	288,165	74.2	5.0	3.3	10.7	1.1
Family income:						
Under $5,000	199,710	65.2	10.5	3.8	9.6	1.9
$5,000 to $9,999	249,207	71.4	6.7	4.0	11.5	1.3
$10,000 to $14,999	251,453	68.4	5.7	4.0	15.3	.8
$15,000 and over	270,842	70.0	4.9	3.8	14.3	1.8

[1] Includes all other places of visits.
[2] Includes unknown income.

Source: Health—United States, 1975, Public Health Service, U.S. Department of Health, Education, and Welfare, 1975.

Information obtained from the National Ambulatory Medical Care Survey shows that the number of office visits to physicians increases with age. Higher levels of visits are recorded for females and whites and in metropolitan areas. For the whole population, over half of the visits are for conditions which the physician judges to be not serious while for the aged only one-third are for nonserious problems. Close to half of the office visits involve some form of drug therapy (including prescription and nonprescription drugs) while over a third of such visits involve a general history or examination. Sixty-one percent of the patients are told to return to the physician at a specified time while 21 percent are told to return if necessary. For 13 percent no followup care is planned. Referrals and hospital admissions are rare.

TABLE 28.—*Rate of visits to physicians offices by patient's age, according to patient's sex and color and region and location of visit: United States, May 1973–April 1974 (from National Ambulatory Medical Care Survey)*

[Number of visits per person]

Sex and color and region and location of visit	Total	Age				
		Under 15 yr	15 to 24 yr	25 to 44 yr	45 to 64 yr	65 yr and over
Color and sex:						
Total	3. 1	2. 3	2. 6	3. 2	3. 8	4. 9
Male	2. 5	2. 3	1. 9	2. 1	3. 2	4. 5
Female	3. 7	2. 2	3. 4	4. 2	4. 3	5. 2
White	3. 2	2. 4	2. 7	3. 1	3. 8	5. 0
Male	2. 6	2. 5	2. 0	2. 1	3. 2	4. 6
Female	3. 7	2. 3	3. 4	4. 1	4. 3	5. 3
All other	2. 6	1. 5	2. 4	3. 4	3. 7	4. 0
Male	2. 0	1. 4	1. 3	2. 1	3. 4	3. 7
Female	3. 2	1. 6	3. 3	4. 3	4. 0	4. 2
Region:						
Northeast	3. 1	2. 4	2. 8	3. 3	3. 6	4. 3
North Central	3. 0	2. 2	2. 6	3. 0	3. 6	4. 9
South	3. 1	2. 4	2. 6	3. 2	3. 8	4. 8
West	3. 2	1. 9	2. 6	3. 3	4. 2	6. 2
Location of visits:						
Metropolitan area	3. 4	2. 3	2. 8	3. 6	4. 2	5. 4
Male	2. 7	2. 4	2. 0	2. 3	3. 5	5. 0
Female	4. 0	2. 3	3. 7	4. 7	4. 8	5. 6
Nonmetropolitan area	2. 5	2. 1	2. 2	2. 2	2. 9	4. 1
Male	2. 2	2. 2	1. 6	1. 6	2. 5	3. 6
Female	2. 9	1. 9	2. 8	2. 8	3. 2	4. 5

Source: Health—United States, 1975, Public Health Service, U.S. Department of Health, Education, and Welfare.

TABLE 29.—*Percent distribution of visits to physicians offices by seriousness of patient's principal problem, according to patient's sex, color, and age, and region and location of visit: United States, May 1973–April 1974 (from National Ambulatory Medical Care Survey)*

[Percent distribution]

Sex, color, age, region, and location of visit	Office visits per person per year	Seriousness of patient's principal problem				
		Total	Very serious	Serious	Slightly serious	Not serious
All patients	3. 1	100. 0	3. 2	16. 0	30. 4	50. 5
Sex:						
Male	2. 5	100. 0	3. 8	18. 1	31. 9	46. 2
Female	3. 7	100. 0	2. 8	14. 6	29. 4	53. 2
Color:						
White	3. 2	100. 0	3. 1	15. 7	30. 5	50. 6
All other	2. 6	100. 0	3. 3	18. 2	29. 5	49. 0
Age:						
Under 15 yr	2. 3	100. 0	1. 5	10. 2	29. 4	58. 9
15 to 24 yr	2. 6	100. 0	1. 7	10. 7	26. 0	61. 6
25 to 44 yr	3. 2	100. 0	2. 7	14. 0	29. 4	54. 0
45 to 64 yr	3. 8	100. 0	3. 9	20. 1	32. 2	43. 9
65 yr and over	4. 9	100. 0	6. 3	25. 0	34. 7	33. 9
Region:						
Northeast	3. 1	100. 0	3. 7	17. 8	28. 7	49. 8
North Central	3. 0	100. 0	2. 8	13. 8	31. 6	51. 7
South	3. 1	100. 0	2. 6	13. 8	29. 5	54. 1
West	3. 2	100. 0	4. 0	20. 5	32. 3	43. 2
Location of visit:						
Metropolitan	3. 4	100. 0	3. 4	16. 4	29. 5	50. 7
Nonmetropolitan	2. 5	100. 0	2. 5	14. 7	33. 1	49. 7

Source: Health—United States, 1975, Public Health Service, U.S. Department of Health, Education, and Welfare.

TABLE 30.—Percent of visits to physicians' office's by treatment and services ordered or provided, according to patient's sex, color, and age, and region and location of visit: United States, May 1973–April 1974 (from National Ambulatory Medical Care Survey)

[Percent of visits with specified treatment or service][1]

Sex, color, and age, and region and location of visit	None	Treatments/services ordered or provided								
		General history/exam	Lab procedure/test	X-rays	Injection/immunization	Office surgical treatment	Drug therapy[2]	Psychotherapy/therapeutic listening	Medical counseling/advice	Other
All patients	5.3	35.9	19.6	7.1	18.6	8.9	49.4	4.3	19.7	8.8
SEX										
Male	5.2	36.8	16.0	8.2	19.4	11.0	47.2	3.8	19.1	8.6
Female	5.4	35.4	22.0	6.4	18.1	7.6	50.8	4.6	20.1	9.0
COLOR										
White	5.4	35.8	19.5	7.3	18.5	9.2	48.3	4.5	20.2	9.2
All other	4.9	37.1	20.8	5.8	19.5	6.6	58.5	2.6	15.3	5.4
AGE										
Under 15 years	6.0	41.2	13.0	4.0	26.0	7.8	46.2	.8	19.6	5.4
15 to 24 years	6.5	35.6	21.3	5.7	14.0	11.0	45.2	3.1	17.3	9.9
25 to 44 years	5.7	33.8	21.2	7.6	14.1	8.8	47.6	8.0	19.2	8.8
45 to 64 years	4.2	34.6	20.7	9.3	19.6	8.6	51.7	5.0	20.7	10.6
65 years and over	4.6	35.4	22.0	8.0	19.5	9.1	56.9	2.6	21.4	6.9
REGION										
Northeast	4.0	43.3	16.7	6.9	17.4	8.4	50.0	7.2	22.1	10.0
North-central	5.2	32.8	18.2	7.0	21.6	8.6	48.6	2.4	18.3	8.2
South	6.1	37.9	22.5	6.4	19.4	8.5	51.4	3.2	17.5	7.6
West	6.0	27.5	20.4	8.7	14.2	10.9	46.4	5.0	22.3	10.2
LOCATION OF VISIT										
Metropolitan	4.9	36.3	19.6	7.8	17.4	9.3	48.5	5.2	20.9	9.4
Nonmetropolitan	6.7	34.8	19.6	5.1	22.1	7.8	52.2	1.6	16.1	7.0

[1] Percents will not add to 100 because many patients visits required the provision of more than 1 treatment or service.
[2] Includes prescription and nonprescription drugs.

Source: Health—United States, 1975, Public Health Service, U.S. Department of Health, Education, and Welfare.

C. DENTAL VISITS

There were an estimated 342 million dental visits in 1974 or an average of 1.7 visits per person per year. The rate recorded has shown a slight increase since 1972. Females continued to have more visits than males with females seeing a dentist at the rate of 1.8 visits per person per year while the comparable rate for males was 1.5 visits. Rates for both sexes declined after age 65. Approximately 49.3 percent of the population had seen a dentist during the preceding year.

TABLE 31.—*Dental visits for civilian noninstitutionalized population 1971–74*

	1971	1972	1973	1974
Number per person per year_____	1. 5	1. 5	1. 6	1. 7
Percent of persons with visits in the past year_	47. 1	47. 3	48. 9	49. 3

Source: "Current Estimates From the Health Interview Survey, United States, 1974 " U.S. Department of Health, Education, and Welfare, National Center for Health Statistics, DHEW publication No. (HRA) 76–1527, September 1975.

TABLE 32.—*Number of dental visits and number of dental visits per person per year, by age and sex: United States, 1974*

[Data are based on household interviews of the civilian, noninstitutionalized population]

Sex	All ages	Under 17 years	17 to 24 years	25 to 44 years	45 to 64 years	65 years and over
Number of dental visits, both sexes (in thousands):						
Both sexes_____	342, 293	100, 999	50, 445	89, 542	76, 687	24, 620
Male_____	150, 137	47, 394	20, 284	38, 700	34, 526	9, 233
Female_____	192, 156	53, 605	30, 161	50, 842	42, 161	15, 387
Number of dental visits, both sexes (per person, per year):						
Both sexes_____	1. 7	1. 6	1. 7	1. 7	1. 8	1. 2
Male_____	1. 5	1. 5	1. 4	1. 6	1. 7	1. 1
Female_____	1. 8	1. 7	2. 0	1. 9	1. 9	1. 3

Source: "Current Estimates From the Health Interview Survey, United States, 1974," U.S. Department of Health, Education, and Welfare, National Center for Health Statistics, DHEW publication No. (HRA) 76–1527, September 1975.

TABLE 33.—*Percent distribution of persons by time interval since last dental visit according to sex and age: United States, 1974*

Sex and age	Total population	Time interval since last dental visit			
		Under 1 yr	1 to 4 yrs	5 yrs and over	Other [1]
Both sexes:					
All ages	100. 0	49. 3	25. 1	13. 8	11. 8
Under 17 yrs	100. 0	49. 9	16. 7	1. 3	32. 2
17 to 24 yrs	100. 0	57. 5	31. 5	5. 8	5. 1
25 to 44 yrs	100. 0	54. 6	30. 9	11. 7	2. 8
45 to 64 yrs	100. 0	46. 7	27. 6	23. 7	2. 1
65 yrs and over	100. 0	28. 6	22. 3	47. 6	1. 6
Male:					
All ages	100. 0	47. 5	26. 1	13. 7	12. 7
Under 17 yrs	100. 0	48. 7	17. 2	1. 4	32. 7
17 to 24 yrs	100. 0	53. 6	34. 2	6. 4	5. 7
25 to 44 yrs	100. 0	51. 5	32. 2	13. 1	3. 1
45 to 64 yrs	100. 0	45. 3	28. 2	24. 3	2. 2
65 yrs and over	100. 0	26. 9	23. 1	7. 9	2. 0
Female:					
All ages	100. 0	51. 0	24. 2	13. 9	11. 0
Under 17 yrs	100. 0	51. 0	16. 1	1. 3	31. 7
17 to 24 yrs	100. 0	61. 1	29. 1	5. 3	4. 6
25 to 44 yrs	100. 0	57. 4	29. 6	10. 4	2. 5
45 to 64 yrs	100. 0	48. 0	27. 0	23. 2	1. 9
65 yrs and over	100. 0	29. 6	21. 6	47. 4	1. 4

[1] "Other" includes "never" and "unknown."

Note: Numbers may not add due to rounding.

Source: "Current Estimates From the Health Interview Survey, United States, 1974" Department of Health, Education, and Welfare, National Center for Health Statistics, DHEW publication No. (HRA) 76–1527, September 1975.

The number of times an individual sees a dentist during a year differs according to several demographic variables. Whites, females, metropolitan area residents, and those in higher income families average more dental visits per year than their counterparts.

TABLE 34.—*Number of dental visits per person per year, by age and selected demographic characteristics, 1973*

	Under age 6	Ages 6 to 16	Ages 17 to 44	Ages 45 to 64
Sex:				
Male			1. 4	1. 5
Female			1. 9	1. 9
Color:				
White	0. 6	2. 3	1. 8	1. 8
Black	. 4	. 8	1. 1	1. 0
Region:				
Northeast		2. 5	2. 1	2. 2
North Central		2. 1	1. 7	1. 6
South		1. 5	1. 4	1. 4
West		2. 7	1. 8	1. 9
Residence:				
Metropolitan		2. 3	1. 8	1. 9
Nonmetropolitan		1. 6	1. 4	1. 4
Family income:				
Under $5,000	NA	1. 1	1. 5	1. 2
$5,000 to $9,999	. 3	1. 4	1. 4	1. 4
$10,000 to $14,999	. 5	2. 2	1. 6	2. 0
$15,000 or more	1. 2	3. 1	2. 1	2. 2

Source: Health: United States, 1975, Public Health Service, U.S. Department of Health, Education, and Welfare, 1975.

D. Utilization of Preventive Care Services

Persons living in metropolitan areas are more likely to have had preventive care examinations within the past 2 years than their nonmetropolitan counterparts. High-income persons are more likely to have had preventive health care than the low-income, though even in the highest income categories the lack of basic health care exams is notable for a certain percentage of the population.

TABLE 35.—*Percent of population with preventive care examination within the past 2 years by selected demographic characteristics: United States, 1973*

Demographic characteristic	Routine physical, under 17 yr	Eye examination, 3 yr and over	Chest X-ray, 17 yr and over	Pap smear, females 17 yr and over	Breast examination, females 17 yr and over	Electrocardiogram, 40 yr and over	Glaucoma test, 40 yr and over
All persons [1]	62. 4	56. 6	43. 8	57. 6	59. 5	33. 0	33. 3
Age:							
3 to 16 yr	57. 7	71. 3					
17 to 24 yr		55. 9	39. 1	58. 1	59. 9		
25 to 44 yr		46. 2	44. 7	74. 7	73. 7		
45 to 64 yr		54. 5	47. 2	52. 0	54. 8	32. 7	34. 8
65 yr and over		48. 4	41. 5	30. 1	36. 9	37. 3	34. 0
Sex:							
Male	64. 6	56. 3	44. 5			36. 3	31. 1
Female	60. 2	56. 9	43. 2	57. 6	59. 5	30. 2	35. 2
Color:							
White	62. 7	57. 0	42. 4	57. 8	59. 8	33. 1	34. 0
All other	61. 1	53. 8	54. 8	56. 0	57. 4	31. 4	27. 2
Geographic region:							
Northeast	72. 6	62. 0	42. 2	52. 7	57. 5	34. 2	35. 2
North central	62. 3	57. 1	43. 5	57. 9	58. 0	31. 1	31. 5
South	56. 4	52. 6	44. 6	57. 7	59. 7	32. 4	31. 8
West	60. 5	55. 7	45. 3	63. 9	64. 5	35. 3	36. 2
Residence:							
Metropolitan	66. 7	58. 0	46. 4	59. 4	62. 0	35. 4	35. 8
Nonmetropolitan	53. 3	53. 2	38. 0	53. 4	53. 8	27. 7	28. 1
Family income:							
Under $5,000	55. 4	50. 2	42. 4	42. 9	46. 6	31. 9	27. 6
$5,000 to $9,999	59. 0	53. 8	42. 4	58. 1	59. 3	31. 1	30. 9
$10,000 to $14,999	63. 7	58. 0	43. 5	64. 9	65. 6	31. 0	33. 6
$15,000 and over	69. 0	63. 0	47. 6	66. 2	68. 7	37. 9	42. 0

[1] Includes unknown income.

Source: Health: United States, 1975, Public Health Service, U.S. Department of Health, Education, and Welfare.

An important component of preventive health care is the administration of certain vaccines during the early years of life. However, a significant percentage of children are not adequately protected. Of particular significance is the decline in the percentage of persons protected against polio. Less than half of the minority children under age 5 have received the necessary vaccines. While the number of persons with rubella vaccine has increased from 1970 to 1974, less than two-thirds of children aged 1–4 have been vaccinated to prevent the spread of the disease. The percent of persons with protection against measles and diptheria-typhoid-pertussis has remained relatively constant over the past 5 years.

TABLE 36.—*Percent of persons with 3 or more doses of polio vaccine by race and age, 1965–74, and by geographic division and age, 1974: United States*

Year and race	Age in years—			
	1 to 4	5 to 9	10 to 14	15 to 19
1965:				
Total	73. 9	89. 9	92. 1	88. 3
White	76. 6	91. 4	93. 1	89. 2
All other	59. 6	81. 3	85. 9	82. 1
1966:				
Total	70. 2	88. 2	90. 0	86. 4
White	72. 9	89. 6	90. 9	87. 4
All other	56. 6	79. 8	85. 0	79. 1
1967:				
Total	70. 9	88. 3	89. 7	82. 5
White	73. 1	89. 8	90. 7	83. 5
All other	60. 2	80. 5	83. 5	75. 5
1968:				
Total	68. 3	84. 9	87. 8	81. 3
White	71. 0	86. 3	89. 2	82. 5
All other	54. 5	77. 0	79. 3	73. 2
1969:				
Total	67. 7	83. 6	85. 7	79. 8
White	70. 7	85. 4	87. 7	81. 4
All other	53. 6	73. 6	74. 8	69. 6
1970:				
Total	65. 9	82. 3	85. 3	77. 8
White	69. 2	83. 8	86. 6	79. 5
All other	50. 1	74. 8	76. 7	67. 7
1971:				
Total	67. 3	81. 2	83. 9	77. 0
White	70. 5	82. 8	85. 9	79. 0
All other	51. 9	72. 9	71. 9	65. 0
1972:				
Total	62. 9	78. 9	81. 8	75. 4
White	66. 3	81. 6	83. 7	77. 3
All other	45. 2	64. 7	71. 5	63. 7
1973:				
Total	60. 4	71. 4	69. 3	59. 1
White	64. 4	73. 5	71. 1	61. 0
All other	39. 8	60. 3	59. 0	47. 8
1974:				
Total	63. 1	73. 5	69. 8	60. 2
White	66. 7	76. 0	71. 8	62. 1
All other	45. 0	60. 4	59. 1	49. 3
1974—Geographic divisions:				
New England	71. 4	79. 6	73. 4	59. 6
Middle Atlantic	64. 1	71. 8	67. 7	56. 0
East north central	59. 0	66. 2	61. 6	53. 2
West north central	61. 4	71. 9	66. 0	57. 3
South Atlantic	63. 1	74. 5	70. 7	59. 9
East south central	57. 9	73. 4	70. 9	66. 1
West south central	67. 3	81. 1	79. 7	71. 6
Mountain	62. 9	75. 1	71. 9	68. 5
Pacific	63. 9	77. 2	76. 3	64. 1

Source: Health: United States, 1975, Public Health Service, U.S. Department of Health, Education, and Welfare, 1975.

TABLE 37.—*Percent of persons with history of rubella vaccine by race and age, 1970-74, and by geographic division and age, 1974: United States*

Year and race	Age in years—		
	1 to 4	5 to 9	10 to 12
1970:			
Total	37. 2	46. 5	29. 5
White	38. 3	47. 4	29. 0
All other	31. 8	41. 7	32. 0
1971:			
Total	51. 2	63. 2	47. 3
White	51. 8	63. 5	46. 7
All other	48. 2	61. 6	51. 2
1972:			
Total	56. 9	66. 8	55. 2
White	57. 8	67. 4	54. 8
All other	52. 6	63. 7	57. 7
1973:			
Total	55. 6	64. 9	54. 1
White	57. 0	65. 8	54. 0
All other	48. 5	59. 8	54. 2
1974:			
Total	59. 8	68. 0	57. 5
White	61. 0	69. 0	57. 9
All other	53. 6	62. 9	55. 2
1974—Geographic division:			
New England	57. 1	66. 8	53. 7
Middle Atlantic	66. 5	73. 5	63. 2
East north central	59. 9	67. 7	57. 5
West north central	58. 2	73. 9	63. 5
South Atlantic	59. 7	70. 2	57. 2
East south central	55. 9	61. 4	50. 8
West south central	58. 3	67. 9	60. 0
Mountain	52. 8	61. 6	56. 6
Pacific	59. 0	61. 6	50. 3

Source: Health: United States, 1975, Public Health Service, U.S. Department of Health, Education, and Welfare, 1975.

TABLE 38.—*Percent of persons with history of measles vaccine and/or measles infection by race and age, 1974, United States*

Year and race	Age in years		
	1 to 4	5 to 9	10 to 13
1974:			
Total	66. 6	80. 8	81. 1
White	68. 6	82. 4	83. 2
All other	56. 3	72. 4	69. 4

Source: Health: United States, 1975, Public Health Service, U.S. Department of Health, Education, and Welfare, 1975.

TABLE 39.—*Percent of persons with 3 or more doses of diphtheria-typhoid-pertussis vaccine by race and age, 1974: United States*

Year and race	Age in years—		
	1 to 4	5 to 9	10 to 13
1974:			
Total_____	73. 9	84. 7	85. 5
White_____	76. 8	86. 7	87. 5
All other_____	59. 6	74. 2	74. 8

E. UTILIZATION OF MENTAL HEALTH CARE AND MENTAL RETARDATION FACILITIES

Both the number and the rate of patient care episodes in mental health facilities more than doubled between 1955 and 1973. A significant decline occurred in the proportion of inpatient episodes (from 77.4 percent of 35.3 percent of the total) with a comparable increase in the percentage of outpatient episodes (22.6 percent to 63.7 percent). The rates of inpatient care episodes reached their peak in 1969; outpatient rates showed a steady increase over the period. There were 2.5 million admissions to psychiatric services in 1971—1.2 million to inpatient and 1.3 million to outpatient services. Females had higher outpatient than inpatient rates while the reverse was true for males.

TABLE 40.—*Number, percent distribution, and rates per 100,000 population of inpatient and outpatient care episodes, in selected mental health facilities, by type of facility: United States 1955, 1965, 1967, 1969, 1971, and 1973* [1]

Year	Total facilities [1]	Inpatient services of—						Outpatient psychiatric services of—		
		Total inpatient	State and county mental hospitals	Private mental hospitals [2]	General hospital psychiatric service (non-VA)	VA psychiatric inpatient services	Federally assisted community mental health centers	Total outpatient	Federally assisted community mental health centers	Other
Percent distribution:										
1973	4,749,361	35.3	13.7	3.2	10.0	4.4	4.0	64.7	20.7	44.0
1971	4,038,143	42.6	18.5	3.1	13.4	4.4	3.2	57.4	15.4	42.0
1969	3,572,822	47.0	21.5	3.5	15.0	5.2	1.8	53.0	8.1	44.9
1967	3,139,742	52.9	25.5	4.0	18.4	4.1	.9	47.1	3.1	44.0
1965	2,636,525	59.4	30.5	4.8	19.7	4.4	----	40.6	----	40.6
1955	1,675,352	77.4	48.9	7.3	15.9	5.3	----	22.6	----	22.6
Rate per 100,000 population:										
1973	------	2,282.4	807.2	313.3	73.0	228.5	100.2	92.2	1,475.2	472.0	1,003.0
1971	------	1,981.5	847.2	364.9	66.1	265.7	86.9	63.7	1,134.3	305.0	829.3
1969	------	1,797.7	849.6	384.2	62.0	268.2	93.6	41.7	948.1	145.2	802.9
1967	------	1,604.3	847.9	409.5	63.5	295.6	65.5	13.8	756.4	49.7	706.7
1965	------	1,374.0	815.9	419.5	65.4	270.6	60.4	----	558.1	----	558.1
1955	------	1,032.2	798.6	504.5	75.9	163.8	54.4	----	233.5	----	233.5

[1] Omitted from this table are: psychiatric service modes of all types in hospitals or outpatient clinics of Federal agencies other than the VA (e.g., Public Health Service, Indian Health Service, Department of Defense, Bureau of Prisons, etc.); inpatient service modes of multiservice facilities not shown in this table; all partial care episodes, and outpatient episodes in VA hospitals.

[2] Includes estimates of episodes of care in residential treatment centers for emotionally disturbed children.

Source: Health: United States, 1975, Public Health Service, U.S. Department of Health, Education, and Welfare.

TABLE 41.—*Admission rates per 100,000 population to psychiatric inpatient and outpatient services by color and sex, by sex and age, and by diagnosis: United States, 1971*

[Rates per 100,000 population]

Color sex, age, and diagnosis	All inpatient and out-patient services	Inpatient [1]	Outpatient [2]
Color and sex:			
Both sexes	1, 238. 5	596. 7	641. 8
Male	1, 319. 1	658. 9	633. 2
Female	1, 162. 2	512. 3	649. 9
White	1, 173. 2	566. 8	606. 4
Male	1, 241. 4	642. 1	599. 4
Female	1, 108. 3	495. 4	613. 0
All other	1, 696. 2	806. 1	890. 0
Male	1, 871. 4	998. 0	873. 4
Female	1, 534. 4	629. 1	905. 3
Sex and age:			
Both sexes	1, 238. 5	596. 7	641. 8
Under 18 yr	626. 8	123. 8	503. 1
18 to 25 yr	1, 936. 0	879. 8	1, 056. 1
25 to 44 yr	1, 982. 2	1, 017. 3	964. 8
45 to 64 yr	1, 315. 7	811. 5	504. 2
65 yr and over	615. 2	464. 1	151. 0
Male	1, 319. 1	685. 9	633. 2
Under 18 yr	736. 4	127. 7	608. 8
18 to 24 yr	2, 264. 9	1, 167. 5	1, 097. 5
25 to 44 yr	1, 914. 2	1, 121. 9	792. 2
45 to 64 yr	1, 403. 8	962. 2	441. 6
65 yr and over	658. 6	535. 5	123. 1
Female	1, 162. 2	512. 3	649. 9
Under 18 yr	513. 1	119. 7	393. 4
18 to 24 yr	1, 634. 9	616. 6	1, 018. 3
25 to 44 yr	2, 047. 8	916. 4	1, 131. 5
45 to 64 yr	1, 235. 2	673. 9	561. 4
65 yr and over	583. 5	412. 1	171. 4
Diagnosis:			
All diagnoses	1, 238. 5	596. 7	641. 8
Mental retardation	28. 9	7. 4	21. 5
Organic brain syndromes	54. 9	37. 6	17. 3
Schizophrenia	258. 0	161. 1	96. 9
Depressive disorders	216. 9	134. 3	82. 6
Other psychotic disorders	18. 9	9. 8	9. 1
Alcoholism	127. 9	94. 0	33. 9
Drug abuse	43. 1	30. 2	12. 9
All other disorders	401. 1	110. 9	290. 2
Undiagnosed	88. 9	11. 5	77. 4

[1] Excludes residential treatment centers for emotionally disturbed children and other multiservice facilities for which the demographic characteristics of admissions were not available.

[2] Excludes VA hospitals and residential treatment centers for emotionally disturbed children for which the demographic characteristics of admissions were not available.

Source: Health: United States, 1975, Public Health Service, U.S. Department of Health, Education, and Welfare.

In 1971, there were approximately 201,225 patients treated in public institutions for the mentally retarded. The average daily resident caseload was approximately 181,000. Total admissions during the year were 15,370 and net live releases were 17,080.

F. Long-Term Care Utilization

The term nursing home embraces a wide variety of health care facilities from special long-term hospitals providing intensive medical care services to the boarding home providing only the simplest form of supporting services. The term "extended care facilities" (ECF's) was the term initially used by the medicare program for approved facilities providing posthospital nursing care to program beneficiaries. The medicaid program used the term "skilled nursing homes" (SNH's) to designate those approved homes providing skilled nursing care to medicaid recipients. In 1972, ECF's and SNH's were redesignated as "skilled nursing facilities" (SNF's); uniform certification procedures and definition of care were established for both programs. An additional category of nursing home care receiving Federal support is "intermediate care" provided by "intermediate care facilities" (ICF's); such facilities, certified to participate in the medicaid program (but not the medicare program) provide a lesser level of health-related care than do SNF's to patients requiring institutional care above the level of room and board.

There were approximately 1.1 million resident patients in all categories of nursing homes in 1973. Over two-thirds of this population, 70.2 percent, were female. Fifty percent of all nursing home residents received care financed by medicaid (29 percent received SNF care and 21 percent intermediate care) while only 4 percent received care financed by medicare. Measures of utilization for 1972 showed the number of admissions per bed per year was 0.86. Homes certified by both medicare and medicaid had the highest turnover rate and the highest percentage of residents discharged alive. The high turnover rate was attributable to two factors. First, since medicare coverage for SNF care is available only following a hospital stay, many of the residents were recovering from an operation or illness and discharged upon recovery. Secondly, medicare will only pay up to 100 days of skilled care in a medicare-approved home.

The following tables show the major utilization characteristics of U.S. nursing homes. The data are provisional estimates developed by the National Center for Health Statistics from the 1973–74 Nursing Home Survey.

TABLE 42.—*Provisional estimates of selected characteristics of nursing home beds certified for medicare or medicaid: United States, 1973–74*

[Figures may not add to totals due to rounding]

Certification status of bed	Beds [1]		Beds occupied by resident receiving program benefits		Percent of total residents receiving program benefits
	Number	Percent of total beds	Number of beds	Percent occupied night before interview	
ECF beds (medicare)	287, 400	24. 2	45, 200	15. 7	4. 1
SNH beds (medicaid)	538, 900	45. 4	321, 100	59. 6	29. 2
ICF beds (medicaid)	378, 600	31. 9	229, 900	60. 7	20. 9

[1] These figures are not mutually exclusive because some beds have dual certification. For example, a bed certified for medicare may also be certified by medicaid. Since 1 bed may be counted twice, the sum of all certified beds exceeds the actual number of beds (1,188,000). For the same reason, the percent distribution exceeds 100 percent.

Source: Health: United States, 1975, Public Health Service, U.S. Department of Health, Education, and Welfare, 1975.

TABLE 43.—*Provisional number and percent of nursing home residents for 1973-74, and provisional estimates of selected measures of utilization for 1972, by certification status: United States*

[Figures may not add to totals due to rounding]

Certification status of home	Residents in 1973-74				Ad-missions	Measures of utilization for 1972					
	Number	Percent				Number of ad-missions per bed	Annual occu-pancy rate [1]	Discharges			
		Both sexes	Male	Female				Number	Total	Percent	
										Live	Dead
All types of certification	1,098,500	100	29.8	70.2	1,018,300	0.86	88.6	984,600	100	69.3	30.7
Both medicare and medicaid [2]	393,600	100	28.5	71.5	549,400	1.27	83.6	535,400	100	73.0	27.0
Medicaid only	524,800	100	31.0	69.0	362,300	.64	90.4	342,700	100	65.8	34.2
SNH [3]	278,600	100	30.3	69.7	209,700	.71	91.0	194,500	100	67.8	32.2
ICF	246,200	100	31.8	68.2	152,600	.57	89.7	148,200	100	63.2	36.8
Not certified	180,100	100	29.4	70.6	106,700	.55	94.6	106,500	100	61.8	38.3

[1] $\dfrac{\text{Aggregate number of days of care provided to residents in 1972}}{\text{Number of beds}} \times 366 \times 100$

[2] 12 percent of these homes were certified by medicare only.

[3] 46 percent of these homes were also certified as ICF's.

In 1974, the Office of Nursing Home Affairs conducted a scientifically selected sample survey of skilled nursing facilities and their residents for the purpose of developing a national prcfile. The sample survey included 288 facilities certified for participation in medicare and 283,915 medicare and medicaid beneficiaries in those homes. The demographic characteristics and health status of these patients is considered fairly representative of the nationwide population of medicare and medicaid residents in such facilities. The survey did not include ICF's where a larger number of mentally retarded and developmentally disabled are found.

Approximately 78 percent of the SNF patients surveyed were over 65 year of age and almost 50 percent were 80 years or over. Women outnumbered men by more than 2 to 1; only 27.1 percent were male compared with 72.9 percent female. Slightly less than 10 percent of the patients represented minority groups with the largest proportion—7 percent—of the black race. Less than one out of every eight patients was married at the time of the survey with the largest proportion, 60.6 percent, widowed (51.4 percent widows and 9.2 percent widowers). About 30 percent of all patients had less than 8 years of schooling while an additional 22.1 percent had only completed 8 years. Less than 9 percent of all patients had ever attended college. The educational levels were in turn reflected in the patients' occupational patterns with only 7.6 percent having been employed as professional workers. Almost one-third had been employed as farmers, skilled service or clerical workers, with an additional one-fifth employed as unskilled laborers. More than one-fourth had been homemakers and over 13 percent had never been employed. Very few patients in SNF's were currently in the labor force. While close to 70 percent were participants at one time, 64 percent were retired. Over 95 percent were not employed and not seeking employment. Patient and family incomes cf SNF residents was very limited. Over 68 percent of all family income was less than $3,000 with an additional 22 percent having no income. This indicates that over 90 percent were below the poverty level. Tables 44–46 highlight the major characteristics of medicare and medicaid SNF patients reported in the survey.

TABLE 44.—*Number and percent distribution of survey patients in skilled nursing facilities by age*

Age group(s)	Number	Percent
Total	283,915	100. 0
Under 20	4,838	1. 7
20 to 64	58,048	20. 4
65 to 69	15,139	5. 3
70 to 74	28,384	10. 0
75 to 79	35,954	12. 7
80 to 84	52,984	18. 7
85 to 89	56,769	20. 0
90 and over	31,799	11. 2

Source: U.S. Dept. of Health, Education, and Welfare, Public Health Service, Office of Nursing Home Affairs. Long Term Care Facility Improvement Study—Introductory Report. July, 1975.

TABLE 45.—*Number and percent of survey patients by sex and race*

Race(s)	Both sexes total		Male total		Female total	
	Number	Percent	Number	Percent	Number	Percent
All races_____	283,912	100. 0	76,845	27. 1	207,067	73. 0
White_____	256,827	90. 5	66,691	23. 5	190,136	67. 0
Negro/black_____	19,952	7. 0	7,417	2. 6	12,535	4. 4
Spanish American_____	4,419	1. 6	1,899	. 7	2,520	. 9
Asian American_____	940	. 3	120	. 0	820	. 3
Other_____	1,774	. 6	718	. 3	1,056	. 4

NOTE: Uniform procedures were used in computations; there may be a minor difference between the sum total figure and the total obtained when the subtotals are added together.

Source: U.S. Department of Health, Education, and Welfare, Public Health Service, Office of Nursing Home Affairs. Long Term Care Facility Improvement Study—Introductory Report. July 1975.

TABLE 46.—*Number and percent of survey patients by sex and family income*

Family income totals	Both sexes		Male sex		Female sex	
	Number	Percent	Number	Percent	Number	Percent
All incomes_____	283, 917	100. 0	78, 186	27. 6	205, 731	72. 4
$15,000 or more_____	2, 075	. 7	1, 437	. 5	588	. 2
$10,000 to $14,999____	1, 132	. 4	254	. 1	878	. 3
$7,000 to $9,999_____	1, 754	. 6	522	. 2	1, 232	. 4
$5,000 to $6,999_____	4, 962	1. 7	2, 009	. 7	2, 953	1. 0
$3,000 to $4,999_____	15, 107	5. 4	6, 141	2. 2	8, 966	3. 2
Less than $3,000_____	194, 949	68. 7	46, 417	16. 4	148, 532	52. 3
No income_____	63, 988	22. 5	21, 406	7. 5	42, 582	15. 0

Source: U.S. Department of Health, Education, and Welfare, Public Health Service, Office of Nursing Home Affairs. Long Term Care Facility Improvements Study—Introductory Report. July 1975.

The HEW sample survey also examined the health status of the sample population group. An assessment of the patient needs for care showed the high degree of dependence on the nursing staff for activities of daily living. Almost 94 percent required assistance with bathing; 72 percent required the services of another person when dressing; 50.1 percent required assistance in order to eat; and 68 percent needed assistance with their toileting. Approximately half of all patients were incontinent of either urine (54.7 percent) or feces (50.1 percent). Long-term patients with limited mobility are prone to have pressure sores; however, only 9.2 percent were found to have bedsores.

The effects of developmental disabilities, chronic illness, and aging on mental functions are complex and have a wide variation among individuals. In response to simple questions, over half of all patients showed some degree of difficulty in their awareness of the existing situation with reference to time, place, and identity of self. One-seventh of the patients had no awareness of their environment at any time or were comatose. Appropriateness of patients' behavior patterns with respect to the nursing home environment was also examined. Behavior was suitable to the environment for 58.4 percent while 41.1 percent had inappropriate behavior. In this latter group patients were about equally divided between those who were passive, those who were disruptive, and those with other detrimental behavior. Most patients in the survey were able to communicate their needs either verbally (74.5 percent) or nonverbally (6.9 percent).

The majority of the surveyed patients (70.4 percent) had sight impairments including 2.6 percent who were legally blind and 52.7 percent who wore corrective lenses or glasses. Hearing impairments occurred in 32.9 percent of the patients; 32 percent had speech difficulties. Observations on the dental status showed only 8.1 percent with no missing teeth. A significant percentage, 38.1 percent, required teeth replaced, including full dentures, but had none.

Age was an important factor in the diagnostic profile of the SNF patients. The primary diagnoses for two-thirds of those under age 65 was pathology of the nervous system—neurological disease, mental retardation, neuroses and psychoses, stroke, and chronic brain disease. Alternatively, for two-thirds of the aged, primary diagnoses were cardiovascular and cerebrovascular disease, senility, and accidents. Age differentials were also reflected in the total diagnostic profile. For the younger population group, 42 percent had an identified neurological disease; 26.8 percent were mentally retarded: and 20.5 percent had a neuroses or psychoses. For the aged, 43.1 percent had heart disease, 32.7 percent chronic brain disease, 24.9 percent generalized arteriosclerosis or hypertension, 21.4 percent arthritis, and 19.1 percent stroke. Of the total postadmission diagnoses recorded, one in three for the aged and two out of five for those under 65 generally related to institutionalization and prolonged bed rest. Tables 47–49 provide a diagnostic profile of the survey population.

TABLE 47.—*Primary diagnoses of survey population recorded on admission by diagnostic group and by age*

Diagnoses	All ages		Under 65		65 and over	
	Number	Percent	Number	Percent	Number	Percent
Total	283, 300	100. 0	50, 400	100. 0	232, 900	100. 0
Heart disease	44, 300	15. 6	2, 500	5. 0	41, 900	18. 0
Chronic brain disease	39, 200	13. 8	3, 700	7. 3	35, 500	15. 2
Stroke	30, 300	10. 7	3, 900	7. 7	26, 400	11. 3
Fractures	24, 800	8. 8	1, 700	3. 4	23, 100	9. 9
Neurological disease	19, 000	6. 7	9, 600	19. 0	9, 500	4. 1
Generalized arteriosclerosis and hypertension	17, 300	6. 1	1, 300	2. 6	16, 000	6. 9
Neuroses and psychoses	15, 200	5. 4	5, 700	11. 3	9, 500	4. 1
Diabetes	14, 300	5. 0	1, 700	3. 4	12, 600	5. 4
Diseases of musculoskeletal system	13, 400	4. 7	2, 000	4. 0	11, 300	4. 9
Mental retardation	9, 300	3. 3	9, 000	17. 9	400	. 2
Neoplasms	8, 400	3. 0	1, 800	3. 6	6, 600	2. 8
Diseases of respiratory system	6, 600	2. 3	800	1. 6	5, 700	2. 4
Diseases of digestive system	6, 500	2. 3	600	1. 1	6, 000	2. 6
Diseases of genito-urinary system	3, 700	1. 3	500	1. 0	3, 200	1. 3
Diseases of eye and ear	3, 300	1. 2	600	1. 1	2, 700	1. 2
Other	27, 700	9. 8	5, 000	10. 0	22, 700	9. 7

Source: U.S. Department of Health, Education, and Welfare. Public Health Service, Office of Nursing Home Affairs. Long-Term Facility Improvement Study—Introductory report. July 1975.

TABLE 48.—*All diagnoses of survey population recorded on admission by diagnostic group and by age*

Diagnoses	All ages		Under 65		65 and over	
	Number	Percent [1]	Number	Percent [2]	Number	Percent [3]
Heart disease	108, 200	38. 1	7, 800	15. 2	100, 400	43. 1
Chronic brain disease	83, 000	29. 2	6, 900	13. 5	76, 100	32. 7
Generalized arteriosclerosis and hypertension	64, 800	22. 8	6, 800	13. 3	57, 900	24. 9
Diseases of musculoskeletal system	55, 800	19. 7	6, 100	11. 9	49, 700	21. 4
Stroke	51, 300	18. 1	6, 900	13. 5	44, 400	19. 1
Fractures	46, 200	16. 3	4, 400	8. 6	41, 800	18. 0
Neurological disease	43, 800	15. 4	21, 500	42. 0	22, 300	9. 6
Diabetes	40, 700	14. 3	6, 100	11. 9	34, 600	14. 9
Neuroses and psychoses	34, 100	12. 0	10, 500	20. 5	23, 600	10. 1
Diseases of digestive system	30, 700	10. 8	4, 000	7. 8	26, 700	11. 5
Diseases of genito-urinary system	29, 600	10. 3	5, 500	10. 7	24, 100	10. 4
Diseases of eye and ear	28, 400	10. 0	5, 900	11. 5	22, 500	9. 7
Diseases of respiratory system	21, 400	7. 5	3, 400	6. 6	18, 000	7. 7
Neoplasms	15, 800	5. 6	3, 300	6. 4	12, 500	5. 4
Mental retardation	14, 900	5. 2	13, 700	26. 8	1, 200	([4])
Other [5]	52, 700	18. 6	11, 600	22. 7	41, 100	17. 7

[1] Percentages are based on a total of 283,900 patients.
[2] Percentages are based on a total of 51,200 patients.
[3] Percentages are based on a total of 232,700 patients.
[4] Less than 0.1 percent.
[5] Includes major surgery, endocrine disease (other than diabetes mellitus), anemias, nutritional disease, and decubitus ulcers and other skin disorders.

Note: Percentages add up to more than 100 because of multiple diagnoses recorded on admission for same patients.

Source: U.S. Department of Health, Education, and Welfare. Public Health Service, Office of Nursing Home Affairs. Long-Term Facility Improvement Study—Introductory Report. July 1975.

TABLE 49.—*Rank order of most common diagnostic groups of survey population by time of recording and age group*

Rank order	Primary diagnoses on admission		All diagnoses on admission		All diagnoses postadmission	
	Under 65	65 and over	Under 65	65 and over	Under 65	65 and over
1	Neurological disease	Heart disease	Neurological disease	Heart disease	Diseases of respiratory system.	Diseases of genito-urinary system.
2	Mental retardation	Chronic brain disease	Mental retardation	Chronic brain disease	Decubitus ulcers and other skin diseases.	Diseases of eye and ear.
3	Neuroses and psychoses	Stroke	Neuroses and psychoses.	General arteriosclerosis and hypertension.	Diseases of digestive system.	Decubitus ulcers and other skin diseases.
4	Stroke	Fractures	Heart disease	Diseases of musculo-skeletal system.	Diseases of genito-urinary system.	Diseases of musculo-skeletal system.
5	Chronic brain disease	General arteriosclerosis and hypertension.	Chronic brain disease	Stroke	Diseases of eye and ear.	Heart disease.
6	Heart disease	Diabetes	Stroke	Fractures	Fractures.	Fractures.
7	Diseases of musculo-skeletal system.	Diseases of musculo-skeletal system.	General arteriosclerosis and hypertension.	Diabetes	Heart disease.	Diseases of digestive system.
8	Neoplasms	Neuroses and psychoses.	Diseases of musculo-skeletal system.	Diseases of digestive system.	Diseases of musculo-skeletal system.	Diseases of respiratory system.
9	Diabetes	Neurological disease	Diabetes	Diseases of genito-urinary system.		
10	Fractures	Neoplasms	Diseases of eye and ear.	Neuroses and psychoses.		

Source: U.S. Department of Health, Education, and Welfare. Public Health Service, Office of Nursing Home Affairs. Long-term Facility Improvement Study—Introductory Report. July 1975.

Sixty percent of the survey residents had been examined by a physician within a month prior to the survey, and an additional 17 percent between 1–2 months prior to the survey. Nine percent of the patients who had been in the homes in excess of a year had not been examined by a physician for at least a year.

Approximately 41 percent of the nursing home patients receive intensive care, 32 percent routine nursing care, and 16 percent personal nursing care.

TABLE 50.—*Numbers and percent distribution of nursing home residents by length of time since current admission according to interval since last saw physician: United States, 1973–74*

Interval since last saw physician	All residents	Length of stay since current admission				
		Under 6 mo	6 mo to 1 yr	1 to 3 yr	3 to 5 yr	5 yr or more
Number of residents	1,074,500	258,800	155,500	357,200	149,600	153,400
Percent distribution:						
All intervals	100. 0	100. 0	100. 0	100. 0	100. 0	100. 0
Less than 1 mo	60. 1	70. 6	63. 1	56. 8	55. 1	52. 1
1 to 2 mo	16. 8	13. 8	17. 3	17. 8	18. 4	17. 4
3 to 5 mo	11. 9	6. 2	12. 8	12. 9	14. 2	15. 8
6 mo to 1 yr	3. 2	---------	4. 7	3. 9	3. 6	5. 2
1 yr or more	4. 7	--------------------		7. 3	7. 5	8. 3
Not since admission	3. 4	9. 3	2. 2	1. 4	1. 3	1. 2

Source: Health: United States, 1975 Public Health Service U.S. Department of Health, 1975.

TABLE 51.—*Number and percent distribution of nursing home residents by age and sex according to level of nursing care received: United States, 1973–74*

Level of nursing care received [1]	All residents	Age				Sex	
		Under 65 yr	65 to 74 yr	75 to 84 yr	85 yr and over	Male	Female
Number of residents	1,074,500	114,200	162,900	384,400	413,000	317,800	756,60 0
Percent distribution:							
All levels	100. 0	100. 0	100. 0	100. 0	100. 0	100. 0	100. 0
Intensive nursing care	41. 0	35. 5	37. 0	41. 1	44. 1	37. 6	42. 5
Limited nursing care	9. 8	9 5	11. 0	10. 2	9. 1	10. 1	9. 7
Routine nursing care	32. 3	30. 0	33. 8	33. 2	31. 5	33. 6	31. 7
Personal nursing care	16. 0	24. 1	17. 1	14. 5	14. 7	17. 5	15. 4
No nursing care	. 9	------	1. 0	1. 0	. 6	1. 1	. 8

[1] Intensive nursing care includes: full bed bath, catheterization, oxygen therapy, intravenous injections, tube feeding, or bowel/bladder training; limited nursing care includes sterile dressings, irrigation, or hypodermic injections; routine nursing care includes enemas, blood pressures, and temperature, pulse, or respiration checks; and personal nursing care includes a rub or massage, a special diet, medication or other treatment, or assistance in personal hygiene or eating. A resident receiving multiple types of services, was classified at the higher level of nursing care.

Source: Health: United States, 1975, Public Health Service, U.S. Department of Health, Education, and Welfare.

The survey demonstrated that there was a significant gap between the percentage of the SNF population needing specialized rehabilitative services and the percentage actually receiving them. An estimated 47 percent of the patients needed physical therapy services, 35 percent needed occupational therapy, and 13 percent needed speech therapy. However, of the numbers requiring care, only 30.7 percent actually received physical therapy, 10.9 percent received occupational therapy, and 10.8 percent received speech therapy.

Chapter 8
Public Programs

There are hundreds of federally sponsored, federally supervised health care programs operating in the United States. Veterans, Indians, military personnel, and federal prisoners, to name a few, have special federal health programs designed to meet their needs. Two programs of particular relevance to national health insurance are included here: Medicare and Medicaid. They are frequently cited as sources of valuable experience by those in favor of and in opposition to national health insurance. Some see them as bold, largely successful social measures to deal with the problems of the medically disadvantaged. Others see them as wasteful and inefficient, serving acquisitive doctors, hospitals, and laboratories more than the needs of those they serve. Over fifty million people are currently enrolled in these programs and the operation of their administration provides a body of experience that will undoubtedly affect the manner in which any national health insurance proposal is implemented. The following brief descriptions serve as background and introduction to the Medicare and Medicaid public programs. Hearings, reports, and staff studies conducted by the Senate Finance Committee, the House Ways and Means Committee, and HEW's Social Security Administration provide further details. See, for instance, the Senate Finance Committee's "Medicare and Medicaid: Problems, Issues, Alternatives," which is a staff report issued February 9, 1973; and the *Social Security Bulletin*, "Early Effects of Medicare on the Health Care of the Aged," April 1971.

MEDICARE ([34], pp. 405–410)

Background

Medicare legislation had been considered for many years before its enactment in 1965. Bills to provide hospital insurance and related health benefits as part of the national social insurance system were first introduced in the Congress as early as 1952 and received active consideration beginning in 1958. The program which finally evolved—including major amendments in 1968 and 1972—represents almost a quarter century distillation of differing and conflicting views of many people and organizations.

Medicare is a federally administered program providing hospital and medical insurance protection for almost 24 million people—those 65 and older, people under age 65 who have been receiving cash benefits under the social security or railroad retirement programs for 2 years because they are disabled, and certain chronic kidney disease patients under 65.

The medicare program is under the overall direction of the Secretary of Health, Education, and Welfare. Within the Department, the Bureau of Health Insurance of the Social Security Administration is responsible for policy and administrative control of the program, with much of the day-to-day operational work of the program performed under contract by some 130 commercial insurance companies and Blue Cross-Blue Shield plans. These organizations have the responsibility for reviewing claims for benefits and making payments. In fiscal year 1975, these organizations processed 27 million bills from hospitals and other participating facilities and 81 million bills for physicians' and other medical services.

Over $14 billion in medicare benefits were paid in fiscal year 1975, approximately 13 percent of the Nation's total health care bill. In each State, health officials assist the Federal Government in determining whether facilities that wish to provide services to medicare beneficiaries meet the conditions for participation in the medicare program. These conditions relate to the quality of patient care and various health and safety requirements. There are about 16,000 health care facilities—hospitals, skilled nursing facilities, home health agencies, and independent laboratories participating in medicare.

Description of Program

The medicare program consists of two parts—the hospital insurance plan (part A) and the supplementary medical insurance plan (part B). Hospital insurance benefits include: (a) inpatient hospital services for up to 90 days in a benefit period, plus a lifetime reserve of 60 additional days of hospital care after the 90 days have been exhausted; (b) posthospital extended care in a skilled nursing facility for up to 100 days in a benefit period; and (c) posthospital home health services for as many as 100 home health visits. A benefit period begins with the first day an individual is furnished inpatient hospital or skilled nursing facility services, and does not end until he has not been an inpatient in either a hospital or a skilled nursing facility for 60 consecutive days.

Supplementary medicare insurance benefits (part B) include: (a) physicians' and surgeons' services, certain nonroutine services of podiatrists, limited services provided by chiropractors, and the services of independently practicing physical therapists; (b) certain other medical and health services such as diagnostic services, diagnostic X-ray tests, laboratory tests and other diagnostic services, X-ray, radium and radioactive isotope therapy, ambulance services, and additional medical supplies, appliances, equipment, and prostheses; (c) outpatient hospital services; (d) home health services (with no requirement of prior hospitalization) for 100 visits during a calendar year; and (e) outpatient physical and speech therapy services furnished by approved providers.

Both the hospital insurance and medical insurance plans contain limitations on program benefits in the form of deductible and coinsurance amounts for which the beneficiary is responsible. The most important of these are a variable deductible—now $104—with respect to part A hospital services and a $60 deductible and 20-percent coinsurance amount with respect to most part B services.[1]

Hospital insurance (part A) coverage is available to: (a) all people 65 and over who are entitled to receive social security cash benefits or railroad retirement benefits; (b) social security beneficiaries under age 65 who have been entitled to social security or railroad retirement benefits for at least 24 consecutive months on the basis of a disability; (c) otherwise ineligible persons,

---

[1] The current monthly premium (paid by people enrolled in the medical insurance part of the program) is also sometimes thought of as a form of cost sharing. The medical insurance premium is discussed later in this chapter.

65 and older, who elect to enroll in the hospital insurance program and to pay the full cost of their coverage, $45 a month now, increasing in the future as costs increase; (d) almost all people under 65 who suffer from chronic kidney disease; and (e) those who were 65 or nearly that age when the program was enacted in 1965 but who were not eligible for cash benefits.

Supplementary medical insurance is available to all hospital insurance beneficiaries and to all other people 65 and over, except recent immigrants.

Payment of medicare benefits is on the basis of (1) reasonable cost in the case of hospitals and other institutional providers and (2) reasonable charges in the case of physicians and other noninstitutional suppliers of services.

Reasonable costs are determined on the basis of actual costs incurred by the individual provider in furnishing covered services to beneficiaries. The principles of reimbursement provide that all necessary and proper costs which maintain the operation of patient care facilities and activities will be included in the computation of medicare reimbursement. A provision in the Social Security Amendments of 1972 now permits establishment of upper limits of "reasonableness" of costs by hospital category or type of service.

The determination of the reasonableness of charges is made by carriers (private organizations with which the Secretary has contracted for the payment of benefits) pursuant to policy guidelines issued by the Social Security Administration, which are established within the framework of general statutory instructions. In determining reasonable charges, the carrier must take into consideration the customary charges for similar services by the physician or other person furnishing the services, as well as the prevailing charges in the locality for similar services. The prevailing charge for a service is limited to the 75th percentile of the customary charges in an area. The 75th percentile amount is increased over time by a factor which takes into account increased costs of practice and increases in earnings levels in the area.

The hospital insurance part of the program is financed primarily through social security payroll contributions paid by employees, employers, and self-employed people covered under social security. The contribution rates are the same for self-employed persons, employees, and employers, and are paid on annual earnings up to the same limit that applies to contributions for the cash benefit program—$15,300 in 1976. Hospital insurance benefits for the present aged who qualify on the basis of the special transitional insured status provision are financed from general revenues. Hospital insurance benefits for aged persons not otherwise eligible are financed through monthly premiums (currently $45) paid by those who voluntarily enroll in the hospital insurance program.

The supplementary medical insurance (SMI) part of the program, in which participation is voluntary, is financed from premiums paid by aged, disabled, and chronic renal disease enrollees and from Federal funds. Under the law the Secretary of Health, Education, and Welfare is required to review the premium rate and to promulgate in December of each year the rate to be in effect for the following fiscal year. Increases in the rate are to be directly related to the expected increase in program costs, but cannot be increased in the future by a proportion higher than the proportionate increase of cash social security benefits resulting from a general benefit increase. The current premium rate is $7.20.

Of the some 23 million people age 65 and older in the United States, 22.3 million—about 95 percent—had hospital insurance protection on January 1, 1975. About 21.6 million aged people were enrolled in the voluntary supplementary medical insurance plan. On January 1, 1975, 2.0 million disability beneficiaries were enrolled in the hospital insurance program and 1.9 million were enrolled in the supplementary medical insurance program. Eleven thousand other persons were enrolled in the medicare program because they were suffering from chronic kidney disease.

ADMINISTRATION

Under the hospital insurance part of the program, groups or associations of providers, on behalf of their members, may nominate a national, State, or other public or private agency or organization to serve as intermediary in the claims process. A member of an association is free, however, to receive payment from an approved intermediary other than its association's nominee, if approved by the Secretary and agreeable to the intermediary selected. In addition, a provider may deal directly with the Social Security Administration.

The Secretary may enter into an agreement with a nominated organization if he finds this to be consistent with effective and efficient administration of the hospital insurance program. The intermediary makes payments to providers for covered items and services on the basis of reasonable cost determinations and assists in the application of safeguards against unnecessary utilization of covered services. The agreement may also call for (1) furnishing consultative services to assist providers to establish and maintain necessary fiscal records and otherwise qualify as providers of services, (2) serving as a center for communicating with providers, and (3) making audits of provider records. Hospital insurance intermediaries also make payments for home health and outpatient hospital services covered under medical insurance.

Requests for medicare payment for covered services generally are submitted by the provider of services; they must be signed by the beneficiary (or someone for him, if he is unable to do so). The provider is reimbursed on the basis of reasonable costs of covered services and bills the beneficiary for deductible and coinsurance amounts as well as for services not covered by the program.

In some instances, hospitals may bill the program for physician services rendered to inpatients. In these cases, payment is made by the hospital insurance intermediary. Depending on the nature of the billing, funds are transferred from the supplementary medical insurance trust fund to the hospital insurance trust fund to cover the cost of these services, or are paid directly from the supplementary medical insurance trust fund.

The intermediary selected by the provider reviews claims for payment and pays the provider. Actual payment is made on the basis of an interim rate established between the provider and the intermediary. Final settlement for each provider's operating year is made on the basis of a cost report submitted by the provider, and subject to an independent audit.

No payments can be made to Federal facilities except for emergency services, unless the provider serves as a community institution. In addition, payment cannot be made to a provider for those services it is obligated to render at public expense under Federal law or contract.

Under the medical insurance program, the Secretary of Health, Education, and Welfare may enter into contracts with carriers for the performance of specified administrative functions. The carriers' principal function is to determine whether charges are allowable (reasonable) and to make payment. Carriers also have the authority and responsibility to determine, in a given case, whether a claim is for a covered service and to deny claims for noncovered or excluded items or services. In addition, carriers are to assist in the application of safeguards against unnecessary utilization of services.

The law requires that in determining allowed (reasonable) charges, carriers should take into account the customary charges of physicians and other suppliers of medical services and the prevailing charges in the locality for similar services. The law also specifies that the allowed (reasonable) charge for a service may not exceed the charge applicable for a similar service and under comparable circumstances to the carrier's own policyholders and subscribers. The allowed charge, therefore, is a charge for a service which in the absence of unusual circumstances or medical complications is the lowest of the following: (1) the actual charge of the physician or other person rendering the service, (2) the charge the physician or other person customarily makes for similar services, or (3) the prevailing charges in the locality for similar services.

Claims for payment of supplementary medical insurance benefits may be submitted to the carrier either by the patient or by the physician or other supplier of services. If the patient submits a claim (an itemized bill) directly to the carrier, he receives direct payment of benefits for covered services: he remains responsible for the physician's (or supplier's) bill. The patient may assign the benefits to a physician or other supplier of services willing to accept assignment. In this case, the physician (or supplier) agrees that the allowed or reasonable charge determined by the carrier is the total charge. The physician (or supplier) submits the bill and is reimbursed. In this situation, the patient remains responsible for the remaining 20 percent of the allowed charges for covered services and the $60 deductible (if applicable to the current bill).

TABLE 1.—*National data on the medicare program* [1]

Item	1968	1969	1970	1971	1972	1973	1974	1975
Persons enrolled as of Jan. 1 for:								
Hospital insurance (HI)	19,465,411	19,750,572	20,173,819	20,588,456	20,966,267	21,374,693	[2] 23,924,000	24,311,731
Supplementary medical insurance (SMI)	18,021,125	18,854,607	19,329,363	19,738,504	20,145,286	20,544,688	[2] 23,167,000	23,503,227
HI and/or SMI	19,495,512	19,815,300	20,278,398	20,732,693	21,154,498	21,601,315	[2] 24,201,000	22,549,181
Amounts reimbursed during the fiscal year:								
HI: Total (in thousands)	$3,736,322	$4,654,000	$4,804,243	$5,442,971	$6,109,139	$6,749,000	[3] $8,118,439	----
SMI: Total (in thousands)	$1,389,622	$1,644,842	$1,979,288	$2,034,999	$2,255,069	$2,439,500	[3] $3,119,598	----
HI: Amount per HI enrollee	$192	$236	$240	$264	$291	$316	[3] $339	----
SMI: Amount per SMI enrollee	$77	$87	$103	$103	$112	$119	[3] $135	----
Participating facilities as of July:								
Number:								
All hospitals	6,865	6,825	6,776	6,745	6,726	6,757	6,773	6,773
Short-stay	6,221	6,182	6,153	6,153	6,131	6,132	6,102	6,107
Tuberculosis	118	113	105	95	80	65	56	43
Psychiatric	341	344	341	335	346	352	357	385
Other long-stay	185	186	177	162	169	208	218	238
Skilled nursing facilities		4,849	4,656	4,287	4,041	3,977	3,952	3,932
Beds:								
All hospitals	1,164,931	1,176,656	1,199,030	1,188,013	1,155,982	1,148,428	1,143,664	1,140,395
Short-stay	781,990	798,652	815,244	834,514	850,070	864,786	882,496	901,787
Tuberculosis	23,903	23,263	21,712	18,995	15,065	13,048	11,303	6,823
Psychiatric	318,896	313,519	320,709	300,696	259,329	236,550	215,513	198,802
Other long-stay	40,142	41,222	41,365	33,808	31,518	34,044	34,352	33,013
Skilled nursing facilities		341,735	333,630	307,548	291,636	287,606	294,000	287,479
Beds per 1,000 HI enrollees:								
Short-stay hospitals	40.1	40.4	40.4	40.5	40.5	41.6	41.7	41.7
Skilled nursing facilities		17.3	16.7	13.9	13.9	13.8	13.9	13.3
Home health agencies	2,093	2,209	2,350	2,284	2,222	2,211	2,248	2,242
Independent laboratories	2,566	2,670	2,684	2,751	2,873	2,929	3,029	3,048

[1] Includes United States and all outlying areas.
[2] Persons enrolled as of July 1, 1974.
[3] Amounts reimbursed during the calendar year 1974.

Source: Social Security Administration.

MEDICAID ([33], pp. 487–495)

I. Legislative Background of Medicaid

A. DEVELOPMENTS BEFORE MEDICAID

Federal participation in the cost of providing medical care to needy persons began when the Federal Emergency Relief Administration between 1933 and 1935 made available to the States funds to pay the medical expenses of the needy unemployed. The Social Security Act of 1935 set up the public assistance programs and, while no special provision was made for medical assistance, the Federal Government paid a share of the monthly assistance payments, which could be used to meet the cost of medical care. However, the payment was made to the assistance recipient rather than to the provider of medical care.

It was in 1950 that Congress first authorized "vendor payments" for medical care—payments from the welfare agency directly to physicians, health care institutions, and other providers of medical services. Federal sharing was liberalized in subsequent amendments, and by 1960 four-fifths of the States made provision for medical vendor payments. In 1951, vendor payments for medical care totaled slightly more than $100 million; by the end of the decade, they had increased to over one-half billion dollars. More than half of the total was spent under old-age assistance.

A new category of assistance recipient was established by Congress in 1960: the "medically needy" aged, whose incomes were greater than that which would have qualified them for cash assistance payments, but who needed help in meeting the costs of medical care. The Federal Government paid from 50 to 80 percent of the cost of this new program of Medical Assistance for the Aged, established under the new Kerr-Mills Act, and provision was made for liberalized Federal sharing in vendor payments for medical care under old-age assistance.

Between 1960 and 1965, total medical vendor payments more than doubled, from about $.5 billion to $1.3 billion. Increases in vendor payments under old-age assistance and the new Kerr-Mills program accounted for almost all of the increase.

B. ENACTMENT OF MEDICAID

In 1965, a new medical assistance (medicaid) program was enacted as part of the Social Security Amendments of 1965 (Public Law 89–97, which also enacted medicare). The medicaid program had these features:

1. It substituted a single program of medical assistance for the vendor payments under the categorical cash assistance and medical assistance for the aged programs, with a requirement that beginning in January 1970 Federal sharing in vendor payments would be provided only under the medicaid program;

2. It offered all States a higher rate of Federal matching for vendor payments for medical care;

3. It required each State to cover all persons receiving cash assistance;

4. It permitted States to include medically needy aged, blind, disabled, and dependent children and their families at the option of the State; and

5. It required that States include inpatient and outpatient hospital services, other laboratory and X-ray services, skilled nursing home services, and physicians' services, and permitted other forms of health care at State option.

Six States began operation of their medicaid programs in January 1966, the earliest possible date. California began its program in March 1966, with New York initiating medicaid in May. By the end of 1966, 26 States had plans in operation. Another 11 began their medicaid programs during 1967. All States, with the exception of Arizona, now have medicaid programs in operation.

C. EARLY FISCAL OPERATIONS OF MEDICAID

The Department of Health, Education, and Welfare had estimated at the time Congress was considering the legislation that the medicaid program would cost the Federal Government an additional $238 million in its first full year of operation. In fact, the Federal share of vendor payments for calendar year 1966 was precisely $238 million more than in calendar year 1965—but only six States had programs in operation during the full year.

It soon became clear that the medicaid program would be more expensive than originally contemplated. But just how much more expensive it would be was not known until later.

In January 1967, the President's budget predicted that 48 States would have medicaid programs in operation by July 1, 1968, and that total payments would be $2.25 billion in fiscal year 1968. By January 1968—midway through the fiscal year—only 37 States had medicaid programs in operation, but the vendor payment cost estimate for fiscal year 1968 had risen to $3.41 billion. Actual expenditures, with 37 States having medicaid programs, turned out to be $3.54 billion.

D. AMENDMENTS TO MEDICAID AFTER ORIGINAL ENACTMENT

Congressional concern over rapidly rising medicaid costs led to legislative action in 1967. The Congress chose as its basic method of cost control limiting the definition of "medically needy" (for purposes of Federal matching) to persons whose income did not exceed 133⅓ percent of the maximum payments for similar size families under programs of Aid to Families With Dependent Children (Public Law 90–248).

In December 1967, the House and Senate conferees were told by the Department of Health, Education, and Welfare that Federal medicaid costs would total $1.9 billion in fiscal year 1969 and $3.1 billion by fiscal year 1972, if there were no change in the law. The restrictions in the 1967 amendments, the conferees were told, would reduce these estimates to $1.6 billion in 1969 and $1.7 billion in 1972.

Scarcely a month later, the President's budget was released allocating $2.1 billion in Federal funds for medicaid in fiscal year 1969—$200 million more than had been previously estimated without changing the law, and one-half billion dollars more than the estimate with the 1967 amendment. Fiscal year 1969 Federal costs totaled $2.3 billion—almost 50 percent more for that year than the estimate of the Department of Health, Education, and Welfare in December 1967.

The 1967 amendments also included an amendment designed to focus on the health needs of medicaid children. Specifically States were required by July 1969 to implement early and periodic screening, diagnosis, and treatment (EPSDT) programs for children under 21. Implementing regulations were delayed until November 1971 (and required full coverage was delayed until 1973) because of the substantial fiscal impact such a requirement would have on the already limited State budgets.

Congressional concern with the operation of the medicaid program continued in 1969. The Department of Health, Education, and Welfare was forbidding the States from reducing the scope of their medicaid programs as a fiscal response to the sharply rising costs of health care. An amendment was enacted by the Congress (Public Law 91–56) to allow the States to make orderly retrenchment in their medicaid programs, provided (1) the States did not reduce their fiscal efforts ("maintenance of effort"), (2) the modifications were not undertaken for the purpose of enabling larger payments to be made to providers of services still covered by the plan, and (3) cost control plans were implemented by the States. The amendment also suspended for 2 years, till July 1, 1971, the time States would have to take action toward expanding their medicaid programs and postponed for 2 years, till July 1, 1977, the goal for comprehensive medicaid programs.

In 1971, Congress provided for the transfer of the administration of the intermediate care facility program from the welfare programs to medicaid. Under an amendment included in Public Law 92–223 such facilities were made subject to the standards set by the Secretary and services in such facilities were made available (at State option) to the medically needy.

Increasing congressional concern with the rapidly escalating costs of the medicaid program as well as with the quality of care provided recipients led to an extensive review of the entire program. In October 1972, legislation was enacted (Public Law 92–603) which contained a substantial number of amendments designed to control costs, strengthen program administration, and improve the delivery and review of services. Cost control amendments included provisions limiting Federal participation for capital expenditures not approved by planning agencies, establishing limitations on prevailing charge levels, repealing the "maintenance of effort" and comprehensive goal requirements, and instituting mandatory and optional patient cost-sharing requirements. Amendments designed to improve program administration included provisions increasing Federal matching for installation and operation of management information systems, establishing penalties for fraudulent acts and false reporting, and assigning responsibility for the establishment and maintenance of health standards to the State health agency.

Public Law 92–603 also included several provisions directed toward expanding the scope and improving the delivery of services. Amendments were included which mandated the provision of family planning services (at 90 percent Federal matching), included institutional mental health care for children as an optional service, and facilitated a State's ability to contract with health maintenance and related organizations. Penalty provisions were included for States which failed to provide the required EPSDT or family planning services.

Major emphasis was directed toward improving the quality of long-term care services. Public Law 92–603 provided for a single definition of care and coordination of certification procedures for facilities participating in both medicaid and medicare. It supported enforcement of long-term care standards by banning payment to substandard facilities through the cash grant program and by providing full Federal financing for 2 years for the costs of State inspectors.

The Congress also focused attention on improvements in existing utilization review programs, Public Law 92–603 established incentives for States to establish effective utilization review activities under medicaid and required coordination of these activities with those required under medicare. The

Congress was particularly concerned that existing utilization controls had been ineffective and that rising costs were in part attributable to the provision of medically inappropriate services. It therefore included a provision providing for the establishment of professional standards review organizations (PSRO's), formed by organizations representing substantial numbers of physicians in local areas, to undertake comprehensive and ongoing review of services under medicaid and medicare. PSRO's are to determine whether services are medically necessary and provided in accordance with professional standards.

Public Law 92–603 also established a supplemental security income program (SSI) which, effective January 1, 1974 replaced Federal/State welfare programs for aged, blind, and disabled individuals. States were permitted (and in certain cases required) to establish programs supplementing the basic Federal payment. Medicaid eligibility determinations for these individuals could no longer be tied to eligibility under the old Federal/State cash assistance programs. Subsequent legislation (Public Law 93–66 and Public Law 93–233) specified the requirements for mandatory and optional coverage. Aged, blind, or disabled individuals on the medicaid and welfare rolls in December 1973 were generally protected against a loss in medicaid eligibility. A State was provided certain options (generally based on its previous coverage levels) in determining the extent of coverage for other persons receiving Federal SSI benefits and/or State supplementary payments.

E. FISCAL IMPACT ON THE STATES

Increasing medicaid costs have had a particularly severe fiscal impact on the States. Welfare costs typically constitute one of the largest items in the State budget, and vendor payments for medical care have represented an increasing share of welfare costs. In fiscal year 1965, just before medicaid's enactment, medical assistance represented 25 percent of total Federal, State, and local welfare costs (excluding administrative costs). Looking at State and local funds only, medical vendor payments have risen from $764 million for medical vendor payments in fiscal year 1965 to an estimated $4,455 million in fiscal year 1974—a 583-percent increase in 10 years.

Medicaid program costs

[In thousands of dollars]

	Fiscal year—		
	1973 actual	1974 estimate	1975 estimate
Total_____	9, 110, 552	10, 526, 038	11, 830, 337
Medical vendor payments_____	8, 713, 587	9, 956, 678	11, 194, 791
Federal_____	4, 782, 888	5, 502, 059	6, 230, 826
State and local_____	3, 930, 699	4, 454, 619	4, 963, 965
Administrative costs_____	396, 965	569, 360	635, 546
Federal_____	214, 798	322, 030	361, 308
State and local_____	182, 167	247, 330	274, 238

NOTE: State figures derived from "total" and "Federal" figures.

Source: "The Budget of the United States Government, Fiscal Year 1975, Appendix."

Persons receiving medical assistance

[In millions]

	1973 actual	1974 estimate	1975 estimate
All recipients_____	23. 5	27. 2	28. 6
Aged 65 or over_____	4. 0	5. 2	5. 1
Blind_____	. 1	. 2	. 2
Disabled_____	2. 0	2. 4	2. 4
Children under 21_____	10. 8	12. 1	12. 9
Adults in AFDC families_____	6. 6	7. 4	7. 9

NOTE: Totals may not add due to rounding.

Source: "The Budget of the United States Government, Fiscal Year 1975, Appendix."

Average medicaid benefit payments per recipient

	1973 actual	1974 estimate	1975 estimate
Average benefit payment per recipient_____	$187	$202	$215
Aged 65 and over_____	385	400	467
Blind and disabled_____	476	470	521
Children under 21_____	90	98	99
Adults in AFDC families_____	132	143	142

Source: "Special Analyses, Budget of the United States Government, Fiscal Year 1975."

Federal medical assistance percentages by State (promulgated for the 2-year period beginning July 1, 1973)

	Percent
Alabama	75. 93
Alaska	50. 00
Arizona	[1] 61. 92
Arkansas	76. 31
California	50. 00
Colorado	57. 22
Connecticut	50. 00
Delaware	50. 00
District of Columbia	50. 00
Florida	60. 95
Georgia	66. 96
Guam	50. 00
Hawaii	50. 00
Idaho	69. 50
Illinois	50. 00
Indiana	57. 01
Iowa	59. 72
Kansas	55. 37
Kentucky	72. 12
Louisiana	72. 80
Maine	70. 03
Maryland	50. 00
Massachusetts	50. 00
Michigan	50. 00
Minnesota	57. 37
Mississippi	80. 55
Missouri	59. 94
Montana	66. 08
Nebraska	57. 86
Nevada	50. 00
New Hamsphire	62. 05
New Jersey	50. 00
New Mexico	72. 01
New York	50. 00
North Carolina	70. 01
North Dakota	70. 12
Ohio	53. 59
Oklahoma	68. 07
Oregon	59. 04
Pennsylvania	55. 14
Puerto Rico	50. 00
Rhode Island	55. 37
South Carolina	75. 00
South Dakota	70. 25
Tennessee	72. 28
Texas	63. 53
Utah	69. 95
Vermont	65. 38
Virgin Islands	50. 00
Virginia	61. 58
Washington	53. 13
West Virginia	73. 52
Wisconsin	60. 02
Wyoming	60. 99

[1] Not applicable. No Medicaid program in the State.

Source: *Medicaid Newsletter,* U.S. Dept. of Health, Education, and Welfare, November 1972.

Federal medicaid obligations, by State, year ending March 1974 [1]

	Amount
Alabama	$57, 622, 231
Alaska	3, 468, 662
Arizona	------------
Arkansas	52, 041, 891
California	644, 090, 040
Colorado	49, 996, 172
Connecticut	64, 639, 186
Delaware	6, 761, 564
District of Columbia	34, 177, 187
Florida	61, 151, 298
Georgia	131, 082, 033
Guam	520, 840
Hawaii	15, 848, 087
Idaho	12, 794, 514
Illinois	307, 551, 241
Indiana	81, 979, 656
Iowa	31, 330, 187
Kansas	39, 158, 062
Kentucky	61, 505, 535
Louisiana	70, 736, 435
Maine	35, 182, 357
Maryland	95, 788, 914
Massachusetts	233, 878, 671
Michigan	255, 118, 988
Minnesota	123, 991, 108
Mississippi	68, 738, 417
Missouri	47, 046, 656
Montana	12, 253, 056
Nebraska	28, 006, 005
Nevada	6, 915, 942
New Hampshire	12, 253, 388
New Jersey	148, 494, 548
New Mexico	16, 937, 972
New York	1, 158, 997, 333
North Carolina	92, 293, 746
North Dakota	11, 957, 473
Ohio	144, 044, 790
Oklahoma	93, 625, 832
Oregon	34, 142, 996
Pennsylvania	218, 806, 447
Puerto Rico	30, 000, 000
Rhode Island	33, 340, 706
South Carolina	33, 507, 005
South Dakota	12, 270, 101
Tennessee	59, 434, 328
Texas	237, 567, 934
Utah	20, 525, 149
Vermont	18, 452, 734
Virgin Islands	805, 199
Virginia	86, 580, 966
Washington	72, 926, 014
West Virginia	18, 281, 874
Wisconsin	141, 252, 702
Wyoming	2, 632, 085
Total	5, 334, 602, 223

[1] Includes grants for both medical assistance and administration. Amounts shown equal sum of individual quarterly awards. Fractions of dollars deleted.

Source: Department of Health, Education, and Welfare.

Medical assistance: Federal share of medical vendor payments, and State and local administration and training; by State; fiscal years 1973–75

States and territories	Fiscal year—		
	1973 actual	1974 estimate	1975 estimate
Alabama	$70, 419, 345	$100, 873, 000	$114, 965, 000
Alaska	1, 866, 595	3, 283, 000	4, 540, 000
Arizona	(1)	(1)	(1)
Arkansas	39, 920, 671	52, 312, 000	59, 564, 000
California	648, 708, 799	692, 531, 000	706, 981, 000
Colorado	52, 455, 512	58, 682, 000	69, 774, 000
Connecticut	59, 997, 854	63, 012, 000	70, 019, 000
Delaware	6, 103, 645	7, 959, 000	11, 369, 000
District of Columbia	33, 724, 621	38, 663, 000	44, 824, 000
Florida	64, 005, 084	92, 991, 000	108, 154, 000
Georgia	131, 454, 189	147, 479, 000	165, 861, 000
Guam	485, 108	484, 000	473, 000
Hawaii	14, 213, 434	17, 120, 000	18, 515, 000
Idaho	12, 026, 004	14, 437, 000	16, 317, 000
Illinois	271, 988, 261	321, 983, 000	354, 549, 000
Indiana	73, 289, 327	87, 500, 000	98, 089, 000
Iowa	22, 649, 582	43, 609, 000	52, 099, 000
Kansas	41, 685, 480	46, 271, 000	54, 970, 000
Kentucky	61, 758, 660	80, 964, 000	105, 431, 000
Louisiana	60, 913, 978	89, 414, 000	104, 026, 000
Maine	30, 285, 023	34, 988, 000	38, 673, 000
Maryland	84, 620, 620	84, 565, 000	93, 830, 000
Massachusetts	194, 884, 627	254, 551, 000	257, 085, 000
Michigan	233, 833, 574	280, 130, 000	340, 589, 000
Minnesota	110, 742, 556	146, 276, 000	168, 280, 000
Mississippi	54, 175, 533	76, 287, 000	93, 934, 000
Missouri	42, 197, 771	52, 929, 000	65, 917, 000
Montana	12, 250, 984	16, 891, 000	16, 776, 000
Nebraska	28, 857, 134	32, 015, 000	35, 281, 000
Nevada	6, 265, 872	9, 319, 000	10, 784, 000
New Hampshire	7, 533, 159	15, 899, 000	17, 809, 000
New Jersey	133, 734, 516	181, 671, 000	199, 633, 000
New Mexico	16, 593, 063	23, 460, 000	25, 928, 000
New York	1, 125, 037, 928	1, 229, 180, 000	1, 353, 115, 000
North Carolina	91, 841, 922	112, 219, 000	143, 876, 000
North Dakota	11, 433, 288	13, 899, 000	16, 935, 000
Ohio	122, 114, 821	168, 438, 000	192, 756, 000
Oklahoma	88, 228, 059	100, 629, 000	106, 799, 000
Oregon	28, 631, 669	38, 227, 000	43, 019, 000
Pennsylvania	193, 796, 481	238, 227, 000	276, 121, 000
Puerto Rico	29, 228, 739	30, 010, 000	30, 000, 000
Rhode Island	30, 036, 305	35, 433, 000	38, 534, 000
South Carolina	32, 973, 309	43, 445, 000	55, 651, 000
South Dakota	10, 917, 312	13, 172, 000	17, 769, 000
Tennessee	55, 618, 935	81, 919, 000	136, 002, 000
Texas	240, 803, 830	348, 696, 000	362, 478, 000
Utah	20, 227, 567	22, 565, 000	23, 895, 000
Vermont	17, 644, 443	19, 907, 000	22, 030, 000
Virgin Islands	704, 458	1, 000, 000	1, 000, 000
Virginia	73, 948, 701	96, 050, 000	116, 843, 000
Washington	64, 997, 490	76, 529, 000	82, 002, 000
West Virginia	19, 902, 470	36, 176, 000	39, 793, 000
Wisconsin	113, 167, 205	162, 459, 000	188, 889, 000
Wyoming	2, 799, 930	3, 650, 000	4, 196, 000
Total State requirements	4, 997, 685, 503	6, 040, 379, 000	6, 776, 742, 000

See footnote at end of table.

Medical assistance: Federal share of medical vendor payments, and State and local administration and training; by State; fiscal years 1973–75—Continued

States and territories	Fiscal year—		
	1973 actual	1974 estimate	1975 estimate
Adjusted State requirements _____	+$202, 216, 000	----------	----------
Used to complete fiscal year 1972 requirements _____	+9, 116, 000	----------	----------
Used to forward fund fiscal year 1974 requirements _____	+552, 227, 000	−$552, 227, 000	----------
Subtotal _____	5, 761, 244, 503	5, 488, 152, 000	$6, 776, 742, 000
Management initiatives _____		−110, 000, 000	−110, 000, 000
Program changes _____		−179, 000, 000	−273, 000, 000
Supplemental security income impact _____		+56, 635, 000	+198, 392, 000
Total _____	5, 761, 244, 503	5, 255, 787, 000	6, 592, 134, 000

[1] No State program under title XIX.

Chapter 9
Health Care Costs in
the United States

In this chapter, the structure of health care costs, both public and private, is described and recent trends are reported. These data provide the base of the expenditure level upon which proposed national health insurance programs will have an impact. Even without any federally supported national health insurance program, the people of the United States are spending $100 billion per year for health care. The costs are rising dramatically each year and, some argue, the quality of care purchased is declining. As indicated in Chapter 2, much of the economic impact of national health insurance will be to shift the manner of payment for health care from the private consumer economy into the public sector. The three documents reprinted here are derived from Executive branch sources. The 1975 health "yearbook" ([5]), prepared by the Health Resources Administration of HEW, contains a report on recent trends in health care costs. This is followed by the February 1976 *Social Security Bulletin* ([7]), prepared by the Social Security Administration, which reports on national health expenditures for 1975—both public and private. Finally, the health care portion of the OMB special analysis of the FY 1977 federal budget ([15]) is included to offer more detail on the federal government's ongoing expenditures. These three documents supply key facts for understanding and analyzing health care costs in the United States at mid-decade.

RECENT TRENDS ([5], pp. 151, 409, 152–162)

National Health Expenditures

Total national expenditures for health care more than quadrupled between 1960 and 1974, rising from $25.9 billion to $104.2 billion. Health expenditures are increasing more rapidly than the Gross National Product: National health care expenditures grew from 5.2% of the GNP in 1960 to 7.7% in 1974. (See Exhibits III-1 and III-2.)

The percentage of national health expenditures coming from public (that is, governmental) sources[1] increased from 25% in 1960 to 40% in 1974.

---

[1] Public health expenditures include both direct governmental payments and payments made by the government to private insurers who act as intermediaries for Medicare and Medicaid payments.

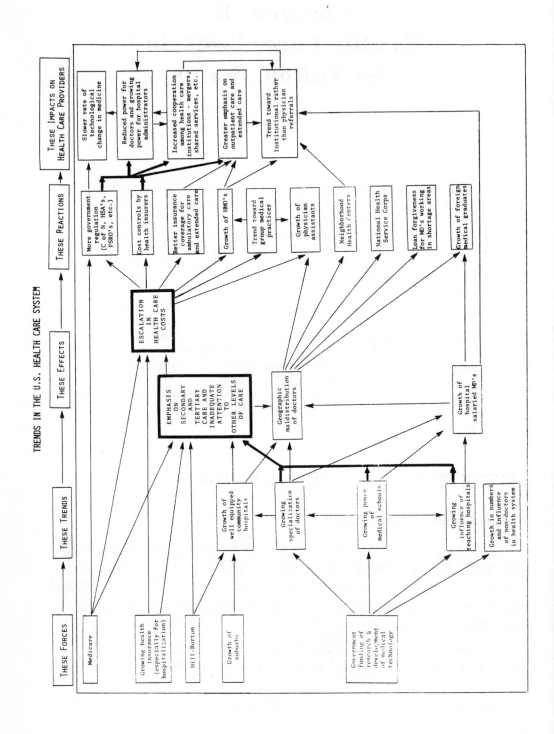

TRENDS IN THE U.S. HEALTH CARE SYSTEM

Exhibit III - 1

NATIONAL HEALTH EXPENDITURES: SELECTED YEARS 1950-1974

Type of Expenditure	1950 Amount ($ millions)	1950 Percent of Total	1955 Amount ($ millions)	1955 Percent of Total	1960 Amount ($ millions)	1960 Percent of Total	1965 Amount ($ millions)	1965 Percent of Total	1970 Amount ($ millions)	1970 Percent of Total	1974(prel.) Amount ($ millions)	1974(prel.) Percent of Total
Health and Medical Services												
Public Expenditures	$ 2,470	20.5%	$ 3,862	22.3%	$ 5,346	20.7%	$ 7,641	19.6%	$22,576	33.2%	$ 37,369	35.8%
Private Expenditures	8,710	72.4	12,529	72.3	18,816	72.8	28,023	72.1	40,492	59.5	59,815	57.4
Total Expenditures	11,180	92.9	16,391	94.6	24,162	93.4	35,664	91.7	63,068	92.6	97,184	93.2
Medical Research												
Public Expenditures	$ 73	0.6%	$ 139	0.8%	$ 471	1.8%	$ 1,229	3.2%	$ 1,653	2.4%	$ 2,479	2.4%
Private Expenditures	37	0.3	55	0.3	121	0.5	162	0.4	193	0.3	205	0.2
Total Expenditures	110	0.9	194	1.1	592	2.3	1,391	3.6	1,846	2.7	2,684	2.6
Medical Facilities Construction												
Public Expenditures	$ 522	4.3%	$ 419	2.4%	$ 578	2.2%	$ 665	1.7%	$ 1,003	1.5%	$ 1,463	1.4%
Private Expenditures	215	1.8	325	1.9	524	2.0	1,172	3.0	2,166	3.2	2,909	2.8
Total Expenditures	737	6.1	744	4.3	1,102	4.2	1,837	4.7	3,169	4.7	4,372	4.2
Total Public Expenditures	$ 3,065	25.5%	$ 4,421	25.5%	$ 6,395	24.7%	$ 9,535	24.5%	$25,232	37.1%	$ 41,311	39.6%
Total Private Expenditures	$ 8,962	74.5%	$12,909	74.5%	$19,461	75.3%	$29,357	75.5%	$42,851	62.9%	$ 62,929	60.4%
Total National Health Expenditures	$12,027	100.0%	$17,330	100.0%	$25,856	100.0%	$38,892	100.0%	$68,083	100.0%	$104,239	100.0%
% of GNP Spent on Health	4.6%		4.6%		5.2%		5.9%		7.1%		7.7%	
% of Health and Medical Services from:												
Public Expenditures	22.1%		23.6%		22.1%		21.4%		35.8%		38.5%	
Private Expenditures	77.9		76.4		77.9		78.6		64.2		61.5	
% of Medical Research from:												
Public Expenditures	66.4%		71.6%		79.6%		88.4%		89.5%		92.4%	
Private Expenditures	33.6		28.4		20.4		11.6		10.5		7.6	
% of Medical Facilities Construction from:												
Public Expenditures	70.8%		56.3%		52.5%		36.2%		31.7%		33.5%	
Private Expenditures	29.2		43.7		47.5		63.8		68.3		66.5	

Sources: U.S. Department of Commerce, Bureau of the Census, Statistical Abstract of the United States, 1974 (Washington, D.C.:
U.S. Government Printing Office, 1974), Table 99.

Nancy Worthington, "National Health Expenditures, 1929-74," Social Security Bulletin, Feburary, 1975, p. 9.

Note: Totals do not always add up precisely due to rounding.

Exhibit III - 2

NATIONAL HEALTH EXPENDITURES AND PERCENT OF GROSS
NATIONAL PRODUCT: SELECTED FISCAL YEARS 1950-1974

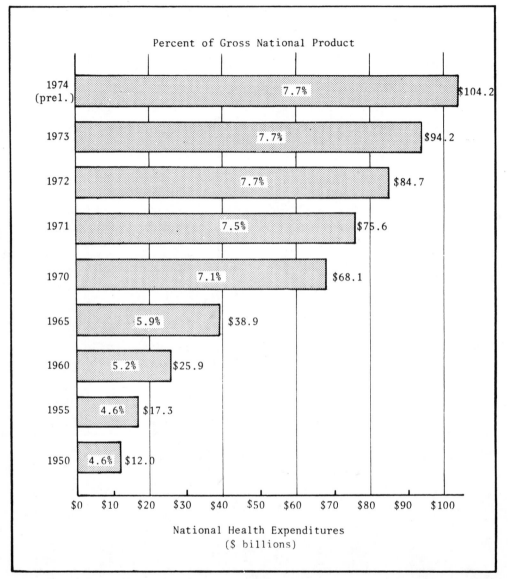

Percent of Gross National Product

Year	Percent of GNP	National Health Expenditures
1974 (prel.)	7.7%	$104.2
1973	7.7%	$94.2
1972	7.7%	$84.7
1971	7.5%	$75.6
1970	7.1%	$68.1
1965	5.9%	$38.9
1960	5.2%	$25.9
1955	4.6%	$17.3
1950	4.6%	$12.0

$0 $10 $20 $30 $40 $50 $60 $70 $80 $90 $100

National Health Expenditures
($ billions)

Sources: U.S. Department of Commerce, Bureau of the Census, Statistical Abstract
of the United States, 1974 (Washington, D.C.: U.S. Government Printing
Office, 1974), Table 99.

Nancy Worthington, "National Health Expenditures, 1929-74," Social
Security Bulletin, February 1975, p. 9.

Conversely, the portion of health expenditures financed by private sources (consumers,[1] philanthropy, and others) has shrunk from 75% in 1960 to 60% in 1974. This shift is due primarily to soaring government expenditures for health and medical services since the introduction of Medicare and Medicaid in 1966. The government's share in the financing of health services rose from 22% in 1960 to 38% in 1974. Government financing of medical research has also grown, climbing from 80% of total research costs in 1960 to 92% in 1974. In contrast, public financing of medical facility construction declined from 52% of the total in 1960 to 33% in 1974 as health facilities were able to finance a growing portion of their construction costs with commercial loans.

The objects of our health expenditures are changing as much as the sources of funds, as can be seen in Exhibit III-3. A growing portion of our health dollar is going to hospitals and nursing homes. Whereas hospitals consumed 31% of national health expenditures in 1950, they absorbed 40% in 1974. Nursing homes took only 1.5% of our health dollar in 1950 but 7.1% in 1974. The percentage of the health dollar going to physicians and dentists has declined somewhat, and the percentage going for drugs and sundries dropped from 13.6% in 1950 to 9.3% in 1974. The changing distribution of our health dollar is the result of different growth rates in per capita expenditures for different health services. Total per capital expenditures for hospital care shot from $24.09 in 1950 to $190.44 in 1974, while total per capita expenditures for nursing home care climbed from $1.16 in 1950 to $34.69 in 1974. These increases are far greater than the increases in per capita expenditures for doctors and dentists, as can be seen in Exhibit III-4.

The shift in the objects of our health expenditures reflects the growing role of institutions in our health system as our increasingly sophisticated medical technology requires that more and more care -- outpatient as well as inpatient -- be provided where elaborate equipment is available. The doctor's black bag can no longer hold the tools needed for medical care. The changing age distribution of our population has also increased the demand for both hospital beds and nursing homes. The hospital has become the kingpin of the health care system, and the government is becoming its chief financier.

Consumer Costs

The government funds pouring into health care have not kept consumers from feeling the impact of skyrocketing costs. Directly and indirectly (through out-of-pocket expenditures and health insurance premiums), the consumer is digging ever deeper into his pocket to pay for health care. Total

---

[1] Health expenditures by consumers include both out-of-pocket payments and payments made by individuals to private insurers for insurance coverage of health expenses.

Exhibit III - 3

SOURCES AND OBJECTS OF NATIONAL HEALTH EXPENDITURES:
1950, 1960 AND FISCAL YEAR 1974

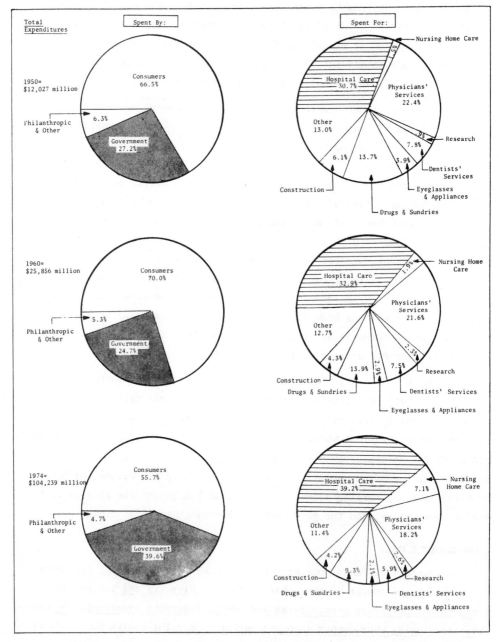

Sources: U.S. Department of Commerce, Bureau of the Census, Statistical Abstract of the United States, 1974 (Washington, D.C.:
U.S. Government Printing Office, 1974), Table 100.

Nancy Worthington, "National Health Expenditures, 1929-74," Social Security Bulletin, February 1975, pp. 9, 13.

Exhibit III - 4

PER CAPITA EXPENDITURES FOR SELECTED HEALTH
SERVICES: SELECTED YEARS 1950-1974

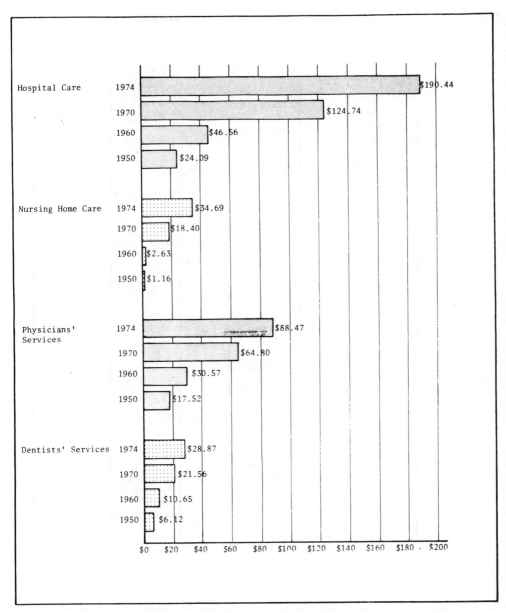

Source: Nancy Worthington, "National Health Expenditures, 1929-74," Social Security Bulletin,
February 1975, p. 13.

Exhibit III - 5

PERSONAL CONSUMPTION EXPENDITURES BY PRODUCT:
1950, 1960 AND 1973

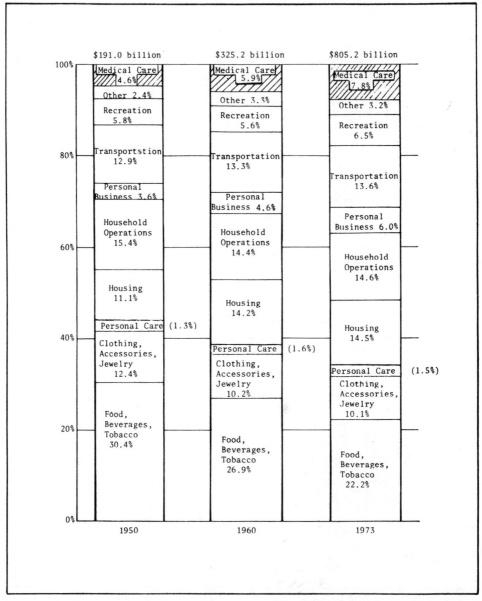

Sources: U.S. Department of Commerce, Bureau of the Census, Statistical Abstract of the United States, 1974 (Washington, D.C.: U.S. Government Printing Office, 1974), Table 605.

U.S. Department of Commerce, Office of Business Economics, Survey of Current Business, Vol. 54, No. 7, July 1974, Table 2.5.

private consumption expenditures for health and medical care were $62.9 billion in 1974, more than three times the $19.5 billion spent in 1960. (See Exhibit III-1.) Health care is not only costing the private sector more; it is also absorbing a higher percentage of consumers' income. As can be seen in Exhibit III-5, the percentage of total private consumption expenditures that went to medical care rose from 5.9% in 1960 to 7.8% in 1973. On a per capita basis, private expenditures for health services and supplies climbed steadily from $54.47 in 1950 to $102.44 in 1960 to $281.95 in 1974.[1]

Prices for medical care have risen steadily since World War II. Like prices for services generally, medical care prices have risen faster than the overall consumer price index. (See Exhibit III-6.) The price controls in effect from August 1971 to April 30, 1974 slowed down the inflation in health care costs, but these costs resumed their upward march as soon as controls were lifted. The charges of physicians and other health professionals have climbed at roughly the same rate as prices for all services, but hospital costs have gone through the ceiling: The cost of a semi-private room in a hospital soared 229% between 1967 and April 1975, while operating room charges rose 235% during that period. The graph in Exhibit III-7 illustrates the disparity between the price increases for hospital care and the rise in consumer prices generally.

While much more of Americans' income is going to health care, Americans to some extent are also receiving more. The number of active non-federal physicians in patient care rose from 123 per 100,000 population in 1965 to 131 in 1973,[1a] and the percentage of the population that had seen a doctor some-time during the year rose from 65% in 1963 to nearly 75% in 1973. On the other hand, the number of physician visits per year per person was the same in 1973 as it had been in 1957-59. The number of dentists per 100,000 popu-lation dropped from 50 in 1950 to 47 in 1972, but the percentage of the popu-lation that had seen a dentist sometime during the year rose from 40% in 1957-59 to nearly 49% in 1973.[2]

The average daily census in all U.S. hospitals dropped from 1.4 million in 1965 to 1.2 million in 1973, as more and more patients were moved out of long-term institutions for the care of those with mental problems or tuber-culosis. However, the average daily census in non-federal, short-term hospi-

---

[1]U.S. Department of Commerce, Statistical Abstract...1974, op. cit., Table 101; and Nancy Worthington, "National Health Expenditures 1929-74," Social Security Bulletin, February 1975, pp. 13 and 16. These figures include the cost of prepayment and administration of health insurance.

[1a]See Exhibit IV-19 in Chapter IV.

[2]U.S. Department of Commerce, Statistical Abstract...1974, op. cit., Table 107; and Exhibit I-7 in Chapter I.

Exhibit III - 6

CONSUMER PRICE INDEXES OF SELECTED ITEMS: 1950-1975

(1967 = 100)

Year	All Items	All Services	Total Medical Care	Hospital Care			Professional Services					
				Hospital Daily Service Charges (Jan. 1972 = 100)	Semi-Private Room Rates	Operating Room Charges	Physicians' Fees	Obstetrical Cases	Tonsillectomy and Adenoidectomy	Dentists' Fees	Optometric Examination and Eye Glasses	Drugs and Prescriptions
1950	72.1	58.7	53.7	NA	30.3	NA	55.2	51.2	60.7	63.9	73.5	88.5
1955	80.2	70.9	64.8	NA	42.3	NA	65.4	68.6	69.0	73.0	77.0	94.7
1960	88.7	83.5	79.1	NA	57.3	NA	77.0	79.4	80.3	82.1	85.1	104.5
1965	94.5	92.2	89.5	NA	75.9	82.9	88.3	89.0	91.0	92.2	92.8	100.2
1966	97.2	95.8	93.4	NA	83.5	88.6	93.4	93.0	94.9	95.2	95.3	100.5
1967	100.0	100.0	100.0	NA	100.0	100.0	100.0	100.0	100.0	100.0	100.0	100.0
1968	104.2	105.2	106.1	NA	113.6	111.5	105.6	105.2	104.9	105.5	103.2	100.2
1969	109.8	112.5	113.4	NA	128.8	128.7	112.9	113.5	110.3	112.9	107.6	101.3
1970	116.3	121.6	120.6	NA	145.4	142.4	121.4	121.8	117.1	119.4	113.5	103.6
1971	121.3	128.4	128.4	NA	163.1	156.1	129.8	129.0	125.2	127.0	120.3	105.4
1972	125.3	133.3	132.5	102.0[a]	173.9	168.6	133.8	133.8	129.9	132.3	124.9	105.6
1973	133.1	139.1	137.7	105.6[a]	182.1	179.1	138.2	138.1	132.8	136.4	129.5	105.9
Apr.1974	143.9	147.9	145.6	110.7[a]	192.0	191.4	145.8	144.1	138.0	142.9	135.2	107.6
Apr.1975	158.6	164.1	165.8	129.3[a]	228.8	234.6	166.2	163.6	160.2	159.7	148.1	117.5
% Increase 1955-1965	+18.0%	+30.0%	+38.0%	NA	+ 79.0%	NA	+33.0%	+30.0%	+50.0%	+44.0%	+21.0%	+ 6.0%
1965-1975	+68.0%	+78.0%	+85.0%	+27.0%[b]	+201.0%	+183.0%	+90.0%	+84.0%	+76.0%	+73.0%	+60.0%	+17.0%

Sources: U.S. Department of Commerce, Bureau of the Census, Statistical Abstract of the United States, 1974 (Washington, D.C.: U.S. Government Printing Office, 1974), Tables 98, 665, and 666.

"Medical Care: Rising Cost in a Peculiar Marketplace," Federal Reserve Bank of Richmond Economic Review, March/April 1975, p. 11.

Boston Office of the U.S. Bureau of Labor Statistics.

[a] January 1972 = 100.
[b] Percent change 1972-75.

NA = Not Available.

Exhibit III - 7

CONSUMER PRICE INDEXES OF SELECTED ITEMS: 1950-1975

(1950=100)

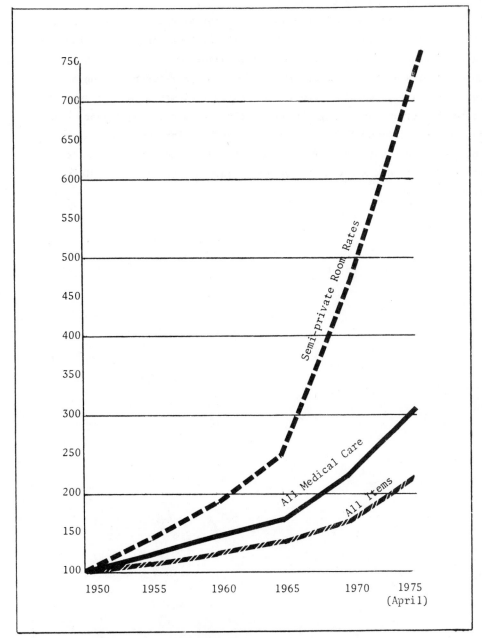

Sources: U.S. Department of Commerce, Bureau of the Census, _Statistical_
           Abstract of the United States, 1974 (Washington, D.C.: U.S.
           Government Printing Office, 1974), Tables 98, 665 and 666.

           "Medical Care: Rising Cost in a Peculiar Marketplace," _Fed-_
           eral Reserve Bank of Richmond Economic Review, March/April 1975,

           p. 11. Boston Office of the U.S. Bureau of Labor Statistics.

tals rose from 530,000 in 1963 to 680,000 in 1973, a 28% increase in a decade.[3]   The use of hospital outpatient facilities has grown at an even more accelerated pace, doubling between 1963 and 1973.[4]   The number of residents of nursing and personal care homes rose from 491,000 in 1963 to 1,076,000 in 1971, an increase of 119%.[5]

In sum, the increases in the amount of medical and dental care received in this country are relatively small, but the utilization of short-term hospitals and especially of nursing homes has climbed rapidly. And whether in a hospital or a doctor's office, the patient is generally receiving more specialized care given with more sophisticated equipment. And, thanks in part to the better care being given, our citizens are living longer -- and requiring more care by doctors, hospitals, and nursing homes than earlier generations required. But consumers, faced with today's health bills, must sometimes wonder if the improvements in health care are growing as rapidly as health care costs.

---

[3] American Hospital Association, Hospital Statistics: 1974 Edition (Chicago, Ill.: 1974), p. 7.

[4] Ibid.

[5] U.S. Department of Commerce, Statistical Abstract...1974, op. cit., Table 121.

NATIONAL HEALTH EXPENDITURES, FISCAL YEAR 1975
([7], pp. 3–21)

by MARJORIE SMITH MUELLER and ROBERT M. GIBSON*

According to preliminary estimates of the Nation's health spending in fiscal year 1975, health expenditures reached $118.5 billion, or $547 per person. Total health spending showed a 14-percent rise, significantly higher than the increase in 1974 when price controls in the health industry were in effect for most of the year. The acceleration of health spending during 1975 was accompanied by a slackening in the growth of the gross national product. Expenditures for this purpose, as a share of the GNP, thus rose significantly to 8.3 percent. Public spending grew two and one-half times as fast as private spending in 1975, mainly because of the continuing expansion of Medicare and Medicaid. Third parties financed an estimated two-thirds of all personal health care spending, with the government share 40 percent and that of private insurance 27 percent.

AMERICANS SPENT a total of $118.5 billion for health care in fiscal year 1975 through public and private funds—an average of $547 a person. The amount spent in 1975, the first full year after the economic stabilization program ended, was up 14 percent from the 1974 total.

The acceleration in health expenditures was accompanied by a slackening in the growth of the gross national product (GNP) in 1975 (chart 1). Accordingly, health care outlays as a proportion of GNP rose significantly to 8.3 percent, after a 3-year period in which the share of GNP had leveled off at about 7.8 percent. If the GNP had grown at its 1974 rate, the share for health care outlays would have been about 8.0 percent.

The data reported for 1973 and 1974 in last year's article in this series have been revised, as more reliable data have become available.

EXPENDITURES IN FISCAL YEAR 1975

The Nation's $118.5 billion expenditure for health care is a function of prices of goods and services, per capita utilization, supply of facilities and health manpower, and the quality and quantity of inputs including the cost of new health care technology (table 1). Price increases continue to be the major contributor to the rise in expenditures. Medical care prices as reflected by the consumer price index greatly accelerated in 1975, according to the data shown below, in

| Fiscal year | Percentage increase | | | | | |
	CPI, all items	Medical care, total	Hospital service charges [1]	Hospital semi-private room charges	Physicians' fees	Dentists' fees
1965	1.3	2.1		5.3	3.1	2.9
1966	2.2	2.9		6.1	3.9	2.9
1967	3.0	6.5		17.3	7.4	4.5
1968	3.3	6.4		15.9	6.1	5.2
1969	4.8	6.5		13.5	6.1	5.8
1970	5.9	6.4		12.8	7.2	6.8
1971	5.2	6.9		13.3	7.5	6.0
1972	3.6	4.7		9.4	5.2	5.7
1973	4.0	3.1	3.2	5.0	2.6	3.1
1974	9.0	5.7	7.9	6.0	5.0	4.4
1975	11.0	12.5	15.4	16.4	12.8	10.8

[1] The index for this component began in January 1972; comparable data for earlier years not available.

Source: Bureau of Labor Statistics, *Consumer Price Index.*

marked contrast to the relatively moderate fiscal year increases observed while the economic stabilization program was in effect (August 1971–April 1974).

Types of Expenditures

Hospital care continues to represent the major share (39.3 percent) of spending for health purposes (table 2). Approximately $46.6 billion, 16.6 percent more than the amount a year earlier, was spent for care in hospitals. The increase, which accelerated sharply from the 10.5-percent rise in the previous year, is attributable for the most part to increases in costs; utilization was a less important factor. As the tabulation that follows indicates, hospital expenses per adjusted patient day, as reported by the American Hospital Association, jumped 15.8 percent in 1975—compared with rises of 1.5 percent in the number of inpatient days and 1.8 percent in admissions and with no change in the average length of stay (after slight declines in the previous 5 years).

Outlays for physicians' services ($22.1 billion),

| Fiscal year | Community hospitals | | | | | | |
	Admissions (in thousands)	Inpatient days (in thousands)	Average length of stay (in days)	Occupancy rate (percent)	Outpatient visits (in thousands)	Total expenses (in millions)	Expense per adjusted patient day [1]
	Number or amount in year						
1966	26,831	203,741	7.6	76.4	94,083	$9,721	$43.58
1967	27,048	214,454	7.9	78.0	100,301	11,510	49.22
1968	27,465	221,971	8.1	78.2	108,150	13,967	56.24
1969	28,027	227,633	8.1	78.5	113,805	15,965	63.66
1970	29,238	231,601	7.9	77.8	126,404	18,669	73.14
1971	30,312	234,413	7.7	77.1	142,582	21,418	82.70
1972	30,706	232,892	7.6	75.1	152,571	23,925	92.48
1973	31,483	235,984	7.5	75.0	163,481	26,589	101.05
1974	32,752	242,393	7.4	75.4	170,584	30,115	110.77
1975	33,331	245,940	7.4	75.3	183,623	35,610	128.26
	Percentage change from preceding year						
1967	0.8	5.3	3.9	2.1	6.6	18.4	12.9
1968	1.5	3.5	2.5	.3	7.8	19.0	14.3
1969	2.0	2.6	.0	.4	5.2	16.6	13.2
1970	4.3	1.7	−2.5	−1.9	11.1	16.9	14.9
1971	3.7	1.2	−2.5	−.9	12.8	14.7	13.1
1972	1.3	−.6	−1.3	−2.6	7.0	11.7	11.8
1973	2.5	1.3	−1.3	−1.3	7.2	11.1	9.3
1974	4.0	2.7	−1.3	.5	4.3	13.3	9.6
1975	1.8	1.5	.0	−.1	7.6	18.2	15.8

[1] Adjusted to account for the volume of outpatient visits.

Source: "Hospital Indicators," *Hospitals,* midmonth issues, and unpublished data from the American Hospital Association.

the second largest category of health expenditures, showed a sharp rise from 1974 (12.9 percent, compared with 8.8 percent in the preceding year). The rate of increase in expenditures for physicians' services was about the same as the rate of increase before price controls were instituted—13.3 percent in 1970 and 12.3 percent in 1971.

Expenditures for nursing-home care reached $9 billion in 1975, up 20.8 percent from 1974. The rise was nearly one and three-fourths times the

* Division of Health Insurance Studies, Office of Research and Statistics, Social Security Administration.

rate of increase in 1974. All levels of nursing-home care are included in expenditures for this category. The rapid growth of expenditures over the past 9 years, as well as trends in sources of funding, is shown below. The share from public

Fiscal year	Amount (in millions)			Percentage distribution		
	Total	Private	Public	Total	Private	Public
1967	$1,751	$844	$907	100.0	48.2	51.8
1968	2,360	894	1,466	100.0	37.9	62.1
1969	3,057	1,354	1,703	100.0	44.3	55.7
1970	3,818	2,145	1,673	100.0	56.2	43.8
1971	4,890	2,919	1,971	100.0	59.7	40.3
1972	5,860	3,395	2,465	100.0	57.9	42.1
1973 [1]	6,650	3,477	3,173	100.0	52.3	47.7
1974 [1]	7,450	3,574	3,876	100.0	48.0	52.0
1975 [2]	9,000	3,799	5,201	100.0	42.2	57.8

[1] Revised.
[2] Preliminary.

funds reached a peak in 1968, shortly after the advent of the Medicare and Medicaid programs. After 1968, tightened controls on the utilization of skilled-nursing facilities resulted in a drop in Medicare outlays for this type of care. Public spending started to rise again in fiscal year 1972 when Medicaid began paying (beginning January 1, 1972) for services in intermediate-care facilities. The public share has grown steadily, particularly in the past 3 years, mainly due to increased Medicaid spending for this purpose—rising from 47.7 percent in 1973 to 57.8 percent in 1975.

Source of Funds

The accelerated growth rates in public expenditures particularly during the past 2 years—public

spending increased almost twice as fast as private spending in 1974 and two and one-half times as fast in 1975—have changed the previously relatively stable relationship of the two sources of funds. In fiscal year 1975 public funds were the source of 42.2 percent of all health care spending; they were about three-fourths as large as the amount coming from private funds (in 1973, they were a little less than two-thirds of the private spending).

Public funds for health care came from all levels of government—Federal, State, and local. The Federal share of total public spending has always been the larger. With the advent of Medicare and Medicaid it has become dominant, jumping from 42 percent in fiscal 1966 to 60 percent in 1967, the first full year of the two programs. In 1975, the Federal share was 67.5 percent.

Private health expenditures consist mainly of direct payments by consumers for health care and insurance payments made in their behalf. The remainder comes from philanthropy and industry expenditures for the maintenance of in-plant services, capital expenditures for construction of medical facilities or their renovation or expansion, and some outlays for research by private foundations. Consumer expenditures—direct payments and insurance benefits—totaled $63.8 billion in 1975—$5.6 billion or 9.5 percent higher than in 1974. Other private spending, including philanthropy and amounts spent by industry for in-plant health services, totaled $4.8 billion or about 3 percent lower than in fiscal year 1974.

Private dollars for health care were spent in a different way from public funds. Almost a third

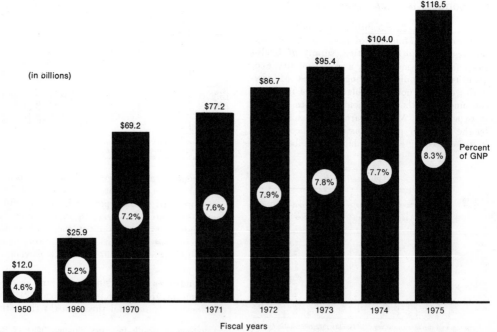

CHART 1.—National health expenditures and percent of gross national product, selected fiscal years 1950–75

(in billions)

$118.5
$104.0
$95.4
$86.7
$77.2
$69.2
$25.9
$12.0

8.3% Percent of GNP
7.7%
7.8%
7.9%
7.6%
7.2%
5.2%
4.6%

1950   1960   1970   1971   1972   1973   1974   1975

Fiscal years

TABLE 1.—Aggregate and per capita national health expenditures, by source of funds, and percent of gross national product, selected fiscal years, 1929–75

Fiscal year	Gross national product (in billions)	Health expenditures								
		Total			Private			Public		
		Amount (in millions)	Per capita	Percent of GNP	Amount (in millions)	Per capita	Percent of total	Amount (in millions)	Per capita	Percent of total
1929	$101.0	$3,589	$29.16	3.6	$3,112	$25.28	86.7	$477	$3.88	13.3
1935	68.7	2,846	22.04	4.1	2,303	17.84	80.9	543	4.21	19.1
1940	95.1	3,863	28.83	4.1	3,081	22.99	79.8	782	5.84	20.2
1950	263.4	12,028	78.35	4.6	8,962	58.38	74.5	3,065	19.97	25.5
1955	379.7	17,330	103.76	4.6	12,909	77.29	74.5	4,421	26.46	25.5
1960	495.6	25,856	141.63	5.2	19,461	106.60	75.3	6,395	35.03	24.7
1965	655.6	38,892	197.75	5.9	29,357	149.27	75.5	9,535	48.48	24.5
1966	718.5	42,109	211.56	5.9	31,279	157.15	74.3	10,830	54.41	25.7
1967	771.4	47,879	237.93	6.2	32,057	159.30	67.0	15,823	78.63	33.0
1968	827.0	53,765	264.37	6.5	33,727	165.84	62.7	20,040	98.54	37.3
1969	899.0	60,617	295.20	6.7	37,682	183.51	62.2	22,937	111.70	37.8
1970	954.8	69,202	333.57	7.2	43,964	211.92	63.5	25,238	121.65	36.5
1971	1,013.6	77,162	368.25	7.6	48,558	231.74	62.9	28,604	136.51	37.1
1972	1,100.6	86,687	409.71	7.9	53,398	252.37	61.6	33,289	157.33	38.4
1973	1,225.2	95,384	447.31	7.8	58,995	276.66	61.8	36,389	170.65	38.2
1974	1,348.9	104,030	484.53	7.7	62,152	294.03	60.7	40,879	190.33	39.3
1975 [1]	1,424.3	118,500	547.03	8.3	68,552	316.46	57.8	49,948	230.57	42.2

[1] Preliminary estimates.

of private payments went for hospital care and about a fourth for physicians' services; dental bills and drugs accounted for another fourth of private expenditures. Only 4 percent of private dollars were used for research and construction.

More than half of the public spending, on the other hand, went for hospital care and a little more than one-fourth for physicians' services and nursing-home care. Government allocated 7 percent of its spending to public health activities and 9 percent for research and medical-facilities construction.

Government spending for medical research and construction represented three-fifths of all spending for this purpose. There was a 16-percent increase in expenditures for research and a 26-percent increase in construction expenditures. Federal funds were concentrated on research (79 percent), State and local expenditures on construction (93 percent). Similar patterns of distribution for this category had existed in 1974.

There is a caveat to be observed in pursuing the above analysis by source of funds. Outlays under government programs reflect enrollee contributions—under the Medicare program, for example. This classification conforms with that of social insurance in the Social Security Administration social welfare expenditure series. Admittedly, it tends to slightly understate the private share.

To illustrate: In 1975, premium payments by enrollees (excluding those paid by Medicaid) accounted for almost 10 percent of Medicare receipts. If these premium payments were classified as private expenditures, the private share of national health expenditures would be raised from 57.8 percent to 59.3 percent.

Total Medicare receipts amounted to $16.9 billion in 1975; total expenditures were $14.8 billion. The percentage distribution of these receipts, by source of funds—payroll tax, premium payments by enrollees, premium payments by Medicaid, general revenues, and interest—is shown below for 1973, 1974, and 1975.

Source of funds	1973	1974	1975
Total Medicare receipts	100.0	100.0	100.0
Percent from—			
Payroll tax	68.7	69.4	67.6
Premium payments by enrollees	11.3	9.9	9.9
Premium payments by Medicaid	1.3	1.1	1.3
General revenues	16.5	16.4	16.9
Interest	2.2	3.1	4.3
Hospital insurance receipts	100.0	100.0	100.0
Percent from—			
Payroll tax [1]	92.5	92.2	90.9
General revenues	5.1	4.3	4.2
Interest	2.4	3.5	4.9
Supplementary medical insurance receipts	100.0	100.0	100.0
Percent from—			
Premium payments by enrollees	43.9	40.3	38.7
Premium payments by Medicaid	5.2	4.5	4.9
General revenues	49.4	53.3	53.9
Interest	1.6	2.0	2.4

[1] In 1974 and 1975 includes small amounts paid in HI premiums by persons previously uninsured.
Source: Unpublished Treasury reports keyed to *Final Statement of Receipts and Expenditures of U.S. Government.*

Expenditures Under Public Programs

Government spending—Federal, State, and local—for health services and supplies totaled $45.6 billion in 1975. Almost $31 billion came from Federal sources, the remaining $15 billion from State and local governments.

Each government program is listed in table 3 along with amounts spent during fiscal years 1973, 1974, and 1975, by type of health care service and administrative costs. Federal and State/local payments are shown separately to distinguish between programs financed solely by Federal funds, those by State and local funds, and those by both. These programs and their outlays are also reported in the annual BULLETIN article on social welfare expenditures.

Expenditures by governments for health services and supplies rose $8.3 billion in 1975, an increase of 22.4 percent over 1974—almost double the 12.5-percent rise in the previous year. The increase is due to the rapid inflation since the lifting of price controls, plus expansion in public programs, particularly Medicare and Medicaid. Medicare program expenditures expanded 30.3 percent in 1975, compared with a rise of only 19.7

percent in fiscal year 1974. The Medicaid program expanded even more rapidly than Medicare did in 1975 (25 percent)—at double the rate of expansion in 1974 (12.6 percent).

The Medicare and Medicaid programs accounted for 72 percent of the overall rise in public spending. The Medicare program spent almost $15 billion—mostly for hospital care and physicians' services. The Medicaid program spent nearly $13 billion, chiefly for hospital and nursing-home care and physicians' services.

The accelerated expansion of the Medicare program was due in part to the increase in the number of disabled persons who received Medicare benefits and in the number who were beneficiaries because of chronic kidney disease. As of January, 1975 the number of disabled persons eligible for Medicare hospital insurance had increased to 1.9 million, including 10,000 with renal diseases; 1.7 million of the disabled were also eligible for supplementary medical insurance. Approximately 9 percent of all Medicare hospital reimbursements and about 11.5 percent of Medicare suppplementary medical insurance payments were in behalf of this group in 1975.

Although coverage of the disabled by Medicare became effective in July 1973, the program was not fully implemented during that first year,

TABLE 2.—National health expenditures, by type of expenditure and source of funds, fiscal years 1973–75

[In millions]

Type of expenditure	Total	Source of funds					
		Private			Public		
		Total	Consumers	Other	Total	Federal	State and local
1975 [1]							
Total	$118,500	$68,552	$63,784	$4,768	$49,948	$33,828	$16,119
Health services and supplies	111,250	65,665	63,784	1,881	45,585	30,776	14,808
Hospital care	46,600	20,957	20,413	544	25,643	18,264	7,380
Physicians' services	22,100	16,245	16,230	15	5,855	4,262	1,593
Dentists' services	7,500	7,085	7,085		415	255	160
Other professional services	2,100	1,591	1,551	40	509	342	167
Drugs and drug sundries	10,600	9,695	9,695		905	478	427
Eyeglasses and appliances	2,300	2,198	2,198		102	57	45
Nursing-home care	9,000	3,799	3,767	32	5,201	2,982	2,220
Expenses for prepayment and administration	4,593	3,389	2,845	544	1,204	997	207
Government public health activities	3,457				3,457	1,201	2,256
Other health services	3,000	706		706	2,294	1,939	355
Research and medical-facilities construction	7,250	2,887		2,887	4,363	3,052	1,311
Research [2]	2,750	235		235	2,515	2,418	97
Construction	4,500	2,652		2,652	1,848	634	1,214
Publicly owned facilities	1,266				1,266	68	1,198
Privately owned facilities	3,234	2,652		2,652	582	566	16
1974 [3]							
Total	$104,030	$63,152	$58,224	$4,928	$40,879	$27,484	$13,395
Health services and supplies	97,214	59,972	58,224	1,748	37,243	24,913	12,330
Hospital care	39,963	18,639	18,126	513	21,324	14,626	6,698
Physicians' services	19,571	14,834	14,820	14	4,737	3,420	1,318
Dentists' services	6,783	6,450	6,450		333	215	118
Other professional services	1,927	1,576	1,538	38	351	225	126
Drugs and drug sundries [2]	9,612	8,862	8,862		750	410	340
Eyeglasses and appliances	2,160	2,070	2,070		90	50	40
Nursing-home care	7,450	3,574	3,544	30	3,876	2,314	1,562
Expenses for prepayment and administration	4,501	3,342	2,814	528	1,159	995	164
Government public health activities	2,625				2,625	959	1,666
Other health services	2,622	625		625	1,997	1,699	298
Research and medical-facilities construction	6,816	3,180		3,180	3,636	2,571	1,065
Research [2]	2,389	219		219	2,170	2,078	92
Construction	4,427	2,961		2,961	1,466	493	973
Publicly owned facilities	1,167				1,167	209	958
Privately owned facilities	3,260	2,961		2,961	299	284	15
1973 [3]							
Total	$95,384	$58,995	$54,213	$4,782	$36,389	$24,280	$12,109
Health services and supplies	88,941	55,846	54,213	1,633	33,095	21,793	11,302
Hospital care	36,155	17,113	16,642	471	19,042	12,793	6,249
Physicians' services	17,995	13,861	13,849	12	4,134	3,008	1,126
Dentists' services	6,101	5,780	5,780		321	218	104
Other professional services	1,781	1,440	1,406	34	341	224	117
Drugs and drug sundries [2]	8,987	8,272	8,272		715	387	328
Eyeglasses and appliances	1,986	1,905	1,905		81	45	35
Nursing-home care	6,650	3,477	3,449	28	3,173	1,849	1,323
Expenses for prepayment and administration	4,299	3,418	2,910	508	881	704	177
Government public health activities	2,152				2,152	911	1,241
Other health services	2,835	580		580	2,255	1,654	601
Research and medical-facilities construction	6,443	3,149		3,149	3,294	2,487	807
Research [2]	2,298	208		208	2,090	2,002	88
Construction	4,145	2,941		2,941	1,204	485	719
Publicly owned facilities	967				967	262	705
Privately owned facilities	3,178	2,941		2,941	237	223	14

[1] Preliminary estimates.
[2] Research expenditures of drug companies in "drugs and drug sundries" excluded from "research expenditures."
[3] Revised estimates.

mostly because of delays in filing claims and payment lags. As a result, expenditures for this group were abnormally low in fiscal year 1974. Thus, Medicare expenditures for the disabled were 75 percent larger in 1974 than expenditures in 1973, as the data that follow show.

Medicare expenditures for hospital care rose

Source of funds	Benefit expenditures for the disabled (in millions)	
	1974	1975
Total	$382.4	$1,742.0
Hospital insurance	249.6	905.1
Supplementary medical insurance	132.8	836.9

33 percent from 1974 to 1975. This increase reflected an increase in the unit costs of hospital care and increased utilization of hospital services (Medicare hospital admissions went up 5 percent from 1974 to 1975). In addition, the Medicare expenditures for hospital services in 1974 were understated by approximately $300 million: Obligations paid that year were reduced by the amount of current financing payments recovered

by the Social Security Administration.[1] If this amount were to be included with the hospital expenditures for 1974, the increase would be reduced to 25 percent. The rises in expenditures for physicians' services and nursing-home care were in the same magnitude as this adjusted increase—27.8 percent and 26.6 percent, respectively. The sharpest rise in spending was for other professional services—from $342 million to $509 million, a 75.1-percent increase reflecting largely the greater utilization of home health services. Expenditures for other professional services, however, represented only about 1 percent of total Medicare program outlays.

Probably the major factor in the steep rise in Medicare hospital benefits was the switch in fiscal year 1975 by many providers—following repayment of outstanding current financing funds in fiscal year 1974—to the "periodic interim payment" method of financing. Payments under this

---

[1] For a fuller explanation of current financing payment recoveries, see Marjorie Smith Mueller and Robert M. Gibson, "Age Differences in Health Care Spending, Fiscal Year 1974," *Social Security Bulletin*, June 1975, page 9.

TABLE 3.—Expenditures for health services and supplies under public programs, by program, type of expenditure, and source of funds, fiscal years 1973–75

[In millions]

Program and source of funds	Total	Hospital care	Physicians' services	Dentists' services	Other professional services	Drugs and drug sundries	Eye glasses and appliances	Nursing-home care	Government public health activities	Other health services	Administration
					1975 [1]						
Total	$45,584.7	$25,643.3	$5,855.4	$414.8	$508.7	$904.6	$102.2	$5,201.3	$3,457.0	$2,293.6	$1,203.8
Health insurance for aged and disabled [2][3]	14,781.4	10,710.6	2,967.1		186.1			257.0			660.6
Temporary disability insurance (medical benefits)[4]	73.3	53.6	17.0		1.2	0.8	0.7				
Workmen's compensation (medical benefits)[4]	1,830.0	922.6	777.7		56.4	36.6	36.7				
Public assistance (vendor medical payments)[5]	12,968.0	4,270.5	1,685.7	337.1	224.8	836.6		4,782.4		349.7	481.2
General hospital and medical care	5,491.7	5,369.7	13.9	3.2		1.6				103.3	
Defense Department hospital and medical care (including military dependents)[5]	3,011.0	1,903.8	216.8	10.8			9.7			848.3	21.6
Maternal and child health services	540.0	81.9	49.8	12.3	40.2	11.8	16.1			323.3	4.6
School health [6]									3,457.0		
Other public health activities	3,242.3	2,253.6	32.4	51.4			7.5	30.7	161.9	669.0	35.8
Veterans' hospital and medical care	190.0	77.0	95.0					18.0			
Medical vocational rehabilitation											
Office of Economic Opportunity [7]											
Federal	30,776.3	18,263.5	4,262.3	254.8	342.0	477.6	57.1	2,981.8	1,201.0	1,939.0	997.2
Health insurance for aged and disabled [2][3]	14,781.4	10,710.6	2,967.1		186.1			257.0			660.6
Workmen's compensation (medical benefits)	50.6	32.9	12.6		3.0	1.0	1.1				
Public assistance (vendor medical payments)[5]	6,966.4	2,288.6	903.4	180.7	120.5	448.3		2,562.9		187.4	274.6
General hospital and medical care	1,089.6	967.6	13.9	3.2		1.6				103.3	
Defense Department hospital and medical care (including military dependents)[5]	3,011.0	1,903.8	216.8	10.8			9.7			848.3	21.6
Maternal and child health services	277.0	42.8	37.6	8.7	32.4	9.5	10.4			131.0	4.6
Other public health activities	1,201.0								1,201.0		
Veterans' hospital and medical care [5]	3,242.3	2,253.6	32.4	51.4			7.5	30.7	161.9	669.0	35.8
Medical vocational rehabilitation	157.0	63.6	78.5					14.9			
Office of Economic Opportunity [7]											
State and local	14,808.4	7,379.8	1,593.1	160.1	166.7	427.0	45.1	2,219.5	2,256.0	354.5	206.6
Temporary disability insurance (medical benefits)[4]	73.3	53.6	17.0		1.2	0.8	0.7				
Workmen's compensation (medical benefits)[4]	1,779.4	889.7	765.1		53.4	35.6	35.6				
Public assistance (vendor medical payments)[5]	6,001.7	1,981.9	782.3	156.5	104.3	388.3		2,219.5		162.2	206.6
General hospital and medical care	4,402.1	4,402.1									
Maternal and child health services	263.0	39.1	12.2	3.6	7.8	2.3	5.7			192.3	
School health [6]											
Other public health activities	2,256.0								2,256.0		
Medical vocational rehabilitation	33.0	13.4	16.5					3.1			

See footnotes at end of table.

TABLE 3.—Expenditures for health services and supplies under public programs, by program, type of expenditure, and source of funds, fiscal years 1973–75—*Continued*

[In millions]

Program and source of funds	Total	Hospital care	Physicians' services	Dentists' services	Other professional services	Drugs and drug sundries	Eye glasses and appliances	Nursing-home care	Government public health activities	Other health services	Administration
					1974 [5]						
Total	$37,242.6	$21,324.1	$4,737.4	$332.8	$351.0	$750.3	$89.9	$3,876.3	$2,625.3	$1,997.0	$1,158.5
Health insurance for aged and disabled [2][3]	11,347.5	8,049.1	2,321.9		106.3			203.0			667.2
Temporary disability insurance (medical benefits)[4]	70.7	52.0	16.1		1.1	0.8	0.7				
Workmen's compensation (medical benefits)[4]	1,560.0	785.5	664.3		47.9	31.2	31.1				
Public assistance (vendor medical payments)[3]	10,371.9	3,617.6	1,401.3	258.4	159.0	695.7		3,548.0		258.4	433.5
General hospital and medical care	5,061.0	4,965.5	11.5	3.8		1.6				78.6	
Defense Department hospital and medical care (including military dependents)[5]	2,741.0	1,738.3	157.6	14.5		4.5				803.8	22.3
Maternal and child health services	493.4	74.8	45.5	11.2	36.7	10.8	14.7			295.2	4.5
School health [6]											
Other public health activities	2,625.3								2,625.3		
Veterans' hospital and medical care	2,786.6	1,967.2	25.8	44.9		5.7		25.7	125.3	561.0	31.0
Medical vocational rehabilitation	185.2	74.1	93.4				17.7				
Office of Economic Opportunity [7]											
Federal	24,913.2	14,626.4	3,419.7	215.3	224.9	409.9	49.9	2,314.5	959.0	1,698.8	994.8
Health insurance for aged and disabled [2][3]	11,347.5	8,049.1	2,321.9		106.3			203.0			667.2
Workmen's compensation (medical benefits)	36.1	23.5	9.0		2.2	0.7	0.7				
Public assistance (vendor medical payments)[5]	5,833.4	2,025.1	784.5	144.7	89.0	389.4		1,986.2		144.6	269.8
General hospital and medical care	821.0	725.5	11.5	3.8		1.6				78.6	
Defense Department hospital and medical care (including military dependents)[5]	2,741.0	1,738.3	157.6	14.5		4.5				803.8	22.3
Maternal and child health services	234.7	36.1	31.8	7.4	27.4	8.0	8.7			110.8	4.5
Other public health activities	959.0								959.0		
Veterans' hospital and medical care [5]	2,786.6	1,967.2	25.8	44.9		5.7		25.7	125.3	561.0	31.0
Medical vocational rehabilitation	154.0	61.6	77.6				14.8				
Office of Economic Opportunity [7]											
State and local	12,329.5	6,697.7	1,317.8	117.5	126.1	340.3	40.0	1,561.8	1,666.3	298.2	163.8
Temporary disability insurance (medical benefits)[4]	70.7	52.0	16.1		1.1	0.8	0.7				
Workmen's compensation (medical benefits)[4]	1,523.9	762.0	655.3		45.7	30.5	30.4				
Public assistance (vendor medical payments)[5]	4,538.7	1,592.5	616.9	113.7	70.0	306.2		1,561.8		113.8	163.8
General hospital and medical care	4,240.0	4,240.0									
Maternal and child health services	258.7	38.7	13.7	3.8	9.3	2.8	6.0			184.4	
School health [6]											
Other public health activities	1,666.3								1,666.3		
Medical vocational rehabilitation	31.2	12.5	15.8				2.9				
					1973 [8]						
Total	$33,094.5	$19,042.0	$4,134.3	$321.4	$340.8	$714.6	$80.8	$3,172.6	$2,151.7	$2,255.1	$881.1
Health insurance for aged [2][3]	9,478.8	6,768.2	2,015.9		83.0			173.0			438.7
Temporary disability insurance (medical benefits)[4]	69.8	52.0	15.3		1.1	0.7	0.7				
Workmen's compensation (medical benefits)[4]	1,335.0	672.4	568.3		41.0	26.6	26.7				
Public assistance (vendor medical payments)[5]	9,208.7	3,474.0	1,137.4	220.4	149.9	652.5		2,892.1		291.0	391.3
General hospital and medical care	4,712.5	4,624.1	8.5	2.2		1.3				76.4	
Defense Department hospital and medical care (including military dependents)[5]	2,468.0	1,548.0	159.7	25.6		6.4				708.0	20.3
Maternal and child health services	455.3	68.9	41.9	10.4	33.8	10.0	13.5			272.1	4.7
School health [6]	300.0									300.0	
Other public health activities	2,151.7								2,151.7		
Veterans' hospital and medical care	2,587.3	1,767.3	21.6	55.2		4.9		23.0	107.5	581.7	26.1
Medical vocational rehabilitation	175.0	67.1	91.0				16.9				
Office of Economic Opportunity [7]	152.4		74.7	7.6	32.0	12.2				25.9	
Federal	21,792.9	12,792.8	3,008.0	217.7	223.9	386.0	45.4	1,849.2	911.0	1,653.7	704.3
Health insurance for aged [2][3]	9,478.8	6,768.2	2,015.9		83.0			173.0			438.7
Workmen's compensation (medical benefits)	32.3	21.0	8.1		1.9	0.6	0.7				
Public assistance (vendor medical payments)[5]	4,997.4	1,884.3	616.9	119.6	81.3	353.9		1,568.7		158.2	214.5
General hospital and medical care	804.7	716.3	8.5	2.2		1.3				76.4	
Defense Department hospital and medical care (including military dependents)[5]	2,468.0	1,548.0	159.7	25.6		6.4				708.0	20.3
Maternal and child health services	221.0	34.0	29.8	7.5	25.7	7.6	8.2			103.5	4.7
Other public health activities	911.0								911.0		
Veterans' hospital and medical care [5]	2,587.3	1,767.3	21.6	55.2		4.9		23.0	107.5	581.7	26.1
Medical vocational rehabilitation	140.0	53.7	72.8				13.5				
Office of Economic Opportunity [7]	152.4		74.7	7.6	32.0	12.2				25.9	
State and local	11,301.6	6,249.2	1,126.3	103.8	116.9	327.7	35.4	1,323.4	1,240.7	601.4	176.8
Temporary disability insurance (medical benefits)[4]	69.8	52.0	15.3		1.1	0.7	0.7				
Workmen's compensation (medical benefits)[4]	1,302.7	651.4	560.2		39.1	26.0	26.0				
Public assistance (vendor medical payments)[5]	4,211.3	1,589.7	520.5	100.9	68.6	298.6		1,323.4		132.8	176.8
General hospital and medical care	3,907.8	3,907.8									
Maternal and child health services	234.3	34.9	12.1	2.9	8.1	2.4	5.3			168.6	
School health [6]	300.0									300.0	
Other public health activities	1,240.7								1,240.7		
Medical vocational rehabilitation	35.0	13.4	18.2				3.4				

[1] Preliminary estimates.

[2] Includes premium payments for supplementary medical insurance by or in behalf of enrollees.

[3] Includes duplication in the Medicare and Medicaid amounts where premium payments for Medicare are financed by Medicaid for cash assistance recipients and, in some States, for the medically indigent.

[4] Includes medical benefits paid under public law by private insurance carriers and self-insurers.

[5] Payments for services outside the hospital (excluding "other health services") represent only those made under contract medical care programs.

[6] Beginning in 1974, data not separable from total education expenditures.

[7] Beginning in 1974, included with "other public health activities."

[8] Revised estimates.

method, which are based on estimated costs and utilization, were 65 percent greater than they were in fiscal year 1974 and accounted for half the increase in hospital benefits. The rise in Medicare medical insurance benefits was largely the result of catch-up increases in physicians' fees after the economic stabilization program ended. Medicare placed a limit of 55 percent on fee increases in determining its calendar-year base for payments for fiscal year 1974; the amounts paid physicians in fiscal year 1975 were based on prevailing and customary charges, derived from actual charges in calendar year 1973.

Medicaid payments totaled $13.0 billion in fiscal year 1975. The 25-percent rise in expenditures was attributable to increases in the number of recipients as well as to rising hospital care costs and physicians' fees. Preliminary estimates indicate that the number of Medicaid recipients went up from 21.9 million in fiscal year 1974 to 24.3 million in 1975, an increase of 10.7 percent. Dental care expenditures and outlays for other professional services also rose substantially.

Medicaid expenditures include amounts paid as premiums into the Medicare supplementary medical insurance trust fund in behalf of aged and disabled persons who either receive public assistance cash payments or are medically indigent. These premium payments are used by Medicare to finance services under the supplementary medical insurance program. Since they are reported as expenditures by both the Medicaid and Medicare programs, a small amount of duplication results and public expenditures are thus slightly overstated. The amounts of premiums that have been paid by States for this "buy-in" coverage are as follows:

Fiscal year	Amount (in millions)
1967	$32.1
1968	53.0
1969	75.8
1970	97.2
1971	131.5
1972	137.9
1973	149.3
1974	171.0
1975	213.1

The next largest category of public health spending—general hospital and medical care—also accelerated in 1975, reacting to inflationary pressures. The rise was 8.5 percent, compared with a rise of 7.4 percent in 1974. Direct medical services are provided by the Federal Government primarily through Public Health Service hospitals and Indian health services. State and local spending—80 percent of the total in this category—represents primarily funds expended for the operation of State or local psychiatric hospitals.

Expenditures for State and local school health and the Federal Office of Economic Opportunity (OEO) programs are shown only for fiscal year 1973. Estimates of school health outlays in 1974 and 1975 were not available separately from the education category. The health activities of OEO were transferred in fiscal year 1974 to the Department of Health, Education, and Welfare and

are currently included in "government public health activities."

Fifty-six percent of all public spending for health care was for hospital care, with the share of the total for this purpose declining from 57 percent in 1974 and 58 percent in 1973. Almost one-fourth of public funds went for physicians' services and nursing-home care. In 1974, spending for these categories amounted to 23 percent of the total; in 1973 it was 22 percent.

For the various types of health care, the share of total expenditures differs with the program and, of course, reflects the program focus. Ninety-eight percent of the outlays from the general hospital and medical care program were for hospital care, for example, and 93 percent of Medicare expenditures went for hospital care and physicians' services. The medical vocational rehabilitation program, on the other hand, spent half its funds on physicians' services. Seventy percent of Veterans Administration expenditures went for hospital costs. Department of Defense health expenditures were also mainly for hospital care (63 percent). Expenditures by State temporary disability programs and State and Federal workmen's compensation programs reflected their emphasis on both hospital and medical care: 95 percent of the expenditures under temporary disability insurance were for these services; workmen's compensation programs allocated 50 percent for hospital care and 43 percent for physicians' services.

Federal outlays for administration of Medicare decreased 1 percent—from $667.2 million in 1974 to $660.6 million in 1975. Administrative costs amounted to 4.5 percent of total Medicare expenditures.

Medicaid administrative costs were 3.3 percent of the total program expenditures ($13 billion) by the States and the Federal Government. The Federal administrative cost ratio was 3.9 percent; the State and local government ratio was 3.4 percent.

Medical Education

As a category, "medical training and education" is not included in the estimates of total health expenditures. Some components of this category, however, are included—mainly training outlays that cannot be separated from hospital expenses and medical research. Most of these expenditures are made by the Department of Defense and the Veterans Administration. Shown below are data on Federal spending for medical

[In millions]

Agency	Fiscal year		
	1973	1974	1975
Total	$1,218	$1,146	$1,324
Department of Health, Education, and Welfare	745	767	860
Department of Defense	131	191	219
Veterans Administration	146	167	223
Department of Labor	156	4	5
Environmental Protection Agency	14		
Other agencies	26	17	17

Source: *Special Analysis, Budget of the United States Government, Fiscal Year 1975*, page 157, and *Fiscal Year 1976*, pages 194–195, Office of Management and Budget, 1975.

TABLE 4.—Aggregate and per capita national health expenditures, by type of expenditure, selected fiscal years, 1929–75

Type of expenditure	1929	1935	1940	1950	1960	1965	1966	1967	1968	1969	1970	1971	1972[1]	1973[1]	1974[1]	1975[2]
							Aggregate amount (in millions)									
Total	$3,589	$2,846	$3,863	$12,027	$25,856	$38,892	$42,109	$47,879	$53,766	$60,617	$69,202	$77,162	$86,687	$95,384	$104,030	$118,500
Health services and supplies	3,382	2,788	3,729	11,181	24,162	35,664	38,661	44,343	49,802	56,327	64,065	71,762	80,548	88,941	97,214	111,250
Hospital care	651	731	969	3,698	8,499	13,152	14,245	16,921	19,384	22,356	25,879	29,133	32,720	36,155	39,963	46,600
Physicians' services	994	744	946	2,689	5,580	8,405	8,865	9,738	10,734	11,842	13,443	15,098	16,527	17,995	19,571	22,100
Dentists' services	476	298	402	940	1,944	2,728	2,866	3,158	3,518	3,920	4,473	4,908	5,364	6,101	6,783	7,500
Other professional services	248	150	173	384	848	989	1,140	1,139	1,217	1,298	1,385	1,509	1,634	1,781	1,927	2,100
Drugs and drug sundries	601	471	621	1,642	3,591	4,647	5,032	5,480	5,865	6,482	7,114	7,626	8,239	8,987	9,612	10,600
Eyeglasses and appliances	131	128	180	475	750	1,151	1,309	1,514	1,665	1,743	1,776	1,810	1,878	1,986	2,160	2,300
Nursing-home care			28	178	480	1,271	1,407	1,751	2,360	3,057	3,818	4,890	5,860	6,650	7,450	9,000
Expenses for prepayment and administration	101	91	161	290	807	1,234	1,446	1,818	1,939	2,066	2,115	2,405	3,645	4,299	4,501	4,593
Government public health activities	89	112	155	351	401	671	731	884	1,001	1,195	1,437	1,698	2,075	2,152	2,625	3,457
Other health services	90	63	92	534	1,262	1,416	1,620	1,940	2,119	2,368	2,625	2,685	2,606	2,835	2,622	3,000
Research and medical-facilities construction	207	58	134	847	1,694	3,228	3,448	3,536	3,964	4,290	5,137	5,400	6,139	6,443	6,816	7,250
Research			3	110	592	1,391	1,545	1,606	1,800	1,790	1,846	1,850	2,058	2,298	2,389	2,750
Construction	207	58	131	737	1,102	1,837	1,903	1,930	2,164	2,500	3,291	3,550	4,081	4,145	4,427	4,500
							Per capita amount[3]									
Total	$29.16	$22.04	$28.83	$78.35	$141.63	$197.75	$211.56	$237.93	$264.37	$295.20	$333.57	$368.25	$409.71	$447.31	$484.35	$547.03
Health services and supplies	27.48	21.59	27.83	72.83	132.35	181.34	194.24	220.36	244.88	274.30	308.81	342.48	380.69	417.10	452.61	513.56
Hospital care	5.29	5.66	7.23	24.09	46.56	66.87	71.57	84.09	95.31	108.87	124.74	139.03	154.64	169.55	186.06	215.12
Physicians' services	8.08	5.76	7.06	17.52	30.57	42.74	44.54	48.39	52.78	57.67	64.80	72.05	78.11	84.39	91.12	102.02
Dentists' services	3.87	2.31	3.00	6.12	10.65	13.87	14.40	15.69	17.30	19.09	21.56	23.42	25.35	28.61	31.58	34.62
Other professional services	2.01	1.16	1.29	2.50	4.65	5.03	5.73	5.66	5.98	6.32	6.68	7.20	7.72	8.35	8.97	9.69
Drugs and drug sundries	4.88	3.65	4.66	10.70	19.67	23.63	25.28	27.23	28.84	31.57	34.29	36.39	38.94	42.15	44.75	48.93
Eyeglasses and appliances	1.06	.99	1.34	3.09	4.11	5.85	6.58	7.52	8.19	8.49	8.56	8.64	8.88	9.31	10.06	10.62
Nursing-home care			.21	1.16	2.63	6.46	7.07	8.70	11.60	14.89	18.40	23.34	27.70	31.19	34.69	41.55
Expenses for prepayment and administration	.82	.70	1.20	1.89	4.42	6.27	7.26	9.03	9.53	10.06	10.19	11.48	17.23	20.16	20.96	21.20
Government public health activities	.72	.87	1.16	2.29	2.19	3.41	3.67	4.39	4.92	5.82	6.93	8.10	9.81	10.09	12.22	15.96
Other health services	.73	.49	.69	3.48	6.91	7.20	8.14	9.64	10.42	11.53	12.65	12.81	12.32	13.30	12.21	13.85
Research and medical-facilities construction	1.68	.45	1.00	5.52	9.28	16.41	17.32	17.57	19.49	20.89	24.76	25.77	29.01	30.22	31.73	33.47
Research			.02	.72	3.21	7.07	7.76	7.98	8.85	8.72	8.90	8.83	9.73	10.78	11.12	12.69
Construction	1.68	.45	.98	4.80	6.04	9.34	9.56	9.59	10.64	12.18	15.86	16.94	19.29	19.44	20.61	20.77

[1] Revised estimates.
[2] Preliminary estimates.
[3] Based on January 1 data from the Bureau of the Census for total U.S. population (including Armed Forces and Federal civilian employees overseas and the civilian population of outlying areas).

education and training compiled by the Office of Management and Budget. These Federal expenditures include, principally, direct support for health professional schools and for student assistance through loans and scholarships. Training is funded for a wide variety of health professionals, including physicians, dentists, nurses, mental health and other health professionals, research personnel, and paramedical personnel.

A study by the Institute of Medicine of the National Academy of Sciences presents estimates of the total cost of education for eight health professions.[2] The study reports that $3.1 billion was spent for the education of more than 300,000 students in 1972. About 25 percent ($765 million) of this expenditure was financed by unrestricted Federal and State government funds. The remainder was financed through private sources or through other types of Federal and State support.

TRENDS IN HEALTH EXPENDITURES

Health expenditures for Americans have increased on an average of 12 percent per year since 1965 (table 4). During this 10-year period health spending has more than tripled—from $38.9 bil-

lion in 1965 to $118.5 billion in 1975—and its share of the GNP has risen from 5.9 percent to 8.3 percent. Apart from inflationary prices within the health care industry, other factors—mainly greater utilization and improvements in quality of care—have interacted to bring this about.

Technological developments in areas such as equipment and drugs, as well as improved treatment procedures and new techniques—all have added substantially to the health care bill in recent years.[3]

In addition to the effect of price increases and technological change, aggregate spending levels are influenced by population growth and by changes in per capita utilization resulting from changes in both demand and supply factors. Although per capita expenditures eliminate the effect of population growth, health expenditures still registered substantial increases from 1965 to 1975. During this period, per capita expenditures rose from $198 to $547, an average annual increase of 10.7 percent. Since this increase is only slightly less than the 11.8-percent average annual rate for aggregate expenditures, it appears that population growth has had relatively little effect on aggregate expenditures. In general, with the decline in the population growth rate in the late 1960's and the 1970's, the effect of rising population on the increases in health expenditures has continued to dwindle.

[2] National Academy of Sciences, Institute of Medicine, Costs of Education in the Health Professions: Report of a Study, Parts I and II, 1974. The eight professions studied are medicine, osteopathy, dentistry, optometry, pharmacy, podiatry, veterinary medicine, and nursing.

[3] Nancy L. Worthington, "Expenditures for Hospital Care and Physicians' Services: Factors Affecting Annual Changes," Social Security Bulletin, November 1975.

What has been the proportionate effect of these factors on the increasing expenditures for health care? As seen in chart 2 and in the following tabulation, population growth has had a rapidly

Source of increase	1950–75	1950–65	1965–75
	Amount of increase (in billions)		
Total	$92.7	$23.0	$69.7
Price	44.9	10.2	36.9
Population	13.9	4.9	6.1
Other	33.9	7.9	26.7
	Percentage distribution		
Total	100.0	100.0	100.0
Price	48.4	44.3	53.0
Population	15.0	21.5	8.7
Other	36.6	34.2	38.3

diminishing effect in the past 10 years. Only an estimated 9 percent or $6.1 billion of the $69.7 billion increase from 1965 to 1975 can be attributed to population growth. Price rises alone account for an estimated 53 percent or $36.9 billion of the rise during that period. The remaining 38 percent ($26.7 billion) can be attributed to greater utilization and improvements in the qual-

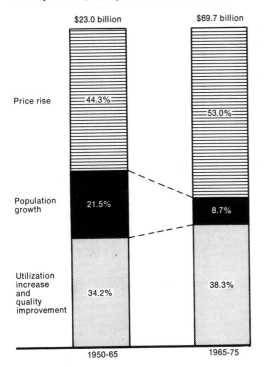

CHART 2.—Factors affecting increases in personal health care expenditures, fiscal years 1950–65 and 1965–75

ity of care. In contrast, during the period 1950–65, population change accounted for 22 percent of the increase, price rises were the source of 44 percent of increased expenditures, and the remaining 34 percent was attributable to increased utilization and quality-of-care improvements.

THIRD-PARTY PAYMENTS

Private health insurance paid $27.3 billion in benefits to consumers in 1975 (15.3 percent more than in the previous year). The amounts paid in claims by insurance companies, Blue Cross-Blue Shield plans, and independent plans (community, employer-employee-union, individual and group practice, and other) are almost triple the private health insurance benefits of 10 years ago. The depth of coverage, however, remains a problem. Table 5 and chart 3 show that, although private insurance payments covered 35.8 percent of hospital costs and 39.0 percent of physicians' fees, the consumer had only minimal help from insurance for his dentist bills, prescription drugs and drug sundries, and all other health services. Thus, 61 cents of every insurance claim dollar goes for

TABLE 5.—Amount and percentage distribution of personal health care expenditures met by third parties, by type of expenditure, fiscal year 1975

Type of expenditure	Total	Direct payments	Third-party payments			
			Total	Private health insurance	Government	Philanthropy and industry
	Aggregate amount (in millions)					
Total	$103,200	$33,599	$69,601	$27,340	$40,924	$1,337
Hospital care	46,600	3,736	42,864	16,677	25,643	544
Physicians' services	22,100	7,618	14,482	8,612	5,855	15
Dentists' services	7,500	6,347	1,153	738	415	
Drugs and drug sundries	10,600	9,011	1,589	684	905	
All other services [2]	16,400	6,887	9,513	629	8,106	778
	Per capita amount					
Total	$476.40	$155.10	$321.30	$126.21	$188.92	$6.17
Hospital care	215.12	17.25	197.87	76.99	188.38	2.51
Physicians' services	102.02	35.17	66.85	39.76	27.03	.07
Dentists' services	34.62	29.30	5.32	3.41	1.92	
Drugs and drug sundries	48.93	41.60	7.34	3.16	4.18	
All other services [2]	75.71	31.79	43.91	2.90	37.42	3.59
	Percentage distribution					
Total	100.0	32.6	67.4	26.5	39.7	1.3
Hospital care	100.0	8.0	92.0	35.8	55.0	1.2
Physicians' services	100.0	34.5	65.5	39.0	26.5	.1
Dentists' services	100.0	84.6	15.4	9.8	5.5	
Drugs and drug sundries	100.0	85.0	15.0	6.5	8.5	
All other services [2]	100.0	42.0	58.0	3.8	49.4	4.7

[1] Preliminary estimates.
[2] Includes other professional services, eyeglasses and appliances, nursing-home care, and other services not elsewhere classified.

hospital bills, 31 cents for physicians' services, 3 cents for the dentist, 3 cents for drugs and drug sundries, and the remaining 2 cents for private-duty nursing, vision care, nursing-home care, visiting-nurse service, and other types of care.

Third-party payments are those made by private health insurance, government, philanthropy, and industry. The contribution of third parties to personal health care financing—expenditures for health services and supplies—though climbing rapidly in recent years, particularly in government spending, still leaves the consumer with direct out-of-pocket expense for a third of his health care bills. Although third parties accounted for 92 cents of every hospital care dollar

CHART 3.—Percentage distribution of per capita personal health care expenditures, by type of expenditure and source of funds, fiscal year 1975

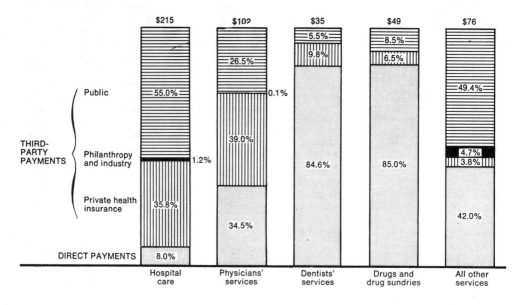

spent, the consumer paid directly more than a third of his charges for physicians' services, 85 percent of his dentist bills, 85 percent of the cost of drugs, and 42 percent of the charges for all other health care services.

The upward trend in third-party payments that began with the advent of the Medicare and Medicaid programs in 1967 has continued steadily with the expansion of those programs and with the slow but steady growth of private insurance benefits (table 6). In 1967, third-party payments represented more than half of all personal health care expenditures for the first time. By 1970, government and private health insurance, with a small contribution from philanthropy and private industry, paid three-fifths of these costs; by 1975, they paid two-thirds. As a result, the consumer's direct share of costs has inched downward from 45 percent in 1967 to 33 percent in 1975. The consumer's expenditures in dollars—because of inflationary pressures, improvements in technology, and other factors—have more than tripled, however, since 1950 and were a third higher in 1975 than in 1970.

The relative shares paid by the various third parties have been fairly stable since the early years of Medicare and Medicaid. In 1950, before private health insurance had seen any real growth, consumers were paying almost 70 percent of their health bills directly, with third parties picking up less than a third of the costs. Insurance met only 8 percent of costs, philanthropy and industry covered only 3 percent, and government funds met the remaining 20 percent.

As a result of the rapid growth of the health insurance industry, by 1965 insurance payments met 25 percent of health care costs, public spending remained at about 21 percent, and consumer

bills were down to 52 percent of total costs. Following enactment of Medicare and Medicaid, public spending surged upward and the share paid by private insurance dropped slightly. In 1975 government paid for almost 40 percent of all personal health care expenditures, but private insurance had leveled off at less than 27 percent, leaving consumer direct payments at about a third of total outlays.

Third-party payments have mainly affected hospital care expenditures (table 7). In 1950, consumers' payments accounted for a little more than a third of all hospital expenditures. The growth in private insurance coverage of hospital care was rapid in the 1950's and early 1960's, and by 1965 private insurance paid 42 percent of hospital costs and consumer payments dropped to 18 percent. After Medicare and Medicaid came into full swing, the share of private insurance dropped to about 35 percent, and government spending for hospital care rose to more than 50 percent. In 1975, public funds accounted for 55 percent of hospital care expenditures and insurance benefits paid for 36 percent, leaving the consumer to finance directly only 8 percent of hospital care outlays.

The impact of third parties on expenditures for physicians' services has been less dramatic, though substantial. Before its swift growth, private insurance paid only about 10 percent of doctor bills. The consumer paid directly 85 percent of all expenditures for physicians' services, and government picked up the remaining 5 percent. By 1965, insurance payments took care of 30 percent of physicians' bills and the consumer's share was reduced to 63 percent. Once Medicare and Medicaid became firmly established, however, the government share had risen to about 22 percent and insurance payments were slowly rising, with consumer direct payments down to less than 50 percent. In 1975, direct payments represented about one-third of the total and covered a little less than two-thirds of expenditures for physicians' services: insurance met 39 percent, government 26 percent.

Despite these increases in third-party financing of hospital and physicians' services, the consumer still pays directly a large share of the outlays for all other health services—dentists and other professional services, drugs and drug sundries, eyeglasses and appliances, nursing-home care, and other health services. As of 1975, little private insurance had been written to cover such services; consequently, private insurance paid only 6 percent of these costs. Government spending (mostly for Medicaid) accounted for 27 percent, leaving the consumer to make direct payments for almost two-thirds of these bills.

DEFINITIONS, METHODOLOGY, AND SOURCES OF DATA

Estimates of national health expenditures are compiled by type of expenditure and source of funds. For 1974 and 1975, the data for the public sector represent the outlays of 10 categories of government health programs.[4] In previous years, 12 such categories were shown, but for two of these categories—school health and OEO programs—data are no longer shown separately. For several Federal health programs, the data are taken from the Office of Management and Budget special analysis of health programs.[5] For the remainder, the data are supplied by the various agencies.

In the private sector, the data are estimated first on a calendar-year basis by type of expenditure and are then converted to fiscal-year figures on the basis of price and utilization change during 6-month periods. The general method is to estimate the total outlays for each type of medical service or expenditure and then to deduct the amounts paid to public and private hospitals, physicians in private practice, etc., under the public programs reported in the social welfare expenditure series. The fiscal-year figures for each public program are allocated by type of expenditure on the basis of published and unpublished reports for each program. In general, the consumer expenditures are residual amounts, derived by deducting philanthropic and government expenditures from the total spent for each type of service.

---

[4] For a description of the public programs, see Barbara S. Cooper and Nancy L. Worthington, *Personal Health Care Expenditures, by State*, Vol. 1: *Public Funds, 1966 and 1969*, Office of Research and Statistics, 1973.

[5] See "Special Analysis K: Federal Health Programs," *Special Analyses, Budget of the United States Government, Fiscal Year 1976*, Office of Management and Budget, 1975.

Hospital Care

The estimates of expenditures for hospital care are derived chiefly from American Hospital Association data on hospital finances, increased slightly to allow for osteopathic hospitals. Expenditures for the education and training of physicians and other health personnel are included only where they are not separable from the costs of hospital operations.

Expenditures by the Veterans Administration and the Department of Defense for physicians' services (except under contract medical care programs) are included as part of hospital care expenditures. Services of salaried physicians in psychiatric, tuberculosis, and general hospitals—whether public or private—are part of hospital care, but self-employed physicians' services in hospitals are not counted as hospital expenditures. The costs of drugs used in hospitals are also included with hospital care. Anesthesia and X-ray services are sometimes classified as hospital care expenditures and sometimes as expenditures for physicians' services, depending on billing practices.

Federal expenditures for hospital care represent total expenses for care in Federal hospitals (less any patient payments) plus vendor payments under government programs to non-Federal hospitals. Similarly, State and local expenditures include net expenses for care in State and locally owned hospitals as well as vendor payments to nongovernment hospitals. Consumer payments for hospital care represent total hospital revenues less all government payments and estimated receipts from philanthropy.

Services of Physicians and Other Health Professionals

Estimated expenditures for the services of physicians and dentists in private practice are based on the gross income from self-employment practice reported by physicians and dentists to the Internal Revenue Service (and shown in its report, *Statistics of Income—Business Income Tax Returns*). Gross receipts are totaled for practitioners in sole proprietorships and partnerships. The total also includes the estimated gross income of corporate offices, that portion of gross receipts of medical laboratories estimated to represent patient payments, and the estimated expenses of group-practice prepayment plans in providing physicians' services (to the extent that these are not included in physicians' income from self-employment), as well as those of group-practice dental clinics. Estimated receipts of physicians for life insurance examinations are deducted.

The gross receipts of physicians and dentists represent total expenditures for these services. Consumer payments are estimated by deducting vendor payments under government programs and estimated payments to physicians and dentists from philanthropic agencies.

TABLE 6.—Amount and percentage distribution of personal health care expenditures,[1] by source of funds, selected fiscal years, 1929–75

Fiscal year	Total	Source of funds						
		Private				Public		
		Total	Direct payments	Insurance benefits	Other	Total	Federal	State and local
		Aggregate amount (in millions)						
1929	$3,165	$2,882	[2] $2,800	----------	$83	$282	$85	$197
1935	2,585	2,204	[2] 2,134	----------	70	382	89	293
1940	3,414	2,891	[2] 2,799	----------	92	523	133	389
1950	10,400	8,298	7,107	$879	312	2,102	979	1,124
1955	15,231	11,762	8,992	2,358	412	3,469	1,583	1,886
1960	22,729	17,799	12,576	4,698	525	4,930	2,102	2,828
1965	33,498	26,540	17,577	8,280	683	6,958	2,840	4,118
1966	36,216	28,324	18,668	8,936	720	7,892	3,349	4,542
1967	41,343	28,883	18,786	9,344	753	12,461	7,471	4,991
1968	46,521	30,322	19,098	10,444	780	16,200	10,401	5,797
1969	52,690	33,987	20,957	12,206	824	18,705	12,283	6,421
1970	60,113	39,568	24,272	14,406	890	20,545	13,403	7,142
1971	67,228	43,999	26,307	16,728	964	23,229	15,401	7,827
1972 [3]	74,828	47,796	28,141	18,620	1,035	27,032	18,126	8,906
1973 [3]	82,490	52,428	30,348	20,955	1,125	30,062	20,178	9,884
1974 [3]	90,088	56,630	31,310	24,100	1,220	33,459	22,959	10,499
1975 [4]	103,200	62,276	33,599	27,340	1,337	40,924	28,578	12,345
		Per capita amount						
1929	$25.72	$23.42	$22.75	----------	$0.67	$2.29	$0.69	$1.60
1935	20.02	17.07	16.53	----------	.54	2.96	.69	2.27
1940	25.47	21.57	20.89	----------	.69	3.90	.99	2.90
1950	67.75	54.05	46.30	$5.73	2.03	13.69	6.38	7.32
1955	91.19	70.42	53.84	14.12	2.47	20.77	9.48	11.28
1960	124.50	97.50	68.89	25.73	2.88	27.00	11.51	15.49
1965	170.32	134.95	89.37	42.10	3.47	35.38	14.44	20.94
1966	181.96	142.30	93.79	44.90	3.62	39.65	16.83	22.82
1967	205.45	143.53	93.35	46.43	3.74	61.92	37.13	24.80
1968	228.75	149.10	93.91	51.35	3.84	79.66	51.14	28.50
1969	256.59	165.51	102.06	59.44	4.01	91.09	59.82	31.27
1970	289.76	190.73	117.00	69.44	4.29	99.03	64.61	34.43
1971	320.84	209.98	125.55	79.83	4.60	110.86	73.50	37.35
1972 [3]	353.66	225.90	133.00	88.00	4.89	127.76	85.67	42.09
1973 [3]	386.84	245.87	142.32	98.27	5.28	140.98	94.63	46.35
1974 [3]	419.44	263.66	145.78	112.21	5.68	155.78	106.89	46.79
1975 [4]	476.40	287.48	155.10	126.21	6.17	188.92	131.92	56.99
		Percentage distribution						
1929	100.0	91.1	88.5	----------	2.6	8.9	2.7	6.2
1935	100.0	85.3	82.6	----------	2.7	14.8	3.4	11.3
1940	100.0	84.7	82.0	----------	2.7	15.3	3.9	11.4
1950	100.0	79.8	68.3	8.5	3.0	20.2	9.4	10.8
1955	100.0	77.2	59.0	15.5	2.7	22.8	10.4	12.4
1960	100.0	78.3	55.3	20.7	2.3	21.7	9.2	12.4
1965	100.0	79.2	52.5	24.7	2.0	20.8	8.5	12.3
1966	100.0	78.2	51.5	24.7	2.0	21.8	9.2	12.5
1967	100.0	69.9	45.4	22.6	1.8	30.1	18.1	12.1
1968	100.0	65.2	41.1	22.5	1.7	34.8	22.4	12.5
1969	100.0	64.5	39.8	23.2	1.6	35.5	23.3	12.2
1970	100.0	65.8	40.4	24.0	1.5	34.2	22.3	11.9
1971	100.0	65.4	39.1	24.9	1.4	34.6	22.9	11.6
1972 [3]	100.0	63.9	37.6	24.9	1.4	36.1	24.2	11.9
1973 [3]	100.0	63.6	36.8	25.4	1.4	36.4	24.5	12.0
1974 [3]	100.0	62.9	34.8	26.8	1.4	37.1	25.5	11.6
1975 [4]	100.0	60.3	32.6	26.5	1.3	39.7	27.7	12.0

[1] Includes all expenditures for health services and supplies other than (a) expenses for prepayment and administration; (b) government public health activities.
[2] Includes any insurance benefits and expenses for prepayment (insurance premiums less insurance benefits).
[3] Revised estimates.
[4] Preliminary estimates.

The salaries of physicians and dentists on the staffs of hospitals and hospital outpatient facilities are considered a component of hospital care. The salaries of physicians and dentists serving in field services of the Armed Forces are included in "other health services." Where they can be separated, expenditures for the education and training of medical personnel are considered as expenditures for education and are excluded from health expenditures.

The Internal Revenue Service also provides data on the income of other health professionals in private practice. Estimated salaries of visiting nurses are added to the private income of other health professionals. Deductions and exclusions are made in the same manner as for expenditures for physicians' and dentists' services.

Drugs, Drug Sundries, Eyeglasses, and Appliances

Expenditures in these categories include only the spending for outpatient drugs and appliances and exclude those provided to inpatients. The basic source of the estimates for drugs and drug sundries and for eyeglasses and appliances is the report of personal consumption expenditures in the Department of Commerce national income accounts in the Survey of Current Business. To estimate the consumer portion, workmen's compensation payments are subtracted. The Department of Commerce counts this expenditure as a consumer expenditure, but the Office of Research and Statistics considers it an expenditure of government. Total expenditures for drugs and appliances represent the sum of these consumer expenditure estimates and the expenditures under all public programs for these products.

Nursing-Home Care

Expenditures for nursing-home care encompass spending by both private and public sources in all facilities providing some level of nursing care. Included are all nursing homes certified by Medicare and/or Medicaid as skilled-nursing facilities and those certified by Medicaid as intermediate-care facilities and all other homes providing some level of nursing care even though they are not certified under either program.

Expenditure estimates are based on periodic surveys of nursing homes conducted by the National Center for Health Statistics of the Department of Health, Education, and Welfare. The estimates for total expenditures are derived from survey data on utilization and charges for a total

universe of nursing-care homes and personal-care homes with nursing, as defined by the Center.[6] Estimates for intervening years (for which no data are available) are based on available economic and other indicators.

Consumer expenditures in nursing homes represent the difference between total nursing-home expenditures and expenditures from philanthropic and government sources for services in skilled-nursing facilities and intermediate-care facilities.

Expenses for Prepayment and Administration

Prepayment expenses represent the difference between the earned premiums or subscription in-

[6] For a complete definition, see *Monthly Vital Statistics Report*, vol. 23, No. 6, Supplement, National Center for Health Statistics, 1974, pages 11–12.

TABLE 7.—Amount and percentage distribution of personal health care expenditures, by type of expenditure and source of funds, selected fiscal years, 1950–75

Type of expenditure and fiscal year	Total	Source of funds				Public
		Private				
		Total	Direct payments	Insurance benefits	Other	
Aggregate amount (in millions)						
Hospital care:						
1950	$3,698	$2,008	$1,265	$610	$133	$1,690
1955	5,689	3,075	1,344	1,560	171	2,614
1960	8,499	4,931	1,583	3,124	224	3,568
1965	13,152	8,222	2,434	5,488	300	4,930
1966	14,245	8,840	2,628	5,892	320	5,405
1967	16,921	8,484	2,084	6,063	337	8,437
1968	19,384	9,080	2,009	6,731	340	10,304
1969	22,356	10,503	2,313	7,842	348	11,853
1970	25,879	12,727	3,174	9,182	371	13,152
1971	29,133	14,006	2,962	10,644	400	15,127
1972 [1]	32,720	15,087	2,892	11,768	427	17,633
1973 [1]	36,155	17,113	3,608	13,034	471	19,042
1974 [1]	39,963	18,639	3,366	14,760	513	21,324
1975 [2]	46,600	20,957	3,736	16,677	544	25,643
Per capita amount						
Hospital care:						
1950	$24.09	$13.08	$8.24	$3.97	$0.87	$11.01
1955	34.06	18.41	8.05	9.34	1.02	15.65
1960	46.56	27.01	8.67	17.11	1.23	19.54
1965	66.89	41.82	12.38	27.90	1.53	25.08
1966	71.59	44.43	13.20	29.60	1.61	27.17
1967	84.09	42.16	10.36	30.13	1.67	41.93
1968	95.31	44.65	9.88	33.10	1.67	50.67
1969	108.87	51.15	11.26	38.19	1.69	57.72
1970	124.74	61.35	15.30	44.26	1.79	63.40
1971	139.03	66.84	14.14	50.80	1.91	72.19
1972 [1]	154.64	71.31	13.67	55.62	2.02	83.34
1973 [1]	169.55	80.25	16.92	61.12	2.21	89.30
1974 [1]	186.06	86.78	15.67	68.72	2.39	99.28
1975 [2]	215.12	96.74	17.25	76.99	2.51	118.38
Percentage distribution						
Hospital care:						
1950	100.0	54.3	34.2	16.5	3.6	45.7
1955	100.0	54.1	23.6	27.4	3.0	45.9
1960	100.0	58.0	18.6	36.8	2.6	42.0
1965	100.0	62.5	18.5	41.7	2.3	37.5
1966	100.0	62.1	18.4	41.4	2.2	37.9
1967	100.0	50.1	12.3	35.8	2.0	49.9
1968	100.0	46.8	10.4	34.7	1.8	53.2
1969	100.0	47.0	10.4	35.1	1.6	53.0
1970	100.0	49.2	12.3	35.5	1.4	50.8
1971	100.0	48.1	10.2	36.5	1.4	51.9
1972 [1]	100.0	46.1	8.8	36.0	1.3	53.9
1973 [1]	100.0	47.3	10.0	36.1	1.3	52.7
1974 [1]	100.0	46.6	8.4	36.9	1.3	53.4
1975 [2]	100.0	45.0	8.0	35.8	1.2	55.0

See footnotes at end of table.

TABLE 7.—Amount and percentage distribution of personal health care expenditures, by type of expenditure and source of funds, selected fiscal years, 1950–75—*Continued*

Type of expenditure and fiscal year	Total	Source of funds				Public
		Private				
		Total	Direct payments	Insurance benefits	Other	
Aggregate amount (in millions)						
Physicians' services:						
1950	$2,689	$2,556	$2,279	$270	$7	$133
1955	3,632	3,392	2,587	797	8	240
1960	5,580	5,218	3,685	1,524	9	362
1965	8,405	7,878	5,315	2,554	9	527
1966	8,865	8,267	5,502	2,756	9	598
1967	9,738	8,323	5,415	2,898	10	1,415
1968	10,734	8,378	5,148	3,220	10	2,356
1969	11,842	9,170	5,407	3,753	10	2,672
1970	13,443	10,512	6,034	4,468	10	2,931
1971	15,098	11,800	6,620	5,169	11	3,298
1972 [1]	16,527	12,878	7,113	5,754	11	3,649
1973 [1]	17,995	13,861	7,290	6,559	12	4,134
1974 [1]	19,568	14,834	7,214	7,606	14	4,734
1975 [2]	22,100	16,245	7,618	8,612	15	5,855
Per capita amount						
Physicians' services:						
1950	$17.52	$16.65	$14.85	$1.76	$0.05	$0.87
1955	21.75	20.31	15.49	4.77	.05	1.44
1960	30.57	28.58	20.18	8.35	.05	1.98
1965	42.75	40.06	27.02	12.99	.05	2.68
1966	44.56	41.55	27.64	13.85	.05	3.01
1967	48.39	41.36	26.91	14.40	.05	7.03
1968	52.78	41.20	25.31	15.83	.05	11.58
1969	57.67	44.66	26.33	18.28	.05	13.01
1970	64.80	50.67	29.08	21.54	.05	14.13
1971	72.05	56.31	31.59	24.67	.05	15.74
1972 [1]	78.11	60.87	33.62	27.20	.05	17.25
1973 [1]	84.39	65.00	34.19	30.76	.06	19.39
1974 [1]	91.12	69.07	33.59	35.41	.07	22.04
1975 [2]	102.02	74.99	35.17	39.76	.07	27.03
Percentage distribution						
Physicians' services:						
1950	100.0	95.1	84.8	10.0	0.3	4.9
1955	100.0	93.4	71.2	21.9	.2	6.6
1960	100.0	93.5	66.0	27.3	.2	6.5
1965	100.0	93.7	63.2	30.4	.1	6.3
1966	100.0	93.3	62.1	31.1	.1	6.7
1967	100.0	85.5	55.6	29.8	.1	14.5
1968	100.0	78.1	48.0	30.0	.1	21.9
1969	100.0	77.4	45.7	31.7	.1	22.6
1970	100.0	78.2	44.9	33.2	.1	21.8
1971	100.0	78.2	43.8	34.2	.1	21.8
1972 [1]	100.0	77.9	43.0	34.8	.1	22.1
1973 [1]	100.0	77.0	40.5	36.4	.1	23.0
1974 [1]	100.0	75.8	36.9	38.9	.1	24.2
1975 [2]	100.0	73.5	34.5	39.0	.1	26.5

See footnotes at end of table.

TABLE 7.—Amount and percentage distribution of personal health care expenditures, by type of expenditure and source of funds, selected fiscal years, 1950-75—Continued

Type of expenditure and fiscal year	Total	Source of funds				
		Private				Public
		Total	Direct payments	Insurance benefits	Other	
Aggregate amount (in millions)						
All other services:[3]						
1950	$4,013	$3,734	$3,562	(4)	$172	$279
1955	5,910	5,295	5,062	(4)	233	615
1960	8,650	7,650	7,308	$50	293	1,000
1965	11,941	10,440	9,828	238	374	1,501
1966	13,106	11,217	10,538	288	391	1,880
1967	14,684	12,076	11,178	492	406	2,609
1968	16,403	12,864	11,823	611	430	3,540
1969	18,492	14,314	13,092	756	466	4,180
1970	20,791	16,329	14,904	916	509	4,462
1971	22,997	18,193	16,544	1,096	553	4,804
1972[1]	25,581	19,831	18,136	1,098	597	5,750
1973[1]	28,340	21,454	19,450	1,362	642	6,886
1974[1]	30,554	23,157	20,730	1,734	693	7,398
1975[2]	34,500	25,074	22,245	2,051	778	9,426
Per capita amount						
All other services:[3]						
1950	$26.14	$24.32	$23.20	....	$1.12	$1.82
1955	35.38	31.70	30.31	....	1.40	3.68
1960	47.38	41.90	40.03	$0.27	1.60	5.48
1965	60.72	53.08	49.97	1.21	1.90	7.63
1966	65.85	56.36	52.92	1.45	1.96	9.49
1967	72.97	60.01	55.55	2.44	2.02	12.96
1968	80.66	63.25	58.14	3.00	2.11	17.41
1969	90.05	69.71	63.76	3.68	2.27	20.36
1970	100.22	78.71	71.84	4.42	2.45	21.51
1971	109.75	86.82	78.95	5.23	2.64	22.93
1972[1]	120.90	93.73	85.72	5.19	2.82	27.18
1973[1]	132.90	100.61	91.21	6.39	3.01	32.29
1974[1]	142.26	107.82	96.52	8.07	3.23	34.44
1975[2]	159.26	115.75	102.69	9.47	3.59	43.51
Percentage distribution						
All other services:[3]						
1950	100.0	93.0	88.8	....	4.3	7.0
1955	100.0	89.6	85.7	....	3.9	10.4
1960	100.0	88.4	84.5	0.6	3.4	11.6
1965	100.0	87.4	82.3	2.0	3.1	12.6
1966	100.0	85.6	80.4	2.2	3.0	14.4
1967	100.0	82.2	76.1	3.4	2.8	17.8
1968	100.0	78.4	72.1	3.7	2.6	21.6
1969	100.0	77.4	70.8	4.1	2.5	22.6
1970	100.0	78.5	71.7	4.4	2.4	21.5
1971	100.0	79.1	71.9	4.8	2.4	20.9
1972[1]	100.0	77.5	70.9	4.3	2.3	22.5
1973[1]	100.0	75.7	68.6	4.8	2.3	24.3
1974[1]	100.0	75.8	67.9	5.7	2.3	24.2
1975[2]	100.0	72.7	64.5	5.9	2.3	27.3

[1] Revised estimates.
[2] Preliminary estimates.
[3] Includes dentists' services, other professional services, drugs and drug sundries, eyeglasses and appliances, nursing-home care, and other health services.
[4] Included in "physicians' services"; data not available separately.

come of health insurance organizations and their claims or benefit expenditures (or expenditures for providing such services in the case of organizations that directly provide services). In other words, it is the amount retained by health insurance organizations for operating expenses, additions to reserves, and profits. It is considered a consumer expenditure.

Data on the financial experience of health insurance organizations are reported annually by the Office of Research and Statistics in an article on private health insurance. Data for 1974 will appear in the March 1976 BULLETIN.

The administration component includes the estimated amounts expended by philanthropic organizations for fund-raising activities. In addi-

tion, it includes administrative expenses (where they are reported) of federally financed health programs. Such data were available for Medicare and Medicaid and for the Veterans Administration and Department of Defense contract medical care programs.

Government Public Health Activities

The category "government public health activities" is the same as the "other public health activities" category in the social welfare series of the Office of Research and Statistics. The Federal portion consists of outlays for the organization and delivery of health services, the prevention and control of health problems, and similar health activities administered by various Federal agencies, chiefly the Department of Health, Education, and Welfare. The data for these programs are taken from the Special Analyses of the Budget.

The State and local portion represents expenditures of all State and local health departments and intergovernment payments to the States and localities for public health activities. It excludes expenditures of other State and local government departments for air-pollution and water-pollution control, sanitation, water supplies, and sewage treatment. The source of these data is *Government Finances* (annual publication of the Bureau of the Census).

Other Health Services

Items of expenditure that could not be classified elsewhere are brought together in the category "other health services." It includes, for each public program, the residual amount of expenditures not classified as a specific type of medical service. In addition, it includes the following: (1) Industrial in-plant services, (2) school health services, before 1974, and (3) medical activities in Federal units other than hospitals.

Industrial in-plant services consist of amounts spent for maintaining in-plant health services and are based on estimates made by the National Institute for Occupational Safety and Health of the Public Health Service.

Until 1974, expenditures for school health were estimated by the Office of Education and reported as a separate item in the social welfare expenditure series. As of 1974, separate estimates for this item were no longer available and, although expenditures for this purpose continue to be included in the social welfare expenditure series as part of total expenditures for education, school health is no longer included as a health expenditure.

Medical activities in Federal units other than hospitals are residual amounts that represent primarily the cost of maintaining outpatient facilities (separately from hospitals) and field and shipboard medical stations.

Expenditures for private voluntary health agencies, included in the "other" private outlays, are the expenditures that remain after amounts for hospital care, physicians' services, etc., have been distributed. They represent the amounts spent for health education, lobbying, fundraising, etc.

Medical Research

Expenditures for medical research include all such spending by agencies whose primary object is the advancement of human health. Also included are those research expenditures directly related to health that are made by other agencies, such as those of the Department of Defense or the National Aeronautics and Space Administration. Research expenditures of drug and medical supply companies are excluded, since they are included in the cost of the product. The Federal amounts represent those reported as medical research in the Special Analyses of the Budget. The amounts shown for State and local govern-

ments and private expenditures are based on published estimates that have been prepared by the National Institutes of Health—primarily in the annual publication, *Basic Data Relating to the National Institutes of Health.*

Construction of Medical Facilities

Expenditures for construction represent "value put in place" for the hospitals, nursing homes, medical clinics, and medical research facilities but not for private office buildings providing office space for private practitioners. Excluded are amounts spent for construction of water-treatment or sewage-treatment plants and Federal grants for these purposes.

The data for "value put in place" for construction of publicly and privately owned medical facilities in each year are taken from the Department of Commerce report, *Construction Review.* Amounts spent by Federal and State and local governments for construction are subtracted from the total. The residual represents the amount coming from private funds.

FEDERAL HEALTH BUDGET, FISCAL YEAR 1977 ([15], pp. 192–218)

Overview.—Federal spending for health programs will total almost $46 billion in 1977, an increase of $3.5 billion or 8.1% over 1976. Federal health outlays continue to assume a growing share of the Federal budget, as shown in Table K–1.

Table K–1. **FEDERAL OUTLAYS FOR HEALTH COMPARED TO THE TOTAL FEDERAL BUDGET (dollars in billions)**

	Actual					Estimated		
	1971	1972	1973	1974	1975	1976	TQ	1977
Total Federal outlays	$211.4	$231.9	$246.5	$268.4	$324.6	$373.5	$98.0	$394.2
Federal health outlays	$20.2	$24.5	$26.0	$29.2	$36.8	$42.5	$10.9	$45.9
Health as percent of total outlays	9.6	10.6	10.6	10.9	11.3	11.4	11.1	11.7

Table K–2 summarizes and distributes Federal health outlays by major category for 1975 through 1977. Expenditures for financing or providing health services, primarily through medicare and the proposed Financial Assistance for Health Care program, account for $38.8 billion in 1977.

Table K-2. **FEDERAL OUTLAYS FOR MEDICAL AND HEALTH-RELATED ACTIVITIES BY CATEGORY** (in millions of dollars)

	Outlays			
	1975 actual	1976 estimate	TQ estimate	1977 estimate
Development of health resources, total	5,108	5,721	1,356	5,983
Health research	2,459	2,826	711	3,048
Training and education	1,384	1,477	322	1,217
Construction	949	1,082	240	1,309
Health planning and statistics	316	336	83	409
Provision of hospital and medical services, total	30,450	35,416	9,169	38,681
Direct Federal services	5,567	6,046	1,490	6,285
Indirect services	24,883	29,370	7,679	32,396
Prevention and control of health problems, total	1,232	1,349	337	1,270
Total, health programs	**36,790**	**42,486**	**10,862**	**45,935**

National Health Care Trends

Over the last quarter century, one of the most prominent trends in the health sector has been the increase in both private and public spending for health. Total expenditures for health have grown from $12 billion in 1950 to $119 billion in 1975, or from $78 to $547 per capita. Spending by Federal, State, and local governments has also increased dramatically during this period—from $3 billion to $50 billion, or from 26% to 42% of the total—primarily due to the enactment of the medicare and medicaid programs in 1965. Figure K-3 illustrates both the increase in public financing and the increase in total expenditures from 1965 to 1975.

Public and Private Health Expenditures

K-3

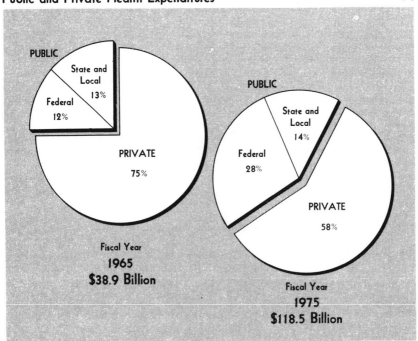

PUBLIC

State and Local
13%

Federal
12%

PRIVATE
75%

Fiscal Year
1965
$38.9 Billion

PUBLIC

State and Local
14%

Federal
28%

PRIVATE
58%

Fiscal Year
1975
$118.5 Billion

In the 5 years from 1970 to 1975, spending for health services and supplies has grown from $64 billion—6.7% of the gross national

product (GNP)—to $111 billion—7.8% of the GNP. Per capita health
services expenditures rose from $309 to $514 during the same period.
Annually these sums purchase over 1 billion physician visits by
the U.S. civilian population, approximately 33 million hospital
stays averaging over 7 days, 2.5 billion drug prescriptions, and other
health services.

Factors which contribute to this growth in spending include an
increased demand for health services by the public, payment mechanisms that reduce out-of-pocket expenditures by individual consumers, changes in medical therapies, and expansion of health
resources. Figure K–4 depicts health care expenditures per capita for
different age groups and financing sources in 1974.

Personal Health Care Expenditures Per Capita   K - 4

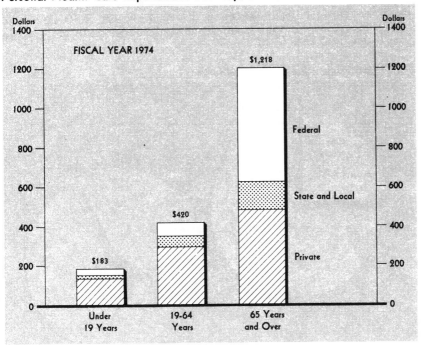

A second significant trend in the health sector is the rapid growth
in health resources, such as the supply of health professionals, biomedical researchers, hospitals, and other health facilities. The Nation's
supply of hospital beds, for example, has expanded from 730,000 in
1963 to 912,000 in 1974, or from 3.9 per 1,000 population to 5.0 per
1,000 population. In addition, the number of active physicians has
risen from 272,000 in 1963 to an estimated 378,000 in 1975 (Chart
K–5). During the same time, the number of active registered nurses
has grown from 582,000 to about 906,000. Presently, more than 4.4
million persons are employed in health-related careers—about 4%
of the civilian labor force. Health workers comprise the third largest
occupational grouping in the United States.

Physicians and other health professionals in the United States are
not evenly distributed geographically. Among the States, the number
of active, non-Federal physicians per 100,000 population in 1973
ranged from 218 in New York and 201 in Massachusetts, to 79 in
Mississippi and 73 in South Dakota. Chart K–6 shows the tendency
for physicians to locate in metropolitan rather than rural areas.
Approximately one quarter of the Nation's 25,000 psychiatrists, for
example, practice in the New York, Boston, and Washington, D.C.,
metropolitan areas. General practitioners are found in somewhat
larger proportions in nonmetropolitan counties.

Active Physicians, Domestic and Foreign Trained

K-5

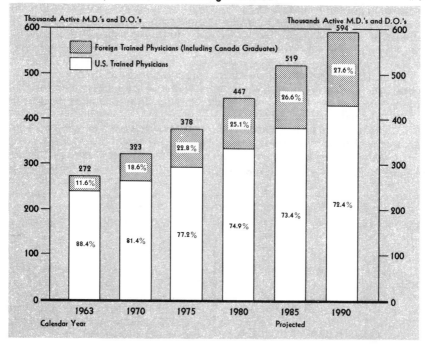

Active M.D.'s Per 100,000 Population in Metropolitan and Non-metropolitan Counties, 1973

K-6

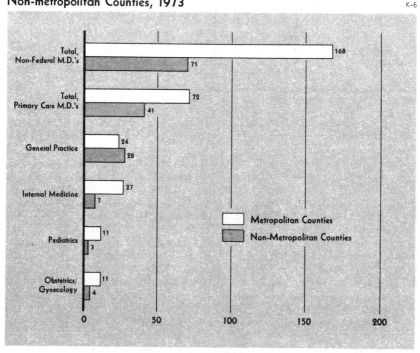

HEALTH STATUS

There has been a significant decrease in the death rate in the United States since the beginning of the twentieth century. This decrease has taken place during a period of significant economic and social change, as well as advances in health research and medical practice. Knowledge about the causes, prevention, and treatment of certain infectious diseases has led to their virtual elimination. These advances have lengthened life for many persons. On the other hand, the degenerative processes of aging have resulted in the increased prevalence of chronic diseases, which are generally more difficult and costly to treat than acute and infectious diseases.

Table K–7. SELECTED HEALTH STATUS INDICATORS (annual rates)

	1950	1960	1970	1974
Birth rate (per 1,000 population)	24.1	23.7	18.4	15.0
Death rate (per 1,000 population)	9.6	9.5	9.5	9.1
Average life expectancy at birth in years	68.2	69.7	70.9	72.0
Infant mortality rate (deaths under 1 year of age per 1,000 live births)	29.2	26.0	20.0	16.5
Leading causes of death (per 100,000 population):				
Diseases of the heart	355.5	369.0	362.0	353.1
Cancer	139.8	149.2	162.8	169.5
Cerebrovascular disease	104.0	108.0	101.9	97.2
Accidents	60.6	52.3	56.4	48.9
Tuberculosis, all forms	22.5	6.1	2.6	1.8
Kidney diseases, all forms	20.8	11.9	8.4	6.4
Diabetes	16.2	16.7	18.9	17.4
Cirrhosis of liver	9.2	11.3	15.5	16.0

Despite the decline in the U.S. death rate in the twentieth century, the recent growth in U.S. health resources, and the highest per capita health expenditures in the world, the health status of Americans, as measured by conventional standards, does not appear to be much different from that of other advanced industrialized nations. Average U.S. life expectancy rates, for example, are not significantly better than those of a number of Western European countries and Canada.

Table K–8. LIFE EXPECTANCY BY SEX AT SELECTED AGES, BY SELECTED COUNTRIES: 1970

Country	Age in years					
	35		55		65	
	Male	Female	Male	Female	Male	Female
Sweden	40	44	22	26	14	17
Canada	38	44	21	25	14	17
France	37	44	20	26	13	17
Italy	38	43	20	24	13	16
United Kingdom: England and Wales	37	42	19	24	12	16
Germany: Federal Republic	36	41	19	23	12	15
United States:						
Total	36	42	20	25	13	17
White	37	43	20	25	13	17
Other	33	39	19	23	13	16

The uneven distribution of health personnel is frequently cited as a reason that this country's health status is not better in relation to other countries. The relationship between the availability of physicians and life expectancy—a common indicator of health status—is, however, ambiguous. Life expectancy rates are generally no higher in States with more physicians per capita than in States with fewer physicians per capita (Chart K–9). For example, the life expectancy rate is virtually the same in Arkansas, Ohio, and New York, even though the number of physicians varies from 80 per 100,000 population in Arkansas to 116 in Ohio and 198 in New York.

The availability of health care is only one factor among many that bear upon health status. Other important determinants of health status are heredity, the quality of the natural environment, social and economic well-being, working conditions, housing, sanitation, nutrition, and personal lifestyle.

Physician Supply and Life Expectancy in Selected States, 1970

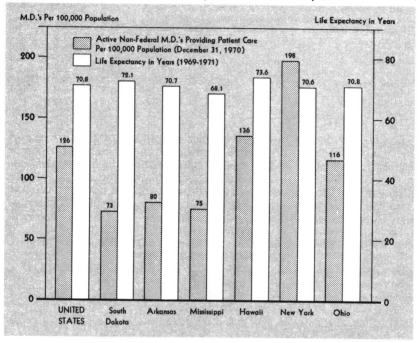

K-9

THE FEDERAL ROLE IN THE HEALTH SECTOR

Federal health programs attempt to improve the health status of Americans by adding to the knowledge of human disease, translating research findings into accepted medical practice, regulating known health hazards, improving financial and physical access to health professionals and facilities, and reforming the existing health care service system.

Health resources.—Federal programs for the development of health resources encompass support for health research, health professions training and education, construction of health care facilities, and health planning and statistics. The combined outlays for these programs, as shown in Table K–10, will be $5,975 million in 1977, an increase of $254 million from 1976.

Table K–10. **FEDERAL OUTLAYS FOR THE DEVELOPMENT OF HEALTH RESOURCES** (in millions of dollars)

	Outlays			
	1975 actual	1976 estimate	TQ estimate	1977 estimate
Health research (excluding research facilities)	2,459	2,826	711	3,048
Training and education	1,384	1,477	322	1,217
Construction	949	1,082	240	1,309
Health planning	316	336	83	409
Total	5,108	5,721	1,356	5,983

Health research.—Through the support of both basic and applied research, Federal biomedical and behavioral research programs attempt to provide new knowledge for use in the prevention, diagnosis, and treatment of disease. Paralleling the increasing incidence of chronic diseases in the United States, Federal research support places emphasis upon degenerative illnesses, such as cancer and cardiovascular disease, and upon environmentally induced health problems. Table K–12 indicates the allocation of Federal funds among research fields and includes funding for construction of research facilities.

Funds for Medical Research and Development

K-11

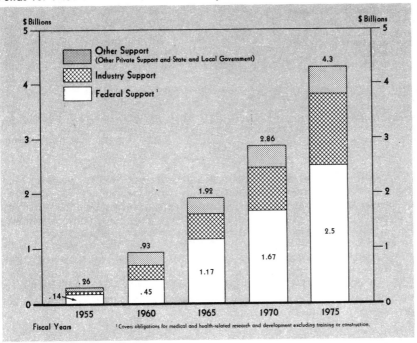

Fiscal Years   ¹ Covers obligations for medical and health-related research and development excluding training or construction.

Table K–12. **FEDERAL OUTLAYS FOR HEALTH RESEARCH AND RESEARCH FACILITIES**

(In millions of dollars)

	Outlays			
	1975 actual	1976 estimate	TQ estimate	1977 estimate
Cancer	499	572	128	666
Cardiovascular	266	286	62	311
Mental health	110	127	26	113
Neurological and visual	155	174	50	188
Population and family planning	58	73	18	65
Environmental health	300	408	122	528
Aging	53	49	13	63
Metabolic diseases	137	197	32	188
Child health	72	105	25	96
Infectious diseases	130	153	57	160
Pulmonary	48	53	12	56
Dental	42	46	10	57
Health services research and development	79	65	32	51
Other research and development	507	519	123	507
Research facilities	80	36	5	26
Total	2,539	2,862	716	3,074

Federal outlays for health research have risen over the past decade, from $1,369 million in 1967 to $3,074 million in 1977. The Federal

Government currently funds almost 60% of all biomedical research in this country.

The National Institutes of Health (NIH), within the Department of Health, Education, and Welfare, is the largest Federal biomedical research agency, and will administer 64% of the total Federal health research funds in 1977. NIH conducts an extensive research program in its own laboratories and clinical facilities, in addition to its research grant and contract activities. The Department of Health, Education, and Welfare also conducts and sponsors substance abuse and health services research to improve the organization, delivery, quality, and financing of health care.

Other Federal agencies support and conduct health research in support of their program missions. The three largest are the Energy Research and Development Administration, the Department of Defense, and the Veterans Administration. Together, these agencies account for 15% of all Federal biomedical research expenditures.

Training and education.—Over 40% of the revenues of the Nation's medical schools are derived from Federal grants or contracts. Table K–13 shows the Federal funds provided to medical schools from selected agencies. These outlays do not include payments for medical services from medicare and medicaid.

Table K–13. **FEDERAL FUNDS TO MEDICAL SCHOOLS**

(In millions of dollars)

Agency	Outlays			
	1975 actual	1976 estimate	TQ estimate	1977 estimate
Department of Health, Education, and Welfare_____	1,191	1,213	216	1,242
Research and development_____	(808)	(884)	(125)	(909)
Education and training_____	(283)	(263)	(73)	(234)
Construction_____	(100)	(66)	(18)	(99)
Department of Defense_____	13	23	9	58
Education and training_____	(11)	(16)	(8)	(19)
Veterans Administration:				
Education and training_____	4	37	8	35
National Aeronautics and Space Administration:				
Research and development_____	4	4	1	4
Energy Research and Development Administration:				
Research and development_____	13	14	3	16
Other agencies:				
Research and development_____	10	12	2	11
Total_____	1,235	1,304	239	1,365
Research and development_____	(837)	(915)	(131)	(941)
Education and training_____	(298)	(316)	(89)	(288)
Construction_____	(100)	(72)	(18)	(137)

The Federal Government will spend a total of $1,217 million in 1977 for health training and education, as shown in table K–14. The principal programs of direct support for health professions schools, which are administered by HEW, include:

- institutional operating cost support grants tied to conditions designed to improve geographic and specialty distribution of health professionals;
- special projects to demonstrate educational reforms and innovations in such areas as improving access to health professions education for the disadvantaged, developing new types of health workers, stimulating the practice of family medicine, and integrating medical education with health care delivery in medical scarcity areas.

A program of national health service scholarships—funded at a level of $35 million in 1977—will support approximately 4,600 medical, osteopathic, and dental students in return for periods of service to

Table K-14. **FEDERALLY AIDED HEALTH TRAINING AND EDUCATION**

(In millions of dollars)

	Outlays			
	1975 actual	1976 estimate	TQ estimate	1977 estimate
Degree or certificate training	1,186	1,278	272	1,035
Research personnel	(114)	(112)	(14)	(90)
Physicians	(491)	(560)	(127)	(485)
Dentists	(86)	(96)	(25)	(74)
Nurses	(155)	(144)	(38)	(104)
Mental health professionals	(51)	(44)	(7)	(24)
Other health professionals	(145)	(161)	(26)	(114)
Paramedical personnel	(144)	(161)	(35)	(144)
All other training	197	199	50	182
Total	**1,384**	**1,477**	**322**	**1,217**

meet public needs. This program helps to meet student financial needs, as well as Federal requirements for health professionals to staff programs such as the Indian Health Service. It also addresses the problem of geographic maldistribution of health personnel by placing physicians and dentists as private practitioners in provider scarcity areas or through such Federal programs as the National Health Service Corps.

The National Health Service Corps seeks to demonstrate the ability of health care provider shortage areas to support health personnel. The program will locate 676 health professionals in underserved areas in 1977.

Construction of health care facilities.—The Nation is well supplied in the aggregate with medical facilities. Chart K–15 suggests that the less populous States are relatively well endowed with hospital beds in contrast to the distribution of health professionals. This geographic distribution of hospital beds reflects in part the impact of over 30 years of Federal hospital construction assistance through the Hill-Burton program. Under its statutory formula, which favored the less populous and poorer areas, the Hill-Burton program allocated more than $4.4 billion in grants to the States.

General Hospital Beds Per 1,000 Population in Selected States, 1974   K-15

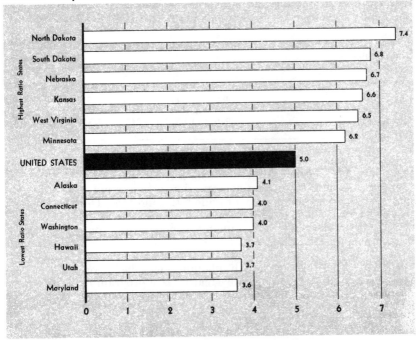

The basic goal of the Hill-Burton program—to improve the supply of health facilities in shortage areas—has been largely accomplished. Hill-Burton program expenditures have declined from 13% of the total $1.5 billion national medical facility construction expenditures in 1963 to 2.4% of the total estimated $4.6 billion construction expenditures in 1975. The vast majority of medical facility construction is now financed through long-term debt service of loans from the private capital markets.

Depreciation costs and debt servicing are legitimate expenses included in reimbursements from health insurance. In the 6 years from 1969 to 1975, for instance, the percentage of private nonprofit hospital construction being financed by debt service increased from 40% to 60%. This trend offsets reductions in the share of construction costs borne by government, philanthropy, and the hospitals themselves through depreciation funds.

Federal programs for the construction of health care facilities include the support of both community facilities to serve the general public, and facilities operated by Federal agencies for special beneficiary groups. In 1977, Federal outlays for the construction of health care facilities, including environmental health facilities, are estimated at $1,300 million.

Table K–16. HOSPITAL AND HEALTH FACILITY CONSTRUCTION

(In millions of dollars)

	Outlays			
	1975 actual	1976 estimate	TQ estimate	1977 estimate
Federally supported construction:				
Hospitals, new	55	60	12	21
Hospitals, modernized and replaced	91	109	11	85
Long-term care facilities	23	21	7	15
Research facilities	80	36	5	26
Environmental health facilities	159	159	50	244
Ambulatory care facilities	53	52	13	34
Health professions educational facilities	174	129	5	111
Other facilities	34	49	11	47
Total, federally supported	669	615	115	582
Federal hospitals and health facilities:				
Hospitals, new	51	95	3	34
Hospitals, modernized and replaced	159	267	80	529
Long-term care facilities	8	8	2	11
Research facilities	15	29	8	37
Environmental health facilities	39	46	11	36
Ambulatory care facilities	6	5	17	22
Other facilities	3	16	2	57
Total, Federal	281	467	125	727
Total, construction	949	1,082	240	1,309

In 1977, States will be able to use a portion of their Financial Assistance for Health Care block grant funds for construction of health care facilities. Federal assistance for the construction of community health facilities will also continue to be provided through the Department of Housing and Urban Development, which funds mortgage insurance for construction of hospitals, nursing homes, and group practice facilities.

Health planning.—Funding for health planning will be incorporated into the new Financial Assistance for Health Care program in 1977. Inclusion of health planning reflects the traditional State and local responsibility for planning.

Other agencies besides HEW will spend a total of $196 million in 1977 on health planning activities, including statistical programs. Nearly $160 million of these funds are for health planning activities in other countries supported by the State Department and the Agency for International Development.

Table K–17. **FEDERAL OUTLAYS FOR HEALTH PLANNING AND STATISTICS**

(In millions of dollars)

	1975 actual	1976 estimate	TQ estimate	1977 estimate
Financing of health planning, total_____	245	253	63	329
State-wide health planning_____	(46)	(29)	(8)	(43)
Substate health planning_____	(86)	(68)	(13)	(83)
Other health planning_____	(113)	(155)	(42)	(203)
Direct planning of Federal health activities_____	30	34	8	30
Health statistical activities, total_____	41	49	12	50
General purpose statistics_____	(20)	(26)	(7)	(26)
Federal program management statistics_____	(21)	(23)	(5)	(24)
Total, health planning activities_____	**316**	**336**	**83**	**409**

FINANCING AND PROVIDING MEDICAL SERVICES

Since enactment of the medicare and medicaid programs in 1965, public funds have become a major source of financing for most health services, particularly hospital and nursing home care. Chart K–18 indicates the relative importance of public funds, which account for over 42% of national health expenditures.

The impact of increased public spending for health care for the low-income population is reflected in changing utilization patterns for health services. The number of physician visits and hospitalizations per capita has increased across the board in the past decade. In addition, the low-income population is now using these health resources

Sources of Health Expenditures

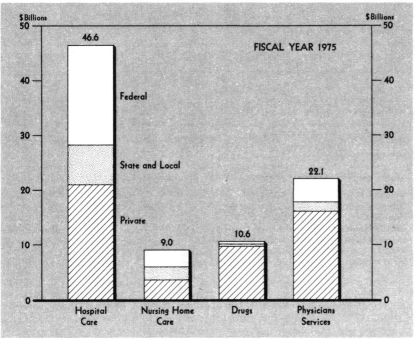

at higher rates than the nonpoor population (see Table K–19). This development stems largely from increased Government financing of medical services through the medicare and medicaid programs for the aged, disabled, and low-income.

Table K–19. **ANNUAL U.S. DOCTOR VISITS PER PERSON, 1964 AND 1974**

	1964		1974	
	Poor	Not poor	Poor	Not poor
All ages	4.3	4.6	5.4	4.9
Under 17 years	2.3	4.0	3.6	4.3
17 to 44 years	4.1	4.7	5.5	4.7
45 to 64 years	5.1	5.1	6.3	5.4
65 years and over	6.0	7.3	6.4	7.3

Federal programs to finance or provide hospital and medical services include medicare and the proposed Financial Assistance for Health Care program—which account for 74% of outlays for these purposes—as well as programs for health services directly administered by the Department of Defense, the Veterans Administration, and HEW. Table K–20 shows Federal expenditures for financing and providing hospital and medical services.

Table K–20. **FEDERAL FINANCING AND PROVISION OF HEALTH SERVICES**

(In millions of dollars)

	Outlays			
	1975 actual	1976 estimate	TQ estimate	1977 estimate
Financing of indirect hospital and medical services:				
General hospital inpatients	15,792	18,386	4,667	20,107
Psychiatric hospital inpatients	360	393	107	452
Long-term care inpatients	2,833	3,321	904	3,473
Outpatient mental health services	521	444	81	399
Outpatient services	3,887	4,817	1,305	5,382
Other services	1,490	2,009	616	2,584
Total, financing of indirect services	24,883	29,370	7,679	32,396
Provision of direct hospital and medical services:				
General hospital inpatients	3,045	3,285	796	3,367
Psychiatric hospital inpatients	652	796	176	761
Long-term care inpatients	177	194	48	210
Outpatient mental health services	37	44	11	50
Outpatient services	1,444	1,579	393	1,645
Other services	212	245	66	251
Total, provision of direct services	5,567	6,046	1,490	6,285
Total, financing and provision of services	30,450	35,416	9,169	38,681

Medicare and the proposed Financial Assistance for Health Care block grant are the Federal Government's largest health activities. In 1977, they will account for $28.6 billion, or 62%, of Federal health outlays.

Medicare.—Medicare finances health care for the aged, disabled, and persons suffering from chronic kidney disease. It includes both hospital insurance (HI)—which pays for inpatient care, posthospitalization skilled nursing home care, and home health benefits—and supplementary medical insurance (SMI)—which pays for physician and other outpatient services.

HI is financed largely through social security taxes on earnings, while SMI is financed by premiums from enrollees—currently $6.70 per month—and contributions from general tax revenues. Both insurance components are administered primarily through private insurance companies under contract with the Social Security Administration.

Medicare has increased rapidly in cost in recent years—rising 123% from 1972 to 1977, even excluding proposed savings of $2.2 billion in 1977. Estimated outlays of $19.6 billion in 1977 will provide average benefits of nearly $2,200 for the 5.9 million persons receiving HI benefits, and over $400 for the 14.2 million persons receiving SMI benefits.

Proposed legislation, the Medicare Improvements of 1976, will provide protection against catastrophic health care costs and make other reforms in medicare cost-sharing provisions. The catastrophic health insurance proposals would establish a limitation on beneficiary cost-sharing of $500 per year for HI benefits and $250 per year for SMI benefits. These limits will reduce cost-sharing by a total of $538 million for over 3 million persons with high medical expenses. Cost-sharing proposals include coinsurance equal to 10% of charges above the deductible for all HI-covered services, and an SMI deductible adjusted with increases in social security cash benefits. These provisions will improve patient incentives for economical use of health services.

The 1977 budget also proposes legislation to limit increases in medicare reimbursement rates. The legislation sets upper limits of 7% on annual increases in hospital per diem payments and 4% on annual increases in physician charges for 1977 and 1978. These limits are designed to slow health cost inflation and restrain the growth of program outlays.

The HI trust fund is currently underfinanced. The proposed legislation will improve the balance of trust fund income and outlays, as well as permit funding of catastrophic insurance. The following table shows the budgetary impact of the proposed legislation in 1976–78.

Table K–21. **MEDICARE IMPROVEMENTS OF 1976** (in millions of dollars)

	Outlays		
	1976 est.	1977 est.	1978 est.
Catastrophic insurance:			
Hospital insurance ($500 limit)	+15	+330	+420
Supplementary medical insurance ($250 limit)	--------	+208	+634
Subtotal	+15	+538	+1,054
Cost-sharing reforms:			
Hospital insurance (10% coinsurance)	−330	−1,730	−2,020
Supplementary medical insurance:			
Dynamic deductible ($77 on January 1, 1977)	--------	−111	−255
Coinsurance on hospital-based services	--------	−19	−38
Subtotal	−330	−1,860	−2,313
Reimbursement limits:			
Hospital insurance (7% per diem)	--------	−730	−1,905
Supplementary medical insurance (4% charges)	--------	−179	−301
Subtotal	--------	−909	−2,206
Total	−315	−2,231	−3,465

The following table displays basic data concerning the medicare program coverage, benefits, and administration.

Table K–22. **MEDICARE COVERAGE, BENEFITS, AND ADMINISTRATION**

(Dollars in millions)

	1975 actual	1976 estimate	1977 estimate
Hospital insurance (HI):			
Persons with protection (millions)	23.7	24.3	24.9
Beneficiaries receiving services (millions)	5.5	5.7	5.9
Benefit payments	$10,353	$11,869	$12,960
Administrative expenses	$259	$327	$321
Claims received (millions)	10.3	11.9	12.7
Supplementary medical insurance (SMI):			
Persons with protection (millions)	23.3	23.9	24.6
Beneficiaries receiving services (millions)	12.6	13.2	14.2
Benefit payments	$3,765	$4,687	$5,804
Administrative expenses	$405	$550	$561
Claims received (millions)	97.5	107.8	121.1

Although medicare offers identical benefits to all enrollees, its reimbursements differ substantially in various regions of the country. These differences reflect variations in resource availability, utilization practices, and service costs. Table K–23 summarizes information on these patterns for 1974.

Table K–23. **MEDICARE UTILIZATION AND REIMBURSEMENT BY GEOGRAPHIC REGION**

	North- east	North Central	South	West
Hospital insurance (HI):				
Hospital beds per 1,000 population [1]	4.4	4.8	4.3	3.9
Hospital admissions per 1,000 enrollees [1]	290	350	360	330
Average length of hospital stay (days) [1]	13.9	11.9	10.7	9.2
HI reimbursement per enrollee	$400	$350	$290	$360
Supplementary medical insurance (SMI):				
Physicians per 100,000 population	161	112	109	148
SMI reimbursement per enrollee	$150	$110	$120	$170

[1] Excludes specialty hospitals.

Financial Assistance for Health Care.—The proposed Financial Assistance for Health Care program will consolidate 16 categorical health programs, including medicaid, into a new block grant to the States. The $9 billion in outlays in 1977 will be used primarily to help provide health services to the low-income. Up to 10% of the funds will be available for other health-related purposes.

Other support for health services.—The Federal Government assists in the provision of health services through a variety of activities in addition to medicare and the proposed Financial Assistance for Health Care program.

Limited support is provided to health maintenance organizations (HMOs) in order to help demonstrate the HMO concept in the delivery and organization of health services. Health maintenance organizations deliver comprehensive medical care and disease prevention services on a prepaid basis.

A total of $482 million will be provided for drug abuse treatment, rehabilitation, prevention, and research activities in 1977, an increase of $27 million over 1976 (Table K–24). Most of the federally supported drug abuse activities are funded by HEW through the Social and Rehabilitation Service and the National Institute on Drug Abuse (NIDA) within the Alcohol, Drug Abuse, and Mental Health Administration. NIDA funding will increase from $222 million in 1976 to $248 million in 1977. Drug abuse treatment capacity will be expanded in 1977 and priority given to treating that drug abuse most costly to society. Defense and VA will continue efforts to remedy drug problems among military personnel and veterans. Within the Department of Justice, the Bureau of Prisons administers drug abuse treatment and rehabilitation services for Federal prisoners, the Drug Enforcement Administration conducts education and research programs, and the Law Enforcement Assistance Administration supports a broad range of community efforts to prevent the abuse of drugs. Drug abuse law enforcement activities are discussed in Special Analysis N.

The Federal Government also finances or provides medical services for certain special categories of beneficiaries, particularly American Indians and Alaska Natives; armed forces personnel, dependents, retirees, and veterans; and Federal Government employees.

Table K–24. **ESTIMATED OBLIGATIONS FOR DRUG ABUSE PREVENTION PROGRAMS (in millions of dollars)**

	Obligations			
	1975	1976	TQ	1977
Treatment and rehabilitation (total)	320.4	344.7	65.9	372.8
Department of Health, Education, and Welfare:				
Alcohol, Drug Abuse, and Mental Health Administration	122.4	139.9	13.9	162.8
Social and Rehabilitation Service [1]	79.0	88.0	23.0	94.0
Office of Human Development	8.8	8.8	2.2	9.4
Department of Defense	48.2	47.4	11.5	46.0
Veterans Administration	33.2	35.1	9.1	36.4
Department of Housing and Urban Development	2.8	4.0	.9	4.7
Department of Justice	21.9	20.4	5.1	18.6
Department of Transportation	.1	.1	--------	.1
Other [2]	3.9	.9	.2	.8
Prevention, education, and information (total)	69.6	52.4	4.5	50.5
Department of Health, Education, and Welfare:				
Alcohol, Drug Abuse, and Mental Health Administration	48.7	36.0	1.0	36.2
Office of Education	4.0	2.0	--------	--------
Department of Defense	9.9	8.9	2.2	9.1
Veterans Administration	.4	.4	.1	.4
Department of Housing and Urban Development	.1	.1	--------	.1
Department of Justice	2.3	2.6	.7	2.5
Department of Transportation	.1	.1	--------	.1
Other [2]	4.2	2.3	.5	2.1
Research (total)	43.8	39.7	5.0	40.1
Department of Health, Education, and Welfare:				
Alcohol, Drug Abuse, and Mental Health Administration	34.0	31.6	3.6	34.0
Department of Defense	3.7	2.4	--------	.2
Veterans Administration	1.0	1.0	.2	1.0
Department of Justice	1.6	2.7	.7	2.6
Department of Transportation	.6	.5	.1	.8
Other [2]	2.9	1.5	.4	1.5
Planning, Evaluation, and Coordination (total)	24.3	18.3	3.7	18.9
Department of Health, Education, and Welfare:				
Alcohol, Drug Abuse, and Mental Health Administration	14.7	14.5	2.8	15.2
Department of Defense	2.2	2.6	.6	2.5
Veterans Administration	.2	.2	--------	.2
Department of Justice	.8	.7	.2	.6
Other [2]	6.4	.3	.1	.4
Total	458.1	455.1	79.1	482.2

[1] In 1977, drug abuse treatment funds in this agency would be included in the proposed Financial Assistance for Health Care program.
[2] Includes drug abuse prevention activities within the Departments of Labor, State, and Agriculture; the terminated Special Action Office for Drug Abuse Prevention; and other agencies.

Indian health services.—The funding level for Indian health services and facilities will rise to $355 million in 1977, a $24 million increase over 1976. These funds are used to provide comprehensive health care, with an emphasis on ambulatory care, as well as to construct hospitals, clinics, personal quarters, and sanitation facilities.

Over the last quarter century, the health status of Indians and Alaska Natives has greatly improved. Since 1950, for example, there has been an increase in Indian average life expectancy of 4.6 years or 8%, a 78% decline in infant mortality, and a 72% decline in deaths due to diseases such as influenza and pneumonia. In recent years, the overall health status of Indians and Alaska Natives has come closer to that of the general U.S. population, as indicated in Table K–25. Differences in health status remain, however, especially in connection with causes of death associated with reservation social conditions. Efforts to further improve the health status of American Indians will continue in the coming years.

Based on an eligible federally recognized Indian population of 518,000 in 1977, spending by the Indian Health Service in 1977 will result in over $685 per beneficiary, or over $2,740 per Indian family of four. This includes over $40 million for the construction of Indian hospitals, clinics, sanitation projects, and staff housing for Indian Health Service personnel, but does not include spending from other Federal sources for the same beneficiary group.

Table K–25. **SELECTED INDICATORS OF HEALTH STATUS OF AMERICAN INDIANS AND THE GENERAL U.S. POPULATION** (annual rates)

	Indians and Alaska Natives				General population	
	1950	1960	1970	1974	1970	1974
Birth rate (per 1,000 population)	36.2	42.7	32.6	30.8	18.4	15.0
Death rate (per 1,000 population)	12.9	9.1	7.7	7.2	9.5	9.1
Average life expectancy at birth (years)	60.0	61.7	64.0	64.6	70.9	72.0
Infant mortality rate (deaths under 1 year of age per 1,000 live births) [1]	85.8	50.3	23.8	18.7	20.0	16.5
Leading causes of death (per 100,000 population):						
Heart	148.8	135.5	142.0	133.4	362.0	353.1
Accidents	125.9	155.2	157.1	140.5	56.4	48.9
Influenza and pneumonia	108.0	95.0	38.6	29.7	30.9	25.7
Certain diseases of early infancy	77.3	66.7	29.6	21.0	21.3	13.2
Cancer	60.3	65.2	62.6	66.6	162.8	169.5
Cirrhosis of liver	7.7	20.7	45.5	46.2	15.5	16.0

[1] Excludes Alaska Natives.

Medical care to active and retired military personnel and their dependents.—In 1977, DOD will operate 180 hospitals directly and will contract with community facilities to provide additional care for its beneficiaries. Outlays for these services will be $3.8 billion in 1977, or $326 million more than in 1976.

Medical care to veterans.—The Veterans Administration (VA) will operate 172 hospitals, 107 long-term care facilities, and 229 outpatient clinics. It will provide VA inpatient care for 1.3 million veterans and will fund over 15.7 million outpatient medical and dental visits to VA facilities. It also will finance care for 92,000 inpatients, and 2.4 million outpatient medical visits in non-VA facilities. Total VA outlays for health activities, including construction of health care facilities, will be $4.5 billion in 1977—an increase of $379 million over 1976.

Health insurance for Federal employees.—Health benefits are provided to 3.1 million Federal civilian employees and annuitants and their 6.2 million dependents under the Federal employees health benefits programs managed by the Civil Service Commission. In 1977, Federal payments to finance these programs will increase by $40 million to a total of $383 million.

Tax expenditures.—After the proposed Financial Assistance for Health Care block grant and medicare, the largest Federal support for health care results from special provisions of the tax laws. The exclusion of employer health insurance contributions from the taxable income of employees is estimated to result in a $4.2 billion tax subsidy for employees in 1977. An additional $2.1 billion in revenue loss will result from itemized deductions that individuals take in their income tax computations for certain health expenditures and insurance premiums.

Distribution of health care outlays by age group and economic status.—Table K–26 distributes Federal outlays for the financing and direct provision of hospital and medical services among three major age groups and between indigent and nonindigent persons. Federal funds for the development of health resources and for prevention and control of health problems are excluded from the table, since they are not normally distributed by population group or income. Unlike other tables in this special analysis, Table K–26 does not include funds for health care provided to foreign nationals, since poverty levels in other countries differ from the U.S. poverty level.

The Financial Assistance for Health Care program will require that 90% of the funds be used by States to provide personal health services. Table K–26 and other tables in this special analysis assume that Financial Assistance for Health Care funds will initially be spent along the same general lines as the grant funds they replace.

Table K–26. **ESTIMATED FEDERAL HEALTH CARE OUTLAYS BY POPULATION AND INCOME GROUPS (in millions of dollars)**

	Outlays			
	1975 actual	1976 estimate	TQ estimate	1977 estimate
Total, all recipients	30, 425	35, 364	9, 154	38, 611
Aged (65 and over)	16, 888	19, 660	5, 111	21, 759
Other adults (19–64)	10, 722	12, 411	3, 179	13, 331
Children and youth (0–18)	2, 816	3, 292	864	3, 521
Indigent persons, total	9, 002	10, 531	2, 632	11, 038
Aged (65 and over)	3, 851	4, 663	1, 161	4, 856
Other adults (19–64)	4, 122	4, 696	1, 162	4, 996
Children and youth (0–18)	1, 029	1, 172	308	1, 187
Nonindigent persons, total	21, 423	24, 833	6, 522	27, 573
Aged (65 and over)	13, 036	14, 998	3, 949	16, 903
Other adults (19–64)	6, 600	7, 715	2, 017	8, 335
Children and youth (0–18)	1, 787	2, 120	556	2, 334

Prevention and Control of Health Problems

The Federal Government supports programs to prevent and control health problems, mainly in the areas of communicable disease control, occupational health, consumer safety, environmental control, accident prevention, and foreign health assistance. Table K–27 shows Federal outlays for the prevention and control of health problems, which are estimated at $1,270 million in 1977.

Disease prevention and control.—The Federal Government supports various programs to prevent diseases and injuries through research, regulatory activities, provision of preventive services, and

Table K–27. **FEDERAL OUTLAYS FOR THE PREVENTION AND CONTROL OF HEALTH PROBLEMS (in millions of dollars)**

	Outlays			
	1975 actual	1976 estimate	TQ estimate	1977 estimate
Disease prevention and control_____	460	462	98	366
Mental illness prevention and control_____	124	135	32	98
Environmental control_____	51	70	22	79
Consumer safety_____	424	471	126	477
Occupational safety and health_____	173	211	58	251
Total, prevention and control_____	**1,232**	**1,349**	**337**	**1,270**

public education. Categorical Federal grants for State and local activities in disease prevention and control will be consolidated into the new Financial Assistance for Health Care program.

The 1977 budget places priority on efforts to detect and eliminate hazards in the workplace. Outlays for these activities will increase by $40 million to $251 million in 1977. An increased number of occupational safety and health standards will be developed and promulgated by HEW and the Departments of Labor and the Interior.

The Alcohol, Drug Abuse, and Mental Health Administration will continue to support clearinghouses, media campaigns, and other activities to help reduce mental illness in 1977. These efforts assist States and localities in developing mental health programs and provide the public with accurate information about mental health and substance abuse problems.

Consumer safety.—In 1976, outlays of $477 million will be spent on efforts to protect the public from unsafe foods, drugs, and other products, and to reduce injuries from automobile accidents.

The Food and Drug Administration (FDA) in HEW will expand its efforts to help assure the quality and safety of drugs, medical devices, and foods. FDA and the Environmental Protection Agency will continue support of long-term studies of the effects of low concentrations of chemicals in the environment and foods.

In 1977, the Consumer Product Safety Commission will continue research, information dissemination, and regulatory measures to protect consumers from unreasonable risks from certain consumer products. The Department of Transportation will also work to prevent automobile accidents and reduce injuries from accidents through various motor vehicle and highway design safety standards. In 1974, about 46,000 deaths resulted from motor vehicle accidents, a 17% reduction from the 56,000 deaths in 1973. Much of the decline is thought to be related to lower speed limits on highways.

Environmental control.—The major Federal effort in environmental control is administered by the Environmental Protection Agency, which maintains surveillance of the effects of environmental pollution on the health of the American people, promulgates environmental standards, and monitors compliance.

Foreign Health Assistance

In 1977, the United States will provide $291 million for health assistance to other nations. These funds will support efforts by the Agency for International Development, the Peace Corps, and international agencies to which the United States contributes financially, such as the World Health Organization and the Pan American Health Organization. The funds are distributed across all categories of health activities.

EXPENDITURES FOR HEALTH ACTIVITIES BY AGENCY

The following tables distribute the health-related outlays of Federal agencies by the categories used in this analysis. Health activities of HEW, the Consumer Product Safety Commission, and parts of the Civil Service Commission and the Departments of Agriculture, Housing and Urban Development, Interior, and Labor are included under the health function (550) in Part 5 of the budget document. Health-related outlays of all other agencies are, because of their major missions, assigned to other functions. The following tables, therefore, indicate the predominant budget functional code for each agency. Other special analyses such as those on research and development, education, and work force also include some of the same outlays in their tabulations.

Table K–28. FEDERAL OUTLAYS FOR MEDICAL AND HEALTH-RELATED ACTIVITIES BY AGENCY, 1975 (in millions of dollars)

	Functional code	Health research	Training and education	Construction	Health planning activities	Direct Federal hospital and medical services	Indirect Federal hospital and medical services	Prevention and control of health problems	Total
Department of Health, Education, and Welfare (total)	550	1,867	928	542	162	255	23,002	639	27,396
Health Services Administration	551	9	28	48	11	208	578	153	1,035
Health Resources Administration	550	58	528	369	126		6	12	1,099
Alcohol, Drug Abuse, and Mental Health Administration	550	114	152	31		43	515	96	950
Center for Disease Control	553	42	2					111	154
National Institutes of Health	550	1,598	177	82				33	1,889
Food and Drug Administration	553	27		1				172	201
Assistant Secretary for Health	550	4		2	21	4	11	2	45
Social Security Administration	551				1		14,781		14,781
Social and Rehabilitation Service	551	2			3	1	6,876		6,879
Other HEW	550	13	42	9			235	59	361
Department of Defense	051	104	231	96	22	2,261	567	26	3,285
Veterans Administration	703	93	198	122	38	3,018	211		3,665
Department of Housing and Urban Development	451			164			1		203
Department of Agriculture	350	47		1				259	307
Environmental Protection Agency	304	20							20
National Aeronautics and Space Administration	250	59						3	62
Energy Research and Development Administration	251	143		6				95	244
Department of Labor	553	1	9					81	91
Department of State	150		7		12		1	24	44
National Science Foundation	250	44							44
Department of the Interior	300	35	2	3			8	2	48
Department of Transportation	400	15			10	9		23	60
Department of Justice	750			3		23	3	3	32
Other agencies		31	8	13	71		40	77	239
Agency contributions to employee health funds	551						1,050		1,050
Total outlays for health, 1975		2,459	1,384	949	316	5,567	24,883	1,232	36,790

Table K–29. FEDERAL OUTLAYS FOR MEDICAL AND HEALTH-RELATED ACTIVITIES BY AGENCY, 1976 (in millions of dollars)

	Functional code	Health research	Training and education	Construc-tion	Health planning activities	Direct Federal hospital and medical services	Indirect Federal hospital and medical services	Preven-tion and control of health problems	Total
Department of Health, Education, and Welfare (total)	550	2,109	939	512	160	280	27,047	664	31,711
Health Services Administration	551	14	32	80	12	222	712	144	1,217
Health Resources Administration	550	33	558	340	116		5	9	1,062
Alcohol, Drug Abuse, and Mental Health Administration	550	134	127	36		53	425	105	880
Center for Disease Control	553	43	1					113	157
National Institutes of Health	550	1,837	173	47				39	2,095
Food and Drug Administration	553	28		3				191	222
Assistant Secretary for Health	550	7		1	25	5	16	5	59
Social Security Administration	551						17,433		17,433
Social and Rehabilitition Service	551	1				1	8,220		8,222
Other HEW	550	13	47	5	6		235	59	365
Department of Defense	051	114	249	171	23	2,404	549	29	3,517
Veterans Administrations	703	97	253	191	23	3,326	251		4,142
Department of Housing and Urban Development	451			168			14	5	209
Department of Agriculture	350	59		6				286	351
Environmental Protection Agency	304	63							63
National Aeronautics and Space Administration	250	67						3	70
Energy Research and Development Administration	251	173		10				117	300
Department of Labor	553	3	14					103	119
Department of State	150		8		13		1	27	49
National Science Foundation	250	43							43
Department of the Interior	300	39		4			9	2	54
Department of Transportation	400	24	2	1	8	10	4	26	70
Department of Justice	750	2		2		24		3	36
Other agencies		35	13	15	109		46	84	302
Agency contributions to employee health funds	551						1,450		1,450
Total outlays for health, 1976		2,826	1,477	1,082	336	6,046	29,370	1,349	42,486

Table K–30. FEDERAL OUTLAYS FOR MEDICAL AND HEALTH-RELATED ACTIVITIES BY AGENCY, TRANSITION QUARTER

(In millions of dollars)

	Functional code	Health research	Training and education	Construction	Health planning activities	Direct Federal hospital and medical services	Indirect Federal hospital and medical services	Prevention and control of health problems	Total
Department of Health, Education, and Welfare (total)	550	517	180	74	41	83	7,059	140	8,095
Health Services Administration	551	3	9	17	3	65	181	26	306
Health Resources Administration	550	25	118	41	31	---	2	2	218
Alcohol, Drug Abuse, and Mental Health Administration	550	30	17	6	---	17	75	25	170
Center for Disease Control	553	16	---	---	---	---	---	31	47
National Institutes of Health	550	434	28	8	---	---	---	6	476
Food and Drug Administration	553	7	---	1	---	---	---	49	57
Assistant Secretary for Health	550	1	---	---	6	1	5	1	15
Social Security Administration	551	---	---	---	---	---	4,562	---	4,562
Social and Rehabilitation Service	551	---	---	---	---	---	2,230	---	2,230
Other HEW	550	---	---	---	---	---	4	---	14
Department of Defense	051	29	67	26	1	603	135	8	867
Veterans Administration	703	25	65	74	6	795	61	---	1,026
Department of Housing and Urban Development	451	---	---	54	---	---	6	2	62
Department of Agriculture	350	15	---	3	---	---	---	80	98
Environmental Protection Agency	304	16	---	---	---	---	---	---	16
National Aeronautics and Space Administration	250	20	---	---	---	---	---	1	21
Energy Research and Development Administration	251	51	---	3	---	---	---	31	85
Department of Labor	553	1	3	---	---	---	---	28	31
Department of State	150	---	4	---	11	---	---	22	37
National Science Foundation	250	11	---	---	---	---	---	---	11
Department of the Interior	300	10	---	---	---	2	---	---	13
Department of Transportation	400	10	---	---	2	2	---	4	19
Department of Justice	750	---	---	---	---	6	---	1	9
Other agencies		6	3	6	23	1	10	20	66
Agency contributions to employee health funds	551	---	---	---	---	---	405	---	406
Total outlays for health, transition quarter		711	322	240	83	1,490	7,679	337	10,862

Table K-31. FEDERAL OUTLAYS FOR MEDICAL AND HEALTH-RELATED ACTIVITIES BY AGENCY, 1977 (in millions of dollars)

	Functional code	Health research	Training and education	Construction	Health planning activities	Direct Federal hospital and medical services	Indirect Federal hospital and medical services	Prevention and control of health problems	Total
Department of Health, Education, and Welfare (total)	550	2,187	656	360	213	204	29,634	531	33,792
Health Services Administration	551	2	23	56	10	143	608	104	946
Health Resources Administration	550	26	388	241	151	—	4	8	819
Alcohol, Drug Abuse, and Mental Health Administration	550	128	62	27	—	55	343	72	687
Center for Disease Control	553	38	—	—	—	—	1	88	127
National Institutes of Health	550	1,955	151	38	—	—	—	44	2,188
Food and Drug Administration	553	29	—	4	—	—	—	194	227
Assistant Secretary for Health	550	8	1	1	46	5	—	20	81
Social Security Administration	551	—	—	—	1	—	8,980	—	9,062
Social and Rehabilitation Service	551	—	—	—	5	—	19,646	—	19,646
Other HEW	550	1	30	1	—	—	34	—	53
Department of Defense	051	125	246	325	—	2,512	585	47	3,841
Veterans Administration	703	97	271	308	23	3,532	301	—	4,521
Department of Housing and Urban Development	451	—	—	265	—	—	33	11	308
Department of Agriculture	350	60	—	5	—	—	—	307	371
Environmental Protection Agency	304	80	—	—	—	—	—	—	80
National Aeronautics and Space Administration	250	72	—	—	—	—	—	4	76
Energy Research and Development Administration	251	253	1	19	—	—	—	142	415
Department of Labor	553	6	20	—	—	—	—	99	125
Department of State	150	—	8	—	17	—	—	34	59
National Science Foundation	250	49	—	—	—	—	—	—	49
Department of the Interior	300	40	—	2	9	—	—	2	53
Department of Transportation	400	48	2	1	—	21	—	20	101
Department of Justice	750	2	—	2	—	26	4	3	37
Other agencies		29	14	15	148	—	37	70	312
Agency contributions to employee health funds	551	—	—	—	—	—	1,793	—	1,793
Total outlays for health, 1977		**3,048**	**1,217**	**1,309**	**409**	**6,285**	**32,396**	**1,270**	**45,935**

Bibliography

PUBLIC DOCUMENTS

The bibliography of public documents comprises the body of documentary material examined for this compilation. It was prepared by the Public Documents Series editors and represents the significant, publicly available government documents pertaining to the scope of this book. The time period covered is from 1970 to 1976.

1. Department of Health, Education, and Welfare. *A Comparison of the Costs of Major National Health Insurance Proposals,* by Gordon R. Trapnell Associates. Executive summary prepared by Saul Waldman. October 1976. 50 pp.
2. Department of Health, Education, and Welfare. *Estimated Health Expenditures Under Selected National Health Insurance Bills: A Report to the Congress.* Washington, D.C., 1974. 75 pp.
3. Department of Health, Education, and Welfare. Health Resources Administration. Bureau of Health Manpower. *Impact of National Health Insurance. The Case of the Comprehensive Health Insurance Plan: An Issue Paper,* by Larry W. Lacy. Report no. 75-139. March 20, 1975. 20 pp.
4. Department of Health, Education, and Welfare. Health Resources Administration. National Center for Health Statistics. *Health–United States 1975.* DHEW publication no. HRA 76-1232. Washington, D.C.: GPO, 1976. 612 pp.
5. Department of Health, Education, and Welfare. Health Resources Administration. Public Health Service. *Trends Affecting U.S. Health Care System.* Prepared by the Cambridge Research Institute. (Health Planning Information Series, 1). HRA 76-14503. October 1975. 430 pp.
6. Department of Health, Education, and Welfare. National Institutes of Health. Bureau of Health Manpower Education. *Assessment and Evaluation of the Impact of Archtypal National Health Insurance Plans on U.S. Health Manpower Requirements.* Prepared by Lien-fu Huang and Elwood W. Shomo. Washington, D.C., February 1974.
7. Department of Health, Education, and Welfare. Social Security Administration. *National Health Expenditures, Fiscal Year 1975.* DHEW publication no. SSA 76-11703. February 1976. 21 pp.
8. Department of Health, Education, and Welfare. Social Security Administration. Office of Research and Statistics. *Compendium of National Health Expenditures Data.* Compiled by Barbara S. Cooper, Nancy L. Worthington, and Mary F. McGee. DHEW publication no. SSA 76-11927. January 1976. 113 pp.
9. Department of Health, Education, and Welfare. Social Security Administration. *Health Insurance Administrative Costs,* by Ronald J. Vogel, and Roger D. Blair. DHEW publication no. SSA 76-11856. Staff paper no. 21. Washington, D.C.: GPO, 1975. 123 pp.

10. Department of Health, Education, and Welfare. Social Security Administration. *National Health Insurance Proposals: Provisions of Bills Introduced in the 94th Congress as of February 1976*. Compiled by Saul Waldman. Washington, D.C.: GPO, 1976. 210 pp.

11. Department of Health, Education, and Welfare. Social Security Administration. *National Health Systems in Eight Countries*, by Joseph G. Simantis. DHEW publication no. SSA 75-11924. Washington, D.C.: GPO, 1975. 107 pp.

12. Department of Health, Education, and Welfare. Social Security Administration. *Public Attitudes Toward Social Security: 1935–1965*, by Michael E. Schlitz. Research report no. 33. Washington, D.C.: GPO, 1970. 231 pp.

13. Office of the President. 1969–1974 (Nixon). "Comprehensive Health Insurance Plan." The president's message to Congress. February 6, 1974. *Weekly Compilation of Presidential Documents*, vol. 10, no. 6, pp. 178–185.

14. Office of the President. 1974–1976 (Ford). Office of the White House Press Secretary. "Financial Assistance for Health Care Act." Supplemental fact sheet. Washington, D.C. February 25, 1976. 9 pp.

15. Office of the President. Office of Management and Budget. *Special Analysis: Budget of the United States Government, Fiscal Year 1977*. March 1976.

16. U.S. Congress. Congressional Budget Office. *Budget Options for Fiscal Year 1978: A Report to the Senate and House Committees on the Budget*. February 1977. 202 pp.

17. U.S. Congress. *Congressional Record*, 94th Cong., 1st sess., January 14, 1975. pp. H40–H42.

18. U.S. Congress. *Congressional Record*, 94th Cong., 1st sess., January 15, 1975. pp. S42–S45.

19. U.S. Congress. *Congressional Record*, 94th Cong., 1st sess., April 22, 1975. pp. H3117–H3118.

20. U.S. Congress, *Congressional Record*, 94th Cong., 1st sess., October 3, 1975. pp. S17449–S17457.

21. U.S. Congress. House of Representatives. Committee on Interstate and Foreign Commerce. Subcommittee on Health and the Environment. *National Health Insurance–Major Proposals*. Hearings on consideration of the major proposals relating to national health insurance. Vol. 1. December 8, 9 & 10, 1975. Serial no. 94-60. Washington, D.C.: GPO, 1976. 1162 pp.

22. U.S. Congress. House of Representatives. Committee on Interstate and Foreign Commerce. Subcommittee on Health and the Environment. *National Health Insurance–Major Issues*. Hearings on consideration of the major issues relating to national health insurance. Vol. 2. February 3, 4, 5, 9, 10, 11, 17, 18, 19, 23, 24 & 25, 1976. Serial no. 94-90. Washington, D.C.: GPO, 1976. 828 pp.

23. U.S. Congress. House of Representatives. Committee on Interstate and Foreign Commerce. Subcommittee on Health and the Environment. *National Health Insurance–Major Issues*. Hearings on consideration of the major issues relating to national health insurance. Vol. 3. February 3, 4, 5, 9, 10, 11, 17, 18, 19, 23, 24, 25 & 26, 1976. Serial no. 94-91. Washington, D.C.: GPO, 1976. 760 pp.

24. U.S. Congress. House of Representatives. Committee on Ways and Means. *National Health Insurance*. Hearings. Vol. 1. April 24, 1974. Washington, D.C.: GPO, 1974. 560 pp.

25. U.S. Congress. House of Representatives. Committee on Ways and Means. *National Health Insurance*. Hearings. Vol. 2. April 24 (continuation), 25 & 26, 1974. Washington, D.C.: GPO, 1974. 475 pp.

26. U.S. Congress. House of Representatives. Committee on Ways and Means. *National Health Insurance*. Vol. 3. May 3, 10 & 17, 1974. Washington, D.C.: GPO, 1974. 487 pp.

27. U.S. Congress. House of Representatives. Committee on Ways and Means. *National Health Insurance*. Hearings. Vol. 4. May 23 & 31, 1974. Washington, D.C.: GPO, 1974. 527 pp.

28. U.S. Congress. House of Representatives. Committee on Ways and Means. *National Health Insurance*. Hearings. Vol. 5. June 7 & 14, 1974. Washington, D.C.: GPO, 1974. 417 pp.

29. U.S. Congress. House of Representatives. Committee on Ways and Means. *National Health Insurance*. Hearings. Vol. 6. June 21, 1974. Washington, D.C.: GPO, 1974. 289 pp.
30. U.S. Congress. House of Representatives. Committee on Ways and Means. *National Health Insurance*. Hearings. Vol. 7. June 28, 1974. Washington, D.C.: GPO, 1974. 461 pp.
31. U.S. Congress. House of Representatives. Committee on Ways and Means. *National Health Insurance*. Hearings. Vol. 8. July 1, 2 & 9, 1974. Washington, D.C.: GPO, 1974. 313 pp.
32. U.S. Congress. House of Representatives. Committee on Ways and Means. *National Health Insurance*. Hearings. Vol. 9. Material submitted for the record. Washington, D.C.: GPO, 1974. 398 pp.
33. U.S. Congress. House of Representatives. Committee on Ways and Means. *National Health Insurance Resource Book*. April 11, 1974. Washington, D.C.: GPO, 1974. 574 pp.
34. U.S. Congress. House of Representatives. Committee on Ways and Means. *National Health Insurance Resource Book*. Revised edition. August 30, 1976. Washington, D.C.: GPO, 1976. 505 pp.
35. U.S. Congress. House of Representatives. Committee on Ways and Means. Subcommittee on Health. *National Health Insurance*. Panel discussions. July 10, 11, 17 & 24; September 12, 1975.
36. U.S. Congress. House of Representatives. Committee on Ways and Means. Subcommittee on Health. *National Health Insurance*. Public hearings. Parts 1, 2 & 3. November; December 1975. Washington, D.C.: GPO, 1976.
37. U.S. Congress. Library of Congress. Congressional Research Service. *Key Facts About Private Health Insurance*, by Susan Bailey. Multilith 76-73 ed. February 26, 1976. Revised April 5, 1976. 6 pp.
38. U.S. Congress. Library of Congress. Congressional Research Service. *National Health Insurance*, by Edward Klebe. Educational and Public Welfare Division. Issue Brief IB73015. December 8, 1973. Updated July 15, 1976. 6 pp.
39. U.S. Congress. Library of Congress. Congressional Research Service. *National Health Insurance: A Summary of Major Legislative Proposals Introduced into the 94th Congress*, by Kay Cavalier. January 5, 1976.
40. U.S. Congress. Library of Congress. Congressional Research Service. *Summary of Health Legislation, 1959 through 1975: 85th Congress-94th Congress, 1st session*, by Susan Bailey, and Richard Price. Multilith no. 75-261 ed. Revised January 7, 1976. 29 pp.
41. U.S. Congress. Senate. Committee on Finance. *National Health Insurance*. Hearings. May 21, 22 & 23, 1974.
42. U.S. Congress. Senate. Committee on Labor and Public Welfare. *National Health Insurance*. Hearings. on S. 4323 and S. 3830. September 23, 1970. Part 1.

SELECTED REFERENCES ON HEALTH INSURANCE IN OTHER COUNTRIES

This bibliography was compiled from two sources: *National Health Systems in Eight Countries* ([11], pp. 104–107), an HEW Publication, and *National Health Insurance Resource Book* ([33], pp. 401–402), prepared by the House of Representatives' Ways and Means Committee.

Abel-Smith, B, *An International Study of Health Expenditures, and Its Relevance for Health Planning*, Public Health Paper No. 32, World Health Organization, Geneva, 1967.

Anderson, Odin, *Health Care, Can There Be Equity? The United States, Sweden, and England*, John Wiley and Sons, New York, 1972.

Charron, K.C., *Health Services, Health Insurance, and Their Inter-Relationship--A Study of Selected Countries,* Department of National Health and Welfare, Ottawa, 1963.

Fry, John and Farndale, W.A.J., *International Medical Care,* Washington Square East, Wallingford, Pa., 1972.

Fry, John, *Medicine in Three Societies--Comparison of Medical Care in the USSR, USA and UK,* American Elsevier Pub. Co., Inc., New York, 1970.

Fulcher, Derick H., *A Study of Some Aspects of Medical Care Systems in Industrialised Countries,* International Labour Office, Geneva, 1973.

Glaser, W.A., *Paying the Doctor,* Johns Hopkins Press, Baltimore, 1970.

Health Services Financing, British Medical Association, 1970.

Hogarth, J., *The Payment of the Physician.* Macmillan Company, New York, 1963.

Langendonck, J. van, *De harmonisering van de sociale verzekering voor gezondheidszorgen in de E.E.G.,* Catholic University of Leuven, 1971.

National Health Insurance Resource Book, Part III, *Health Financing and Delivery Systems of Selected Foreign Nations,* U.S. Govt. Print. Off., Washington, 1974, pp. 275-428.

Public Health Reports, *Health Insurance Programs and Plans of Western Europe,* Govt. Print. Off., Washington, vol. 62, No. 11, Mar. 14, 1947.

_____, *Voluntary Health Insurance in Western Europe,* Govt. Print. Off., Washington, vol. 62, No. 21, May 23, 1947.

Roemer, M.I., *The Organization of Medical Care Under Social Security,* International Labour Office, Geneva, 1969.

Schoeck, H. (ed.), *Financing Medical Care,* Caxton Printers, Ltd., Caldwell, Idaho, 1962.

World Health Organization, Regional Office of Europe, *Health Services in Europe,* Copenhagen, 1965.

AUSTRALIA

Dewdney, J.C.H., *Australian Health Services,* John Wiley and Sons, New York, 1973.

"Health Insurance--Planning Committee Report," Australian Government Publishing Service, Canberra, 1973.

Kewley, T.H., *Social Security in Australia,* Sydney University Press, 1965.

Ryan, J.G.P., "General Practice in Australia," *International Journal of Health Services,* vol. 2, No. 2, 1972, pp. 273-284.

CANADA

Detweiler, I.F., *Health Care Through Government,* Office of Health Care Finance, Sydney, N.SW., Australia, 1972.

Fisher, Peter, *Prescription for National Health Insurance*, North River Press, Inc., Croton-on-Hudson, 1973.

Hastings, J.E.F., *Monograph on the Organization of Medical Care Within the Framework of Social Security*, International Labour Office, Geneva, 1968.

_____, "Federal-Provincial Insurance for Hospital and Physician's Care in Canada," *International Journal of Health Services*, vol. 1, No. 4, 1971, pp. 398-414.

Health and Welfare Canada, *National Health Expenditures in Canada, 1960-1971 With Comparative Data for the United States*, Ottawa, 1973.

McWhinney, I.R., "General Practice in Canada," *International Journal of Health Services*, vol. 2, No. 2, 1972, pp. 229-237.

Taylor, Malcolm, "The Canadian Health Insurance Program," *Public Administration Review*, January-February 1974 p. 36.

FRANCE

Bridgman, R.F., "Medical Care Under Social Security in France," *International Journal of Health Services*, November 1971, p. 334.

Foulon, A., Comptes Nationaux de la Santé, CREDOC, Paris, 1972.

Ministère de la Santé Publique, *Tableaux-Santé et Securité Sociale*, Paris (editions for selected years).

Rosch, G., et al., *Elements de Economique Médicale*, Flammarion Medecine-Sciences, Paris, 1973.

FEDERAL REPUBLIC OF GERMANY

Kastner, F., *Monograph on the Organization of Medical Care Within the Framework of Social Security*, International Labour Office, Geneva, 1968.

Pflanz, M., "German Health Insurance: The Evolution and Current Problems of the Pioneer System," *International Journal of Health Services*, November 1971.

Sozialbericht, Annual report by the Bundesiminister für Arbeit and Sozial Ordnung, Bonn (for various years).

NETHERLANDS

Kapteijn, J.C.O., et al., "The General Practitioner in the Netherlands--General Outlines of Health Care," *International Journal of Health Services*, vol. 2, No. 2, 1972, pp. 263-271.

Stolte, J.B., "Health Services in the Netherlands," *World Hospitals*, vol. VI, No. 3, July 1970, pp. 147-156.

NEW ZEALAND

Bernstein, Arthur H., "No-Fault Compensation for Personal Injury in New Zealand," *Report of the Secretary's Commission on Medical Malpractice, Appendix,* U.S. Department of Health, Education, and Welfare, 1973, pp. 836-853.

"Social Security in New Zealand," *Report of the Royal Commission of Inquiry,* Wellington, 1972.

Ward, J.T., and Tatchell, P.M., "Health Expenditure in New Zealand," *Economic Record,* vol, 48, No. 124, December 1972, pp. 500-516.

SWEDEN

Andrews, Joseph L., "Medical Care in Sweden--Lessons for America," *Journal of American Medical Association,* vol. 223, No. 12, Mar. 19, 1973, pp. 1367-75.

_____, "Primary Medical Care in Sweden," *Rhode Island Medical Journal,* vol. 55, No. 5, May 1972, pp. 152-172.

Sosial Sikkerheit i de Nordiske Land, Grondahl and Son, Oslo (annal reports of various years).

Swedish Health Services System, Lectures from the A.C.H.A.'s Twenty-Second Fellows Seminar, Stockholm, 1969. American College of Hospital Administrators, Chicago, 1971.

Werkö, Lars, "Swedish Medical Care in Transition," *The New England Journal of Medicine,* Feb. 18, 1971, pp. 360-366.

UNITED KINGDOM

Battistella, Roger M., and Chester, Theodore E., "The 1974 Reorganization of the British National Health Service--Aims and Issues," *The New England Journal of Medicine,* vol. 289, No. 12, Sept. 20, 1973, pp. 610-615.

Daniels, Roberts S., "The British National health Service," *Hospitals,* vol. 45, June 16, 1971, pp. 39-44.

ILO Social Security Branch, *Monograph on the Organization of Medical Care Within the Framework of Social Security,* International Labour Office, Geneva, 1967.

Mechanic, David, "General Medical Practice in England and Wales," *New England Journal of Medicine,* vol. 279, No. 13, Sept. 26, 1968, pp. 680-688.

Mencher, Samuel, *British Private Medical Practice and the National Health Service,* University of Pittsburgh Press, 1968.

UNITED KINGDOM (from [33])

Simanis, J.G.: Medical care expenditures in seven countries. Soc. Secur. Bull. 36: 39-42, 1973.

Great Britain, Department of Health and Social Security, National Health
Service Reorganization: England (Command Paper 5055). London. Her
Majesty's Stationery Office, 1972.

Great Britain, Department of Health and Social Security, Management Arrangements for the Reorganized National Health Service in Wales (Grey
Book). London. Her Majesty's Stationery Office, 1972.

Great Britain, House of Lords, National Health Service Reorganization
Bill, November 15, 1972, London. Her Majesty's Stationery Office,
1972.

Great Britain, National Health Service, Ministry of Health. The Administrative Structure of the Medical and Related Services in England and
Wales (Green Paper). London. Her Majesty's Stationery Office, 1968.

Great Britain, National Health Service, Department of Health and Social
Security. The Future Structure of the National Health Service (Green
Paper). London. Her Majesty's Stationery Office, 1970.

Great Britain, Department of Health and Social Security. National Health
Service Reorganization (Consultative Document). London. Department of
Health and Social Security, 1971.

Great Britain, Department of Health and Social Security. Report on the
Working Party on Medical Administrators (Hunter Report). London. Her
Majesty's Stationery Office, 1972.

Silver, G.A.: The community-medicine specialist--Britain mandates health
service reorganization. N. Engl. J. Med. 287: 1299-1301, 1972.

Great Britain, House of Commons. Parliamentary Debates (Hansard). March
26, 1973. Vol. 853, No. 85, Cols. 923-1053. London. Her Majesty's
Stationery Office, 1973.

Great Britain, House of Commons. Parliamentary Debates (Hansard). March
27, 1973. Vol. 853, No. 86, Cols. 1101-1234. London. Her Majesty's
Stationery Office, 1973.

Editorial, Manchester Guardian. June 6, 1973, p. 14.

Appendix 1
List of Acronyms

AALL: American Association for Labor Legislation

AAMC: Association of American Medical Colleges

ADA: American Dental Association

AFDC: aid to families with dependent children

AFL-CIO: American Federation of Labor/Congress of Industrial Organizations

AHA: American Hospital Association

AMA: American Medical Association

AMPAC: American Medical Political Action Committee

AOA: American Osteopathic Association

CAASI: Canadian Association of Accident and Sickness Insurers

CBO: Congressional Budget Office

CCMC: Committee on the Cost of Medical Care

CHIP: Comprehensive Health Insurance Plan

COPE: Committee on Political Education

CPA: Certified Public Accountant

CPI: Consumer Price Index

DHEW: Department of Health, Education, and Welfare

DM: Deutsche Mark

DOD: Department of Defense

ECF: extended care facilities

EHI: employee health insurance

EPSDT: early and periodic screening, diagnosis, and treatment

ESP: Economic Stabilization Program

FDA: Food and Drug Administration

FMG: graduate of foreign medical school

FTC: Federal Trade Commission

FTE: full time employees

FY: fiscal year

GAO: General Accounting Office

GNP: gross national product

GP: general practicioner

HCC: health care corporation

HEW: Department of Health, Education, and Welfare

HI: hospital insurance

HIAA: Health Insurance Association of America

HMO: health maintenance organization

HPS: Armed Forces Health Professions Scholarships

HRA: Health Resources Administration

HSA: Health Systems Agencies

ICF: intermediate care facilities

JAMA: Journal of the American Medical Association

LCME: Licensed Colleges of Medical Education

LPN: licensed practical nurse

NAIC: National Association of Insurance Commissioners

Note: This list was compiled by the editors of the Public Documents Series.

NCHS: National Center for Health
   Statistics
NHI: national health insurance
NHS: National Health Service
NIDA: National Institute on Drug Abuse
NIH: National Institutes of Health
NSF: National Science Foundation

OEO: Office of Economic Opportunity
OMB: Office of Management and Budget
ORS: Office of Research and Statistics
OTC: over-the-counter

PHS: Public Health Service
PSRO: Professional Standards Review
   Organizations

RN: registered nurse

SHC: State Health Commission
SMI: supplementary medical insurance
SMSA: standard metropolitan statistical
   area
SNF: skilled nursing facilities
SNH: skilled nursing homes
SRS: Social and Rehabilitation Service
SSA: Social Security Administration
SSI: supplemental security income

TDI: temporary disability insurance
TQ: third quarter

UAW: United Auto Workers
UR: Utilization Review

VA: Veterans Administration
VNA: Visiting Nurses Association

Appendix 2
National Health Insurance
Bills Introduced

This appendix contains detailed descriptions of the four congressional health measures addressed in Chapter 1 of this volume, as well as summaries of other similar bills. The four are: (1) the Kennedy-Corman Health Security Act of 1975 (S. 3/H.R. 21); (2) Ullman's National Health Care Services Reorganization and Financing Act of 1975 (H.R. 1); (3) Fulton's Comprehensive Health Care Insurance Act of 1975 (H.R. 6222); and (4) the Long-Ribicoff/Waggonner Catastrophic Health Insurance and Medical Assistance Reform Act (S. 2470/H.R. 10028). These bills, and others treated in summary form, are further described in Waldman's "National Health Insurance Proposals" ([33]).

FOUR PRINCIPAL APPROACHES ([33], pp. 1–3)

This report includes the 18 national health insurance bills introduced in the 94th Congress as of February 1976. For this report, a national health insurance program is defined as one which would at least (1) establish a plan by law or provide substantial incentives for its voluntary establishment, (2) use some type of insurance or tax mechanism, and (3) potentially affect all or most of the population.

To aid in comparison, the plans have been grouped according to their general approach as follows:

        (1) Mixed public and private

        (2) Mainly public

        (3) Tax credit

        (4) Catastrophic protection

Classifying the proposals into these groups necessarily involves a degree of arbitrariness. Plans which fall into the tax credit and catastrophic protection categories are classified as such and all other plans are divided between the mixed public and private and the mainly public groups, based on consideration of the degree of government involvement in the plans. It might be noted that while the two catastrophic plans both limit their benefits for the general population to persons with unusually high health expenses, they both also provide basic health benefits for the low-income population. Also, the Fulton bill which is included in the tax credit group incorporates both a tax credit mechanism and a mandated employer plan.

Table A lists the bills by name, bill number, first sponsor in the House and Senate, and indicates any announced support by major national organizations. A comparison is also made of these bills with those introduced in the 93rd Congress indicating that most of them are identical to or are

TABLE A.--LISTING OF NATIONAL HEALTH INSURANCE BILLS INTRODUCED IN THE 94th CONGRESS, BY TYPE OF PROPOSAL, FEBRUARY 1976

Type and name of bill	First sponsor		Bill number		Supported by national organization	Comparison with bills introduced in the 93rd Congress
	House	Senate	House	Senate		
Mixed public and private						
The National Health Care Services Reorganization and Financing Act.	Ullman	...	H.R. 1	...	American Hospital Association.	
The National Health Care Act of 1975.	Burleson	McIntyre	H.R. 5990	S. 1438	Health Insurance Association of America.	Modified.
The National Health Standards Act.	...	Fannin	...	S. 2644	U.S. Chamber of Commerce.	Modified.
The Comprehensive Health Insurance Act of 1974.	Carter	...	H.R. 4747	...	...	Similar to Administration-supported bill.1/
National Comprehensive Health Benefits Act of 1975.	Staggers	...	H.R. 2049	...	...	Identical.
National Family Health Protection Act.	Lujan	...	H.R. 3672	...	...	Identical.
Mainly public						
The Health Security Act.	Corman	Kennedy	H.R. 21	S. 3	AFL-CIO, Committee for National Health Insurance.	Modified.
The Health Security Act.	Matsunaga	...	H.R. 3674	...	...	New.2/
National Health Insurance Act.	Dingell	...	H.R. 94	...	...	Identical.
Comprehensive National Health Care Act of 1975.	Young	...	H.R. 10888	...	...	New.
National Voluntary Medical and Hospital Services Insurance Act of 1975.	Ketchum-Lagomarsino	...	H.R. 3252	...	...	Modified.
Tax credits						
Comprehensive Health Care Insurance Act of 1975.	Fulton	...	H.R. 6222	...	American Medical Association.	Modified.
Health Care Insurance Act of 1973.	Downing	...	H.R. 363	...	...	Identical to Fulton-Broyhill bill in 93rd Congress.
Health Care Insurance Act of 1975.	Bennett	...	H.R. 93	...	...	Identical to Fulton-Broyhill bill in 92nd Congress.
Medical Expense Tax Credit Act.	...	Brock	...	S. 600	...	Modified.
Basic Health Insurance Tax Credit and Medical Assistance Act.	Clawson	...	H.R. 10562	...	...	New.
Catastrophic protection						
Catastrophic Health Insurance and Medical Assistance Reform Act.	Waggonner	Long-Ribicoff	H.R. 10028	S. 2470	...	Modified.
National Catastrophic Illness Protection Act of 1975.	Roe	...	H.R. 1373	...	...	Identical.

1/ The Administration has not introduced a national health insurance bill in the 94th Congress.
2/ Similar to Corman-Kennedy bill.

modifications of bills introduced in the last session. Of the bills supported by major national organizations, five have been reintroduced, all of them in modified form. A bill similar to the Administration bill in the 93rd Congress has been reintroduced by Representative Carter (H.R. 4747). This bill was not introduced on behalf of the Administration which has not proposed any national health insurance bill in this session.

To facilitate analysis and comparison, the provisions of all the bills have been presented in a manner which provides information on the following subjects:

(1) General concept and approach

(2) Coverage of the population

(3) Benefit structure

(4) Administration

(5) Relationship to other government programs

(6) Financing

(7) Standards for providers of service

(8) Reimbursement of providers of service

(9) Delivery and resources

Many of the bills include provisions specifically designed to effect changes in the methods of delivery of health care services or to increase the supply of health resources. These provisions are included in the category of delivery and resources. Of course various other provisions of the bills, especially those concerning standards for providers and methods of reimbursement, could often have significant effects on health delivery and resources.

PUBLIC SECTOR APPROACHES ([34], pp. 464–469)

The Health Security Act of 1975 (H.R. 21; S. 3): Kennedy-Corman

Date introduced.—January 14, 1975.
Chief sponsors.—Representative James C. Corman and Senator
Edward M. Kennedy.
Earlier versions.—91st Congress, S. 4297 (Aug. 27, 1970); 92d
Congress, S. 3 (Jan. 25, 1971), H.R. 22 (Jan. 22, 1971); 93d
Congress, S. 3 (Jan. 4, 1973), H.R. 22 (Jan. 4, 1973).

A. General Approach

The proposal would provide for the establishment of a national health insurance program covering the entire population and offering a broad and comprehensive range of services. For covered services there would be no cutoff dates, no coinsurance, no deductibles, and no waiting periods. The program would be financed by a Federal payroll tax on employers and employees, a tax on unearned income and self-employment earnings, and by Federal general revenues. The bill would create an administrative structure within the Department of Health, Education, and Welfare to be charged with the administration of the program. The proposal includes provisions which are intended, through study and evaluation as well as through economic incentives and grants and loans, to reorganize and improve the delivery of health care services, to alleviate shortages and maldistribution of health personnel and facilities, and for the development of community home care programs designed to maintain chronically ill or disabled persons in their own homes, in lieu of institutional care.

B. People Covered

All residents of the United States would be eligible for benefits, including aliens admitted as permanent residents or for employment. No history of contributions to the program would be required. The bill would allow for reciprocal and "buy-in" agreements to cover certain nonresident aliens and in some cases, U.S. residents traveling abroad.

C. Scope of Benefits

A comprehensive range of health services would be covered under the program, with no payment required of the patient for those services covered in full and without limitation. Limitations would be applied primarily in the area of psychiatric care, nursing home care, dental services, and prescription drugs, as noted in the following list of covered services:

Institutional services

General hospital inpatient and outpatient care, including pathology and radiology services.

Psychiatric care in a general or psychiatric hospital—limited to 45 consecutive days of active treatment during a benefit period.

Skilled nursing home care—restricted to 120 days per benefit period. Period may be extended, however, for (1) nursing homes owned or managed by a hospital if payment for care is made through the hospital's budget, and for (2) all homes depending on the availability of funds.

Ambulance services, by regulation.

Practitioner services

Physicians' services (nonpsychiatric): includes physical checkups, immunizations, well-child care, and family planning services.

Physicians' psychiatric services—limited to 20 visits during a benefit period, except when benefits are provided through group practice organizations, hospital outpatient departments, or comprehensive mental health care organizations, in which case there is no limitation.

Dental services—exclusive of most orthodontia and restricted at the program's inception to children under the age of 15, with the covered age group extended annually by two years until all those under age 25 are covered. However, the Health Security Board is authorized to expand dental benefits more rapidly if availability of resources permit. Within 7 years of the effective date of the legislation, the Board would be required to establish a timetable for phasing in dental benefits to the entire population.

Optometrists and podiatrists services.

Other services

Home health agency services.

Diagnostic services of independent pathology laboratories, and diagnostic and therapeutic radiology furnished by independent radiology services.

Care of a psychiatric patient in a mental health day care service—covered for up to 60 days.

Services of free-standing ambulatory drug abuse and alcoholism centers, family planning centers, and rehabilitation centers.

Supporting services—psychological, physiotherapy, nutrition, social work, and health education are covered services if they are part of institutional services or are furnished by a group practice organization, individual practice association, or certain public or non-profit agencies.

Prescription drugs—limited to those provided through hospital inpatient or outpatient department, through skilled nursing homes, or through organized patient care programs, such as group practice organizations and individual practice associations. For other patients, coverage would extend only to drugs from an approved list, as required for specified chronic illnesses or conditions requiring prolonged or costly drug therapy.

Medical appliances—therapeutic devices, appliances, and equipment (including eyeglasses, hearing aids, and prosthetic appliances) from an approved list. Expenditures to be limited to 2 percent of total program expenditures if possible.

D. Administration

At the Federal level, the program would be administered within the Department of Health, Education, and Welfare. A five-member Health Security Board, appointed by the President with the consent of the Senate, would be responsible for general administration of the program, including policy and regulation, control of expenditures, standards and reimbursement for providers of services, initiation of studies as to the adequacy of the financing of the program, quality, and costs of services, etc. An Executive Director would serve as Secretary to the Board and chief administrative officer of the program.

A National Health Security Advisory Council would assist the Board by advising on policy and evaluating operation of the program. The Council would include the Chairman of the Health Security Board and 20 additional members, including representatives of consumers (who would constitute a majority) and providers of health services.

A Commission on the Quality of Health Care would be established in the Department to recommend to the Secretary and to the Board standards pertaining to the quality of health care provided under the program. The Commission would consist of seven representatives of providers of health services or of nongovernmental organizations engaged in development standards for health care, and four representatives of consumers of health care. The Commission would be responsible for monitoring providers for compliance with established standards of care.

HEW regional offices and local health service area offices would be responsible for administering the program at their respective levels. Regional and local advisory councils, similar in composition to the National Advisory Council, would advise the regional and local offices. Individuals or providers with grievances would be entitled to hearings, appeals, and judical review in Federal courts.

No private health insurance organizations would be used under the plan.

E. Financing

The program would be financed through a Health Security Trust Fund. Income to the fund would be derived from the following sources:

1. A 3.5 percent tax on employers' payrolls;
2. A 1 percent tax on employees' wages up to $20,000 a year;
3. A 2.5 percent tax on self-employed income and on unearned income up to $20,000 a year;
4. Contributions from Federal general revenues equal to the total amount collected through health security taxes.

Persons over age 60 would be allowed to exempt the first $5,000 in unearned income from the 2.5 percent health security tax. The Internal Revenue Code would be amended to disallow income tax deductions for medical care covered by the program.

Through collective bargaining, employers could agree to pay part or all of their employees' required contribution. Employers would not be relieved by enactment of the program of any existing contractual or other nonstatutory obligation to provide or pay for health services to present or former employees. If an employer's existing obligations for the purchase of health benefits for his employees are greater than 3.5 percent of payroll, the excess would be applied toward the 1 percent which would otherwise be withheld from an employee's wages.

F. Payments to and Standards for Providers of Services

Each year, a national health budget for the coming year would be established. The budget could not exceed the estimated total receipts for that year from health security taxes and general revenues but could be modified if later estimates of program experience indicated that tax receipts or expenditures differed significantly from the estimates or if an epidemic or similar event required higher expenditures.

Funds would be allocated by the Board to each region on a per capita basis for institutions, physicians' services, dental services, drugs, appliances, and other professional and miscellaneous services. Regional funds would be further allocated on a similar per capita basis to the local health service areas. Authorization is provided to eliminate unwarranted differences in average costs of health services among the regions by curtailing increases in funds to high expenditure regions and increasing the availability of services in low expenditure regions.

Providers of health services would be compensated directly by the Health Security Board; individuals would not be charged for covered services. Hospitals, nursing homes, and home health agencies would be paid on the basis of approved prospective budgets designed to pay reasonable costs. Independent practitioners such as physicians, dentists, podiatrists, and optometrists could elect to be paid by various methods, including fee-for-service, capitation, salary, and supplemental stipends for practitioners locating in remote or medically-deprived areas. A medical or professional society could administer the fee-for-service reimbursement on the basis of fee schedules or relative value scales prescribed by regulation.

Group practice organizations and individual practice associations would be paid a basic capitation rate multiplied by the number of eligible enrollees; these organizations could then reimburse affiliated providers of services by methods which they chose to arrange among themselves. A group practice organization or individual practice association would be entitled to share in up to 75 percent of any savings which are achieved by reduced utilization of institutional services by its enrollees—provided (1) that the Board finds that the services furnished have been of high quality and adequate to the needs of its enrollees; and (2) that the average utilization of hospital or skilled nursing services by the enrollees is less than the use of such services by comparable population groups not so enrolled.

The bill includes various provisions designed to ensure the quality of health care provided under the program. National standards for participation by providers of services would be established similar to those required under medicare, but more exacting. At the start of the program, independent practitioners would be eligible to participate if they were licensed in at least one State and met the program's requirements for continuing education. For practitioners licensed after the start of the program, new national standards established by the Board would also apply. A State-licensed practitioner who met national standards would be considered qualified to provide services in any other State. Nurses and other health professionals would also be required to meet national standards (including a requirement for licensure in at least one State). Major surgery and certain other specialist care would be covered only when furnished by qualified specialists and generallly only upon referral from a primary care practitioner.

Hospitals and other institutions would be eligible to participate if they meet national standards and if they establish utilization review and affiliation arrangements. Special conditions of participation would apply to group practice organizations and individual practice associations.

G. Effect on Other Government Programs

Medicare would be terminated and the assets and liability of both medicare trust funds would be transferred to the health security fund. Federal aid to the States for medicaid and other Federal programs, such as vocational rehabilitation and maternal and child health, would also cease, except to the extent that benefits under such programs are broader than under the health security program. The bill does not affect current provisions for personal health services under the Veterans Administration, temporary disability or workmen's compensation programs, the Department of Defense, or institutions of HEW serving merchant seamen, Indians and Alaskan Natives. The bill does, however, provide for a study of methods of coordinating HEW and veterans programs with the proposed plan.

H. Other Major Provisions

Financial, professional, and other incentives are provided in order to stimulate the establishment of group practice organizations; to encourage the training continuing education, and effective utilization of health personnel, particularly those in short supply; to encourage linkages between physicians and specialists and other patient-care resources such as health institutions; and to develop new community-based home health care programs designed to maintain chronically ill or disabled persons in their own homes, in lieu of institutional care. A special resources development fund would be established to commence operation for the period between enactment and when health security benefits began, in order to prepare the system for the anticipated greater demands to be placed upon health facilities and providers.

Major New Features

1. *Catastrophic protection* is specifically recognized in the preamble of the bill.

2. The terms *"group practice organization"* and *"individual practice association"* have been substituted in all references to what had previously been termed "health maintenance organization" and "professional foundation."

3. Professional services of *optometrists* have been delineated to include "examination, diagnosis, and treatment of conditions of the vision system."

4. *Optometrists and podiatrists* have been defined as "physicians" when furnishing certain covered services under the program.

5. *Free-standing* ambulatory alcoholism and drug abuse centers, free-standing family planning centers, and free-standing rehabilitation centers would be recognized as providers of services.

6. An amendment on *employment rights* (including collective bargaining) in health institutions is incorporated into the new bill.

7. The Internal Revenue Code would be amended to disallow *income tax deductions* for medical services covered by the health security program.

8. The *exemption* from health security taxes of the first $3,000 in unearned income for persons over age 60 has been *raised to $5,000.*

9. The *ceiling* on payroll and individual taxes for the health security program has been *raised from $15,000 to $20,000* (or 150 percent of the social security wage base).

10. The new bill establishes a Federal grant program for development of community programs designed to maintain disabled or chronically ill persons in their own homes, in lieu of institutional care. *Personal care services* included in such a program could include homemaker and home help services, home maintenance, laundry services, meals-on-wheels, and other nutrition services, assistance with transportation and shopping, etc. (The old bill provided grants for "conducting tests and demonstrations into the feasibility" of such home care programs.)

11. New provisions authorize the Secretary to *establish a staff* of up to 50 positions for the Health Security Board and up to 25 positions for the Commission on the Quality of Health Care.

12. The planning, resource development, and administration sections of the new bill have been revised to coordinate with provisions of the recently enacted *title XV of the Public Health Service Act* (Public Law 93–641—the National Health Planning and Resources Development Act of 1974).

Summaries of H.R. 21/S. 3 and Other Bills ([33], pp. 10–13)

Mainly public--CORMAN-KENNEDY BILL

Subject	Provisions
General concept and approach--------------	A program administered by Federal Government and financed by special taxes on earned and unearned income and by Federal general revenues. Supported by Committee for National Health Insurance and AFL-CIO.
Coverage of the population----------------	All U.S. residents.

Benefit structure------------------------	Benefits with no limitations, except as noted. No cost sharing by patient.
	    Institutional services:
	        Hospital.
	        Skilled nursing facility: 120 days.
	    Personal services:
	        Physicians.
	        Dentists: For children under age 15; scheduled extension to age 25;
	          eventually to entire population.
	        Home health services.
	        Other health professionals.
	        Laboratory and X-ray.
	    Other services and supplies:
	        Medical appliances and ambulance services.
	        Eyeglasses and hearing aids.
	        Prescription drugs needed for chronic illness and other specified
	          diseases.

Administration---------------------------	Federal Government: Special board in DHEW, with regional and local offices to operate program.
Relationship to other Government programs-	Medicare: Abolished. Medicaid and other assistance programs: Would not pay for covered services. Other programs: Most not affected.
Financing-------------------------------	Special taxes: On payroll (1.0% for employees and 2.5% for employers), self-employment income (2.5%) and unearned income (2.5%). Income subject to tax: Amount equal to 150% of earning base under social security (i.e., $22,950 in 1976). Employment subject to tax: Workers under social security and Federal, State, and local government employment. Federal general revenues: Equal to amount received from special taxes.
Standards for providers of services-------	Same as Medicare, but with additional requirements: Hospitals cannot refuse staff privileges to qualified physicians. Skilled nursing facilities must be affiliated with hospital which would take responsibility for quality of medical services in home. Physicians must meet national standards; major surgery performed only by qualified specialists. All providers: Records subject to review by regional office. Can be directed to add or reduce services and to provide services in a new location.

Reimbursement of providers of services----	National health budget established and funds allocated, by type of medical services, to regions and local areas.
	    Hospitals and nursing homes: Annual predetermined budget, based on reasonable cost.
	    Physicians, dentists, and other professionals: Methods available are fee-for-service based on fee schedule, per capita payment for persons enrolled, and (by agreement) full- or part-time salary. Payments for fee-for-service may be reduced if payments exceed allocation.
	    Health maintenance organizations: Per capita payment for all services (or budget for institutional services). Can retain all or part of savings.

Delivery and resources--------------------	Health planning: DHEW responsible for health planning, in cooperation with State planning agencies. Priority to be given to development of comprehensive care on ambulatory basis. Health resources development fund: Will receive, ultimately, 5 percent of total income of program, to be used for improving delivery of health care and increasing health resources. Health maintenance organizations: Grants for development, loans for construction, and payments to offset operating deficits. Manpower training: Grants to schools and allowances to students for training of physicians for general practice and shortage specialties, other health occupations, and development of new kinds of health personnel. Personal care services: Demonstration projects to provide personal care in the home, including homemaker, laundry, meals-on-wheels, transportation, and shopping services.

Mainly public--DINGELL BILL

Subject	Provisions
General concept and approach---------------	Program providing health benefits, administered at Federal, State, and local levels and financed by payroll taxes.
Coverage of the population-----------------	All U.S. residents.

Benefit structure--------------------------	Benefits with no cost sharing or limitations, except as noted.
	Institutional services:
	  Hospital: 60 days of care.
	
	Personal services:
	  Physicians.
	  Dentists.
	  Home health services.
	  Laboratory and X-ray.
	  Other health professionals.
	Other services and supplies:
	  Medical appliances and eyeglasses.
	  Prescription drugs: Unusually expensive drugs.
	Specified benefits may be delayed in a State if resources are inadequate.

Administration-----------------------------	Federal Government: Special board in DHEW with overall supervision of program. State: Under contract with Federal Government, would establish State plan to operate program at the local level.
Relationship to other Government programs--	Medicare: Continues to operate, but study to be made of methods of incorporating it into the national plan. Medicaid and other assistance programs: Would not pay for services under the national plan. Other programs: Most not affected.
Financing----------------------------------	Tax on wage and self-employment income similar to social security tax. Total tax for employers and employees combined would be 4 percent.
Standards for providers of services--------	Must meet State standards. If no State standards, they would be established by national board.
Reimbursement of providers of services-----	Hospitals and other institutions: Reasonable cost of services, but subject to a maximum rate. Physicians and other professionals: Fee for service (based on fee schedule), per capita (for persons enrolled with a practitioner), or salary.
Delivery and resources---------------------	Grants to students and educational institutions for training in health occupations.

Mainly public--YOUNG BILL

Subject	Provisions
General concept and approach--------------	A program administered by the Federal Government and financed by special taxes on earned and unearned income.
Coverage of the population----------------	All U.S. residents.

Benefit structure-------------------------	No limits on benefits, except where indicated. No cost sharing for the patient.
	  Institutional services:
	    Hospital inpatient and outpatient.
	    Skilled nursing facilities: 180 days per year.
	  Personal services:
	    Physicians.
	    Dentists.
	    Laboratory and X-ray.
	    Home health services: 180 visits per year.
	    Health exams, maternity care, and well-child care.
	  Other services and supplies:
	    Prescription drugs: For specified conditions.
	    Medical supplies and equipment.
	    Eyeglasses and hearing aids (and eye and ear exams).

Administration---------------------------	Administered by an independent SSA in manner similar to Medicare program.
Relationship to other Government programs-	Medicare and Medicaid abolished. Other programs: Most not affected.
Financing--------------------------------	Special taxes: On payroll (2% for employee and 6% for employer), self-employment (5%), unearned income (5%), and SSI and AFDC payments (2% for recipient and 6% for government). Income subject to tax: Total income (no earnings base). Employment subject to tax: Workers under social security and Federal, State, and local employment. Tax credits: For individuals, one-half of contributions to a maximum of $250 for individual returns and $500 for joint returns. For employers, one-half of contributions to a maximum of $750 per employee. Federal excise taxes on alcohol, tobacco, and firearms would be diverted to, and earmarked for, the program.
Standards for providers of services-------	Standards similar to Medicare. Major surgery and other specialized services only covered on referral and when performed by a qualified specialist.
Reimbursement of providers of services----	Institutions: Reimbursed according to prospective payment methods to be developed by SSA. Practitioners: Fee schedule approved by SSA.
Delivery and resources--------------------	Regulation of providers: Services, facilities, and capital expenditures of institutions must be approved by State and local planning agencies. Professional Standards Review Organization (PSRO): Applies to all services under program. Health resources development: 1% of receipts of program allocated to help finance costs of health facility construction authorized under title 16 of the Public Health Service Act.

Mainly public--KETCHUM-LAGOMARSINO BILL

Subject	Provisions
General concept and approach---------------	A national program administered by the Federal Government, permitting coverage on a voluntary basis, and financed by enrollee premiums and Federal general revenues.
Coverage of the population-----------------	All U.S. residents could voluntarily enroll. Employers could voluntarily enroll their employees.

Benefit structure--------------------------	Following benefits, with no limits on amount of services and no cost sharing by the patient.
	    Institutional services:
	      Hospitals, nursing homes, alcohol and drug centers.
	    Physicians services (including psychiatric) and diagnostic services.

Administration-----------------------------	Administered by new independent Federal agency.
Relationship to other Government programs--	Federal funding would be terminated under Medicare and Medicaid for services covered by new program.
Financing----------------------------------	Premium contributions (including employer contributions, if any): $15 monthly for each adult and $7.50 for child. Premiums reduced for families with income under $10,000. Federal general revenues: Amount equal to premiums collected. Funds allocated as follows: 67% for hospital benefits, 30% for medical benefits, and 3% for administrative costs.
Standards for providers of services--------	Providers of service must be approved by the administering agency.
Reimbursement of providers of services-----	Hospitals: Per diem rates based on hospital's financial statements and projected budget. Physicians: Fee schedule based on usual, customary and reasonable fees in area, established after consultation with medical society. Physicians may charge more than scheduled amount, but must disclose extra fee in advance to patient and report it to the agency. Consolidated payments: Claim forms designed for computer processing and audit. Providers receive monthly consolidated payments.
Delivery and resources---------------------	Malpractice claims: Must be submitted to arbitration board whose decision could be appealed to courts. Capital expenditures of hospitals: Must be approved by agency to be recognized for reimbursement. Utilization review: Agency would contract with medical societies or PSRO's to assist with or conduct utilization review. Where provider guilty of abuses, payments could be reduced or suspended, or provider excluded from program.

MIXED PRIVATE AND PUBLIC SECTOR APPROACHES ([34], pp. 457–464)

The National Health Care Services Reorganization and Financing Act of 1975 (H.R. 1): Ullman

Date introduced.—January 14, 1975.
Chief sponsor.—Representative Al Ullman.
Earlier versions.—92d Congress, H.R. 14140 (Mar. 28, 1972); 93d Congress, H.R. 1 (Jan. 9, 1973).

A. General Approach

The bill would establish a program of comprehensive health care benefits for all U.S. residents, phased in over a 5-year period, and would provide for creation of Health Care Corporations (HCC's) to cover every geographic area of the country. Employers would be required to provide specified private health insurance for their employees and their families. A federally financed plan would provide health insurance for the aged, low-income, and medically indigent, administered through Federal contracts with insurance carriers. The self-employed and others not eligible for Federal coverage could enroll voluntarily under plans made available by the States at reasonable group rates.

Initially, medicare parts A and B would be merged, the part B premium eliminated, and catastrophic coverage added to the program. These expanded medicare benefits would be extended to low-income groups, to be financed through Federal general revenues. Concurrently, employers would be required to provide their employees with at least this new medicare level of benefits and to contribute at least 75 percent of the premium cost. After the first 4 years of the program, comprehensive health care benefits (CHCB's) broader than the new medicare level, would be mandated for all three plans.

Newly created State health commissions (SHC's) would be responsible for a large part of the program's administration and for setting up health care corporations within each State. HCC's would be community-based, nonprofit organizations capable of providing comprehensive health services to all residents in a given geographic area. The bill would also consolidate all Federal health programs within a new Department of Health and would make available grants, loans, and other incentives to reorganize and improve the delivery of health services.

B. People Covered

Effective 6 months after enactment of the bill, the aged and low-income would be covered under the combined medicare program. Concurrently, all employers subject to the social security tax (including nonprofit organizations and other employers who have elected social security on a voluntary basis) would be required to provide their employees and dependents with the same level of coverage through private insurance plans. The coverage requirement would not apply to the Federal Government as an employer, but would apply to State and local governments. Three years after enactment, the medically indigent would become eligible for federally contracted coverage.

C. Scope of Benefits

Initially, the program would cover the level of benefits currently provided under medicare, plus additional catastrophic coverage which would take effect after health expenditures, by or on behalf of an individual or family, reached a specified limit graduated according to income. Medicare deductibles and co-insurance would not be applicable to low-income groups. At the end of the 5-year phase-in period, the following comprehensive health care benefits would be required of the employer-employee plans, the federally contracted coverage for the aged, low-income, and medically-indigent, and the voluntary plans for the self-employed:

I. Periodic health evaluations

    a. Screening tests and exams.

    b. All immunizations.

    c. Well-baby care to age 5, with number of covered visits decreasing with age of child.

    d. Dental services for children to age 7; once child is covered, benefits continue to age 12.

        1. One free routine exam per year.

        2. Extractions, fillings, etc.—20 percent copayment.

    e. Vision services for children to age 12.

        1. One free routine exam per year.

        2. Prescription eyeglasses—20 percent copayment.

II. Physicians' services and services of other qualified health professionals and allied health personnel

    a. Services on outpatient basis in any appropriate setting (including the home) by physician or allied personnel under his supervision—10 visits per year with $2 copay per visit.

    b. Outpatient disgnostic procedures—20 percent copayment.

    c. Hospital or outpatient center services.

    d. Supplies, materials, use of facilities and equipment, including drugs used or administered in connection with outpatient services.

    e. Ambulance services—20 percent copayment.

III. Other outpatient services

    a. Outpatient institutional care program for physical disability, mental illness, alcoholism, drug abuse—$2 copayment per day.

    b. Day car or other part-time services for physical disability, mental illness, alcoholism, drug abuse—3 visits or sessions in lieu of each day of inpatient hospital care allowable during a benefit period.

    c. Drugs, prosthetic devices, and equipment—$1 copay per prescription, 20 percent copayment for devices and equipment.

    d. Home health care services—a total of 200 days in any benefit period, with a $2 copay per visit for the following:

        1. Intensive home care services, involving coordination by a registered nurse;

        2. Intermediate home care services through an affiliated home health agency provider;

        3. Basic home health services to individuals requiring "palliative and terminal" care.

IV. Inpatient services

    a. Hospital care—90 days per benefit period, $5 copayment per day.

    b. Extended care services—30 days per benefit period, $2.50 copayment per day.

    c. Nursing home care—90 days per benefit period, $2.50 copayment per day.

d. Physicians' services to inpatients—$2 copayment per visit of attending physician only; copayment of 10 percent of charges in cases where a single combined charge is made for services such as surgery, pregnancy, etc.

V. *Catastrophic expense benefits*

For low-income persons (e.g., individuals with annual income below $2,000, a family of four with income less than $6,000), catastrophic benefits would become effective immediately. For medically indigent persons and all other income classes, benefits would become effective after medical expenses (including amounts paid for premiums, copayments on covered services, etc.) reached a special expenditure limit graduated according to income. For example, a family of four with income of $10,500 would be required to incur $750 in out-of-pocket medical expenses before catastrophic benefits would take effect. Once the expenditure limit is reached, all copayments on covered services would cease, and restrictions on the number of physician visits, hospital stays, etc., would be removed. However, outpatient care for mental illness would be limited to cases in which active medical treatment is provided and psychoanalysis would be excluded except when used for treatment of severe functional disability.

D. ADMINISTRATION

All Federal health programs would be consolidated within a new Department of Health. The Federal Government would administer the insurance program for the aged and low-income and would contract directly with carriers or HCC's to provide covered benefits. The Federal Government could use the State as its agent in negotiating contracts. Employer-employee plans would be administered through approved carriers or NCC's. New independent State health commissions (SHC's) would be established in each State to designate geographic service areas for HCC's, authorize incorporation of HCC's, enforce regulations pertaining to providers, control premium rates charged by carriers, HCC's, and nonaffiliated providers, approve charges for institutional and noninstitutional providers of services, approve expansion of health facilities and services, etc. The Department of Health would assume functions of a State health commission in any State which failed to establish one. Private insurance carriers approved by the SHC's would issue qualified insurance policies, collect premiums, administer claims, and reimburse providers in accordance with Federal and State guidelines.

E. FINANCING

The Federal insurance program for the aged would be financed through payroll taxes and general revenues, with some cost-sharing for services. Government insurance for the poor and medically indigent would be financed through general revenues with some cost-sharing and premium contributions required of the medically indigent. Employers would be required to pay at least 75 percent of the premium cost for employee plans, with employees responsible for the remaining 25 percent. Federal general revenues would also be used to cover the cost of a 10 percent premium subsidy for anyone registering with a health care corporation. Federal tax credits would be made available to employers with less than 10 employees whose required contributions for CHCB's exceeded 4 percent of average wages paid to those employees. Similar tax credits would be available to the self-employed and certain other individuals.

Individual taxpayers would be allowed to deduct 100 percent of the amounts paid by them as premiums for approved CHCB contracts, without regard to the dollar limitation currently applicable under existing Federal income tax law. This amount would be reduced by any amount allowed to self-employed and certain other individuals as a tax credit for such health insurance coverage.

F. Payments to and Standards for Providers of Services

State health commissions would be responsible for determining premium rates to be used by private insurers and health care corporations for mandated comprehensive health care benefit packages. SHC's would also approve on a prospective basis all charges for services provided by HCC's and all other health providers, whether or not affiliated with an HCC. State health commissions would review the activities and performance of HCC's and nonaffiliated providers to assure that providers were meeting their obligations under the bill. Federal regulations would prescribe methods to be used in determining reasonable operating costs and sufficient capital payments for HCC's and institutions; and reasonable fees, salaries, or other compensation for individual providers or groups of providers. The Department of Health would also prescribe standards for providers relating to quality, safety, personnel, etc.; as a minimum, providers would be expected to meet existing medicare requirements.

A health card account would be established by an approved carrier for each individual enrolled under the carrier's plan. These accounts would be similar to credit card accounts and would serve as the basis for reimbursement of providers of service. Payments would be made from these accounts by carriers directly to providers of service for covered items and services at the applicable payment rates approved by State health commissions. The provider would be reimbursed the full amount of the approved charge and the carrier would then bill the enrollee for any applicable copayment amounts.

G. Effect on Other Government Programs

Medicare for the aged would be replaced by the new program. Federal financing of medicaid would eventually be limited to services not covered under the new program. Federal financial assistance under the maternal and child health program would be limited to noncovered services for persons covered by federally contracted insurance.

H. Other Major Provisions

The bill provides that, in accordance with Federally approved State plans, every geographic area within a particular State would be covered by at least one nonprofit health care corporation (HCC), charged with responsibility for making available and furnishing to all residents within the assigned area all the comprehensive health care benefits mandated under the bill. The concept of an HCC would allow for organizational flexibility. The only definitional requirement in the bill is that the organization assure all area residents of CHC benefits. The ownership, organizational form, methods of payment, modes of medical practice, choice of participating providers, etc., would be left to community preference. Initially, health care corporations would develop around existing providers. The bill provides that, as rapidly as possible, HCC's develop a system of outpatient care centers, with empahsis on health maintenance, home care, medical social services, mental health clinics, etc., and undertake a program of continuing health education of HCC registrants. HCC's could be paid on any appropriate prospective or prior-budgeted basis; however, capitation payments would be encouraged through the use of financial incentives to consumers who register with HCC's and would be mandated as an option after the first 5 years of operation of the HCC. Federal grants and contracts would be available to facilitate the planning, organizing, developing, and establishing of HCC's. Federal grants would also be authorized for (1) State health commissions to cover all or part of the necessary cost of developing and preparing State health plans, and (2) development and initial operation of home health care agencies.

Major New Features

1. The reimbursement provisions have been amended to establish a *health card* system (similar to the health credit card provision contained in H.R. 12684—the administration's bill in the 93d Congress). Carriers would be required to establish a credit account for each individual enrolled with them. Payments would be made by carriers from these accounts directly to the providers of services for the full amount of the charge prospectively approved by the State health commissions. Carriers would then bill the enrollee for any applicable copayment amount. This system would apply both to HCC's and non-HCC providers.

2. The term "health-related custodial care" has been changed to *"palliative and terminal care."*

3. The new bill includes a statement of congressional findings that *philanthropic support* for health care should be continued and that nothing in the bill is intended to eliminate or limit such support.

4. The definition of the term "State" has been expanded to include the *Virgin Islands* and *Guam*.

5. The new bill includes *State and local governments* under the definition of "employer" for purposes of the program. However, Federal Government employees would still remain outside the program. (Under the previous bill, the term "employer" was not applied to Federal, State, or local governments.)

6. The previous bill had contained a Federal subsidy feature for small employers whose costs for required CHCB coverage for employees exceeded 4 percent of wages. This feature has been eliminated and replaced with a *tax credit for employers* with 10 or fewer employees, whose premium costs exceed 4 percent of wages paid to those employees. A similar tax credit provision would be available to the self-employed and certain other individuals.

7. Benefits for outpatient services have been expanded to include "outpatient institutional care *programs for physical disability*" and "day care or other part-time services for rehabilitation of the physically disabled" on the same basis and subject to the same terms and cost-sharing applicable to such programs for treatment of mental illness, alcoholism, and drug abuse.

8. The term "ancillary health care" (as included in the benefit structure under covered physicians' services) has been changed to "services of *other qualified health professionals* and allied health personnel."

9. The previous bill had limited inpatient hospital care for *treatment of mental illness* to a period of 45 days, with 90 days allowed to enrollees of a health care corporation. The new bill omits this special limitation, thereby allowing 90 days of hospital care regardless of the mental or physical condition and irrespective of enrollment with an HCC. However, inpatient treatment of mental illness would only be covered if the patient were in an acute phase and subject to "active medical treatment," as defined in item 13.

10. The new bill provides that expenses incurred for *outpatient treatment of physical disability* could be included among the amounts applied toward satisfaction of the special expenditure limit applicable to catastrophic benefits.

11. The old bill had excluded expenses for inpatient or outpatient *treatment of mental illness* from those expenses which could be credited toward satisfaction of the catastrophic deductible. The new bill omits this provision.

12. The new bill provides that outpatient care for *mental illness*, when provided as part of catastrophic expense benefits, must be characterized by "active medical treatment," as defined in item 13.

13. The term *"active medical treatment,"* for purposes of both inpatient and outpatient treatment of mental illness, means a "written and individualized plan that is based on diagnoses; based on goals relative to arrest, reversal, or amelioration of the disease process or illness and aimed at restoring the individual's adaptive capacity to the maximum extent possible; based on objectives relating to such goals; comprised of defined services and activities; specific as to the means to measure the progress or outcome; and clear as to periodic review and revision of the plan.

14. The new bill directs the Secretary of Health, in considering regulations pertaining to the definition of services to be included under outpatient institutional care programs for the physically disabled, to give consideration to inclusion of *appropriate transportation services*.

15. The new bill describes extensively the three different concentrations of home health care services covered under the program. The old bill had contained a more narrow definition of such services. The new definition would include——

a. *Intensive home care services*, involving the professional coordination of a registered nurse, including:

    1. Part-time or intermittent nursing care;

    2. Physical, respiratory, occupational or speech therapy;

    3. Medical social services;

    4. Services of a home health aide, in accordance with regulations;

    5. Diagnostic and therapeutic items or services, furnished by a hospital or outpatient center;

    6. Drugs, medical supplies, appliances, and equipment;

    7. Hospital or outpatient center physicians' services;

    8. Medical services of an intern or resident provided in patient's home or hospital outpatient center; and

    9. Ambulance or other special transportation services to and from the patient's home and the provider institution, when indicated by the patient's condition and when involving the use of equipment which cannot be made available in the patient's home.

b. *Intermediate home health care services*, provided either directly or through an affiliated home health agency, including:

    1. Part-time or intermittent nursing care;

    2. Physical, occupational, or speech therapy;

    3. Medical social services;

    4. Services of a home health aide, as permitted in regulations;

    5. Medical supplies (other than drugs) and use of medical appliances and equipment;

    6. Medical services of an intern or resident in an affiliated home health agency provider; and

7. Any of the foregoing items or services provided on an outpatient basis, under arrangements made by an HCC or home health agency, at a hospital, skilled nursing facility, or rehabilitation center, and which involve the use of equipment which cannot be made readily available in the patient's home; transportation would not be included except for ambulance service when other transportation is contraindicated by the patient's condition.

c. *Basic home health services*, furnished either directly or through an affiliated home health agency to persons requiring "palliative and terminal care," as follows:

1. Part-time or intermittent nursing;

2. Medical social services including counseling;

3. Part-time or intermittent home health aid services, assigned and supervised by a registered nurse; and

4. Medical supplies (other than drugs) and use of medical appliances and equipment.

16. The new bill authorizes the Secretary to prescribe standards for *systems of accounting* that can provide guidance to State health commissions in developing such systems adapted to individual State needs and also to set standards for a *national system of reporting and billing*.

17. In determining *financial requirements of health care corporations* and other providers, the new bill authorizes the Secretary to consider provisions to assure that gifts, grants, loans, endowments, etc., will not be deducted from operating costs when computing reimburseable costs unless (1) such amounts are designated for specific operating costs, (2) such amounts were not restricted as to use and are commingled with other funds, in which case the income derived from investment of such funds may be deducted from interest expense when computing reimbursable costs. The Secretary must also assure that gifts, etc., are not utilized for facilities which have not been granted a certificate of need.

18. The new bill expands the grant authority of the Secretary to include grants to health care corporations, or public or nonprofit providers affiliated with an HCC, for the initial operation of new or *expanded home health care agencies*.

19. The new bill broadens the requirements for approval of a State health plan to include a requirement that the State develop and implement, consistent with the Secretary's regulations, *a system of uniform accounting*, reporting, and billing to be utilized by providers, carriers, and the State health commission within that State.

20. The new bill contains a description of the methods which may be used by State health commissions for purposes of *prospective reimbursement* of providers, including budget review, negotiated rates, target rates, formulas, and others.

21. The new bill provides that rates of providers prospectively approved would be applicable to a "particular fiscal period," rather than the "12-month period" specified in the old bill.

Summaries of H.R. 1 and Other Bills ([33]) pp. 4–9)

Mixed public and private--ULLMAN BILL

Subject	Provisions	
General concept and approach-------------	A 3-part program including: (1) a plan requiring employers to provide private coverage for employees, (2) a plan for individuals, and (3) federally contracted coverage for the poor and aged. State establishes a health care plan, supervises carriers and insurers, and promotes a system of health care corporations (HCC). Supported by American Hospital Association.	
	Private plans	Plan for low income and aged
Coverage of the population--------------	Employees of employers under social security and of State and local governments. Also, individuals who elect coverage.	Low-income and medically indigent families, and aged persons.

Benefit structure------------------------	Benefits phased in over 5-year period. Final benefits:
	  Institutional services:
	    Hospital: 90 days, $5 copayment per day.
	    Skilled nursing facility: 30 days, $2.50 copayment per day.
	    Nursing home: 90 days, $2.50 copayment per day.
	  Personal services:
	    Physicians: 10 visits per year, $2 copayment per visit.
	    Laboratory and X-ray: 20 percent coinsurance.
	    Home health services: 200 visits per year, $2 copayment per visit.
	    Dental services: Children age 7-12: 1 exam per year, other services,
	      20 percent coinsurance.
	  Other services and supplies:
	    Prescription drugs: Limited to specified conditions, $1 per prescription.
	    Medical equipment and appliances and ambulance service: 20 percent
	      coinsurance.
	    Eyeglasses: Children to age 12, 1 set per year, 20 percent
	      coinsurance.
	  Catastrophic coverage: Payable when certain noncovered expenses reach a
	    specified limit, which varies by family income and age; would remove
	    the cost sharing on all benefits and the limitation on number of hospital days and physicians' visits.	

Administration---------------------------	Administered by private insurance carriers under State supervision, according to Federal guidelines.	Federal Government would contract with private insurance carriers who issue policies to eligible persons.
Relationship to other Government programs--	Medicare: Abolished. Medicaid and other assistance programs: Would not pay for covered services. Other programs: Mostly not affected.	
Financing--------------------------------	Employee-employer premium payments, with employer paying at least 75 percent. Federal subsidy of premium for low-income workers and certain small employers, and 10 percent subsidy for HCC enrollees. Individuals pay own premium.	Financed in part by premium payments by medically indigent, but with no premium for lowest income group. Balance of cost financed by Federal general revenues and the payroll taxes of the present Medicare program.
Standards for providers of services--------	All institutions and HCC's must meet Medicare standards. Skilled nursing facilities must be under supervision of a hospital medical staff or have its own organized staff. Use of paramedical personnel must meet Federal standards. All providers and HCC's must establish systems of peer review, medical audit and other procedures to meet Federal-State requirements on quality and utilization of services.	
Reimbursement of providers of services-----	Institutions and HCC's: State commission would establish prospective payment methods and review proposed charges. Physicians and other professionals: Reasonable fee, salaries, or other compensation, as approved by State commission.	
Delivery and resources---------------------	State health commission: Establishes a State health plan, including provisions for regulation of providers and insurance carriers. Takes responsibility for health planning and must approve, in advance, proposed capital expenditures of providers. Health care corporations: State commissions would incorporate system of HCC's, approved to operate in designated geographical areas. HCC must furnish all covered services through its own facilities or affiliated providers (and permit all qualified practitioners to furnish services for it). Would be required to hold open enrollment for public and eventually offer services on a capitation basis. Federal grants provided for HCC's for planning, development, outpatient centers, medical and data equipment, and to cover initial operating deficits.	

Mixed public and private--BURLESON-McINTYRE BILL

Subject	Provisions	
General concept and approach---------------	A 3-part plan including a voluntary employee-employer plan and a plan for individuals, under which contributors would receive tax advantages, and a State plan for the poor. All plans administered through private insurance carriers and provide same benefits. Supported by the Health Insurance Association of America.	
	Private plans	**State plan**
Coverage of the population-----------------	Employee-employer plan includes employees (and their families) of employers who voluntarily elect a qualified plan. Individual plan includes persons who voluntarily elect.	Low-income families.

Benefit structure-------------------------	Benefits phased-in over a 8-year period, final benefits as follows:
	  Deductible of $100 per person and 20% coinsurance, except where noted.
	    Institutional services:
	      Hospital.
	      Skilled nursing facility: 180 days.
	    Personal services:
	      Physicians.
	      Dentists.
	      Home health services: 270 days.
	      Laboratory and X-ray: No cost sharing.
	      Health exams and family planning. Well-child care with no cost sharing.
	    Other services and supplies:
	      Medical appliances.
	      Eyeglasses.
	      Prescription drugs.	

	Annual limit for all cost sharing of $1,000 per family.	Reduced cost sharing and family maximum, according to family income.
Administration---------------------------	Insurance administered by private carriers under State supervision. Treasury Department determines tax status of plan.	Insurance administered by private carriers under agreement with the State. Regulations for program established by DHEW.
Relationship to other Government programs--	Medicare: Continues to operate. Medicaid and other assistance programs: Would not pay for services under programs. Other programs: Most not affected.	
Financing-------------------------------	For employee-employer plan, premium paid by employers and employees, as arranged between them, but contributions of low-income workers limited according to their wage level. For individual plan, policyholder pays entire premium. Employees and individuals who itemize deductions can take entire premium as deduction on income tax return.1/ Employers can take their entire premium as normal business deduction as under present law (but contributions to nonqualified plans would not be deductible).	No premium required for lowest income group; for others, premium paid by enrollees, varying according to family income. Federal and State governments pay balance of costs from their general revenues, with Federal share 70 to 90 percent, depending on State per capita income.
Standards for providers of services--------	Same as Medicare.	
Reimbursement of providers of services-----	Hospitals and other institutions: Prospectively approved rates for various categories of institutions. Hospitals prepare budgets and schedule of charges which are reviewed by a State commission which approves or disapproves charges, subject to DHEW review of rate levels. Physicians and dentists: Reasonable charges, based on customary and prevailing rates.	
Delivery and resources--------------------	Health planning: Planning agency approval required for capital expenditures to be recognized for reimbursement. Health maintenance organizations: Must be made available as an option to persons enrolled in State plan. Ambulatory health centers: Grants, loans, and loan guarantees for construction and operation of centers. Health manpower: Increases loans and grants for students, with special provisions for shortage areas.	

1/ Under present law, deduction of premium is limited to one-half the premium cost up to a maximum of $150.

Mixed public and private--FANNIN BILL

Subject	Provisions	
General concept and approach---------------	A 2-part program including (1) a plan requiring employers to offer health insurance coverage to their employees and (2) a State plan for low-income families. Supported by U.S. Chamber of Commerce.	
	Employer-employee plan	**Low-income plan**
Coverage of the population-----------------	Full-time employees, including employees of Federal, State, and local governments.	Low-income families.

Benefit structure--------------------------	No limit on amount of benefits, except where indicated:
	    Institutional services:
	        Hospital.
	        Skilled nursing facility: By regulation.
	    Personal services:
	        Physicians.
	        Laboratory and X-ray.
	    Other services and supplies:
	        Prescription drugs.
	        Medical supplies and appliances.	

	Deductible of $100 per person and 25 percent coinsurance, but total limit to $2,600 annually per family. Actuarially equivalent benefits may be substituted for specified ones.	10-percent coinsurance, but limited to 5 percent of annual family income.
Administration-----------------------------	Private health insurance carriers (or self-insured arrangements) supervised by the States, under Federal regulations.	Administered by States through private carriers.
Relationship to other Government programs--	Medicare: Continues. Medicaid: Abolished. Other programs: Most not affected.	
Financing----------------------------------	Employee-employer premium payments, with employer required to pay at least 50 percent of cost. Special pools for small employers and self-employed.	Premium payments from enrollees according to family income, with none for lowest income group. Balance of cost from Federal general revenues.
Standards for providers of services--------	Same as under Medicare.	
Reimbursement of providers of services-----	Institutions: Prospective budgets with uniform payment rates per specified period of time (e.g. per day) for all patients. Physicians: Usual and customary charges.	
Delivery and resources---------------------	Health maintenance organizations: Under both plans, option available to enroll in approved HMO's. Professional Standards Review Organization (PSRO): Would apply to all services under program. Regulation of providers: Proposed and existing capital facilities and services must be approved by local planning agency.	

Mixed public and private--CARTER BILL

Subject	Provisions		
General concept and approach----	A 3-part program including: (1) a plan requiring employers to provide private health insurance for employees, (2) an assisted plan for the low-income and high medical-risk populations, and (3) an improved Federal Medicare program for the aged. The States would supervise providers of health service and insurance carriers, under Federal guidelines. Supported by the Administration in the 93rd Congress.		
	Employee plan	Assisted plan	Plan for aged
Coverage of the population------	Full-time employees, including employees of State and local governments.	Low-income families, employed or nonemployed. Also, families and employment groups who are high medical risks.	Aged persons insured under social security.

Benefit structure---------------	No limits on amount of benefits listed below, except where indicated:
	Institutional services:
	  Hospital inpatient and outpatient.
	  Skilled nursing facility: 100 days per year.
	Personal services:
	  Physicians.
	  Dentists: For children under age 13.
	  Laboratory and X-ray.
	  Home health services: 100 visits per year.
	  Family planning, maternity care, and health examinations; by regulation.
	Other services and supplies:
	  Prescription drugs.
	  Medical supplies and appliances.
	  Eyeglasses and hearing aids (and eye and ear exams): For children under age 13.		

	Deductible of $150 per person and 25 percent coinsurance, but total cost sharing limited to $1,500 annually per family ($1,050 for individuals).	Maximum cost sharing provisions are same as employee plan, but reduced according to individual or family income.	Deductible of $100 per person and 20 percent coinsurance, but total cost sharing limited to $750 per person annually. Reduced cost sharing according to individual income for low-income aged.
Administration------------------	Insurance through private carriers (or self-insured arrangements) supervised by States, under Federal regulations.	Administered by States, using private carriers to administer benefits, under Federal regulations.	Administered by Federal Government in way similar to present Medicare program.
Relationship to other Government programs-----------------------	Medicare: Program continues as the Federal plan for the aged. Medicaid: No Federal matching funds for covered benefits (or for premiums or cost sharing) under new program, but continues for specified noncovered services (such as intermediate-care facilities).		
Financing----------------------	Employer-employee premium payments, with employer paying 75 percent of premiums (65% for first 3 years). Temporary Federal subsidies for employers with usually high increases in payroll costs. Special provisions to assure coverage for small employers.	Premium payments from enrollees according to family income (none for lowest income groups). Balance of costs from Federal and State general revenues, with State share varied according to State per capita income.	Continuation of present Medicare payroll taxes and premium payments by aged (but no premiums for low-income aged). Federal and State general revenues used to finance reduced cost sharing and premiums for low-income aged.
Standards for providers of services----------------------	Similar to Medicare, with additional standards for participation of physicians' extenders.		
Reimbursement of providers of services----------------------	Reimbursement rates established by States, according to Federal procedures and criteria. Providers of service who elect as "full participating" would be paid the State-established rates, including the cost sharing, as full payment of their charges. Providers who elect as "associate participating" could charge more than the State rate for employee plan patients, but must collect the extra charges and cost sharing from the patients. However, all hospitals and SNF's must be full participating providers.		
Delivery and resources----------	Prepaid practice plans: Under all plans, option available to enroll in approved prepaid group or individual practice plans (which meet special standards). Regulation of insurance carriers: By State, including approval of premium rates, enforcement of disclosure requirements, annual CPA audit, and protection against insolvency of carriers. Regulation of providers: By State, including standards for participation in program, approval of proposed capital expenditures, and enforcement of disclosure requirements. Professional Standard Review Organization (PSRO): Applies to all services under program.		

Mixed public and private--STAGGERS BILL

Subject	Provisions	
General concept and approach---------------	A 3-part program: (1) a plan requiring employers to provide private cover-age for employees, (2) a plan for individuals, and (3) federally contract-ed plan for the poor and aged. State establishes a health care plan, supervises carriers and insurers, and promotes a system of health main-tenance organizations (HMO's).	
	Private plans	Plan for low income and aged
Coverage of the population-----------------	Employees and their families of employers subject to the social security tax. Also, other persons who elect coverage.	Low-income and medically indigent families, and aged persons.

Benefit structure-------------------------	Benefits phased in over 6-year period. Final benefits:
	Institutional services:
	  Hospital: 60 days, $5 copayment per day.
	  Skilled nursing facility: 30 days, $2.50 copayment per day.
	  Nursing home: 60 days, $2.50 copayment per day.
	Personal services:
	  Physicians: 50 visits per year, $3 copayment per visit.
	  Laboratory and X-ray: 20 percent coinsurance.
	  Home health services: 100 visits per year, $2 copayment per visit.
	  Dental services: Children age 7-12: 1 exam per year; other services, 20 percent coinsurance.
	Other services and supplies:
	  Prescription drugs: Limited to specified conditions, $1 per prescrip-tion.
	  Medical equipment and appliances and ambulance service: 20 percent coinsurance.
	  Eyeglasses: Children to age 15, 1 set per year, 20 percent coinsurance.
	Catastrophic coverage: Payable when certain noncovered expenses reach a specified limit, which varies by family income and age; would remove the cost sharing on all benefits and the limitation on number of hospi-tal days and physicians' visits.	

Administration----------------------------	Administered by private insurance carriers under State supervision, according to Federal guidelines.	Federal Government would contract with private insurance carriers who issue policies to eligible persons.
Relationship to other Government programs--	Medicaid and other assistance programs: Would not pay for covered services. Other programs: Most not affected.	
Financing--------------------------------	Employee-employer premium payments, with employer paying at least 75 percent. Federal subsidy of pre-mium for low-income workers and certain small employers; and 10 percent subsidy for HMO enrollees. Individuals pay own premium.	Financed in part by premium payments by medically indigent, but with no premium for lowest income group. Balance of cost financed by Federal general revenues.
Standards for providers of services-------	All institutions and HMO's must meet Medicare standards. Use of para-medical personnel must meet Federal standards. All providers must meet Federal-State quality and disclosure requirements.	
Reimbursement of providers of services-----	Institutions and HMO's: State commission would prospectively approve charges based on review of budget and schedule of proposed charges. Physicians and other professionals: Reasonable fee, salaries, or other compensation, as approved by State commission.	
Delivery and resources---------------------	State health commission: Establishes a State health plan, including pro-visions for regulation of providers and insurance carriers. Takes responsibility for health planning and must approve, in advance, proposed capital expenditures of providers. HMO's: State commissions would regulate a system of approved HMO's. HMO must furnish all covered services through its own facilities or other providers (including arrangements with medical groups or individual practice associations). Would be required to hold open enrollment for public and must eventually offer services on a capitation basis. Federal grants provided for planning, development, outpatient centers, and initial operating expenses.	

Mixed public and private--LUJAN BILL

Subject	Provisions
General concept and approach---------------	A plan under which the Federal Government would issue certificates to families to purchase private health insurance.
Coverage of the population-----------------	All U.S. residents.
Benefit structure--------------------------	No limits on amount of benefits and no cost sharing, except where indicated: Institutional services: Hospital: Extended care facility: } No cost sharing for 120 days; afterward, 20 percent to 50 percent of cost. Personal services: Physicians: $50 deductible, maximum of $5 per visit. Laboratory and X-ray. Home health services. Other services and supplies: Medical equipment and supplies. Maternity care: $100 deductible.
Administration-----------------------------	Families would apply for a health protection certificate on their Federal income tax return. The certificate would be accepted by carriers as full premium payment for a qualified health insurance policy.
Relationship to other Government programs--	Medicare: Abolished. Medicaid: Abolished. Other government programs: Not affected.
Financing----------------------------------	Financed by a 5-percent surcharge on Federal personal income taxes. Federal Government would redeem certificates from carriers for their actuarial value.
Standards for providers of services--------	Same as under Medicare.
Reimbursement of providers of services-----	Institutions: Same as Medicare.
Delivery and resources---------------------	No provisions.

FINANCING THROUGH TAX CREDITS ([34], pp. 487–491)

The Comprehensive Health Care Insurance Act of 1975 (H.R. 6222): Fulton

Date introduced.—April 22, 1975.

Chief sponsor.—Representative Richard Fulton.

Earlier versions.—None—bears some similarity to Administration bill (H.R. 12684) and "Medicredit" proposal (H.R. 2222) in 93d Congress.

A. General Approach

The bill would require employers to provide employees with comprehensive health care insurance coverage purchased from qualified private health insurance carriers. Employers would have to pay at least 65 percent of the premium cost; acceptance of coverage by the employee would be optional. Federal subsidies in the form of cash payments or tax credits would be available to employers who experienced substantial cost increases as a result of complying with the requirement for health insurance coverage.

Federal income tax credits would be utilized to provide health care insurance protection for the non-employed, self-employed, and elderly. The amount of the credit would be scaled according to income tax liability; those persons who have no tax liability would be eligible to receive a certificate or voucher with which to purchase qualified private coverage.

Benefits would be comprehensive in scope and would not be subject to payment of a deductible; however, 20 percent coinsurance would be applied to covered services, with the total amount of coinsurance in any one year limited according to income.

B. People Covered

All employers, including Federal, State, and local governments, would be required to make health insurance coverage available to all their full-time employees (who work at least 20 hours a week on a continuing basis) and their employees' families. Acceptance of coverage would be optional on the part of the employee, although the employee's decision would have to be rendered within 30 days of beginning employment or during an open enrollment period.

Nonemployed or self-employed U.S. residents and their families who are not eligible for an employer-sponsored plan would be eligible for the tax credit provisions of the bill. Individuals eligible for medicare would also be entitled to the tax credit provisions or for health insurance certificates for coverage supplemental to medicare.

Temporarily unemployed persons receiving Federal or State unemployment compensation benefits would be eligible for a federally financed program paying the full premium for continuation of the qualified health care insurance previously furnished through the employer and in effect at the time employment was terminated. Coverage under the Federal program for the temporarily unemployed would continue until the employee became reemployed or until 30 days following the expiration of unemployment compensation benefits.

C. Scope of Benefits

A qualified health insurance plan for purposes of either the employer-sponsored coverage or Federal tax credits for the nonemployed, self-employed, and elderly would have to provide as a minimum the following benefits during any policy year:

    1. 365 days of inpatient hospital care.

    2. 100 days of skilled nursing facility care.

    3. All home health services to an individual under a physician's care.

    4. All emergency and outpatient services normally provided by a hospital, including X-rays, lab tests, etc.

    5. All diagnostic, therapeutic, and preventive medical care by a doctor of medicine or osteopathy, where ever provided including but not limited to physical exams, immunizations and inoculations, well-baby care, services for pregnancy, diagnostic X-rays and lab services, psychiatric care, etc.

    6. Routine dental care (including diagnosis, therapy, and treatment) initially for children ages 2 through 6, with the covered age group gradually to be expanded to include children through age 17.

    7. Emergency dental services and oral surgery for all ages.

    8. Medically necessary ambulance service.

No deductible would be applied to covered benefits. However, an individual or family would be liable for 20 percent coinsurance on all covered items and services, with the total amount of coinsurance in any year limited according to income. The poor would pay no coinsurance; for all others, the ceiling on coinsurance would rise gradually. For example, a family of four would pay no coinsurance unless its income exceeded $4,200, at which point its ceiling would be 10 percent of the excess over $4,200. At the $5,000 level, for example, the maximum coinsurance for a year would be $80 ($5,000 less $4,200 times 10 percent). Regardless of income, the coinsurance ceiling would not be more than $1,500 for an individual nor more than $2,000 for any family. The coinsurance ceiling would trigger catastrophic expense protection. All benefits under the insurance policy would thereafter continue for the remainder of the policy with no further obligation for coinsurance.

D. Administration

Private insurers offering qualified health insurance plans would directly administer claims for benefits and payments to providers. The Federal Government would continue to administer the medicare program as it now does, through carriers and intermediaries. State governments would continue to regulate insurance within the State; an appropriate State agency (generally the State insurance department) would be responsible for approving private carriers for participation in the program.

A 15-member Health Insurance Advisory Board would be created at the Federal level to prescribe regulations for the program as necessary, establish Federal standards for use by State insurance departments in regulating insurance companies, consult with carriers, providers and consumers in planning and developing programs for quality medical care, etc.

In order to be qualified for participation in the program, private insurance carriers would have to be authorized by the appropriate State agency, agree to participate in an assigned risk pool, provide qualified health care insurance as defined in the bill, and provide specified open enrollment periods. Carriers would be required to offer assistance to individuals in preparing and filing applications for certificates of entitlement (to a health insurance premium subsidy) and to provide prompt health insurance coverage to such individuals pending issuance of the certificate. Carriers would also be required to identify medical expenditures in accordance with a classification system and to assure confidentiality of medical records.

E. Financing

The mandated employer plans would be financed through premium contributions from the employer and employee, with the employer required to pay at least 65 percent of the premium. The amount of the premium would be negotiated between the employer and the carrier. Premiums for employee groups of up to 100 persons, and for the self-employed, could not exceed 125 percent of the average premiums in the State for employee groups of more than 100 persons.

Employers whose payroll costs increase by more than 3 percent as a result of purchasing mandated coverage for employees would be eligible for Federal assistance in the form of cash payments or tax credits for the first 5 years of the program. The Federal subsidy would range from 80 percent in the first year to 40 percent in the fifth year of the amount by which the total payroll cost increase exceeds 3 percent of the total payroll costs of the employer. A continuing study by HEW would determine the need for any future subsidies.

Health insurance for the nonemployed and self-employed would be financed through premium payments to private insurers, for which the insured individual would be eligible for either a Federal tax credit or a federally issued health insurance certificate acceptable by the private insurer in payment of the health insurance premium. The amount of Federal premium assistance in each case would be determined on the basis of income tax liability. Persons with no tax liability would receive a Federal contribution equal to 100 percent of the health care insurance premium. For others, Federal assistance would range, between 99 percent and 10 percent of the premium. For example, a family of four with a $6,000 income resulting in a $159 tax liability would be entitled to have 84 percent of the premium paid by the Federal Government.

Nontaxable income would be included in the income computation in determining the amount of Federal premium assistance on the following basis: for each $100 of such nontaxable income (exclusive of the first $4,000 of pension or social security income), the amount of Federal premium assistance otherwise applicable (either as a tax credit or certificate) would be reduced by 1 percentage point.

An employed person entitled to coverage under an employer plan could not elect coverage under the program for the nonemployed. As an equalizer, however, he could claim a tax credit (or apply for a certificate) in the amount by which his share of the premium as an employee exceeded what he would pay as a nonemployed person under the subsidy program. The bill also specifically allows self-employed persons to claim as a business expense 65 percent of the premium cost of qualified health insurance; normally, tax law does not allow self-employed persons to qualify as employees for purposes of business expenses related to health insurance.

Nonemployed persons aged 65 and over who are eligible for medicare would also be eligible for a Federal subsidy under this program on the same basis and in the same manner as described above for self-employed and non-employed persons under age 65. However, the subsidy in this case would be applicable only to a premium for "qualified supplemental coverage" designed to equalize the available benefits for the elderly as for all others. Such supplemental insurance would be the same in content as the full insurance policy for persons under 65, but would contain a clause excluding payment for all benefits obtainable by medicare eligibles under parts A and B of medicare. The supplemental insurance would not be allowed to cover medicare deductibles and coinsurance and would be required to make its supplemental benefits available without any deductible or coinsurance payments on the part of the insured individual.

Premium payments for the temporarily unemployed would be paid by the Federal Government from general revenues to cover periods of unemployment, until the individual became newly employed or until expiration of his unemployment compensation benefits. Once unemployment compensation benefits were exhausted, the individual would become eligible for Federal assistance to the nonemployed, with full subsidy of the premium for the remainder of the calendar year.

F. Payments to and Standards for Providers of Services

Physicians' services would be reimbursed on the basis of "usual and customary or reasonable charges" for covered services; payment for hospital services would be determined by an appropriate State agency, after consultation with providers, on a reasonable cost basis under "acceptable methods of reimbursement including appropriate prospective rate determination systems" (e.g., budget review, negotiated rates, target rates, formula negotiations, etc.). Other costs would be paid on either a reasonable cost or reasonable charge basis, as appropriate.

The Health Insurance Advisory Board at the Federal level would consult with carriers, providers, and consumers to plan, review, and develop programs to maintain the quality of medical care and the effective utilization of available financial resources, health manpower, and facilities through utilization review, peer review, and other means providing for the participation of carriers and the providers of services.

G. Effect on Other Government Programs

Medicare would continue to cover the aged and disabled as at present; the program would allow medicare eligibles to obtain private coverage supplemental to medicare and receive tax credits or certificates of entitlement toward the costs of such private coverage. Although the bill itself does not amend the Social Security Act to eliminate the title XIX (medicaid) program, the intent of the program is to eliminate the need for medicaid by covering medicaid eligibles under private health insurance plans, either through a mandated employer plan or the tax credit/certificate of entitlement provisions for the nonemployed

H. Other Major Provisions

The bill provides that, in an action for damages against a medical provider, no liability would be recognized with respect to the costs of health care which are payable under this program or any other health care program under the Social Security Act.

Summaries of H.R. 6222 and Other Bills ([33], pp. 14–18)

Tax credits--FULTON BILL

Subject	Provisions	
General concept and approach--------------	A 2-part plan including (1) a plan requiring employers to offer private health insurance to employees and (2) a plan making available private insurance for the nonemployed and self-employed, with Federal subsidies of the premium provided through tax credits or subsidy certificates. Supported by American Medical Association.	
	Employee plan	Plan for nonemployed and self-employed
Coverage of the population---------------	Full-time employees of private employers and of Federal, State, and local governments (including persons under Medicare) and workers receiving unemployment insurance.	Low-income families, self-employed, and all others not under an employee plan (including persons under Medicare).

Benefit structure------------------------	No limits on benefits, except where indicated:
	  Institutional services:
	    Hospital inpatient and outpatient.
	    Skilled nursing facilities: 100 days.
	  Personal services:
	    Physicians services.
	    Dental care: Initially for children age 2-6, later extended to age 17.
	    Home health services.
	    Laboratory and X-ray.
	    Health exams, maternity care, and well-child care.
	  Other services and supplies:
	    Medical supplies and equipment.
	  Cost sharing: 20% coinsurance, with maximum limit of $1,500 for individuals and $2,000 for families; cost sharing reduced or eliminated for low-income and unemployed families.
	  Medicare beneficiaries: Same benefit coverage, but policy excludes the benefits provided by Medicare.	

Administration---------------------------	Insurance provided through private carriers, supervised by the States under regulations issued by a new Federal board.	
	Employers purchase insurance from carriers.	Family purchases insurance from carriers.
Relationship to other Government programs-	Medicare: Continues to operate. Medicaid: Would not pay for covered services.	
Financing--------------------------------	Employee-employer premium payments, with employer paying at least 65% of cost. Special maximum limit on amount of premium costs for small employers. Federal subsidies for all employers with large increases in payroll costs. Premium for unemployed persons paid by Federal Government.	Federal subsidy of premium ranging from 100% to 10% of premium costs, varied according to annual tax payment of family; this subsidy is taken as income tax credit or by obtaining a subsidy certificate from DHEW. State insurance pools established to assure coverage.
Standards for providers of services-------	Standards could be issued by a new Federal board.	
Reimbursement of providers of services----	Hospitals: Reimbursement determined by State governments, based on prospective payment or other methods. Physicians: Payment on basis of usual and customary or reasonable charges.	
Delivery and resources--------------------	Studies to be conducted by new Federal board.	

Tax credits --DOWNING BILL

Subject	Provisions
General concept and approach----------------	Would provide credits against personal income taxes to offset the premium cost of qualified private health insurance providing specified benefits. Also, would require employers to provide qualified policies to retain favorable tax treatment.
Coverage of the population------------------	All U.S. residents, on voluntary basis.

Benefit structure--------------------------	Tax credits of 10 to 100 percent of cost of qualified health insurance policy, depending on annual tax payments. Voucher certificates issued to persons with little or no tax liability.
	Institutional services:
	  Hospital: 60 days cf care; $50 deductible per stay.
	  Skilled nursing facility: Substituted for hospital days on 2 for 1 basis; $50 deductible per stay.
	Personal services:
	  Physicians: 20 percent coinsurance.
	  Dental care: Initially for children age 2-6. Later extended up to age 17.
	  Home health services: 20 percent coinsurance.
	  Laboratory and X-ray: 20 percent coinsurance.
	Other services and supplies:
	  Ambulance services: 20 percent coinsurance.
	Catastrophic coverage: Unlimited hospital days, an additional 30 days in a skilled nursing facility, prosthetic devices, and blood (after 3 pints) covered after corridor deductible (out-of-pocket payment) which varies according to income.
	Total coinsurance for physicians, laboratory and X-ray combined limited to $100 per family; separate limit of $100 for hospital outpatient, home health, and ambulance; and separate limit of $100 for dental care.
	Medicaid program would pay all cost sharing for cash assistance recipients.

Administration----------------------------	Private insurance carriers issue health insurance policies. State insurance departments certify carriers and qualified policies. DHEW issues voucher certificates. A new Federal board establishes standards for program.
Relationship to other Government programs--	Medicare: Continues to operate. Medicaid and other assistance programs: Would not pay for services under program. Other programs: Most not affected.
Financing---------------------------------	Tax credits financed from Federal general revenues. Employers must provide qualified policies as a condition of taking the full premium cost as a normal business deduction.
Standards for providers of services--------	No provisions.
Reimbursement of providers of services-----	Usual and customary charges.
Delivery and resources---------------------	No provisions.

Tax credits--BENNETT BILL

Subject	Provisions
General concept and approach---------------	Would provide credits against personal income taxes to offset the premium cost of qualified private health insurance providing specified benefits. Also would require employers to provide qualified policies to retain favorable tax treatment.
Coverage of the population-----------------	All U.S. residents, on voluntary basis.

Benefit structure--------------------------	Tax credits of 10 to 100 percent of cost of qualified health insurance policy, depending on annual tax payments. Voucher certificates issued to persons with little or no tax liability.
	Institutional services:
	  Hospital: 60 days of care; $50 deductible per stay.
	  Extended-care facility: Substituted for hospital days on 2 for 1 basis; $50 deductible per stay.
	Personal services:
	  Physicians: 20 percent coinsurance.
	  Laboratory and X-ray: 20 percent coinsurance.
	Catastrophic coverage: Additional hospital days, 30 nursing facility days, and prosthetic devices covered after corridor deductible (out-of-pocket payment) which varies according to income.
	Total coinsurance (for physicians, laboratory and X-ray) limited to $100 per family. Additional limit of $100 for hospital outpatient services.

Administration-----------------------------	Private insurance carriers issue policies. State insurance departments certify carriers and qualified policies. DHEW issues voucher certificates. The new Federal board establishes standards for program.
Relationship to other Government programs--	Medicare: Continues to operate. Medicaid and other assistance programs: Would not pay for services under program. Other programs: Most not affected.
Financing---------------------------------	Tax credits financed from Federal general revenues. Employers must provide qualified policies as a condition of taking the full premium cost as a normal business deduction.
Standards for providers of services--------	No provisions.
Reimbursement of providers of services-----	Usual and customary charges.
Delivery and resources---------------------	No provisions.

Tax credits--BROCK BILL

Subject	Provisions
General concept and approach----------------	The proposal would provide tax credits against personal income taxes when medical expenses exceeded a specified percent of family income.
Coverage of the population------------------	All U.S. residents, on voluntary basis.
Benefit structure---------------------------	The credit against income taxes would be payable if medical expenses exceeded 15 percent of modified adjusted gross income. The credit would be equal to 85 percent of the excess amount. Adjusted gross income would be modified by subtracting the amount of personal exemptions ($750 for each exemption) and adding certain excluded capital gains and interest income. The definition of medical expenses would be similar to that used for the present medical expense income tax deduction.
Administration------------------------------	Persons would be required to file an income tax return. The full amount of the tax credit would always be payable without regard to the amount (if any) of taxes.
Relationship to other Government programs---	The President would study the possibilities of ending, reducing, or changing the Medicare, Medicaid, and other Federal programs.
Financing-----------------------------------	The proposal would be financed from Federal general revenues. The present medical expense deduction would be repealed.
Standards for providers of services---------	No provisions.
Reimbursement of providers of services------	No provisions.
Delivery and resources----------------------	No provisions.

Tax credits--CLAWSON BILL

Subject	Provisions
General concept and approach------------------	The proposal would provide tax credits and revised medical deductions in connection with health insurance and expenses.
Coverage of the population--------------------	All U.S. residents, on voluntary basis.
Benefit structure----------------------------	The taxpayer could take a tax credit against personal income taxes equal to 100% of the premium cost of private health insurance. The full tax credit would always be payable without regard to the amount of taxes (if any). The present medical expense deduction would be revised to include medical expenses which exceed $500 in the year for all taxpayers. The definition of medical expenses for both the tax credit and tax deduction would be the same as under present law.
Administration-------------------------------	Person would be required to file an income tax return to claim credits or deductions and the proposal would be administered through the tax system.
Relationship to other Government programs----	The President would study the possibilities of ending, reducing, or changing Medicare, Medicaid, and other Federal medical programs.
Financing------------------------------------	The proposal would be financed from Federal general revenues.
Standards for providers of services----------	No provisions.
Reimbursement of providers of services-------	No provisions.
Delivery and resources-----------------------	No provisions.

PROTECTION AGAINST CATASTROPHE ([34], pp. 494–502)

The Catastrophic Health Insurance and Medical Assistance Reform Act (S. 2470/H.R. 10028): Long-Ribicoff-Waggonner

Date introduced.—October 3, 1975.

Chief sponsors.—Representive Joe Waggonner, Senators Russell Long and Abraham Ribicoff.

Earlier versions.—93d Congress, S. 2513 and H.R. 14079 (Oct. 2, 1973).

A. GENERAL APPROACH

The bill would provide catastrophic health insurance protection for all legal U.S. residents through one of the following plans: (1) a federally administered public plan for the unemployed, welfare recipients, the aged, and persons who do not opt for private insurance coverage, and (2) a private catastrophic insurance plan allowed an an option for employers and the self-employed, who would be required under the terms of the bill to provide and pay the full cost of such catastrophic protection for their employees. Benefits would be similar to those currently covered under medicare, but would be subject to payment by the beneficiary of the first 60 days of hospital care and the first $2,000 in medical expenses. The program would be financed through a 1-percent tax on the payroll of employers, with 50 percent of the amount paid as payroll tax allowed as a tax credit. Employers opting for a private plan would have the amount of their premiums deducted from their 1 percent payroll tax liability. They would also be eligible for a 50 percent tax credit on *both* the total amount of premiums paid for catastrophic coverage and any remaining Federal payroll tax liability after the premiums have been deducted.

In addition, the bill would replace medicaid with a uniform, national program of medical benefits for low-income persons, administered by the Department of Health, Education, and Welfare. The bill further provides for a voluntary Federal certification program for basic private health insurance to encourage private insurers to make such basic coverage (supplemental to the catastrophic program) available in all areas of the country. If private insurers failed to make certified basic private health insurance available in any State, the Secretary of HEW would be empowered, 3 years after the enactment of the program, to offer a standard health insurance policy to individuals and families living in that State.

B. PEOPLE COVERED

Under the catastrophic health insurance plan, every individual who is a resident citizen or a lawfully admitted resident alien would be entitled to catastrophic health insurance benefits under either the public plan or the private plan for employers and the self-employed. All employers, including Federal, State, and local governments, would be required to provide for all their full-time employees (who work more than 25 hours per week) and their employees' spouses and dependent family members the health insurance protection as specified in the bill. At their option, employers could also include part-time and temporary employees. An employer would be obligated to continue coverage for 90 days after an employee left his employment unless the employee obtained coverage under another employer plan. Federal, State, and local governments would be considered employers for purposes of the catastrophic program.

The unemployed, welfare recipients, the aged, and all others not covered under an employer or self-employed private catastrophic plan would be covered under the public plan.

The *medical assistance plan* for low-income persons would be available to all persons eligible for medicaid benefits during the period from January to July 1977 and all individuals and families having an annual income at or below the following levels: $2,400 for an individual; $3,600 for a two-person family; $4,200 for a three-person family; $4,800 for a four-person family; and $400 additional for each additional family member.

Families with incomes above these levels would become eligible if they spent enough on medical care to reduce their income to the eligibility levels. Thus, a family of four with an income of $5,000 would become eligible if it spent $200 for medical care.

C. Scope of Benefits

The *catastrophic plan* would cover the same kinds of services as currently provided under parts A and B of medicare, except that there would be no upper limitation on hospital days or home health visits. Present medicare coverage under part A includes 90 days of hospital care, plus an additional lifetime reserve of 60 hospital days; 100 days of posthospital extended care; and 100 home health visits during the year following discharge from a hospital or extended care facility. Part B coverage includes physicians' services, 100 home health visits annually, laboratory and X-ray services, outpatient physical therapy services, and other medical and health services such as medical supplies, appliances and equipment, and ambulance services.

Benefits excluded from medicare would also be excluded under this program. Medicare's limitation on skilled nursing care would also be retained. The catastrophic plan would apply different limits on inpatient and outpatient mental health services than those currently applicable under medicare (i.e., 190-day lifetime maximum in psychiatric hospitals, $250 maximum payable for outpatient mental health care); the catastrophic plan would cover (1) unlimited inpatient services, consisting of a course of active care and treatment provided in an accredited medical institution, (2) unlimited mental health care services provided on a partial hospitalization basis by an accredited medical institution or qualified community mental health center, (3) unlimited outpatient services provided by a qualified community mental health center, and (4) 5 visits to a privately practicing psychiatrist during any 12-month period, unless additional visits have been approved in advance by an appropriate professional review mechanism on the grounds that the patient would require institutional care in the absence of such additional outpatient visits.

Unlike medicare, which provides *basic* insurance coverage, the catastrophic health insurance program would provide institutional benefits only after an individual had first been hospitalized for a total of 60 days in one year (this feature of the program is called the "hospital deductible"), and medical benefits only after an individual or a family had incurred medical expenses of $2,000 for physicians' services, home health visits, physical therapy services, laboratory and X-ray, and other covered medical and health services (this "medical deductible" would be dynamic in character, ajdusted annually to reflect changes in the Consumer Price Index and other economic factors). The plan would have a deductible carryover feature under which days spent in a hospital in the last 3 months of one calendar year could be counted toward satisfaction of the hospital deductible in the following calendar year; similarly, covered medical expenses incurred in the last 3 months of one calendar year could be counted toward meeting the $2,000 medical deductible for the next year. Once the hospital and medical deductibles had been met, the individual would not be charged for services covered under the program. However, following the first period of any 90 consecutive days during which the individual incurred *less* than $500 in medical expenses, catastrophic benefits would temporarily terminate until such time as the individual once again satisfied the medical deductible by incurring $2,000 in additional medical expenses. Similarly, following the first consecutive 90-day period during which an individual was neither an inpatient in a hospital nor an inpatient in a skilled nursing facility, the individual would once again be liable for the 60-day hospital deductible applicable to catastrophic benefits.

The *medical assistance plan* for the low-income would cover the following benefits, generally without any limit on the amount of services or any cost-sharing required, except as indicated:

Inpatient hospital services—60 days in benefit period.

All medically-necessary skilled nursing facility care, intermediate facility care, and home health services.

Physicians' services—$3 copayment for each of first 10 outpatient visits per family, except no charge for visits for well-baby care, family planning, and periodic exams for children under age 18.

Laboratory and X-ray services.

Prenatal and well-baby care.

Family planning, counseling, and supplies.

Periodic screening, diagnosis, and treatment for children under age 18.

Outpatient physical therapy.

Immunizations and Pap smears.

Medical supplies and appliances.

Ambulance services.

Mental health care services as follows: (1) on an inpatient basis—if provided in an accredited institution, services are included in the hospital inpatient benefit if the service constitutes active care and treatment; (2) on a partial hospitalization basis—if provided by an accredited institution or accredited institution or qualified community mental health center; (3) on an outpatient basis—without limit if provided by community mental health center, limited to 5 visits if provided otherwise (e.g., by a psychiatrist) with additional visits subject to approval by a professional review organization. Benefit includes approved drugs when necessary to avoid hospitalization.

The medical assistance plan would also pay the medicare part B premium for eligible individuals and would reimburse an individual for one-half of the amount of the actuarial value of catastrophic health insurance coverage paid by such individual under a self-employed plan or deducted as taxes from his self-employment income.

A special copayment requirement would also apply to individuals who are not a member of a family, after the 60th continuous day spent in a long-term facility. The amount of this copayment would be equal to the amount of the patient's monthly income, less $50. (A similar requirement would apply in a situation where all members of a family have a stay exceeding 60 days.)

D. ADMINISTRATION

The public *catastrophic insurance plan* would be administered by the Social Security Administration in a manner parallel to the administration of medicare. The private catastrophic plan would be administered by a qualified private insurance carrier of the employer's choice. The Secretary of HEW would be responsible for approving the employer plans and the self-employed plans administered through private carriers. To be approved as a carrier for private catastrophic insurance, an insurance carrier would have to comply with various Federal requirements, including a requirement that the carrier establish claims determination procedures which comply with section 503 of the Employee Retirement Income Security Act of 1974 and are consistent with those procedures employed by the carrier in its noncatastrophic health insurance business; to assist carriers in meeting this requirement, the Secretary would allow carriers reasonable access to claims data developed under medicare's hospital insurance program. Carriers would also be exempted from certain antitrust laws as they might otherwise pertain to a group of carriers entering into a pool, reinsurance, or other residual market arrangement.

The *medical assistance plan* for the low-income would be administered by the Secretary of HEW. Individuals eligible for benefits under the program would be issued a health benefits card indicating that their application for benefits had been filed and approved for a given benefit period. The Secretary would utilize private carriers as fiscal intermediaries responsible for administration of claims and payments to providers of services. The bill also provides that the Secretary could require the consolidation of the activities of these carriers in areas with small populations if necessary to improve quality and efficiency. Three years after the enactment of the program, no private carrier or other organization could be utilized under the medical assistance plan or medicare unless it was approved and certified under the voluntary certification program established under the bill.

E. Financing

The *catastrophic insurance plan* would be financed through a 1-percent tax on the payroll of employers and the income of the self-employed now subject to the social security tax. No employee contribution would be allowed. Amounts collected as taxes would be deposited in a Federal catastrophic health insurance trust fund. An employer or self-employed individual who opted for a private, rather than public, catastrophic health insurance plan would have the amount of the premium for private coverage deducted from his 1-percent payroll tax liability; he would, however, remain liable for payment to the Federal Government of any difference between the amount paid as premium for a private plan and the 1 percent Federal tax liability. Publicly insured employers and self-employed individuals would be eligible for a catastrophic health insurance tax credit equal to 50 percent of the amount paid as payroll tax liability. Similarly, privately insured employers and self-employed persons would also be eligible for a 50-percent tax credit on the amount paid for private catastrophic insurance premiums, as well as a 50-percent tax credit on any additional amount paid to meet the 1-percent Federal payroll tax liability.

Employers and self-employed persons opting for private coverage would pay premiums directly to the carriers. The bill requires that the employer plans administered through private carriers must make available to the employer certain arrangements for the pooling of risks among various employee groups of different employers, so that premiums can be determined on a class, rather than an individual, basis.

Each year, a five-member Federal Actuarial Committee would prepare a table of values of catastrophic health insurance coverage for the following year, indicating the actuarial value of 1 year's catastrophic health insurance coverage for one individual. This table could be used by the employer as a guideline by which to evaluate the actuarial value of catastrophic health insurance coverage (and the premium charged therefor) offered through private carriers. The Committee would also review the marketing and rating practices of private carriers providing employer and self-employed plans for catastrophic insurance.

The *medical assistance plan* would be financed from general revenues, just as the Federal share of the current medicaid program is now financed, and also with State funds. A medical assistance trust fund would be established to make payments for benefits under the program. States would contribute a fixed amount which would be equivalent to their total expenditures from State funds under medicaid for the types of benefits covered under this plan during the year prior to the effective date of this program. Additionally, a State would also pay 50 percent of the estimated amount that the State and local governments had expended in the same base year for provision of these types of services to people not covered under medicaid who would, however, be covered under the new medical assistance plan. State contributions in future years would be limited to the initial contribution amount.

To encourage States to offer optional services not covered under the medical assistance plan, the State contribution would be reduced by an amount equal to one-half the amount expended by the State from non-Federal funds in providing types of services not covered under this program, but which would have been matched under the medicaid program (such as drugs, dental services, etc.), provided, however, that the State had actually included such types of services under its medicaid plan prior to the effective date of the new program.

F. Payments to and Standards for Providers of Services

Providers of services under the catastrophic insurance plan and the medical assistance plan would be reimbursed on the same basis as under medicare. Reimbursement controls would include the payment of audited "reasonable costs" to participating institutions and agencies, and "reasonable charges" to practitioners and other suppliers. Payments to skilled nursing facilities and intermediate care facilities would be reimbursed on a "cost-related" basis.

Payments made under the medical assistance plan, along with any required copayment from the patient, would have to be accepted by providers and practitioners as payment in full for the services rendered, and no persons accepting such payment could charge additional amounts for these services.

Both programs would apply the same standards for providers of services as under medicare. Both plans would also incorporate the quality, health and safety standards, and utilization controls which exist in the medicare program, including review of services by institutional utilization review committees and professional standards review organizations (PSRO's).

G. Effect on Other Government Programs

The catastrophic insurance plan would supplement benefits provided under medicare for persons covered by that program. The medical assistance plan would replace the existing medicaid program. The catastrophic insurance plan would always be the primary payor in cases where an individual was also entitled to have payment made under either medicare or the medical assistance plan. Nor could payments under the catastrophic plan be denied or reduced because benefits for services covered under that plan were also payable, or had been paid, under any other public or private insurance or health benefits plan.

H. OTHER MAJOR PROVISIONS

1. Voluntary certification program for private basic health insurance—The bill establishes a program whereby private health insurers could, at their option, submit one or more basic health insurance policies to HEW for certification. Certification would be based upon certain minimum criteria with respect to adequacy of coverage, conditions of eligibility, actual availability of the policy, and reasonableness of premiums to expenses. State agencies could also be used for certification of basic health insurance policies in States having an approved basic health insurance facilition program. In addition to offering certified basic policies, a private carrier, in order to be "approved," would have to employ effective procedures designed to assure appropriate utilization and cost controls with regard to health services insured under its policies.

Three years after the start of the program, no insurer could serve as a carrier or intermediary for either medicare or the new medical assistance plan unless it offered one or more certified policies to the general public in each geographic area or service area in which it did business. The bill would facilitate establishment of insurance pool arrangements in order to make such certified policies available to the general public with a proportionate sharing of risks and rewards among participating insurers.

2. Government-sponsored standard health insurance policies on a cost basis.— Three years after the start of the program, the Secretary of HEW would be required to offer a standard health insurance policy providing basic health benefits to individuals and families living in any State which had neither a basic health insurance facilitation program nor approved basic health insurance policies actually available through private carriers. Premiums charged for such policies would be designed to cover costs, including administrative costs and reserves.

3. Amendments to medicare.—Makes several amendments to existing medicare program, designed to (*a*) allow coverage of immunizations on a scheduled allowance basis, (*b*) increase the dollar amount payable for mental health services under part B, (*c*) adjust the amount of premiums for hospital insurance coverage payable for uninsured individuals not otherwise eligible for Medicare, (*d*) clarify provisions relating to payment for extended care services on a cost-related basis, and (*e*) extend coverage under the renal disease program to all individuals with kidney disease, regardless of insured status for purposes of social security benefits.

4. Philanthropic support for health care.—Includes provisions designed to encourage philanthropic support for health care, especially in support of experimental and innovative efforts to improve the delivery system.

MAJOR NEW FEATURES

TITLE I—CATASTROPHIC HEALTH INSURANCE PROGRAM

1. Option to purchase private coverage.—The new bill allows an option to employers and the self-employed to purchase private catastrophic health insurance coverage (meeting Government standards) in lieu of the publicly administered plan; persons taking advantage of the private option would still be liable for the full amount of the 1 percent payroll tax used to finance the plan, but amounts paid as premiums for private catastrophic coverage would be deducted from the actual payroll tax liability.

2. Financing provisions.—The old bill had provided for partial employee financing of the program; the new bill provides for total employer (and self-employed) financing of a 1 percent payroll tax with 50 percent of that amount allowed as a tax credit to the employer or self-employed individual.

3. Benefits.—The new bill eliminates the old bill's provision for 20 percent patient coinsurance on covered medical benefits after satisfaction of the $2,000 medical deductible; the new bill applies no cost-sharing to either covered hospital or medical benefits once the applicable deductible has been satisfied. Mental health benefits have been broadened over last year's bill; the old bill had applied medicare's limit on inpatient and outpatient mental health benefits, i.e., 190-day lifetime limit for care in psychiatric hospitals, $250 maximum payment for outpatient care.

4. Eligibility.—The old bill had linked eligibility for the program to social security status; the new bill extends entitlement to virtually every U.S. resident, without requirements for a history of contributions, etc.

TITLE II—MEDICAL ASSISTANCE PLAN

1. Eligibility.—Income determinations for purposes of eligibility would be based on actual income of individual or family for the *2-month* period immediately preceding the date of filing of an application and the prospective income for the 2-month period immediately following such filing date; under the previous bill, income determinations would have been based on actual income of the *past year*, unless the amount of prospective income for the coming year would be much greater or lesser than the past year's income.

2. Benefits.—(a) Eliminates copayment on periodic exams for persons under age 18; (b) change in relationship to new catastrophic program would now reimburse one-half of the actual value of catastrophic health insurance coverage for individual eligible under title XIX and covered under a catastrophic plan for the self-employed.

3. Payment for health services.—Applies "reasonable cost-related" reimbursement provisions, in accordance with regulations of the Secretary, to skilled nursing facilities and intermediate care facilities.

4. Administration.—Under the old bill, responsibility for administration of the new title XIX program had been delegated to the Social Security Administration; the new bill vests responsibility directly in the Secretary of HEW.

5. Optometrists' services.—The new bill contains a provision which would include optometrists' services as part of covered "physicians' services" in States which had been providing payment for such services under their title XIX programs during all or part of the 2-year period preceding the effective date of the new program.

6. Income definition.—The new bill omits from the definition of income for purposes of determining eligibility under the program the following items: "prizes and awards," "proceeds of life insurance policies exceeding the lesser of expenses for last illness and burial or $1,500." The new bill also excludes from income cash gifts of less than $240; the old bill had limited the gift exclusion to gifts of less than $100.

7. Definition of health care expenses.—The new bill under "health care expenses" for purposes of the spend-down provision includes one-half of the amount of insurance premiums paid by or on behalf of an individual for catastrophic health insurance coverage under a self-employed plan; *"medical and other health services"* definition has been broadened to include outpatient rehabilitation services.

8. Definition of intermediate care services.—Has been broadened to include services in a public institution for the mentally retarded or persons with related conditions.

9. Definition of mental health care services.—Amended to include services provided on a partial hospitalization basis by an accredited medical institution or qualified community mental health center.

10. Definition of outpatient rehabilitation services.—The old bill had not included such services under its definition of medical and other health services, as noted in item 8 above; the new bill does cover such services and provides a lengthy definition of what would be included for purposes of title XIX.

TITLE III—PRIVATE BASIC HEALTH INSURANCE CERTIFICATION PROGRAM

1. Authority to offer basic Government health insurance plan.—The new bill contains an entirely new provision which directs the Secretary of HEW to make available individual and family health insurance policies on a cost basis in any State which does not have a basic health insurance facilitation program (as described below) and in which there is not actually and generally available one or more basic health insurance policies approved through the Government certification program. Such Government policies would not be offered until 3 years after the enactment of the program.

2. Basic health insurance facilitation program.—The new bill contains an entirely new provision which would encourage States to facilitate the offering of certified basic health insurance policies through enactment, amendment, or enforcement of various insurance laws and regulations.

3. State certification of insurance plans.—State agencies in those States having a basic health insurance facilitation program could be utilized by the Secretary for the purpose of certifying basic health insurance policies.

4. Approval of carriers.—The new bill stipulates an additional condition pertaining to carrier approval—carriers must employ effective procedures and practices designed to assure appropriate cost and utilization controls with regard to covered health services.

5. Antitrust exemption.—The new bill has broadened this exemption, as it applies to private carriers offering certified policies, to include (in addition to an "insurance pool") "reinsurance or other residual market arrangements."

Summaries of H.R. 10028/S.2470 and Other Bills ([33], pp. 19–20)

Catastrophic protection--LONG-RIBICOFF--WAGGONNER BILL

Subject	Provisions		
General concept and approach---------------	Proposal includes (1) a catastrophic illness insurance program for the general population provided through a federally administered plan or alternatively under approved private plans and (2) a Federal medical assistance program for the poor and medically indigent. Also includes provisions for Federal certification of qualified private basic health insurance.		
	Catastrophic insurance		Medical Assistance Plan
	Government plan	Private plans	Without regard to age or employment, low-income families and families qualifying under "spend-down" provisions.
Coverage of the population----------------	All U.S. residents, except persons under private plans.	Employees (and their families) of employers who voluntarily elect private plan. Self-employed who voluntarily elect.	
Benefit structure------------------------	After person spends 60 days in the hospital, following benefits become available: Additional hospital days, skilled nursing facility (100-day limit), and home health services. After family spends $2,000 on medical expenses, following benefits become available to all members of family: Physicians services, laboratory and X-ray, home health services, medical supplies and appliances. No limit on amount of services (except SNF) and no cost sharing.		No limits on services and no cost sharing except as indicated: Institutional services: Hospital (60 days), skilled nursing and intermediate care facilities. Personal services: Physicians ($3 a visit for first 10 visits), laboratory and X-ray, family planning, maternity, and exams for children. Other: Medical supplies and appliances.
Administration---------------------------	Similar to Medicare program.	Employers and self-employed purchase approved private insurance from approved carriers. DHEW supervises program.	Similar to Medicare program.
Relationship to other Government programs--	Catastrophic benefits payable without regard to coverage under other government programs or private plans. Medical assistance benefits secondary to all other programs and plans. Medicare program continues and Medicaid abolished.		
Financing-------------------------------	Payroll tax of 1% on employers, including Federal, State, and local governments; employers allowed a credit against their Federal income tax of 50% of the tax. Similar provisions for self-employed.	Employers are subject to regular 1% payroll tax, but this tax is reduced by the actuarial value of their private coverage; also receives the 50% tax credit. Similar provisions for self-employed.	Financed by Federal and State general revenues. State share is fixed annual amount based on State cost under Medicaid for types of services under new program, with some additions and subtractions.
Standards for providers of services--------	Same as Medicare.		
Reimbursement of providers of services-----	Same as Medicare.	Determined by carrier.	Same as Medicare, but physicians must accept plan's payment as payment in full.
Delivery and resources--------------------	Government catastrophic program and medical assistance plan incorporate HMO and PSRO provisions now applicable to Medicare.		
Encouragement of basic insurance-----------	Under provisions designed to encourage improved basic health insurance, DHEW would certify private policies meeting specified standards (including coverage of 60 hospital days and first $2,000 in medical services). States would arrange marketing of this insurance through pools and reinsurance arrangements. DHEW would offer certified insurance in States where not available.		

Catastrophic protection--ROE BILL

Subject	Provisions
General concept and approach---------------	Program which would pay medical expenses when they exceed a specified amount. Administered by private insurance companies under State super-vision and financed by private premium payments and Federal subsidy.
Coverage of the population-----------------	All U.S. residents, on voluntary basis.
Benefit structure--------------------------	All services eligible as medical expense deductions under the income tax law may be covered after family medical expenses exceed a specified amount (the deductible) which varies according to family income and size. There is no deductible for low-income families but the deductible rises rapidly as income increases. Expenses paid by other private insurance or govern-ment programs can be counted toward the deductible.
Administration-----------------------------	Private insurance carriers would issue and administer the insurance policies. Each State would design and establish a plan. DHEW would establish regulations for the program.
Relationship to other Government programs--	Medicare: Continues to operate. Medicaid and other assistance programs: Would not pay for services covered under the program. Other programs: Most not affected.

Financing----------------------------------	Policyholders would pay premium.
	  Premium rate: DHEW would determine actuarial value of policies, but could set a premium rate lower than the actuarial value to encourage widespread enrollment. It would pay carriers (from general revenues) the difference between the actuarial value and the premium rate.
	  Reinsurance: DHEW would arrange a reinsurance mechanism. The carrier would pay the reinsurance premiums.

Standards for providers of services--------	No provisions.
Reimbursement of providers of services-----	No provisions.
Delivery and resources---------------------	No provisions.

Index of Included Documents

Arranged by Issuing Agency

Index of Subjects and Names